# The Rise and Development
# of Western Civilization

# The Rise and Development of Western Civilization

PART II: 1300 to 1850

Second Edition

JOHN L. STIPP
*Knox College*

C. WARREN HOLLISTER
*University of California, Santa Barbara*

ALLEN W. DIRRIM
*San Fernando Valley State College*

John Wiley & Sons, Inc., New York · London · Sydney · Toronto

*To our Parents*

*COVER:* Michelangelo, St. Peter's Cathedral. Cross section engraving by Dupérac. Prints Division, New York Public Library.

**Library of Congress Cataloging in Publication Data:**

Library of Congress Catalog Card Number: 72-2661

Stipp, John L., Hollister, C. Warren and Dirrim, Allen W.
  The Rise and Development of Western Civilization.
2nd ed., 3 vols., pbk.
New York    John Wiley and Sons

Fall 1972    4-14-72

Printed in the United States of America.

10 9 8 7 6 5 4 3 2 1

# Preface to the Second Edition

This edition of *The Rise and Development of Western Civilization* presents the last three chapters of revised Volume I and the first five chapters of revised Volume II of the original work of the same title. Companion parts of this new series, one from earliest times to 1500, the other devoted to life in the West (and, particularly for the twentieth century, the East) are available for use in appropriate term courses.

Textbooks, like any academic endeavor, periodically need re-examination. A college generation has passed since publication of the first edition of *The Rise and Development of Western Civilization,* and some recasting is in order. Although the book's fundamental structure and substance have not been radically altered, necessary changes have been made.

One change has involved the occasional shifting or clarification of emphases. In Volume I, for example, the original section on the late Roman Empire too easily gave the impression, despite contrary cautionary remarks, of a sudden collapse of that empire. In this edition material has been added to underscore the innovative sanctions and alterations of Diocletian and Constantine. Similarly, significant parts of the complex of chapters dealing with post-medieval and early modern times have been reworked. The same treatment, where needed, is given to material in Volume II. There, for example, exposition of the background of the Russian Communist Revolution underemphasized the role of precommunist theoreticians and revolutionaries; accordingly, a fairly substantial section of new matter has been included. On the other hand, some material has been deleted where its inclusion has come to seem unnecessary in a survey account of Western civilization; an example of this kind of change is the excision of the section on the New Deal.

Many comments sent in by users of one or both volumes have motivated other changes. Examples of the latter are the addition of a section on the nature and use of history, the reordering of the sequence of units of Crete and Greece, and the addition of new maps.

v

There is neither point to, nor practicability in, listing exhaustive details of the range of suggestions; but reference should be made here to the citation, in the *Acknowledgments* section, of some critic-reviewers whose comments and suggestions have been especially helpful. The authors will be pardoned if they also express their understandable gratification to those respondents who plainly and sometimes very forcefully asserted that any wholesale tinkering with the text would almost certainly spoil it for them.

Naturally, major events and developments that have occurred since the appearance of the first edition are given attention in this one. To make room for such new material several units have been abridged.

But despite all the additions, changes, deletions, and other modifications, the book retains its original nature and purpose. It seeks now, as it did in the original edition, to present the basic characteristics of our heritage thematically and graphically.

JOHN L. STIPP
C. WARREN HOLLISTER
ALLEN W. DIRRIM

*April, 1972*

# Acknowledgments

We wish to express appreciation to a number of fellow historians who have carefully read portions of the manuscript and made many helpful suggestions. They are not, of course, to be held accountable for any errors of fact or interpretation, for which we bear sole responsibility.

Klaus Baer, University of California (Berkeley)
R. Davis Bitton, University of California (Santa Barbara)
William J. Bouwsma, University of California (Berkeley)
Gene A. Brucker, University of California (Berkeley)
Sidney A. Burrell, Boston University
Mortimer Chambers, University of California (Los Angeles)
Ann D. Kilmer, University of California (Berkeley)
Gordon Leff, University of Manchester
William G. Sinnigen, Hunter College

In preparing the present edition we have profited from wide-ranging comments sent in from many users of the text whose classroom experience with it give to their suggestions a special weight and influence. Of this group we should like to give particular credit to the following:

Robert P. Barnes, Central Washington State College
Miles W. Campbell, New Mexico State University
Samuel E. Dicks, Kansas State Teachers College
Walter S. Hanchett, State University of New York (Cortland)
Lee N. Layport, Jr., Santa Ana College, California
F. Darrell Munsell, West Texas State University
H. L. Oerter, Miami University (Ohio)
Terence P. O'Neill, Ventura College (California)
Wallace Sokolsky, Bronx Community College
Edith C. Tatnall, Metropolitan State College, Denver, Colorado
Warren L. Vinz, Boise State College, Idaho

We wish to express our deep appreciation for the helpful suggestions from Alfred Andrea at the University of Vermont.

We also wish to express our collective debt to Jere Donovan of *Time Magazine*, whose maps have made portions of this work instructive beyond the power of words. We are deeply obliged to our chief editor, Carl E. Beers, for his careful over-all supervision of this new edition. We further wish to express our appreciation to Arthur Vergara for his in-depth editing and to Marjorie Graham for her valuable help in the selection and arrangements of illustrations and maps. For his encouragement and guidance throughout the long period of gestation of the original edition, William L. Gum deserves our continuing appreciation. Each of us is under special obligation to particular individuals. We should like to express this obligation in the following separate statements.

Grateful acknowledgments are made to: Elizabeth B. Wilson for critically reading most of the material of the first six chapters of Part I and for making countless helpful suggestions; my wife, Cleo, not only for patient understanding throughout, but for skillful help in preparation of portions of the manuscript; Jo Ann Ooiman, typist extraordinary and, more importantly, perceptive critic; Mark Lawrence and other members of the Seymour Library staff for their inestimable assistance; and Mary Mangieri and Kathy Freise for their competent handling of seemingly endless typing chores.

J.L.S.

# Contents

# List of Maps

MAPS BY
J. DONOVAN

*xiii*

# The Rise and Development
## of Western Civilization

*Historians are not the only tellers of the story of man. Besides the scholar—and perhaps beyond him—there is the artist, working in many media, telling the story directly.*

*It would be impossible, in the compass of a few pages, to capture anything but a hint of man's artistic heritage. Still, the pictures that follow show man at his most revealing; for whereas in the arts he has also treated the objects of his love, hate, and worship, here man poses for himself. Thus the pictures that make up this study, which ranges over centuries, are humanity's changing—but always recognizable—self-portrait.*

RIGHT: *Christian prince subduing heretic. Carolingian ivory. Museo Nazionale del Bargello, 9th c.*
**EDITORIAL PHOTOCOLOR ARCHIVES**

BELOW: Bayeux Tapestry. *Detail showing Saxon foot soldiers confronting Norman cavalry. Town Hall, Bayeux, France, ca. 1075.*      SCALA

*Ambrogio Lorenzetti (1300?–1348):* Good Government. *Detail of fresco from the Palazzo Pubblico, Siena.* SCALA

Smead

Cy Chapitre contient le
cas ? ? la destruction de la cité de Jhe-
rusalem et du peuple des Juifs.
De l'oroison ou latin. Adhuc:
dum supplicatione et ?

Et qui estoy-
e pensif et cuma-
ge et par desdaing
coururoie con-
tre les hommes
gloutons. Je te
noye mon vi-
saige et ma pe-
see deuers la charoingne du glou-
ton empereur Aulus Victellus:

qui dedans les ondes du tybre flot-
toit plus ? plus la. Et ainsi com-
me ie tour noye ma pensee et mon
visaige contre la charoingne de Victellus ie vy si grant nombre de
maleureux qui par tourbeaulx
s'amouuient vers moy que ie ne
auoie pas que nature mere de tou-
tes choses en eut tant engendre:
Tous ces hommes acouru's
deuers moy disoient qu'ilz descen-
dirent iadis du noble et saint pa-
triarche iacob le pere du peuple:
d'israel. Ilz gemissoient tous ilz
estoient couuers de douloureuses

TOP: *Grape harvesting;* BOTTOM: *farmer plowing fields. Historiated initials from manuscript, 15th c.*

TOP: *Fruit and vegetable market;* BOTTOM: *tailor shop. Frescoes from Castello d'Issogne, Val d'Aosta, late 15th c.* EDITORIAL PHOTOCOLOR ARCHIVES

*Benozzo Gozzoli (1420–1498):* **Procession of the Magi.** *Detail showing Lorenzo the Magnificent, fresco from Palazzo Medici Riccardi, Florence.* SCALA

*Quentin Massys (1466?–1530):* Contract of Marriage. *São Paulo Museum of Art.*

*Emanuel de Witte (1617?–1692):* Interior of the Old Church at Amsterdam.
*Mauritshuis, The Hague.* SCALA

*Pieter de Hooch* (1629–1683): Interior of a Courtyard in Delft. *Mauritshuis, The Hague*                                                    SCALA

*Anonymous:* Bread and Fowl Market at the Quai des Augustins, Paris, around 1670. *Musée Carnavalet, Paris.* EDITORIAL PHOTOCOLOR ARCHIVES

*Jean Antoine Watteau (1684–1721): Flute Player. Galleria degli Uffizi, Florence.*

*Pietro Longhi (1702–1785):* The Hairdresser and the Lady. *Ca' Rezzonico, Venice.*

SCALA

*Sir Thomas Gainsborough (1727–1788): Mr. and Mrs. Andrews. The National Gallery, London.*

*William Hogarth (1697–1764):* The Shrimp Girl. *The National Gallery, London.*

*Lie-Louis Périn (1753–1817):* The Little Queen [Marie Antoinette]. *Musée Saint-Denis, Reims*

SCALA

*Francisco de Goya (1746–1828):* The Wounded Mason. *Museo del Prado, Madrid.* Joseph Martin/SCALA

# CHAPTER I

# The Renaissance: 1300—ca.1520

## A. The Meaning of Renaissance

### WHY WE USE THE WORD *RENAISSANCE*

"Renaissance" means rebirth. Its usage in the fourteenth and fifteenth centuries derives from Italian literary scholars who believed that the centuries following the Fall of Rome had been dominated by barbarians. By way of contrast, their own age marked a wonderful revival of classical learning and art. By 1435 Matteo Palmieri, a patriotic Florentine advocate of republican activism, was thanking God for having been "born in this new age, so full of hope and promise." This optimism rested not only on the recent attainments of the Italian city-states but also on a new way of looking at the past. Equating the urban civilization of antiquity with the civic revival of their own times, they provided later Western historians with the idea that a "medieval" period of darkness had followed the glories of the ancient world. Modern authors who have shared these Italians' disdain for the Middle Ages have extended the concept of rebirth to apply to almost all phases of human activity during this era. In 1860 the German-Swiss historian Jacob Burckhardt popularized this view in a famous book, *The Civilization of the Renaissance in Italy.* He believed that the Renaissance was a "golden age" of beauty and individualism, when esthetic considerations so dominated the minds of men that even making war or building a state became a work of art. "The Renaissance," his follower J. A. Symonds wrote, "was the liberation of the reason from a dungeon, the double discovery of the outer and the inner world."[1] Modern Protestant historians have extended this interpretation to include the claim that the Renaissance formulated a concept of elitist individualism that the Reformation, in making every man his own priest, subsequently democratized for the masses.

[1] Alfred Pearson, *A Short History of the Renaissance in Italy Taken from the Work of John Addington Symonds* (New York: Henry Holt & Co., 1894), p. 6.

1

Post-Reformation historians steeped in classical educations along lines first laid down by Renaissance scholars have also argued persistently that a new civilization —one no longer medieval, but recognizably modern—came into being during the fourteenth and fifteenth centuries. Their influence on historical writing has been so strong that even those who think that the modern world was not born so early usually use the term *Renaissance* in the same sense as a matter of convenience. But many historians reject it for northern Europe because they consider society there to have been essentially medieval until after the closing date for this chapter (ca. 1520).

## The Rebirth Disputed

Nineteenth-century romantics who idolized the Middle Ages, as well as a good number of medievalists who admire that epoch, have tried to deny that a rebirth actually occurred and to prove that earlier significant rebirths occurred during the Middle Ages. Especially as science and technology rather than classical education appears to have become the touchstone of modernity, historians have attempted to disprove Burckhardt's interpretation. On close examination, they say, the break with the Middle Ages was not so sharp as Renaissance Italians and the Burckhardtian school thought. In fact, to assert that a rebirth occurred is to assert a false view of history, for men now know

that one cannot break abruptly with the past. Medievalists have found a long train of predecessors for the alleged innovations of the Renaissance, and they have made their point: medieval ways and institutions had great staying power. For example, the aristocracy, which had dominated medieval institutions, proved resilient enough to overcome the challenge of the urban middle classes. But in order to prevail, the aristocracy had to adopt new ways and to rely on new, more authoritarian governments. Thus the Renaissance was an age of transition, and some of its changes anticipated more recent events.

In order to study that transition we shall examine in turn the changes that occurred in three important areas. First, we shall trace in some detail the major developments in learning and the arts—those parts of civilization that are the most pliable in men's hands, where changes are highly visible. It is only in this area that we can apply the concept of Renaissance without reservation. Scholars and artists self-consciously used classical models to express new attitudes toward learning, man, society, and nature. Second, we shall study the great secular institutions and activities, the Renaissance economies, societies, states, and politics. Changes in that area during the two centuries were gradual and, for the most part, slighter. Third, we shall examine the grave problems affecting the Church, for conditions leading to a religious explosion—the Reformation—were created during the Renaissance.

## B. Cultural and Artistic Developments

## LETTERS AND LEARNING

The revival of classical philosophy, law, and science had made substantial advances in the High Middle Ages; during the Renaissance, revival also spread to rhetoric, poetry, and especially to history. But whereas the medieval revival of classical studies had been undertaken by churchmen, the vastly broadened revival that took place during the Renaissance was mainly the work of laymen. In either case we call these scholars humanists because they were devoted to the humanities or liberal arts, especially the moral philosophy of the classics. Renaissance humanists propagated secular classical, moral, and esthetic standards as the code of an educated and social elite. The strongest lay influence, however, came not from humanists but from those officials of the territorial and dynastic states who were trained in law. Although their outlooks were not drastically different from earlier jurists trained in Roman law, their burgeoning numbers in positions of power enhanced their role in Renaissance society. It was these men who also censored the new printing press which, had it been free of political and religious controls, might have extensively democratized literary culture.

### Vernacular Literature and Literary Naturalism

The cultural unity of medieval Europe rested on the use of a common language of learning, administration, and liturgy: ecclesiastical Latin. As we have seen in Part I, Chapter XI, certain dialects, or vernaculars—usually the language of political administration and the royal court—achieved literary stature as competitors with Latin in the thirteenth and fourteenth centuries. In the Spanish kingdoms Castilian—a blend of Germanic, Latin, and some Moorish elements—gained ascendancy as the language of affairs. English, a composite of Anglo-Saxon and Norman French as spoken in Middlesex, was required in the courts of law and used in most official documents by the middle of the fourteenth century.

The most influential late medieval vernacular was Parisian French. Although local dialects vied with it, as the language of the French court it became the literary pacesetter and the language of much commerce as well. Later, Tuscan—the spoken Latin of the northern Italian peninsula and the language of the most advanced commercial areas of the Middle Ages—began to set literary standards. German was slower to crystallize, but after the middle of the fourteenth century High Saxon was used by most local princely courts. Except for a temporary period of Czech religious and political agitation during the late fourteenth and fifteenth centuries, the Slavic and Ural-Altaic languages of eastern Europe failed to achieve literary status until the nineteenth century.

Early vernacular literatures incorporated the themes and content of oral traditions: from the courts of the French nobility came heroic epics, troubadour songs, and lyric poetry; from the townsmen came anticlerical tales, called *fabliaux*, often touched with barnyard bawdiness; from them too came secularized church dramas, didactic devotional tracts, and stories of cunning such as *Reynard the Fox*. Learned vernacular writers sought to popularize in poetry the science and theology of the universities, while popular writers drew upon peasant, bourgeois, and noble themes. Stirred by an interest in classical literature, such men as Dante (1265–1321), Petrarch, and Boccaccio developed local tongues—in this case Tuscan—into highly influential mediums of expression.

In the previous chapter we saw Dante's use of the vernacular as the climax of medieval poetry.* Dante's life span and works are often seen as bridging the Middle Ages and the Renaissance. His greatest work, *The Divine Comedy*, was medieval in that it was a religious allegory in which natural science (and many Florentine businessmen) were relegated to the inferno. But he put Pope Boniface VIII there too. Dante also gave expression to the notion that feminine beauty and goodness could exercise a regenerative influence. It was an idealized woman, Beatrice, who led him into paradise. But Beatrice was a symbol of a virtue, of holy rather than carnal love, that kindled Dante's hope, faith, charity, and assurance of his own salvation.

Dante's claim to fame was advertised, and the Tuscan tongue further developed, by Francesco Petrarch (1304–74) and Giovanni Boccaccio (1313–75). Although both were humanists dedicated to classical learning, their principal literary impact

* See Part I, pp. 500–501.

came from Petrarch's poetry and Boccaccio's *Decameron*. In the person of Laura, Petrarch continued Dante's theme of feminine inspiration, and it is to her that his sonnets are dedicated, lyrics that became classic models imitated in Italy and the rest of Europe. The uneasiness that Petrarch felt in breaking with older, more ascetic norms was not shared by his friend Boccaccio. The Paris-born illegitimate son of a Florentine merchant, Boccaccio witnessed the horrors of the Black Death, which provides the *Decameron*'s setting. Seven fashionable young men and women from Florence pass their time in a secluded refuge relating tales that Boccaccio culled from popular lore. Satirical, witty, full of situations involving the artful defenses of virtue and the more frequent yieldings to temptation, Boccaccio's "Human Comedy" set down the realism, actual or touched up, of Florence. In common with other bourgeois writers of the time, he pilloried the Church and the clergy for their hypocrisy. In one tale the idea of the equal validity of Christianity, Judaism, and Muhammadanism is introduced. In another a Jew returning from a trip to Rome is converted to Christianity on the grounds that any institution so degenerate at its core could have survived so long only with divine assistance. Like other urban anticlerics Boccaccio made no formal break with the Church; in fact, he later regretted the *Decameron*'s tone, which nevertheless struck popular fancy by artfully handling subjects more often discussed than written. Boccaccio's naturalistic tone found echo throughout Europe in the writings of Chaucer, Rabelais, and many others.

Italian, like other modern vernaculars, developed under the tutelage of classical Latin. However, after Boccaccio Italian humanists directed almost all of their energies into the rarefied field of classical letters, style, and antiquities, disdaining the vulgar tongue of commoners. Until close to the end of the Renaissance only a few gifted individuals, not many of them humanists, continued to write in polished Italian prose and verse. Meanwhile, as Italian society became more aristocratic, Northern feudal themes found expression in popular literature. When Italian of any influence reappeared in the early sixteenth century, it was dominated by crusading adventures, Italianized versions of the French *Song of Roland* (for example Ariosto's *Orlando Furioso*), and manuals of the art of being a proper courtier.

Italian served as a model for subsequent Northern vernacular naturalism. In the Middle English of London and the court Geoffrey Chaucer (1340–1400) drew on a busy life of public affairs, French and Italian literary contacts, and late medieval lore to produce *The Canterbury Tales*. Chaucer set his tale-tellers on a pilgrimage in the course of which some of them related episodes equaling Boccaccio in anticlericalism and naturalism; others defended matrimony and honorable clerks (clerics). Chaucer initiated the first tradition of vernacular English realism, a tradition that culminated in Shakespeare in the sixteenth century.

French chronicles and poetry tended toward chivalric and generally medieval subject matter. But secular elements of love, anticlericalism, and even the debunking of crusades and fraudulent relics were represented. After the Hundred Years' War, François Villon (1431?–63) left both a great and a small *Testament* of the world of thieves and harlots, of sickness and want, of death, dungeons, and the expectation of execution. A century later such lower-class naturalism had yielded to the aristocratic erudition of court and polished letters, represented by Margaret of Navarre and François Rabelais (1494?–1553).

Margaret, sister of Francis I and patron of French humanism, imitated Boccaccio's *Decameron*, but her tone was more mystical and moralizing. French vernacular literature reached its maturity in Rabelais, as much a child of humanism as of popular naturalism. German vernacular was represented by Sebastian Brant (1458–1521), who satirized social foibles in the *Ship of Fools*. He also pioneered the use of popular tracts which flooded Germany during the early Reformation. In Spain, where governments had first used a written version of the spoken language for administrative records, the emergence of a distinctly modern literary masterpiece was delayed until the early seventeenth century, when Cervantes's *Don Quixote* appeared.

The evolution of different local spoken languages into written literary vehicles increased the diversification of cultures. Political boundaries tended to become linguistic frontiers, while patriotic impulses helped shape the development of local language patterns. As rivals to ecclesiastical Latin—to which must be added the revival of classical Latin—vernacular languages threatened the hold of the Church on culture. And since the themes of works in these tongues were frequently naturalistic, they similarly threatened the standards of ideal and absolute values that the Church historically represented.

## The Decline of Scholastic Universalism

The breakdown of medieval linguistic universalism also had parallels in academic thought. Thirteenth-century schoolmen headed by Thomas Aquinas had met the challenge of Aristotelian philosophy and science—much of it handed on to Europeans by the Arabs—by subordinating its natural reason to Christian revelation and the divine authority of the Church. Nevertheless Aquinas considered Aristotle to be "the philosopher" because he came so close to perfection in his use of

*Theology lecture at the Sorbonne in Paris of the kind that repulsed humanists.*

natural reason. The Thomists—Aquinas's followers—believed that ultimate reality consisted of universal concepts grasped by both reason and revelation; provided that proper premises—universals—were used, they could deduce from these the nature of particular things by means of logical syllogisms. As we saw in the preceding chapter, this method undergirded the Church's claims to universal obedience and the medieval idea of a single commonwealth of Christendom, but during the Renaissance both theory and practice were attacked by nominalist philosophers, Augustinian theologians, and empirical scientists.

Scholars working in the tradition of St. Augustine held that only knowledge of divine things secured in the pursuit of salvation constituted real wisdom; they never accepted Aquinas's "Aristotelianized" Christianity. In the universities, particularly among Franciscan

teachers, *nominalist* scholastics followed the Augustinian tradition. They attacked Thomist universals as mere names (*nomina*) and found ultimate reality only in individual things. The most forceful fourteenth-century nominalist was William of Ockham. Like Augustine he denied that reason could either penetrate divine mysteries or demonstrate the dogmas of the Church. Reason, for example, could not uphold the doctrine of the Trinity, since reason required that there be either one or three gods. For Ockham the Trinity was a divine mystery; logic could not explain it. It had to be accepted on the basis of revelation, faith, and authority. Moreover, the sovereign will of God was not circumscribed by reason; God could save the wicked and damn the virtuous as he chose.

In theology, nominalists encouraged non-rational faith, mysticism, and unquestioned obedience to authority. But for the study of nature they advocated direct observation or experiment rather than deduction from given universal principles. At fourteenth-century Oxford and Paris this empirical approach to nature led to a rethinking of Aristotle's physics. Although the nominalists hardly dared deny that the universe was directed by spirits they nevertheless found Aristotle's explanation of motion untenable. Deficiencies and inadequacies in instruments, mathematics, and conceptual tools probably accounted for their failure to achieve a scientific revolution. But their conclusions were carried to Italy, where the soil for scientific advances proved to be more fertile; there the universities were not dominated by theology, nor had scholastic theology taken deep root. In addition, Archimedes' methods had been rediscovered, and manuscripts edited by humanists demonstrated that not all of the ancients had agreed with the Aristotelians. Professors at the Venetian university of Padua studied Aristotle without the theological trappings of supernatural causation that Thomists had added to his philosophy; they sought only natural causes for natural phenomena. Leonardo da Vinci—the foremost empirical scientist of the Italian Renaissance—and, later, Copernicus and Galileo were in intimate contact with this scientific tradition. Aided by significant advances in mathematics during the Renaissance the tradition bore fruit in the scientific revolution of the seventeenth century.

Italian natural scientists agreed with the nominalists that current religious doctrines could not be demonstrated empirically; hence they often agreed with the nominalists and Augustinians that reason was not a proper tool for theology. The nominalists, however, did not persist in their quest for an empirical science of nature; they abandoned it for a theology based on faith and revelation, engaging in complicated disputes with the Thomists

and each other at stratospheric levels of abstraction. This, too, weakened the hold of scholastic universalism.*

## Italian Humanism

Theological wrangling generated robust skepticism concerning the meaningfulness of all scholastic hairsplitting. This was especially true for laymen of the Italian city-states who came to find a better treatment of their personal problems in classical Roman and Greek texts than by academic philosophers and theologians. Urban rather than feudal, practical rather than metaphysical, Italian society first supported a corps of scholars devoted to the revival of ancient, pagan moral philosophy produced by similar societies of antiquity. Thus the range of its interests far exceeded the Christian humanism of the High Middle Ages.

Consistent with the belief that their age marked a new departure from the medieval past, the Italian humanists heralded a "revival of learning" held up in conscious opposition to scholasticism. Classical humanism rapidly became a movement whose contagiousness grew among the many educated laymen hungering for a secular, practical ethic. For them, neither the medieval monastic ideal nor the timeless, abstract philosophical doctrines of the scholastics seemed livable. Medieval scholars had also used the classics widely, but they had subordinated them to theology and scholastic philosophy or else had borrowed legal and scientific data from them as final, authoritative statements. Humanists whose manuscript discoveries

* But it should not be assumed that scholastic universalism was dead; rather, it continued to coexist with humanism in the universities. Revived during the religious controversies of the 1500s and disseminated more widely than ever by the new printing presses, it continued to thrive at least until the eighteenth century.

immensely expanded the body of available classical writings approached them with a different intent and purpose. The "revival of learning" was thus not so much the discovery of a new set of authorities as a different appreciation of the meaning and usage of pagan antiquity.

Generally recognized as the first to give classical studies a new turn was Petrarch (Petrarca), a notary living in the Florentine colony at papal Avignon. As a youth he broke from legal studies to take up the classics, and as an adult he spurned the "crazy and clamorous set of scholastics." In classical literature, especially in Cicero's writings, he found his model of literary style and moral philosophy. Noting that Cicero had been an active statesman forced against his will to become a reclusive Stoic philosopher, Petrarch turned his attention to "civic humanism." Here he made a lasting contribution to the moral philosophy of involvement in political affairs, for Cicero taught that the primary task of man is action in, and service to, the community. Henceforth Cicero became the object of the kind of enthusiasm previously directed toward Aristotle; but Petrarch was not himself a political activist. His enthusiasm for the ancients encouraged him to hunt down manuscripts for his library, to woo fame by writing a long Latin epic poem in imitation of Virgil, and to urge the recovery of Greek language and literature. His *Familiar Letters* and *Lives of Illustrious Men* displayed a new depth of classical scholarship and a preoccupation with historic personalities whose lives might serve as models for living in civic society.

Since Petrarch conceived of religion as moral philosophy rather than knowledge of doctrine, he saw no conflict between Cicero and Christ. But the quest for fame and the exaltation of ideal womanhood in his vernacular sonnets brought him into conscious conflict with traditional ascetic ideals. He set down the tensions gen-erated by this conflict in his *Soul's Secret*, an imaginary exchange of letters with St. Augustine, who himself had abandoned classical wisdom for doctrinal and institutional Christianity. Petrarch agreed with the great otherworldly theologian on many points but insisted on living in one world at a time. "There is a certain justification of my way of life," he writes to Augustine.

"It may be only glory that we seek here, but I persuade myself that so long as we remain here, that is right. Another glory awaits us in heaven and he who reaches there will not wish even to think of earthly fame. So this is the natural order, that among mortals the care of things mortal should come first; to the transitory will then succeed the eternal; from the first to the second is the natural progression."[2]

Although Petrarch affirmed the value of contemplation, he praised civic activity more than anyone since Roman times. His successors, inflamed by his enthusiasm for classical studies, lent increasing emphasis to Augustine's "earthly city" as against his "heavenly" one.

It was Boccaccio who transmitted Cicero's civic humanism and standards of style to Florence, where they found their fullest development between 1375 and 1450. After Boccaccio's death, in 1375, prominent Florentines formed study groups to reexamine the classics. They collected libraries and manuscripts and, beginning with Coluccio Salutati (1331–1406), installed a succession of distinguished humanist chancellors. The development of republican Florentine humanism coincided with the victory of the woolen guild masters over the lower classes in 1382. It reached a peak shortly thereafter as Florence defended itself

[2] Quoted by James Harvey Robinson and Henry Winchester Rolfe, *Petrarch. The First Modern Scholar and Man of Letters* (New York: G. P. Putnam's Sons, 1914), p. 452.

against Milan, seat of an aggressive despotism. Rather surprisingly this venture of Florence into civic humanism did not particularly encourage businessmen or lower-class elements to exploit it in order to gain a higher place in society. Instead it served as a rationale for the Florentine elite to use their talents and leisure for the advancement of the commonweal of the republic. For the most part their ideals were culled from the study of classical history and moral philosophy. Preeminent among them was the development of the well-rounded man of universal accomplishments, strength of character in adversity, possession of fortune or luck's favor, and the ability to wield power.

Florentine civic humanism became most secular and utilitarian at the hands of Leonardo Bruni (1370–1444), a biographer of Cicero. As chancellor he promoted educational practices designed to create citizens rather than scholars. For patriotic purposes he wrote a legend-purged history of the city that looked for human political and economic causes for events of the past. However worthy such efforts were, civic humanists could flourish only in a republic; thus when Florence became a Medicean principality the institutional support for their ideology withered. Sixteenth-century Venice, whose leading families belatedly adopted humanism, preserved some aspects of its outlook. For the most part civic humanism was a transient phenomenon of the Renaissance confined to one city, Florence, and even there it lasted less than a century. Moreover in many parts of Italy classical humanists supported despots whose conquest of all Italy would presumably put an end to the peninsula's constant wars.

While activist republican humanism was running its course classical scholarship matured in method and achievement to the point where it became a potentially explosive cultural and intellectual force. Boccaccio contributed to a deeper knowledge by compiling biographies of famous men and women, a genealogy of the gods, and a classical geography. With all the enthusiasm of prospectors caught up in the fervor of a gold rush, traveling scholars combed monastic libraries and Eastern cities for manuscripts of classical Latin and Greek authors. Their energies were devoted variously to inscriptions, archaeology, architecture, and coinage. Visiting Eastern Orthodox church dignitaries taught Italians Greek philosophy, especially Platonic philosophy.* In addition to learning Latin and Greek in their ancient styles, humanist scholars, the better to cope with deviating texts and copyists' errors, developed historical philology and a respect for original sources. Unlike the scholastics, who used multiple allegorical meanings for passages picked out of historical context, they learned to rely upon a single literal, historical meaning within a specific context.

Enamored of the clarity and forcefulness of ancient expression as compared with contemporary "barbarous" Latin, the humanists became zealous advocates of pure classical style. But the implications of their method and knowledge reached much deeper than the mere training of stylists. The career of Lorenzo Valla (1405–57) illustrates this. As a young teacher, rhetorician, and philologist, he was employed in 1433 by King Alfonso of Naples who, like many other princes, was an enemy of the pope. Before he had long been at his job Valla conclusively demonstrated from internal evidence that the Donation of Constantine, a purported cession of central Italy to the papacy in the fourth century was in fact a fabrication of the ninth century. Retained thereafter by the hu-

---

* They also taught some northern Italian humanists the Greek language, but in southern Italy and Sicily a Greek-speaking populace had preserved a knowledge of that language throughout the Middle Ages. Thus the humanists' study of Greek was not entirely new.

manist pope Nicholas V as his secretary, Valla followed this exposé (which others had anticipated) with a demonstration that the Apostles' Creed originated in Nicene rather than apostolic times and that other popular authorities were similarly antedated or fraudulent. Having access to Vatican codices, he also treated the Bible as a historical document and called attention to numerous errors in the Latin Vulgate edition of the New Testament.

Valla's method of going to the sources undercut much traditional authority, and it epitomized the birth of a new sense of historical consciousness among the humanists. No longer were the ancients treated as timeless oracles. Rather, the humanists were aware of the span of time that separated them from the ancients. It was precisely that historical perspective which enabled them to enter into the thoughts of the ancients as living men trying to solve real human problems in the context of their own times. This new sense of historical perspective and the use of evidence introduced the novel idea of *anachronism,* something utterly foreign to most previous thought which had dealt with timeless universals and authority. To the idea of going back to pure sources was linked that of returning to a period of ecclesiastical or ethical purity as a standard or model. Long the practice of religious reformers, this primitivism soon became a revolutionary tactic of the Protestant Reformation. Historical consciousness was a real revolution of the Renaissance, but because its implications were too sensitive for so many cherished beliefs, it was centuries before they were followed up thoroughly. As a result numerous humanists and historians, instead of pursuing the new principles to their logical conclusions, put themselves to the composition of idylls and the depiction of Arcadias, or ideal country life, utterly detached from contemporaneous reality.

In addition to the employment of a revolutionary method, Italian humanists differed from traditional theologians and scholastics in posing a different set of significant questions. Most of them totally ignored metaphysics, formal theology, and preoccupation with death. Instead they were concerned with practical questions of human relationships. Language (rhetoric) was basic because it was the means of social communication, of moving and directing human will and actions. Because they ignored theology the humanists found no conflict between ancient pagan philosophers and Christianity. Although they taught rational restraint, they considered nature good and worthy of enjoyment and artistic imitation. Religion was seen to be a part of nature, therefore while all but a few denounced monasticism or monastic vows, rarely did the humanists break formally with the Church. They found divinity less in sacrament and priest than in wordly and classical beauty. To most Northern humanists as well as to later religious reformers, whether Catholic or Protestant, the esthetic, political, and social morality of the Italian humanists appeared pagan.

Whatever evaluation is made, the Italian humanists formulated a lay ethic rivaling the monastic ideal—which, it should be remembered, the Church never intended to apply to society as a whole. Moreover, the Renaissance papacy and hierarchy tended increasingly to accept classical humanism's standard of values. To the extent that they did, the Church's authority was undermined for all those who believed in the preeminence of doctrine and traditional ideals. Wherever doctrinal religion recovered ascendancy, classical studies were again subordinated to the role that they had played in the Middle Ages.

Italian humanists made their greatest impact as educators. If they were mistrustful of logic and abstract philosophy, they were downright scornful of law and science.* For these disciplines they substituted rhetoric, grammar, poetry, history, and purified classical languages. Mathematics, physical education, and music also received attention. The emphasis on classical languages and perfected style tended to make humanist scholarship a cult with high admission requirements, particularly as these scholars began to look down on vernacular languages. As late as the nineteenth—even the twentieth—century, classical education was a mark of achievement and status in Western countries.

Obviously not all products of humanist schools became scholars. The fact that humanism became a movement of general social importance is probably best explained by the availability of positions open to men trained in style and rhetorical persuasion. Most young men with classical educations found employment with states, prelates, or private patrons. Many were employed as the equivalent of modern press agents to present their employers' cases persuasively. As historians they frequently wrote commissioned and biased accounts, gracing their patrons' heroic deeds with impossible classical perorations.

The nature of patronage and of educational opportunities helped shape the course of late Italian humanism. The Church, the princes, and the aristocracy were the principal patrons. As republics declined, civic humanism waned or adjusted to courtly surroundings. In Florence Cosimo de' Medici founded a formal school of philosophy—the Platonic Academy—headed successively by Marsilio Ficino and Pico della Mirandola. Although

both championed free will and the dignity of man, both also exalted the contemplative life above the active. Rising despotism and a feeling of helplessness in the face of foreign invasion after 1494 made faith in man's ability to use institutions for human improvement difficult to sustain.

In Florence the powerful popular preacher Savonarola (1452–98) tried to turn back the tide with a blend of civic democracy and Christian fundamentalism. Gaining a following among the Florentines when his prophecies of repeated disasters seemed to be fulfilled, he became the leading figure behind an attempt to restore Florentine republicanism when the Medici were driven out by an invading army in 1494. For four years his sermons steered the Florentine republic, whose citizens were moved to burn their immoral books and works of art. His puritanism and his attacks on Pope Alexander VI made him many enemies, however; in 1497 he was excommunicated by the pope, and in the following year the Florentine government executed him. After a short interlude, the Medici regained control over the city. Temporary as it was, Savonarola's career demonstrated how slight a hold the humanists had on Florence.* Witch-hunts during the fifteenth century exposed the same weakness. This humanistic elitism, with its requirements of wealth, leisure, and political participation in an oligarchic society, had confined the values of humanism to a narrow cult.

As defeated Florentine republicans became disillusioned cynics, the typical ideal that emerged from the Italian Renaissance was that of the refined, well-rounded courtier, witty in repartee, appreciative of feminine beauty, and adept

* Nevertheless they contributed heavily to the development of both science and law. Their emphasis on mathematics in the schools and their recovery of classical texts from antiquity aided the scientific revolution that culminated in the seventeenth century. Some of them—notably Valla—turned their critical philology to the historical understanding of legal texts with eventually revolutionary effects.

* The conversion of no less a humanist than Mirandola testifies to the persuasive power of this reformer, by whose message Michelangelo was also deeply affected.

*Savonarola preaching, 1496.*

at arms. Count Baldassare Castiglione (1478–1529), a product of the polished courts and diplomatic service of Milan, Mantua, and Urbino, gave definitive and much-imitated expression to the new courtly ideal of the secular, classically educated chivalric gentleman in *The Courtier*. Translated into northern tongues, his work more than any other of the Renaissance provided a ready definition of the all-accomplished gentleman, the universal man of polite courtly society that characterized the ideals of Europe's educated aristocracy in the following century.

## Northern Humanism

By the end of the Renaissance the more aristocratic and religiously oriented parts of Europe outside Italy were receptive to the force of the contemplative, religious, and chivalric humanism that the Italians had evolved. But Northern humanism did not become a mere copy of Italian models

—local traditions and the vagaries of individual humanists filtered and modified their impact; therefore Northern humanism had many different facets. In general it was less esthetic than Italian humanism; in particular, philology and the content of the classics were more subordinated to religion and metaphysics. Northern humanists were also less antagonistic toward scholasticism and the study and practice of Roman law.

In Spain tradition blunted the impact of secular humanism. There, philological and linguistic studies, which spread rapidly during the reign of Ferdinand and Isabella, were strictly subordinated to theology. This diluted brand of humanism culminated in the career of Cardinal Ximénes, Queen Isabella's confessor, head of the Spanish Inquisition, and regent on Ferdinand's death.* Ximénes was responsible for the founding and reform of several universities, notably Alcalá. The fa-

* See p. 47.

culties of these schools devoted a third of their instructional time to language and literature as auxiliaries to theology. Ximénes's crowning philological achievement was a Polyglot Bible. To facilitate textual comparison the Scriptures were presented in different early languages set up in parallel columns. Other Spanish humanists such as Juan Luis Vives (1492–1540) proved more receptive to the advanced doctrines of Eramus of Rotterdam. But under pressure of the Inquisition to conform to scholastic tradition, they either emigrated or were silenced. As political master of Italy during the Catholic Reformation, Spain also served to stifle Italian humanism.

Ultimately France, the hearth of medieval scholasticism, responded more creatively to Italian humanism, especially after the French invasion of Italy in 1494. The royal court of Francis I and especially of his sister, Magaret of Navarre, patronized the "new learning." Most of its early devotees sought a fusion of traditionalism, religious mysticism, and classical forms. Prominent among them were Lefèbvre d'Étaples; Guillaume Briçonnet, bishop of Meaux; and Guillaume Budé, all of whom flourished around the turn of the sixteenth century. They spurned secularism and devoted their energies to religion based on the classics and Scripture. In particular they deemphasized the sacraments and exalted conduct as the essence of Christianity. In phrases such as "salvation by faith alone," they seemed to anticipate a Protestant theme. In fact, their fundamental assumptions concerning human dignity and free will were quite different from the Augustinian premises of the depravity and bondage of the will held by Luther and Calvin.

Alongside this strain of French thought ran the secular naturalism of Francois Rabelais, physician and humanist who relished emancipation from the "thick Gothic night" of the Middle Ages. His *Gargantua and Pantagruel* pilloried scholasticism and proposed an ideal coeducational "monastic" system in which universal learning and disciplined willpower would set all the rules. Stoicism, which identified virtue with happiness and wisdom with prudence, was also widespread in French humanist circles.

German humanism had roots in a variety of institutions: the imperial court of the fifteenth century, the schools of the Brethren of the Common Life, and the elite families of the imperial cities. Colored by romantic cultural nationalism, this humanism refuted the Italian charge that Northern barbarians had ruined classical culture during the Middle Ages. Some German humanists upheld scholasticism and were trained in civil or canon law or both; most were primarily interested in religious reform. Although they usually conceived religion more as deeds than creeds, they rejected the "paganism" of the Italian Renaissance. The most accomplished German humanist was Johann Reuchlin (1455–1522), a jurist and professor who mastered not only Greek and Latin but also Hebrew literature. Influenced by Hebraic studies, especially the esoteric mystical interpretations of scriptures known as the *Kabbalah*, Reuchlin's works touched off a celebrated controversy with anti-Semitic traditionalists who indicted him (unsuccessfully) before the Inquisition. In his defense a small group of radical humanists under the leadership of Ulrich von Hutten* satirized the ignorance, credulity, and petty doctrinal preoccupations of Reuchlin's monkish opponents in the *Letters of Obscure Men,* two series of which appeared in 1515 and 1517. The Reuchlin affair was soon overshadowed by the creedal conflicts of the Reformation that fractured German humanism.

England also developed a strain of re-

* See pp. 83–84.

ligious humanism that drew inspiration from the late Italian Renaissance. John Colet returned from Italy to lecture after 1496 on the Scriptures, particularly the letters of St. Paul. Of greater fame was another English townsman, Thomas More (1478–1535), a lawyer and classically educated layman who served Henry VIII. An ascetic more devoted to redemptive religion than to the classics, More published a mocking satire on contemporary England, *Utopia*, which showed that non-Christian people could create a near-perfect society. In this and other writings, More advocated partial tolerance, a warm sympathy for the lower classes, and a concept of limited government. As an official, he did not always act in conformity to his theoretical views. Caught up by the religious controversies of the Reformation, he became an anti-Protestant polemicist. Ultimately he had to choose between loyalty to Henry VIII as head of the English church and loyalty to the Roman church. Preferring the latter, he became a martyr and was canonized in the twentieth century.

## Erasmus

Far overshadowing the reputations and influence of all other contemporary Northern and Italian humanists, with most of whom he kept in some contact, was the cosmopolitan "prince of the humanists," Erasmus of Rotterdam (1467?–1536).

An orphaned illegitimate son of a priest educated at the Deventer school of the Brethren of the Common Life, Erasmus was sent by guardians to a monastery. Thereafter he became an episcopal secretary, a student of theology at the University of Paris, and a nomadic scholar. Attracted early by the classics and the works of Lorenzo Valla, he rejected contemporary scholasticism (but not Thomas

Aquinas) and—with a papal dispensation—spent the remainder of his life outside cloister walls. A visit to England in 1500 yielded contacts that produced uninterrupted patronage as well as the friendship of Thomas More and John Colet, who encouraged him to follow a career of religious scholarship. When he returned to the continent he began a prolific publishing career, editing the early Church Fathers, beginning with St. Jerome, and a Greek edition of the New Testament. Textbook selections from the classics for purposes of style and reference, works of satirical criticism, personal letters, and paraphrases from the New Testament followed and attained wide popularity. They mostly dealt with literary history and a specific educational reform program and had very little to do with scholastic theology and philosophy.

Among Erasmus's publications were the *Adages,* a selection of classical quotations, and the *Colloquies,* a reader much used in schools. From inspired pagans who were thought to have anticipated Christianity he sought to gain knowledge of all that was known of the arts of war and peace, poetry, writing, speech, and science. "Good letters"—training in classical literature and moral philosophy—were essential to virtue, for love without knowledge he held to be blind. For Erasmus classical scholarship could never be an end in itself. Although he constantly revised his immense personal correspondence in order to achieve literary excellence, he chided "Ciceronian" stylistic purists and decried Italian "paganism." Indeed, he subordinated classical scholarship to a broad educational and religious reformation that was to be rooted in the New Testament and the early Fathers of the Church.

Although Erasmus wrote on theological subjects, he deemphasized ritual, doctrines, and external observances in favor of a Christian ethic defined by the letters

Erasmus *by Hans Holbein the Younger.*

of Paul and the Sermon on the Mount, which he described as "the philosophy of Christ." He worked to reform Christianity so that it might rest on texts, institutions, and practices purged of corruption. His "social gospel" involved a drastic social transformation, but his method was marked by gradualism and nonviolent education rather than by force. His publication of critical editions of the Greek New Testament was intended as the basis for vernacular translations that he hoped would eventually be read and sung by the simplest laymen, male and female alike. Most of his publishing efforts were devoted to the printing of the early Church Fathers' writings, which appealed to him not only because they represented primitive uncorrupted Christianity but also because they differed sharply from one another on doctrines that had become hardened orthodoxy in the medieval Church. Toward controverted or unverified dogmas, Erasmus was tolerantly skeptical; for the purposes of his classical moral Christianity, they were beside the point. In his first edition of the Greek New Testament, for example, he omitted, on literary and historical grounds, the proof text for the Trinity. He was supported by Pope Leo X, but he nevertheless lived in fear that an aggressive, intolerant doctrinal resurgence by "the monks" would turn to force and destroy his reform by education.

Founder of neither a church nor a state to perpetuate and circulate his writings, Erasmus became known to posterity primarily as a satirical critic who tried to take an independent course through the confessional wrangles of the early Reformation. Best known of his writings has been *The Praise of Folly,* a tract in which Folly, a laconic woman, twits the foibles of society, clergy, businessmen, and—so alive and honest was Erasmus's sense of humor—even scholars. More devastating was *Julius Excluded from Heaven,* an anonymous tract.* In it he depicts Julius II, the "warrior pope," boasting to St. Peter of his manipulation of Church councils and threatening to take heaven's gates by military storm if refused admission. In other writings Erasmus associated war with savagery and held that it should be prevented among Christians by arbitration between judicious princes—a rare lot, he said, for princes, like fools, needed only to be born! His satirical criticism extended to relics, indulgences, domination of clerical posts by nobles, pilgrimages, invocation of saints, and sundry other aspects of external popular piety then current. His satire and his pacific humor were intolerable to both doctrinal Protestants and traditionalist Catholics; for Erasmus they were a means of laughing his opponents out of

court, much preferable to reliance on force. The latter course he accurately predicted would lead to generations of religious warfare rather than to peace and unity under reformed institutions.

Always writing in Latin (with the exception of the Greek New Testament, to which was joined a fresh Latin translation), Erasmus believed in a cosmopolitan aristocracy of talent that should practice and develop a social as well as an individual moral gospel. To others he left the task of translating and implementing his humanistic reform program; however, after 1517 its fate became inextricably bound up with the confessional conflicts of the Reformation, a consequence that we shall consider in the following chapter.

## Jurists and Political Theorists

Humanists have usually been considered the truest representatives of the Renaissance, but in their own day jurists and officials commanded more prestige. During the late Renaissance four concepts of the state were formulated: the Roman law—or absolutist—conception; the divine-right theory; the humanistic idealism of Erasmus; and the political realism of Machiavelli and Guicciardini.

The study of Roman law as preparation for service in governments and the Church was the surest path to power, fortune, and prestige. As secular governments curbed the jurisdiction of ecclesiastical canon law, Roman civil lawyers gained preeminent influence. For example, their foremost Renaissance teacher, Andrea Alciati (1492–1550) of Pavia, was renowned throughout western Europe.

Roman law in its late absolutist, or Justinian, form* was revived ca. 1100, when Irnerius of Bologna began teaching the subject to mature students. Townsmen

---

* Erasmus may not have written this, but contemporaries attributed it to him, and with good cause.

* See Part I, pp. 510–11.

found congenial its recognition of, and legal support for, absolute property rights (as distinct from feudal tenure and manorial rights of use) as well as contractual obligations basic to a commercial, capitalistic society. Other parts of the law were used by kings as a rationale for centralizing power in the hands of state officials rather than delegating it to feudal tenants.* In late imperial Rome the will of the prince (or council) had become law. Now in the late Renaissance, growing authoritarianism gave rise to comparable law, important for effecting the transition from decentralized feudalism to the centralized, absolute state of the late Renaissance. As oligarchies tightened and monarchs undermined the nobles' political power, existing authorities laid exclusive claim to the secret "mysteries of state."

Clergymen reinforced and extended Roman law absolutism with the doctrine of the divine right of kings: kings were accountable to God alone; resistance to them was a cardinal sin. As the pope had been exalted by many canonists, especially in the thirteenth and fourteenth centuries, divine-right princes were now exalted above the law and representative assemblies. Their courts, councils, and officials combined legislative, executive, and judicial functions; still, in practice, they shared authority with the Church. By the beginning of the sixteenth century, all wielders of power—magisterial, ecclesiastical, patrimonial—constituted a separate "estate," a privileged status group within the traditional social hierarchy. The members of this estate were too numerous and often too obscure to warrant mention by name here.

Quite different from the viewpoints of Roman lawyers and theological theorists of divine-right monarchy were those of the Erasmian humanists. For Thomas More and Erasmus, the ruler was neither

* Often, however, royal officials exploited these powers to benefit themselves rather than the ruler.

possessor of the kingdom nor above the law. Rather he was a steward subject to deposition by "freemen"—that is, by the aristocracy. In his *Institution of a Christian Prince* Erasmus subsumed politics under ethics as defined by the New Testament. The prince's first duty was to care for the commonweal of his subjects. He ought to tax the luxuries rather than the necessities of life and to promote peace, education, and the practical arts. In matters of taxation and peace Erasmus was advocating nothing less than a complete reversal of political trends then current. Although he wrote guides for existing rulers, his critiques of princes frankly implied republicanism.

The humanist concept of government existing for the commonweal was very widespread on the eve of the Reformation; but religious controversies restored the notion that Christian magistrates must secure the salvation of souls by enforcing doctrinal purity. Its enforcement need not, however, coincide with the mundane general welfare. Erasmian influences remained strongest in republican towns, the Low Countries, and in England. Although critics have tended to dismiss Erasmus's thought as an impracticable return to medieval political theory, more recently he has assumed the position of an intellectual godfather to the European Economic Community and to other attempts to secure international peace and cooperation.

The most significant approach to politics during the Renaissance was the realism of Machiavelli and Guicciardini. Niccolò Machiavelli (1469–1527) became one of the most celebrated political theorists of all history. Born into a prominent Florentine family and given a gentleman's education (which included the Roman classics), he entered public service in 1498 while Florence's rulers, the Medici, were in exile. After serving as secretary of the secret committee for military affairs, in the chancery, and on the highest council, he was sent as a diplomatic agent to France,

Germany, Switzerland, and various parts of Italy. His letters show that he was particularly impressed with Ferdinand of Spain, Cesare Borgia, Julius II, and the armed citizenry of the Swiss Confederation. When the Medici returned in 1512, he was recruiting peasant subjects for a citizens' army with which to recover rebellious Pisa.

This experience served him well, but it was his literary gifts, not his reputation as an administrator, that made Machiavelli famous. Politically suspect to the restored Medici, he spent the remainder of his life writing political commentaries, history, satirical drama, and even a piece of devotional literature. Apart from his *Art of War*, which advocated the restoration of a citizens' army, his most significant political works were *The Discourses on the First Ten Books of Titus Livy* and *The Prince*. His writing reflected secular humanism, but he included topics that most humanists omitted: conspiracies, assassinations, and the calculated use of terror. His announced intention was to create a science of statecraft based on classical learning. He tried to do for politics what others did for art, medicine, and jurisprudence: to clarify and codify the principles that antiquity, especially Rome, had followed. With instructive examples and maxims drawn from the repetitiveness of history——a record forever marked by the depravity of man—perhaps men could foresee events and prevent future errors. Many critics consider him the first empiricist in modern political science, although one not without his doctrinaire prejudices.

Machiavelli followed civic humanists in rejecting religious justification for the state. He conceived the state as having its own rules apart from social or individual morality and from divine or natural law. In a wicked world, moral rulers failed. Statebuilding required force, fraud, and deceit to advance security of the state; in both foreign and domestic policies

*Niccolo Machiavelli.*

"reason of state"—concern exclusively for the security of the state—should determine political action. Machiavelli's state is not irreligious, however. Princes and heads of republics should uphold religion, keep their people pious, and esteem miracles as the means of increasing their own authority and keeping the state well ordered and united. But ultimate human values should be concerned with the preservation and growth of the state. "I love my native city more than my own soul," wrote Machiavelli, thus chastizing the Church for making men soft, indolent, and unfit for battle. In common with most officials and diplomats of the time, he advocated state supremacy over the Church.

In Machiavelli's age, society was rigidly stratified and gentle birth highly honored, but he was an antiaristocratic advocate of a popular regime. In his scheme of things the heroic virtues would supplant gentility, for at all times force was decisive in human affairs. For extraordinary crises he advocated despotic tyranny. In *The Prince* we find the ideal nature of his autocrat: he is both feared and loved—but mostly feared. By concentrating cruelties in short periods and extending well-advertised liberality over longer times he maintains an aura of goodness. He kills opponents rather than confiscates their property, for heirs are grateful for the inheritance and not permanently alienated as dispossessed persons. He keeps the faith—when it serves his interest to do so.

*The Prince* lends itself to varying interpretations. In the seventeenth century men of such diverse political philosophies as the French monarchist Richelieu and the English Radical Republican Whig James Harrington found it congenial to their positions. The work is sometimes taken for Machiavelli's attempt to gain the favor of the Medici, sometimes for a sincere exposition of realistic politics. A few scholars have seen it as tongue-in-cheek satire. They argue that Machiavelli's republican contemporaries could not have sanctioned the despotic prince. Yet many Italian classical republicans did indeed approve of temporary tyrannies under unusual circumstances. Whatever its author may have intended, *The Prince* offered a rationale for power politics in a world of competing states. Often, however, Machiavelli was condemned as immoral by statesmen and clergy who nevertheless subordinated religion to secular rule and who approved Machiavellian tactics when these advanced their own religious viewpoint.

Equally pessimistic and cynical about human nature and the violent basis of all state power was Machiavelli's contemporary, Francesco Guicciardini (1483–1540), Florentine diplomat, professor of law, and civil servant. A partisan of the aristocratic Medicean clique, he was ousted when Florence fell to Spain in 1527. Spurning Machiavelli's classical maxims and precedents as unrealistic romanticism, Guicciardini nevertheless agreed that opportunism based on expediency was the most rational and desirable policy for the efficient state. When Italy collapsed before Northern conquerors, he advised each individual to enrich himself as best he could (whereas Machiavelli had held that seeking after wealth was evil). In retirement he penned histories of Florence and Italy that bristled with unmerciful psychological analyses of individuals and societies, writings that are more deserving of the label "scientific" than Machiavelli's writing. But until his unpublished history of Florence was brought to light in the nineteenth century, Guicciardini's influence was slight.

## The Impact of Printing with Movable Type

All types of Renaissance letters and learning were profoundly affected by the major technological innovation of the era, the invention of the printing press. Heretofore all forms of thought and expression had been dependent on handwritten manuscripts and "books" printed with carved wooden blocks. But now editions or printings of a single work or broadside could easily go into thousands of copies, and governments could rapidly publicize laws and decrees and circulate instructions to their officials and subjects.

Technologically, printing brought together the skills and inventions of craftsmen—goldsmiths, silversmiths, metallurgists, paper makers—and artists who had developed oil-based paints suitable for pressurized application to paper. Transition from wood-block printing to movable type may have been developed simultaneously in two or more cities, but

*German handwriting and printing of the late Renaissance.*

the first printing shop known to the book trade was that of Johann Gutenberg (whose contribution to the technology of printing is obscure). He set it up in Mainz, Germany, slightly before 1450. From Mainz printing establishments spread rapidly. By 1500 the Low Countries had at least 50, Venice and Paris more than 150. England had only two, but the number rapidly increased. Presses were also located in all the large towns of Spain and in some towns of eastern Europe outside Russia.

Mass-produced books implied the democratization of culture. Now, for example, the goal of Erasmus and Martin Luther to have biblical texts in the hands of the simplest layman was possible of achievement. But printing in itself extended neither literacy nor the amount of leisure available for reading and learning. Most early books* were traditional in content. The great majority of them were devotional works or treatises. Books on the art of dying, apocalyptic themes, and prophecy had greater circulation than reports of new geographical discoveries or business techniques, especially in Germany.

Churchmen and political authorities quickly realized the power of the press to influence public opinion—educated opinion. They moved early to control heresy and sedition, particularly after the religious schism of the sixteenth century. Where this control was weak, as in parts of pre-Reformation Germany, large numbers of popular tracts gave impetus to revolutionary social movements. Throughout Europe, including all of Germany after 1525, censorship became a function of

---

* Books produced before 1500 are called *incunabula*. Since printed books were considered inferior to fine manuscripts, printers tried to imitate as closely as possible the appearance of manuscript books.

government. Only in periods of tension did censorship break down (as in England during the 1640s, or in France during the religious wars of the second half of the sixteenth century), at which time large quantities of critical materials circulated in the vernacular. These periods were preludes to revolution.* Degrees of censorship varied in different times and places, but relative freedom of the press was primarily the work of nineteenth-century liberals. Where they failed to gain power, as in eastern Europe, political and ecclesiastical authorities have an unbroken record of control over the written word. Thus, although the invention of printing was able to revolutionize the means of communication, it could not of itself revolutionize modern culture.

*Late fifteenth-century printing press.*

## THE FINE ARTS

Renaissance thinkers were self-consciously certain that their age had broken sharply with the medieval past. They could point not only to the revival of classical literature and philosophy but also to vast accomplishments in the fine arts. In his *Lives of the Painters, Sculptors, and Architects* Giorgio Vasari reveled in this decisive break even though progress might not continue into the future. He wrote of the "rebirth" of naturalism and classicism, describing how they gained ascendancy over post-Roman "barbarian" and Christian philosophies. Although his generalizations would not apply to many areas of fourteenth- and fifteenth-century life, his judgments on esthetic expression (he might have included literature) have been upheld. Without question, there was a "renaissance" in art.

* Two longer-term exceptions were the Dutch Republic after the seventeenth century and England's North American colonies during the eighteenth. English censorship was also relaxed after the revolution of 1688.

### Gothic Realism

In its naturalism Renaissance art was partly an outgrowth of Gothic art. Medieval artists had used allegorical symbols, not seeking to imitate nature. But the same spirit of "naturalism" that came to prompt new forms of literature, new methods of philosophy, and new views of theology, also eventually worked changes in art. Gothic painters and sculptors began to portray individuals rather than types. In northern France of the thirteenth century they began to master the techniques of realistic detail, evident in the late statuary on the Cathedral of Chartres. At the Burgundian court, the Low Country sculptor Claus Sluter (d. 1406) achieved fleshlike verisimilitude with painted stone. The van Eyck brothers, especially Jan (1370?–1440), painted almost photographic altar pieces with oil paint, a new medium permitting greater detail. Although they achieved marked realism, northern Gothic artists, like the architects

*Flemish realism:* The Crucifixion *by Hubert van Eyck.*

of Gothic cathedrals, multiplied picturesque details without achieving consistency of form; nor did they master the portrayal of natural space. Despite the fact that lay patrons commissioned some works from them, these artists did mostly death and crucifixion scenes for traditional, didactic purposes.

This Gothic realism became universal during the Renaissance. It was the preeminent art form of the era, especially in northern Europe. Prior to 1500 only Italy produced a competing style; and there, too, the plastic arts were dominated by Gothic realism until the fifteenth century. But during the quattrocento (1400s) Italy became the heart of a scientific realism that displayed mastery of the rules of linear perspective, and Italian artists turned to classical expression.

Medieval Italian art owed much to Byzantine forms, particularly to the flat iconography of the Eastern church, which did not give the illusion of depth. But under French influence an Italian form of Gothic painting reached a peak that established norms in the wet plaster (fresco) paintings of Giotto (d. 1336). He transformed the style of Byzantine painting by arranging figures more naturally in space, foreshortening them to give the illusion of depth, and using expressive postures and gestures to indicate emotions. His themes were religious—the most famous of his works is the *Life of Christ* on the walls of the Arena Chapel at Padua—but he abandoned abstract symbolism to portray emotions of joy, sorrow, hope, and despair. According to a contemporary chronicler, Giotto's figures "live and breathe." His paintings could be valued apart from their religious content, and they constituted a model for such of his successors as Fra Angelico and Fra Lippo Lippi. Until the fifteenth century Italian Gothic painters strove for prettiness of detail and exactness of representation but had no formal rules of perspective.

*Italian Gothic realism in fresco: Giotto's* Kiss of Judas, *a detail from his* Life of Christ.

## Scientific Naturalism and Classicism in Italy

When Italy's artists departed from the Gothic style they were influenced in their new directions both by scientific naturalism and by Roman classicism. Contemplating Roman ruins, architects were the first to turn to classical forms. Since Renaissance artists were not usually specialized—one and the same man was often shop-trained in sculpture, painting, goldsmithery, and architecture—boundaries between disciplines were fluid. Classical forms spread rapidly, first to sculpture, later to painting.

Science and classicism often merged in the careers of fifteenth-century artists. The work of Brunelleschi, architect and sculptor, is illustrative. He was the first both to work out mathematical laws of linear perspective and influentially to

*Brunelleschi's Dome, Cathedral of Florence.*

*Alberti, interior of S. Andrea at Mantua.*

LEFT: *Naturalism and pathos: Masaccio's* Adam and Eve.

*Classical realism at its peak: Donatello's* David.

*Leonardo's* The Madonna of the Rocks.

TOP RIGHT: *Botticelli's return to mystical allegory:* The Birth of Venus.

BOTTOM RIGHT: *A page from Albrecht Dürer's scientific treatise on human proportions, 1528.*

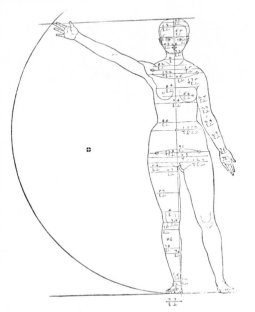
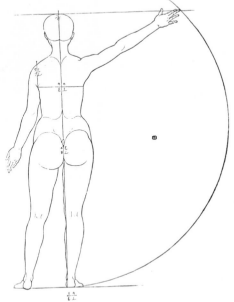

*Religious naturalism and quizzical cherubs:* Sistine Madonna *by Raphael.*

TOP RIGHT: *Realism and power:* The Creation of Adam (*Sistine Chapel*) *by* Michelangelo.

BOTTOM RIGHT: *Manneristic sensuousness: a nude by Titian.*

*A giant to kill a giant: Michelangelo's* David.

emulate classical styles of building. Disliking Gothic, he studied in Rome, a veritable museum of ancient, earthbound architecture. Commissioned to remodel Florence, he introduced round columns, rounded arches, pilasters, and domes. He refrained, however, from copying buildings of antiquity. Another architect and theorist, Leon Battista Alberti (1405–71), soon developed a more imitative classicism and proposed to make architecture a mathematical science of balance and proportion as well as the most utilitarian of the arts.

In 1401 Brunelleschi competed with Ghiberti, Jacopo della Quercia, and others for the commission to cast sculptured bronze doors for the Baptistery of Florence. Ghiberti won. He spent a decade executing the project, which Michelangelo later described as worthy of being the gates of paradise. Ghiberti put the biblical story of Isaac into a natural setting, using light and shade to give dramatic impressions of depth. His student, Donatello (d. 1466), who excelled in obtaining balance between scientific realism and classical models, cast a bronze *David* designed to stand alone in a garden. A combination of grace, reserve, mathematically conceived proportions, and naturalism, *David* was presumably chosen to kill the giant because of his natural perfection, not because of his piety. In another feat of symmetry and balance, Donatello cast at Padua one of the first equestrian statues since antiquity (*Gattamelata*). In this work, the movements of the horse and rider are in perfect harmony. Other sculptors, such as Verrocchio, equaled or surpassed Donatello in specific projects, but at his best Donatello came closer than any other to achieving perfection as it was then defined.

As an art for which no antique models survived, painting was slow to respond to classical stimulation. But Masaccio, who died in 1428 at the age of 27, introduced mathematical laws of perspective. He was realistic without being Gothic; imitating nature rather than his masters, he worked out the perspective of the human body. His figures exist in three-dimensional space, so that the viewer feels able to touch them. In the expressions of the two lifelike nudes, *Adam and Eve,* he portrayed the pathos of man's expulsion from the Garden of Eden. Before Masaccio, Florence had been the fountainhead of Renaissance sculpture and architecture. Now it also became the center of painting's "rebirth."

Realism in painting made the canvas a transparent windowpane with nature on the other side. "That picture is most praiseworthy," wrote Leonardo da Vinci, "which most clearly resembles the thing to be imitated."[3] No paintings better conformed to this dictum than his own. His service as a military and civil engineer for Cesare Borgia and others took precedence over his artistic work; so did his research into anatomy, physiology, botany, geology, and mechanics. But these pursuits were also closely related to his art. In whatever he did da Vinci sought to derive rational, mathematical laws from empirical reality. He noted hitherto unobserved color and line aberrations in ocular perception and combined these with the use of light and shade to secure a better illusion of perspective. His adherence to imitation was selective. He tempered his realism with a classical sense of decorum, carefully picking elements of ideal beauty from his environment. Classical repose and dramatic tension coexist in the few paintings he completed, which include *St. John the Baptist, St. Jerome, The Madonna of the Rocks,* and *The Last Supper.* Even when scientifically conceived, Italian realism was usually selective and strove for an ideal form.

Just as contemporary humanists sought

[3] Quoted by Erwin Panofsky, *Renaissance and Renascences in Western Art* (Copenhagen: Russack and Co., 1961), p. 162.

to describe a perfect literary style, so artists sought to temper realism with classical balance, harmony, proportion, and decorum. While Northern artists concentrated on desolate scenes of death and crucifixion, Italian artists, painting both secular and religious works, dealt with life, natural beauty, and the spectrum of human emotions. At the peak of classical realism man became the measure of all things; his dignity, perfection, or fame replaced metaphysical principles as the measure of values; his struggles with himself replaced the struggle between heaven and hell as the chief concern of artist and humanist; and the enjoyment of life, which art enhanced, was seen to be more divine than the contemplation of death and salvation. In tracts on architecture, sculpture, painting, mathematics, natural science, family life, law, and religion the civic humanist and universally accomplished Florentine Leon Battista Alberti summed up this blend of humanism and realism.

During the second half of the fifteenth century artists began to draw more on classical literature than on contemporary life. The realistic imitations of da Vinci and Alberti gave way to Greco-Roman gods, heroes, battles, and myths painted by such artists as Mantegna and Piero de Cosimo. Other painters such as Botticelli were influenced by the philosophy of Neoplatonism. His *Allegory of Spring* and *Birth of Venus* combine a command of scientific realism and a return to allegorical symbolism (classical rather than religious); both depict hierarchies of spirits, types of soul, and forms of love. Following Botticelli, artists of the High Renaissance no longer considered themselves recorders of external nature; rather they were creative geniuses inspired by divine spirit. Having developed the ability to reproduce nature in almost photographic detail, they began to look away from their immediate environment for new themes with which to experiment.

## The High Renaissance

Idealized classical form rather than fidelity to nature as recorded by the senses characterized the art of the High Renaissance, a short period of two or three decades following 1500. Compared to the youthful realism of the previous century, High Renaissance art emphasized grandeur, perfection of form, and self-assurance. Artists now often worked in greater-than-life proportions, and were encouraged in this by the patronage of monarchs in Rome, northern Italy, and France—successful bidders for the greatest artistic skills. Increasingly art's purpose became one of glorifying these ruling patrons and attaining immortal fame for both them and the artist. By 1500 the major artists were no longer merely respected guildsmen but were highly rewarded individuals of great prestige and affluence who traveled from one court to another, at least until Spanish influence reduced the status of most of them.

The most ambitious patron of the High Renaissance was Pope Julius II, who called Bramante, Raphael, Michelangelo, and others to Rome. Bramante was a student of Roman architecture who brought principles of mathematics and physics to bear on his work. Julius commissioned him to build St. Peter's Basilica in the capital of Christendom, a grandiose project whose completion required more than a century. Raphael also worked on the design of St. Peter's, but his fame rests primarily on paintings of idealized madonnas—for example, his *Sistine Madonna*—and of various classical themes. His madonnas were generally more human than pious in appearance, but they conveyed an abstract humanity of grace and dignity rather than an individuality. Like other late Renaissance painters Raphael drew on philosophical and classical themes in the *School of Athens,* an assemblage of savants of the past, and in *Parnassus,* an anachronistic combination of classical antiquity, the classical present, and inventive imagination.

The crowning jewel of Julius's assemblage of talent was Michelangelo, a Florentine-trained sculptor. The pope set him to work from 1508 to 1512 on frescoes of the Sistine Chapel and later on the plans of St. Peter's. Working on his back for four years in order to paint 300 figures on the wet plaster of the Sistine Chapel ceiling, Michelangelo displayed both dependence on and independence of Florentine scientific naturalism. Departing from mathematical laws of perspective, he consciously used distortion to awake a heightened sense of perspective and to convey a feeling of power. Ideal beauty he found in the nude human form, which he used in his depictions of creation and of man's early biblical history. He included no crucifixion or judgment scenes until Pope Paul III pressed him into doing a wall on the chapel entitled the *Last Judgment* (1535–41).

Michelangelo was primarily a sculptor rather than a painter or architect. For the Medici he built tombs portraying the family head as a victor in greater-than-life size and flanked by symbolic figures whose meaning is debatable. His most classical work was *David*, a relaxed and serene but powerful giant who could self-assuredly kill his biblical opponent without miraculous intervention. For the tomb of Julius II he carved another giant, *Moses*, in a psychological state of restrained wrath. In sculpture, as in painting, Michelangelo relied on his own subjective standards and produced art for art's sake. But his inner tranquility was shaken by political and religious crises after 1527, and this is reflected in his art. Rome was sacked in 1527; Italy was conquered by the emperor in 1529; advocates of force replaced Catholic humanists at the papal court in 1541. As his optimistic world of the Renaissance crumbled, Michelangelo turned more and more to mysticism and pious resignation.

The full range of his work is impossible to classify under a single heading: his art styles chronicle successive changes from classical realism to subjective and imitative "mannerism" to, finally, the baroque.

In quantity of works and in grandeur of restrained style the High Renaissance far surpassed the early Italian Renaissance. It was no longer primarily a Florentine or even exclusively Italian phenomenon. Venice rivaled Rome as a center of High Renaissance art. There a school of painters developed whose members relied more on color and oil-painted texture than on light and shade. Founded by Giovanni Bellini (d. 1516) and his student Giorgione (d. 1510), this school was carried to its greatest heights by Titian (1477–1576). Like those of Michelangelo, his works, which run from larger-than-life religious frescoes to sensuous nudes, are too varied to be classifiable by either subject or technique. He helped introduce a new phase of Italian art: *Mannerism*, the imitation of individual masters and the distortion of classical techniques. At the very same time when Italian art began to influence all of Europe, its own foundations of classical and scientific realism were crumbling.

By 1500 an Italian journey had become a necessity for Northern men of culture and learning, and Italian artists were summoned to the Northern courts. Still, High Renaissance influence was uneven outside Italy. France proved receptive to both its art and its letters, but Spain and Germany remained primarily Gothic and religious in a doctrinal sense. Albrecht Dürer (1471–1528) of Nuremberg and Hans Holbein (d. 1543), primarily a portrait painter, utilized Italian techniques of perspective, but neither they nor other Northern artists would adopt the secular esthetic content of the Italian Renaissance. Symbolism and Mannerism eventually proved easier for them to absorb.* The

* The Low Countries produced their own humanistic art without classical standards of beauty.

North, inclusive of England, was also primarily responsible for the development of Renaissance music, which Italy and other countries adopted. Despite much concourse with Italy, Northern artists under continuing Gothic influences did not fully comprehend the language of Italian art and music until that language became baroque and metaphysical during the religious wars of the sixteenth and seventeenth centuries.

## C. Socioeconomic, Political, and Religious Developments

### ECONOMIC AND SOCIAL TRENDS

It used to be a natural assumption that Renaissance culture rested on a continued upsurge of the "commercial revolution" of the eleventh, twelfth, and thirteenth centuries. This economic growth contributed to the rise of towns and a money economy; to territorial expansion and centralizing states; to the erection of cathedrals and the establishment of universities; and to the elaboration of more secular, sophisticated levels of thought. Indeed it must be granted that Renaissance culture is inconceivable apart from this late medieval economic development. But recent economic studies conclusively demonstrate that this culture came not on the crest of growing prosperity but in the slough of a century-long depression. Since recovery was slow, uneven, and in many older commercial centers incomplete, contemporary historians are inclined to explain the Renaissance as a delayed phenomenon of "cultural lag" rather than as the cutting edge of a new, triumphant bourgeois world.

### A Century of Depression

The commercial depression that extended from ca. 1350 to ca. 1450 may have been due in part to previous overexpansion, but famine, plague, war destruction, and domestic turmoil were the more likely causes.

Following a series of severe famines the Black Death (or bubonic plague) killed more than a quarter of Europe's population between 1348 and 1350; in Mediterranean towns the figure was as high as 35 to 65 percent. Thereafter the plague recurred generation after generation.* The decline in population retarded both commerce and industry. With fewer opportunities of profit, entrepreneurs became demoralized, and the rise of newly enriched merchants competing for positions of power and influence diminished. Old banking families such as the Bardi, Peruzzi, and Acciaiuoli of Florence were ruined by the depression. Financial power fell into the hands of a few great banking families or

* The bubonic plague did not cease to be a major urban killer in Europe until the eighteenth century.

*Burial of plague victims at Tournai, 1349.*

individuals including the Medici of Florence, the Fuggers of Augsburg, and Jacques Coeur of France. Such techniques as double-entry bookkeeping at least temporarily secured some of them against losses. Although outstanding as great "individualists" of the age, they commanded fewer total resources than had a greater number of earlier merchant capitalists. And these "few great" increasingly tied their resources to the foremost ruling dynasties and to the papacy.

• Endless warfare also affected trade. In western Europe the Hundred Years' War (1338–1453) between France and England disturbed trade routes, laid waste to considerable parts of France, and led to feuds and dynastic civil war in England. Similarly, endemic warfare in Italy, Spain, Scandinavia, and eastern Europe disrupted trade and destroyed wealth. The invasion of eastern Europe by the Ottoman Turks made Eastern trade more difficult. In approximately 1340 the Mongol Empire, which had policed trade routes from Poland to Korea, began to disin-

tegrate, and Europeans were barred from China by the nativist Ming dynasty. As trade and industry declined, Italian banks, including those of the Medici, often involved in financial military ventures, began to fail.

In the wake of depression and war, peasant and urban revolutions enveloped fourteenth-century Europe. Indeed, domestic disorders continued in some areas, notably Germany, until the sixteenth century. Had these revolts produced a more nearly egalitarian political order they might have contributed to a return of prosperity. But they failed, and the crushing tax burdens, which had in part stimulated the revolts and which the privileged classes escaped, continued to fall exclusively on the productive elements of society, stripping them of purchasing power.

Venice, although it escaped revolution, exemplified many mercantile difficulties of the late fifteenth century. Venetian merchants had dominated Far Eastern trade through the city's commercial empire in the eastern Mediterranean, where Arab caravan and sea routes terminated. But new Ottoman rulers raised the wholesale prices of Oriental spices and cottons by setting up royal monopolies. At the same time Portugal opened up a cheap, all-water transportation route to the Far East around Africa. Italian wars disrupted Venetian commerce as shipments of goods were often confiscated. As a result of these challenges, after 1496 Venetian merchant-nobles intensified their efforts to pursue safer investments. They found some outlets abroad, in England or Spain, but government bonds and real estate gained favor over commercial investment. In the early sixteenth century, war crises caused suspension of interest payments on bonds and deprived owners of the use and the revenues of their estates. Deforestation deprived Venice of necessary raw materials for building new ships, and, although it remained the major shipping and trading city of the Mediterranean, it steadily lost economic vitality and initiative.

The depression might have been arrested sooner had the period been rich in technical inventions. While it is true that earlier discoveries in commerce, industry, and agriculture continued to spread, few innovative changes revitalized basic production and exchange in the Renaissance. There were new industrial processes in paper making, silk throwing, cloth production, glass manufacture, metallurgy, and distilling, but none of these processes involved use of the new sources of motive power that characterized the later Industrial Revolution. The craft guilds, which preserved and transmitted industrial techniques, increased in number. Still, the Renaissance, like societies of the sixteenth, seventeenth, and eighteenth centuries, was as dependent as the Middle Ages on the power furnished by wind, water, animals, and humans. Except in Flanders and northern Italy urban commerce and industry occupied only a minute proportion of the population; the overwhelming majority remained peasants. Substantial changes in the pattern of agricultural production occurred in some areas supplying wool, wines, or garden produce for towns. For the most part, however, agricultural technology made few advances.

## Partial Recovery

As we have noted, recovery from the depression was uneven. Some formerly thriving towns, especially those of eastern Europe, never recovered from the combination of misfortunes that befell them in the fourteenth and fifteenth centuries. Other towns, such as the German centers of Augsburg and Nuremberg, did not reach their former levels of population and economic activity until after 1450.

Substantial commercial expansion occurred in areas along the Atlantic seaboard thanks to the development of three-masted ships, capable of tacking against the wind, which made ocean voyages feasible although still exceedingly dangerous. The peoples along the Atlantic seaboard now secured geographic and economic advantages over the Italian and German cities that had previously dominated Europe's carrying trade. These ships, armed with weapons using gunpowder, were also to give seaboard peoples naval and military superiority over the offshore islands, Africa, the New World, and the Orient. Portugal, soon challenged by Spain and the Low Countries, took the lead in building a commercial empire using Atlantic trade routes to supply Negro slaves, sugar, ivory, gold, and herbs to new markets. Thus a commercial revolution was in the making that would transfer the hub of international trade to Antwerp in the sixteenth century, but it had little impact on most of fifteenth-century Europe. Throughout the greater part of the Renaissance period, commerce stagnated at a lower level than it had reached in the High Middle Ages.

## Urban Revolutions and Reaction

Seen as a whole the Renaissance was marked by the unprecedented prominence of townsmen in affairs. Nevertheless the economic depression and the internal revolutions that followed in its wake undermined the long-term impact of these people as a class on government and society.

The rise of the medieval commercial towns had thrust revolutionary ingredients into the rural, chivalric, manorial, and ecclesiastically oriented society of the Middle Ages. Town life was built on formal legal equality, personal freedom, property ownership, and the goals of commerce. Dominated by merchant oligarchies, town governments overrode rural custom with legislation, taxes, and titled property and rent records. As long as prosperity lasted, the towns provided paths of social mobility upward for the newly enriched, the skilled, and the rural immigrant. Late medieval depression, however, reinforced previous tendencies in the towns to form rigid hierarchies of privilege and power and to restrict the opportunities of "out" groups. Town societies were dominated by cliques of families who intermarried and monopolized positions of power. To a great extent they adopted the social values of the traditional aristocracy in seeking status, coats of arms, luxury, country estates, and offices. Below these elite families were the guildmasters, who closed their ranks to all except their own descendants and who secured the power to forbid their journeymen and apprentices to organize. Below the guildmasters stood their disunited employees and the bulk of the town population, largely engaged in agriculture

or marketing. Instead of providing a common front asserting "middle-class" over against rural aristocratic social ideals, the classes in Renaissance towns were caught up in internal conflicts that weakened their influence and invited authoritarian rule or hostile intervention.

Medieval town life had always been turbulent, but during the economic crises of the Renaissance, social and political tension flared into open revolution in almost every European town. Each revolt had its local peculiarities, but certain patterns were general. Masters of leading craft guilds and some merchants were excluded from power by the closing of patrician ranks, so when economic or military setbacks occurred, both craftsmen and merchants were likely to organize internal dissent, attack ruling oligarchies for mismanagement, and demand the right to fill certain town offices. Guild victories in turn led to restrictive trade laws, the proscription of patrician families, and the continued exclusion from power of the lower classes. Popular urban revolts, frequently joined by neighboring peasants, often followed. The fear of bloodshed by mobs was great, but both patricians and the new business elite were adept at using terror to secure the submission of the disunited lower classes.

Rarely did the masses secure more than momentary concessions, and rarely did these urban revolts result in increased autonomy or prosperity. Each victorious faction sought to strengthen its own position in (and sometimes against) the community and to maintain its power by securing outside help. Frightened by lower-class restiveness, urban patricians invited intervention by princes who grasped these discords as opportunities of appointing their own officials to key urban posts, of breaking town and guild charters, and of assuming responsibility for public peace. The towns of France, England, Spain, and the German states all lost their autonomy

*Draper's market at Bologna, 1411.*

to monarchs during the Renaissance. In Italy, where there were no princes to turn to, single-party or family tyrannies were set up. Both patricians and despots adopted the social outlook of the tradi- tional aristocracy and sought either royal offices or aristocratic marriages and titles.

The continuing but unsuccessful popu- lar resistance to aristocratic control is well illustrated by Florence, the heart of secular

Renaissance culture. With more than 90,000 people in 1300, it was one of the world's largest cities and both a commercial and an industrial center. Probably one-third of its population was employed as "barefoot" (*Ciompi*) wool workers by the masters of the leading craft guilds. In 1282 a revolution had given political rights to the 21 leading guilds and political dominance to the upper seven. To awe the old patricians the new oligarchy used extraordinary police measures and penalties. But financial and political crises after 1338 drove Florence into decline. An exceedingly expensive war to conquer Lucca failed. Edward III of England defaulted on large debts owed to the two leading banking families, the Bardi and the Peruzzi. Plagues that had begun in approximately 1340 and that had continued intermittently came to a climax in the Black Death of 1348. Following a plague and a three-year war against the papal states, in 1378 the Ciompi revolted for political and social rights. After only four years they were put down by a mercenary army hired by the great guildmasters; but the latter's restored oligarchical government was harassed by Milan's aggressive expansion southward into Tuscany.

Following successive military reverses the oligarchy was undermined and finally replaced in 1434 by the city's foremost banker, Cosimo de' Medici, who ruled the city effectively from behind a facade of traditional republican institutions. Under him Florence enjoyed a golden age of subsidized art and scholarship and of luxurious living by the upper classes; anomalously, it also suffered decline, as did the fortunes of the Medici. War, first with Milan as an ally of Venice, and then with Venice as an ally of Milan, failed to gain more than the negotiation of an uneasy "balance of power." In 1469, after a bland interlude under Piero de' Medici, Lorenzo the Magnificent took over the reins of the city and the family bank. When, a few years later, he allied himself with Milan and Venice to prevent the popes from consolidating the papal states, all Italy burst into arms again. Pressed by the failing resources of heavily indebted Florence, Lorenzo managed in 1480 to negotiate peace on the peninsula just as a Turkish expedition was landing at Otranto. Because of the death of the reigning sultan, however, Italy was spared a Turkish invasion. To save the Medici's fortunes after failure of the bank's branches in Bruges and London, Lorenzo established ties with the French royal family.* Similar ties were contracted with the highest Italian aristocratic families and the papacy. Lorenzo, for example, secured the appointment of his 14-year-old son, Giovanni (the future Pope Leo X), as cardinal in 1489.

The political glitter of Medicean Florence was the flicker of a dying candle for Italian republicanism; involving only the leading citizens and rigidly excluding the lower classes, it was always narrowly oligarchical, perhaps too narrowly based to last. During the French invasion of 1494–95, the Medici were driven out by a democratic and theocratic revolution led by Savonarola, under whom the Florentine republicans opposed both the papacy and the Medici oligarchs, until his execution in 1498. Subsequently (1512) the Medici family returned to power because of Giovanni's influence with an invading Spanish army. (He himself was to assume the papal crown in the following year.) Habsburg victories in Italy after 1527 destroyed all hope of reviving representative republican constitutional forms, except in Venice. The republican towns proved to be more resistant to invasion than the princely despotisms, but Florence itself became a hereditary duchy under a branch of the house of Medici after Spanish power in the peninsula became entrenched.

* Likely enough he also helped himself to public funds in Florence for the same purpose.

For the lower class majority and the conquered subjects of ruling towns, this shift from oligarchic republic to despotic government made little difference. Both types of government resorted to heavy indirect taxes on foodstuffs and other common items of consumption, the poor being the most adversely affected. Political and economic organization was prohibited, and the prohibition was enforced. The republics differed from the despotisms primarily in giving, at least, some of the capitalists decisive influence over affairs.

## Aristocratic Recovery and the Decline of the Peasantry

Although the Renaissance saw more government positions held by townsmen than before, its conclusion in most areas was marked by an aristocratic recovery. Monarchs acknowledged the importance of the wealthy bourgeoisie by employing them as officials and by drawing them into diets or parliaments. Instead of imposing urban social standards on the state, however, these officials usually used their talents to secure admission into the aristocracy, whose social traditions they aped. Even in Tudor England, where by reputation the middle classes were supposed to be of decisive influence, they were, in fact, supposed to keep their place well below the aristocracy. In short, the shifting of the most talented townsmen from business to royal service weakened the urban impact on early modern European institutions.

Despite its considerable recovery after approximately 1450, the traditional aristocracy was for a time demoralized by several important innovations. One was the new means of warfare with expensive firearms and mercenary infantry, which they could not afford. Another was the commutation of peasant obligations into fixed money payments whose value was cut by inflation. Still another was the competition of educated burghers for church and state offices. Even so, the aristocracy proved resilient enough to maintain its social dominance. In eastern Europe the ascendancy at this time of the aristocracy and the gentry (aristocratic untitled country squires) is unquestioned; they dominated peasants, townsmen, and kings. Elsewhere noblemen and gentry found compensation for their losses in tighter estate management, well-paying Church positions, and posts at princely courts—often sinecures. Titled nobles were exclusive; they made it difficult for commoners to marry into noble families or otherwise to gain noble status. At the same time they saw to it that their sons secured education sufficient to outbid lower-class competition for offices. Noblemen responded to the creation of infantry armies, financed by kings, by becoming royal officers.

In strong monarchical states the rulers helped the nobility to preserve this caste system. Although monarchs curbed the nobles' political powers, royal courts shared their social outlook and culture, bestowing grants and sinecures once their political rebelliousness was tamed. When kings employed commoners, they usually provided them with privileges or titles and expected them to act as aristocrats. Thus the traditional nobility, the gentry, and a new "service" aristocracy (particularly jurists drawn from the bourgeoisie but no longer part of it) proved to be the most dynamic elements of Renaissance society.

The lower urban and peasant classes, which constituted the bulk of the population, were even more unsuccessful than the bourgeoisie in their bid for social and political recognition. Peasant revolts were endemic during the Renaissance; but only in areas where town life remained active and expansive did the peasants' *legal* position improve. Here the bonds of serfdom disintegrated within a market economy.

*Economically* their gains, if any, were not so clear. New taxes, legal fees, and requisitions by new state officials for civil and military purposes—when added to traditional obligations to church and manorial lords—took the greater part of their income. And in eastern Europe (outside the Ottoman Empire) both the legal and the economic status of the peasant deteriorated as the German-Slavic frontier, which had been an area of relative freedom, became an area of nascent serfdom.

## THE COURSE OF POLITICS

In the traditional view, Renaissance politics were a continuation and culmination of the efforts of medieval monarchs, aided by townsmen invoking the precepts of Roman law, to centralize their kingdoms into "national states." In certain instances this generalization has merit, particularly as it applies to England; but as an overall statement it is misleading. Political loyalties continued to be focused on local provinces that had their own oligarchical representative assemblies, not on the larger unit of nation-states. Despite the invention of the printing press, poor communications continued to retard the growth and effectiveness of central governments. It is true that courts and precepts styled on Roman law emerged prominently in the monarchical states and enhanced the power of the king. But they were in competition with the canon law administered by the Roman Catholic church. They also had to compete with local customary law, which buttressed the privileges of aristocracies and oligarchical townsmen and regulated daily life in the local villages.

With few exceptions royal politics were dominated by dynastic rather than national interests. The right to rule was passed on by inheritance from one ruler to another and was considered to be private: like the royal domain, it could be acquired and transferred. Usually dynasts sought to enlarge their territories by advantageous marriages of their children. However, their domains were often diminished by marriage portions given to daughters, division of inheritance among heirs, and grants of autonomy to princes of royal blood. The result of dynasticism was the personal union of disparate principalities under a single ruler, not the creation of nation-states.

Townsmen served as royal officials, often as aggressive centralizers. Yet, as we have seen, townsmen serving kings failed to make the monarchies after their own image. The social order that the monarchical states served was predominantly aristocratic and traditional.

Nothing better illustrates the hierarchy of the social order than the diets that Renaissance rulers began to call in almost every monarchy of western Europe. Summoned to get influential sectors of society to accept treaties, defy the pope, accept succession settlements, or impose taxes, their composition varied in detail but they were basically similar. Representatives of the clergy and the nobility made up the two highest orders; delegates from privileged towns represented the commoners; rarely was the peasantry—the mass of the population—represented at all. Deliberation was by order or estate, and each estate negotiated separately with the monarch, particularly when its privileges were at stake. In addition to some kingdomwide assemblies such as the English Parliament and the French Estates-General, each provincial part of the continental dynastic kingdoms often maintained its own diet as a guardian over local customs, law, and privileges. None of the diets—provincial or national—constituted a modern legislative assembly, at least not before the seventeenth century, when the English Parliament made that transition.

The most decisive political innovations occurred among the city-states of northern Italy, no one of which encompassed a modern "nation." As in the late Middle Ages, Lombardy and Tuscany served as laboratories for the creation of a territorially compact state subject to a uniform law and administrative system. Resting solely on secular power in their relationships with one another, these city states also developed the first modern system of diplomatic representation. Venice followed suit, creating the most renowned diplomatic corps of the late Renaissance. Although the kingdoms of Europe were incompletely consolidated, in most cases for three centuries or more, nevertheless they became ready converts to Italian-style diplomacy as the Renaissance came to an end.

## The States of Italy: 1300–1527

Italy was a region of many different states. In the extreme south, Sicily—the former centralized, cosmopolitan, and secular imperial headquarters of the Holy Roman Emperor, Frederick II—claimed Naples. Naples was dominated by local feudal barons. Central and parts of northern Italy were controlled by the Papal States, which were in a permanent state of crisis. The popes' residence in Avignon for more than 70 years paralyzed government, and the states had to be reconquered to return them to loyalty to the pope, thereafter to remain an attractive area for mercenary captains bent on carving out states for themselves. The principal victim of the chaos and continued warfare was communal government.

Distinctly different in political evolution were the towns of the Tuscan and Lombard plains, where town life and Roman law had never completely disappeared. Beginning, like other medieval towns, as republican communes, the Lombard and Tuscan towns leagued together

ITALY, ca. 1490

Republics shown by diagonal lines

0    60    120

Map by J. Donovan

and, allied with the papacy, threw off the authority of the Holy Roman Emperor in the twelfth century. Titular imperial governors presided over several of their councils, but thenceforth they retained *de facto* independence. Bankers from Lombardy and Tuscany dominated financial affairs in late medieval courts, fairs, and the Crusades. Two cities, Florence and Venice, gave their stable units of money— the florin and the ducat—to the early modern commercial world.

The commercial rivalry of the various towns led to naval and land wars in which the stronger city-states swallowed their weaker neighbors. In Tuscany, Florence extended her territory to include, among others, Arezzo and Pisa (a port city that had previously reduced her neighbors to submission). In Lombardy, Milan under the Visconti—later under the Sforzas—was the principal expansionist state. Here republicanism gave way to a dynastic monarchy set up by a prominent captain of mercenary troops. Milan's territorial ambitions collided with those of Venice, which abandoned its aloofness from peninsular affairs in the fourteenth century to push its holdings landward for control of the commercial routes extending northward across the Alps.

By the middle of the fourteenth century Italy consisted principally of five major states locked in a relative equilibrium of power maintained by shifting alliances: Naples, the Papal States, Venice, Florence, and Milan.

Constant factional strife and turbulence affected constitutional development among ruling cities, with the exception of Venice.* Elsewhere factionalism that had social and economic roots was a major cause for the failure of Italian republicanism. When the Holy Roman Emperor was the principal enemy, the Ghibellines, or imperialists, were proscribed with their property confiscated. Where the Guelfs (Welfs), or papalists, triumphed, they formed one-party states; but their ruling factions, based on family groupings, were split apart by family rivalries. Newly rich families tried, by revolution if the need arose, to break into the ruling oligarchies. In Venice such efforts were curbed by the creation of a permanent committee of public safety, which preserved the old oligarchy in uneasy power. When Florentine guildsmen came to power in 1282 they proscribed, exiled, or executed their patrician foes. Warfare gave this factionalism another dimension, since military defeats were the most frequent causes for revolution and the outbreak of civil war. But victory also had its dangers: town councils, fearing to arm their own subjects, often hired mercenary troop captains to conduct wars on land. These captains, in Milan and other towns, seized power and set up hereditary dynastic tyrannies, marking a general trend away from oligarchical republican government.

Both republics and despotisms had established territorial states whose law and administration were sovereign within their borders. Establishment of that sovereignty required the eradication of both noble and clerical privileges and jurisdictions. Once the authority of the emperor was removed, the aristocracy, which tended to live in the towns and to engage in commerce, was brought under city law. Similarly the Church was more thoroughly subordinated to secular government in the Italian city-states than in any monarchy, even though the towns had achieved their independence as allies of the papacy. A Visconti of Milan once summed up his powers to an archbishop in this way: "Do you not know, you fool, that here I am pope and emperor and lord in all my lands, and that no one can do anything in my lands save I permit it—no, not even God."[4]

Considerations of power rather than legitimate family claims of succession regulated the relationships among the Italian city-states. Milan originated the practice of sending resident diplomatic agents to neighboring states. Their chief tasks were to acquire intelligence, to mask

---

* At the end of the thirteenth century the leading merchant-nobles consolidated their hold over Venetian affairs. Henceforth only those whose names were inscribed in genealogical "golden books" were eligible to participate in public affairs. Venice's stability under this narrow oligarchy excited the awe of aristocratic factions elsewhere, notably in Florence.

[4] Quoted by Denys Hay, *The Italian Renaissance in its Historical Background* (Cambridge: Cambridge University Press, 1961), p. 105.

aggressive intentions with pacific eloquence, and to secure allies. Other Italian states soon adopted the practice. Mercenary armies and diplomats were inspired by neither religious zeal nor modern nationalism, but solely by the desire to gain expansive domains and political power.

By the middle 1400s, the states of the whole peninsula had achieved a balance of power by means of constantly shifting alliances in which yesterday's enemy became tomorrow's ally. As each state strove to tip that balance in its own favor, allies were sought among the great monarchies, two of which, France and Spain, had conflicting claims to Naples and Milan. Once these giants intervened, however, no individual Italian state could turn them back. In the early sixteenth century the papacy shifted alliances to prevent dominance by either. But by 1527 the Spanish house of Habsburg was in effective control of the peninsula, except for Venice.

More than any other court the Spanish royal house of Habsburg developed an Italian type of diplomatic corps and supported it with immense resources. In this way the secular diplomacy of the Italian city states was grafted onto the foremost divine-right kingship of sixteenth-century Europe.

## The Iberian Kingdoms

In contrast to northern Italy, Spain tended to favor the creation of an empire based on religious rather than secular goals. The country may have been divided among the contending kingdoms of Castile, Leon, and Aragon, but it was united in its long holy war, beginning in the tenth century, to drive out the Moors. After 1230, victory was facilitated by the union of Leon and Castile. Although the Moors continued to hold Granada, the Iberians dashed Moorish hopes of recovery in 1340, and finally achieved their aim

in 1492 with the fall of Granada to the combined forces of Castile and Aragon. Reconquest proceeded in the guise of a holy war inspired by the legend of St. James (Santiago). Erroneously believed to be a brother of Christ who came to Spain, Santiago was considered the peculiar property of Iberian Christians, especially the Castilians. Crusading orders joined the secular clergy in obtaining vast lands, income, and local political powers as the frontiers were pushed southward and colonists settled on confiscated lands. Christian towns and nobles also obtained extensive grants of local authority and autonomy. Thus as the kingdoms of Portugal, Castile, and Aragon expanded territorially, they became administratively and legally decentralized.

Reconquest also bred the idea of a Christian ruling caste, to which Spaniards of rank high and low aspired. Even in the reconquered areas the Moors and Jews furnished most of the technical skills in finance, industry, agriculture, scholarship, and medicine. Rather than imitate the heretic's superior skills most of the conquerors relied on the sword or piety to secure positions of power. Probably no other people in Europe stigmatized manual labor so much as the Castilians. Especially among them honor, religious faith, and arms rather than knowledge and skills became the basis of an "individualism" based on gentle, or even simply Spanish, birth. For all its pious character this code cheerfully allowed defiance of authority and defrauding of the government at every opportunity. In the Middle Ages considerable tolerance, cultural exchange, and intermarriage occurred among Christians, Moors, and Jews. But as the Iberian Christians obtained unquestioned military ascendancy, they turned their sense of divine mission into a drive for empire, total uniformity, and "racial purity."

After military security against the Moors had been obtained, endless dy-

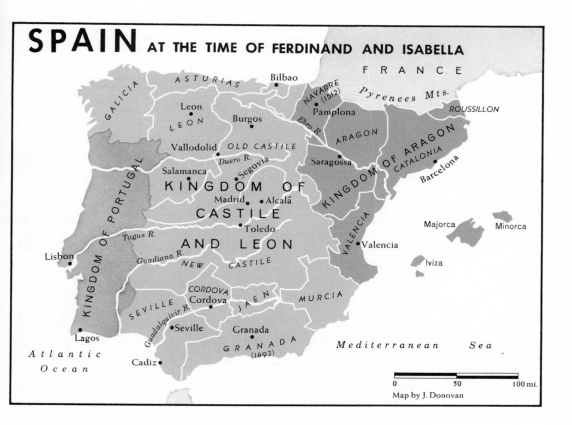

Map by J. Donovan

nastic feuds and civil wars broke out in the fourteenth and fifteenth centuries. Royal weakness provided an opportunity for local estates (*cortes*) to consolidate their power in Aragon, where the diets remained the watchdogs of noble, clerical, and urban privileges rather than legislative chambers responsive to the common welfare. Royal dominance in Castile was easier to maintain because the Castilian Cortes withered when the clergy and nobility ceased to attend. Even though leagues of townsmen usually fought for kingly order against noble lawlessness, the principal beneficiaries of the disorders were the nobles, who gained lands at the expense of the royal domains. Towns, under royal officials who severely taxed commerce, began to decline in the fourteenth century.

Ultimately the joint reign of Ferdinand of Aragon (1479–1516) and Isabella of Cas-

tile (1474–1504), husband and wife, produced order out of chaos through monarchical despotism. Even so, their kingdoms retained their separate identities and constitutions. These Catholic sovereigns enforced domestic peace and set up a system of royal councils, courts, and administration that overrode the political claims of towns, nobles, and clergy, with all towns in Castile coming under firm royal control by 1480. Gentry loyal to the crown (*hidalgos*) were placed in half the towns' offices, town leagues were broken up, and the guild system was spread throughout the kingdom under royal auspices. Ferdinand attempted similar measures in Aragon against fairly effective opposition by the local cortes. Individual townsmen continued to serve in the royal administration, especially as Roman-law jurists; but politically the towns' autonomy was broken and their future prosperity under-

St. Dominic Burning Books—*painted while the Spanish Inquisition was at its height.*

mined by royal taxation and social policies.

Ferdinand and Isabella also stripped the nobility of autonomous political power. Royal police enforced order, dueling and private warfare were forbidden, baronial castles were torn down, and the crown regained part of the lands previously seized from the royal domain. The monarchs relied on councils and courts rather than the cortes, which they seldom called. The Catholic sovereigns also attempted to

*The Renaissance: 1300–ca. 1520*

abolish serfdom, but in Aragon success was limited to the abolition of a few practices such as noble rights to peasant brides. The crown also took over the patronage and income of the three great wealthy crusading orders, which the nobility had controlled. The nobles' political role was further diminished by the Crown's use of churchmen and townsmen as jurists and administrators. But these officials sought and were accorded privileges and status defined by noble social ideals.

Military changes also affected the nobility as Spanish infantrymen and artillery replaced feudal troop levies. Assembled in phalanxes of hollow squares called *tercios,* these troops made Spain dominant on the battlefields of Europe for a century and a half. The monarchs, however, had no intention of making war on the aristocracy as a social class. Except where potential political rivalry was involved the nobility retained and enlarged its wealth, privileges, and social importance. Once noblemen ceased to be a revolutionary danger, they dominated the court, which became the font of further privileges, sinecures, and appointments to high civil, military, and clerical posts.

In establishing royal control over the Roman Catholic church the monarchs removed another rival and made its structure serve their ends. In addition to gaining control of the crusading orders, the Crown dominated another ecclesiastical source of revenue and power, the Spanish Inquisition, established by a papal bull of 1478. Although its procedures were no worse than those of many other secular and clerical courts, the scope of its activity under Tomás Torquemada and Cardinal Ximénes earned it a well-deserved reputation as a secret terrorist agency. The Crown appointed the inquisitors and shared the confiscated property of its victims. Until Christian "deviationists" became suspect during the Reformation, the primary targets were converted and unconverted Jews and Moors.

Ferdinand and Isabella obtained the power to nominate, in addition to the inquisitors, all major ecclesiastics in Castile, Aragon, and Sicily. Not only did they reward loyal servants with ecclesiastical posts, but the state also took a portion of the tithes collected. Themselves technically exempt from secular taxation, the clergy of the wealthy Spanish church acted as zealous agents of the royal treasury. Having achieved their political and financial objectives, the sovereigns had no intention of further despoiling the church. Churchmen such as Cardinal Ximénes, Isabella's confessor and, later, regent on Ferdinand's death, held the most powerful positions in the monarchy. Clerical keepers of the royal conscience played a larger role in Spain than in any other European state.

Although the monarchy's rise to political ascendancy was aided by the towns, its economic policies were detrimental to both merchant capitalism and productive enterprise. Pressed for foreign exchange, which sales of wool would provide, Ferdinand and Isabella confirmed the privileges of the Mesta, a corporation of shepherds whose long sheep drives to and from summer pastures destroyed peasant agriculture. They also increased the *alcabala,* a tax on every commercial transaction. Maintenance of a large army and diplomatic corps increased taxes which, thanks to the exemption granted clergy and nobility, fell primarily on the commoners. In catering to popular prejudices the Inquisition harassed, or secured the expulsion of, the most productive economic groups, the Jews and the Moors. Lacking native capitalists after the Jews were expelled in 1492, the Crown relied for financial support on German and Italian bankers, who in turn secured control of many royal revenues. Internal economic policies favored the privileged, restrictive position of master guildsmen rather than merchant capitalists. Although the Crown's treasury was supplemented by New World metals, most of the revenues for Spain's expansionist policies came from domestic sources. In the sixteenth century the strains of supporting a world empire proved too much for the domestic economy, while imports of bullion from the New World inflated domestic prices to the point that Spain could not compete successfully in foreign markets.

The first decades of the sixteenth century marked the reconciliation of the nobility with royal predominance. When the new Habsburg king, Charles I (1516–56), initially appointed Burgundians* to the highest posts in church and state and increased court expenses tenfold, Castilian nobles joined townsmen in revolt. When the nobles realized that their town allies were hostile to aristocratic privileges, however, they accepted Charles's promise that he would henceforth appoint only Spaniards to office. Thus the nobility again turned to the court as the protector of its privileges. As the Renaissance era drew to a close the nobles found the court lavish in providing the means of securing fortunes. Particularly fruitful for them were the burgeoning expansion of Spain (and Portugal) into the New World and the protracted Habsburg-Valois wars of the sixteenth century.†

## England and France: The Hundred Years' War and After

As in Italy and the Iberian peninsula, the Renaissance period in England and France was marked by both internal and external conflicts, which led to the establishment of authoritarian governments that curbed domestic turmoil and directed aggressive energies outward. Unlike the Iberian and Italian peninsulas, however, England and France had had strong medieval monarchies.

After the Norman conquest of 1066 England had greater legal and economic unity than any other European kingdom. Edward I (1272–1307) reversed feudal decentralization by attaching nobles directly to the king and forbidding them to grant fiefs to underlings owing allegiance to themselves rather than to the monarch. Out of Edward's royal council evolved a Parliament that drew the aristocracy, townsmen, and clergy into the affairs of the entire kingdom. His successor Edward III (1327–77) humbled the barons and wielded an effective (though legally limited) political, judicial, and administrative authority in conjunction with Parliament.

Because English kings held large sections of France (as vassals of the French kings), English power was a constant threat to the security of the French throne, and over a period of 175 years feudal warfare had flared up intermittently between the French Capetians and their overmighty English royal vassals. When the direct male Capetian line died out in 1328, English kings claimed the French throne itself. Anglo-French conflicts went deeper, however, than feudal and dynastic rivalries. France supported Scotland, England's perennial enemy; it also sought to acquire Flanders, the principal market for English wool; and seamen of both countries engaged in piracy and coastal raids. War broke out in 1338 when the French king seized England's feudal property. Thereafter and sporadically for more than 100 years popular passions contributed to wanton destruction, pillage, and the killing of prisoners and noncombatants. Large parts of France were denuded of people and economic resources.

The opening phases of the Hundred Years' War demonstrated the superiority of English ships and the ability of yeomen armed with longbows to win battles such

---

* For Charles's ties to Burgundy see below, p. 53.
† For the Habsburg-Valois wars see below, pp. 76, 90.

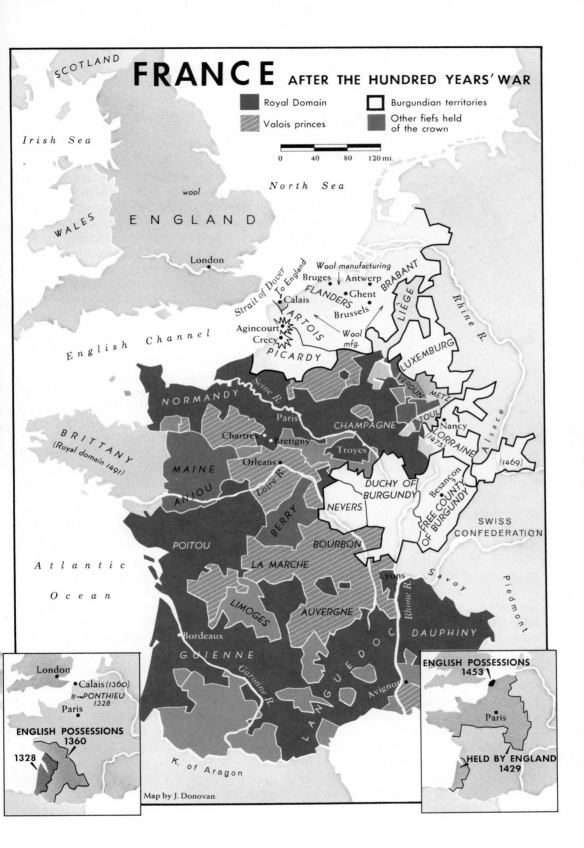

# FRANCE AFTER THE HUNDRED YEARS' WAR

Royal Domain
Valois princes
Burgundian territories
Other fiefs held of the crown

0   40   80   120 mi.

SCOTLAND

*Irish Sea*

WALES   E N G L A N D

London

*North Sea*

wool

*English Channel*

Strait of Dover

To England

Wool manufacturing

Bruges   Antwerp   BRABANT

Calais   FLANDERS   Ghent

ARTOIS   Brussels   LIEGE

Agincourt   Wool mfg.   LUXEMBURG

Crecy   PICARDY

Rhine R.

*Atlantic*

NORMANDY   Seine R.

Paris

BRITTANY
(Royal domain 1491)

Chartres   Bretigny   CHAMPAGNE   VERDUN   METZ

MAINE   Orleans   Troyes   TOUL   Nancy

ANJOU   Loire R.   LORRAINE   Alsace
(1475)

BERRY   NEVERS   DUCHY OF
BURGUNDY   Besancon   (1469)

POITOU   BOURBON   FREE COUNTY
OF BURGUNDY   SWISS
CONFEDERATION

LA MARCHE   Lyons

*Atlantic*   LIMOGES   AUVERGNE   Savoy   Piedmont

*Ocean*   Bordeaux   Rhone R.   DAUPHINY

GUIENNE   LANGUEDOC

Garonne R.   Avignon

K. of Aragon

London

Calais (1360)
PONTHIEU
1328

Paris

**ENGLISH POSSESSIONS**
**1360**

**1328**

Map by J. Donovan

**ENGLISH POSSESSIONS**
**1453**

Paris

**HELD BY ENGLAND**
**1429**

*Early field gun and gunmaster.*

General by collecting war taxes, maintaining a standing army independent of its control, and dealing with select groups of notables rather than the formal representatives of the kingdom. Until approximately 1440 Charles VII, financially assisted by Jacques Coeur, attempted to centralize the entire monarchical structure under royal authority. The king emerged from the war with independent tax powers, a small standing army, control over the French church and, for the period, a substantial bureaucracy. Before the end of the war, however, he was obliged to begin making concessions to local provinces and duchies. Local *parlements* (law courts) were established in many provinces; royal finances were decentralized; and laws were codified locally by estates or assemblies rather than by a national Estates General.

Charles's successor, Louis XI (1461–83), used force to suppress the nobility politically but compensated them with pensions and emoluments so that he became their principal benefactor socially and economically. French constitutional development after the Hundred Years' War was marked by tension between centralized royal authority and the provincial law courts and estates that upheld local autonomy. At the level of central government Louis and his immediate successors (Charles VIII, Louis XII, and Francis I) ignored the Estates General and ruled absolutely. Nevertheless French commoners found "government" and aristocracy to mean very much the same, for provincial authorities maintained their rights in vigorous local estates. Thus French absolutism was still far from absolute.

Because England was spared battle at home during the Hundred Years' War, it suffered less than France; hence its social, political, and constitutional development differed considerably from those of France.

Parliament, for example, retained control over finances, and in 1399 it even

as those of Crécy (1346), Poitiers (1356) and, later, Agincourt (1415). But sufficient resources to conquer and garrison France were lacking, and by the beginning of the fifteenth century France had recovered from early defeats. Henry V's new invasion after 1415 was successful, but it affected the new course of the war only temporarily. In 1428 the French rallied once again, this time under the leadership of Joan of Arc, whom the English burned at the stake in 1431. Finally in 1453 the English made peace, retaining only the port of Calais.

The Hundred Years' War left deep marks on France's constitutional and political development. At first the Estates General was brought into prominence. It represented the privileged clergy, nobles, and commoners who were called to vote taxes, ratify treaties, and deal with crises in which the Crown felt the need of support from its leading subjects. But later French kings undermined the Estates-

deposed a monarch who displayed absolutist tendencies. Instead of representing three estates separately as on the Continent, it evolved into a two-house body. Dissatisfied with their status, the lower clergy withdrew from the lower house, (the Commons); in that house knights and townsmen were joined together, significantly bridging a broad social gulf (an achievement that continental assemblies were never able to effect). The House of Lords represented the titled nobility and prelates. Together the houses of Parliament acted as both a court and a legislature—not a modern legislative body, yet the king's enactments in response to grievances presented by it gave its members a role in legislation that tended to make England a limited constitutional monarchy.

For administration in the counties English kings had no paid bureaucracy comparable to that of the French monarchy. They depended rather on newly created justices of the peace—paid by fees and drawn from prominent local families —who thereafter became the local governors of England, although they were subject to parliamentary statutes applicable to the whole kingdom.

Neither Parliament nor the justices of the peace represented the interests of either the peasantry or the lower urban classes. Following the Black Death, the Statute of Laborers (1351) charged justices of the peace with checking the wage increases that resulted from the shortage of labor. Angered by the egalitarian doctrines of anticlerical priests known as "Lollards" (see p. 595) and reacting to severe poll taxes, in 1381 the peasants and townsmen revolted. Disarmed by the king's false concessions to their demands, including emancipation from serfdom, the revolutionaries were easily suppressed; but their failure did not check the gradual release of English leaseholders from compulsory services, a process completed in the sixteenth century.

Hostile to the wealth of the Church, the revolt of 1381 was evidence of the strong antipapal and often anticlerical sentiments that led to state encroachment on the Church's independence during the Hundred Years' War. As early as 1279 the English Parliament had acted to curtail further transfers of property to the "dead hand" of the Church,* where they no longer produced revenues. But political conditions during the Hundred Years' War favored stronger measures, since the papacy at Avignon was considered a tool of French foreign policy. Until his Lollard followers became embroiled in the revolt of 1381, John Wycliffe (1320?–84) was allowed to attack the validity of sacramental rites performed by miscreant priests and to urge that the Church be stripped of its temporal wealth.† Parliament itself enacted laws that regulated papal appointments, although enforcement by the Crown was not always consistent. Additional laws restricted the papacy's legal jurisdiction and stopped feudal payments to the pope.

Following the Hundred Years' War England was plagued by feuds between private armies. Nobles had assembled bands of warriors under their "livery and maintenance" (i.e., under their colors and at their expense) in the course of the wars with Scotland and France during the fourteenth and fifteenth centuries. Finally these feuds merged in the dynastic Wars of the Roses,‡ from which the first Tudor monarch, Henry VII, emerged victorious in 1485. Fearful of further disorders, Henry established a popular absolutism

---

* Once acquired, property—acquired through wills and gifts—could not be alienated from Church hands; hence, its policy was called *mortmain*—the dead hand.

† For further discussion of Wycliffe and the reasons why secular officials and nobles were favorably disposed toward his doctrines see p. 63.

‡ The conflict is so named because the Lancastrians used the symbol of a red rose, the Yorkists a white rose.

eign power of the state; before his reign it had already been reduced to an echo of whatever military faction was temporarily predominant. By working with Parliament, which represented the major vested interests of the kingdom, Henry wielded greater power than his French counterparts—even though Parliament continued to control taxation and deny the king a standing army. Thrust off the Continent by the Hundred Years' War, Englishmen applied their energies increasingly to commerce, industry, and mercantile expansion.

## The Rise and Fall of Burgundy

The Hundred Years' War roused national passions in England and France, but the framework of politics remained decidedly dynastic, as the rise and fall of Burgundy vividly illustrates. After the last male Capetian duke of Burgundy died of the plague in 1361, the Valois king of France gave Burgundy as an autonomous dependency to a younger son, Philip the Bold, who also received Franche-Comté, a territory between France and the Swiss Confederation, as a fief from the Holy Roman Emperor. Philip immediately contracted an ambitious marriage with the heiress of Flanders—the most industrialized, most urbanized, and richest part of northern Europe. To prevent Flanders from falling to England, on which it was dependent economically for raw wool, the French monarch agreed to Burgundian control. Marriage alliances further extended Philip's control of the Low Countries from the Somme River to the Zuyder Zee. Thereafter a succession of Burgundian dukes played off France and England against each other in the Hundred Years' War. As the leading vassal-rivals of the Valois kings, they built up a dynastic state whose revenues were probably the largest in Europe.

*Chivalric Burgundian shield.*

favorable to the commercial interests and antagonistic to the nobility. His use of the court of Star Chamber (a court made up of certain councillors who met in secret and decided cases more or less arbitrarily), his administrative organization, and his taxation policies were extraordinarily effective in establishing order, removing potential competitors for the throne, and intimidating the old nobility, whose ranks had been thinned by the dynastic wars. Henry retained Parliament as part of the sover-

When Henry V invaded France the Burgundian Duke, John the Fearless, secretly allied with the English forces and brought the archbishopric of Liège, a pioneer area in coal and iron production, under his control. His immediate successor, Philip the Good, openly allied with the English but denied them access to the Low Countries. By separate peace with the king of France at Arras in 1435, he secured royal recognition of his domain in the Low Countries. Philip brought all local principalities in that region directly or indirectly under his control and tried to acquire a royal title commensurate with his power. Burgundian expansion and its threat to the integrity of Louis XI's France reached their peak under Charles the Rash (1467–77). After almost securing royal recognition of Burgundian independence, Charles acquired rights to Alsace and then conquered Lorraine, which directly linked the Burgundian inheritance with the Low Countries. In 1474 he simultaneously allied with England and Aragon to reopen the Hundred Years' war. But instead of attacking France he pushed his troops eastward and southward along the Rhine.

Between 1475 and 1477, however, Charles's dreams of imperial grandeur rapidly faded. Deserted by Burgundy, England made a separate peace. Meanwhile Louis XI supported revolts in Alsace and Lorraine, and the Swiss and the Austrian Habsburgs joined the ranks of Burgundy's enemies. The empire retrieved Alsace, and in 1476 Charles was twice beaten roundly by Swiss pikemen. In 1477 he died in the siege of Nancy, in Lorraine, without leaving a male heir.

Territorial aggrandizement had proceeded more rapidly than political centralization. At Charles's death the duchy of Burgundy was still a personal union of disparate principalities; Louis XI of France thereupon reclaimed it and occupied Franche-Comté. To protect her inheritance Charles's daughter, Mary, married Max-

*Burgundian defense of a beseiged town.*

imilian, son of the Holy Roman Emperor. By this dynastic marriage Burgundy became the cradle of the greatest political coalition of the sixteenth century for, as part of an anti-French diplomatic maneuver, Philip the Handsome, son of Mary and Maximilian, married Joanna the Mad, daughter of Isabella and Ferdinand of Spain. Philip's and Joanna's son Charles in time inherited the Spanish throne as well as the Low Countries and in 1519 was elected to the imperial title. Thereafter the Burgundian inheritance* became part of the Habsburg Empire, but the continued existence of the Low Countries as a political entity separate from France and the

* In 1493 France abandoned claims to the Netherlands and Franche-Comté to Maximilian by treaty; nevertheless, the French monarchy did not give up attempts at recovering Franche-Comté. Quarrels over the Burgundian inheritance became a major cause of the Habsburg-Valois wars of the sixteenth century.

*C. Socioeconomic, Political, Religious Developments*

empire remained as a monument to Burgundy's fleeting existence.

Socially and politically Burgundy was a mirror of the major conflicts of the Renaissance. Drawing revenues from the most advanced urban centers of northern Europe, its court effected a dazzling revival of chivalry. Under its great bourgeois administrators the court consumed immense revenues—and much borrowed money besides—for festive displays, ceremonies, and tournaments. Court etiquette became incredibly complicated and formalized. There was even a hierarchy of kitchen hands. The dukes collected libraries and patronized historians whose writings upheld chivalric values. The court was also the major patron of a Northern, "Gothic" Renaissance in sculpture, painting, drama, and poetry. Such genteel activity, however, did not prevent the dukes from practicing ruthless power politics. They also effectively utilized propaganda to appeal to the lower classes, established universities to train officials, and sponsored the codification of laws in local provinces. Thus a romantic chivalry and a realistic use of administrative power existed side by side.

Eventually this most flamboyant of princely courts collided head on with the social and political aspirations of urban guildsmen and the common people of Ghent, Ypres, and Bruges, already in revolt against the patrician oligarchies of merchants. French kings supported urban revolts in Flanders while Burgundian dukes aided French rebels. But in their own domains the dukes proceeded ruthlessly and successfully against democratic movements in the towns.

## The Holy Roman Empire

Meanwhile the Holy Roman Empire continued to disintegrate into local clerical and secular principalities. Triumph of the more influential princes over the emperors, towns, and papacy was formalized by the Golden Bull of 1356, which remained the basic constitution of the empire until its dissolution in 1806. As declared in the bull, permanent right to elect the emperor was vested in three archbishoprics (Mainz, Cologne, and Trier) and four secular principalities (Saxony, Brandenburg, the Rhine Palatinate, and Bohemia), with the papacy excluded from elections. The bull forbad unauthorized leagues of towns, and until 1489 the imperial cities were not recognized as an estate within the Imperial Diet (Reichstag). On the other hand, the princes constituted a second "house" within the Reichstag. And the third "house," the Electors, whom the emperor had to consult on convening the Reichstag (as well as on other matters), imposed crippling checks on the imperial executive. Lacking administrative officials, taxes, and a fixed capital, the emperor had to depend on the resources of his inherited personal domains to govern imperial affairs.

During the fourteenth century the emperors drawn from the House of Luxembourg failed to check the tide of decentralization and the consolidation of local princely domains. Nor were the Habsburgs, who after 1438 held the imperial title, any more successful, despite their large holdings along the Danube. Authority in the German states centered on local principalities that, because of the absence of primogeniture and inheritance contracts, were divided and redivided among heirs. Thus hundreds of splintered principalities of Germany developed their own systems of officials and courts bringing the local towns, nobility, and churches under varying degrees of dependence.* Over all of these affairs, therefore, the empire had but little control.

During the fifteenth century the empire not only lost border territories but failed to maintain internal order as it had done

---

* Not all of the ecclesiastical states were thus fragmented, however.

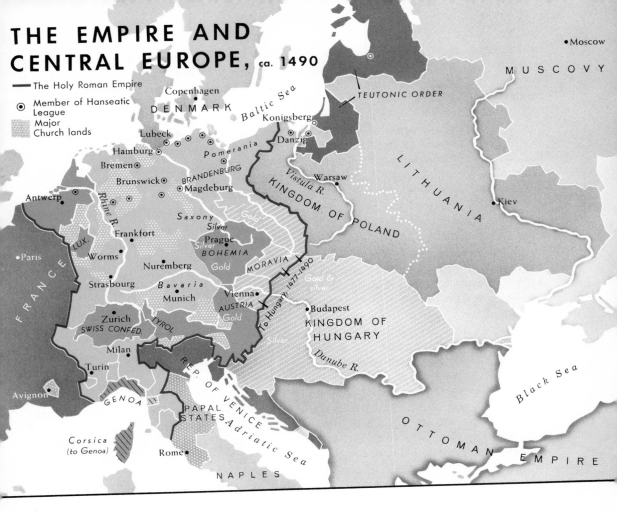

# THE EMPIRE AND CENTRAL EUROPE, ca. 1490

— The Holy Roman Empire

⊙ Member of Hanseatic League

Major Church lands

in the fourteenth century. As we have seen above, Italy had already escaped from imperial control. So had the forest cantons of the Swiss Confederation, whose infantry was more than a match for feudal knights unfamiliar with the mountainous terrain. They achieved almost complete independence in the fourteenth century. In standing off the aggressive designs of the emperor Switzerland remained a republican irritant both to him and to the German princes. On the eastern frontier German penetration (by the Teutonic Knights and colonists) was turned back. Indeed, during the 1420s the Bohemian Hussites* not only repulsed repeated

* See p. 64.

crusades but also in turn ravaged large parts of eastern Germany. Throughout the long inactive reign of Frederick III (1440–93), the empire lost territory to Burgundy and on two occasions the Hungarian king seized Vienna. Internally German society remained as turbulent during the fourteenth century as the western kingdoms. The nobility persisted in waging private warfare and preying on commerce. In 1493 the emperor complained that "the nobility as well as the common man was in great poverty." Ever-new taxes only left the populace restive and left insolvent those governments that were overweighted with military expenditures.

Demands for reform were vocal and

*C. Socioeconomic, Political, Religious Developments*

widespread, but almost invariably they became muted in the din of conflict between the emperor and the princes. A Reichstag at Worms in 1495 tried to provide a constitutional "reformation" by banning private warfare and establishing an imperial high court. Reform was carried further in Cologne in 1512, when local "circles" were organized for defense and the emperor obtained an administrative council. In addition, monopolistic banking and trading companies in the imperial cities were dissolved, at least on paper.

But in practice all these reforms amounted to little. The ban on private warfare was enforced primarily against increasing revolts by townsmen, peasants, and imperial knights, while the major princes continued to fight dynastic battles with impunity. The trading companies were not in fact dissolved. And the court and council could not function effectively without an imperial army and tax system. Chronic differences between princes and emperor made cooperative efforts for reform difficult. The difficulty became especially acute after the Habsburgs secured the imperial election of Charles, already duke of Burgundy and king of Spain. When shortly after this triumph they dispossessed the duke of Wurttemberg (1520), princely tempers flared again. United by growing fears of Habsburg domination, the princes were able to score a resounding victory at the Diet of Worms (1521), where the question of constitutional reform was finally passed upon.*

## The Eastern Frontiers

During the fourteenth and fifteenth centuries eastern Europe absorbed little of the

---

* Although the Diet of Worms is most famous for the appearance there of Martin Luther, the outcome of his case before the Diet, as will be related in the next chapter, is inexplicable apart from the constitutional crisis of the Holy Roman Empire.

culture of the West. Through royal courts, colonization, and commerce, Western sociopolitical institutions filtered into parts of the area—Poland-Lithuania, Bohemia, Hungary, Novgorod—but the vast distance that separated many areas of eastern Europe from the commercial centers of the West retarded the development of a flourishing town life. So did endemic warfare and the hostility of princes and noblemen. For the most part, therefore, the political and social life of eastern Europe was oriented away from the culture of the West. East of the Elbe River peasants began to lose their legal status as independent yeomen, and by the seventeenth century many had become formally bound to soil and master. The critical development for the political evolution of all eastern Europe was the rise of two aggressive, non-Western military autocracies, Muscovy and the Ottoman Empire.

Because of its great size the most striking state in eastern Europe during the Renaissance was the dynastic union of Poland-Lithuania. The dual kingdom extended from the Baltic to the Black Sea, and occasionally as far east as Moscow. Lithuania incorporated most of the medieval Russian state of Kiev. Twice Poland defeated the Teutonic Knights and eventually turned the order into a feudal dependency; but royal power was on the wane. With stubborn persistence nobles and gentry usurped the governing authority, crowded urban merchants out of the diets, and reduced the legal status of the peasantry.

Other strong monarchies in eastern Europe did not survive the Renaissance era. Serbia's empire was destroyed by the Turks and Hungarians in the fourteenth century. Bohemia emerged only briefly into prominence during the Hussite period* of the 1420s and 1430s when it was a center of popular revolution and military

---

* For the Hussites see p. 64.

might. With the Turkish invasion of the Balkan peninsula after 1333, Hungary became a buffer state, a military frontier between Ottoman and Habsburg. It achieved a strong central government only under Matthias Corvinus, after whose death without an heir in 1490 the nobility regained most of its privileges.

On the far northeastern fringes of Europe the princes of Muscovy built a more lasting autocratic state, almost totally outside the reach of Western influence. The part of Kievan Russia that had not been incorporated into Lithuania fell under the suzerainty of the Mongol-led Tartars (1238) until Muscovite princes threw off the "Tartar yoke" and substituted their own authority for it. Under the Tartars these same princes had gained ascendency by collecting tribute and helping to suppress revolts. They also made Moscow the seat of the Russian Orthodox church. The latter's repudiation of both Rome and Constantinople as corrupt centers of Christianity made it easy to identify the divine mission of Moscow—the "Third Rome"—with the Muscovite state.

With full Church support Ivan III and Vasili III pushed Muscovite frontiers to the Baltic Sea and the Ural Mountains by purchase, treaty, and war. Noteworthy victims of their military autocracy were the city-states Novgorod (1478) and Pskov (1510), whose institutional and social developments had closely paralleled those of the city-states of Italy. The czars rooted out their republican institutions and exiled their leading citizens into remote areas. As a consequence Russia, lacking a native middle class, failed to develop a diet or parliament comparable to those of the Renaissance kingdoms of the West. Most Russians, in fact, remained peasants on the estates of the military aristocracy, and for the next two centuries the general trend was toward a uniform level of serfdom.

EXPANSION OF MUSCOV TO 1533

Map by J. Dor

Muscovite expansion cut off Western trade routes and more than ever isolated Russia from the West; but the other Eastern autocracy, the Ottoman Empire, thrust itself into Western affairs, invading by land and sea. Originally mercenaries of the Seljuk Turks from Asia Minor, the Ottomans took possession of Anatolia and turned it into a base for imperialism. Heading the government, the army, and the Church was the sultan, who relied on slaves as administrators and infantrymen. His military machine was further served by fief-holding cavalrymen and by the development of effective artillery. By 1333 the Ottomans had reached the Dardenelles; thereafter they moved into the Balkan peninsula, overrunning Greeks, Serbs, and Bulgarians. Thus they encircled Constantinople, whose empire had degenerated into feudal factions and civil war. In 1453 the old capital of the eastern

*C. Socioeconomic, Political, Religious Developments*

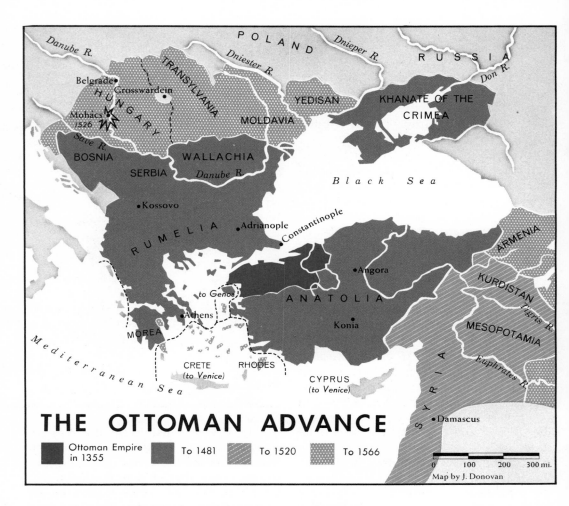

THE OTTOMAN ADVANCE

| | | |
|---|---|---|
| ■ Ottoman Empire in 1355 | ■ To 1481 | ▨ To 1520 |
| ▨ To 1566 | | |

0   100   200   300 mi.

Map by J. Donovan

Roman Empire fell. Until 1480 the Turks pressed their advantage in the Balkans and in the eastern Mediterranean; then Europe received a respite for 40 years. But between 1515 and 1519 the Turks doubled their empire in the Near East by conquering Persia, Mesopotamia, Syria, and Egypt. These victories put the Ottomans in control of the overland trade to the Far East, a commercial advantage that was weakened, however, by Portugal's earlier establishment of a cheaper, all-water route to the Indies around Africa. At the end of the Renaissance the Ottoman Empire was poised to launch a new wave of invasions of Europe.

Ottoman expansion revived talk of crusades in Europe, but the crusading spirit against foreign infidels had been replaced by interest in dynastic conflicts and forceful maintenance of the social status quo. Venice salvaged part of her Mediterranean empire by coming to terms with the Turks. In 1494 Pope Alexander VI sought an alliance with the Turks against France, and in subsequent years France repeatedly allied with them against the Habsburgs. The renewed Turkish attacks after 1520 coincided with the outbreak of religious strife in Germany and the beginning of a long series of Habsburg-Valois conflicts. The impact of this new thrust had serious consequences that we shall consider in the following chapter.

## The Territorial State

Eastern autocracies centralized their states by military conquest. More typical of the West was the growth of bureaucratic governments that partially daunted or displaced the feudal and ecclesiastical authorities, who were already their nominal subjects. Commerce encouraged consolidation by providing a taxable money economy, regular lines of communication, demands for secure trade routes, and economic problems too broad for local authorities. Privileged officials also gave impetus to centralization, but they often employed their increased powers for personal and family gain. More significant for the centralization of authority were the great problems of internal disorder and warfare that confronted every Western state. At some point during the Renaissance private warfare waged by feudal nobles or bands of mercenaries destroyed the internal security of every major state. Civil war shook nearly every town as the lower classes, aided by local peasants, rose against their oligarchical authorities. New taxes imposed on townsmen and peasants to meet the costs of modernized warfare (fought with mercenary troops and guns) commonly caused these revolts.

European responses to these problems varied, but they shared a common pattern in the emergence of authoritarian territorial states. The transition from feudal to national monarchy made the greatest advance in England. By limiting royal power Parliament made its extension over courts, church, towns, military forces, and taxation acceptable to, at least, the propertied classes. French centralization began later and was less complete. Royal officials encroached on the political prerogatives of church and nobility, and the kings relied on the officials rather than cooperate with the Estates General. By circumventing the latter's control of finance, French monarchs achieved absolute control of the army. In the provinces, however, their officials met with local vested interests that they could superintend but not control. Spanish centralization began still later. At the end of the fifteenth century royal absolutism emerged from feudal chaos in Castile, but other kingdoms of the peninsula successfully resisted royal discipline and incorporation into a single territorial unit. In the empire secular princes began to build territorial states, but their dynastic conflicts disrupted public order and weakened the empire's external security. A similar decentralization occurred in Italy, except that the local Italian states achieved unmatched compactness and administrative efficiency.

Everywhere except in the various political entities of northern Italy territorial authority was incompletely centralized—but all of these states legislated economic and social controls and curbed the autonomous power of the Church, the nobility, and the town corporations. This authoritarianism imposed some degree of order and social stability. In international affairs, however, internal consolidation was a prelude to dynastic warfare on an unprecedented scale. This consolidation and conflict naturally posed grave problems for the one institution in Europe whose claims to authority transcended the local territorial states—the Roman Catholic church.

## CRISIS IN THE CHURCH

For the Roman Catholic church the Renaissance was a period of unprecedented crisis. Although its institutional machinery had never been more centrally organized, the areas of its jurisdiction and effective obedience were shrinking. Popular piety may not have been declining, but ecclesiastical influence on culture and secular activities clearly was. Part of the problem concerned the inability to meet the spiritual needs of a great many Europeans; another grew out of the old church-state disputes of the High Middle Ages.

## The Papacy at Avignon

Medieval Church reformers had attempted to wrest control from secular rulers by concentrating authority in the papacy. In elaborating papal claims to spiritual and secular authority canon lawyers developed a full-blown theory of the pope's sovereignty. In the words of a leading fourteenth-century canon lawyer, "The pope is the wonder of the world. . . . He is neither God nor man, just as if he were neuter, he is between the two."[5] Renaissance monarchs were no more inclined than their predecessors to accept papal supremacy over the hierarchy, which included bishops and abbots with political as well as religious functions. In the medieval investiture struggle with the Holy Roman Emperor the papacy had won; but during the pontificate of Boniface VIII (1294–1303), himself a canon lawyer, the Church failed to make good its claims to the right of superintending secular rulers.

In 1296 Boniface forbade laymen to collect levies from the clergy and the clergy to pay them without the pope's authorization. Supported by a new institution—Parliament—Edward I frustrated Boniface by outlawing the clergy. Philip IV of France also defeated this enactment by forbidding the export of money and valuables from the kingdom. Philip and Boniface soon clashed again, however. After Philip's courts charged a bishop with blasphemy, heresy, and treason, Boniface called a council to reform the French government. Buoyed by a successful jubilee in Rome and a Flemish victory over France, Boniface issued a bull in 1302 (*Unam Sanctam*) in which he reaffirmed the old claim of papal supremacy in the most resounding language ever used by a pope. Infuriated, Philip responded with a boldness and brutality that indicated how little regard monarchs felt for the moral authority of the pope. In 1303 Philip assembled a meeting of clergy, nobles, and commons in Paris—France's first Estates General—to increase his support. Then Philip's henchman, the great lawyer Nogaret, went to Italy and invaded the little town of Anagni where the pope was staying, with the object of dragging him to France to depose him. The townspeople prevented that, but Boniface died soon after (1303).

Thereafter Philip secured a total victory, including the exoneration of Nogaret. In 1309 the pope (Clement V) moved the papal see to the little enclave of Avignon in southern France. Here French influence predominated until 1378, giving credence to the belief, in other kingdoms, that the papacy was in "Babylonian Captivity," subservient to the foreign policy of France.

During the years of the Babylonian Captivity the Avignon popes expanded the central administration of the Church, the Curia. The chancery, courts, and diplomatic service of the Church excelled those of all contemporary governments. Particularly elaborate was collection of the pope's revenue. Because some of the traditional sources of income such as tithes had fallen to lay collectors, other resources were developed. In addition to exacting various smaller obligations, the Curia levied a tax on the clergy's net income, which drew tremendous amounts from great prelates unprotected by their rulers. New offices were created and sold, and fees were set for dispensations, absolutions, legal cases, and document services. The sale of in-

[5] Johannes Andreae, *Glossa ad Proemium s. v. papa,* in *Clementis Papae Quinti Constitutiones* (Paris, 1601).

dulgences* also became a major source of income.

The Avignon papacy marked the Church's adjustment to a world of commercial wealth. To handle papal accounts the popes turned to the great banking houses whose services were necessary for the collection and disbursement of funds in diverse currencies. In the eyes of its critics the Avignon papacy was also seen to mark a period in which monetary concerns dominated papal policies. Finance took precedence over other administrative tasks which, due partly to the sale of offices and exemptions (simony), were often in disarray. Moreover, centralization of ecclesiastical courts inevitably led to conflicts between the secular states and the papacy over conflicting jurisdictions. Governments at odds with Avignon curtailed papal courts, taxes, land acquisition, and appointments. Some of them protected heretics who drew wide popular followings, and not a few pitted claims of divine-right kingship against papal claims of divine authority.

## The Great Schism and the Conciliar Movement

In 1378 papal prestige and influence plunged further when part of the College of Cardinals seceded and elected a second pope. Thus arose the Great Schism, with rival popes at Rome and Avignon claiming divine sovereignty, exchanging anathemas, sponsoring polemical propaganda, erecting competing administrative and tax systems, and vying for support of local hierarchies. For the most part, foreign policy considerations determined alignment behind one or the other pope.

* In the fourteenth and fifteenth centuries indulgences were exemptions from temporal punishment of sins in purgatory granted by authority of papally sanctioned writs to penitents or persons representing the dead.

More than the Babylonian Captivity, the Great Schism invited total rejection of the ecclesiastical system and the subordination of local hierarchies to secular rulers.

Since each pope considered himself the only true Vicar of Christ and the apostolic successor to St. Peter, the schism seemed constitutionally insoluble without abandonment of the principle of papal sovereignty. One of the two popes would have to step down; but neither would. The two separate colleges of cardinals offered no solution, for each perpetuated its own line of popes.

To end the Great Schism such University of Paris scholars as Pierre d'Ailly and Jean de Gerson argued the doctrine of conciliarism, which held that Church councils, which princes as well as popes could summon, possessed authority equal to or greater than that of the pope. One recalls that many councils were held since the first ecumenical one at Nicaea in A.D. 325 in order to resolve fundamental problems. In 1409 a new council convened at Pisa. It debated the schism, the urgency of moral and administrative reform, and the spread of heresy. Dealing with the schism first, the council elected a new pope. But alas! Both existing popes denounced the council's authority and refused to give way. So now the Church had three successors to St. Peter, each claiming full papal powers.

Since Pisa resolved nothing, the Holy Roman Emperor Sigismund took the initiative in forcing another council at Constance (1414–18). The problems were still the same: schism, reform "in head and members," and the spreading heresy, especially the Hussite heresy in Bohemia. The dead Wycliffe was anathematized. The leaders of Bohemian dissent, John Hus and Jerome of Prague, were interrogated, condemned, and burned at the stake despite guarantees of safe conduct granted by the emperor. Instead of moderating Bohemian dissent, the executions spurred Bohemia into a national religious revolt.

On constitutional issues the Council of Constance was more assertive and successful than Pisa. In legislation that anticipated acts of the seventeenth-century English Parliament against divine-right kings, the council declared in the decree *Sacrosancta* (1415) that it possessed sovereignty directly delegated by Christ, whence its authority was superior to that of the contesting popes. In 1417 it decreed that regular councils should be held whether or not the pope convoked them. By persuasion and coercion it also secured the resignation of all three existing popes and the reestablishment of a single papal line under Martin V. The Great Schism ended, but Martin V promptly repudiated the conciliar movement that ended it by reaffirming papal sovereignty.

The hostility of the popes delayed any future conciliar action of significance until 1431, when churchmen assembled at Basel (1431–49). The theme of this convocation was the conflict between conciliar and papal powers. The delegates eventually voted to depose Eugenius IV and replace him with another head of the Church. Radicalism divided the council and made enforcement of its decisions impossible; nor could the council abrogate papal taxes or reform papal appointment procedures. Following the collapse of the crusades against the Hussites, the council was obliged to offer them concessions, which constituted a disastrous blow to the council's prestige.

Pope Eugenius outmaneuvered the embarrassed council by calling an official rival council at Ferrara and Florence (1438–45) and by negotiating a much-heralded but empty reunion with the Eastern Orthodox church (1439), whose sees were being overrun by the Turks. More significantly, Eugenius won monarchs away from their support of the council by negotiating concordats with them or by pragmatically sanctioning their curtailment of papal authority. In theory these agreements required that local Church posts be filled in the future by election; in practice they delivered control of ecclesiastical affairs to local rulers. Thus monarchical and papal authoritarianism joined hands for their mutual advantage.

Despite papal hostility the conciliar idea survived, but in 1460 Pius II threatened to excommunicate all who appealed to conciliar authority over the pope. Because any council attempting to reform the papacy would by necessity be subversive of papal sovereignty, reform by council was barred until after the Protestant Reformation made great progress, creating a new and greater crisis for the Church. On the other hand, the Renaissance popes were not free agents to carry out reforms even when they were so minded, for their hands were tied by vested ecclesiastical, noble, and monarchical interests serving the status quo.

## Heresy, Mysticism, and Reform Agitation

Christian teachings had led Europeans to believe that the hallmark of the Church was spiritual purity and Christian solicitude. What they actually saw was something quite different. The vows of poverty, chastity, and obedience were violated with impunity. Wealth was visibly used for the self-gratification of high churchmen, but parishes were poor. Many prelates held several benefices at the same time (pluralism), enjoyed their extra incomes, but were rarely if ever seen in the benefices (absenteeism). Meanwhile poverty was the lot of the vicar who substituted for the absentee churchman. Nepotism, simony, and concubinage were openly practiced. The interests of the aristocracy and wealthy townsmen were given priority over those of the poor by bishops and abbots. Mendicant friars, such as the Spiritual Franciscans who held to apostolic poverty, stimulated popular dissatisfaction with the Church by their denunciations of the worldliness of the secular clergy. It should be understood that anticlericalism was a protest against the intolerable secularism of the clergy; it was not a sign of disbelief in Christianity.

The erosion of confidence in the Church revealed itself in many ways, but the causes were not altogether the worldliness of the clergy. The Black Death (1348–50) was a traumatic event, a spiritual crisis. Occurring during the Babylonian Captivity, the early years of the Hundred Years' War, and the general retrenchment of Europe, it seemed to some a terrible judgment on wayward Christianity. Millenarianism, self-flagellation, apocalyptic prophecy, social revolt, violence, and morbid preoccupation with death (such as the "dance of death" drawings, with their grinning skeletons) were some of the manifestations of a deep fear bordering on hysteria and a spiritual dislocation that endemic plagues only deepened. Here were ample psychological conditions for a diversity of religious expression. At the same time that humanism began to give expression to lay attitudes, a kind of religious epidemic swept Europe.

Of the major heresies of the Middle Ages, Albigensianism had been reduced to impotent fragments. But the Waldensians were still active in parts of France, Italy, and Germany. They proclaimed the priesthood of all believers, denied the efficacy of sacraments performed by priests in states of mortal sin, and used the Bible as authority in opposing the hierarchy's demand for obedience.

During the Hundred Years' War John Wycliffe of Oxford, a popular preacher, writer, and scholar who assisted in the preparation of the government's antipapal enactments of the 1350s, initiated a similar heretical movement in England. Wycliffe relied on the Bible for authority and, as-serting the competence of inspired laymen to understand it, stimulated its translation into English (1380). Disdaining the hierarchical Church at Avignon, he taught that the true Church consisted of all who were predestined to salvation. He denied the miracle of the Mass, in which the priest transformed bread and wine into the flesh and blood of Christ, and from the exercise of which the priest secured his elevated status. In addition, he denounced the temporal possessions and temporal authority of churchmen. He also encouraged poor wandering priests, or "Lollards," to preach throughout the country.

Although Wycliffe taught absolute obedience to secular authority even when it was tyrannical, the royal court eventually had second thoughts about his religious orthodoxy and secured his retirement to a country estate. Wycliffe's teachings continued at Oxford, however, eventually permeating all classes of society. When they reached the lower classes through the Lollards, they became mixed with demands for secular and social reforms. The Peasants' Rebellion of 1381 involved religious radicalism, causing a conservative reaction to set in. A half-century of persecution by the authorities of church and state, during which the burning of heretics was first introduced in England, sufficed to extinguish organized Lollardy, whose ideas nevertheless lingered on until the outset of the English reformation; but as an organized movement, it had all but disappeared by the end of the Hundred Years' War.

Opposition to the affluence and secular power of the prelates, to the practice of simony, and to the sale of indulgences became general during the Renaissance. In Bohemia a heretical reform movement compounded of religious, political, and social grievances burst into widespread revolution. Religious criticism was mixed with a Czech cultural movement that emanated from Prague, the capital of Emperor Charles IV (1346–78). Dissatisfaction with ecclesiastical conditions came to a climax in the writings and teachings of John Hus (1369–1415).

A Czech of humble parentage, he became a professor at the new University of Prague as well as the queen's confessor. Drawing upon the teachings of Wycliffe and Czech predecessors, Hus and popular preachers using the Czech language attacked a host of religious malpractices. The reformers especially denounced simony, clerical immorality, scholastic philosophy, reverence of relics and saints, and the sale of indulgences. Accepting the challenge, the local archbishop excommunicated Hus and placed Prague under interdict. At first King Wenzel resisted the interdict and supported Hus, but the two disagreed over the sale of indulgences, in whose proceeds the king shared. After riots broke out in Prague, Hus retired to a country estate to write. In 1414 his case came before the Council of Constance, which stripped him of his imperial safe-conduct, condemned him for heresy, and handed him over to secular authorities to be burned at the stake.

Instead of ending the Bohemian heresy Hus's betrayal and execution fanned national and religious resistance to the Church and to the German emperor who inherited the Bohemian crown in 1419. Nobles and knights drew up a reform program; and the emperor was turned away from Prague's gates by force. Between 1420 and 1436 a series of Bohemian wars, at once civil and foreign, devastated central Europe as the Czechs turned back repeated German and papal crusades and raided neighboring territories. Internally, the Hussites split between moderate nobles and militant egalitarian radicals (Taborites) who sought the destruction of noble and clerical privileges as well as the abolition of all doctrine not to be found in the Bible. Although the Taborites were ultimately defeated, the Church was obliged to yield to doctrinal deviations that it could not stamp out by force of arms. Thus

Bohemia became the first country to carry out a successful religious reformation.* Had the printing press then been available for the reformers' use, the Hussite movement might have spread to other parts of Europe as Luther's reformation did later.

No less critical of existing conditions in the Church, but uneasily trying to remain within it, were those who deemphasized the role of the priest as mediator between God and man. They exhorted fellow Christians to establish a direct relationship to God either through self-exertion (mysticism) or by divine direction (spiritualism). Both tendencies were old within monasticism. During the Renaissance their principal advocates among the clergy were the Spiritual Franciscans, a branch of the Order of St. Francis that held to apostolic poverty in imitation of Christ and his disciples. Their literal emphasis on poverty embarrassed the popes at Avignon, who condemned them as heretics. On the fringe of the controversies over apostolic poverty was the foremost Franciscan schoolman, William of Ockham, a nominalist philosopher. Protected after 1327 by the emperor, Ockham attacked the Avignon popes and undermined the theology of the late medieval sacramental system. His most telling attack was directed against the doctrine that human reason could fathom divine will and nature; the elaborate arguments he used to undermine rational philosophy were later adopted by many Protestant reformers of the sixteenth century. Ockham was excommunicated in 1328. Moved by the mass misery wrought by the Black Death, many of the Spiritual Franciscans became involved in social revolts, extreme practices such as self-flagellation, and predictions of the imminent end of the world.

More successful in avoiding official con-

---

* Memory of this reformation has largely lapsed, however, because it was completely undone during the 1620s, a victim of the Thirty Years' War.

demnation were the mystic Upper Rhenish "Friends of God" who produced a popular devotional treatise entitled *The German Theology*. In the Netherlands others formed lay brotherhoods called Brethren of the Common Life, founded in the wake of the Black Death by Gerard Groote (1340–84), a scholar-priest from a prominent Deventer family. The Brethren organized laymen of both sexes who dedicated themselves to devotions, education, and preaching in the vernacular without taking irrevocable vows. As mystics they held the complexities of scholastic theology in low esteem and emphasized a simple ethic of humble imitation of the life of Christ. The Brethren achieved great success in educating the townspeople of the lower Rhine, and Deventer became the center of Northern humanism and an important seat of publishing. One of its pupils was Erasmus, who, as we have seen, became the leading humanist of Renaissance Europe. Despite their criticism of the clergy, the Brethren escaped excommunication during the fifteenth century. In the early part of the Reformation many of the people influenced by them apparently became "Sacramentarians," that is, persons who denied any divine miracle in the sacraments. On the other hand Ignatius Loyola, founder of the Society of Jesus during the Catholic Reformation, was significantly influenced by their writings, especially by *The Imitation of Christ*, attributed to Thomas a Kempis.

The spread and influence of the Brethren of the Common Life was only one expression of general lay piety during the Renaissance. More than half of the books published in the first half-century after the invention of printing (1450–1500) were religious, usually devotional tracts. Rites of the Church, many of which would be considered superstitious today, permeated every aspect of life. Towns competed in building churches; and, since indulgences were often granted to those who visited sacred places, crowds thronged to shrines and relic collections. Also, in areas under interdict the clergy were compelled by the laity to continue services. But the Church hierarchy was unable or unwilling to accommodate new forms of piety. After its experience with the Franciscans it refused to authorize the foundation of new orders, and critics who might otherwise not have turned against the Church's authority were forced into heresy by official condemnation.

## The Papacy of the High Renaissance

By 1450 the papacy had won a clear-cut victory over councils as the supreme authority in the Church, but it was clearly losing control over culture, the secular state, and the administrative power to effect reforms. Popular anticlericalism was a clear indication that the tutelage of clergymen, or at least the policies they pursued, were objectionable to large segments of the populace. Intervention by secular rulers to secure relief from papal authority was popularly approved. Even local prelates, especially those who owed their appointments to those rulers, offered little or no protest.

As we noted above in connection with humanism, clerical control of education and culture gradually passed, at least in part, into the hands of laymen. Wealthy patrons were commissioning secular works of art, and town schools and colleges of civil law and medicine were turning out educated laymen; thus the ranks of educated persons who were not clergymen swelled. Among the educated the cult of humanism developed a passion for the secular culture of classical antiquity. Few of these changes threatened the Church's existence, but they narrowed the scope of its accepted jurisdiction.

In the absence of ecclesiastical reform the papacy of the High Renaissance was powerless to check the erosion of its influ-

*Julius II, detail from the* Mass of Bolsena *by Raphael.*

ence. It did move, however, to regain its hold on culture and, at least in Italy, on political affairs. Popes and prelates became foremost patrons, and often even practitioners, of classical arts and letters. They sought to make humanism "safe" by drawing it into the service of religious education and scholarship. Many high churchmen became more concerned with esthetics, learning, and luxurious living than with religious doctrines and administration. Understandably, they alienated fundamentalists preoccupied with salvation, self-denial, and the traditional ideals of the Church. As social conservatives they also frustrated social as well as religious reform. Thus although the higher clergy came to terms with Renaissance arts and letters, they risked social

and doctrinal revolts against their authority.

It was the tragedy of the papacy as a temporal state to be drawn into inescapable political situations that caused it to lose further prestige as a spiritual force. During the Great Schism noble families, mercenary captains, and nearby princes and republics carved up the Papal States into local domains or dependencies. With the restoration of a single line of popes in Rome the task of recovery began. Lacking reliable officials, Renaissance popes distributed offices among their own relatives, a nepotistic device that soon yielded fresh scandals. Alexander VI (1492–1503), for example, attempted to establish his son, Cesare Borgia, at the head of a conquered family principality. Military efforts to reconquer the Papal States reached their peak under Julius II (1503–13). This "warrior pope," a patron of Michelangelo, Bramante, and Raphael, personally led his troops in the field.

Invasion of Italy by France and Spain after 1494 further complicated papal politics. The popes, fearing domination of Italy and the papacy by either France or Spain, organized "holy leagues" against whichever was more threatening at the moment. Thus papal diplomacy became indistinguishable from the secular diplomacy of the Italian city-states, and its spiritual weapons of interdict and excommunication lost all effectiveness. Eventually the papacy failed to prevent the domination of the peninsula by Spain; thereafter papal fortunes were wed to the secular power of the Spanish Habsburgs, who superintended much of the Catholic Reformation of the sixteenth century. Meanwhile the expenses of war, papal patronage of the arts, and clerical luxury alienated non-Italians, on whom fell heavy financial burdens. Particularly roused were the Germans, who had little sympathy with the purposes to which papal revenues were being put.

Failure to effect reforms and a related contest for power between popes and cardinals continued to sap papal prestige. The foremost Italian townsman, Lorenzo de' Medici, was wont to refer to Rome as a moral "cesspool" even when actively seeking ecclesiastical preferments for his son Giovanni (the future Pope Leo X). Responsibility for this reputation was not, however, due to the popes alone. The Curia, especially the cardinals, had heavy vested interests in the status quo. These they sought to extend by wringing advance concessions or "capitulations" from candidates for the Holy See who were preferably older men with short prospective reigns. As papal electors the cardinals did not want to destroy papal sovereignty; they merely sought to use it for their own ends. Alexander VI fought back by

creating 43 new cardinals, almost all from Italy and Spain, including five from his own family. But his successor, Julius II, was obliged to grant further financial and personal privileges to the cardinals. Leo X, pope when the Lutheran issue broke in Germany, let things rest as they were. His reform-minded successor, Adrian VI, the last non-Italian to sit on the papal throne, found resistance to reform too strong to overcome during his brief reign (1522–23). Papal tenure too short to master opposition and assert executive authority continued to be a source of administrative weakness throughout the sixteenth century.

## THE LEGACY OF "THE RENAISSANCE STYLE"

Now that we have surveyed the developments of the fourteenth and fifteenth centuries, let us return to our question of departure: what is the legacy of the Renaissance for the modern world? Some historians claim that "the Renaissance style" subverted tradition and pervaded the Western World, bringing with it new concepts and institutions. Prominent among these were individualism, nationalism, capitalism, the rise of the bourgeoisie as a social class, the secularization and simplification of religion, classical standards of esthetics, and an optimistic, lusty enjoyment of life. The Renaissance did include all of these elements; but to cite them as *the* Renaissance style and to imply that they were ascendant is to underestimate the heavy weight of tradition—especially in eastern Europe, Germany, and Spain—that soon dominated Italy, the hearth of Renaissance secularism. Such a "style" could and did continue to flourish only in those countries where economic and political developments were auspicious (England, the Low Countries, France).

*C. Socioeconomic, Political, Religious Developments*

Seen as a whole, the Renaissance cannot be considered a solo of subsequent modernity. Composed and performed by diverse creators, it was a dissonant symphony of contradictory voices. Nor were its ideals always novel; often they accommodated rather than undermined chivalric tradition. The "universal man," for example, had become a gentleman. But his highest values continued to be medieval: military valor, honor, and the thirst for fame and glory.

Many would measure the Renaissance by the ideals of a few of its shining lights: Lorenzo de' Medici, Leonardo da Vinci, Erasmus. These men epitomized the ideals of the Renaissance, but they did not set the tone of the succeeding age, the Reformation. Still, the humanistic world view, Renaissance esthetics, and the new concepts of state and society survived the passions of the sixteenth century. Combined with new scientific discoveries, they inspired the secular thought of the Age of Reason, thus helping to shape the world view of modern man.

## Selected Readings

*Bainton, Roland H. *Erasmus of Christendom.* New York: Charles Scribner's Sons, 1969.

*The latest and best biography of Erasmus in English. With superb quotes, good illustrations, and an extensive bibliography, it pushes the ecumenical thesis of basic agreement between Erasmus and Luther too far.*

*Berenson, Bernard. *Italian Painters of the Renaissance.* New York: World Publishing Co., Meridian Books, 1957.

*Vivid interpretations of individual painters, especially those who made of two-dimensional canvases "windowpanes" through which appeared the illusion of an external, objective reality.*

*Blunt, Anthony. *Artistic Theory in Italy 1450–1600.* London: Oxford University Press, 1962.

*This sketches with illustrations the purposes for which art was intended from the Middle Ages through the Catholic Reformation.*

Bouwsma, William J. *Venice and the Defense of Republican Liberty: Renaissance Values in the Age of the Counter Reformation.* Berkeley: University of California Press, 1968.

*An extended account of the role that civic consciousness played in Renaissance Venice and its points of collision with the papal monarchy.*

Brucker, Gene A. *Florentine Politics and Society 1343–1378.* Princeton: Princeton University Press, 1962.

*This study portrays the factional turbulence of Renaissance town life within the machinery of a "one-party" state.*

*Burke, Peter. *The Renaissance Sense of the Past.* New York: St. Martin's Press, 1969.

*A heavily documented account of the birth and growth of historical consciousness during the Renaissance.*

Burckhardt, Jacob. *The Civilization of the Renaissance in Italy.* Many editions in English.

*A discovery of the spirit of the Renaissance in the union of the classics and the genius of the Italian people. An extremely influential, controversial, and romantic interpretation of the nineteenth century.*

Bush, Douglas. *The Renaissance and English Humanism.* London: Oxford University Press, 1962.

*These are lectures that emphasize the religious traditionalism in English humanism.*

Carsten, Francis L. *The Origins of Prussia.* London: Oxford University Press, 1954.

*This traces the transition of the German-Slavic frontier from freedom to serfdom. The account goes up to the seventeenth century.*

Chabod, Federico. *Machiavelli and the Renaissance* Cambridge, Mass.: Harvard University Press, 1960.

*Essays assessing Machiavelli's realism as a political reporter and theorist; they conclude with a keen analysis of what was new in the Renaissance.*

Calmette, Joseph. *The Golden Age of Burgundy.* New York: W. W. Norton & Co., 1963.

*A cultural and political account of Burgundy's blending of northern Europe's richest urban culture, dynastic aggrandizement, and sumptuous chivalric display at court.*

*Cheyney, Edward P. *The Dawn of a New Era: 1250–1453.* Rise of Modern Europe Series. New York: Harper & Row, Publishers, 1962.

*A comprehensive summary stressing the emergence of national cultures and concluding with an extensive annotated bibliography.*

Ergang, Robert. *The Renaissance.* Princeton: D. Van Nostrand Co., 1967.

*A new account, excellent in its treatment of literature, that demonstrates the perseverance of the Burckhardtian school.*

*Ferguson, Wallace K. *Europe in Transition: 1300–1520.* Boston: Houghton Mifflin Co., 1962.

*A new standard textbook account that makes the middle of the fifteenth century a turning point from depression and internal disorder to economic improvement and dynastic consolidation.*

Ferguson, Wallace K. *The Renaissance in Historical Thought: Five Centuries of Interpretation.* Boston: Houghton Mifflin Co., 1948.

*Chronicles changing attitudes toward the Renaissance, as informative of later generations as of the Renaissance itself.*

Ferguson, Wallace K. et al. *The Renaissance: Six Essays.* New York: Harper & Row, Publishers, 1962.

*Interpretative essays by representative authorities on politics, economics, art, literature, science, and religion.*

Garin, Eugenio. *Italian Humanism, Philosophy, and Civic Life in the Renaissance.* Translated by Peter Munz. New York: Harper & Row, Publishers, 1965.

*An English translation of an influential Italian work that traces the Italian*

Renaissance up to the seventeenth century, placing considerable emphasis upon philosophy and science.

Gilbert, Felix. *Machiavelli and Guicciardini: Politics and History in Six-teenth-Century Florence.* Princeton: Princeton University Press, 1965.

This study contrasts subjects' political theory with humanist writing of history and relates it to the actual conditions of practical politics, including the partisan factions to which each belonged.

*Gilmore, Myron P. *The World of Humanism: 1453–1517.* Rise of Modern Europe Series. New York: Harper & Row, Publishers, 1962.

A general history of all Europe and its contacts with other civilizations.

Hay, Denys. *The Italian Renaissance in its Historical Background.* Cambridge: Cambridge University Press, 1961.

A readable survey based on the most recent scholarship.

*Hexter, J. H. *Reappraisals in History.* New York: Harper & Row, Publishers, 1961.

A collection of articles on early modern European history that provocatively challenges such commonly accepted clichés as "the rise of the middle class."

Huizinga, Johan. *The Waning of the Middle Ages.* Garden City: Doubleday & Co., 1954.

A perceptive cultural history (based on the Low Countries) that fails to find evidence of revolutionary changes during the Renaissance.

Leff, Gordon. *Heresy in the Later Middle Ages: The Relation of Heterodoxy to Dissent ca. 1250—ca. 1450.* 2 vols. New York: Barnes & Noble, 1967.

A brilliant account of the mystics and heretics of the Renaissance period with apt conclusions about the role official repression played in driving dissenters to extremes.

*Lucki, Emil. *History of the Renaissance 1350–1550.* Salt Lake City: University of Utah Press, 1963–65.

A textbook arranged according to subject in five small volumes, emphasizing continuity rather than change.

Mariéjol, J. H. *The Spain of Ferdinand and Isabella.* New Brunswick, N. J.: Rutgers University Press, 1961.

A translation of a nineteenth-century French account still fresh and valuable.

Martines, Lauro. *The Social World of the Florentine Humanists: 1390–1460.* London: Routledge and Kegan Paul, 1963.

A sociological investigation of the leading Florentine humanists and their family connections, placing them among the ruling elite.

Mattingly, Garrett. *Renaissance Diplomacy.* London: Jonathan Cape, 1955.

A masterful combination of institutional analysis and political events that traces the origin and spread of the sending of diplomatic envoys and characterizes Renaissance politics as dynastic rather than national.

*Mollat, G. *The Popes at Avignon: 1305–1378*. New York: Harper & Row, Publishers, 1965.

> *A detailed classical French account of the Church's "Babylonian Captivity" and the efforts of the papacy to recover the Papal States.*

*Perroy, Edouard. *The Hundred Years' War*. New York: G. P. Putnam's Sons, Capricorn Books, 1965.

> *An English translation of the best account of the war, including its social history as well as the military and political aspects.*

*Pirenne, Henri. *Early Democracies in the Low Countries*. New York: Harper & Row, Publishers, 1963.

> *An opinionated but rare treatment of conflicts leading to the loss of urban autonomy in the Low Countries.*

*Roover, Raymond de. *The Rise and Decline of the Medici Bank 1397–1494*. New York: Norton & Co., 1966.

> *Probably the best work in English on banking institutions, this account of the leading Renaissance bank is highly revealing with respect to economic trends and sources of wealth.*

Smith, Preserved. *Erasmus*. New York: Frederick Ungar Publishing Co., 1962.

> *A sympathetic biography of the "prince of the humanists," which finds in him roots of a twentieth-century nondogmatic religion.*

Taylor, Henry O. *Thought and Expression in the Sixteenth Century*. 2d rev. ed., vol. 1. New York: Frederick Ungar Publishing Co., 1959.

> *A literary history that, despite its title, begins with the early Italian humanists of the fourteenth century.*

Asterisk (∗) denotes paperback.

# CHAPTER II

# The Confessional Age: The Reformation of the Sixteenth Century

## A. The Protestant Reformation

Before an aggressive Catholic Reformation checked their progress, several churches successfully broke from Rome between 1520 and 1560. Their success tore Western religious unity further asunder and laid the basis for prolonged religious warfare in the following century. Their zealous rivalry produced a confessional age, which attempted to restore the primacy of revealed religion as the norm for society, government, and truth.

In the past, overt heresy within Christendom had been recurrent and heated, but force and persuasion had succeeded in preventing most heresies from causing lasting schisms.* Nevertheless, following 1054 the schism between the Greek Orthodox and Roman Catholic churches had become quite clear and almost irreparable. Also the Bohemian Hussites successfully wrested concessions from the Roman church in the fifteenth century, and remnants of the Waldensians managed to survive persecution by the Inquisition. But in the main schismatic threats had been checked by crusades and reforms. In the sixteenth century the papacy failed to check dissenting religious leaders, who were supported by many local princes and governments, from establishing rival organizations.

The religious schism of the 1500s has often been described as a simple rift between traditional Catholicism and emergent Protestantism. This is hardly satisfactory, for it obscures divisions and changes within Catholicism and attributes to the Protestant reformers a unity that they did not possess. Moreover it ignores other traditions—neither orthodox nor Protestant by sixteenth-century standards—such as the Erasmian humanists and the sectarians who

---

* Technically heresy is the belief in any doctrine contrary to that taught by the Church, whereas schism simply means visible separation from the ecclesiastical framework of the Church. The two need not go together, but the Roman Catholic church taught that schismatics would almost necessarily become heretics, since they had abandoned the infallible, true chruch.

*Illustrations from a German tract of 1508, prophesying disasters to come.*

broke away from the Protestant reformers. The intensity and passion with which these varied groups fought one another remind the modern student of the fierce conflicts between rival totalitarian and social ideologies of our own day. But to give exclusive emphasis to these differences, uppermost though they were in sixteenth-century minds, is to conceal their dependence on common authorities.

The founders of new religious movements in the sixteenth century were primarily theologians preoccupied with new interpretations of old authorities revered by their Roman Catholic opponents. For this reason the historian must consider divergent schools of theology as critically important. Harder to assess but everywhere present and equally critical were the religious passions of the common people. In addition to the ultimate terror of death, their lives were made doubly uncertain by new diseases, large-scale warfare, famine, and plague—scourges for the partial control of which they lacked the science and institutions of more recent,

less religiously oriented men. Whether Catholic, Protestant, or sectarian Anabaptist, they sought solace in supernatural salvation along paths prescribed by revelation and tradition. Religious faith was the principal focus of their loyalties and concerns, and for it most were willing even to kill as instruments in the hands of God.

Thus theology and popular faith were constant ingredients of the Reformation era, but they alone do not satisfactorily explain the success or failure of specific religions in specific areas. Social, economic, and especially political movements became an inextricable part of both the religious controversies and their eventual outcomes. Except for sectarians of the radical left of the Reformation movement, religious thinkers of the sixteenth century did not conceive of a separate church and state. Indeed, most theologians used religious principles to buttress the existing order, for changes in the status quo inevitably meant changes in the administration, if not in the doctrine, of the Church.

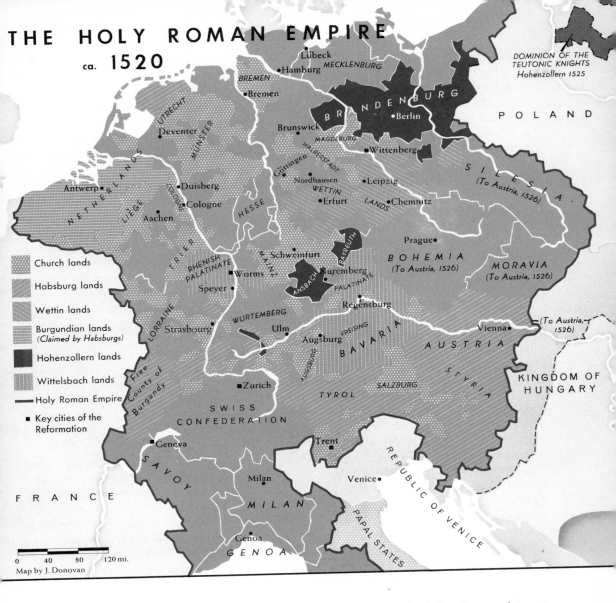

# THE HOLY ROMAN EMPIRE
## ca. 1520

DOMINION OF THE
TEUTONIC KNIGHTS
Hohenzollern 1525

Lübeck
Hamburg
MECKLENBURG
BREMEN
Bremen
BRANDENBURG
Berlin
POLAND

Deventer
UTRECHT
MÜNSTER
Brunswick
MAGDEBURG
HALBERSTADT
Wittenberg
SILESIA
(To Austria, 1526)

Antwerp
NETHERLANDS
LIÈGE
Duisberg
COLOGNE
Cologne
Aachen
HESSE
Göttingen
Nordhausen
WETTIN
Erfurt
LANDS
Leipzig
Chemnitz
Chemnitz

TRIER
RHENISH
PALATINATE
Worms
Schweinfurt
MAIN
BAYREUTH
Nuremberg
ANSBACH
PALATINATE
Prague
BOHEMIA
(To Austria, 1526)
MORAVIA
(To Austria, 1526)

LORRAINE
Speyer
Strasbourg
WURTEMBERG
Ulm
AUGSBURG
Augsburg
FREISING
Regensburg
BAVARIA
AUSTRIA
STYRIA
Vienna
(To Austria, 1526)

KINGDOM OF
HUNGARY

Free
County
of
Burgundy
Zurich
SWISS
CONFEDERATION
TYROL
SALZBURG
Trent

Geneva

SAVOY
Milan
Venice
REPUBLIC OF VENICE

FRANCE

MILAN
Genoa
GENOA
PAPAL
STATES

### Legend

- Church lands
- Habsburg lands
- Wettin lands
- Burgundian lands (Claimed by Habsburgs)
- Hohenzollern lands
- Wittelsbach lands
- Holy Roman Empire
- ■ Key cities of the Reformation

0    40    80    120 mi.

Map by J. Donovan

---

Thus reform programs that supported the existing power structures, particularly "absolutist" princes and councils, received political and military support. By the same token, sectarians and humanists who opposed existing power structures suffered general persecution and frequently extirpation. International politics, such as the alliance of Catholic France with German Protestants in the 1530s, was also involved. How well a given government could suppress religious dissent depended on how much support it had. But when dissenters had foreign assistance, attempts to suppress them involved international as well as domestic conflict.

## THE GERMAN REFORMATION

### The Secular Background

Soon after Martin Luther sparked the theological dispute in Germany in 1517, eastern Europe was under attack by

Turkey. The empire was also engaged in wars between the houses of Habsburg and Valois (1521–59) over the Burgundian inheritance and over the possession of Milan and Naples. Also, various political and economic crises complicated its domestic affairs. The empire became a network of interaction between the conflicting religious, political, economic, and social interests that characterized the Reformation.

The Church exercised exceptionally great power under the Holy Roman Empire. Not only did the papacy draw far more revenues from it than the emperor, but certain clerical states—chiefly the electorates of Mainz, Cologne, and Trier, as well as numerous principalities of bishops, abbots, and commanders of the Teutonic Knights—were provocatively prominent in public affairs. Some local princes, it is true, had restricted clerical courts, papal appointments, the accumulation of property by the clergy, and the outward flow of clerical taxes. But until the Reformation more decisively subordinated church to state, the lack of an effective central government in the empire left the Church stronger there than in the territorial states of Italy or the more centralized monarchies of France and England.

The Church's immense power fed anticlerical movements at every level of society. At the imperial diets princes presented their grievances, or *gravamina*, against Rome and demanded redress through the imperial government. Popular feeling ran also against the clergy for failure to conform to its professed moral code. Guildsmen and merchants protested clerical exemptions from property taxes, excises, and tolls; they also naturally resented direct economic competition with privileged churchmen in milling, craft production, and retail sales. Especially in towns under clerical rulers revolts often led to armed attacks on the clergy.

The principal weakness of the German church, however, was not so much popular anticlericalism as the dynastic and economic ambitions of princely families. The same princes who complained vociferously of Roman power shared the proceeds from sales of indulgences and secured leading Church posts for members of their families, often young boys. Albert of Hohenzollern was appointed Archbishop of Mainz (his third major church post) even before he came of age. Members of the Wittelsbach family of the Palatinate held or administered bishoprics in Speyer, Utrecht, Freising, Naumburg, Regensburg, and many remunerative cloisters. But reaping spoils from the Church did not guarantee these families' loyalty to Rome. During the early Reformation the Palatinate wavered in religious allegiance and eventually became Protestant. The head of the house of Hohenzollern was one of the first German princes to espouse Lutheranism. Another member of the Hohenzollern family converted the holdings of the Teutonic Knights in East Prussia into a hereditary Lutheran fief of Poland in 1525.

Whether they remained Catholic or became Protestant, German princes and town councils extended their control over ecclesiastical affairs. This was part of a larger consolidation of local territorial governments that deprived the emperor as well as the pope of effective, direct authority. In the absence of Church reform, the secular governments reorganized monasteries, took control of schools, and enacted stringent laws governing lay and clerical morality.

In their striving for local autonomy, princes went much further than curbing the Church. Through newly established chanceries they worked to replace semiautonomous nobles with a new corps of paid officials. They also changed the composition of law courts by putting Roman law jurists (with incomes from salaries, fees, and bribes) on the benches. In the name of the "commonweal" (a universal but ambiguous slogan) lawyers and officials systematically overrode local custom. In effect, a legal-administrative revolution from above—of which the Reformation was but one part—was under way during the late fifteenth and early sixteenth centuries. Out of the changes came assurance of social privilege—but not political rights—for aristocrats. For chartered guildmasters and merchants came guarantees of monopoly. The peasantry and unprivileged townsmen had to bear the burden of supporting these social and economic advantages; for most of them, channels of appeal were closed. In peasant villages, for example, appointed officials replaced traditional assemblies and courts. These officials, whose decisions in practice were not subject to appeal, collected dues and services in the name of the prince.

Economic pressure from authoritarian governments was one of several factors intensifying social revolutionary movements that came to a climax in the "Peasants' Revolt" of 1524–26. Accelerating prices after 1450 depressed real wages. Population increase led to the division of estates into smaller parcels and jeopardized livelihood, especially after short harvests. English and Flemish competition made deep inroads in the German textile market at the expense of native producers. Small traders, lenders, and mine operators were supplanted by large monopolizing commercial and banking firms in Augsburg and Nuremberg. These firms, such as the Fuggers, Welsers, Hochstetters, and Peutingers, were supported by the emperor and the papacy. Meanwhile, upon the very people who could barely subsist the Church continued to lay heavy obligations. And almost intolerable governmental taxation—probably outweighing all other sources of economic strain—increased with endemic public disorder. Local governments tried to stabilize their shaking economic foundations by protective measures, while popular leaders sought to overcome German woes

*A Bundschuh rebel, as pictured by a hostile tract of 1513.*

by leading revolts against the Church and the princes, against landlord nobility in the country and patrician oligarchy in the cities.

These uncoordinated revolts of the fourteenth and fifteenth centuries continued into sixteenth-century Germany. In the towns there was conflict between guildsmen and patrician oligarchs. Revolutionaries accused officials of improper behavior, demanding an end to financial corruption, nepotism, and government by secret manipulation. They also sought to prevent the legal system from making justice too expensive for common people to obtain. Above all, they protested the increasing indirect taxation on items of consumption and commerce. Between 1509 and 1512 there were revolts in scores of towns.

At the same time, in the southern countryside, peasant uprisings occurred. These *Bundschuh* revolts (named after the thonged peasant boot which they adopted as their emblem) were sometimes directed toward a return to communal authority and old customs. The latter had certainly not been based on equality and justice, but many felt that it was a far easier kind of oppression to live under. Sometimes the revolutionaries aimed at establishing a standard of divine justice that would render serfdom unchristian. Nevertheless these revolts failed: the oppressed had access to no political lever with which to pry concessions from the ruling powers. Furthermore, their uprisings were disorganized and disconnected from one another. Of course, there had arisen among the privileged classes the fear that these eruptions would lead to a general revolution and to the establishment of a social order akin to that of Switzerland where villagers and townsmen had gained a greater degree of personal liberty. But not until the early Reformation did such fears coincide with actual developments. By then the revolutionaries were united in a general anticlerical feeling. After the emergence of Luther and the early reformers they were spurred on by a common conviction that their standard of justice was supported by God.

## The Emergence of Luther

For a short time the different levels of German discontent were knit together by the activities and writings of Martin Luther (1483–1546) in Saxony and Ulrich Zwingli in Zurich. Although their main appeal was religious, their early attack on the status quo was sufficiently broad to bring together divergent, even contradictory, bodies of dissent under common slogans.

Born a younger son of a copper-smelting family of peasant stock, Luther grew up while his family's fortunes were rising. Educated in urban schools, he obtained a bachelor's and a master's degree in liberal arts at Erfurt University. At his parents' urging he began the study of Roman law, the most promising path to power and prestige. Fulfilling a vow taken in a moment of terror, young Martin sud-

denly switched his career, broke with his father, and joined an Augustinian cloister at Erfurt in 1505. His personal account of this decision, taken in the anguish of a search for religious identity, later endeared him to generations of German Protestants who were preoccupied with the question of the salvation of their souls. Zealous but dissatisfied as a monk, Luther was directed by his superiors to obtain a doctorate in theology at the new university founded at Wittenberg by Elector Frederick the Wise of Saxony. There, as a professor of theology, Luther resolved his personal longings for certainty of salvation in the course of preparing his lectures. More than a personal discovery, his solution formed the basis of a revolutionary assault on the hierarchy of the Roman Catholic church. It also led him to a career of religious reform that, without his intending it, brought him greater influence with the Elector than was enjoyed by any contemporary lawyer.

Despite Luther's rapid rise within monastic orders, he later reported that he experienced great anxiety and dissatisfaction with monastic rules as a religious way of life leading to salvation. Despairing of ever meriting through his own works, grace from an angry, incomprehensible, and predestining God, he found an escape from eternal damnation in St. Paul and St. Augustine. Salvation was not to be found in pious acts or ethical behavior but in a God-implanted faith that alone served to justify man. On his own, man remained immutably and impotently depraved. Authority for this doctrine of "faith alone" he found not in the papacy or tradition of the Church but in the Scriptures. Luther's changing subjective moods made him a volatile and sometimes inconsistent theologian; but he was confident that whatever position he took in a given situation represented faith in an objective, revealed creed that anyone not blinded by the Devil could find for himself in Scripture.

Luther began his career of reform with

Martin Luther *by Lucas Cranach the Elder.*

the curriculum of Wittenberg University. At the university he met and befriended Melanchthon, an accomplished classical scholar and nephew of Reuchlin. Melanchthon became Luther's lifetime ally and the systematizer of his doctrine. Together they excluded the traditional scholastic disciplines from Wittenberg's course of study, giving Luther a reputation for being an Erasmian. But his theology opposed that line of thought as much as it opposed scholasticism. Erasmians were concerned with replacing ignorance with reason and with encouraging men to behave ethically. Luther was preoccupied with religious justification and with opening people's hearts to the experience of faith. For him reason and ethics were helpful only under the direction of that faith; otherwise reason was the "Devil's harlot" and ethical conduct a lure to heresy.

The Wittenberg monk became a public figure when, on October 31, 1517, he posted his Ninety-Five Theses attacking abuses in the sale of indulgences. In neighboring territories the Dominican friar Johannes Tetzel was proclaiming an indulgence to raise money for Albert of Hohenzollern, who had become heavily indebted to the papacy and the Fuggers in the acquisition of the archbishopric of Mainz, his third major ecclesiastical post. Luther's ire was raised when pilgrims visiting Frederick the Wise's relic collection confronted him with Tetzel's indulgences, for he believed that writs of indulgence inculcated a false sense of religious salvation. Although Luther did not deny the principle of indulgences, his theses argued that only God could forgive sins; the pope could forgive only punishments he himself had imposed. Luther posted his theses for an academic debate that never took place, but they were translated, printed, and circulated throughout Germany. Unlike his earlier more radical attack on scholasticism, his theses against indulgences appealed to popular resentment against financial exactions from Rome, and their popularity threatened to dry up a fruitful source of papal revenue.

Luther did not attack the principle of indulgences as such until 1520, but in the meantime he attacked the Church in tracts and debates. He went so far as to call for a new general Church council, an excommunicable offense. Later he questioned the infallibility of past councils. Pope Leo X tried to curb Luther's attacks, but political complications—namely Leo's efforts to prevent the powerful Charles of Spain from becoming emperor in 1519—delayed decisive action. Meanwhile the monk ignored papal rulings. Finally in 1520 Leo X issued a papal bull excommunicating Luther and his associates.

Because Luther originally believed himself a loyal son of the Church, he had not forseen conflict with the hierarchy. Yet since he placed Scripture above the authority of tradition, such conflict was inevitable, however unforseen. Debating Johann Eck at Leipzig in 1519, Luther had declared both popes and councils fallible. He elaborated on this declaration in a series of tracts the following year. His *Address to the Christian Nobility of the German Nation* was directed to the princes, calling on them to reform the Church if clerics would not. Luther further argued for the "priesthood of all believers." With this principle (introduced earlier by Waldensians and others) he could justify state intervention: since princes were also priests, they could reform the Church. In the same tract he advocated congregational control over pastors and Church property. (This demand would later be repeated by the Peasants' Revolt and the Anabaptist movement.) He also called for reform in secular affairs. In *The Babylonian Capitivity of the Church*, written in Latin since it was addressed to the clergy, Luther argued that only baptism, the Liturgy of the Lord's Supper and, perhaps, penance were based on Scripture. (Later he decided that penance was not scriptural and therefore not a sacrament.) All other so-called sacraments had been added by papal antichrists and deserved destruction. A third tract, *On the Freedom of a Christian*, was intended for both the papacy and the general populace. In it Luther—who had already denounced the merit of all good works and the saving efficacy, by themselves, of sacraments, liturgies, acts of charity, and the like—developed more fully his concept of the efficacy of faith and God's grace as well as the priesthood of all believers. He set freedom apart from the secular world, defining it as wholly internal and spiritual.

Often considered Luther's primary reformation writings, these tracts established his emergence as an Old Testament type of prophet for Germans who felt oppressed by the papal yoke. In full rebellion against the secularization of the Renaissance Church and society, he operated in an apocalyptic framework: either the Church was to be reformed by itself or by the princes or the end of the world was at hand. Luther always opposed the use of violence to advance his gospel, but as a prophet he cared little for Erasmus's irenic secular wisdom of not provoking violent opposition, at least at first. He was fond of quoting Christ, who had "not come to preach peace, but the sword." On December 10, 1520, he defied authority by burning both the papal bull condemning him and collections of the canon law, the basis of the Church's legal system. Feeling that he had rediscovered the historical core of revelation, the unique work of God in Christ, Luther was prepared to court martyrdom even though he was to be plagued by self-doubts for the rest of his life. Luther expected God to secure the victory of His Gospel over its Roman foes, but at the same time he made the fullest use of humanist scholarship and the printing press to advance it and to discredit the papacy. A powerful penman in both Latin and the vernacular, he kept up a continuous output of tracts, treatises, commentaries, sermons, and letters for the rest of his life. His literary gifts, armed with his convictions, enabled him to grasp leadership of the German reformation. Other provincial reformers gained wide reputations, but it was Luther, a national hero of anti-Roman Germans, who was summoned to the Diet of Worms in 1521. Not only did he impress many of his contemporaries as a prophet; he has continued to inspire more literature, pro and con, than any other figure of modern times.

## The Diet and Edict of Worms

So long as Church and state cooperated as in the past, excommunication and condemnation for heresy were preludes to secular outlawry and execution. Thus Luther's case, which popular agitation had made a major German issue, came before the first diet that the young Emperor Charles V attended. More was at stake than the fate of an individual condemned by the Church, for his case involved the question whether the German princes would continue to put secular force at the disposal of the Church.

For both ruler and assembly, Luther's hearing was secondary to more pressing problems. With the help of generous bribes and concessions to the princes, Charles had become emperor in 1519. Although he was now the greatest dynast Europe had yet beheld, his vast holdings were threatened by revolts in Spain and an imminent war with France and the Turks. Understandably, he was primarily concerned with securing tax grants and a new military organization for the empire. These the princes refused. Princes and emperor also clashed on the question of creating a central appellate court and an executive Regency Council to maintain order in Charles's absence. Both institutions were established, but the contest over control of them seriously weakened their authority. The Diet also enacted "antitrust" laws against the great southern German trading companies. These laws Charles would soon undermine, for they threatened the very interests that financed him as emperor.

This rivalry between the princes and the emperor was important for Luther's case. Charles backed the pope, but not all of the princes were prepared to enforce Luther's excommunication and brand him an outlaw; they were aggrieved with the papacy and fearful of Charles's power. They handed their grievances to Aleander, papal legate to the assembly, and de-

*German lampoon depicting Luther with seven heads.*

such as the rulers of ducal Saxony* and Bavaria did enforce it, but they did not begin to coordinate their efforts until the spring of 1524. Meanwhile Luther had been spirited away for safekeeping to Wartburg Castle by agents of Frederick the Wise. Under Frederick's protection Luther continued to work. He translated the New Testament into idiomatic German from Erasmus's Greek and Latin texts and continued to pen influential tracts. In one particularly powerful piece he appealed to monks and nuns to leave their cloisters. Luther's revolt was characterized by considerable personal courage, but for its success it depended on the simultaneous revolt of the German princes and city councils against the emperor and Rome.

manded either a general or a German council to reform the Church. Some of them feared that suppression of Luther would provoke a general revolution. Even during the Diet, Worms, the scene of an anticlerical revolution only seven years before, seethed with discontent. Aleander feared for his life as Luther received a rousing welcome from the townsmen; still, he was able to secure the emperor's condemnation of the excommunicated monk. Together, emperor and legate were able to prevent him from arguing the details of his position. After some delegates had departed, they pushed through a proclamation—the Edict of Worms—outlawing Luther, his followers, and his books.

But this edict was to go generally unenforced. At Nuremberg the newly established Regency Council, nominally representing the emperor's authority, simply ignored the Edict while the emperor was preoccupied elsewhere. A few princes

## Pamphlets, Agitation, and Revolts

Meanwhile, Luther's religious appeal had swept through Germany, gaining influential converts, especially among the clergy. Personal contacts and students supplemented the written word in converting such future Protestant leaders as Martin Bucer, who became the reformer of Strassbourg and an influence on Calvin's thought. Monks leaving their cloisters provided a constant flow of new recruits. Led by local clergymen and converts in city councils, numerous local towns began to introduce the Reformation and to depose Roman Catholic officials. In their rapid expansion, however, Luther's doctrines were popularized so that they meant different things to people with different religious or social grievances. The best evidence of this confusion is preserved in the popular tracts that circulated while the lines of confessional allegiance among the anti-Romanists were still fluid.

* Ruled by Duke George, a vociferous opponent of Luther, ducal Saxony was separate and distinct from Luther's electoral Saxony, ruled by Frederick the Wise.

In these tracts Luther was mistakenly identified with anticlerical causes more radical than he was prepared to support.

Luther and his followers took their cause directly to literate laymen with tracts printed in the German language. Between 1517 and 1525—when censorship confined discussion to government approved polemics—thousands of tracts circulated. Luther was most influential in setting their initial theme, but other writers, many of them anonymous, soon developed positions from which he rapidly backed away. In attributing German woes solely to clerical greed, sophistry, and obscurantism, he had kept religious reform separate from, although conjoined with, secular change. But fellow pamphleteers, such as Martin Bucer, combined social and religious reform in a "social gospel," an anticipated reorganization of society based on divine justice and Scriptural text. Many of them insisted that the Gospel was about brotherhood and justice, basic reform meaning the transformation not only of the Church but of society as well. Deep strains of antiintellectualism and utopianism ran through these writings, lifting people from the depths of despair to heights of exultant expectations. At the same time, some writers addressed themselves to the practical problem of achieving social and political as well as religious reforms.

The chief objects of their attack were the existing authorities, many of whom were prince-bishops and prince-abbots. On this issue Luther was ambiguous. He denounced clerical rule as illegitimate and castigated princes hostile to his Gospel, but he soon deferred to friendly princes, allowing them to take all initiative in introducing ecclesiastical changes. For those living under hostile rulers he gave no practical advice prior to his development of a doctrine of passive obedience. According to this, a Christian was obligated to obey the existing authorities even though they be infidels. But not all the reformers were so willing as Luther to accept the prevailing political and social system. An influential anonymous tract, probably written by Martin Bucer, went further in urging the peasants—whom these pamphlets venerated as superior in religious judgment to Roman prelates—to "use their flails" to coerce authorities into accepting reform without overt revolution. In Zurich, Ulrich Zwingli denounced tithes and called for resistance to ungodly governments. In Saxony Thomas Müntzer preached revolution against princes who barred the Gospel's path. To be sure all these positions had revolutionary implications, but there was no agreement on the path to reform, especially in territories ruled by clerical or aggressively Catholic princes.

After 1521 the slogans of the major reformers penetrated the lower classes. Often led by former monks, urban masses attacked the existing order and the partial reforms of the authorities who owed allegiance to Luther. They pressed for more stringent regulation of morality as well as for changes in rites and doctrine. Congregations in some places made faltering attempts to control pastors, properties, and alms; in widespread areas peasants began to withhold tithes, dues, and services.

In 1522 reform erupted into violence on a major scale with the revolt of the imperial knights led by Franz von Sickingen. Eclipsed in wealth by trading companies and in political power by princes, the knights desired to regain their old position of power and eminence serving directly under the emperor. Their leader Sickingen had commanded a mercenary army for the emperor in the Low Countries and terrorized towns and weak principalities by extorting indemnities. In so doing he could count on the sympathy of many provincial nobles restive under princely rule. Acting as publicist for the Knights' Revolt was Ulrich von Hutten, a nationalist humanist and pamphleteer who published Valla's *Donation of Constantine* in Germany in 1519. When Sickingen set out to seize the archiepiscopal electorate of Trier in 1522, Hutten portrayed the attack as a step toward religious reform, a characterization that Luther felt compelled to repudiate. But other rising leaders of the German Reformation accepted Hutten's judgment and applauded it. They collected at Sickingen's castle and supported him by siring anonymous popular tracts. Instead of assisting the revolt, however, the religious issue served to divide the dissident nobility. Nor was Hutten and Sickingen's circle of popular pamphleteers able to gain allies from the towns and peasantry. In 1523 Sickingen was surrounded in his castle by the princely armies of Saxony, Hesse, and the Palatinate. Their guns pierced his fortifications and mortally wounded him. Although some knights were to participate in the Peasants' Revolt of 1524–26, the Knights' Revolt collapsed, leaving the princes in control of southwestern Germany.

After a poor harvest in 1524, the condition of the peasant and urban lower classes of southwestern Germany was rife with deprivation and discontent. Their hostility, which clerical and secular rulers had nurtured by trying to enforce the Edict of Worms, spilled over into what is known in German history as the Great Peasants' War. Revolutionary townsmen of the major cities adopted articles condemning clerical and peasant economic competition. Most of these revolts, however, were inspired by a common program of reform, *The Twelve Articles of the German Peasantry,* which swept northward through the clerical states of central Germany. In 1525 they joined another center of revolt in Saxony. The Articles, written in the form of a contract to which local rebel "hosts" sought to secure their lords' assent, asserted that society and politics should rest on Scripture unadulterated by human invention and that con-

gregations should have the right to elect and depose their own clergy. It would be further agreed that communal property seized illegally by present authorities should be returned. Common people would have hunting and fishing rights. Serfdom would be abolished. Tithes not mentioned in the Bible would be forgotten. And the legal system would be renovated.

Counting on divine assistance rather than overt revolution, the rebels sought to enforce these contracts by withholding dues, tithes, and services from the authorities. Thus deprived, governments collapsed, and large numbers of local nobles and churchmen signed the Articles. Townsmen, radical clergymen, and sometimes nobles joined the revolt and provided leadership. In Franconia such leaders drew up a formal military organization and proposed an abortive liberal constitution to be implemented by a parliamentary government. In place of princely absolutism, urban oligarchies, and the traditional social hierarchy, the peasant hosts universally proclaimed a society based on "Christian brotherhood"—a civic equality similar to the *fraternité* sought in the French Revolution of 1789.

The initiative taken by the rebellious lower classes, their demand for civic equality or brotherhood, and their ecclesiastical congregationalism collided squarely with the existing order. They also challenged the position of Luther and his followers, who were veering sharply toward authoritarian absolutism. Raising charges of anarchy and communism, local leagues of princes organized loyal nobles, townsmen, and mercenary troops into an aggressive counteroffensive determined to make sanguinary examples of those who dared to revolt. In meeting this counterattack, the rebels destroyed large numbers of castles and monasteries but seldom resorted to bloodshed. One by one the "peasant" hosts were isolated and annihilated, usually in flight from the point

*Two armed peasants from a tract of 1524.*

of confrontration with the princes' armies. Divine assistance was not forthcoming. In routing the "peasant" hosts the lords' armies seldom lost more than two or three men. Financing their expeditions as far as possible by booty and indemnities, the princes were believed by some contemporaries to have killed or executed 300,000 men; 100,000 would probably be closer to the truth. Only in Tirol, where peasants and townsmen had military strength and could fight on their own ground, were concessions retained. Elsewhere the "prewar" power structures were restored after indemnities and destruction were made good.

Roman Catholicism had made its first major recovery. The rebels had not only been soundly defeated but bitterly disillu-sioned. They had assumed (except in Saxony) that they were acting in accord with Luther's wishes, but in the closing days of the revolt Luther himself preached a crusade of extermination against them. Terrified by the anarchical implications of their uprising, he came to believe that they had perverted the spiritual Gospel for "fleshly" gain.* Already disillusioned with Rome, the rebels of 1525 were now

---

* Luther later took credit for the suppression of the revolt, even though his tract *Against the Robbing and Murdering Bands of Peasants* did not appear until the eve of the peasants' rout at Frankenhausen in Thuringia, one of the last encounters of the revolt. Similarly, he attributed the whole uprising to his archenemy in Saxony, Thomas Müntzer, an opinion that documentary evidence fails to substantiate.

*A. The Protestant Reformation*

disenchanted with Wittenberg. Many returned to Roman Catholicism. Others either resigned themselves to their lot or joined the burgeoning Anabaptist movement that swept across Germany from Switzerland on the heels of the revolt's suppression.

## THE SHATTERING OF REFORMATION UNITY

Luther's premise that scriptural authority would produce a single, objectively revealed creed that every person could quickly discover for himself soon ran into trouble. Erasmian humanists abhorred his precipitate actions and repudiated his Augustinian predestinarian doctrines as subversive of morality. Radical Evangelicals and humanists opposed his social and political authoritarianism. The rebels of 1525 learned the hard way that they and Luther held different concepts of scriptural authority and Christian brotherhood. Reformers in southern German towns, such as Martin Bucer in Strassbourg and Oecolampadius in Basel, maintained varying degrees of independence from Luther's leadership; one of them, Ulrich Zwingli of Zurich, became an acknowledged leader of a rival creed and organization. Thus the common front against existing Catholicism soon dissolved into a number of competing creeds and organizations seeking consolidation and control over local areas.

### Zwinglian Reform in Zurich

Ulrich Zwingli (1484–1531) became a public figure of reform in Zurich at about the same time that Luther became famous in Saxony. An outspoken opponent of indulgences, he also attacked dietary regulations and clerical celibacy in theory and practice. Nor did tithes and infant baptism escape his criticism—at first. A former chaplain attached to Swiss mercenary troops in Italy in 1515, he excoriated the ruling oligarchy of Zurich for selling the services of Swiss mercenaries to foreign powers. Theologically Zwingli had much in common with Luther, from whom he derived some of his doctrines. They agreed on the absolute sovereignty and inscrutability of God from whom fallen man was separated by a gulf unbridgeable except by divine grace. Although both affirmed the principle of biblical authority, Zwingli treated the Liturgy of the Lord's Supper as a memorial service rather than a supernatural sacrament. He also offended Luther's followers by justifying revolution.

Zwingli established a state church in Zurich, a republican state controlled largely by the guilds from whom Zwingli drew most of his political support. His urban republican reformation spread among the townsmen of southern Germany, and in this, too, he differed from and antagonized Luther, who leaned heavily on princely support and authoritarian urban governments. "Sacramentarians," as Zwinglians were called, were soon proscribed by Saxon laws. Thus both theologically and politically a basis for cooperative efforts between northern and southern reformers was lacking. Although Philip of Hesse, an energetic early Protestant prince, was able to bring Luther and Zwingli together at Marburg in 1529, Luther refused to discuss what he considered to be Zwingli's use of reason in matters of revelation. Shortly thereafter Zwingli was killed in a war between Zurich and the Swiss Catholic cantons that resisted Zwinglian proselytism. His mantle fell to Heinrich Bullinger, who eventually secured agreements with John Calvin rather than the Wittenbergers. Bullinger's many writings were also translated into English and exerted considerable influence upon the English reformation after 1558.

## Sectarians and the Radical Reformation

Whatever their differences on other questions, both Luther and Zwingli, like the Roman Catholics they opposed, relied on coercion to secure their religious authority. Both set up established or state churches binding on all members of the political community. In Zurich the state church was directed by the city council, which heard debates and legislated new doctrine and rites. Working through it, Zwingli reinstated infant baptism and tithes and made state intervention in religious affairs common practice. Rejection of the state's authority in enforcing the Gospel was denounced by Zwingli as sedition and blasphemy.

Certain radical reformers soon proved "blasphemous" and "seditious." Like the Erasmian humanists, they insisted that doctrine must be judged by its adherents' behavior, that a creed was acceptable only if its observance meant living by New Testament ethics, and that the priesthood of all believers required voluntary religious participation and tolerance. In 1524 Conrad Grebel, a Zurich humanist, led a secession from Zwingli's ranks. He and his followers refused to obey government regulations concerning religion, thus following the example of Christians as recorded in the Acts of the Apostles. For example, they insisted that only adult or adolescent converts had the faith requisite for baptism and that converts baptized in older confessions had to be baptized a second time. Joined by other dissenters from established churches (whether Protestant or Catholic) they thus launched the Radical Reformation. Quite naturally, this was denounced by all established clergy— Protestant and Catholic—as sedition, heresy, and blasphemy. The very name applied to them—Anabaptists (rebaptizers) —reflects this animosity, for under the Justinian code rebaptism was a capital offense.

The Anabaptists found their model in the early persecuted Church recorded in the Acts; for them, the true Church was not an invisible body or the political community at large, but rather a voluntary association of baptized believers whose purity of conduct was maintained through admonition and expulsion. Their measure for both creed and society was the New Testament, especially the Sermon on the Mount. Most Anabaptists refused to take oaths and disavowed the taking of human life by any state or individual, although some, like the south German preacher Balthasar Hubmaier, defended the use of the sword. The ruling concerns of their common life were Christian brotherhood and the distribution of alms; they were not much preoccupied with distinctions of rank and sex. Those who fled to Bohemia for sanctuary practiced a form of consumption communism or communitarianism. Although humanists and persons of high social status occasionally joined or led their congregations, most Anabaptists were petty craftsmen and peasants. From the Anabaptist point of view the Reformation that relied on the state to enforce uniformity offered no improvement over the previous order: it still relied on compulsion rather than individual faith. Their ranks in Germany rapidly swelled after the suppression of the Peasants' Revolt, but Protestant and Catholic churchmen, viewing them as a revolutionary threat to established society, subjected them to bloody persecution. As their leadership fell, adversity tended to encourage their belief that the end of the world was at hand.

Until very recently historians have been content to recount Catholic and Protestant charges against Anabaptists as unimpeachable truth. According to this reading of history, the real spirit of Anabaptism was revealed by an action that occurred in the Westphalian episcopal city of Münster in 1534 and 1535. A few radicals who had fled from the terror of the Inquisition in the Low Countries and had taken over the city tried desperately to hold out against the bishop's army, which was reinforced by the troops of neighboring princes. In their desperation they made a drastic transition from New Testament pacifism to Old Testament theocracy: with Anabaptist leaders in charge, they invested the kingship in a tailor, introduced polygamy, and established a form of "war communism."*

When Münster fell the Anabaptist leaders were executed. Their remains were placed in a basket at the city's gates, where they stayed until the nineteenth century. After the Münster episode, Menno Simons led Anabaptists in the Low Countries back to the sober, pacific tradition that marked most of their history in the sixteenth century; one group of Anabaptists—the Dutch Mennonites, prominent in business and agriculture—obtained tolerance there in 1572. But elsewhere persecution continued. As a minimal penalty, Anabaptists were excluded from urban trades. At the maximum, many paid with their lives.

Other radicals were lumped together under the derogatory Anabaptist label. In the main they tried to reconstitute the early New Testament Church and to emphasize a humanitarian ethic. In Germany, Spain, Italy, and the Low Countries anti-Trinitarian biblicists (heavily influenced by Erasmus) tried to practice their beliefs. Those who survived fled to Poland or other pockets of temporary toleration. The German historian and former Lutheran pastor Sebastian Franck (1499–1542) developed an individualistic mysticism that emphasized personality rather than doctrine and that rejected all existing churches, including the Anabaptists, for being sectarian. However, these radical reformers of the sixteenth century were "hunted heretics," not founders of influential movements; not until after the

* That is, all resources were commandeered for the common defense and support of the city.

fury of the religious wars was spent would they succeed at all in "reforming the Reformation."

## The Consolidation of Lutheran Territorial Churches

While Charles V was proccupied with the Turks and wars with France, and while the Roman Catholic church was paralyzed by the princes' failure to support it, Lutheran princes and town councils took control of religious affairs. Charles V had decisively won over Francis I at Pavia in 1525, but just before the first Diet of Speyer (1526) the papacy, the northern Italian states, and Henry VIII of England joined with Francis to expel Charles's forces from Italy. At the same time, a Turkish army of 100,000 was moving into Hungary where it killed the king of Bohemia and Hungary and routed his forces at Mohács at the end of August 1526. This weakened Charles's influence over his German states, some of which had already become Lutheran. After the Peasants' Revolt several German princes prominent in its suppression—Landgrave Philip of Hesse, Elector John of Saxony, and Margrave Casimir of Brandenburg—had become converts to Lutheranism, finding it more effective than Catholicism in maintaining public order; and several imperial cities also adopted Lutheranism or a modification of it. The Diet of Speyer (1526), over which the emperor had little control, resolved to leave each prince free until a general council should be called to interpret the Edict of Worms subject to his readiness "to answer before God and His Imperial Majesty."

Philip of Hesse seized this opportunity to install Lutheran clergymen in his towns and to confiscate all church property and endowments. Under Luther's advice, he brushed aside proposals for a representative church structure and personally took all initiative in reforming the church,

# EUROPE IN 1526

**DYNASTIC POWER RIVALS**

- France (Valois)
- Dominions of Charles V (Habsburg)
- Holy Roman Empire
- Ottoman Empire

K. OF SCOTLAND

IRELAND

North Sea

K. OF DENMARK

Baltic Sea

K. OF ENGLAND (Tudor)

London

Antwerp

Münster

NETHERLANDS

Wittenberg

THE EMPIRE (Habsburg)

Worms

Speyer

KINGDOM OF POLAND (Jagellon)

GRAND DUCHY OF LITHUANIA (Jagellon)

SILESIA

BOHEMIA

Prague

Paris

KINGDOM OF FRANCE

Atlantic Ocean

Zurich

Geneva

SWISS CONFED.

MILAN

Pavia 1525

Venice

Vienna

AUSTRIA

HUNGARY

Transylvania

Moldavia

Mohács 1526

Wallachia

Danube R.

Black Sea

OTTOMAN EMPIRE

REP. OF VENICE

Genoa

Florence

PAPAL STATES

Rome

KINGDOM OF NAPLES

Corsica

Madrid

SPAIN

Aragon

KINGDOM OF

Balearic Is.

Granada

SARDINIA

Mediterranean

K. OF SICILY

Sea

Crete (Venice)

making minor concessions to townsmen and nobles in allowing them, for example, to retain their patronage in the appointment of local clergy. But to peasants nothing was conceded; they now had to pay the state all obligations previously owed the church and were forbidden to compete with urban guilds. Most former church incomes now went to Philip's treasury, and after a military attack against the Archbishop of Mainz in 1528, Philip seized control over all ecclesiastical jurisdictions. Cramped by Luther's passive attitude toward politics, Philip soon turned to Zwingli and Martin Bucer for theological advice. His precedent in establishing princely control over a territorial church was soon followed in Saxony, Brandenburg, Prussia, Denmark, Sweden, Wurttemberg, and other principalities. Everywhere the chief beneficiaries were the privileged orders of town and country and the "Christian magistracy"—usually a prince or king, considered by Lutherans as the father of an extended family. To him as head of the family—or to the city council—the Lutheran church taught passive obedience as the first requirement of piety, and the clergy relied on him to root out all remnants of Roman Catholicism as well as all new heresies, especially Anabaptism. New state-appointed clergy undertook the strict enforcement of creedal uniformity in which only true believers could exhibit their religious faith. To dissenters—Zwinglians, Calvinists, Anabaptists, spiritualists, papists, and others—they applied various civil penalties, including corporal punishment and execution. The German and other reformations had substituted the Christian magistracy for the humanists' concept of a secular commonweal. Opposition to Lutheranism, in other words, had become a crime worse than murder.

The German magisterial reformers emphasized that their work was purely spiritual and uncorrupted by material motives. Most of their changes were confined to doctrine and liturgy: the number of sacraments was reduced to two—baptism and the Liturgy of the Lord's Supper; monasticism was suppressed; and in worship, but not in scholarship, the vernacular language was used. Also, to church services the reformers added more sermons and congregational singing. Otherwise they followed tradition. Luther, unlike Calvin and the radical sectarians, taught that only those traditions directly in conflict with Scripture should be abolished. The rest were to be retained.

For a generation these changes took place without imperial intervention, for the emperor was not strong enough to oppose them, fend off the Turks, and fight France all at the same time. Although he was at first content to seek a political compromise, nevertheless in 1529 and 1530, backed by alarmed Catholic princes (who were building their own territorial churches), he regained enough power to threaten the Lutherans. Having won a new war with Francis I in 1529, Charles secured an order from the second Diet of Speyer in the same year to halt all further innovations. The Lutheran princes and 14 imperial cities *protested* formally (hence, the name Protestant, which did not apply to the sectarians), but in vain.

In 1530 Charles V, freshly strengthened by the defeat of the Turks at Vienna, attended the Diet of Augsburg in person. Failing to get a compromise between the Lutherans (for whom Melanchthon drew up the conciliatory Augsburg Confession) and the Catholics, and profiting from the doctrinal divisions separating northern from southern Protestants, Charles ordered a return to the traditional faith. Led by Philip of Hesse, the Lutheran princes organized the League of Smalkald for defense against a Catholic League and the emperor. Hostilities were postponed, however: both sides entertained some hope of working together on common religious reforms. In 1532 a temporary truce was arranged, but in 1541 a final effort at religious reconciliation collapsed at Regensburg. From then on papal policy became more uncompromising and aggressive. Meanwhile German Protestantism, aided and supplied by Francis I, continued to expand by court revolutions, conversions, and the military conquests of Philip of Hesse.*

The emperor was again busy with foreign affairs. In 1536 a new Habsburg-Valois war broke out. At the same time, the Turks were still threatening Hungary and Charles's recent inheritance—central Europe. From 1542 to 1544 Charles warred against a French-Ottoman alliance. The peace concluded with France in 1544 at Crépy freed his hands to proceed against the Protestants, but not until 1546, after the first session of the Council of Trent had opened, was he able to launch a military and diplomatic offensive. In 1547 at the battle of Mühlberg he checked the superior Protestant forces, but his victory was temporary. Unable to secure ecclesiastical concessions from the pope or from the Council of Trent and failing in his own efforts to settle the German religious dis-

* Philip captured Wurttemberg, Brunswick, and other territories for the Reformation, but he embarrassed the cause by taking a second wife. Luther approved this secret bigamous marriage as preferable to divorce.

pute,* Charles was forced in 1552 to strike a truce with the Protestant princes, temporarily recognizing their territorial state churches. In the same year, war with France broke out again. In 1555, in the Peace of Augsburg, the Lutheran states forced Charles to tolerate their existence and grant them equal rights within the empire. Neither Calvinism, Anabaptism, nor any other religious group secured toleration.

Thus the German princes wrested religious autonomy from the German emperor. Exhausted and disillusioned with the task of ruling his vast dynastic empire, Charles retired as a private person to a monastery in 1556. He abdicated the Spanish crown to his son Philip and the eastern Habsburg lands to his brother Ferdinand, who became the new emperor. Relationships between Lutherans and Catholics in the empire remained tense but, strange to say, there followed the longest period of peace in Germany since the Reformation. The major German wars of religion did not break out until 1618.

# ENGLAND
# SECEDES FROM ROME

The Reformation in England was quite different from the German experience because religious doctrine and popular protest movements had little to do with it; what doctrinal disputes there were concerned papal supremacy and the English translation of the Bible. The English Catholic clergy were not scandal-free, but popular resentment did not force England's secession from Rome; on the contrary, the only major popular protest movement was directed against the king's break with Rome. Initially the English reformation was mainly an act of state, a change of administration led by the king himself. Because papal authority in England had long

* See below, p. 111.

been checked by secular controls, this change seemed at first more an evolutionary mutation than a clean break with the past.

## Henry VIII and
## the Succession Crisis

In 1509 Henry VIII inherited his father's throne, a well-stocked treasury, and an efficient administration. By then that administration had wrested obedience to the King and Parliament from the nobility. Fond of display, arbitrary in action, and ambitious beyond his means in foreign policy, Henry quickly drained the treasury surplus with few international gains to show for it. In domestic affairs he was mainly concerned with the growth of royal power, in which he was more successful. Within a few years he had won for the monarchy supreme control over both church and state.

The process of bringing church and state under a single head was initiated by Thomas Wolsey, Henry's lord chancellor from 1515 to 1529. Not only was he the chief governmental administrator and diplomat, but he also held important church positions throughout northern and western England and was the archbishop of York. The only absentee holder of many bishoprics in England, Wolsey also—with the king's assistance—became a cardinal and a papal legate. Although a favorite of the King, Wolsey was hated by nobles and churchmen for his enormous wealth and power. In 1526 he was given certain duties by the King that exceeded his capabilities and brought his downfall.

Of the children born to Henry and his queen, Catherine of Aragon, only his daughter—Mary—survived, whereas Henry wanted a male heir to prevent renewed dynastic civil war on his death. Furthermore, he had tired of Catherine and was transferring his favor to Anne Boleyn, the daughter of a recently elevated peer. He ordered Wolsey to secure a papal annulment of his long marriage, which itself had been effected under papal dispensation, since Catherine had first been the wife of Henry's older brother. Wolsey filed the plea for annulment in 1527, aware that such requests from monarchs had been granted before by the papacy. But the pope, Clement VII, was prisoner of Charles V, Catherine's nephew and a dominant force in Italian affairs and papal policy. Thus Wolsey's petition was denied. Henry, to whom the request was urgent for personal as well as dynastic reasons, stripped Wolsey of all authority in 1529 and set about getting the annulment on his own by intimidation.

Henry gained authorization from Parliament in 1529 to investigate the clergy; in 1531 he extorted a huge fine of £100,000 from the clergy for having accepted Wolsey (his own nominee) as legate. In 1532 he persuaded Parliament to abolish *annates*—payments to Rome approximately equal to the first year's income of a new bishop. (They were restored after the king became head of the Anglican church.) When these measures failed Henry named a new archbishop of Canterbury, Thomas Cranmer, a Cambridge scholar and an advocate of royal supremacy in all matters. In haste and secrecy Cranmer nullified Henry's marriage to Catherine and pronounced her daughter, Mary, illegitimate. Anne Boleyn, soon to be a mother, was proclaimed queen in 1533. In 1534 a succession act required that all subjects swear to the legitimacy of Henry's new marriage and made dissenters guilty of high treason. Still the King's problem was not solved: Anne also produced a daughter, Elizabeth. Following her in the marriage bed were Jane Seymour and a succession of new queens. Meanwhile the state church of England had become a permanent institution.

Secession from Rome was formalized in 1534 by the Act of Supremacy, which proclaimed the king head of the church; henceforth no authority outside England was recognized. Although no doctrinal issue except papal supremacy was at stake, Henry nevertheless enforced this administrative revolution with statutes of treason. The executions of Bishop John Fisher and Sir Thomas More served notice of the penalties that resistance, even merely oral resistance, entailed.

## The Reformation Settlement of Henry VIII and Edward VI

Henry VIII's break from Rome proved to be a wedge with which to force further changes. In 1535 he commissioned Thomas Cromwell, who replaced Wolsey as lord chancellor, to investigate the cloisters. These monasteries were no longer playing a major social or economic role in society; rather, they served mainly as inns and centers of alms distribution. Cromwell gave an exaggerated account of their degeneration, submitting a detailed report on their assets and revenues. Parliament responded by ceding the smaller cloisters to the king, and monks, nuns, and other cloister workers were either transferred or sent home. A new centralized court administered this additional royal income and proceeded on its own to sequester further properties, and in 1539 Parliament sanctioned the dissolution of all cloisters. The redistribution of property that followed was more far-reaching than any other since the Norman Conquest. The recipients of this property, local gentry families and royal favorites, now had a vested interest in Henry's reformation that his Roman Catholic daughter, Mary, would later be unable to shake when she temporarily returned England to Roman jurisdiction (1553–58). Perhaps even more significant, the redistribution opened church lands to progressive economic exploitation. Historians frequently cite this as a crucial step toward England's emergence as the foremost commercial and

*Henry VIII in Parliament.*

industrial country of eighteenth-century Europe.

The English reformation catered for latent antipapal sentiments, but the dissolution of church holdings did not please the lower classes of the countryside. In northern England they joined with old believers in the Pilgrimage of Grace (1536) to petition the king to preserve the monasteries, resume papal jurisdiction, and abolish penalties of treason against opposing clergymen; they also sought to curb consolidation of so much power in the hands of the king. But the Pilgrimage of Grace, like other resistance to the king and Parliament, came to naught, and after its participants had disbanded voluntarily their leaders were condemned by the courts and executed.

In breaking with Rome, Henry VIII had no intention of bringing England into conformity with continental Protestant doctrines. He worked to repress the influence of William Tyndale, whose Protestant-oriented translation of the New Testament was nevertheless absorbed into the official English translation of the Bible. The Six Articles of Faith, passed by Parliament in 1539 and for which the king was primarily responsible, upheld clerical celibacy, private masses for the dead, auricular confession, and the transubstantiation of sacramental bread and wine into the body and blood of Christ—all of these being orthodox Roman Catholic positions. Lutherans were sent to the stake in the later part of Henry's reign, and his will affirmed the existence of purgatory and the validity of private masses for the dead. Nevertheless he did not cut off all Protestant growth, for his heir was reared in that tradition.

Henry was succeeded by Edward VI, a boy of ten whose regency was dominated until 1550 by his uncle, the earl of Hereford (then duke of Somerset), who allowed the English reformation to veer more toward continental Protestantism; he relaxed the heresy and treason laws and permitted the clergy to marry. In 1549 Parliament proclaimed an Act of Uniformity, introducing the first Book of Common Prayer. It failed to affirm transubstantiation, and it contained Protestant prayers by Archbishop Cranmer, one of the most influential men during the regency. Opposition to the Prayer Book arose in Devonshire and Oxfordshire, but the action of Protestant mobs in destroying relics and images indicated that Protestant doctrines were reaching into the consciousness of the general population.

## Social Tension, Revolt, and Reaction

Somerset's government faced difficult economic and social problems rooted in the preceding reign. Despite income from the confiscation of the cloisters, Henry VIII had left the treasury empty and in debt. To meet financial needs, the regency continued and expanded expedients used by Henry: debasement of the coinage and further confiscation of church and corporate properties; it also expropriated chantries (special funds for private masses for the dead), other endowments, and guild welfare treasuries that were intended for both welfare and religious purposes. Henry's confiscations had struck primarily the old clergy, but these expropriations affected many laymen as well; funds were drained from the schools, poor relief, and the guilds. And promises to use the proceeds for schools and charity went unredeemed. The principal beneficiaries were the king's treasury and, as before, the gentry.

The people hurt worst by these confiscations and the debased money were already the victims of other social and economic miseries. Of these, enclosures of common lands for sheep pasturage and more profitable cultivation were the most detested because they revoked cottagers' and tenants' rights to common village lands. Peasants', and especially cottagers', tenure rights to village lands were replaced by terminable leases so that rents could be raised. Economic pressures on the poor were further increased as prices spiraled while wages remained fixed. Somerset sympathized with the plight of the lower classes and launched an investigation of enclosures, whose continuance he forbade. In Norfolk and nearby counties an estimated 16,000 peasants, participating in "Kett's Rebellion," rose up against the enclosures and plundered—but seldom killed—the gentry. Blamed for causing the abortive uprising, Somerset was displaced by the Earl of Warwick (later duke of Northumberland), who threw the weight of law and administration behind the gentry. Former heresy and treason laws were restored, and the gentry was allowed to determine tenants' needs as common lands were enclosed. Resistance by 40 or more peasants was defined as treason, by 12 to 39 as simply a felony.

Northumberland carried the Reformation still further toward Protestantism, but both his power and English Protestantism were jeopardized by the imminent succession of a Roman Catholic monarch—Mary. In 1552 a second Book of Common Prayer

Mary Tudor, *portrait by Antonio Moro.*

omitted references to the mass and the altar. The regency council then adopted a Protestant definition of faith in the Forty-Two Articles. The failing health of Edward VI made these changes tenuous, for Henry VIII's will designated Catherine of Aragon's daughter Mary—a fervent Catholic—as his heir. From Edward VI (but not from Parliament) Northumberland secured a new will passing the throne to Lady Jane (Grey) Dudley, a Tudor who had married Northumberland's son. However when Edward died in 1553, Mary eluded Northumberland's grasp and raised an army. In his desperate bid for power, Northumberland failed to command the loyalty necessary to precipitate a new dynastic war for the throne, and Mary became queen—with the intention of restoring Roman Catholicism.

Mary (1553—58) achieved gradual but only partial success in restoring Catholicism, and this success was in its turn jeopardized by a prospective Protestant successor, Elizabeth. While Mary's first parliament returned the religious question to the status quo at the end of Henry VIII's reign, it refused to persecute non-Catholics, to restore confiscated church properties, and to revert to papal authority. Against her will, the queen remained head of the English church until she could secure a more pliant parliament. She also failed to gain support for her alliance with Spain (sealed by her marriage to Philip II, the son of her cousin Charles) against France and the papacy. As a result, Mary lost much of her popularity, and England lost Calais, the last British foothold on the Continent. Finally, however, a parliament was returned that restored papal authority and enacted laws against the Protestant heretics. But under this persecution, which led more than 300 to the stake, Protestant resistance stiffened: its exiles to the Continent imbibed deeply of a more strident Protestantism, with which they returned after Mary's death in 1558, at which time the Catholic cause in England was lost. Her successor—Elizabeth, daughter of Anne Boleyn—was necessarily Anglican, for in Catholic eyes she was illegitimate. A single short reign by a Catholic monarch proved insufficient to reverse the English religious revolution.

## THE CALVINIST REFORM

Except among the sectarians, most religious revolutionaries were not interested in missionary attempts to universalize their faith. Anglicanism was particularly a national religion. Lutheranism remained German, Scandinavian, and East European; its passive obedience to existing authorities appealed to the city governments and paternal courts of Eastern Europe, many of which adopted it. The reformation initiated by John Calvin (1509–64), however, constituted an aggressive "international" movement that threatened existing governments with armed revolution and Roman Catholicism with a "visible," disciplined, rival church whose ideal state-church relationship closely resembled the ideal church-state relationship which several medieval popes had dreamt of and worked toward but never fully realized. As militant Roman Catholics became aware, Calvin's combination of the moral zeal of the sectarians with the conscious use of political and military power in carrying out "the will of God" made Calvinism the most serious threat to the religious status quo of Europe during the sixteenth and seventeenth centuries.

## John Calvin, Would-be Reformer of France

John Calvin, (Jean Cauvin) was born into a rising middle-class family of artisan ancestry in the French cathedral city of Noyon. His half-cleric, half-layman father was secretary for secular affairs to the bishop—the *seigneur* ("lord")—of the city. At an early age he was pointed by his father toward the priesthood, but he never became a priest, although he began drawing church revenues at the age of 12. Educated among the notables of Noyon, the boy went to the College of Montaigu in Paris. Among his classmates was Ignatius Loyola, later to found the Jesuit order. The rigorous rules of the college, which had repelled Erasmus, may have provided Calvin with a disciplinarian model for his later reorganization of Geneva.

After his father was charged with mishandling funds, Calvin, under parental direction, turned from Paris and the study of theology to Roman law at Orléans and Bourges. Both schools had come under the influence of humanist philology and historical interpretation of the Justinian code. Calvin pursued law only so long as his

*John Calvin.*

father lived; with the elder Calvin's death in 1531, he returned to Paris and the study of the classics. For these languages, and later Hebrew, he had the best teachers in France—teachers who also happened to be Protestant in outlook. His first book, a commercial failure, was a humanist commentary on Seneca's Stoicism, emphasizing morality and a sense of sin yet quite different in tone from the biblical and God-centered theology to which he devoted his life after 1533. Although his study of law was brief, marks of the legalist remained strong in his systematic theology and in his refutation of opponents.

Calvin was one of several in a circle of humanists patronized by the royal family and defended by them against the Sorbonne's indictments. Part of this group eventually abandoned humanism to adopt the pessimistic Protestant view of man's moral and religious capabilities. Unlike Luther, Calvin left few detailed personal reminiscences about his conversion to Protestantism. Probably it occurred in or before 1533, for in the following year he resigned his ecclesiastical sinecures. It is certain that he considered his conversion the work of a sovereign God who directed all of his subsequent actions and whose honor was at stake whenever he, Calvin, was criticized or contradicted. A second-generation reformer, Calvin never passed through a transient radical or liberal period during which he committed himself, as had Luther, to the freedom of the individual conscience.

Calvin's conversion came ten years after the first Protestant heretic had been burned in Paris at the instigation of the university, and it coincided with a new wave of suppression, precipitated by outbreaks of iconoclasm and the appearance of anti-Roman placards. Unsafe as a Protestant, Calvin wandered about France and then fled early in 1535 to Basel, a Protestant but humanist city. There he drafted the first edition of *The Institutes of the Christian Religion,* the most influential handbook of Protestant doctrine produced in the sixteenth century. To the *Institutes* Calvin appended a prefatory letter to Francis I in which he exonerated French Protestants from charges of anarchy and attributed such charges to malicious rumors. His plea failed to secure tolerance for French Protestants, but it projected its author, an exile, into leadership of the French Reformation. Before the *Institutes* appeared in print in Basel, Calvin wandered further to Italy, back to Noyon, and from there to Geneva en route to Strassbourg. Asked to remain in Geneva by William Farel, reformer of Berne and Geneva, Calvin thus acquired accidentally a very fortunate base for the implementation of his ideas.

The *Institutes,* repeatedly revised and enlarged and eventually published in French as well as Latin, contained few novelties, but its clarity and precision made it the cutting edge of expanding Protestantism. In asserting the absolute sovereignty of a predestining God and the total, immutable depravity of man, Calvin was in agreement with Luther, on whom he depended heavily. Pessimistic as to man, he was optimistic with respect to divine providence, individual predestination, and the revealed goal of history.

Rather than conduce to gloom or uncertainty, predestination served to give the parishioner confidence of salvation by divine election and to stimulate a communal feeling of "God-chosedness." Men need not live as doomed reprobates predestined to eternal hell. In Calvin's system all aspects of life—economic activity, politics, worship services, and family relationships—were subordinated to the literal, absolute standard of scriptural revelation. All that was not sanctioned by Scripture was forbidden. Morality he defined as the advancement of the kingdom of God on earth or God's honor; if familial or humanitarian considerations conflicted with this objective, they were denounced as blasphemies. Calvin emphasized the progressive evolution of revelation from the Old Testament to the New; but Old Testament concepts undergirded his concept of politics and society and his justification for the use of force. In addition to denouncing works as a means of salvation, Calvin emphasized that love and charity originated from faith. But the boundaries of the religious brotherhood or commonweal were set by the boundaries of doctrinal orthodoxy. The toleration of blasphemers—those who impugned the honor of God by defying His revealed doctrine—he made tantamount to blasphemy itself.

For authority, Calvin used the Scripture, but he interpreted it more narrowly than Luther. Custom unsupported by the Word of God he rejected in principle, although not always in practice; the Church should be governed as the early Church was—by pastors, elders, and deacons whose duties were spelled out in the text. He agreed with Luther in reducing the sacraments to two, but he denied the effective physical presence of the body and blood of Christ in the Liturgy of the Lord's Supper, a denial that precipitated acrimonious exchanges with various Lutherans. In the same way, Calvin's scripturalism cut away more of the supernatural and magical tradition of Christianity than Luther's; but the parts of that tradition which he did retain, including belief in witchcraft, were rigidly enforced.

In theory, Calvin—like Luther—advocated the Christian's freedom from binding laws. But like Bucer, he reconstituted in practice both laws and enforcement procedures that regulated private life to the minutest degree. Although he did not impose celibacy, dietary regulations, or formal works of grace, Calvin tried to establish a universal monastic standard; thus all laymen were to take the sacrament weekly and submit themselves to daily sermons. Legislation of morals was equally stringent in Lutheran, Anglican, and Calvinist areas, but Calvin and his followers enforced their laws with particular zeal by threatening excommunication and sending teams of elders and clergymen into all homes annually to ferret out any religious or moral nonconformists.

Unlike the Anglican and Lutheran established churches, the Calvinist church was not subservient to secular authority. Calvinism adopted a system of synods representing clergy and elders. Through them the state was to serve as the handmaiden of the church, its primary task the prevention of blasphemy. Far from introducing a separation of church and state, Calvin sought to reassert the authority of the clergy and elders over the social and political order.

Politically a sharp difference separated Calvinism from the Anglican and Lutheran churches. Both of the latter taught obedience to the existing authorities as a matter of conscience. Declaring doctrinal orthodoxy the only legitimate basis of government, Calvin proselytized even when hostile secular governments forbad him to do so. Faced with royal suppression of his gospel in France, he abandoned the obedience originally offered to Francis I and justified resistance to that monarchy when it was led by the "lesser magistrates"—nobles, town councillors, and jurists. In France and other areas Calvin attracted powerful political forces of dissidence that potentially constituted alternate governments. Thus his followers laid the groundwork for the civil and international wars of the second half of the century.

## The Holy Commonwealth of Geneva

Calvin never succeeded in converting more than a small minority of his French countrymen. But following his accidental appearance in Geneva—which he interpreted as an act of divine providence—he turned that city into his own religious kingdom.

A commercial city of about 13,000 people, Geneva had been in political turmoil for 20 years prior to Calvin's arrival. Nominally ruled by bishops (usually young boys from the neighboring house of Savoy), the city was striving to establish its independence from both bishop and Savoy. The first thrust toward that independence was engineered by William Farel, an iconoclastic French Puritan. Farel came to Geneva from Berne, where he had been part of a Protestant reformation in 1528 and had played a role in the expulsion of the prince-bishop of Lausanne. In Geneva he instigated disputations and riots that finally led to an official but precarious and unorganized Protestant reformation in 1535. Soon thereafter he convinced the city council to hire John Calvin as a teacher. Almost immediately, the youthful Calvin introduced a program of religious reorganization.

Calvin wanted to establish an autonomous church wielding the power of excommunication and moral censorship, but the ruling city council, which had become a closed oligarchy in the fifteenth century and assumed the bishop's former powers in 1535, resisted the French re-

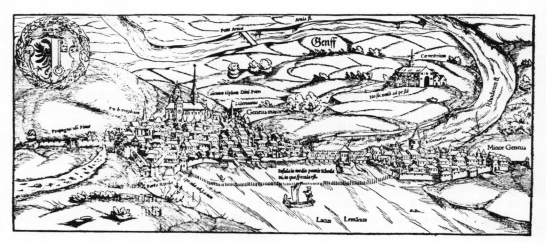

*View of Geneva.*

former. In 1538 opponents of Calvin and Farel gained control of the city's executive offices. Farel left the city permanently for Neuchâtel; Calvin emigrated to Strassbourg. There, as pastor of the French refugee colony between 1538 and 1541, he observed Jakob Sturm's reformed educational system at work, became more familiar with Martin Bucer's liturgy and ecclesiastical discipline, and introduced the singing of psalms in service. Here also in a singularly unromantic union he married, upon Bucer's recommendation, the widow of a converted Anabaptist. Meanwhile his opponents in Geneva had discredited themselves by an unfortunate foreign policy, and the city fathers asked him to return and reorganize the church. Although Calvin was never to obtain all that he wanted from the councils, he did succeed in gaining a permanent and increasing hold on city affairs, both religious and secular.

The Ecclesiastical Ordinances enacted by the councils of Geneva in 1541 were basically his; but the city magistrates retained their right to confirm appointments of pastors, teachers, elders, and deacons, and only they could name the elders who met every Thursday with the "Venerable Company" of ministers. (The fate of citi-

zens who breached either church doctrine or the city's moral code was decided at these meetings.) The councils also reduced Calvin's proposed weekly communion to four times a year, and they jealously guarded the city's authority in legal affairs by denying the clergy the power to pronounce civil penalties. Although the secular authorities retained these legal prerogatives, the clergy still gained considerable autonomy of action. And Calvin, who until 1559 was not a citizen, became, as the interpreter of the "Word of God," the city's most powerful political figure until his death.

Calvin's political power, absolute by 1555, derived from two sources: an unshakable belief in his own righteousness —accompanied by limitless zeal—and the numerical strength of his following. He was unalterably determined to overcome all obstacles to the execution of God's will, and all opponents, personal and political, he denounced as enemies of God. An influx of refugee pastors and other exiles contributed significantly to his following, which outnumbered that of the divided Genevan opposition.

In 1547 the elections went against Calvin. His supporters organized popular demonstrations and kept the new government under a continuous fire of criticism until they at last prevailed, whereupon leading men of the opposition were beheaded. Tortured and banished were theological critics who had attacked Calvin's predestination doctrine on the grounds that it made God a tyrant. In 1551 the Genevans countered Calvin's ascendancy by making a 25-year residency requirement for citizenship. Two years later, however, in the events that surrounded the case of Michael Servetus, Calvin routed and broke his opposition. "Holy terror" thus served to consolidate the reformer's position.

Michael Servetus (1511–53) was a Spanish physician and humanist scholar, who, following Erasmus's method of philological criticism, denied the doctrine of the Trinity on biblical grounds. Like the Anabaptists, he desired the restitution of the early Church, the exclusion of coercion from religion, and a humanitarian definition of Christian ethics. He lived under a pseudonym in France until his true identity was discovered. Then he was prosecuted by the Inquisition on the basis of evidence provided by one of Calvin's colleagues in Geneva. Escaping prison, Servetus made his way to Geneva for reasons unknown. Here he was recognized, taken into custody, and tried for heresy. He probably counted on aid from Calvin's foes, but the reformer successfully pressed the prosecution and used Servetus's heresy to discredit his opposition. In 1553, in an action approved by most of the Protestant clergy on the Continent, Servetus was burned at the stake. Protests came from Erasmian humanists such as Sebastian Castellio, but he, like Calvin's other opponents, was obliged to seek physical safety outside Geneva. The Holy Commonwealth, solicitous of the welfare of the disinherited as well as of the industrious within its communion, held out only destruction by divine wrath to those who challenged the authority or accuracy of its leading interpreter of Holy Writ.

## The Calvinist International

Often identified as a forerunner of modern nationalism, Calvinism was in fact the most international of the major Protestant reformations. Although Calvinists in every area were preoccupied with the establishment of their own "New Jerusalem," common aims and coordination from Geneva held their efforts together at least so long as Calvin lived. Had he succeeded in becoming head of a successful French reformation, his church might have become identified politically with France; but as a religious body of refugees in Geneva, it was never connected with the foreign policy of a major state.

Calvinism varied only slightly from place to place. Its adherents accepted a common doctrine, performed the same liturgy, and organized their churches according to the Genevan model. Everywhere Calvin's *Institutes*, clarified and extended by his personal correspondence, were the guide. Missionaries and pastors were trained almost exclusively in Geneva, and their orthodoxy was assured before they were allowed to fill teaching or pastoral posts; in some instances the work of missionaries was kept under surveillance. Most of the Genevan students were from other lands, such as France, Scotland, England, and Germany. In 1559 the Genevan consistory—a court composed of ministers and lay elders—established a college headed by Theodore Beza, Calvin's eventual successor, to enlarge and systematize the training of the Calvinist clergy.

This uniform and well-controlled Calvinism spread widely in Europe. Only Spain and Spanish-dominated areas such as Italy were exempt from its impact. Penetrating the Swiss Confederacy, in 1549 the Calvinists reached an agreement with Heinrich Bullinger in Zurich; they also made inroads into Germany, especially the southern and Rhenish states. In 1580 the Lutheran evangelical churches res-

*Anti-Reformation woodcut depicting Calvin, Luther, and Beza as its primary villains.*

ponded to this "reformed" encroachment with the Formula of Concord, which made Calvinists heretics; however they failed to check the spread of Calvinism.

Under conditions of relative tolerance, Calvinist missionaries gained followings in Bohemia, Hungary, Poland, and Transylvania. Calvinism also grew in the Low Countries where it was less under Genevan control. Trained at Geneva, John Knox returned to Scotland and carried out a political and religious revolution there. Calvinist influences became perceptible also in England during and after the reign of Edward VI. Everywhere radical, armed Calvinist reformers were striving for total control over the machinery of state, and thus they precipitated violent reactions from kings and traditionalist religious opponents. Except where they were in full control or else too weak to challenge existing authority, the growth of their influence was the prelude to civil war. During the religious-political wars of the sixteenth century, the Calvinist clergy preached solidarity against the common Roman Catholic enemy, whose internationalism it rivaled.

## B. The Humanist between Confessional Fronts

Men educated in the classics were involved on all sides of the Reformation, but the followers of Erasmus came to occupy a middle ground from which they mediated the violent extremes. After religious wars had taken heavy tolls, Erasmians gained influence on both sides; but at the outset they were despised all around. To traditional Catholics their appeals for reform were heresy. Their opposition to schism and vituperation also alienated them from the Protestants. In the midst of brutality and authoritarianism they and a few humane but powerless sectarians stood alone for diversity, tolerance, and for a humanitarianism that placed the commonweal above religious differences.

### The Break between Luther and Erasmus

When the Reformation began, Protestant reformers were commonly identified with Erasmian critics of the Church; indeed, their criticisms coincided at many points, and such Protestants as Melanchthon and Zwingli were also humanist scholars of philology and Church history. Yet humanism and early Protestantism proved incompatible; the fundamental differences between them came to light in the irreparable break (1525) between Erasmus and Luther.

As early as 1517, Luther, for whom all wisdom consisted of knowing about sin, grace, and the revealed path to salvation, had complained that Erasmus was too secular and too preoccupied with human concerns. For his part, Erasmus feared that Luther's inflammatory popular writings could produce violence and counterviolence. To forestall tumult, Erasmus urged moderation on the reformers while he strove to prevent the traditionalists from indicting Luther for heresy without redressing his grievances. In 1520 Luther undercut Erasmus's mediation by attacking the sacraments and burning canon law. The humanist began to fear that the reformer would destroy the cause of peaceful reform and cultural renaissance in an abortive doctrinal and doctrinaire revolution.

As Luther and Erasmus became more familiar with each other's reform programs, they recognized gulfs between themselves that could not be bridged. Neither their temperaments nor their methods agreed. In Luther's theology of predestination the human will was totally without merit; free exercise of it led to sin. Without divine grace—that is, without professing Luther's creed—the doer of good works was doomed to eternal damnation. To Erasmus, preoccupied with ethics and the overcoming of ignorance and violence, Protestant denial of free will weakened man's sense of morality and made God a tyrant who kept men bound to evil. This quarrel pitted Luther the theologian against Erasmus the moralist. The moralist deemphasized the sacraments and was skeptical of the theologian's "revealed" and absolute dogmas. In 1525 the two exchanged polemical pamphlets on the nature of the human will. Erasmus upheld the dignity and capabilities of man; Luther asserted man's total immutable depravity and denied that he had a free will. As this quarrel grew heated, Erasmian humanists drew back from Luther. Melanchthon, who stayed with him, nevertheless retained enough confidence in human initiative to be denounced as a "crypto-Calvinist" in Saxony after Luther died in 1546.*

In adopting "Calvinism" as a derogatory synonym for Erasmus's philosophy, the Lutherans were greatly oversimplifying. Erasmians found Geneva no more hospitable than Wittenberg; as we have seen, Sebastian Castellio, among others, was obliged to flee Geneva for his life. Theodore Beza, Calvin's successor, frankly wrote that he preferred tyranny to religious individualism and that "the freedom of conscience is the devil's principle of faith"—it allowed everyone to chose his own path to hell. Eventually such humanists did influence Protestantism, especially in England, the Netherlands, and to a lesser extent in southern Germany. But the Protestants who opened themselves to humanist influence were not the major continental reformers of the sixteenth century.

## The Expulsion of Humanists from Catholic Reform

Meanwhile Catholic traditionalists attacked Erasmus and his followers for

* This attack on Melanchthon was particularly inappropriate because Calvin denied human initiative even more systematically than did Luther.

aiding and abetting the Protestant enemy. Led by Girolamo Aleander, papal nuncio to the emperor, and the Spanish Dominicans, they argued that unconditional obedience was due to the papal church whatever its shortcomings, because it was commissioned by God. Nonconforming humanists and their books were burned in the Low Countries as early as 1522 and 1523, and Erasmus complained of being "stoned by both sides." Between the fronts of intolerant "integralist" Protestantism and militant Catholic traditionalists, Erasmians were caught in the crossfire of denunciation and physical jeopardy. Until aggressive conservatives gained control within the Roman church, however, most humanists retained some hope of effecting their kind of reformation within it. Their optimism soared briefly under Pope Adrian VI (1522–23), who conceded to the German diet at Nuremberg the necessity of drastic reform. Time was too short and resistance was too strong for Adrian, however; his successor, Clement VII—a Medici—dropped this approach.

The sacking of Rome in 1527 by the unpaid German troops of Charles V indicated how badly things were going for the traditionalists. Spanish humanists applauded it as a forerunner of reform, but their position became untenable when they came under heavy attack by the Inquisition. Of course, the pope could still have called a council had he not feared that he would lose papal prerogatives to any council he did not tightly control. A further force militating against this decision was the continuing conflict between Valois and Habsburg, the two leading Catholic dynasties.

In the absence of leadership from Rome or a general council, Catholic reform began at the local level; in fact, many small reform movements had existed before the Protestant Reformation began. Early in their history a struggle developed between advocates of persuasion and advocates of force: the Brethren of the Common Life advocated tolerance and humanitarian brotherhood; in Spain reformers led by Cardinal Ximénes often relied on coercion; in Italy some reformers followed the Venetian nobleman, Gasparo Contarini, an apostle of conciliation, while others supported Giovanni Pietro Caraffa—equally dedicated to changes, but by inquisitional methods. As both these men were appointed by Pope Paul III to successively higher posts, they came to epitomize the two conflicting trends in the Catholic Reformation.

Paul commissioned a body including cardinals Contarini and Caraffa to draw up a general proposal for regenerating the Church. In 1537 they returned their report. It so frankly indicted the clergy for avarice and irresponsibility in high places that when it leaked out German Protestants circulated it as propaganda for their own cause. Other cardinals and secular rulers, however, opposed the calling of a council to act on the report. So Contarini and Caraffa proceeded along their own rival paths of reform.

Contarini equated Christianity with freedom. He denied the theory of absolute papal authority and refused to exalt the papal monarch above canon law. He also pursued a course of conciliation with the Protestants. At the Imperial Diet of Regensburg (Ratisbon) in 1541, he followed a very liberal interpretation of Catholic dogma in order to seek agreements with Bucer and Melanchthon, the more flexible Protestant reformers. In so doing, he overrode Catholic traditionalists and exceeded his instructions from the pope. But he failed to reach a general agreement with the Protestants: the Colloquy of Regensburg—the last attempt to heal the religious schism—fell apart, and negotiators on both sides were denounced in their respective camps as heretics. Rapidly losing influence, Contarini died in 1542. His demise marked a milestone in the disappearance of Erasmian influence on the Catholic Reformation.

While Contarini was at Regensburg his rival reformer, Caraffa (who became Pope Paul IV in 1555), had helped institute the Roman Inquisition and an extensive *Index of Prohibited Books*. Although classical studies as well as humanist philology and educational techniques were used by subsequent reformers, particularly those in the Society of Jesus, it was symptomatic of the spirit of Catholic reform henceforth that all of Erasmus's writings appeared on the early *Index*, where most of them remained until the twentieth century.

## The Continued Vitality of Humanism

Wherever rigid doctrinal orthodoxy was enforced as in Spain, most of Italy, Geneva, Scotland, and the German principalities, Erasmian humanism could survive only when expressed in nonverbal disciplines; talents not in accord with the prevailing creed were more safely expressed in music or painting. Though exceptional, pockets of toleration continued to exist. After 1555 the Austrian Habsburgs were influenced by Erasmian humanists, but their toleration aimed at an eventual restoration of religious unity. In other areas, notably France, England, and the Low Countries, latitudinarian religious policies* or toleration necessitated by religious pluralism left greater room for the continuation of the "Northern Renaissance." Most productive of new viewpoints within the humanist tradition were the French and the Dutch.

French humanists developed a notable secularization of thought and new methods for studying society. They laid

---

* Latitudinarians drew up vague creeds for state churches that were intended to encompass the beliefs of most of the population.

the basis for a political faction, the *politiques,* that shunned both the militant Calvinist and Catholic sides during the French wars of religion (1562–98) because they considered the commonweal or security of life more important than creedal orthodoxy. The most original of these humanists was Jean Bodin (1530–96), who is best known for developing the theory of the absolute sovereignty of the secular state. But he was no less significant for applying a comparative empirical approach to theology and law. In theology it led him to conclude that different religions share a common or natural core, an assumption that provided the basis for deism during the eighteenth-century Enlightenment. In law he denied the validity of the Justinian codes for all times and places; rather he considered them a composite of historical laws, applicable to specific conditions in the past and subject to such local influences as climate. Thus he undermined the revival of Roman law which had become basic to the legal systems of most European countries earlier in the sixteenth century. Bodin's empiricism resulted in a curious paradox: it led him to accept the testimony of women that they were witches and at the same time to argue for social reform based on accumulated knowledge. Bodin's method and his idea of progress, which Erasmus

had developed, gained wide circulation during the Enlightenment of the eighteenth century when the Baron de Montesquieu mined his works for their content and methodology.

A parallel humanist evolution developed in the Netherlands. Dirck Coornhert (1522–90), for example, developed an ethical code based on religious sectarianism and the social philosophy of Cicero that had been so inspiring to the civic humanism of the Italian Renaissance. He too conceived of a natural religion whose rites and dogmas could vary from one environment to another. His humanism and denial of predestination attracted a following of Dutch burghers (the Arminians) who resisted the religious and political objectives of both orthodox Calvinists and the Spanish Inquisition. Although it was nominally a Calvinist movement, Arminianism itself was a humanistic religion, for it emphasized the compatibility of reason and faith, deemphasized dogmas and sacraments, and asserted some human initiative in achieving salvation.

Humanism was narrowed and restricted by the competing orthodoxies it tried to temper, reform, or stand against. After surviving the religious wars, it became a rallying point for many who were weary of fanaticism and violence in the late sixteenth and early seventeenth centuries.

## C. The Catholic Reformation

By the middle of the sixteenth century Protestantism's rapid growth in northern Europe posed a graver crisis for Roman Catholicism than had the papal schism and heretical movements of the Renaissance. England, Scandinavia, numerous principalities and cities of the Holy Roman Empire, and parts of the Swiss Confederation had defected. Under the leadership of John Knox, a Geneva-trained Calvinist, Scotland followed in 1560. Tightly organized Calvinist minorities were forming in the Low Countries and in France. And in the empire the militant Calvinists were displacing the Lutherans in the territories along the Rhine, even Bavaria and Austria were

*Woodcut showing the "true" Roman church surrounded by heretical devils.*

eigns with the popular support to meet Protestantism by force. At the same time, the protracted Habsburg-Valois wars were temporarily suspended (1544) and terminated for more than half a century in 1559 by the Treaty of Cateau-Cambrésis. These lulls in warfare between the two major Catholic dynasties permitted Charles V to launch military and diplomatic offensives against German Protestants. They also gave Catholic leaders the confidence to attempt a general council, the Council of Trent (1545–47, 1551–52, 1562–63). Moreover the Treaty of Cateau-Cambrésis, which recognized Spanish dominance in Italy, was signed in the same year as that in which the last outspoken anti-Spanish pope, Paul IV, died. Thereafter the leading secular power in the Catholic Reformation and the model for its institutions and procedures was Habsburg Spain.

## New Religious Orders

In medieval crises brought on by moral and administrative decay, the founding of new monastic orders had refurbished the Church's reputation and released its wasted energies. Such had been the origins of the Cluniacs, the Cistercians, and the mendicant Franciscans and Dominicans. New orders had been rejected during the Renaissance, but in the sixteenth century new orders and reform movements within existing ones again heralded fresh vigor in the Roman church.

At about the same time that Luther was becoming famous in Germany, reformers —clergy and lay aristocrats of diverse religious views—were organizing in Italy. They founded Oratories of the Divine Love—small societies dedicated to prayer, frequent reception of the sacraments, and acts of charity. Among their ranks were leading Catholic reformers of the following generation: Jacopo Sadoleto, Giovanni Pietro Caraffa (later Pope Paul IV), and

tottering in allegiance while their proximity to Protestant territories weakened Rome's control over the thought of their clergy. Only Spain, where a state-directed Reformation had already occurred, and—to a lesser degree—Italy, remained impervious to the Protestant onslaught.

Instead of submitting to a rout, the Roman Catholic church began to muster forces to check the Protestant tide and, in subsequent decades, to regain lost or wavering territories. Barriers to the foundation of new religious orders collapsed. Following the lead of the Society of Jesus a host of new orders emphasizing education, social welfare, and pastoral work labored to counteract heresy and inculcate piety. These were most effective in mobilizing the emotional religious passions of the masses behind tradition and ingrained patterns of religious life; and these passions provided Catholic sover-

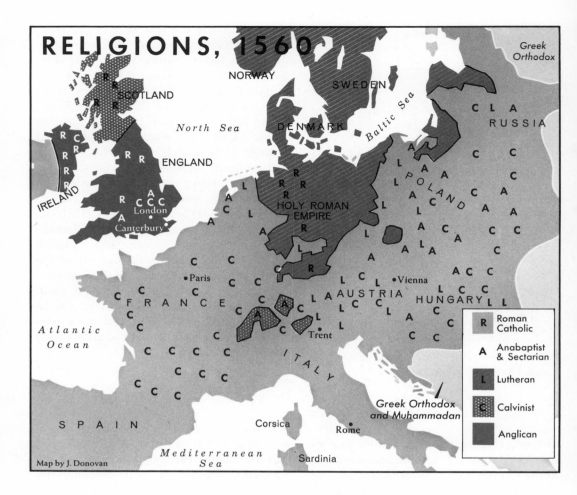

RELIGIONS, 1560

**Legend:**
- R — Roman Catholic
- A — Anabaptist & Sectarian
- L — Lutheran
- C — Calvinist
- Anglican

Greek Orthodox

Map by J. Donovan

Gaetano di Thiene. Thiene founded another new order in 1524, the Theatines; like most of the orders that followed, it adjusted old ideals of monasticism to the needs of a new generation. These "clerks regular" did not withdraw from the world but combined methodical prayer with secular activism. Like the mendicant friars, they owed allegiance directly to the papacy, and their clerical members were bound by formal vows; but they were neither friars nor monks. Although they were exceedingly few in number, the Theatines (who took their name not from Thiene but from Caraffa's bishopric) enforced Caraffa's severe discipline against clerical neglect, concubinage, and other abuses by personal visitations and provided the papacy with more than 200 bishops during the remainder of the sixteenth century. In addition to the Theatines, Italy produced similar orders, including the Somaschi and the Barnabites. In both Italy and France, new women's orders, beginning with the Ursulines, were also organized to care for the poor and especially to teach the young.

Within the existing order, Franciscans began another influential reform movement, the Capuchins. As disappointed with their order as Luther was with his, they tried to go back to the purity of St. Francis rather than destroy the monastic tradition. In origin the Capuchins were the offspring of the Italian populace; their direct approach to the masses made them the principal agents in regaining and holding the loyalty of the Italian lower classes. In 1542 they were shaken by the desertion of their leading popular preacher and third vicar-general, Bernardino Ochino, to the Unitarians, but they recovered rapidly. In France, where the Spanish background of their Jesuit competitors was suspect, the Capuchins gained positions of power and influenced the court.

Far exceeding the other new orders in total efforts and effectiveness was the Society of Jesus, the "shock troops of the Counter Reformation," founded by a disabled Spanish soldier, Ignatius of Loyola (1491–1556). A young nobleman serving in the Habsburg-Valois wars, Loyola was wounded while campaigning in Navarre in 1521. While recuperating, he experienced a mystical religious conversion comparable in impact to Martin Luther's revelation of salvation by faith alone, and from chivalry he turned to "spiritual knighthood." In 1523 he set out on a pilgrimage via Rome and Venice to the Holy Land. Returned to Barcelona in 1524, he decided that he lacked sufficient education to be an efficient instrument of God. With the city's school children he attended grammar school; thereafter he attended the universities of Alcalá, Salamanca, and Paris. It was at Paris that he gathered around him ten disciples who became the Society's early nucleus. He demanded of them a disciplined will and unconditional obedience to higher authority. He strongly encouraged their higher education and urged that they foster the zeal to work (in the words of his personal motto) "to the greater glory of God."

After going to Rome, where their frequent religious observances had made them suspect, the Jesuit initiates received official papal approval as a new order on the recommendation of Cardinal Con-

*Ignatius of Loyola.*

tarini in 1540. There they took permanent vows of poverty, chastity, and obedience to the papacy, and were commissioned soldiers of God to propagate doctrine and faith by public preaching, acts of charity, and especially public education. Until 1544 the order was limited to 60 members but, freed of this restriction, it expanded rapidly, especially in the Iberian kingdoms and their colonial empires. The Jesuits' zeal for missionary work proved as intense as that of the Franciscans and Dominicans. One of the original founders, Francis Xavier (1506–52), is credited with hundreds of thousands of converts in India, China, Malaya, and Japan.

The Jesuits did not limit their missionary efforts to the Iberian colonial empires; they also moved into those areas of Europe jeopardized by Protestantism. Many parts of western and southern Germany were recovered for the Roman church by Peter Canisius of Nimwegen (1521–97). An educator and Jesuit administrator, he competed hard and effectively against Protestant preaching. Supported by the rulers of Bavaria and Poland during the second half of the century, the Jesuits almost totally restored religious conformity there by persuasion and force.

Among primitive peoples, the Jesuits usually secured little more than acceptance of the sacraments as a sign of conversion. But in Europe their goals were political and power-oriented as well as spiritual, and their methods, both admired and feared by their enemies, were highly sophisticated. Aside from pastoral work, Jesuits devoted great attention to higher education, founding colleges to train and indoctrinate the elite of both church and state. These colleges and their faculties became an integral part of the Catholic resurgence, enjoying reputations that attracted non-Catholics as well. More controversial were the strivings of Jesuit confessors to influence rulers' policies. The order was committed to papal supremacy in spiritual affairs, but nothing prevented its members from trying to influence secular events. In the eyes of its Protestant opponents, the Society of Jesus was a centralized papal conspiracy. The members persuaded receptive kings that their religious ends justified the use of political means. Thus a large Protestant literature denouncing Jesuit casuistry grew up during the religious wars. In itself, the heat of the Protestant reaction was a strong indication of the Jesuits' effectiveness.

## The Council of Trent

Jesuit zeal and scholarship were not the only indication that the carefree days of the Renaissance papacy had come to an end. After disastrously long delays, prelates, theologians, canonists, generals of the mendicant orders, and papal legates assembled with other dignitaries of the Roman church at the city of Trent. This council faced the serious business of refuting Protestantism and purifying the Church of the abuses that had helped the Protestant influence to spread.

More than vested interest in the status quo had caused the council to be postponed until the eleventh hour. Although the pope and the Curia had surely feared that a general council would usurp their prerogatives, the wars between Francis I and Charles V had nevertheless made an ecumenical council impossible. Following the truce in 1544 the papacy entered into a military alliance with Charles under the terms of which a papal army was dispatched to help fight the German Protestants. It was hoped that the convening of the council would coincide with a military victory.

Politically the moment seemed auspicious for the council to enforce a religious settlement after the Protestants' defeat, but this strategy was frustrated by an incomplete military victory and by disagreement among the Catholics. Pope Paul III set highest priority on refuting Protestant doctrines. Fearing nothing more than rigid doctrinal proclamations that would make peace in Germany impossible, Charles V wanted immediate reform of abuses. Charles's political priorities alarmed the pope, and as their alliance expired, the pope withdrew the remnants of his army from Germany and approached France diplomatically. Meanwhile Charles also became disillusioned with the council because it followed papal leadership in promulgating uncompromisingly traditional religious doctrines before carrying out reforms.

From the start, legates instructed by the pope were in command of the council so that it did not become a threat to papal sovereignty. They secured the restriction of voting rights to the higher clergy, set the agenda, and reserved for the pope the exclusive right to promulgate, interpret, and execute the council's decrees. Opposition to the legates, although divided, was heated, and the council did not conform completely to papal wishes. Giving ear to the opinions that "only reform can save Germany for the Church,"[1] the assembled fathers agreed to deal simultaneously with doctrines and reforms. In practice, however, the council offended Charles V, for reform proposals were delayed by long debates and divisions, whereas rigid doctrinal decrees passed rapidly with near unanimity.

Rather than cataloging Catholic doctrine comprehensively, the doctrinal decrees uncompromisingly reaffirmed Catholic dogmas that unnamed Protestants had attacked. In opposition to Protestant reliance on scriptural authority alone—which no Protestant reformer maintained consistently for long—the council declared the parity of unbroken apostolic tradition with the Bible. It also affirmed the Church as the sole interpreter of Scripture and established prepublication censorship over all theological works. Repudiating the humanists' criterion of textual purity, the council approved only the Latin Vulgate edition of the Bible on the grounds that its long use by the Church established its authenticity. Another decree rejected the Protestant dogma that man was totally and immutably depraved as a result of original sin, to remedy the effects of which—concupiscence and death—Trent relied on the sacraments. The debate on original sin, the longest of the entire council, inexorably compelled participants to grapple with Luther's fundamental doctrine of unmerited salvation by faith alone. The council avoided rigid personal predestination and asserted the necessity of human free will to opt for salvation through the sacraments, which had to be supplemented by faith, love, hope, and good works. The emphasis on sacraments included a denunciation of Anabaptists as well as Protestants. Logically this position on original sin required another decree that affirmed the seven sacraments, the greater number of which Protestants had denounced as human inventions.

The council took major steps to restore the authority of bishops over their dioceses, and to produce a more competent clergy. In order to make clergymen capable of public preaching, bishops and monastic orders were required to provide them with instructors in theology. Another decree attacked the central problems of administrative disorder: absenteeism, pluralism—the holding of several church posts simultaneously—the use of offices as sinecures, and exemptions from episcopal visitation. With few exceptions the council ordered heavy penalties for absentee prelates. The price of this reorganization was not only greater clerical discipline; papal revenues derived from dispensations from the canon law also shrank. Meanwhile in other moves against the prelates' affluence, the pope suspended the sale of indulgences and reduced the sale of offices.

The first sessions terminated following Paul III's rift with Charles V. Dismayed by the council's doctrinal decrees and unable to prevent the pope's removal of the council to Bologna, where it ended, Charles in 1548 proclaimed a religious settlement for Germany on his own authority. This "Interim" permitted the continuance of married priests in their functions and the dispensation of Communion to the laity in both bread and wine until the council resumed. The Interim divided the German Protestants but failed to bridge the confessional gap in the empire.

Pope Julius III (1550–55) reassembled the council again in 1551–52. This time Protestant representatives were invited, but instead of contributing to conciliation, they demonstrated the breadth of the schism by insisting on the nullification of

[1] Quoted by Hubert Jedin, *A History of the Council of Trent*, vol. 2, *The First Session at Trent* (St. Louis: B. Herder Book Co., 1961), p. 36.

all previous actions. Little was accomplished also because Protestant forces, aided actively by France, defeated the emperor and threatened to overrun Trent itself. The council hastily disbanded. Subsequently the Peace of Augsburg (1555), which placed religious affairs in the hands of ruling German princes, provided a settlement the council had failed to reach.

The council did not reconvene until 1562. Caraffa, reigning as Pope Paul IV from 1555 to 1559, preferred autocratic rule as an instrument of reform. His successor, Pius IV, called the final assembly. It amplified and extended previous decisions, creating the basic legislation by which the Roman Catholic church has subsequently been governed. To curtail commercialization of religion the council forbade the sale of indulgences and regulated the cult of saints and the veneration of relics. Reacting against Renaissance naturalism, the fathers issued some puritanical decrees. As one result, second-rate artists painted loincloths on the frescoes of Michelangelo and other great Renaissance painters.

The council ordered the redistribution of parish incomes and dictated in detail the content of eduction in the seminaries. At the same time a host of dispensations and privileges were abolished; Spanish, French, and imperial bishops sought and were denied greater prerogatives for themselves. The fathers elaborated on the sacraments, especially holy orders and matrimony, and they espoused the teachings, though not the rationalism, of Thomas Aquinas, proclaiming him the authoritative interpreter of Christianity. To inculcate the approved doctrines, the council ordered that clerical and popular catechisms be prepared. The *breviary* (daily prayers of the priesthood), the official lives of the saints, and the *missal* (prayers of the Mass) were also to be revised. Charles Borromeo, archbishop of Milan and director of the final session at Trent, supervised these tasks.

## The Implementation of Catholic Reform

To legislate reforms was one thing; to enforce them over the opposition of vested political and clerical interests was another. Catholic reform depended heavily on papal leadership, since the pope reserved for himself all rights of implementing the council's decrees. His power outside Italy, however, was narrowly circumscribed by the Catholic monarchs, whose predecessors had established a tradition of royal control over the local churches. Now they refused to let the papacy with its reform rulings encroach on their jurisdiction: they quite simply vetoed whatever rulings they wished not to adopt or tolerate. Thus the implementation of Catholic administrative reform depended on the policies of Catholic rulers, especially the Spanish Habsburgs, who commanded the most formidable military forces during the wars of religion.

In the decades after 1559 most of the popes made Catholic revival their primary concern. Pius IV began work on the Catechism, *Breviary*, and the *Missal*, projects which were completed under his successor, Pius V (1566–72). A former monk and inquisitor-general, Pius V applied the Inquisition rigorously and commanded a puritan standard of morality for Rome. The actions of these two popes made Rome a less attractive place for seekers of fortune and pleasure. Another noteworthy reformer-pope was Gregory XIII (1572–85), a canon lawyer who revised the canon law, encouraged the rapid growth of the Society of Jesus and its colleges, and issued the revised Gregorian calendar. The succession of reforming popes continued into the middle of the seventeenth century.

Catholic reformers relied heavily on persuasion, but the popes had at their disposal two instruments of coercion initiated by Cardinal Caraffa, the Roman

*Didactic Reformation art: Detail from* Seven Deadly Sins *by Hieronymous Bosch, an earlier Flemish artist (d. 1516). Bosch's works were widely reproduced, especially in Spain.*

Inquisition and the *Index of Prohibited Books.*

The Inquisition served as an extraordinary court for the extirpation of heresy.*

* The Roman Inquisition had a medieval predecessor founded in the thirteenth century to stamp out heresy on the Continent, but it fell into disuse during the Renaissance. In 1478 the papacy approved the establishment of the Spanish Inquisition, which Caraffa observed and admired, imitating it in the foundation of the Roman Inquisition in 1542.

Proceedings were secret, torture was used on both the accused and the witnesses, and suspects were imprisoned without recourse to counsel or confrontation with witnesses. Although the Inquisition functioned as a confessional tribunal in which mercy was normally extended to those who confessed guilt and begged forgiveness, the inquisitor-generals were empowered to override the jurisdiction of local bishops, to pronounce judgments,

113    C. *The Catholic Reformation*

and to turn the condemned over to the secular authorities for punishment. Since most secular governments preferred their own tribunals or autonomous inquisitions, the Roman Inquisition in practice functioned little outside Italy, where it played a heavy and controversial role. It succeeded in crushing heresy in the Italian cities, but in so doing it has since been held accountable for creating an atmosphere of intellectual stagnation. In this regard, however, it was scarcely more repressive than many secular tribunals.

Cardinal Caraffa's other innovation, the Index, initially banned all the works of Erasmus as well as those of the Protestant reformers. Under Caraffa's original orders, too, thousands of books were burned; this Index of 1559 established categories of prohibited offensive works: all the books of certain outlawed authors, anonymous heretical writings, works of specific printers, and all vernacular translations of the New Testament. The Council of Trent ordered a revision of the Index that led to its modification, but at the same time more efficient machinery for its enforcement was set up, including a system of prepublication censorship. The Index, a powerful tool of thought control during the Reformation, proved to be a lasting institution; however more recent revisions have restricted its scope—for example, no works of Erasmus appear in the latest compilation, and the list of specific works permission to read which has still to be secured is confined to matters relating solely to faith and morals. Recently, after the Second Vatican Council, all penalties relating to the Index were removed.

At the last meeting at Trent the major Catholic princes agreed to cooperate with reform under papal leadership, but no Catholic sovereign followed suit; and the kings retained their control over Church affairs. Occasionally some of them with subjects of differing faiths outrightly resisted Trent's decrees on doctrine. The Austrian Habsburgs, for example, attempted to maintain domestic peace by offering concessions to the Protestants. Similarly, the French house of Valois, which was on the threshhold of a long religious civil war, sought a more tolerant solution to doctrinal controversies than the final assembly at Trent provided.

Resistance to the doctrinal decrees was slight, however, compared to resistance to administrative decrees and to the Inquisition. For the monarchs to comply with these meant that they surrendered control over the higher clergy and would further lose their power to reward favorites with sinecures and ecclesiastical revenues. Their favorites, the local aristocracy, would in turn lose a major source of family income. Moreover, the local churches in both Catholic and Protestant kingdoms were beginning to espouse the principle of divine-right monarchy. Profiting from the doctrine drawn from the Epistle of St. Paul to the Romans, that he who resists constituted authority resists God himself,* rulers were adamant against returning to papal overlordship. No secular government, least of all the Most Catholic King of Spain, fully accepted the administrative reforms of the Council of Trent. Outside the clerical archbishoprics few German principalities ever adopted them, and the French church was not reformed administratively until the revolution of 1789.

Catholic resurgence was a reality, especially in producing a more highly educated clergy and in establishing a host of new orders engaged in social work as well as acts of piety. But the locus of power remained not in the papacy or Church councils but in the hands of secular rulers who had broken from Church control prior to the Reformation. For them religion was subordinate to the interests of power.

* "Let every person be subject to the governing authorities. For there is no authority except from God, and those that exist have been instituted by God. Therefore he who resists the authorities resists what God has appointed, and those who resist will incur judgment" (13: 1–3).

## D. Eastern Europe and the Reformation

By the mid-1500s the Protestant Reformation had spread into Roman Catholic central Europe, where it became entangled in the political conflicts within Bohemia, Hungary, and Poland-Lithuania; but the Balkan countries, Greek Orthodox by tradition and ruled by Muhammadans, were impervious to its creeping influence. So was Muscovy, the only independent principality with an Orthodox population. Muscovite Orthodoxy, isolated from developments in the West by barriers of both geography and tradition, remained devoted to antiintellectualism, monasticism, and an authoritarian political state. Therefore the Reformation never went beyond western and central Europe.

### Bohemia, Hungary, and Poland-Lithuania

At the beginning of the Protestant Reformation the borderlands of eastern Europe were governed by the Jagellon family. Under military pressure from both east and west, these rulers (who were failing to produce male heirs) lost extensive territory to neighboring kingdoms. They also yielded internal authority to aristocrats and gentry who, in the absence of central authority, exercised considerable "local option" in religious affairs. At Mohacs in 1526 the Turks killed Louis, the childless Jagellon king of Bohemia and Hungary, whereupon the Habsburgs took possession of his throne. They also had designs on Poland-Lithuania, the last surviving Jagellon state, which at this time was under attack from the east by Turks, Tartars, and Muscovites. Its leaders sought maximum internal unity to stand off the encircling threats, and in 1569 they effected the Union of Lublin. The state, once jointly governed by Polish and Lithuanian dynasts, now came under a single, elective kingship and a common diet, the latter dominated by the nobles and gentry. When the last Jagellon king died, factions of the nobility and the gentry competed with one another and with various foreign influences for the ruling power.

These conditions of political instability were conducive to religious dissent, which political power-seekers used for their own advantage. Supported by Lutherans, Calvinists, and anti-Trinitarians (Unitarians), they defied traditional authority then embodied in Sigismund I (1506–48). In vain he and his successors tried to suppress these heresies—their decrees went unacknowledged. A diet of 1556 demanded comprehensive religious reforms, and in 1573 Henry of Valois (temporarily king of Poland before becoming king of France) was obliged to extend religious toleration. Following 1550, soon after the rise of Calvinism in Poland, the Jesuits launched a Counter-Reformation. Sigismund III (1587–1632) utilized their services to almost wholly extirpate dissent from Polish religious life.

Events followed a somewhat similar course in Habsburg Bohemia, where first Lutheranism and then Calvinism became an important movement of political and religious revolt. There the native Hussite tradition was dominant although divided between conservative Utraquists, who had gained the Church's permission for extending Communion to the laity under species of both bread and wine (*utra* = L. "both"), and the more radical Czech Brethren, who had replaced revolutionary fervor with pacifist pietism. Persecution of the Czech Brethren between 1548 and 1552 failed to check religious dissent, and Maximilian II (1564–76) permitted extensive toleration.

Compared with Bohemia, which was neither invaded nor beset with civil war, Hungary's reformation was much more chaotic. After 1526 the Ottoman Turks held the eastern two-thirds of that kingdom, and the Habsburgs occupied the remainder. Against these two powers Transylvanian nobles led a movement for Hungarian autonomy. Denouncing the authority of the Church as well as of the state, they espoused Calvinism and Lutheranism, and after 1560 anti-Trinitarianism also became an important force in their revolt. In 1564 all three new religions were recognized as legally equal with Catholicism. Unlike the Roman resurgence in Poland and Bohemia, the Catholic Reformation in Habsburg Hungary never entirely suppressed religious dissent.

## Greek Orthodoxy and the Turks

Several times in the sixteenth century Lutherans and Calvinists both sought active cooperation with the Greeks against Rome. One patriarch of Alexandria and Constantinople actually published a Calvinist-like confession of faith in Geneva in 1602, but he was thoroughly repudiated by official synods in the East. Differences between Greek Orthodoxy and the West, Catholic and Protestant, were deep-rooted. Protestant hopes of uniting with the East against Rome proved illusory.

For the continued schism splitting Orthodoxy from the West, not only different religious traditions but Turkish tolerance was responsible. When the Ottoman Turks conquered Asia Minor and the Balkans in the late fourteenth century they brought almost all Greek Orthodox peoples except the Muscovites under Muhammadan rule. But even the shock of conquest and government by the foreign infidel created no more than temporary ties between Eastern and Western Christianity. The sultans moved the Patriarch of Constantinople from Santa Sophia, which was converted to a mosque, and deposed refractory patriarchs; however they did not disestablish the popularly supported Greek Orthodox clergy. Instead they profited from selling high church offices to the highest bidder. By the sultan's religious toleration, political stability was fostered.

Nor did the common threat of renewed Turkish invasion in the sixteenth century heal splits within the West. Idealists and kings talked of, or even committed themselves to, joining crusades against the Ottoman power, but in fact most Europeans feared their own neighbors more than the infidel. Only once, in 1571, was an effective joint crusade launched under papal leadership, resulting in the naval victory of Lepanto. Even then the Venetians, whose territories were in jeopardy, were as wary of Spanish as of Ottoman predominance in the Mediterranean. Crusading zeal during the Reformation period was directed not so much toward the Turks as toward the Indian population of the New World, overrun by Spanish conquistadores.

The Ottomans, often as allies of Francis I, made repeated invasions along the

*Panel of icons for Russian Orthodox services, Moscow, late fifteenth century.*

Danube, distracting the German emperor and keeping him from working against domestic and religious uprisings. Their influence in eastern trade was considerable, too. They imposed tolls and transfer fees, all to the commercial advantage of the Atlantic seaboard states, whose traders had meanwhile opened all-sea routes to the Indies. After 1566 the efficiency of Ottoman rule declined—but up to then the Turks made a distinctive impact on events in western Europe.

## Muscovy

With the expansion of Muscovy went extension of the Russian Orthodox church, which added monastic frontier colonies to its vast but taxed holdings. In its social organization the Duchy of Moscow had much in common with east-central Europe, and its subordination of religion to politics was paralleled in many countries in western Europe after the Reformation. But from the intellectual ferment of the Reformation, Muscovy was a world apart: while other heads of state were engaged in conflicts over the subtleties of theology, Ivan IV (the Terrible,

1533–84) was waging more primitive wars. Reared in a setting of palace violence, he was brought up to rule a society shamelessly dominated and exploited by the traditional aristocracy, the *boyars.* Although a literate and educated man, he monopolized and wielded power in a way that led exiles to portray him as a madman.

To keep the land-hungry nobility occupied while he broke their strength, Ivan contrived constant warfare. His forces conquered almost the whole of the Volga River Valley and the watersheds of the Don and Donetz rivers as well as the territory along the Ural Mountains. Against the Teutonic Knights of Livonia and their Polish protectors he loosed a "human sea" of warriors from 1558 to 1583.

To break the boyars' monopoly, Ivan established a special bodyguard, the *streltsy,* which he enlarged to garrison the cities. Suddenly in 1564 he opened a veritable war on the boyars, whom he accused of treason. He confiscated their estates and transferred them to new areas while the confiscated lands went into the hands of favorites directly dependent upon him. This redistribution of land and destruction of custom took place in about half of the state—furthered by secret police, torture, and liberal application of the executioner's ax. In the other half of the duchy traditional practices were continued. Ivan also called Russia's first representative assembly, the *zemsky sobor*, two and one-half centuries after parliaments had appeared in western and central Europe; but thereafter Russian development did not follow the Western constitutional pattern.

## E. The Reformation and the Modern World

The Reformation made only a shallow impact on eastern Europe, but it became a lasting part of the western European heritage. Until very recently, most Catholic and Protestant historians have identified heroes and culprits according to their doctrinal affiliations, and both sides have condemned the Erasmian humanists and the radical sectarians. In the nineteenth century as nationalism, industrial capitalism, secular science, and the idea of evolutionary progress came to influence Reformation historians, they began to abandon doctrinal polemics for assessments of the Reformation's contributions to the modern world.

Some Roman Catholic writers continued to denounce the "Protestant Revolt" as a catastrophic opening of society to further revolutions, schisms, and secularization. But secular and many Protestant historians began to discover the roots of the modern world in the Protestant Reformation. They portrayed the reformers as purveyors of individualism, tolerance, nationalism, and a capitalistic economy. Some historians, on the other hand, have been impressed with the reformers' traditionalism and have questioned the evidence on which the equations of Protestantism with progress have been based. Others, mainly "Neo-Orthodox" theologians, assert that the early reformers were spokesmen for an other-worldly religion based on pessimism about the earthly capabilities and future of man. Scholars studying sectarian movements that advocated and practiced tolerance and religious individualism have also raised doubts about the interpretation of major reformers as liberal nationalists. They point to reformers such as Luther who tried determinedly to stamp out the very views that have been attributed to him. The role of the Reformation in shaping the modern world is thus a matter of dispute. Because theological ways of thinking have declined, most twentieth-century Western peoples have difficulty projecting themselves into the arguments of the sixteenth century. But discussion of some consequences or alleged consequences of the Reformation should help us assess its controversial role in shaping the modern world.

## Individualism

Since Luther proclaimed every man his own priest, the Protestant Reformation has been widely interpreted as a major step toward the recognition of individual judgment or conscience. In theory, the assertion of a direct relationship between man and God was a powerful fillip to the idea of individuality, for which past heretics had struggled in vain. Nothing was further from the reformers' minds, however, than the submission of divine revelation to private judgment or interpretation. For Holy Church they substituted Holy Writ, which each reformer in his own way held to be concretely and objectively revealed. To assert that the individual should take any initiative in his own salvation was to derogate the absolute sovereignty of God. Faith came from hearing or reading the Word, but its reception was a divine miracle for which the individual person was totally unworthy. Inwardly a person could believe what he would—faith could not be forced—but the honor of God required the magistrates to enforce external conformity, including church attendance and submission to the sacraments. For this reason mystics, sectarians, and humanitarian humanists accused the reformers of forcing dissenters to be hypocrites. In reality, Protestants of the sixteenth century adopted a new absolute authority; they found "freedom of conscience" quite compatible with the persecution of nonconformists.

The Catholic Reformation, especially the Council of Trent, had no such ambiguities as the "priesthood of all believers" to deal with. It categorically denounced religious individualism and substantially narrowed the tolerable range of diversity in thought. Like the Protestants, but to a lesser degree, the Catholic reformers also curbed individual expression in the arts.

## Toleration

Expression of individual religious judgment was inseparable from the question of tolerance. Luther at first opposed the use of force and the burning of books to deal with religious dissent. But he came to equate religious dissent from his reformation with political rebellion and insisted that princes maintain uniformity. Soon he and other Protestant writers were trying to justify coercion and to reconcile it with the repeated assertion that a man could not be compelled to believe. Ultimately the Protestant Reformation contributed indirectly to tolerance in certain areas and circumstances, but its immediate impact was the creation of several intolerant creeds, each maintained by the force of local political authorities.

Because they believed in predestination—that a sovereign God had selected the elect and damned the rejected before earthly time began—the Protestant reformers, unlike the Roman inquisitors, could not justify persecution on the grounds that it could lead to the heretic's salvation. They found sufficient other bases for it, however. One was scriptural authority as interpreted by St. Augustine —a favorite theologian of the Protestants— who had sanctioned persecution of North African heretics. Another was the Protestants' concept of heresy: deviations from their own version of divine revelation could only be the work of Satan. Persecution of Satan's legions (the heretics) upheld the honor of God and protected the faithful who were incapable of recognizing the Devil's snares. Still another justification was political. The reformers shared the traditional Roman Catholic belief that no state divided in religion could survive and that it was the magistrate's commission from God—from whom all legitimate authority flowed—to maintain the morality and orthodoxy of his subjects. The alternative, they believed, was civil war. Until religiously pluralistic

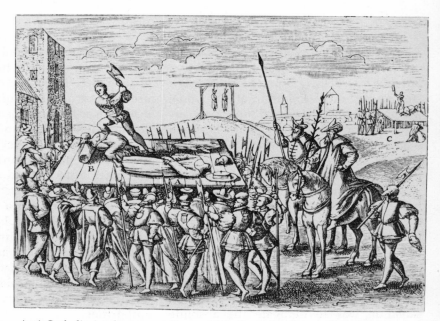

*Anti-Catholic intolerance of Henry VIII: the beheadings of John Fisher (cardinal-bishop of Rochester), Thomas More, and the Countess of Salisbury are included in one illustration.*

states began to survive in peace and demonstrate that coexistence was possible—an expedient for the security of life and property—the secular premises of religious persecution went unchallenged except among sectarians, radical humanists, and state-church minorities too small to attempt a seizure of power.

Such sectarians as the Anabaptists advocated separation of church and state and the exclusion of force from religious affairs. They and the most avidly read publicist on behalf of toleration in the sixteenth century, Sebastian Castellio, shared the belief that, besides faith, Christianity required the imitation of Christ. They could not sanction the bloody acts of Old Testament kings whose precedent the reformers invoked against humanitarianism when doctrine was at stake. Where sectarians were numerous they pressured rulers into granting at least toleration and at most equal religious rights.

Erasmian humanists, on the other hand,

were latitudinarians; regarding many contested dogmas as conflicts over nonessentials, they usually worked to make official creeds flexible enough to be acceptable to a majority of the population.

Eventually the Reformation tended in Protestant and religiously divided states to diminish the intolerance that it had initially generated. By substituting secular for clerical judges, state-church Protestantism turned religious disputes over to laymen, who were not as meticulous on the fine points of theology as the clerics, but who nevertheless dealt out harsh penalties to dissenters. However in both Catholic and Protestant states where nonconformist minorities were too large to be easily exterminated, jailed, or banished, expediency dictated compromise and limited toleration as alternatives to civil war. The religious diversity produced by the Reformation also produced some doctrinal relativity as reflected in the adage "orthodoxy is my doxy." But the establishment of toleration based on political —and sometimes commercial—expediency drastically altered the authoritarianism on which the Protestant reformers had based their politics. Rather than an outgrowth of Protestantism, toleration was more often the result of religious, civil, and international wars. People came to choose diversity over the devastation and turmoil of war.

## Political Ramifications

Churchmen, Protestant and Catholic alike, usually sought the support of secular governments; thus they were invariably involved in politics and with political theory. To separate church and state was inconceivable to all except the radicals. Most Reformation thinkers were very much concerned to define the role of the magistrates in reforming the Church, and they devoted considerable thought to the problems of a ruler whose religion differed from that of the majority or sizable minorities of his subjects.

By attempting to restore the primacy of religion in affairs of state the Reformation inaugurated an era of "Christian princes." Rulers gained extensive additional powers by controlling or intervening in religious affairs. No religious reform succeeded without the direction, or at least the approval, of the government; and no government supported reform without acquiring more power for itself in the process. In the Protestant (non-Calvinist) states of the early Reformation princes held the main legislative and executive powers within the churches. The Peace of Augsburg (1555) recognized this state of affairs by legally authorizing them to make their states Catholic or Lutheran. Clergymen cast these reforming princes as Old Testament ruler-priests, agents of an inscrutable deity to whom alone they were accountable. This divine warrant did not give Protestant rulers absolute control over religious affairs, however: they were subject to Holy Writ. If they transgressed this limitation, Lutheran and Anglican divines sanctioned passive resistance against them. But as we have already seen, according to Romans XIII active resistance was no less than resistance to God.

Thus many Protestant churches encouraged the notion of divine-right kingship. Defending the old order, Roman Catholic spokesmen also advocated rule by divine right as well as timid obedience to constituted authority. But the aggressive Calvinists actively defied traditional governments, and by the middle of the sixteenth century they began to collide violently with Roman Catholics made desperate by the extent of their losses. Civil wars followed in France, the Netherlands, and England, exceeding all bounds of diplomacy and all conventional restraints on warfare. These conflicts, whose course will be sketched in the following chapter, were between factions that sought to impose their religious positions on a state by seizing the machinery of its government. In France, for example, Calvinists sanctioned revolution by "lesser magistrates," whereas Jesuits appealed democratically to the majority of the population. Both viewpoints reflected a broader appeal to people than was characteristic of the past, and to this degree the Reformation released forces that were "democratic" but not liberal in the sense of protecting individual rights or establishing constitutional processes for government by persuasion.

Because the Reformation focused political loyalties on divine-right kings or councils that acknowledged no earthly limitation, it has often been hailed as the forerunner of modern nationalism. In particular, Calvinist "New Jerusalems" resembled the fervent nationalist states of the last two centuries. A kind of nationalism did characterize the foreign policy of Spain and other governments that the Spanish Jesuits—who formulated and encouraged adherence to a theory of international law—tried in vain to influence. But irresponsible state sovereignty lodged in divine-right kings or in the magistrates of "God's chosen people" was not a distinct creation of the Reformation. It was probably more clearly enunciated in the messianism of czarist Russia: Ivan claimed that Muscovy was the "Third Rome," the only pure representative of Christianity on earth, with a world mission to perform. Certainly the Reformation coincided with the disruption of Western Christendom into individual states, each claiming a divine head equal in authority to the pope or else acting totally without reference to the papacy. But how far this disruption was the result of political forces already in operation before the Reformation, and how much the Protestant reformers were responsible for it, are moot questions. It is certain, however, that religious innovations contributed as often to irreconcilable divisions within existing states as they did to a new basis for national unity.

## Social and Economic Repercussions

The Reformation was a revolution that stopped short of a general social upheaval. Apart from religious practices, the lives of the great majority of the population—the peasantry and the lower townsmen—were little changed. Only for the clergy—one of the two privileged medieval estates—was it a partial social revolution. Sectarian anticlericals were prevented from removing the clergy as officers of the state or as wards of noble patrons, but in resources and positions of power the Protestant clergy declined far more precipitously than the Catholic clergy. In Protestant states the economic power previously commanded by clergymen was transferred to secular governments and laymen. In some instances the transfer of property from the corporate "dead hand" of the Church to laymen contributed to more rapid economic development. According to some historical sociologists, Protestants, especially Calvinists and sectarians, made religious virtues of economic attitudes. Thus they stimulated the growth of capitalism and contributed to the transfer of the most active trading centers from Catholic to Protestant territories.

Protestants made drastic changes in the status and role of the clergy. They removed its prestige as unique agent in transforming the bread and wine into the body and blood of Christ in the Eucharist; they suppressed monasticism and discouraged clerical celibacy. In dress, social status, and political obligations, the Protestant clergy became less distinguishable from ordinary subjects. Their profession came to resemble most other occupations and, as in other fields, the sons began to follow the calling of their fathers. Exemptions of clergy from secular justice and from taxes, tolls, and guild regulations usually lapsed; clerical representation in territorial diets dwindled; courts staffed in part by clergymen still ruled on family affairs such as legitimacy, marriage, divorce, and wills, but they functioned only in special departments of government. Pastors were considered officials of the state as well as of the Church, but they seldom served as leading ministers or diplomatic representatives of princes. What is perhaps most significant, the higher clergy no longer received large revenues. Former obligations of peasants and townsmen to the Church were not canceled, but they were diverted to recipients other than prelates. Costly projects such as relief, education, and building now required *state* support or administration.

In some respects the Catholic Reformation took a course diametrically opposed to that of the Protestants; in others there were distinct similarities. The Council of Trent spurned all pleas for clerical marriage and legislated strict enforcement of clerical celibacy. It reasserted the role of the priest as sharply separated from that of the laity, and the prelates retained their political role as the first estate in the territorial diets. In most Roman Catholic states of the late Reformation, the Church regained its position as a major landholder, and monasticism flourished. The clergy generally lost their exemptions from civil penalties, but they retained more of their privileges than their Protestant counterparts. The Protestant and Catholic reformations paralleled one another in the gradual creation of an educated clergy charged with preaching, teaching, and pastoral care. Both also curtailed commercialized religion and the sale of offices.

According to some historians the Protestant reformers not only secularized society and weakened clerical influence over it but also played a major role in advancing modern capitalism. Noting apparent correlations of Protestant and nonconformist religion with individual and group business success, nineteenth- and twentieth-century historians and historical sociologists have sought an explanation of this association in the social ethic of Protestantism, Judaism, and such sectarian minorities as the Anabaptists, Quakers, Baptists, and Wesleyans. At the end of the nineteenth century Max Weber, a German sociologist, published a classic thesis, *The Protestant Ethic and the Spirit of Capitalism,* to demonstrate this connection. He argued that the positive attitude of Protestants, especially Calvinists and sectarians, toward hard work, self-denial, and the holiness of secular callings was *one* factor in the development of the spirit of capitalism. He defined that spirit not as the desire for unlimited accumulation of wealth but as the rational organization of men and material to produce recurrent profits. Paradoxically he found that the practice of ascetic otherworldliness, which repudiated the aristocracy's ostentatious

displays of wealth, contributed to constructive social and individual economic success.

Weber's thesis is not immune from serious criticism in several details, and incautious popularizers have distorted his case by exaggeration. Therefore some qualification of the reckless associations of Protestantism and economic progress is in order. Before the Reformation capitalism flourished in Catholic Italy and Flanders. In the nineteenth century Catholic Belgium industrialized rapidly while a distinctly medieval economic organization persisted in large parts of Lutheran Germany. Furthermore the fact that Calvin sanctioned the taking of interest does not mean that he was a pioneer of an unregulated economy. The five percent interest which he approved was below rates already current. Finally, orthodox Calvinist sermons from seventeenth-century England and the Netherlands—the two areas of greatest economic development and the period from which Weber drew much of his evidence—indicate that capitalism eventually influenced Calvinist doctrines rather than vice versa.*

Nevertheless certain Protestant and sectarian practices had undeniable significance for economic growth where resources and other requisites were present. The creation of a literate laity is one case in point, although this was not achieved by all Protestants; the devotion of nonconformists (barred from aristocratic and royal favors) to productive economic activity and to the building of reputations for business integrity is another. The social attitudes of radical Protestantism helped to dissolve traditions

* More recently Weber's method has been used with equally ambiguous results to assert a Protestant, especially Calvinist, encouragement of science by emphasizing the idea of a divine universal order purged of much superstition. Consideration of the rise of scientific approaches to nature is deferred, however, to the following volume.

wherever they were maintained. But—as Weber, although unfortunately not all his popularizers, knew—these attitudes in themselves do not completely explain the complex interaction of material and human resources that increased per capita production and distribution. According to some historians, the major reason that Protestantism came to be associated with capitalism was that it was less hostile than rejuvenated Roman Catholicism to the needs of business.

As in other aspects of life, the Protestant assault on tradition, which varied widely from confession to confession, helped open the path to innovations that the reformers themselves did not intend or necessarily promote. The immediate sequel to the Reformation, however, was not the immediate blossoming of the modern world but rather a series of crises that challenged the very bases of Western civilization.

## Selected Readings

*Bainton, Roland. *Here I Stand: A Life of Martin Luther.* Nashville: Abingdom Press, 1950.

*A leading critical but sympathetic biography with excellent bibliography. Unlike many biographies of Luther, it includes details of his later life.*

*————. *The Travail of Religious Liberty.* New York: Harper & Row, Publishers, 1951.

*A series of biographical sketches treating victims and practitioners, Catholic and Protestant, of religious persecution. In effect it presents the Reformation as a highly intolerant age.*

Brandi, Karl. *The Emperor Charles V.* London: Jonathan Cape, 1954.

*A lengthy standard political biography concerned mainly with Charles's government of the Holy Roman Empire.*

Breen, Quirinus. *John Calvin: A Study in French Humanism.* 2d ed. Hamden, Conn.: Archon Books, 1968.

*An excellent study of Calvin's humanist background and the basis of his break with the humanists. It provides references to other biographies of Calvin and their points of view.*

*Burns, Edward McNall. *The Counter-Reformation.* New York: Van Nostrand Reinhold Company, 1964.

*A recent short, critical account with major documents in an appendix.*

Butterfield, Herbert. *The Whig Interpretation of History.* London: G. Bell & Sons, 1931.

*A devastating critique of nineteenth-century liberal-national history, which rebuts popular Protestant interpretations of the Reformation.*

*Chadwick, Owen. *The Reformation.* Baltimore, Md.: Penguin Books, 1964.

*An excellent nonpartisan survey concentrating on religious developments; especially good for the Reformation's impact on the clergy as a social class.*

*Dickens, A. G. *The Counter Reformation.* London: Thames & Hudson, 1968.

*A sympathetic account of the Catholic Reformation that finds saints among its mystics. Lucid and superbly illustrated, it exaggerates the cultural unity of a Europe confessionally divided.*

———. *Thomas Cromwell and the English Reformation.* London: English Universities Press, 1959.

*A political biography of the leading lay architect of the English Reformation.*

*Elton, Geoffrey R. *Reformation Europe. 1517–1559.* New York: World Publishing Co., Meridian Books, 1964.

*One of the author's many works on the Reformation, emphasizing the role of politics in determining its outcome.*

Evenett, H. Outram. *The Spirit of the Counter-Reformation.* Cambridge: Cambridge University Press, 1968.

*A series of sympathetic, insight-filled lectures that capture what was new and distinctive in the piety of the Catholic Reformation.*

Franklin, Julian H. *Jean Bodin and the Sixteenth-Century Revolution in the Methodology of Law and History.* New York: Columbia University Press, 1963.

*This traces French humanist origins of new comparative and empirical methods in sixteenth-century studies of society. It is basic for understanding differences between humanist and religious approaches to society and politics.*

Gelder, Herman Arend Enno van. *The Two Reformations of the 16th Century.* The Hague: Martinus Nijhoff, 1961.

*A development of the controversial thesis that the major reformation of the sixteenth century was not Protestant but humanist.*

Grimm, Harold J. *The Reformation Era: 1500–1650.* 2d ed. New York: The Macmillan Co., 1965.

*A factual, standard textbook treating all aspects of the period.*

Hillerbrand, Hans J., ed. *The Reformation: a Narrative History Related by Contemporary Observers and Participants.* New York: Harper & Row, Publishers, 1964.

*A collection of vivid sources related to major personalities and events.*

Holborn, Hajo. *A History of Modern Germany.* Vol. 1, *The Reformation.* New York: Alfred A. Knopf, 1959.

*A definitive political, cultural, and religious history of Germany from about 1500 to 1648.*

Hughes, Philip. *A Popular History of the Reformation.* Garden City, N.Y.: Doubleday & Co., 1960.

*A balanced summary by a Roman Catholic authority on the English Reformation.*

Janelle, Pierre. *The Catholic Reformation.* Milwaukee: Bruce Publishing Co., 1949.

*A Catholic version that treats the Catholic Reformation as a spontaneous movement and omits reference to the Inquisition.*

Jedin, Hubert. *A History of the Council of Trent.* 2 vols. St. Louis: B. Herder Book Co., 1957–61.

> *An exhaustive account of the Church councils of the Renaissance and Reformation by a German Catholic scholar. These volumes reach only the first session at Trent.*

Kidd, B. J. *The Counter-Reformation: 1550–1600.* London: Society for Promoting Christian Knowledge, 1958.

> *Emphatically Protestant, this reverses the interpretation of Janelle.*

*McNeil, John T. *The History and Character of Calvinism.* New York: Oxford University Press, 1957.

> *This sympathetically and comprehensively relates the origins, nature, and spread of Calvinism.*

*Mosse, George L. *The Reformation.* New York: Holt, Rinehart & Winston, 1953.

> *A short, balanced account of the entire Reformation; excellent as an introduction.*

Nelson, Benjamin N. *Idea of Usury.* Princeton, N.J.: Princeton University Press, 1949.

> *This restates the Weber-Tawney thesis for Calvinism by investigating the psychological background of prohibiting usury and provides rare detail on the anticapitalistic attitudes of the early German Reformation.*

Philips, Margaret Mann. *Erasmus and the Northern Renaissance.* London: Hodder and Stoughton, 1949.

> *This study presents Erasmus as the formulator of an independent religious and secular reform movement. Publication of Erasmus's later correspondence has forced modification of this interpretation—at least of the older Erasmus. (See Bainton listing in previous chapter.)*

*Ridley, Jasper. *Thomas Cranmer.* New York: Oxford University Press, 1962.

> *A definitive biography of the leading cleric of the English Reformation which finds his consistency in belief in the divine right of kings.*

Ritter, Gerhard. *Luther, His Life and Work.* New York: Harper & Row, Publishers, 1963.

> *This treats Luther in the role of a prophet of the Germans, breaking the bonds of medieval piety but not as a man who wished to secularize the world in any way.*

*Rupp, Gordon. *Luther's Progress to the Diet of Worms.* New York: Harper & Row, Publishers, 1964.

> *An appreciative sketch by a prominent English scholar on Luther.*

Schapiro, Jacob S. "Social Reform and the Reformation," Ph. D. dissertation, Columbia University, 1909.

> *The only collection in English of documents on the German Peasants' Revolt; it includes penetrating commentaries that find the origins of liberalism within the revolt rather than among the reformers.*

Tavard, Georges H. *Holy Writ or Holy Church: the Crisis of the Protestant Reformation*. New York: Harper & Row, Publishers, 1960.

*A description of the differing bases of authority used by sixteenth-century Catholics and Protestants, tracing the origins of the latter.*

*Tawney, Richard H. *Religion and the Rise of Capitalism*. New York: New American Library, 1950. *Weber, Max. *The Protestant Ethic and the Spirit of Capitalism*. New York: Charles Scribner's Sons, 1958.

*Both advance the classic thesis—in vulnerable form—that Protestants, especially Calvinists and sectarians, stimulated capitalism by fostering ascetic renunciation of luxury and dedication to secular work.*

Trevor-Roper, H. R. *Religion, the Reformation, and Social Change*. New York: Harper & Row, Publishers, 1968.

*Two of these essays, one on witchcraft and one on the rise of capitalism, concern this chapter. The author provides the best rejoinder to Weber and Tawney thus far.*

Williams, George Hunston. *The Radical Reformation*. Philadelphia: The Westminster Press, 1962.

*This makes heavy use of recently published documents on the Anabaptists and other sectarians to reevaluate the defamed radicals of the Reformation. Heavily theological in tone.*

Asterisk (*) denotes paperback.

# CHAPTER III

# The Century of Crises: 1560–1660

Facing new realities with old ideas, Europeans passed through a century of terrible crises from 1560 to 1660. It was not a simple matter for them to adjust to the new religious and political pluralism, the recent intellectual, spiritual, and social upheavals, and the enormous new geographical world. Their traditions and experiences had not taught them how to cope with ideological ferment on such a colossal scale, or how to form a new conception of the world that shattered their familiar biblical view of three continents inhabited by the three races of men, descendants of Shem, Ham, and Japheth. Europeans became global men for the first time, and immediately projected their internal conflicts on a world stage. As population growth outstripped subsistence at home, they fought for such of the world's wealth as could be fed into the engines of war to give an advantage to one side or another. Seething with religious hatreds, Europeans fought one bloody ideological war after another among themselves until they were forced by sheer exhaustion, after the Thirty Years' War (1618–48), to try to reorganize their civilization as a family of coexisting nations.

## A. Empires and Mercantilism

### EUROPE'S TERRITORIAL EXPANSION

From the time of the Crusades Europeans had been expanding territorially, but in the late Renaissance that expansion entered a new phase: states along the Atlantic seaboard had extended and consolidated their economic and political influences on overseas territories. Looking at developments from a worldwide perspective, we see that western Europe was rapidly emerging as the most dynamic and powerful area in the world. Not many people directly participated in this expansion, and only a few of these people appreciated its implications. Nevertheless, vast numbers of European villagers and townspeople were significantly affected in their economic and political life by the activities of merchants, seamen, officials, and intellectuals.

Why should European expansion have entered such a dazzling phase in the sixteenth century? The answer is partly that European technology and institutions were more advanced than those in other parts of the world. With superior arms and ships and with advanced knowledge of navigation and naval warfare, western Europeans could control the seas: their fleets could strike coastal targets at will and could retreat in relative safety; with this advantage they could dominate commerce. Where they were forced to strike out far beyond the range of their ships, their command was less sure. Their conquests on land often failed to equal their prowess on the sea. Still, Europeans did wrest vast territories from "less civilized" peoples who could not combat Western organization and technology. Strong, highly structured societies in Asia effectively barred European penetration, and climate and disease repulsed Western moves into the interior of Africa. On the African coast, however, the European triumphed, forcing the populations into slavery. In the New World he triumphed again, even more impressively, for the Indian had neither iron weapons, nor horses, nor extensive political organization. From him the European could take an entire virgin continent.

People from Europe seized control of the New World by more than sheer force of arms. Powerful commercial companies, officially backed by home governments, sold cheaply produced wares to primitive peoples who had almost no concept of economic organization and whose craving to acquire fascinating but economically useless gadgets like mirrors and equally fascinating but not so harmless products like alcohol hastened their subjection. Even more devastating were the white man's diseases such as smallpox or measles, which wracked many colonial peoples and destroyed their power to resist.

It seems, too, that European civilization had developed within it a strong drive for dominance. With conquerors and traders came missionaries to propagate the faith and education. Already convinced that they were sent by divine providence to subjugate and convert God's enemies, the Europeans saw in the natives' acceptance of Christianity certain proof that Western expansion had divine sanction. Missionaries like Bartolomé de Las Casas (1474–1566) had more humanitarian ideas, but all in all, the more advanced European societies were convinced of their superior right to dominate the globe.

Nevertheless, cultural exchange between Europe and the outside world was reciprocal. To the dependent populations of the New World, Europeans brought animals, crops, technology, learning, social and political institutions, the printing press, and religion. From overseas they gained wealth and adopted new products, some of which eventually had a profound impact on Europe. Spices, tea, chocolate, and tobacco became common consumption items even though they lacked the medicinal qualities claimed for them by their early promoters. The potato was a gift from the New World, and American plantations soon became the primary source of sugar. The consumption of both of these foods would increase over the centuries until they became vital to Europeans' survival. The New World also opened new horizons of experience: contact with other civilizations slowly eroded European parochialism and reinforced the idea that men could live in a state of nature under natural law without the sanctions of supernatural religion. However, before 1660 beliefs like these were confined to narrow intellectual circles.

*Confrontation of Europeans and Indians in Mexico.*

## Portugal's Commercial Empire

At the end of the fifteenth century the kingdoms along the Atlantic seaboard were beginning to build worldwide empires. They had at their disposal the skills, knowledge, and financial resources of the Italians who had built Mediterranean empires during the High Middle Ages and the Renaissance. The first Atlantic explorations that led to durable overseas empires were made by the Portuguese. With a long history as a seafaring people, they ventured into Africa in the course of waging war against the Moors; once there, they established important trading contacts.

From 1418 until his death in 1460 Prince Henry ("the Navigator") sent out an expedition almost yearly. His policy plunged the royal family heavily into debt, but it also created for the Portuguese kingdom the most advanced geographical knowledge and the best navigational equipment of the times. At first Portuguese sailors sought to explore the western coast of Africa. Later, spurred on by reports of lucrative trade opportunities in India, Henry sent navigators to find a route eastward around Africa. The famous voyage of Vasco da Gama at the very end of the century proved that it was profitable as well as possible to trade with India by sea. With their new route to the East the Portuguese outflanked the Ottoman Turks who, by their monopolies and tolls, had until then frustrated Venetian trade with the Orient. In 1509 a Portuguese fleet defeated an Arabic and Egyptian fleet off Diu on the west coast of India, putting Portugal in a position to monopolize the spice trade with Europe. From Goa, their base in India, the Portuguese flung out a series of trading stations: Java and Sumatra (1511), the Moluccas (1512), Formosa (1542), Japan, and later Macao on the coast of China. The Portuguese empire in the Far East was strictly commercial; the only Portuguese who went to the colonies were traders rather than settlers. Spices were the main commodity of the empire, but the Portuguese did not even market the spices in Europe; rather they turned that business over to an Antwerp monopoly. In the vast Portuguese empire only Brazil— which was of little economic significance before the establishment of sugar plantations using African slaves—was to become a major colonial settlement to which the Portuguese emigrated in considerable numbers.

## Spain's Bid for Colonial Wealth

Portuguese supremacy did not go long unchallenged. Da Gama had no sooner preempted the route around Africa than Castilian venturers embarked on their own imperial search. The voyage of the Genoese captain Christopher Columbus in 1492 was Spain's first bid in the overseas competion. Columbus, as everyone knows, was sailing west in the hope of finding a direct trade route to the Far East (hence, the name West Indies for the islands lying off the coast of the New World). The Spanish were still effectively cut off from the profitable Eastern trade, but the gold and silver they found in South America was compensation.

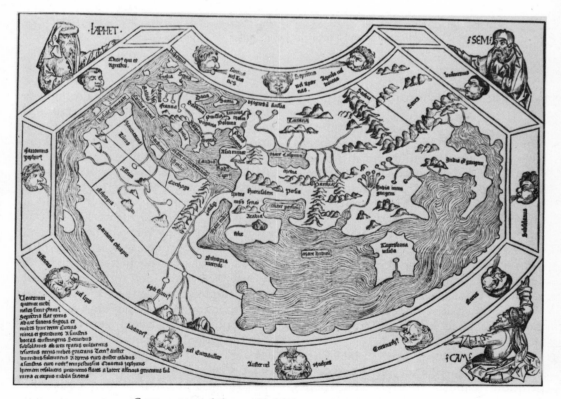

*German map of the world, 1493.*

*World map of 1529, reflecting the age of discovery.*

Spanish conquerors and explorers fanned out from the West Indies to subjugate Aztec, Inca, and Central American Indians. The gold and, particularly, the silver mines yielded phenomenal wealth. In 1545 the richest mine of all, the Potosí mine in Peru, was brought into production; in 1600 precious metals constituted 90 percent of all European imports from Spanish America. Meanwhile Magellan's voyage around South America in 1519 had opened a route to the Far East, but the Pacific crossing was so hazardous that, except for trade with the western coast of South America, the new route was of little commercial value. Content to rule the Philippines (first settled in the reign of Philip II) indirectly through Mexico, the Habsburgs left the Portuguese commercial monopoly in the Far East undisturbed.

The Spanish tried, but largely failed, to transplant their institutions to American soil. By the end of the sixteenth century their New World colonies were in serious decline. Fortune-hunting noblemen were superb conquerors but inept administrators. When the rulers of Spain replaced Columbus, Pizarro, Cortes, and other conquistadores with their own appointees, New World affairs passed into the hands of men who were seldom capable and usually uninterested. These royal appointees, who often bought their offices, made many mistakes. Castilians tried to harness Indian labor, but the natives died so rapidly from European diseases, such as smallpox, that by 1600 their population had dwindled from an estimated 11 million to 2 million. African slaves were imported, but they too were subject to disease. After 1576 the history of the Spanish Empire is a history of economic depression and the breakdown of order. Colonial officials lost control over the hinterlands of the empire to cattlemen on the continent and buccaneers on the islands who defied their authority. The buccaneers were particularly lawless: by selling provisions to foreign interlopers they undermined Spain's monopoly of commerce. By the early seventeenth century, when the flow of gold and silver from the colonies became a trickle, Europe began to feel the decline of Spain's empire in America.

## Empire Building
## by Northern Europeans

Meanwhile English and French explorers staked out claims to North America (Cabot for England, 1497–98, and Verrazano—also Italian—for France in 1524). They found scant riches, established no permanent colonies, and failed to find a new commercial route to the Far East. In the 1550s, however, Englishmen did succeed in opening Russia to western trade by sailing around Norway. In the same century the English also began to encroach on Spain's colonial trade—especially the profitable slave trade—eventually bringing on a prolonged Anglo-Spanish conflict. Throughout most of this century France was too occupied with civil wars to develop her imperialism; for both England and France the establishment of empires in the New World awaited the dawn of the seventeenth century.

At first the Dutch were far more successful empire builders than the English and the French. Like the Italians, they already had solid experience in fishing, shipping, banking, and manufacturing. When Phillip II of Spain acquired the poorly defended Portuguese empire in 1580, the Dutch (having revolted against the Habsburgs in 1566) were still at war with Spain. Soon they sought to establish a direct link with the Far East. By organizing the East India stock company they eliminated competition among themselves and, in the first years of the seventeenth century, outbid Portuguese merchants in the East Indies, Formosa, and Japan. Like the Portuguese before them, the Dutch monopolists carefully controlled supplies for the European spice market. They also dealt in silk, chinaware, sugar, coffee, tea, cocoa, precious metals, Japanese copper, and Indian cloth. Even more lucrative was the local Far Eastern carrying trade, which shipped cargoes from India around Malaya and the East Indies to Japan. East India Company officials like Jan Pieterszoon Coen ruthlessly eliminated native competitors and maintained an exclusive preserve closed to all other European shippers. The Eastern trade lured fortune hunters not only because it yielded a high return on investment but also because company employees could smuggle private cargoes of such prized commodities as opium and slaves. For a while Batavia (in what is now Indonesia) was the most profitable post in the Dutch commercial chain; but during the Thirty Years' War its richness was rivaled by trade centers in Persia, especially those that supplied Europe with silver. Australia, which was discovered by the East India Company in 1627, was a commercial disappointment.

By displacing the Portuguese in the Far East the Dutch accomplished considerably more than they did in competing with rivals in the Atlantic. The West India Company, for example, fell short of its primary objective, the seizure of Brazil. But, by searching for northwestern and northeastern passages to India, the Dutch added to man's store of knowledge about geography. In the course of their search they also secured a place for themselves in the Russian trade and founded a fur-trading settlement colony on the Hudson River.

Closer to home the Dutch were immensely successful. They displaced the Hanseatic League in the carrying trade from the Baltic Sea, and on the Mediterranean they dislodged the Italians. Still, overseas trade made only a small contribution to the general prosperity of the Netherlands, which depended on local trade in fish, Baltic grains, salt, Scandinavian timber, and French wine. Thriving Dutch commerce benefited from adopting advanced techniques in industry, finance, and technology. Especially rewarding was the development of an unarmed sailing ship called the flute (*fluit*) that required few men and offered little resistance to wind and water. By the end of the sixteenth century the Dutch merchant marine had an estimated 10,000 ships.

Sweden prospered from Dutch Baltic trade—the great Swedish export was naval stores—and participated for a brief time in the quest for overseas empire. Russia was a more persistent expansionist once her isolation was broken by contact with English and Dutch traders. From her contacts with the West she appropriated a technology for successful military expansion into Poland and Sweden. At the same time a major market for her furs opened in Europe. The Stroganov family built an enormous fortune from a fur company that sent Cossack trappers across Siberia, established villages, and opened mines.

Russia's eastern expansion produced no rivalry with the major imperial powers, but the other northern peoples' entry into the quest for colonies and overseas wealth intensified Europe's struggles for hegemony of power. These struggles continued to be primarily dynastic and religious, but economic warfare for commercial advantages was beginning to play an increasingly important role in them.

## THE COURSE OF ECONOMIC CHANGE

The establishment of empires overseas was only one facet of Europe's radically changing economic shape in the sixteenth century; the astonishing growth in volume, variety, and value of its long-distance trade was another. Also, the centers of commerce were shifting, for states along the Atlantic seaboard now held the economic initiative and were speedily gaining control. The fruits of European economic expansion were, however, unevenly divided. Once the merchant fleets of Italy had been the greatest in Europe; now they were unable to compete on the high seas. Italians continued to engage in trade in the Mediterranean and on the coast, but

by the 1550s it was clear that profits from the sea would go mainly to the Atlantic states. Spain and Portugal were in the ascendancy in the sixteenth century, but at the same time Antwerp and Lyons were beginning to rival the Italian city-states as centers of banking and exchange. Although bullion flowed directly to Spain and Portugal from the New World at first, the profits of imperial trade were ultimately reaped by others, notably the Dutch, English, and French. Near the end of the sixteenth century Antwerp and Lyons were crippled by religious and civil wars. After 1600, Amsterdam stood as the greatest commercial *entrepôt* of the Western world.

To characterize the century between 1560 and 1660 as an era only of expanding commercial wealth and capitalism is to oversimplify. As with most generalizations, the student of history must acknowledge important exceptions. First, eastern and southern Europe did not participate in this expansion. Italy, which had led the rest of Europe in industrial, agricultural, and financial techniques during the Renaissance, actually experienced a serious decline throughout this period. Capital flowed westward out of Italy, and in Italy itself investment was siphoned out of industry and commerce and diverted to baroque art and architecture, a spendthrift style of life in the courts of the aristocracy, and unprofitable—even wasteful—loans to the Habsburgs. Second, even in the maritime states—England and the Netherlands—commerce apparently entered a long period of general stagnation or decline during the Thirty Years' War, the effects of which were particularly severe in Germany. There the prosperity of commercial towns was throttled and technological innovation decreased. In eastern Europe the devastations of war served to bolster aristocratic domination of overwhelmingly agrarian societies. Eastern European social patterns became rigid, and the populations consisted almost ex-

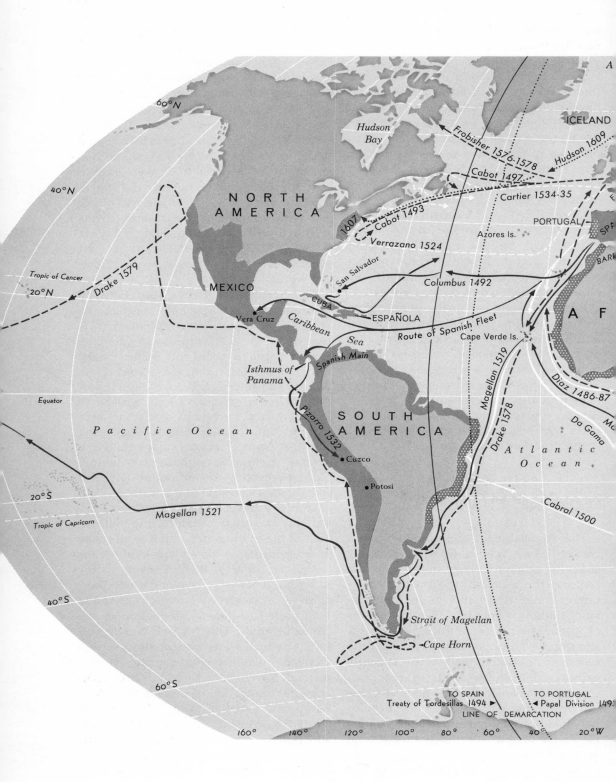

Hudson
Bay

60°N

ICELAND

Frobisher 1576-1578

Hudson 1609

Cabot 1497

40°N

Cartier 1534-35

NORTH
AMERICA

Cabot 1493

PORTUGAL

Azores Is.

1607

Verrazano 1524

SPA

Tropic of Cancer

San Salvador

Columbus 1492

BAR

20°N

Drake 1579

MEXICO

CUBA

A F

Route of Spanish Fleet

Vera Cruz

ESPAÑOLA

Caribbean

Cape Verde Is.

Sea

Spanish Main

Magellan 1519

Isthmus of
Panama

Equator

Pacific   Ocean

Pizarro 1532

SOUTH
AMERICA

Diaz 1486-87

Da Gama

Cuzco

Drake 1578

Atlantic
Ocean

Potosi

20°S

Magellan 1521

Cabral 1500

Tropic of Capricorn

40°S

Strait of Magellan

Cape Horn

60°S

TO SPAIN

TO PORTUGAL

Treaty of Tordesillas 1494 ►

◄ Papal Division 149

LINE OF DEMARCATION

160°     140°     120°     100°     80°     60°     40°     20°W

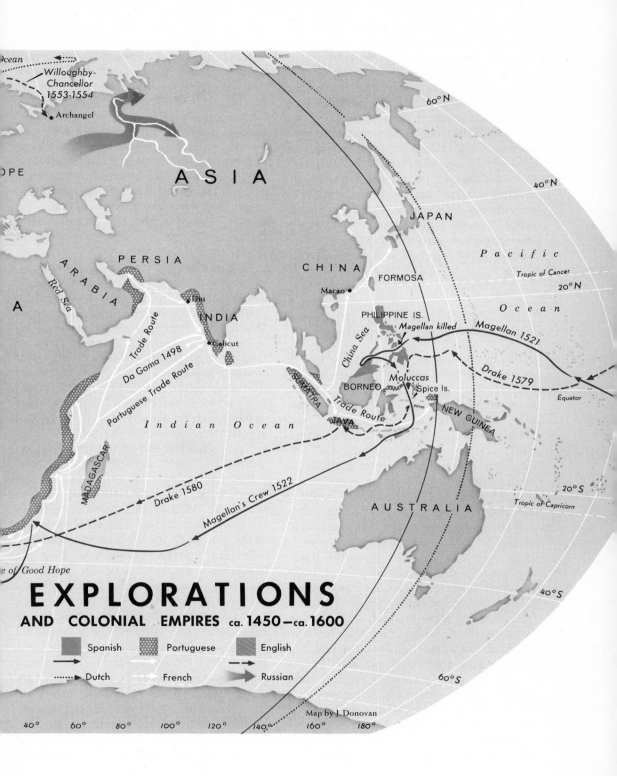

Ocean

Willoughby-
Chancellor
1553-1554

• Archangel

OPE

A S I A

OPE

A

ARABIA

Red Sea

PERSIA

• Diu

INDIA

• Calicut

Trade Route

Da Gama 1498

Portuguese Trade Route

Indian Ocean

MADAGASCAR

Drake 1580

e of Good Hope

Magellan's Crew 1522

CHINA

Macao •

FORMOSA

JAPAN

Pacific

Tropic of Cancer

60°N

40°N

20°N

Ocean

PHILIPPINE IS.

Magellan killed

Magellan 1521

China Sea

SUMATRA

Trade Route

JAVA

BORNEO

Moluccas

Spice Is.

Drake 1579

NEW GUINEA

Equator

AUSTRALIA

Tropic of Capricorn

20°S

40°S

# EXPLORATIONS

## AND COLONIAL EMPIRES ca. 1450—ca. 1600

Spanish ___ Portuguese ___ English

Dutch ___ French ___ Russian

Map by J. Donovan

40°   60°   80°   100°   120°   140°   160°   180°

60°S

clusively of lords and serfs. Lastly, we must recognize that the mere fact of commercial expansion in the maritime states did not assure the general prosperity of their populations. More and more men were becoming rich, but at the same time population increase mainly added to the number of the poor, who were particularly vulnerable to the effects of commercial crises, inflation, and famine. For all except the most favored peoples and classes this century was an era of stark scarcity. To provide for subsistence, trading opportunities, social stability, and military strength most territorial governments extended their regulation of economic activity.

## Commercial Capitalism in the Netherlands and England

Italian merchants had been the first to develop techniques by which capital resources could be pooled and used to underwrite large-scale commercial ventures. During the sixteenth century merchants in the Dutch Netherlands and England adopted these techniques and improved on them. Banking institutions were particularly important, since it was through them that capital savings could be mobilized, foreign exchange provided, private loans negotiated, and notes issued. The Bank of Amsterdam, founded in 1609, rapidly became the model for banks in Sweden, Hamburg, and eventually, London. As the flow of money was organized and capital grew more plentiful, interest rates were lowered and also became stable. During the Middle Ages financial activities had been carried on at fairs; now they were replaced by the *bourses,* which were at once money markets and commodity exchanges. Here goods, public debts, and land—in the form of mortgages—would be represented by documents—pieces of paper that could circulate and become objects of specula-

tion; in short, they could be treated like coinage. People of various classes rushed to put their savings into commercial ventures, and the hope of easy profit often drove men into manias of speculation. In the Netherlands between 1633 and 1637 tulip bulbs were the object of market speculation. Rather than cultivate the exotic oriental import, people invested huge sums in the bulb market. Before the inevitable bursting of the bubble, the craze had engulfed large numbers of both rich and poor. This was, however, an unusual instance. Investments in insurance—of cargoes, of lives, and against fire—were much more reliable.

One of the most significant commercial innovations during this period was the development of the joint-stock company, a method of conducting trade in which Dutch and English merchants soon excelled. The joint-stock company was an outgrowth of the regulated company, a trading organization that had devolved from the Middle Ages. The regulated company was a group of merchants who were usually granted a monopoly of trade in a specific area under a charter. The men who directed the company made arrangements for transportation and shipment, established rules of competition, and decided what the destination of cargoes would be. Within this loose framework the individual traders who were members of the company operated entirely on their own. During the sixteenth century the regulated company was the common means of overseas trade. The Merchant Adventurers, an old English company that sold unfinished cloth to the Low Countries, is a good example of a regulated company; the Muscovy Company, founded in 1554, the Eastland Company (1579), and the Levant Company (1581) are others. Out of the regulated company developed a more centralized business enterprise, the joint-stock company. Particularly well suited to enterprises that required heavy capital, the joint-stock company appeared first in mining. The investors in the joint-stock company did not participate as traders; rather they used their money to purchase shares in the company and, by virtue of their status as shareholders, elected directors who were responsible for managing paid company employees. The joint-stock company bore more resemblance to the corporation as we know it today than to the old regulated companies: shares could be converted to cash, and the death of a shareholder in no way disrupted the company's operations or affected its continuity as would death in a partnership. Naturally, the earliest joint-stock companies were rather crudely organized. At first, the capital invested as well as the profits realized on each specific venture were distributed among shareholders after each undertaking. The idea of continuity took a while to develop, but by 1660 managers of both great pioneer joint-stock ventures (the Dutch and English East India Companies, founded at the beginning of the seventeenth century) were controlling permanent aggregations of capital.

Joint-stock trading companies were often chartered with great powers to wage aggressive economic warfare for the expansion of trade. Grants of monopoly concentrated in the hands of company directors all of the state's economic power in specific areas, with the directors receiving legal and political power to exclude all competitors outside the company. Against foreign rivals they were empowered to wage war with their own ships and troops, and frequently they did this despite the fact that their home governments were at peace. Some of these chartered companies, such as the English East India Company, gained immense power in domestic politics and continued to function as colonial governments until the nineteenth century.

## The Organization of Production

Local craftsmen following traditional methods continued to supply goods for local markets. But where production for distant markets served by trading companies was concerned—and in some branches of domestic industry as well—significant changes took place in business organization and technology.

Since the late Middle Ages the cloth dealers who met the needs of large markets had sought to employ cheap labor and evade the stringent quality controls imposed by the urban guildmasters. The usual method was to distribute raw materials among suburban and rural laborers who bought or rented their own hand-operated machines, although the word

*Domestic carding, spinning, and weaving.*

*machine* is really too modern to apply to these rudimentary devices. After the various steps of production were completed, the entrepreneur (merchant-capitalist) collected the finished cloth and stored it in a *factory* for further shipment or sale. (Thus he was often known as a *factor.*) This method of organizing production revolved about the merchant-capitalist. His main role was to coordinate the various functions of production and distribution, his knowledge of market conditions being crucial for success. The "domestic system," which required that little fixed capital be tied up in productive machinery, allowed merchant-capitalists to adjust output to the demands of rapidly fluctuating markets. As the system was extended during the commercial expansion of the sixteenth century, a large and insecure class of laborers came into existence—men who lived on subsistence wages and who, since their labor could as easily be discarded as purchased, absorbed the shocks and dislocations inevitable in commercial depressions.

Occasionally the entrepreneurial system brought pieces of work together in some finishing process at a single place resembling a modern factory. But centralized production calling for heavy capitalization was required in only a few industries like mining, shipbuilding, cannon founding, and printing. In what we would call "heavy industry" privileged chartered companies or state ownership was common.

Institutional developments—the growth of banks, the rise of new commercial companies, the spread of entrepreneurial middlemen, and the appearance of heavy capitalization in some industries—were signs of an expanding economy. The capital accumulation required for economic growth in the sixteenth and seventeenth centuries has been explained by a variety of factors: profits from urban rents, military spending by governments, expanded markets offered by territorial

*German mine water-pump linkage of the sixteenth century.*

states, increased commercial profits, and the influx of gold and silver from the New World. No one now ascribes the economic expansion of Europe to any single cause, for conditions varied from country to country and from generation to generation. Although no full-scale "industrial revolution" occurred in any part of Europe, it is now believed that technological innovations contributed significantly to economic growth in certain areas, notably England and the Low Countries.

These innovations included the introduction of hand-operated machines like the knit-stocking frame (invented in England in 1589) and the ribbon loom, which could weave several ribbons at once (invented in the Netherlands in 1621). More important in reducing production costs, especially in England, was the substitution of coal for firewood as a source of heat. Coal was inexpensive and readily available, while the scarcity of wood and charcoal made their prices soar. That coal could be used for smelting or transformed into energy was not discovered until the eighteenth century, but long before this, coal as a cheap fuel was exploited in brewing, distilling, sugar refining, glass making, soap making, and the production of salt, gunpowder, and alum. Apart from these developments, however, the most important mechanical means of converting inanimate energy was found in the sailing ship. In the century that we are considering this was so improved as to enable a mere handful of men to manage and direct a force equivalent to the power of many horses. The higher standard of living and the accumulation of wealth for investment in the Netherlands, England, and Sweden were due in no small part to the impressive proportion of the world's shipping fleet that was at the disposal of merchants in those countries.

Despite new developments in commerce and industry, agricultural expansion was still restrained by traditional techniques and the lack of new arable land. Productivity increased in England, in the Netherlands, and in the vicinity of commercial centers. Elsewhere output per acre was limited by the peasants' ignorance how to replenish the fertility of the soil by any means other than letting it lie fallow. Until seed grasses for hay were introduced the scarcity of forage dictated that few cattle could be kept alive over the winter, and in turn the scarcity of cattle meant a shortage of manure for fertilizer. Good weather brought mediocre harvests, and poor weather meant famine, soaring grain prices, starvation, and weakened resistance to disease. Food shortages were general in Italy and Spain. In 1599 and again during the 1630s importation of Baltic grains by Dutch merchants failed to stave off general famines, which were followed by the plague; in other parts of western Europe local famine was endemic. Grain shortages pushed food prices up, accounting for the bulk of consumer expenditures. Famine thus invariably reduced the sale of industrial products and threw workmen in the domestic industries out of work. The combination of war levies, war devastation, and plagues carried by armies produced a similar pattern in theaters of war.

## The "Price Revolution"

Famines struck primarily at the lower classes, but a general inflation of prices penetrated all economic developments and cut across all social levels in the period from 1450 to ca. 1650. At first gradual, this acceleration of prices—often called the "price revolution"—was most rapid in western Europe between 1500 and 1600, during which time prices almost doubled. The timing and intensity of the price inflation varied from country to country and from product to product. In some places the price of grain, hay, and wood increased fifteenfold between 1500 and 1650. Generally the prices of industrial goods rose less than the costs of foodstuffs; this meant that the heaviest burden of the change fell on the poor.

Few contemporaries could offer a rational explanation of the inflation. However modern economic historians, working, we must realize, with incomplete and inaccurate data, attribute it to a shortage of products whose supply was inelastic or declining, combined with the influx of precious metals into the economic system. The population increase heightened the demand both for foodstuffs whose supply was limited because of the stagnation in agricultural productivity and for forestry products whose supply was shrinking.

Prices were inevitably driven upward. At the same time, the introduction of precious metals into the economy, first from the mines of central Europe, then from New Spain, doubled and then redoubled the amount of gold and silver in circulation. Because more money was avilable to buy the same amount of goods and services, prices soared.

The inflationary effects of new bullion supplies were further compounded by governments and speculators. Rulers had to cope with rising expenses while the real money value of the taxes they collected decreased. Generally they debased the value of their coinage, a measure that only further increased the money supply. New sources of silver bullion caused an imbalance in the traditional ratios of gold and silver, and this too unsettled monetary exchanges. In a process described by Sir Thomas Gresham (Elizabeth I's agent at the Antwerp exchange), hoarders and speculators gathered up "dear money."* Monetary confusion injured commerce as it disrupted exchanges and allowed informed speculators to reap quick profits.

Inflation affected various social classes in different ways, but in general it operated to reinforce the distinctions among classes. Hardest hit were the landless laborers whose wages lagged far behind prices. In 1630, according to a detailed study, the real wages of English building craftsmen were less than half what they had been in 1450. Some economic historians have concluded that the growing disparity between prices and wages contributed both to the profits of merchants and entrepreneurs and to the accumulation of industrial capital. But this result did not always follow. As usual, inflation benefited debtors and reduced the value of fixed incomes. Many petty nobles (*hidalgos* in Spain, *hobereaux* in France, *Rittern* in western Germany) who

* A modern dictum has Gresham's law thus: "Bad money drives out good."

were bound by long-term rent contracts with their peasants eventually lost their estates to peasants and townsmen. These newly landless men, together with vagabonds, were ready recruits for mercenary armies. On the other hand, those English gentry who were able to raise their rents often prospered. East of the Elbe River, where local lords exploited their powers over the peasants, serf labor was used to produce market surpluses, but here prosperity was undermined by the wars of the seventeenth century. During the era of inflation the largest fortunes were, on the whole, amassed by merchants, courtiers, officials, lawyers, and commanders of mercenary troops.

## State Economic Policies

The course of economic change created new problems for sixteenth- and seventeenth-century governments. Military expenditures were steadily increasing, but inflation depreciated tax revenues. Commercial expansion enriched some states, but for others it represented an unequal competition that only siphoned off their circulating coinage. As the domestic system spread, the class of insecure subsistence workers grew, and their demands threatened to undermine the traditional social order. Population increase and famine contributed to swell the ranks of the unemployed, vagrant poor, and brigands. In their efforts to secure order in society and to maintain the flow of tax revenues into the coffers of the state, early modern governments intervened directly and participated extensively in economic life.

Bullionism is the term often applied to the fiscal expedients and traditional protectionist measures used by governments that tried to keep coinage in circulation by regulating imports, exports, and exchange rates. Above all, it attempted to prevent the export of precious monetary metals like gold and silver. Often this effort led to attempts to curtail the importation of expensive cloth, such as silk, by restricting its use to the nobility. Usually bullionists upheld the traditional social order by preserving the tax exemptions of the privileged nobility. They also responded to urban complaints about rural competition from domestic workers by instituting restrictive statewide guilds. For revenues kings were expected to support their governments from the royal domains instead of by taxes. To raise money they commonly sold offices, negotiated loans in expectation of future revenues, and granted—or sold—monopolies of such commodities as salt. By this procedure monopolists' profits were in effect shared with court and crown. Despite these measures, income seldom covered expenses. A few rulers—the dukes of Saxony and the Austrian Habsburgs—benefited from locally mined bullion, but no other European kingdoms had significant deposits of gold and silver ores within their own territories. The rest tried to make up for their deficiency of precious metals by legislation protecting their money supply or by gaining an empire.

Castile and Portugal followed bullionist economic policies exploiting their imperial resources and geographical advantages to amass great treasure from colonial mines and trade. But in both kingdoms taxation policies reflected the interests of court, church, and dynastic ambition rather than those of the productive classes. As bullion flowed in from the New World, Spanish prices rose and the kingdom's manufactured goods were priced out of the European markets. Since its wares could not compete at home or abroad, Spanish industry lagged. Thus despite the influx of bullion, Spanish industry did not accumulate capital but fell victim to cheaper imports from abroad. Spanish fiscal difficulties even dealt heavy blows to Italian, German, and Spanish bankers when the government defaulted on loans in 1557, 1575, 1607, 1627, 1647, and 1653.

Eventually the Iberian kingdoms saw their bullion and trade absorbed by other countries, and they finally came to depend on goods imported by Dutch merchants. Since bullionism failed in the Iberian kingdoms, it was discredited as a policy that could achieve self-sufficiency or economic growth. Its most resounding success—the discovery and import of precious metals from the New World—seemed to produce more problems than it solved.

In contrast to continental monarchies where royal officials set fiscal policies and supervised economic activities, Dutch policy was largely formulated and executed by a group of men who formed a merchant oligarchy. Merchants sought and obtained governmental assistance, yet they were subject to a minimum of restrictions on commerce and production. Provincial governments negotiated agreements that opened new markets, preserved old ones, and kept the North Sea open to their ships. Dutch mercantile interest groups, who preferred peace to war and naval warfare to war on land, secured monopoly trading charters and naval protection from the government. When war increased the power of the House of Orange supported by Dutch Calvinists who advocated war on land, the States-General banned trade with Spain and required that merchant ships be armed; but in practice merchants usually ignored such laws. They continued to profit from trade with the enemy. Since the Dutch Republic (the United Provinces)* depended on imported foodstuffs and raw materials, these goods were admitted duty-free, and the export of monetary metals was allowed as a normal part of trade. Thus Dutch mercantile policy and practice deviated significantly from the

* Comprising the seven northern provinces of the Burgundian inheritance, the United Provinces, or Dutch Republic, gained independence under a confederated government, the States General, in a revolt from Spain. See pp. 151–52.

*Dutch warships of the seventeenth century.*

bullionism of its foes, and it prospered.

Instead of encouraging freer trade elsewhere, Dutch commercial dominance only provoked protectionist measures on the part of other states. On the Continent these measures were in most cases traditionalist, bullionist, and defensive. England and France, however, responded with policies that favored native merchants, native producers, and new industries over foreign competitors. The term mercantilism is the general label applied to the policies that aimed to gain power abroad and thus expand wealth at home. Mercantilists continued the bullionists' emphasis on protectionism but went much further in attempting to achieve self-sufficiency and a favorable balance of trade by stimulating native manufactures that would employ the poor, provide a surplus of foreign exchange, and provide tax revenues.

During Elizabeth I's reign, English trade contracted. There were periodic depressions that caused unemployment and food riots, to which the government responded by reforming the coinage and granting charters to new monopoly companies that proposed to exploit new markets. By such regulations as the Statute of Artificers (1563) the growth of the domestic system was checked, while such measures as the Poor Law (1601) represented an effort to provide relief and employment for the indigent and hungry who seemed to be growing more numerous. Elizabeth's leading counselor, Lord Burghley, encouraged English industry: patents were granted for new industries, searches for mineral deposits were sponsored, skilled artisans were imported from the Continent, and the production of gunpowder and naval stores was fostered.

After 1620 serious commercial depressions affected England's traditional export product—woolen cloth. These crises played a part in the formulation of mercantilist economic principles, which were expounded in such treatises as the *Discourse on England's Treasure by Forraigne*

*Trade* by Thomas Mun, a director of the East India Company. The Stuart governments tried to counter the depressions with relief measures; they also pressed commercial companies to buy up domestic cloth production so that employment would be maintained, but this policy did not succeed. In addition they continued to protect English markets and shipping against foreign competition and embarked on a program to expand the navy. Gradually English commerce and production adjusted as Englishmen learned to adopt new products for new markets. The process was facilitated because both the justices of the peace and the central government neglected to enforce traditional industrial regulations.

As the enforcement of domestic regulations grew lax, England was slowly establishing an empire in North America and the West Indies. In 1651 the empire was brought under a comprehensive navigation act that was designed to exclude Dutch competition. By 1660 a strengthened and expanding English fleet was engaged in a series of commercial wars with the Dutch.

French governments at the end of the sixteenth century and at the beginning of the seventeenth century also sponsored new industries and sought to protect native merchants from foreign competition. But the industrial regulations designed to maintain uniform standards of quality grew more and more rigid, and French economic policy, compared with that of England and the Dutch Republic was more explicitly directed to fill war treasuries. French officials could also exercise more initiative because they had direct authority from the crown and because French merchants were timid in taking the initiative in forming new companies. French entrepreneuers continued to be inhibited by social traditions stigmatizing commerce as less noble than investment in land, titles, offices, and state loans.

Economic policies, which varied from state to state, all shared certain fundamental assumptions that constituted the core of "mercantilist" thought. Mercantilists took it for granted that state intervention was necessary to secure prosperity and power, which they believed went hand in glove. They lived in an age of scarcity and thus readily assumed that the world's wealth was relatively static and that one state's gain was another's loss. Hence even in those states where merchant prosperity was identified with the general welfare, a powerful state—or at least a powerful navy—was considered indispensable to maintain and extend prosperity, for mercantilists considered power to be the source of plenty. Nevertheless in the continental monarchies state intervention during this period served to preserve the traditional framework of society more often than it advanced commerce and industry. The kind of mercantilism practiced in the continental monarchies often hewed to traditional bullionist regulations; their rulers did not yet subscribe to Thomas Mun's belief that expanding exports even with the export of bullion was the surest way to national prosperity.

## B. Spain and the Religious Wars

### THE DOMINANCE OF THE SPANISH HABSBURGS

Warfare lay at the heart of the crises of the century between 1560 and 1660. Commercial rivalry inspired few wars; the conflicts that wracked Europe were more often generated by issues of politics and religion. Religious hatreds fed international as well as dynastic civil strife, breeding militant ideologies whose zeal often overrode rational considerations of life, prosperity, and property. Almost all factional leaders were belligerent, but Philip of Spain wielded the preponderant power. He identified his own dynastic ambitions with God's will that all Europe be restored to Roman Catholicism, preferably under Spanish control.

Philip II's father, Emperor Charles V, had bequeathed to him a vast but scattered empire: the Spanish kingdoms, territory in Italy, the Low Countries, the so-called Free County of Burgundy, Spain's possessions in Central and South America, the West Indies, and a claim to the Philippine Islands. By 1560 French resistance to Habsburg dominance in Italy and the Low Countries had waned. The treaty of Cateau-Cambrésis of 1559 terminated a long series of wars and in effect ratified Philip's European hegemony. But his ambitions exceeded his far-flung empire. He wed Mary Tudor in order to bring England into the Catholic Habsburg orbit, but Mary failed to produce a male heir. Following Mary's death he courted Elizabeth Tudor—and suffered a further marital-diplomatic fiasco. Finally he married another Elizabeth, the daughter of the king of France. This connection with the house of Valois in 1559 gave him the opportunity of actively intervening in French affairs. But not until his fourth and last marriage, this time to his Habsburg cousin, Anne of Austria, did Philip succeed in begetting an heir to the throne (Philip III).* This marriage alliance also paved the way for renewed political cooperation with the Austrian branch of the Habsburg family.

In 1580 Philip came closest to satisfying his hunger for empire when he succeeded to the Portuguese throne. The childless king of Portugal had been killed while fighting the Moors in Africa, and, assisted by Castilian noblemen, Philip was able to make good his claim to the throne. He swore to maintain the Portuguese constitution and promised that the country would not be administered by Castile; the Portuguese were to govern themselves and to continue the direction of their commercial empire. But while Philip was technically only an administrator, the territories he "administered"—the Azores, the Canaries, the Madeiras, Cape Verde, posts on the eastern and western African coasts, and trading stations in Sumatra, Java, Ceylon, Burma, China, and Japan—comprised the second greatest world empire in the sixteenth century.

* Don Carlos, his son by his first wife (who was Portuguese), was demented. Philip kept him in confinement where he died under mysterious circumstances in 1568.

*Bust of Philip II.*

## The Government of Philip II

Dynastic tradition legitimized Philip's enlargement of his empire; to maintain it he had the most powerful military machine in Europe; but the practical problems of ruling such extensive lands eventually overwhelmed him. He was unable to maintain communication with his far-flung outposts, and he could hardly pursue policies that served the conflicting interests of all his subjects.

Only in the kingdom of Castile and in the Castilian empire did Philip have an efficient bureaucracy that had the power to impose his will. Outside Castile he ruled through his viceroys and regents, who were obliged to bend to local customs and

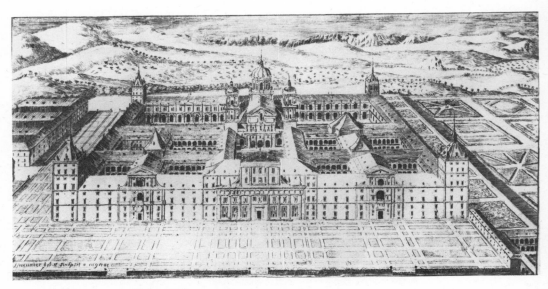

*El Escorial.*

representative assemblies. The Iberian kingdoms in no sense constituted a national "Spanish" state, for in neighboring Aragon Castilians were looked on as foreigners, just as they were in Portugal or in the Low Countries. Philip's empire was a federation of provinces and kingdoms united only by his person. In most of them a separate royal council sat in the capital, but no single council—not even the Supreme Tribunal of the Spanish Inquisition—was capable of exerting authority throughout the king's possessions.

In Castile various royal councils held nominal and legal jurisdiction over colonial trade (a Castilian monopoly), military matters, and other areas of government. The only link and coordination among them was the king, who directed their operations through his powerful royal secretaries. The secretaries dispensed patronage (as they had done under Charles V) and wielded more influence in formulating state policy than the council members. But real control of Castilian policy remained in Philip's hands.

Although suffering from gout and asthma, he was a dedicated and hard-working administrator. Often behaving more like a bureaucrat than a ruler, he applied a phenomenal memory to the minutest details of administrative and military affairs. From his permanent capital in Madrid he exercised close personal control, keeping court factions in check by arbitrary rule whenever he felt his power threatened. He used the magnificent Escorial Palace near the city only as a summer residence and to house dignitaries whom he summoned to court.

Philip had been educated by a bishop and was deeply devout. He placed full confidence in his confessors and theologians, all of whom were advocates of absolute monarchy: according to these clerical advisers he ruled by divine right and could be subject to no institutional checks. Although quick to curb local autonomy in the Low Countries and Aragon, in Castile his absolutism was tempered by solicitude for the Church and for the welfare of the provincial aristocrats, from whose ranks he drew most of his local officials and highest administrators. Traditionally Philip has been represented as a bigoted, humorless champion of the Cath-

*Burning of heretics (auto-da-fé) by the Spanish Inquistion.*

olic Reformation. He was always sensitive to the interests of the Church, and the Church in turn was sensitive to his, providing both substantial revenues and offices to which he could appoint his favorites. But he was not in any way a servant of the papal hierarchy: he ruled the Spanish church quite as authoritatively as Henry VIII ruled the Church of England. His proclamation of "one king, one faith" was perfectly in keeping with all other measures—fiscal, military, political—that he took to preserve the Habsburg power.

One institution was common to all Spanish lands under Philip's rule: the Inquisition. Designed to enforce religious conformity and obedience, it was superbly equipped to ferret out and destroy heretics. In 1559 arrests and burnings snuffed out the first signs of organized Protestantism. Then Philip took further measures to insulate his empire from

Christian heresy: he had an enlarged Spanish edition of the *Index of Prohibited Books* published; he forbad his subjects to attend foreign universities; and he ordered all bookshops searched for subversive material.

Protestants, however, posed less of a threat to Philip's "one faith" than Jews and Moors. Spain had expelled unconverted Jews in 1492, but the converts who remained behind preserved their traditions. They, along with the converted Moors (*Moriscos*), were charged with responsibility for all heresy and evil. The Inquisition enforced a test of "blood purity" that barred them from admission to the state, the Church, and the professions. Numerically the Moriscos were far more significant than the Jews; they, too, defied the laws, retained their old traditions, and were hated for their refusal to assimilate completely. In addition they suffered the stigma of being identified with African pirates and Ottoman forces, who were engaged against Spanish power in the Mediterranean. In 1567, when Philip tried to enforce edicts against Moorish customs and the use of Arabic, the Moriscos in Granada revolted. The struggle, marked by savage atrocities and reprisals on both sides, ended in 1571 when the defeated rebels, 80,000 strong, were deported to Castile and dispersed among Castilian families. They remained there until 1609, when all Moriscos were expelled by Philip III.

Philip's religious policies were closely bound up with his financial measures. King and Church shared all property confiscated from "heretics" condemned by the Spanish Inquisition. By the end of the sixteenth century the Church controlled half the revenues of the kingdom, but from them it made substantial contributions to the crown. Philip accepted this state of affairs, thus proving that, despite grand theoretical statements of divine-right monarchy, social tradition and fiscal expedients played a determining role in his economic policy. Although the flow of bullion imported from America increased, Philip never established a firm structure of finance. Direct taxes levied on Castile were his main source of revenue, but because the aristocracy and clergy were exempt from direct taxation, almost the entire weight of the tax burden fell on peasants and townsmen. Only with the imposition of the *alcabala*—a tax of 10 (later 14) percent on every commercial transaction—as well as a heavy excise (*millones*) were the other social classes forced to contribute to the costs of the state. Still, revenues always failed to cover expenditures, and the monarchy negotiated new loans, debased the coinage, sold royal offices, and disposed of its shares in privileged monopolies.

Disaster ultimately overtook the Castilian economy. By raising prices the alcabala priced Spanish goods out of foreign and domestic markets. As the value of im-

ports exceeded exports many times over, the crown encouraged the raising of merino sheep, hoping that the sale of wool would narrow the gap in foreign exchange. This it did, but the unbalanced extension of sheep pasturage also caused erosion of farm lands. And although the crown extended privileges to sheep raisers' guilds, there was no redress of grievances for the peasants whose crops were destroyed by sheep. Royal policy also diverted to court and Church the income that people might have invested in productive enterprise. The expenses of the court were a major drain on the king's treasury, but the bulk of his dwindling resources went to defend and extend his empire.

## Defense of the Mediterranean

Philip is usually remembered as a militant foe of Protestantism, but for the first 20 years of his reign he was more concerned with Ottoman power on the Mediterranean Sea and with the Moriscos at home. Ottoman naval power was at peak strength under Suleiman the Magnificent (1520–66), whose navy was augmented in the west by corsairs operating from the rapacious pirate states of Tripoli and Algiers. When the peace treaty of 1559 deprived Suleiman of his French ally, Philip turned his newly built galleys against Tripoli—a premature effort in which he suffered serious defeat. After the papacy had helped subsidize more Spanish naval construction, Philip took the offensive again in 1565, at which time he drove the Turks from Malta. This victory broke Ottoman power in the western Mediterranean, but the Turks then invaded Cyprus, a Venetian possession. Determined to end Ottoman conquest, the papacy organized a huge fleet made up mainly of Spanish forces. Its victory at Lepanto in 1571 under Don Juan, a natural brother of Philip who was fresh from triumph over the Moriscos in Granada, was joyously celebrated, but the Turks persisted in Cyprus and continued to dominate the east. Both Spain and the Turks rebuilt and enlarged their navies after Lepanto, but there was to be no second encounter. In 1580 Philip negotiated a truce that proved to be lasting, although it did not put an end to African piracy. In the meantime his attention was diverted westward, where the Low Countries were in revolt and English and Dutch raiders were attacking his lines of communication and challenging his colonies in the Atlantic.

## The Revolt of the Low Countries

The Low Countries constituted the 17 richest provinces of Philip's Burgundian territory. His father, Charles V, had crushed the independence of the towns and executed thousands of religious dissenters, but in the time of Philip the Low Countries still persisted in their defiance of Habsburg absolutism. Many of their provinces were highly urbanized, and among their prosperous towns was Antwerp, the greatest financial center and commercial *entrepôt* of Europe. The domestic textile industry flourished, particularly in Flanders. Literate and well-educated townsmen came under the influence of Erasmian humanism, radical sectarianism, and Protestantism. In the States General at Brussels the Low Countries boasted a representative body that possessed real vitality, although we must remember that only urban oligarchies and rural aristocracies were actually represented. This diet had a long established tradition of collecting taxes as well as voting them. Against royal encroachment it was ready to defend jealously the vested interests of its members, interests that included patronage and control of local church affairs.

Philip became ruler of the Low Countries in 1556. Three years later, when he took up residence in Spain, he appointed a regent—his natural sister, Margaret of Parma. She at once pressed for heavy new taxes and demanded ecclesiastical reorganization, measures that were fiercely resented by Dutch aristocrats as well as the urban oligarchs. The new taxes were intended to fall only on commoners, but from the very outset of her regency Margaret managed to alienate the leaders of society, some of whom were members of her own council of state.

The regency was determined to halt the spread of Calvinism and bring the Church under its control. This proved to be a thorny task. In the French-speaking Walloon provinces, Calvinist preachers set to organizing armed congregations; they were also successful in the larger towns where, by 1566, economic depression was breeding serious social discontent. Even the Inquisition, which operated through local bishops, failed to check the spreading Calvinism. When the nobility resisted all attempts to reorganize the Church, the regency, acting on its own authority, resorted to means of persecution more violent than those practiced by the Inquisition in Spain.

The nobles were hostile to radical Calvinism, but they were even more afraid of Habsburg absolutism. In 1566 they demonstrated unified opposition. Four hundred nobles—whom the regent called "beggars"—petitioned for a moderation of regency policy. They also demanded that royal edicts that encroached on the prerogatives of the States General be repealed. Margaret yielded and issued an order for moderation, but the Calvinists continued their iconoclasm. In 1567 Philip responded by sending the inflexible Duke of Alva with German, Italian, and Spanish mercenaries to reassert royal authority. When Margaret relinquished the regency, Alva reconstituted her council of state as a "council of blood," which set out brutally to reduce all opposition. Public preaching was ruled treasonous; also anyone who denied the king's power to abrogate all

*Flemish protest in Biblical allegory: Pieter Brueghel the Elder,* Massacre of the Innocents.

charters, laws, and privileges was declared a traitor. To define treason thus was to declare war on the aristocracy, and, indeed, two leaders of the aristocrats' resistance—the counts of Egmont and Hoorn—were executed by the council. Thereafter William of Orange, known as William the Silent, became disillusioned with pacific resistance and, until his assassination in 1584, led armed aristocratic resistance. William had a Lutheran upbringing, a Catholic education, and little sympathy for the fanaticism of his Calvinist coreligionists. He enunciated a policy of religious toleration in 1572, hoping to ease conflict and promote unity among the opponents of Spanish rule.

Actually Alva's government was more effective than William in uniting the op-position. When, in imitation of policies in Castile, it imposed taxes on commerce, the whole of the Low Countries, Catholic as well as Protestant, took up arms. William's troops were supplemented by "sea beggars"—privateers who disrupted Habsburg lines of communication at sea and seized coastal towns in Holland and Zeeland. Insurrection spread rapidly. In the same year, 1572, the sea beggars overturned local governments, pillaged churches, and established Calvinist dictatorships in one town after another. Alva's policy may be summed up in his own words. "It is far better," he wrote, "to preserve by war for God and the king, a kingdom that is impoverished and even ruined than, without war, preserve it entire for the benefit of the devil and his disciples, the heretics.''[1] But with his program of terror Alva neither extirpated heresy, disarmed the nobility, nor impoverished the kingdom. In 1573 Philip replaced him with another general, Requesens, who was instructed to repeal the new taxes, dissolve the "council of blood," and proclaim a general amnesty.

Requesens set out to indulge the moderates and wage war to the death against the Calvinists. He succeeded with neither party. The Calvinists supported by southern refugees, gained control over Holland and Zeeland, the two richest provinces of the north. The moderates were effectively alienated in 1576 by the "Spanish Fury," in which Requesens's unpaid troops mutinied, pillaged Antwerp, raped women, and killed several thousand burghers. Delegates from the southern provinces met at Ghent immediately after the "Spanish Fury," and under the terms of a treaty known as the *Pacification of Ghent* the provinces united to expel Spanish troops and try to settle their religious differences by deferring them to a States General. Requesens died in 1576. Obliged to bow to the Pacification of Ghent, Spain's new governor-general, Don Juan of Austria, dispersed his troops.

But the rebels were soon divided again by religious strife. Calvinist refugees returning to Flanders after 1576 set up radical urban governments and persecuted Catholics, who in turn became more reconciled to Spain. In the south Calvinist centers fell one after another. In 1579 the schism within the rebels' ranks was ratified: Calvinists banded together in the Union of Utrecht, and Catholics formed their own League of Arras. With the rebels divided, Spanish troops under the Duke

of Parma were able to reconquer the ten southern provinces. The northern provinces declared their independence in 1581, and, taking advantage of defensible terrain, maintained themselves as the United Provinces (Dutch Republic). Finally, in 1609, after the death of Philip II, the merchants of Holland negotiated a Twelve-Year Truce, but it did not recognize their independence. At the end of the truce the renewed Dutch war for independence merged with a larger struggle, the Thirty Years' War.

Economically the war affected each belligerent in a different way. Subject to Spanish taxation and crippled by Dutch control over the River Scheldt, its major artery of commerce, the southern ten provinces took long to recover. Many of its leading capitalists emigrated. Meanwhile the center of European finance and commerce shifted from Antwerp in the south to Amsterdam in Holland. Castile was drained of men and money, but Dutch pirates, privateers, and merchants prospered; they were beginning to build a commercial empire on the colonies and markets wrested from Portugal. Moreover, the merchants of Holland and Zeeland regained their war expenditures by selling foodstuffs and raw materials to the enemy in return for Spanish bullion. In short, while the southern Netherlands and Spain continued to suffer and their economies to stagnate, the seven United Provinces rapidly recovered from the worst effects of the "price revolution."

Although they were obliged to renew their struggle for independence between 1621 and 1648, the seven United Provinces had succeeded in escaping from the most formidable divine-right ruler in Europe. In their revolt the Dutch broke away from the tradition of "one king, one faith," and Holland—the name of the leading province which contemporaries applied to the whole United Provinces or Dutch Republic—became an enclave of relative lib-

---

[1] Quoted by John Lynch, *Spain under the Habsburgs*, vol. 1, *Empire and Absolutism, 1516–1598* (New York: Oxford University Press, 1964), p. 290. Philip made a similar statement, that he would prefer being king in a desert to being a lord of heretics.

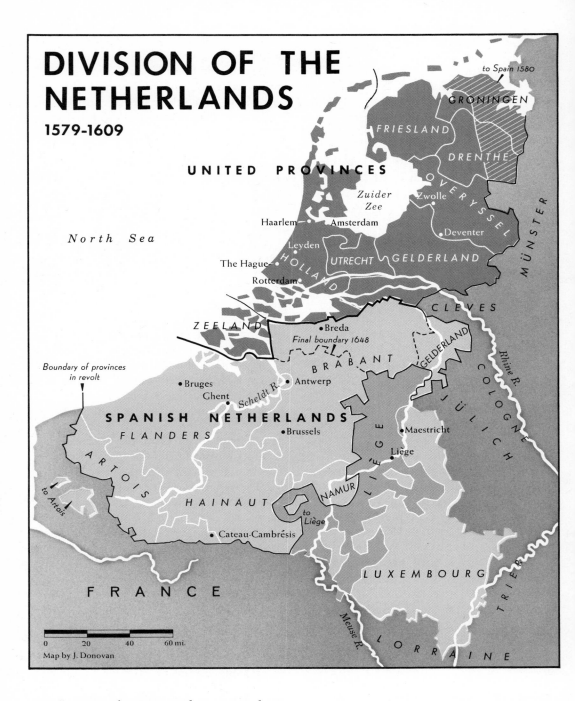

# DIVISION OF THE NETHERLANDS

## 1579-1609

to Spain 1580

**UNITED PROVINCES**

GRONINGEN

FRIESLAND

DRENTHE

OVERYSSEL

MÜNSTER

*North Sea*

*Zuider Zee*

Zwolle

Haarlem •   • Amsterdam

• Deventer

Leyden

The Hague • HOLLAND   UTRECHT   GELDERLAND

Rotterdam •

CLEVES

ZEELAND

• Breda

*Final boundary 1648*

BRABANT

GELDERLAND

Rhine R.

*Boundary of provinces in revolt*

• Bruges   Ghent •   • Antwerp

Scheldt R.

JÜLICH

COLOGNE

**SPANISH NETHERLANDS**

FLANDERS

• Brussels

• Maestricht

LIÈGE

• Liège

ARTOIS

*to Artois*

HAINAUT

NAMUR

to Liège

• Cateau-Cambrésis

LUXEMBOURG

TRIER

**FRANCE**

Meuse R.

LORRAINE

0   20   40   60 mi.

Map by J. Donovan

erty in a sea of seventeenth-century absolutism. Instead of one monarch ruling through his court and councils, governing powers were partitioned among the local oligarchies in the various confederated provinces and a weak States General. Either the ruling oligarchy of the province of Holland or the House of Orange imposed unity, as each in turn predominated in a long contest for power. Although they had led the drive for independence, Calvinists constituted a minority, and a divided one at that. Orthodox Calvinists were counterbalanced by the merchants of Holland and Zeeland, whose religion was not dogmatic. As a result there emerged the first pluralistic society in western Europe, for it was obliged to tolerate religious and secular heterodoxy.

To justify their revolt against a God-anointed king, Dutch leaders appealed to their chartered rights and privileges, which princes, by contractual obligation, were bound to respect; otherwise they were released from obedience to the princes. This was an aristocratic rather than a democratic position; democratic ideas did make a hesitant appearance but were rapidly submerged when urban patricians and the landed aristocracy took over the direction of the revolt. Yet conflicts between those two classes went unresolved and prevented them from forming a solid alliance. Dutch society remained in their control, but they were too much divided to impose a new absolutism.

## Philip II and Tudor England

The success of the Dutch revolt was partially due to Philip's logistical problems. He had to divert resources from the Duke of Parma's forces to his wars with England and to his involvement in the French civil war; meanwhile both England and France gave aid to the rebellious Low Countries. After Elizabeth restored Protestantism to England, Philip tried to recover his influence there by marrying the queen. Failing in that, he became increasingly hostile; his emissaries were implicated in a Catholic uprising in northern England in 1569, and on the Continent his government helped support Catholic colleges for training emigrés who were to bring about a Catholic restoration in England. But the King of Spain refrained from attempting to conquer England so long as Mary Queen of Scots was alive. Prospective ruler of a Catholic England, she was a Guise by birth and a Valois by marriage. Because Philip feared that her accession would lead to a coalition of England and France, he had no intention of conquering England for her benefit even though she was a Roman Catholic.

For Englishmen, Spain and Catholicism were the national enemies. Nationalism reached a peak of ferocity in 1570 when the pope excommunicated Elizabeth, declaring her deposed, and when Catholic plots to assassinate her and her leading counselors were exposed. When the "Sea Dogs" under Francis Drake and John Hawkins ran pirate raids against Spanish naval power, they were widely acclaimed. Eventually Elizabeth sanctioned their deeds. In 1585, when she sent troops to aid the Dutch Republic, she also publicly supported the Protestant rebels in the Low Countries whom for the past eight years she had assisted only covertly.

Once Mary Queen of Scots was executed, Philip had a Catholic martyr to avenge, and he decided that the best and most economical way to protect the coast, colonies, and shipping trade of Spain was to invade England. After many delays the "invincible" Armada was dispatched in 1588, consisting of 130 ships—an imposing number; but they were ill equipped. Philip's plan called for transporting troops from the Netherlands to conquer England, but he neglected to arrange for the shallow-draft vessels needed to transport them from the Dutch coast to the Armada for transport to England. While the Armada waited at anchor for troops that never came, an English fleet composed of private vessels and government warships attacked from the windward side. The outnumbered English effectively deployed fireships and artillery, breaking the elaborate but inflexible formations of the Armada. To return to Spain the Armada was forced to sail northward around Scotland, where the damaged fleet suffered severe losses from storms. England suffered no loss of ships, but about half of the Armada failed to return.

According to common accounts England emerged as mistress of the seas as a result of her defeat of the Armada. In fact no such rapid shift of power occurred. Philip received the bad news impassively and announced that he would build a still larger armada. And he did. New convoy tactics and increased naval construction made Spanish sea power stronger than ever before. Drake and Hawkins had predicted that Philip's supply of New World treasure would be cut off, but for the next 15 years bullion flowed to Spain at an unprecedented rate, and new fortifications of naval bases made them less vulnerable to piracy. Still, costs of defending the Spanish empire were prohibitive. In fact, neither Spain nor England possessed the technology or the requisite number of ships to command the whole Atlantic.

The defeat of the Armada had more significance in European politics. When it occurred, Spain appeared to be at the brink of global dominance; but it proved to spectators all over Europe that the Habsburgs were not omnipotent and that they had no special claim to the blessings of divine providence. Protestant England had escaped being made a Catholic kingdom within the Habsburg empire; no longer could Spain be seen as the instrument that would enforce a uniform Catholic peace on Europe. From the English victory over Spain, Henry III of France took courage and undertook the assassination of his rival, Henry of Guise, the leader of French Catholics who relied on Spanish support. Philip, however, continued to aid Catholic partisans against the Huguenots when their leader, Henry of Navarre, succeeded to the throne as Henry IV in 1589.

Although still unable to defeat his old enemies, Philip had committed himself to taking on new ones. Castile, still the strongest land power in Europe, was nevertheless entering a period of relative decline. Internal economic difficulties, the overcommitment of her resources, and the rise of powerful rivals all hastened the decay of Spanish supremacy.

## The Reign of Philip III (1598–1621)

Monarchy, it has been observed, is a lottery; there is no guarantee that an heir will pursue the policies of his predecessor. When death seemed imminent, Philip lamented that "God who has given me so many kingdoms has not granted me a son fit to govern them." Unlike his diligent father, the sickly Philip III would not concern himself with affairs of state. For more than 20 years the real ruler of Spain was his royal favorite, the Duke of Lerma, who was a descendant of the great king Ferdinand I. In his time state offices were sold en masse for purposes of revenue, the coinage was debased, extravagant festivities marked even the most trivial social event at court, and public funds were embezzled in staggering amounts. Lerma himself accumulated a fortune of incredible size, much of it consisting of fines from the Moriscos, who were expelled in 1609. When his opponents finally insisted on an accounting, Lerma hastily secured a cardinal's hat and papal permission to leave the court, thus escaping punishment and avoiding restitution.

It is to Lerma's credit, however, that he concluded peace with England and the United Provinces. Philip II had already been forced to make peace with France in 1598. Before Spain and England came to terms there was one more encounter, when Castilian troops and ships joined an Irish uprising in 1601. The Spanish were again defeated, although more narrowly than in 1588. Under James I, England's militant policies against Spain were relaxed, and peace was negotiated in 1604. With the Dutch, however, full-scale hostilities on land and sea continued, and the Spanish suffered defeat off Gibraltar in 1607. But then Lerma found a Milanese general, Ambrose Spinola, who was able to drive back the forces of Maurice of Nassau, the son of William of Orange. In 1609 both sides agreed to a truce. By terminating these two wars and by checking French schemes of aggression (this was accomplished by intrigue in Henry IV's court), Lerma gave Spain the time she desperately needed to recuperate. The greatest test of Habsburg power, the Thirty Years' War, was still to come.

## ELIZABETHAN ENGLAND

In the past, French rivalry had checked Habsburg ambition, but after 1560 French strength was drained by civil and religious wars. Meanwhile England, whose smaller population and limited resources hardly seemed to warrant such resistance, stepped into the breach to defy Spanish power, and Elizabeth reluctantly assumed the role of rallying Protestant Europe. Rivalry with Spain, which broke into naval warfare and brought the Armada, also profoundly affected English domestic affairs.

### The Elizabethan Religious Settlement

Elizabeth had little of the religious fanatic in her, but religious questions were central to the political and diplomatic policies of her reign (1558–1603). Her policies concerning religion were tailored to fit political expediency. From her first parliament (1559) she sought only one

measure to overturn Mary's restoration of Catholicism: the reassertion of royal supremacy over the English church. But many of her subjects took their religion far more seriously than that. A strong group in the House of Commons sympathized with the Marian exiles—those laymen and clergymen who had fled England under the persecution of "Bloody Mary." During their residence in Geneva and the cities of Germany these exiles had absorbed Protestant doctrines as well as techniques of propaganda. Their militant supporters in the House of Commons pressed for a return to the religious settlement of Edward VI, and they further demanded punitive measures against Catholics and retribution for past persecution. Elizabeth compromised: she agreed to both an act of royal supremacy and an act of uniformity which imposed a common prayer book on the whole kingdom. Nevertheless the prayer book that was finally published was theologically ambiguous enough to accommodate many diverse opinions. She resolutely refused to persecute nonconformists unless their actions were seditious or treasonable. This compromise between queen and Commons laid the basis for a middle way. What emerged in England was a state church whose strict hierarchy was traditional but whose doctrines were flexible and broad.

Most Englishmen, except for a number of Roman Catholics (and these were dwindling) and a vociferous Puritan minority, adjusted gradually to the Anglican settlement. Deep-rooted Catholic customs were perpetuated in some rural areas, particularly in the north. But without any institutions to rely on, Catholic teachings and ritual practices could now be preserved only in the households of devout gentlemen and lords. Calvinists, or Puritans, on the other hand, began to penetrate the power structure of the state, church, and society; they had partisans in the Queen's Privy Council itself. So long as she was sure of their political support, Elizabeth kept and used them within the church. The spread of Puritanism among the gentry was reflected in the House of Commons, where Puritans attacked what they considered popish survivals in the services authorized by the Elizabethan settlement, such as the wearing of vestments by ministers. They also criticized the queen's leniency toward Catholics, for they were not prepared to be tolerant. In what may be taken as a typical outburst, one of them declared in 1559 that "Maintainers of false religion ought to die by the sword."[2] The Puritans' political influence increased as they became outspoken patriots and vigorously denounced Spain. Eventually the queen came to oppose them. After 1574 she was convinced that they constituted a threat to the stability of the Church of England, and she took steps to limit their power and influence in the church hierarchy. During the latter part of her reign, clashes in the House of Commons between Elizabeth and the Puritans laid bare those issues that would later ignite the civil wars of the seventeenth century.

## Society, Politics, and Constitutional Development

The gentry, whose power and influence grew during the sixteenth century, constituted one of the most important classes in Elizabethan society. They were landed gentlemen whose estates were a main source of income. Membership in this social class was extremely fluid: from below, their ranks absorbed yeomen, wealthy lawyers, officials, and merchants who purchased country estates; in their turn, the gentry—who had no titles—very much wanted to narrow the gap between themselves and the titled nobility.

Although the nobles were forced to share their political and social power with the gentry, they retained tremendous prestige and influence and continued to represent the highest goals of social ambition. Still, some of the wealthiest men in England could be found among the merchants, particularly the narrow coterie of London merchant-bankers who were closely allied with crown and court.

The first half of the sixteenth century was an era of expanding commerce and urbanization. One city—London—dwarfed all other English towns as the center of trade, finance, and marketing. The line between wealth and poverty was drawn more sharply in England as commerce expanded, for as more men became rich, and as rich men grew more affluent, the lower classes became more numerous and in some cases poorer. Church and state subscribed to the social theory of a well-ordered hierarchical society in which each rank had its fixed place; but in reality men were always struggling in ruthless competition to move up the social ladder or to secure a stronghold near the top. Charity and private contributions to education relieved some of the friction between rich and poor, but at the end of Elizabeth's reign the greatest single financial and administrative problem facing English society was the growth of poverty. The Poor Law was one attempt to deal with it.

The Elizabethan Poor Law of 1601 was the last in a series of statutes directed toward regulating the economy and the social system of England. It made local parishes or districts responsible for providing for the destitute. These districts are good places with which to begin a study of Elizabethan government, for the success of all legislation eventually depended on local administration. Almost every traditional executive function of local government was filled by justices of the peace, many of whom were also members of the House of Commons, where they

[2] Quoted by John E. Neale, *Elizabeth I and Her Parliaments 1559–1581* (New York: St. Martin's Press, 1958), p. 117.

helped make the laws that they enforced in the counties. Administering the Poor Law became their largest single task. Recruited from the gentry to serve in their own neighborhoods, they set compulsory tax rates and appointed and supervised the overseers of the poor in each parish. They also served as judges and sheriffs, searched out and penalized Catholic recusants, set wages and prices, enforced craft and trade regulations, and maintained waterways. Many of the educated gentry also had some degree of legal training. Familiarity with the law helped them to secure their own lands as well as carry out their official functions. During the sixteenth century the law became an ever more fashionable and profitable pursuit. The gentry thus exerted enormous power, for fundamental to Elizabethan government was the fact that the queen could carry out only those policies that the gentry supported; to put it another way, the government had no chance of implementing any policies to which the gentry was opposed.

The central government under Elizabeth was little changed from the days of her father, Henry VIII. Her chief counselors—Burghley, Walsingham, and Leicester—made sure that the men appointed as lord lieutenants were usually peers or privy councillors. Since the lord lieutenant in each county nominally supervised administration, this system of appointment gave a semblance of unified central administration to the country; but because his jurisdiction conflicted with that of the justices of the peace, the lord lieutenant's actual power seldom extended beyond military recruitment and training.

During Elizabeth's reign the House of Commons expanded and developed new vigor. Although it could neither initiate legislation nor directly supervise the execution of laws, and although the speaker usually wielded considerable power on behalf of the crown, still, the Commons did initiate tax measures; and no such measure or any other bill could be passed without its assent. Since many new towns were chartered and privileged to send two burgesses to Parliament, the size of the Commons increased. Townsmen did not gain more power, however, for borough elections usually returned gentry to the House of Commons. These latter resided in the countryside and primarily looked after only their own interests. Still, Englishmen possessed more civil rights, and were subject to fewer taxes, than their counterparts living under the monarchies on the Continent. Parliament was representative of an important segment of society, and its continued vitality was in great part responsible for the notable cooperation between ruled and ruler in England. While static continental diets functioned as guardians of class privilege, the Parliament of England assumed an active role in the fiscal and political life of the nation.

On the issue of royal succession Elizabeth's government was perhaps most vulnerable. The sixteenth century was an era of dynastic as well as religious conflict, and the English throne, secured only by the life of a single woman, was a prime target for the Spanish Habsburgs and the French house of Guise. Constantly in fear of the confusion that might ensue if Elizabeth died without an heir, the House of Commons defied her orders to be silent on the subject of marriage and vociferously urged her to wed. But she insisted on remaining single. For as long as it was possible, she played her marital eligibility for all it was worth in the game of diplomacy, trusting to luck that on her death no crisis of internal succession would develop.

## Elizabeth's Foreign Policy

In the Elizabethan era England ceased to be an insignificant factor in European affairs. Its strategic location, economic interests, and unsought role as the champion of

Protestantism thrust it into the power struggles of Europe. To subsequent generations the defeat of the Armada was dramatic evidence of English emergence; but at the same time it was mainly an act of defense. Until 1588 the English position in relation to Spanish power had been extremely precarious. Elizabeth could count on brilliant ministers such as William Cecil (Lord Burghley), who directed one of the most efficient intelligence services in Europe. Until the 1580s she successfully coped with coalitions of powerful foreign enemies without placing heavy strains on the economic resources of her kingdom.

The first major threat came from France and Scotland. Mary Stuart, Queen of Scotland and the wife of Francis II of France, ruled Scotland with the aid of her French mother, Mary of Guise. The queen, who was a Roman Catholic, also had strong claims to the English throne—claims that France strongly supported. Philip II, anxious to thwart Guise ambitions, tried to marry Elizabeth. Fearful of provoking either side, Elizabeth remained noncommittal. In 1559 Protestants in Scotland revolted against French rule. Although the leader of the revolt, John Knox, was a strict Calvinist (as well as the author of a polemic against women rulers), Elizabeth supported him. In 1560 Mary Stuart became a widow, and for a time thereafter—even though she remained Queen of Scotland—she posed a lesser threat to Elizabeth's throne.

Wanting to weaken the house of Guise, Elizabeth supported the Huguenots in the French civil wars between 1562 and 1564. England regained Calais, which it had lost under Mary Tudor, but the venture ended in disaster when the French united temporarily to expel the English. Meanwhile Mary Stuart married another claimant to the Tudor throne, Lord Darnley. Once more it appeared that she intended to displace Elizabeth; but instead (although James, the child of her marriage with Darnley, would eventually rule Scotland and England) Mary lost even her own throne. Darnley grew jealous of her affections for her royal secretary and had him murdered. The very next year (1567) Darnley himself was murdered. When the Queen then married Bothwell, another of her favorites who had been implicated in Darnley's death, the scandal that ensued forced her to seek refuge in England. There she was confined. Serving as the focus of Catholic plots against Elizabeth's life, she was compromised and eventually sacrificed to the executioneer's block in 1587.

The real foe of England was Spain. Elizabeth, however, was reluctant to become involved in a major war against this enemy. When the important English cloth trade with the Low Countries dictated that England support their revolt against Spain, Elizabeth offered herself as bait. By protracted but fruitless marriage negotiations with the younger brother of the king of France, she lured the house of Valois into supporting the Dutch revolt. But after 1584, when William of Orange was assassinated, the French deserted the rebels. Once Elizabeth had openly intervened on the Dutch side, England remained more or less in a state of war for the duration of her reign. Not until a Stuart attained the English throne would there be a settlement with Spain.

## FRENCH CIVIL AND RELIGIOUS WARS

While England united under Elizabeth against Spain, France floundered in civil wars, of which there were eight between 1562 and 1598. Had a strong monarch been at the helm in France as long as Elizabeth ruled in England, these wars might have been avoided; instead, a succession of weak boy-kings undermined the power of the throne. The unsteady control of Catherine de' Medici over her royal sons and the extinction of the Valois male line subjected the kingdom to bitter feuds among aristocratic factions. Less avoidably, it allowed a Calvinist minority to establish an alliance with noble dissidents who were bidding for power.

## Prelude to Religious Revolution

Between 1536 and 1559 French Calvinists (Huguenots) became strong enough to challenge the unreformed French church. Although Francis I considered them anarchists, his alliance with the German Protestants at first forced him to be lenient. After 1540, however, his government began to uproot heresy systematically. His more bigoted successor, Henry II (1547–59), established a special court in the Parlement of Paris, the *chambre ardente,* or "hot box," where summary justice was handed down to Protestants. The Huguenots defied persecution and even increased in numbers, especially in the southern provinces. At Paris in 1559 they held a clandestine "national synod," which drew up a uniform confession of faith. The Huguenot organization in effect provided an alternative government capable of raising money and troops.

Most of the early Huguenots were people of education but little political significance—workingmen, petty tradesmen, professionals, and regular clergy—who resignedly suffered martyrdom. They remained a small minority because Protestants never gained much support among the peasants, but after 1559 highly placed noblemen joined their ranks, compensating for their lack of broad popular support. When these powerful men flocked to the movement, resignation gave way to armed resistance, a course compatible with Calvinist doctrine. Thus Protestantism became involved in the power struggles at the top echelons of the French state. Its involvement further complicated family feuds, court rivalries, and what was

after 1584 a three-cornered struggle among the houses of Valois, Bourbon, and Guise for possession of the French throne.

## The First Seven Wars: 1562–1580

Calvinism grew into a significant political force at a time when the two oldest and most powerful feudal families were arrayed against each other. The Bourbon faction was headed by Anthony of Navarre, who held vast territories in south-central France. The Guise family from Lorraine, whose cardinal-patriarch administered the sees of Rheims, Metz, and Verdun (among other benefices) and the rich abbeys of St. Denis and Clery, led the other faction. Members of a third great family, the Montmorencys, divided their loyalties between Bourbon and Guise.

In 1560 the Huguenots plotted to seize the boy-king, Charles IX, a plot foiled by the court and attributed by the Guise family to the Bourbons and Montmorencys, against whom they swore vengeance. The Queen Mother, Catherine de' Medici, tried to bring peace by calling a religious colloquy and issuing an edict of toleration in 1562. The edict was very much limited and Catherine herself intended it to be temporary; but the Huguenots, for whom toleration was not enough, refused to cooperate. So did the Guise family, which was determined to enforce the doctrines of Trent by fire and sword. Local riots and killings expanded into general war in 1562 when Guise troops slaughtered a Huguenot congregation at Vassy. There followed a complicated series of seven wars punctuated by truces.

As a result of the first war the nobility gained religious toleration, which was anathema to the Guise family. From the second and third the Huguenots won liberty of conscience and four fortified towns, something still more detestable to the Guises. Worse still, the Huguenots' politi-

The Massacre of St. Bartholomew's Day *by Francois Dubois.*

cal spokesman, Admiral Coligny, was given a position of royal confidence. His influence with Charles IX led to the betrothal of the king's sister to Henry of Navarre, son of the leading Huguenot nobleman. This marriage pact threatened Catherine's sway over her son and brought her wrath down on Coligny's head. She plotted his assassination, but the plot miscarried; then she became involved in a conspiracy to kill several prominent Huguenot nobles, including Henry and Coligny. The murderers struck during Henry's marriage celebration on St. Bartholomew's Day, 1572, and assassination turned into massacre. Mob passion led to the slaughter of approximately 20,000 Huguenots in Paris and provincial towns. Coligny was killed, but Henry of Navarre escaped with his life by embracing Catholicism (a momentary conversion, however).

The massacre of St. Bartholomew's Day ravaged the Huguenots' leadership but their organization survived. Determined

to root it out, Henry of Guise accepted Spanish aid, but again in vain. Royal treachery had alienated moderate Catholics from Catherine de' Medici. Moreover, she herself had lost enthusiasm for a Guise victory when she realized that the dashing Henry of Guise could be a dangerous rival to her son. Following the death of Charles IX and the accession of his younger brother, Henry III, Catherine arranged another truce in 1576, which put great sections of France under Guise administration but still contained a provision utterly unacceptable to ardent Catholics: except in the city of Paris, the Huguenots were again to enjoy religious toleration.

## The "War of the Three Henrys": 1585–1589

Disaffected by these concessions to the Huguenots, zealous Catholics organized a Guise-led "Holy League" supported by

Spain and the papacy. Henry III tried to neutralize it as a threat to his power by becoming its head, but Henry of Guise was too domineering an ally. When the king's younger brother—the last direct male heir to the throne since it was obvious that Henry III would not beget a son—died in 1584, the Holy League proposed its own candidate for the throne to prevent its passing to Henry of Navarre, Bourbon leader of the Huguenots, who was next in line. In 1588 the League seized Paris and tried to depose Henry III. (The coup was coordinated with the Spanish Armada's attack on England.) But Henry III escaped and had Henry of Guise murdered. The Guise faction retaliated with a full-scale revolt, which Henry met by enlisting the aid of Henry of Navarre and the *politiques,* a powerful faction of moderates who eventually set the terms that ended the war.

Reacting against foreign intervention and appalled by the destruction of civil war, the politiques set the welfare of France above religious creed—as zealous religious partisans put it, "they preferred the safety of their country to the salvation of their souls." In Languedoc, a province about evenly divided between Catholics and Huguenots, the politiques found a spokesman in the royal governor, Henry of Montmorency-Damville. To prevent further atrocities and destruction, Montmorency enforced toleration; resorting to authoritarian, even despotic, means, he became the "uncrowned king of the south": neither side could hope to win the civil war without his support. After 1584 he threw his weight to the side of Henry of Navarre, who promised him high office in the future.

Henry of Navarre became King Henry IV in 1589 after Henry III was assassinated by a fanatical monk. In the north, especially Paris, Henry faced strong Spanish-supported Catholic opposition. Belatedly following Montmorency's ad-

**RELIGIOUS AND POLITICAL DIVISIONS OF FRANCE** 1585-1598

Map by J. Donovan

Bourbon possessions

Huguenot rule

Guise control (Catholic League)

vice, he removed his religious impediment; "Paris vaut bien une messe!" he is reported to have said.* He announced his (third) conversion to Roman Catholicism, entered the capital, and drove the Spanish troops back to the Netherlands.

Continuing to follow politique guidance, Henry made toleration an official and enforceable policy when he issued the Edict of Nantes in 1598. One other concept had high priority in the politiques' program: the establishment of a strong national monarchy. Henry helped make that concept a political reality as he laid the foundation for subsequent Bourbon absolutism.

* "Paris is well worth a Mass."

## Toleration, Absolutism, and Power

In order to take firm possession of his throne Henry had adopted Catholicism. Now, for the peace of the kingdom, he issued the Edict of Nantes, one of the most advanced programs of toleration of the sixteenth century. By its terms the Huguenots were granted freedom of conscience and were authorized to conduct private and extensive public worship; they could attend schools and universities, establish a limited number of colleges, and hold public office; and, to guarantee their security amid the Catholic majority, they were given complete control over 200 towns, including the seaport of La Rochelle. These walled towns were garrisoned at royal expense, and they boasted more troops than the king himself maintained. Later Cardinal Richelieu would sharply reduce this Protestant "state within a state"; but for the time being it set limits on Bourbon absolutism. By the end of the century the Huguenots had assumed an influential role in French affairs. Meanwhile their great antagonist, the Roman church, had been forced to sell many of its monastic lands (during the reigns of Charles IX and Henry III), and its power was waning.

Throughout the period of protracted civil wars men discussed the right of oligarchs, even of the masses, to resist heretical kings. Not surprisingly, the monarch and his advisors were all advocates of royal absolutism. Henry IV was in theory, and to a certain extent in practice, an absolute monarch. During his reign he convoked no meeting of the Estates General, and with huge sums of money he brought off Catholic leaders who pressed for feudal decentralization. His principal minister, the Duke of Sully, introduced a new official called the *intendant*, who was a direct agent of the crown in the provinces.

*Henry IV, 1589–1610.*

Nevertheless Henry's "absolutism" was a political compromise just as the Edict of Nantes was a religious one. Great lords lost their independence, but their pockets bulged with the king's gold, and institutions that preserved local privileges and autonomy were left intact. Sully cut court expenses and halted peculation of public funds, but as a financial expedient the king permitted some officials to transform their offices into hereditary property by the payment of a special tax, the *Paulette*. Thus many officials gained independence from their royal master. Rather than a political revolution, the Bourbon accession represented a restoration of royal power as it existed under Francis I in the early part of the century. Internal stability was not completely assured, however, and on occasion the kingdom was still rocked by the schemes of dissident court nobles who conspired with Spain.

With domestic peace and some government aid French peasants and tradesmen could recover from the extensive destruction of the wars. The Duke of Sully promoted agriculture, introduced new silk and glassware industries, and built highways and canals. Overseas Champlain was laying the basis for a French empire in Canada. As the economy rapidly recovered, taxes decreased and the royal treasury grew fat.

Although Henry chafed against Habsburg power, he delayed a show of force until 1609. Then he decided to intervene into a dynastic dispute between Brandenburg and the Palatinate over the Rhenish duchies of Cleves and Jülich. Had he moved an army into Germany, a general war would probably have begun, but in 1610 a fanatic's dagger ended both his life and the expedition. All three Henrys had died by assassination, the last of which postponed the confrontation of Habsburg with Bourbon until the middle of the Thirty Years' War. Meanwhile France was again ruled by a boy-king and his queen mother: Louis XIII and Marie de' Medici.

## C. Four Decades of War and Revolution: 1618–1660

### THE ERA OF THE THIRTY YEARS' WAR

At the beginning of the seventeenth century Europe had a respite from war and religious revolution. Philip III made peace with Spain's enemies. Henry IV pacified France and was assassinated before he could shatter the peace of Germany. But peace was too fragile to last; it was the prelude to the worst series of religious, civil, and dynastic wars of the entire century of crises.

#### Origins of the Thirty Years' War

The first of these conflicts, the Thirty Years' War (1618–48), originated in the domains of the German Habsburgs as a response to the Catholic Reformation. Unlike their Spanish cousins, the emperors after Charles V—Ferdinand, Maximilian II (1564–76)—tolerated or even sympathized with Lutheranism, and under their relaxed vigilance Lutherans and Calvinists made heavy inroads among upper townsmen and the nobility who were represented in the provincial diets. Then, in the latter part of Emperor Rudolf's reign (1576–1612) Habsburg leniency began to change toward intolerant rigor. Rudolf himself granted Bohemian Lutherans religious toleration, but his brothers were attempting to depose him. One of them—his successor, Matthias—entered into a family compact with the Spanish Habsburgs, who encouraged him to suppress the Protestants. When his heir-apparent, Ferdinand, the king of Bohemia who became Emperor Ferdinand II in 1619, openly imitated Spanish Catholic rule, the Protestant estates of Bohemia rebelled. In Prague Bohemian noblemen threw the emperor's representatives out of a palace window (the Second Defenestration of Prague), declared the throne vacant, and solicited aid from Protestants throughout Europe.

*Mercenaries in hand-to-hand combat by Holbein.*

The Bohemians primarily counted on assistance from the Protestant estates of the empire. As their new king they chose Frederick V of the Palatinate, the Calvinist head of a German Protestant league (the Protestant Union) and son-in-law of James I of England. German conditions, however, were not auspicious for substantial aid.

German Lutheranism had taken possession of many Catholic lands in northern Germany after the Peace of Augsburg (1555), but the tide turned in 1577 when a Lutheran was elected archbishop-elector of Cologne and was then deposed by the imperial high court. Thereafter Lutherans were preoccupied more with checking the inroads of radical Calvinism than with staying the progress of resurgent Catholicism. "Better popish than reformed" was their watchword as the Calvinists began to spread along the Rhine. In 1580 they drew up a strict common creed, the Formula of Concord, which branded Cal-

vinists as heretics. After this, effective political cooperation between the two creeds became almost impossible. In 1609 they did join in a Protestant Union, in opposition to which the rival Catholic League soon formed, but the Union was paralyzed by conflict between Lutherans and Calvinists; only the Calvinists, who were not recognized by the Peace of Augsburg, actively supported it. Instead of coming to the aid of the Bohemians, Lutheran Saxony used the opportunity of the Bohemian revolt to seize part of the Bohemian crownlands (Lusatia).

From the outset the Bohemian revolt was an international affair, outside forces converging on Austria and Bohemia. Maximilian of Bavaria sent military assistance to the emperor, and Spanish troops and Catholic forces assembled by Poland and the papacy came to the aid of Ferdinand. Bohemia obtained aid from only a few small territories and from Bethlen Gabor, a rebel leader of Transylvania, whose forces twice besieged Vienna before a Turkish attack disabled them. In 1620 troops of the Catholic League, commanded by Baron Tilly—the "monk in arms"—decisively defeated the Bohemians at the Battle of White Mountain, outside Prague. The army of Frederick V was routed in less than two hours.

After Frederick's hasty flight to Holland, the Habsburgs proceeded to wreak revenge on Bohemia, rooting out both the Hussite and Protestant reformations. They executed intellectuals and military leaders, banished some Protestant clergy, and condemned the rest to death. Habsburg dragoons enforced mass conversions of Bohemian Protestants to Catholicism. Refugees—prominent intellectuals among them—swarmed out of Bohemia in numbers that have been estimated from 30,000 to 150,000. About half of all land belonging to the nobility was confiscated and distributed among aristocrats of the Habsburg domains. This policy of redistribution created large landed estates—*latifundia*—worked by serfs, who had heavier duties imposed on them. The extent of the nobility's control over their lives is suggested by the name for their service obligations (Czech, *robota*; Ger. and Eng., *robot*). The men who directed the parceling out of lands, particularly Albert of Wallenstein, grew enormously rich. In 1627 the Habsburgs gave Bohemia a new constitution, which abolished the elective monarchy and placed Bohemian affairs under the direct supervision of the imperial Habsburg court—an arrangement that persisted for more than two centuries. Bohemia would suffer further from the Thirty Years' War when, in its last years, foraging troops again ravaged her countryside.

The collapse of Bohemia spelled doom for Austrian Protestantism. Austria was subjected to a rigorous counterreformation; between 1622 and 1628 Protestants throughout the Habsburg provinces were shorn of all their rights.

## Spread of the Thirty Years' War

After the battle of White Mountain the seat of war moved to the Palatinate. Spanish troops under Spinola and Tilly's forces had systematically devastated Frederick V's home base by 1623. Meanwhile Spain gained possession of important passes through the Alps, a crucial advantage since renewal of the Dutch war of independence in 1621 threatened Spain's lines of communications at sea.

Renewal of the Dutch war was the next major extension of the conflict, carrying it beyond Europe to the colonial empires. Before the Spanish-Dutch truce expired, a revolution in the United Provinces brought to power Calvinists favoring war. The truce of 1609, negotiated by the Arminian lord advocate of Holland, Jan van Oldenbarneveldt, had never been popular with the Calvinists; it was the work of Arminian burghers who denied predestination and advocated a relatively tolerant state church. Calvinists considered it a weak-kneed heresy, and at the synod of Dortrecht (1618–19) they delivered the Arminians a serious theological defeat. Following the synod the victorious Calvinists executed Oldenbarneveldt and began preparations for the war which began again in 1621. When France joined the fray in 1635, the Calvinist-led United Provinces established a firm alliance with it in order to overcome the Habsburgs.

Between 1624 and 1629 Ferdinand II routed the German Protestants, gaining control over the empire more complete than any emperor had held for centuries. Tilly and Wallenstein (whose large private army was now paid by booty and run for profit) won victory after victory as Germany became one great theater of war. During the so-called Danish period,

1625–29, King Christian IV of Denmark led the Protestants to defeat at the hands of Tilly and Wallenstein, who went on to conquer Holstein and to occupy the German coast as far east as Stralsund, not far from the Polish border. Much to the discomfiture of the German princes, Ferdinand II made Wallenstein—a mere upstart—Duke of Mecklenburg. By 1629 Ferdinand was master enough of the empire to order the German Protestant princes, except Saxony, to return to the Roman church all the lands taken since the Peace of Augsburg in 1555.

Ferdinand was so successful that even his allies felt threatened. Just when his Catholic Reformation seemed to be at the crest of victory, the Pope, who had subsidized Ferdinand's armies, deserted him; and Bavaria, fearful that Ferdinand would suppress her autonomy, entered into negotiations with France and forced Wallenstein's dismissal, which Ferdinand accepted in an effort to keep the Catholic forces together. But while German affairs were still unsettled, the war suddenly entered a new phase: partly at French instigation, Gustavus Adolphus, king of Sweden, proceeded to invade Germany as the self-proclaimed deliverer of German Protestantism.

## Swedish and French Intervention

Mercenary warfare allowed small states, if they had sufficient money, to become major military powers. Gustavus Adolphus ruled only about 1,500,000 people, but he successfully invaded the most populous area of Christendom. During his reign war became a successful business: he had an efficient conscription system, his army used revolutionary tactics involving the use of small firearms, and his country had an iron industry to produce artillery. These factors, in addition to heavy subsidies from Cardinal Richelieu of France and some from the Dutch, underlay his success in Germany.

The Swedish invasion of 1630 quickly turned the military situation about. In Saxony, near Leipzig, Gustavus Adolphus's forces met, and nearly annihilated, half of the imperial army under Tilly. Then he swung through the Church states along the Rhine and invaded Catholic Bavaria. To stop Gustavus the emperor restored Wallenstein and granted him extensive personal power. At Lützen (Saxony) in 1632 the Swedes defeated Wallenstein, but in the battle the "snow king" of Sweden was killed. Thereupon Bavaria was cleared of Swedish troops after the battle of Nördlingen in 1634; but Swedish troops remained on German soil for the remainder of the war. Meanwhile Wallenstein negotiated secretly with the Swedish and the French. For this Ferdinand deposed him and had him assassinated. The emperor then took charge of his own army and rapidly gained strength. Once again German Protestantism and the foreign policy of Richelieu, the cardinal architect of Bourbon French opposition to the Habsburgs, were in serious trouble.

Since 1624 Richelieu had been building up France's military and diplomatic power for the day that he could force a showdown with the Habsburgs. In 1635 that day arrived, whereupon he brought France directly into the Thirty Years' War. Central Europe continued to be the principal battleground, but the final phase of the war became a struggle between Habsburg and Bourbon for European hegemony.

The assassination of Henry IV had left France under the nine-year-old Louis XIII with Marie de' Medici as regent. Royal weakness was again the occasion for the nobles to reassert their powers and privileges. In 1614 they secured a summoning of the Estates General (it would be the last until 1789), but the Third Estate opposed the nobility and stalemated the meeting.

*Three of the many sides of Cardinal Richelieu—a triple portrait.*

Louis XIII did not prove to be a strong ruler, but he made up for his deficiencies by making Cardinal Richelieu first minister in 1624. Richelieu was a politique whose ruling passion was to build the authority of the French monarchy at home and extend French influence abroad. In 1626 he destroyed the fortresses of the great nobles and removed them from positions of command in his new navy. In the meantime the Huguenots, who made common cause with the aristocracy, rebelled. By 1628 they were crushed and their political and military rights withdrawn; they retained only religious toleration under the Edict of Nantes. Richelieu further subordinated France to royal authority by extending the power of the *intendants,* bureaucrats who came from the middle class: gradually they assimilated the judicial and financial functions that had once belonged to the aristocratic governors of the provinces. Richelieu followed a typical mercantilist policy in building a navy, expanding the army, founding trading companies and colonies, and allowing the increasing burden of taxes and services to be laid on the non-privileged classes. In addition, tax farmers abused their authority and kept about one-half of all the money collected. But Richelieu overlooked the need for reform in order to devote himself to immediate diplomatic and military tasks.

At first Richelieu believed that France was too weak to risk a direct assault on the Habsburgs and indeed French weakness was displayed both during the Huguenot revolt when Spain seized strategic Alpine passes, and again in 1635 when Spanish invaders nearly took Paris. Richelieu had had to content himself with aiding Protestant allies against the Habsburgs from 1624 to 1635. When France finally entered the war against the Habsburgs in 1635, however, his efforts to mobilize French resources soon began to pay dividends. While Gustavus Adolphus invaded Germany, French troops made major gains in Alsace. Richelieu died in 1642, but French strength continued to grow. In 1643, after the Dutch cut Spanish lines of communication with the Netherlands, French troops defeated the Spanish at Rocroi in the Spanish Netherlands, the first such victory over Spain in more than a century. Following victory at Rocroi so much of the Spanish Netherlands fell to France that the Dutch soon feared their French ally more than distant Spain.

In the German states and Bohemia the effect of active French participation in the Thirty Years' War was to prolong the war devastation for 13 more years.

## The Outcome of the War in Central Europe

As Gustavus Adolphus had noted, the wars of Europe had all been rolled into one. Complexities of the war were so great that they baffled negotiators, who brought it to an end in the Peace of Westphalia in 1648. Peace in Germany was impossible until the two major outside belligerents, France and Spain, were weakened by exhaustion and revolution, nor could Germans unite to expel foreign invaders, for Protestants needed foreign troops to protect themselves against Catholics; and

the princes needed them to maintain their "liberties" against the emperor. Since the papacy could not sanction concessions to heretical Protestants, the negotiators could not all meet at the same place. Protestants met at Osnabrück, Catholics at Münster. This separation, as well as slow communications between Westphalia and distant Spain, slowed the pace of the talks. Westphalia was the first general peace conference in history, and for it there was no body of accepted rules by which precedence and rank could be determined. Such was only one of the difficulties. Not until the alliance system broke down could meaningful talks get under way. This finally happened when Dutch fears of French expansion led to a separate peace between the United Provinces and Spain. By then both France and Spain, torn by internal revolution, were anxious to reduce their foreign commitments.

A compromise on the question of Church property and official recognition of Calvinism resolved the religious wars in Germany. Princes continued to maintain religious uniformity in their territories, but individual Lutheran, Catholic, or Calvinist dissenters were given certain rights to worship privately and to emigrate. After the Peace of Westphalia few princes changed the religion of their states; religious boundaries hardened into a pattern little disturbed until the mass migration of Germans after 1945. France and Sweden made sure that the German princes obtained almost complete sovereignty. Although the princes were not to make war on the emperor, France and other powers promptly began to organize leagues of German princes to challenge the emperor under the pretext of preserving German liberties.

Sweden, France, and France's protegé, Brandenburg, all left Westphalia with substantial territorial gains. France retained the Alsatian bishoprics of Metz, Toul, and Verdun as well as sovereign but vaguely

*North Sea*

UNITED NETHERLANDS

BREMEN *To Sweden*

VERDEN

• Hamburg

HITHER POMERANIA *To Sweden*

FARTHER POMERANIA

• Stettin

*Vistula R.*

BRANDENBURG

MAGDEBURG

KINGDOM OF POLAND

Osnabrück •

MINDEN

• Münster

WESTPHALIA *Weser R.*

HALBERSTADT

Breitenfeld

LUSATIA

• Cologne

Lützen

• Leipzig

SAXONY *Elbe R.*

SILESIA

*Oder R.*

SPANISH NETHERLANDS

White Mountain • Prague

BOHEMIA

MORAVIA

RANCE

Rocroi

PALATINATE

UPPER PALATINATE

• Paris

VERDUN

METZ

*To France*

TOUL

Nördlingen

• Donauworth

BAVARIA

AUSTRIA *Danube R.*

KINGDOM OF HUNGARY

Breisach

*Rhine R.*

Spanish

• Vienna

FRANCHE COMTÉ (Spanish)

SWITZERLAND
*(Independent of the Empire, 1648)*

TYROL

STYRIA

CARNIOLA

OTTOMAN EMPIRE

Church lands

Habsburg lands

Wettin lands

Hohenzollern lands

Wittelsbach lands

Holy Roman Empire

Land ceded by Westphalia

VENETIAN REPUBLIC

*Adriatic Sea*

0   50   100 mi

Map by J. Donovan

defined authority over all of Alsace. Sweden received Western (Hither) Pomerania and territory (towns, bishoprics, or islands) near the mouth of every major river flowing from the empire into the Baltic; these were remunerative toll stations. In their capacities as German princes, the rulers of both France and Sweden became members of the Imperial Diet. With French support the Hohenzollerns of Brandenburg increased their scattered holdings, gaining Eastern Pomerania, the bishoprics of Minden, Halberstadt, and Cammin, and inheritance rights to Magdeburg. The peace also recognized the independence of Switzerland and the United Provinces (the Dutch Republic).

Westphalia began the final breakup of the Holy Roman Empire and sealed the decline of the papacy as a force in international affairs. Although modified by subsequent treaties, it laid the foundation of the European state system that prevailed until the days of the French Revolution. Nationalists would eventually lament the fact that Westphalia divided Germany, but at its inception the treaty was generally hailed as a diplomatic success and a keystone of European order and peace.

This settlement implied that states, no matter how they differed in might, were—at least in theory—equal members of a community of sovereign states. The medieval ideal of universal rule by pope and emperor thus gave way to a new order.

After hostilities were ended central Europe faced an immense task of reconstruction. Although we do not have accurate statistics, the empire as a whole probably lost one third of its population. Some areas in Saxony were barely touched; others, like Henneberg along the Main River, may have lost four-fifths of their people. Depopulation on this scale resulted not so much from military losses as from the plagues that swiftly followed armies and swept through the towns where civilians sought refuge from marauding troops. Under normal conditions human beings are generally able to recover from such losses within a generation, but conditions in postwar Germany were severely abnormal.

German nationalists later exaggerated the destructive effects of the war; but of the serious agrarian crisis that followed in its wake there can be no doubt. Shortages of money and labor led ruling aristocrats to force harsh servitude on lower-class youth and to appropriate much peasant land. Peasants were enserfed at a particularly rapid rate east of the Elbe, where fighting continued for some time. But the shrunken supply of money and workers does not alone account for Germany's failure to recover from the war: central Europe also lost its commercial initiative to the west, largely because its small individual states followed restrictive, protectionist policies of mercantilism. The petty German princelings, desperate for local self-sufficiency and revenues, put so many barriers in the way of commerce that continental trade became extremely difficult. Economically, Germany grew more parochial and sluggish than it had been in the Middle Ages.

## War, Revolution, and Defeat in Habsburg Spain

The Thirty Years' War fatally drained the ebbing resources of the Spanish Habsburgs. And the Peace of Westphalia left Spain to fight alone against France in a war that would last for 11 more years.

At the Habsburg helm during the critical years 1621 to 1643 was the favorite of Philip IV, the Count of Olivares. His career and policies—save for their notable lack of success—ran strikingly parallel to those of Richelieu. Trained for the Church, Olivares became the most powerful minister in Spanish history. He began his career as a reformer, setting out to force officials to disgorge the fortunes that they had embezzled, curb the power of the Church, abolish taxes on necessities, and reduce the size and costs of the court. But the status quo put up too strong a resistance, and as a consequence he was able to accomplish little. Moreover he became an advocate of an aggressive foreign policy, and the war he favored forced him to double the very excises he considered ruinous to Castile.

Bled by the costs of defense and aggression, Castile faced imminent exhaustion of men and money. To save it and to distribute the financial burdens among other parts of the empire, Olivares sought to bring all the Iberian kingdoms under one law and to establish a common army. But the other kingdoms were too firmly wed to their own constitutions, administrations, and privileges to concur in these changes; in their provinces local *cortes* controlled finance, and troops could not be recruited for use outside their own borders. In 1626 Catalonia, Aragon, and Valencia rejected the common army. Valencia and Aragon voted money, but Catalonia, strategically situated on the French frontier, cited past violations of local laws by Castilian viceroys and refused to grant either men or money. Portugal, whose colony of Brazil was being defended by Philip against the Dutch, was no more cooperative.

The rejection by the other kingdoms of "Castilianization" forced Olivares to fall back on the inadequate resources of Castile. He resorted to radical manipulations of the coinage, stamp duties, sales of offices and titles, revival of old feudal obligations of the nobility, and confiscations of dwindling silver shipments from America. None of these exactions averted defeat: in 1638 the fall of Breisach cut land communications with the Spanish Netherlands, and in the following year, in a battle off the English coast, the Dutch destroyed much of the Spanish fleet and blocked Spain's sea communications with the Netherlands. In addition, Castile's colonial trade was faltering. And in 1640 the old foundations of empire gave way.

The first blow was the revolt of Catalonia, which was trapped in a general Mediterranean depression and prodded by tax demands by Olivares at the same time; Castilian exactions after 1637 for the defense of Catalonia against French invasion had offended all social classes. In 1640 revolutionaries killed the Castilian viceroy, proclaimed a republic, and solicited French assistance. Although the revolution lacked unity of purpose and leadership, Castile was unable to suppress it until 1652. When Olivares called on Portugal for assistance against Catalonia in 1640, the Portuguese nobility proclaimed the duke of Braganza king and initiated their own war for independence which, with French and English aid, they eventually secured. Olivares sought to make peace with France and the Netherlands as a way out of his difficulties, but they spurned his offers.

Confronted with two simultaneous revolutions, gyrating prices, and a flagging war effort, Philip IV (1621–65) dismissed Olivares in 1643 and took personal charge of the government. Crisis followed on crisis. In 1647 new revolts against the policies of Castilian viceroys broke out in Sicily and Naples; in that same year—and again in 1653—the treasury, unable to meet its obligations by any expedient, was forced into bankruptcy.

The most remarkable outcome of these crises was that the Habsburg dynasty survived them all. The Habsburgs' greatest asset was that their foes, foreign and internal, were at odds among themselves. In 1647 the United Provinces broke with France (a break largely manipulated by Spain); and at about the same time Catalonia also stopped taking aid from the French, feeling that its autonomy was more threatened by them than by the powers in Madrid. Rebellious forces in Iberia and Italy never broke out of their isolation to cooperate with one another for mutual gains, and class conflicts within the revolutionary ranks proved ultimately irresolvable. The rebel aristocrats were so frightened by the social and political radicalism of their commoner brethren that when Philip IV offered to restore their old privileges, they eagerly cooperated with him. One by one the isolated revolutions collapsed, except in Portugal. The house of Habsburg had survived by appealing to the traditionalism of the nobility; but such reverence for tradition also prevented reform, and the monarchy still tottered on the verge of financial collapse. Probably only a fourth of the tax moneys collected actually reached the treasury. The Peace of the Pyrenees with France (1659) came barely in time to save Philip IV from total insolvency.

Spain accepted the Pyrenees as a boundary, and thus abandoned Roussillon and part of Cerdagne to France; in the Low Countries it ceded Artois. The marriage of Maria Theresa of Spain to Louis XIV sealed the treaty—until the Habsburgs failed to pay her dowry and thus gave Louis an excuse to claim other Spanish lands. From that time onward Spain's role in Europe was limited to defensive efforts against Louis XIV's ex-

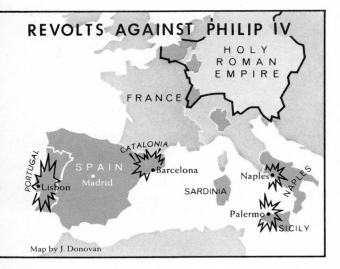

REVOLTS AGAINST PHILIP IV

Map by J. Donovan

deceased, he has changed his age" was very apt.

But unlike Richelieu, Mazarin had no mature king to rely on. He compensated for this somewhat by becoming the queen mother's lover, but her support could not mitigate his widespread unpopularity: the French nobility and upper classes hated him. Not only was he a foreigner building a private fortune at state expense, but also he refused to recognize the aristocracy as tax exempt. Hostile satires (*Mazarinades*) began to circulate, especially when he bestowed state favors on his own family. What popularity he did enjoy derived mainly from his military feats, but even these proved self-defeating. His war policy—which was designed to conquer the whole of the Spanish Netherlands—only caused the Dutch to break with France. And when domestic revolts further strained his control, Mazarin was forced to accept the more moderate gains of the Peace of Westphalia.

In 1648 disaffected jurists of the Parlement (high law court) of Paris and members of royal councils initiated a revolution (the *Fronde*) against Mazarin. Borrowing from arguments used by the English parliamentarians against the Stuarts, the Fronde was a revolt against the whole financial-administrative system of Richelieu and Mazarin. Taxes were to be levied only with the consent of the high law court, extortions by tax farmers were to be investigated, and the land tax was to be reduced and levied solely for purposes of war. The *Frondeurs* also demanded abolition of the office of intendant, approval by the Parlement of all new offices created, and no imprisonment without trial for more than 24 hours. Although these demands might have held great appeal for the masses, the motives behind them were suspect. The leaders of the Fronde were primarily concerned with protecting ennobled officeholders from taxation and with freeing them from the supervision of administrative officials; but such aims

pansionist policies. Spanish predominance had been superseded by French hegemony.

## Mazarin, Revolution, and Peace in France

A major reason why France agreed to peace in 1648 and why Spain was able to hold out successfully so long alone against France was that France, too, was weakened by a revolution that had Spanish diplomatic support.

Both Louis XIII and his chief minister, Richelieu, died before the end of the Thirty Years' War (Richelieu in 1642, Louis in 1643); but French policy changed little. The new king, Louis XIV, was only five years old and the state was controlled by his first minister, Cardinal Mazarin. Handpicked by Richelieu as his successor, the Italian-born Mazarin was a Jesuit-educated international adventurer serving his apprenticeship in war and diplomacy under the papacy when Richelieu noticed him, took him into the French court, and secured for him a cardinal's hat. Mazarin's policies followed Richelieu's so closely that the epigram "the cardinal is not

were too narrow to sustain an effective revolt. The Frondeurs were thus unable to constitute themselves as a representative legislative assembly, and Mazarin undermined them with temporizing concessions and dissimulating intrigues. After a major victory in Artois (1648) he stormed Paris with veteran troops, and in 1649 stubborn resistance in the capital collapsed.

Mazarin's victory satisfied neither nobility nor populace, however. A new revolution, the Nobles' Fronde, broke out in 1649. Supported by Spain, it was aimed simply at overturning Mazarin. But Mazarin overturned it instead. By 1653 his foreign mercenaries had defeated the nobles, whereupon he renounced all his previous concessions to them and set about in earnest to realize the ambitions of Louis XIV to rule absolutely.

Before Mazarin died, in 1661, he negotiated the Peace of the Pyrenees and, by aligning German princes along the Rhine with French foreign policy, laid the groundwork for future French expansion. He also left Louis XIV the corps of officials who made the French monarchy a model of dynastic absolutism. An outstandingly efficient bureaucracy in the service of the crown was one legacy of the seventeenth-century crisis in France.

## Crisis in Eastern Europe

The Swedish invasion of Germany from 1630 to 1648 was only one part of a larger and longer eastern power struggle, mainly instigated by Sweden's imperial ambitions, which was a contest for control of the territories adjoining the Baltic Sea. Between 1655 and 1660 all of Europe was concerned about its outcome. Sweden's rise to power in Europe was impressive, but she did not maintain for very long her role as a leading state. Gustavus Adolphus, until he invaded Germany in 1630, was fighting for the throne of Poland

SWEDEN'S BALTIC EMPIRE

Sweden 1523-1560
Gustavus' Sons 1560-1611
Gustavus II 1611-1632
Christina 1632-1654
Charles X 1654-1660

0    100    200    300 mi.
Map by J. Donovan

and the Baltic Sea coast. While Sweden was engaged in Germany, Russia tried and failed to conquer the Smolensk area from Poland and in 1634 renounced all claims to the Baltic littoral. After Westphalia, Sweden had bases in Germany (Pomerania was an especially vital one) from which to launch new assaults on Poland across Hohenzollern East Prussia.

The first link in the chain of events leading to general war in 1655 was a revolt of seminomadic Cossacks in the Ukraine against their Catholic Polish overlords in 1648. Defeated by Poland, the Cossacks sought Russian protection in 1653. Soon the Ukraine became part of the czars' empire. With the Cossack war chieftains on his side, the Romanov czar, Alexis (1645–1676), renewed war with Poland, captured Smolensk, and proceeded to invade Lithuania. Sweden resisted Russia's push to the Baltic and, taking advantage of

Poland's involvement in the east, invaded that country.

The Northern War (1655–60) soon involved most of Europe. At first the Swedish invasion of Poland was immensely successful. Soon, however, the Poles were antagonized by the invaders' aggressive Protestantism and their capacity for cruelty. Brandenburg, caught between Poland and Sweden, was obliged to become a Swedish ally in 1656. When Denmark entered the war against Sweden, Brandenburg, supported by the emperor, secretly switched sides in return for a promise of sovereignty over East Prussia, which the elector of Brandenburg had held previously as a fief of Poland. In order further to check Sweden, the emperor allied with Poland. Then Mazarin, who was locked in a diplomatic battle with the emperor, prompted the western maritime states—England and the United Provinces—to intervene also. Wanting to establish a balance of power in the northeast, Mazarin secured an international peace conference at Oliva, near Danzig. By the Treaty of Oliva (1660) Sweden lost her wartime conquests with the exception of Livonia (now part of Latvia and Estonia), and the Baltic was opened to the ships of all states.

The peace terms of Oliva proved transitory, but the Northern War left lasting marks on the societies of the Baltic states. Like the Thirty Years' War, it provoked an agrarian crisis that helped to rivet the status of serfdom onto the peasants of east-central Europe; it also cleared new ground in which authoritarianism could take root. The principality of Brandenburg, for example, was so dismayed at its vulnerability to foreign invaders that Frederick William "the Great Elector" had little trouble building a standing army and instituting a military despotism there. The outstanding exception to the despotic social order that took root in the wake of these wars was Sweden, but it, too, passed through a revolutionary crisis after the Thirty Years' War. Gustavus Adolphus's successor, the erratic Queen Christina,

ceded a major portion of the royal domain to the nobility and created a horde of new nobles who claimed state office as an aristocratic privilege. Meanwhile the nobles sought powers commensurate with the German and Polish lords with whom they had made contact in Sweden's new acquisitions along the Baltic. In 1650 a social-constitutional crisis rocked Sweden. Unlike peasants and townsmen in Poland and Germany, the Swedish commoner had well-established legal rights and sent representatives to a diet that possessed considerable vitality. The nobles made impressive gains in power, but the lower orders in the diet—in coalition with lower-ranking officials—were able to check them. In this respect, Swedish social and constitutional development resembled that of England more than the rest of the Continent.

## STUART ENGLAND

By and large, England remained aloof from the struggles on the Continent, but it had its own religious revolution, its own civil wars. As on the Continent, the major source of those conflicts was the growth of a revolutionary Calvinist movement that championed the rights of Parliament and the courts against the absolutist claims of the monarchy.

### Stuart Kings and Parliaments

The aspirations of James I were probably no more despotic than those of Elizabeth, but his insistence on proclaiming the principle of divine-right kingship quickly brought him into conflict with Parliament and the common-law courts. Elizabeth had always managed the House of Commons very diplomatically, but James departed from this policy and asserted that its members owed him obedience as a matter of right and principle—

an obedience that he claimed from all his subjects. Parliament was not amenable to this approach and was particularly recalcitrant in meeting the king's demands for taxes to cover the mounting expenses of the state. In order to raise money, therefore, James was forced back on other expedients: he sold titles and honors wholesale to wealthy men desirous of buying prestige, liquidated large portions of the royal domain, and established and sold monopolies in consumer items. None of these schemes satisfied the financial needs of the state, and all of them detracted from royal prestige and weakened the power of the Crown. The massive sale of titles cheapened the status of men who already had them and weakened their attachment to the Crown. To sell lands from the royal domain was bad economic policy; it meant that the king was living on his capital and transferring his economic power to his wealthier subjects. The monopolies antagonized merchants who were excluded from them and alienated the ordinary consumers who had to pay higher prices. And Parliament was hostile to measures that were designed to circumvent parliamentary control over finance; the Parliament that met in 1614 persisted in discussing constitutional issues rather than voting supplies, and it finally provoked James to dissolve it.

Between 1611 and 1621 James called Parliament only once—in 1614. But a serious depression in the cloth trade from 1620 to 1624 so strained the already flagging royal revenues that James was forced in 1624 to seek new grants of taxes. The House of Commons not only failed to comply, but reasserted some of its ancient prerogatives. In that same year Parliament attacked trading company monopolies, which many independent merchants held responsible for the depression. Now Parliament was no longer staging a defensive struggle against the king; it was claiming the right to initiate legislation and to appoint committees to supervise the execution of the laws it enacted. Although the concept of the modern legislative assembly was yet only dimly perceived, Parliament was gradually assuming the character of a legislature that could call on some degree of popular support. But just as on the Continent in the seventeenth century—where diets defended only the privileges of the aristocracy—so in England at that time popular support meant mostly support from the wealthier classes of society. In the face of his rebellious legislature James I denounced men who presumed "to meddle with anything concerning our government mysteries of state," and at one point he even arrested the leaders of the House of Commons. Nevertheless, he did make some concessions to Parliament.

Although the reign of his successor, Charles I, would end at the executioner's block, it appeared to open auspiciously. As a young prince Charles had opposed his father's pro-Spanish foreign policy, an attitude that gained him considerable popularity. But once on the throne, he soon came into conflict with the same institutions and doctrines that had confronted James. When Charles requested money, Parliament proceeded to proclaim its rights anew and to attack his favorite minister. In his desperate search for new forms of revenue, the king exacted forced loans from his subjects and revived archaic feudal dues. In 1628 Parliament firmly responded with the Petition of Right, a landmark in the history of constitutional government. It declared that no taxation should be levied without parliamentary consent, that no troops should be billeted in private homes, that martial law should not be imposed in peacetime, and that no man should be imprisoned without the cause being shown. As it reaffirmed personal liberty, attacked royal control over a standing army, and claimed the right of Parliament to approve taxation, the Petition of Right significantly challenged the fundamental bases of royal absolutism.

The struggle against the king had religious as well as political roots. English Calvinists had produced a talented and articulate group of propagandists who used the press and pulpit to fullest advantage. The increasing strength of Puritanism was further reflected in the membership of the House of Commons. Puritanism was a social doctrine as well as a religious creed: it established an aristocracy of the predestined elect—"the Godly people"—who were known by their moral code and their religious devotion. Puritan doctrines placed a high premium on individual thought and action and set commitments derived from personal experience above rulings handed down from church hierarchies, and moral responsibility counted for more than formal religious observance. In rituals and traditions of priestly privilege—whether Roman Catholic or Anglican—Puritans saw the embodiment of the devil and superstitious idolatry. They identified their enemies as God's enemies, deserving bitter invective, persecution and, ultimately, death. They were doing God's work and it was his will that they reach their goal. They did not conspire—as Royalists later accused them of doing—to create a revolution. But as they tried to achieve the reforms dictated by their consciences, they followed a course that led, gradually but inexorably, to the overthrow of the monarchy. Certainly James I had never shown a readiness to conciliate them. "If you aim at a Scottish presbytery," he said to them, "it agreeth as well with monarchy as God with the devil." But although harsh measures were taken against the more Puritan clergy and against Separatists, who wanted to break away from the official church, James interfered very little with the religious lives of his subjects. Charles I, however, yielding to Archbishop William Laud, followed quite another policy. By 1629, Laud, whose beliefs seemed to border on Catholicism, had gained substantial influence in Charles's court. He began, through the ecclesiastical court of High Commission (a Tudor creation), to restrict and penalize Puritan practices. After 1630 it seemed all too apparent to Puritans that royal policy offered them only the choices of emigration, conformity, or struggle. Some did emigrate; but eventually most of them took to arms.

In 1629, when the House of Commons disobeyed Charles's command and discussed religious issues, the king locked the chamber and arrested eight of its leaders. Charles then ruled without Parliament from 1629 to 1641, but the conflict did not abate. The Puritans were eager for the king to intervene in the continental religious struggle, but Charles's financial difficulties dictated caution. He was forced to follow a weak and very unpopular foreign policy. At the same time, the laws against Catholics were only casually enforced, which infuriated Puritans who were themselves under legal pressure to conform. But it was the king's attempt to institute an Anglican prayer book and establish an episcopal hierarchy in his Calvinist kingdom of Scotland that finally brought an end to his financial independence of Parliament. The Scottish Presbyterians rose and invaded England in 1640, and Charles was forced to summon a new Parliament. Many Puritans were returned as members, and the body (which has come to be called the Short Parliament) proved so obstreperous that the king hastily dissolved it. Continued pressure from Scotland, however, forced him to call another a few months later. The first session of this "Long Parliament" lasted almost a year, a period of unmatched significance in English legislative history.

Although members of the Long Parliament claimed that the measures they were enacting were merely restoring the old fundamental laws of England, the Long Parliament stripped the king of some of his traditional powers, and some of its enactments did represent constitutional innovations. Charles was forced to assent to an act that authorized Parliament to meet once every three years whether or not summoned by the Crown (the Triennial Act). He was also made to abolish such unpopular prerogative courts as High Commission and Star Chamber and to eliminate all feudal revenue measures. His two closest ministers, Strafford and Archbishop Laud, were impeached; a parliamentary statute was passed demanding Strafford's execution, and the King assented to it. Despite all his concessions, a majority of the members of the House of Commons did not trust Charles with control of the army. The situation came to a head in October 1641 when there was a revolt in Ireland. Parliament voted—by a narrow majority—to assume command of the militia, an act that precipitated civil war, the first that England had known since the Wars of the Roses in the fifteenth century and her last to date.

## The Civil Wars

In every English county there was a contest for loyalty between the king and the revolutionary parliamentarians. Opposing armed camps of Roundheads (parliamentarians) and Cavaliers (royalists) were slowly and reluctantly formed, and war preparations were interspersed with negotiations. While parliamentary and royalist agents jockeyed for control of arms and men, some counties tried to remain neutral. Alliances shifted. Some parliamentarians who had previously opposed the king and voted against him joined Charles now that the choice was between revolution and loyalty to the Crown. The first campaigns of the civil war were half-hearted and inconclusive. Until 1642 the conflict was confined to the members of the ruling aristocracy who feuded among themselves, but once the conflict developed into full-scale hostility, the door was opened to the more radical Puritan minorities to take control of the parliamentary movement and armies.

Heretofore religious opposition to the royalist Cavaliers had been led by Presby-

terians who wanted to abolish the bishops replacing them with a synodal type of Calvinist government of the Scottish variety. Their opposition to the crown was not unanimous or zealous, for most of them were prepared to support the king provided that he introduced the church reforms that they desired. The radical Puritans, however, would go much further. Paramount among these were the so-called Independents (Separatists or Congregationalists) who demanded autonomy for their religious congregations and advocated toleration of at least other Puritan sects. These aims could only be achieved by defeating both the king and the conservative Presbyterians. As the Independent Oliver Cromwell emerged as the leader of the radical Puritans, the civil war began in earnest.

Ever since the seventeenth century men have offered various explanations of the civil wars, and historians still argue about how and why loyalties were divided into warring factions. Royalists attributed the wars to a Puritan conspiracy directed against the rich and the well born. Thomas Hobbes, the political philosopher who formulated a theory of secular absolutism, laid the Puritan revolution that caused the civil wars at the feet of men of the universities and the pulpits whom we would nowadays characterize as "alienated intellectuals." In the nineteenth century historians were dedicated to a "Whig interpretation" whose heroes were the Puritans and parliamentarians. They presented the Roundheads as crusaders who successfully defended the constitutional liberty of Englishmen against Stuart despotism at the same time that they established the foundations for English commercial and imperial power. Recent interpretations of the English civil wars, however, have looked to social factors in an attempt to explain political alignment. No longer are the parliamentarians and the Stuart kings seen solely in terms of black and white. Some historians believe that Stuart social policy was socially useful and that the men who opposed the Stuart kings in Parliament were primarily defending their own class and economic interests. For Marxists, the English civil war represents one stage in the development of capitalism, the "bourgeois revolution," or the phenomenon by which an emerging capitalism frees itself of feudal restraints.

Because in England the ownership of land was the foundation on which all social prestige and, hence, political power was based, the role of the gentry in the upheavals of seventeenth-century England has been subject to intense scrutiny. The term "gentry" itself, although essential, is often misleading, and historians have not been able to agree among themselves what sort of men the term should include. It is not surprising therefore that the role of the gentry should have engendered fierce controversy. One school has held that the gentry as a class was growing rich because its members applied business techniques to farming; they were engaging in a form of capitalist agriculture and—at the expense of a declining nobility—were accumulating land and the political power that went with it. This interpretation has it that the revolutionary civil wars were caused to a large extent by these members of the rising gentry, who were eager to grasp and exercise social and political power commensurate with their economic wealth. Other historians, however, have come to completely opposite conclusions. They believe that the civil wars were brought about by the efforts of a gentry whose fortunes were declining, and they maintain that the radical Independents of the revolution were the men who, because they were in fact losing their lands, turned in desperation against the Stuart kings. Still other historians are convinced by solid evidence that the gentry maintained its status quo and preserved a relatively comfortable position in society, but that great fortunes were made by lawyers, merchants, and courtiers who naturally invested their money in land. This academic battle, which has been de-scribed as a "storm over the gentry,"[3] is not likely to abate, for our knowledge of early seventeenth-century economic history is too meager to be conclusive. One thing, however, is certain: every major faction of the revolution drew its leadership from men of the gentry. How then can we say which factors determined an individual's loyalty? Whether a man chose the side of the king or of Parliament, his decision was probably influenced by his religious feelings and his connections—or lack of connections—at court.

Owing to the structure of economic life in early seventeenth-century England, men who had friends at court were likely to prosper from favors. It was only natural, therefore, that merchants and members of the gentry who had no or only weak court connections blamed their economic difficulties on the court, on the monopolies, and finally on the Crown itself. Small producers, who were suffering from a slump in the export trade of woolen goods, voiced the same kinds of complaint; also, tradesmen in the towns were exposed to radical religion and participated to a marked degree in the Puritan movement.

Religious affiliation was also crucial in defining loyalties, for in the past only Anglicans stood to prosper from court connections and favors. Since the established episcopal church was the main agent of social control, conflict raged over what structure the English church would assume. Should the church be dominated by bishops appointed by the king, should it be organized on the basis of presbyteries under the control of men of substance, or—the most radical suggestion of all—should it consist of independent democratic congregations? These were questions that aroused religious dispute; they also stirred up social conflict. Men of wealth feared that the demands of the lower classes for religious equality were only a prelude to demands for political,

[3] J. H. Hexter, *Reappraisals in History* (New York: Harper & Row, Publishers, 1961), pp. 117–62.

and eventually economic, equality. Nor were these forebodings completely unjustified.

When Oliver Cromwell took command of what would become the nucleus of the national army—the "New Model"—he picked his men for their fighting zeal, a quality that apparently went hand in glove with radical religious views. Under Cromwell and his men the war became an enthusiastic crusade to defeat "papist" royalists and secure toleration for sectarian Puritans. Cromwell's army, "Ironsides," backed by the resources of the wealthier southeastern part of England (now taxed by excises never conceded to Stuart kings), destroyed the main Cavalier army at the decisive battle of Naseby in 1645. The Royalist cause was crushed and Charles I surrendered to the Scots, who delivered him as a prisoner to the parliamentarians.

Once the king was defeated the Puritans in Parliament set about the religious and political reconstruction of the nation, a task that was at once complicated by the sharp disputes that arose between conser-

**ENGLISH CIVIL WARS**

Districts controlled by Parliament (1642)

Districts controlled by King Charles (1642)

Map by J. Donovan

vative Presbyterians and more radical Independents. The Independents drew their support from the victorious army whose members were every day growing more vociferous in their demands. Parliament sought to disband the army, leaving the soldiers' pay in arrears. Led by Cromwell, the army seized power in 1647. It looked as though Presbyterian intolerance had been defeated, but the army itself was divided between the Independents (represented by Cromwell) and more radical sectarians who demanded reforms much more democratic than any Cromwell and his associates envisaged.

The relative freedom of thought and expression permitted under the earlier Cromwellian government was fully exploited by political and social reformers. After 1643 debate became fiercer, and in the years that followed thousands of pamphlets appeared. The Independents soon found themselves challenged by a sectarian movement that was growing more and more radical. One of the most extreme radical sects—the Diggers—claimed the right of every man to use the common lands of England, and they attempted to

*Oliver Cromwell, a contemporary portrait.*

found a communal society. Another sect, known as the Fifth Monarchy Men, believed that the final day of judgment was at hand. A larger, less radical, and more significant group was the Levellers—a name given them by their opponents, who feared that the extension of the franchise they advocated (by no means universal manhood suffrage) would lead to an assault on property rights and the ultimate leveling of all social distinctions. Twentieth-century historians have paid considerable attention to the Levellers, who are often cited—with much justification—as representing the first modern democratic political movement. The Levellers based their political programs on the doctrine of natural rights. They demanded legal equality, a written constitution, annual parliaments, a single-chamber legislature, separation of church and state, the abolition of tithes and excise taxes, and intensive reform of common law that among other things would do away with imprisonment for debt, arbitrary imprisonment, and compulsory self-incrimination. The Levellers were a small minority, and even within the army they had no real opportunity of achieving their objectives. Although Cromwell and his Independents were willing to assent to part of this program, they saw in the most advanced of the Levellers' ideas a threat to public order and an attack on the rights of property. Cromwell finally turned against them and the Leveller leader, John Lilburne, acknowledged political defeat when he joined the Quakers. The Quakers, who were not originally pacifists, were another group that had appeared during the civil war to "reform the Reformation." Later they adopted the technique of nonviolence to achieve humanitarian reform. None of the more radical groups was sufficiently organized or powerful to influence the course of events.

Rather it was Cromwell's army that took the lead in crushing the resurgence of royalism that culminated in the second civil war (1648). Fearful of army radical-ism, Presbyterian parliamentarians in 1647 offered to restore Charles I in return for a temporary establishment of a Presbyterian church. The army forestalled this alliance by taking custody over the king, but he escaped and negotiated a treaty with the Scots recognizing Presbyterianism. As the Scots invaded England, royalists and some Presbyterians rallied to the royalist cause. Under Cromwell's leadership the army united against the counterrevolutionary coalition decisively defeating the Scots at Preston in 1648. Thereafter the army purged Parliament of its Presbyterian members, leaving it—the "Rump"—with only members who supported the army. One of the Rump's first actions was to try Charles Stuart for treason; in 1649 he was executed under conditions that made him a popular martyr of the royalist cause.

## The Commonwealth and the Protectorate

The Rump promptly abolished the monarchy and the House of Lords, proclaiming the sovereignty of the people represented solely by the commons. This action inaugurated the Commonwealth, an experiment in republican government, but the real power of the state was in the hands of the parliamentary commander, Oliver Cromwell, who accepted his victories as evidence that he was now the chosen instrument by which England would become a truly "Godly" society. (That England was also becoming a Protestant imperial power seemed equally a part of divine providence.) Before the end of 1649 Cromwell began the suppression of Ireland, where a royalist-Catholic faction was strong, with calculated military terror, and in 1650 he put down Scottish royalist opposition with his stunning victory at Dunbar. Both Scotland and Ireland were united with England. Under the Commonwealth the Navigation Act of 1651, designed to remove the Dutch from the English carrying trade, was passed, and England conducted a naval war against the Dutch Republic.

But despite his foreign and military successes, Cromwell failed to unify England behind him. When the Rump refused to disband, Cromwell cleared the house with troops, declaring Parliament dissolved. It was replaced by a parliament picked by the council of the army from nominations submitted by Independent congregations. The inexperience and radicalism of this "Barebones Parliament," which set out to disestablish the existing tithe-supported church and made marriage a civil contract, so disappointed Cromwell and his fellow officers that they drew up a new constitution for England, the Instrument of Government of 1653.

The Instrument of Government (England's last written constitution) represents an effort to separate and balance the central powers of government. Thus it did not terminate the tension between the executive and Parliament which England had experienced under the Stuarts. Cromwell rejected the crown for himself, preferring to take the title of Protector, but like the Stuarts whose mantle he spurned he dismissed Parliament for its encroachments on executive powers. The army began again to determine what elected members were eligible to sit, and soon a new house of lords was created to counterbalance the commons' power.

By 1655 real power was lodged in the hands of major generals in command of eleven military districts into which the country was divided, but even with military rule Cromwell was never able to force Englishmen to accept toleration and Puritanism. Instead there was a strong reaction in favor of restoring the son of the martyred Charles I. Cromwell died in 1658 leaving his son Richard as his designated successor, but Richard was completely ineffectual. Control over the army fell to General George Monck who reestablished the Long Parliament of 1640, returning to it those expelled Presbyterians who were still alive. Under his direction the Crown was restored to Charles II. Although a Stuart was once again on the throne, the Crown was stripped of extraordinary prerogative courts, extraparliamentary powers of raising revenue, feudal rights, and rule by royal edict. These were the positive constitutional gains produced by the revolutionary epoch that closed in 1660.

England under Cromwell had experimented with a variety of constitutional systems, but even military rule under a republic did not expunge traditional monarchist sentiment. The failure of the army also meant the failure of Puritanism. As a spiritual force Puritanism continued to survive in England, but, as in the Netherlands, Puritans did not succeed in imposing their political will on the nation. Under the restored Stuarts the Puritans were effectively excluded from political life. Never again would they attempt to overthrow the government in hope of achieving their aims; never again would England know religious fanaticism so strong or pass through a crisis so deep that it would result in civil war.

## D. The Art and Literature of Crisis

### THE AGE OF THE BAROQUE

In a climate of conflict the Renaissance ideals of art and literature were unable to flourish. Humanists and artists of the Italian Renaissance had emulated a classical tradition, aiming at perfect form and style, proportion, naturalism, tempered emotion, and decorous serenity. Italians continued to maintain their artistic and literary preeminence while their own states fell to despots and foreign invaders and while religious controversies set the rest of Europe ablaze. But the model of classical simplicity was supplanted by the colossal grandeur, metaphysical allegory, and emotional subjectivity we characterize as baroque. Traditional classicism and naturalism retained a hold in Venice and spread, except where they were banned by Puritan sentiments, through the mercantile states of northwestern Europe.

Baroque became a pejorative term, connoting extremely ornate and gaudy works. Baroque artists retained classical themes, but adapted them to portray power, spirit, suffering, emotion, and sensuality, the measure of individuality in this kind of art being the extent to which its creator had pressed the rules of classicism. To view most Renaissance works with maximum effect, the eye rests on definite planes and within fixed boundaries. But the baroque characteristically required a visual sweep which knew no bounds and suggested something beyond. In both art and literature baroque artists revived the use of allegory and metaphysical symbolism that had been dominant in the Middle Ages and subdued by the classical realism of the early Italian Renaissance.

Baroque art was a product of the militant Catholic Reformation. It first appeared in Italy, from which base missionaries and armed forces were operating to reinstitute the Catholic faith in Europe. Italian-trained artists went to capitals as far apart as London and Moscow, but they were not always warmly welcomed; populations whose main concern was commerce were unresponsive. Anglicans, German Lutherans, and followers of the Russian Orthodox faith could disregard doctrinal content and yet be moved by the emotional religious quality of the baroque style. But Calvinists were often distinctly hostile. Outside Italy the baroque had its greatest appeal in Habsburg Europe; there Crown, nobility, and Church exploited it to celebrate victories, exalt noble families, and satisfy the emotional hunger of a people beset by war, famine, epidemics, and oppression by a rigid social hierarchy. Baroque art flourished in Spain, Portugal, southern Germany, Flanders, Bohemia, Hungary, Poland, and, to a lesser extent, France. The Iberian kingdoms carried it to their American colonies, where some of its most exotic expressions can still be found today.

## Sculpture and Architecture

The most versatile and influential baroque artist was Giovanni Bernini (1598–1680). After 1629 he was the architect of St. Peter's in Rome. Together with his famous contemporary, Borromini, he worked under papal patronage to make Rome the fittingly ornate capital of a rejuvenated Catholicism. Bernini grew famous as the only worthy successor of Michelangelo. Louis XIV, the English court, and other high powers sought him out for commissions; and he was paid a personal visit by the pope. Although he thought his genius lay in painting, Bernini is best known today for such architecture as the Plaza and Colonnade of St. Peter's and such sculptures as *Daphne and Apollo, Bust of Louis XIV,* and the *Ecstasy of St. Theresa.* He also drew plans to rebuild the Louvre in Paris, but royal ministers rejected them as too expensive. Most of his career was spent in Rome, where he and his large staff of assistants were employed by a series of pontiffs.

Bernini and his Italian contemporaries profoundly influenced architecture and sculpture in Catholic Europe, particularly churches, palaces, and villas that were usually as large as funds permitted—the churches to provide in addition to services and rituals an imposing setting for elaborate decorations and large numbers of worshippers, the palaces and villas to accommodate lavish parties in addition to opera and ballet performances. In the case of the Escorial—the vast structure Philip II built near Madrid (it included a royal palace, a church, a mausoleum, a college, and a monastery)—baroque architecture was a means of exalting the nobility of an entire kingdom. Before Louis XIV created Versailles the Escorial was the outstanding example of monumental and sumptuous construction. Baroque buildings were characterized by curved exterior walls with recesses, twisted columns, massive facades, and ornate (and sometimes grotesque) statuary both inside and out. The rooms were often oval-shaped, and interiors were heavily laden with paintings, tapestries, and massive carved decorations. Ceilings sometimes took on the appearance of infinite sky, an impression that floating figures were designed to convey. Statuary, including altar pieces (Bernini's *Ecstasy of St. Theresa* was designed as such), expressed movement and dynamic emotion. Twisted figures were shown in diagonal positions, and the figures were partially shrouded in blowing drapery to magnify the sense of grandeur or movement.

Not all statuary and architecture in Catholic countries were baroque, and the baroque influence outside Catholic boundaries was limited. Traditional classicism and simple functionalism predominated in England, the United Provinces and, to some degree, in France. In classical architecture the simple lines and pillars of the Venetian architect Andrea Palladio (1518–1580) were widely imitated.

## Painting

Baroque painting reflected the same emotionalism found in baroque statuary, and techniques were as parallel as the different media allowed. Baroque painters covered a wide range of subjects. They frequently portrayed the great religious themes (saints and martyrs were particularly popular), mythological episodes, and grotesque or disfigured persons from the lower classes. Mysterious or eerie lighting effects often gave their works an otherworldly aura. The plethora of canvasses produced in the baroque era defies any attempt to discuss individual examples. We shall limit our study here to representative groups. Italians of Rome and Venice produced most of the baroque art of the seventeenth century, but important baroque painters also appeared in Spain during the reign of Philip IV (El Greco, Velásquez, Murillo, José Ribera), and in Flanders (Rubens and Van Dyck). Classicism and realism were intermingled with the baroque in France by Poussin, Lorrain, and the Le Nain brothers.

That baroque techniques also penetrated the Dutch provinces is demonstrated by the later works of Rembrandt van Rijn (1606–69), the greatest of the Northern masters. He was not alone in portraying religious themes infused with anguish, pity, or passion. But as he became more drawn to these themes—after his famous *Night Watch* of 1641—his commissions declined, and he (and other painters), long dependent on a highly competitive market, fell into poverty. Perhaps as many as 2000 painters were working in the Netherlands. Most of them employed some baroque techniques, but they catered to urban middle-class patrons who preferred art that was less gaudy and not so metaphysical. The works of Hobbema, van Ruisdael, Vermeer, and Hals were painstakingly realistic. Baroque art had little opportunity of flourishing in the Netherlands, for its religious and social requisites were lacking. A landowning aristocracy did not dominate society, nor did the Dutch have a monarch bent on glory and grandeur. And Catholicism, which provided the imagery and emotional content in baroque works, was not a force in the Netherlands. England and the German states produced no notable painters during the heyday of the baroque, and their major commissions went to foreign artists.

*Bernini's* Ecstasy of St. Theresa.

*Bernini's colonnade at St. Peter's.*

*An example of Borromini's work in Rome: S. Carlo alle Quattro Fontane.*

## Music

Italian composers, like other Italian artists, were leaders in their medium in the seventeenth century. Their achievements were rivaled only by the chorale, a notable Protestant contribution. Their chief creations, the oratorio and the opera, both partook of the baroque spirit, having orig-inated in the Renaissance when drama was first set to music—oratorios in the church, and opera on the secular stage. The oratorio remained almost exclusively a Catholic form of music until George Friedrich Handel (1685–1759) popularized it in England. The opera, too, thrived best where other baroque art flourished, notably in Italy at the hands of Claudio Mon-

*Dutch baroque: Rembrandt's* Night Watch.

teverdi, a composer of madrigals exploring new departures in harmony whose first great opera *Orfeo* was performed in Mantua in 1607. Italians attended opera with gusto, but it was also applauded in a few Protestant courts. Eventually Italy lost its lead to Vienna and Versailles. The Habsburg emperors were ardent devotees, as was Louis XIV, who

awarded a monopoly of operatic production to Jean Baptiste Lully. At Versailles the opera, and the ballet that complemented it, were cherished by the monarchy as symbols of prestige, and Lully encouraged his royal master to identify himself and members of his court with the gods and goddesses portrayed on the stage.

Italians also pioneered in developing

new instruments, particularly the church organ and the violin, but of all the arts music proved to be the one most capable of transcending the boundaries of religious confessions. Those instruments were especially congenial to the genius of Heinrich Schütz (1585–1672). Born in Germany and trained in Italy, he played and composed some of the finest baroque music of the period. Baroque organ music eventually culminated in the towering genius of John Sebastian Bach, a fellow German and a contemporary of Handel. As Lutheran choir director at Leipzig, Bach brought the baroque traditions of the seventeenth and eighteenth centuries to a climax in preludes, fugues, and choral preludes, also in over 200 cantatas secular and sacred. The elderly Bach outlived the popularity of the tradition he represented, but later musicians regarded him as their greatest teacher, and his works are still being mined for musical themes today.

## Literature

The baroque literature of the century between 1560 and 1660 is ornate, dramatic, and tense. Baroque writers, playwrights, and poets were influenced by chivalric romance of the late Renaissance, elaborate treatises on courtly behavior, classical mythology, and the Judeo-Christian religious tradition revived during the Reformation. They repudiated the skeptical humanism and robust earthiness of writers like Montaigne, Cervantes, and Shakespeare. Baroque writers saw life governed by two irreconcilable bodies of law: strict secular laws of vengeance and personal honor, and absolute moral laws of obedience to divine commands. Running through their works were themes of violent conflict: in politics, between the rewards and penalties of power; in morality, between the norms of society and the teaching of religion; in art, between the rigid formal rules to which they bowed and the ornateness and complexity of expression that often led them to pile words

on words in great profusion. The best examples of baroque literature are the works of the Spanish poets and dramatists like Góngora (1561–1627), Lope de Vega (1562–1635), Calderón de la Barca (1600–81), and the priest-dramatist Tirso de Molina (1571–1648). Unlike *Don Quixote,* which was written at the beginning of the seventeenth century as a satire on the lingering traditions of Spanish chivalry, their works have seldom been translated, owing to their ponderous formal style, emphasis on aristocratic virtues and dilemmas, and complicated allusions to classical mythology and geography. They are therefore little appreciated today.

To some degree baroque forms did appear in England, France, and the Low Countries. Although his particular genius defies any simplified labeling, Shakespeare shares the emotionalism of the baroque writers and often seems to echo their conclusion that secular life is only an empty illusion. For Macbeth life is "a tale/Told by an idiot, full of sound and fury,/Signifying nothing"; and in *The Tempest* Prospero tells us that

*We are such stuff*
*As dreams are made on, and our little*
*    life*
*Is rounded with a sleep.*

The dominant literary and artistic form developing in northern and western Europe, however, was a neoclassicism adapted to meet the needs of aristocratic society in those areas. Neoclassicists uncovered and tried to honor the formal canons of simplicity, serenity, conciseness, emotional restraint, and brevity that had defined the classical tradition. They sponsored campaigns to standardize the spelling and form of vernacular languages and were supported in such efforts by royal literary societies. But these campaigns were only beginnings, and neoclassicism would not really flower until after the century of crises.

## E. *The Roots of Crisis* RELIGIOUS, MILITARY, AND ECONOMIC TURMOIL

No century of human history has been without crises; however in examining the period between 1560 and 1660, we are forced to the conclusion that few centuries have had simultaneous crises in so many different compartments of human experience. This century was an age of ideological warfare and revolution, of power politics, incredible corruption, famine, inflation, plague, judicial torture, and spreading bondage. Its barbarity has gone unsurpassed until our own day.

The most conspicuous cause of upheaval was an interlocked combination of religious, political, and social discontent. Minorities—ardent Catholics and revolutionary Calvinists—were determined to impose their views by force. The Catholic Reformation became identified with the imposition of absolutist society based on a hierarchy of ranks. Revolutionary Calvinism combined with the dissident nobility that tried to thwart that absolutism by vesting power in parliaments, courts, and councils. The Calvinists also recruited lower-class townsmen pinched by the price revolution. Again and again the outcome was civil war, which was then caught up in the diplomacy of dynastic power politics.

In these wars religious hatreds inspired the use of unrestrained force and represented an important threat to life, property, and domestic tranquility. No government launched a purely religious crusade, but religious ideologies nurtured militancy and were used to justify duplicity and atrocities. Kings, clerics, and laymen cited precedents from the Old Testament to sanction acts of extreme barbarity, taking their victories as proof that divine providence was on their side. Finally, religious differences seriously affected international diplomacy, thwarting negotiations between states whose rivalries were primarily dynastic.

In addition to these obvious roots of disorder, historians now look to concrete social and technical data to understand the depth of this period's crises more fully.

One area of such investigation has been the changing nature of warfare. In 1560 wars were fought by armies of mercenary infantry supplemented by artillery and cavalry. Societies already unable to provide adequate subsistence for the bulk of their populations found that the costs of supplying and equipping mercenary armies could not be sustained by public revenues. Troops were paid through the captains who had recruited them, but armies also maintained themselves by foraging the countryside, imposing taxes and services on peasants under their control, extorting indemnities from towns, seizing booty, and holding prisoners for ransom. Discipline was casual and armies led by the incentive of plunder were often as destructive of friendly as of enemy territory. In the early seventeenth century the Dutch and the Swedish challenged the traditional mode of warfare, effecting what has been called "the military revolution." Maurice of Nassau, the son of William the Silent, and Gustavus Adolphus replaced massed squares of infantry with thin lines of men using firearms; they enforced discipline by increasing the number of officers, establishing regular pay, and introducing distinctive uniforms; and they applied scientific skills and knowledge to the building of fortifications and the use of artillery. Their enemies were unable to imitate these changes immediately; instead, they further increased the size of their traditional armies. Thus the deleterious influence of mercenary warfare only deepened in many areas.

Another line of inquiry has sought to throw light on the underlying economic weakness of the century of crises. Agriculture and commerce were unable to support the growing population, and colonial products and imports from the "new lands" of eastern Europe did not provide sufficient relief. War, famine, plague, and what is so far an unaccountable decline in the birthrate reduced or at least stabilized the European population in the first half of the seventeenth century. But there could be no basic solution to the age-old subsistence problem until agricultural and industrial technology improved drastically—something that did not begin to happen to a sufficient extent until the eighteenth century.

## RENAISSANCE COURTS

Some historians believe that military, religious, and economic explanations cannot satisfactorily account for either the prevalence of religious civil wars or the epidemic of revolutions that swept through the monarchies of Europe as the Thirty Years' War came to a close. They have suggested that states where top-heavy "Renaissance courts" were still to be found suffered from inherent weaknesses that religious conflict and warfare simply increased. The Renaissance court consisted of favorites and noble magnates who clustered about the monarch and who were, to a large extent, maintained by him. The court nobles relinquished their old feudal political rights, but in compensation they were given remunerative posts in the army, diplomatic corps, church, and administration—posts whose powers they exploited for personal and family gain. The cost of their maintenance consumed a large portion of royal revenues even though the bulk of their income came from fees, services, church obligations, monopolies, tolls, bribes, and embezzlement of funds ostensibly collected for public purposes. And they rivaled the king as dispensers of favors and vied with the monarch in determining state policy. Only a very strong king who personally controlled a loyal bureaucracy could triumph over factional intrigues that characterized court life. For the king who was weak, or whose courtiers allied with foreign kings or discontented domestic factions, court politics were dangerous. Further, the fiscal expedients to which kings were driven only served to provoke domestic opposition that often developed into revolution. To raise money kings sold titles, honors and offices. This large-scale "lay simony" cheapened the prestige of the nobility and effectively alienated the older aristocracy and officials. Monarchs endangered their security even more by trying to channel the profits from taxes, patronage, and legal fees out of the hands of local aristocrats and into the royal treasury. Every major revolution and religious civil war during the century involved either factions that competed for power at court or entrenched privileged bodies that resisted all efforts of economic and social reform.

## WITCHCRAFT: TRADITION REAFFIRMED

To understand these crises, contemporaries had only their own immediate experiences, intuitive feelings, and traditions to draw on in order to explain and confront the dilemmas of their age. Many of them, especially the clergy, were swept away by the worst witch-craze in European history. Indeed, the Protestant Reformation had done nothing to diminish the late medieval belief in compacts between Satan and witches and in conspiracies of Satan's legions against those of God; and the religious wars did much to further such beliefs. Trials and executions of witches flourished, especially during the first half of the seventeenth century. Between 1623 and 1631 the Catholic bishop of Würzburg in Germany is alone reported to have had 900 persons burned as witches. Protestant countries took their toll, too, on a smaller scale. Skeptics, largely Erasmian humanists, were persecuted by both sides. The witch-craze would not die until a new cosmology, a new world view in which embattled spirits no longer played a conspicuous part, was accepted. Such a revolution was underway. Copernicus had already offered part of the basis for it in 1543, but for a century it remained confined to narrow intellectual circles that were themselves embattled with the weight of tradition.

## ABSOLUTISM AND THE SEARCH FOR SECURITY

Meanwhile a few contemporaries developed new political and religious ideologies as a response to the breakdown of the old order. Led by Jean Bodin (who had a fair understanding of the causes of inflation but who also believed in witchcraft!), the *politiques* in France formulated the notion of a secular state sovereignty and proposed that the sovereign state, responsible to the commonweal, tolerate religious dissent too strong to be crushed without civil war. The Arminian humanist Hugo Grotius, who wrote in the United

*A contemporary woodcut illustrating the treatment of witches.*

193     E. The Roots of Crisis

Provinces during the Thirty Years' War, outlined a theoretical system of international politics independent of theology, and for this he is credited with having founded the science of international law. Under his system the sovereign state, in its own self-interest, had to accept rational restraints on the conduct of war.

The often disastrous interaction of religion and power politics had helped discredit Reformation doctrines in certain religious circles. Partly as a consequence of this, pietists in Germany and Quakers in England, as well as many other sectarian groups, cultivated religions that set personal morality above formal creeds. Many Roman Catholic reformers such as St. Vincent de Paul (1580–1660) also attached new importance to humanitarian social reform.

Before these humanitarians, the new scientists, and their humanistic popularizers provided alternative ways of thinking, the main response of contemporary people to the crises of the seventeenth century was to establish greater state absolutism. Rulers sought to achieve security from invasion and tried both to eliminate warfare conducted for private profit and to control all military forces within their realms. By 1660 European monarchs had generally adopted disciplined standing armies (although at sea private warfare was still accepted as a normal means of conducting hostilities). The same rulers attempted to control the economy and society by mercantilistic regulations. In their attempt to discipline all aspects of life that had become chaotic during the century of crises they also sought to control the arts, bringing them under the canons of neoclassicism. Religion, too, became a matter of state. Uniformity was the goal, and fanaticism of any kind became suspect. Although the maritime states—England and the Dutch Republic—charted different courses, the immediate sequel of the century of crises for most countries was an age of absolutism.

## Selected Readings

Ashley, Maurice. *The Greatness of Oliver Cromwell.* London: Hodder & Stoughton, 1957.

*An outstanding apologetic biography by the leading English authority on Cromwell's career.*

Ashton, Trevor, ed. *Crisis in Europe: 1560–1660.* New York: Basic Books, 1965.

*Articles from* Past and Present, *an English journal of "scientific history." The contributors agree that a general crisis existed, but they fail to find a single common cause.*

*Burckhardt, Carl J. *Richelieu: His Rise to Power.* Rev. ed. New York: Random House, Vintage Books, 1964.

*An interpretation in political psychology that finds Richelieu's centralized absolutism a prototype of modern democratic society—a controversial thesis useful for its material on court intrigue.*

Cipolla, Carlo M. "The Decline of Italy." *Economic History Review,* 2d series, V (1952–53): 178–87.

*One of many recent articles in that journal, whose conclusions sharply modify older general histories of early modern Europe.*

\*Clark, George N. *The Seventeenth Century.* 2d ed. New York: Oxford University Press, 1961.

> *Perceptive analytical chapters arranged by subject and particularly useful for early modern institutions.*

Clough, Shepard B. *The Economic Development of Western Civilization.* New York: McGraw-Hill Book Co., 1959.

> *Several chapters incorporating recent research are pertinent to this period.*

Davies, D. W. *A Primer of Dutch Seventeenth-Century Overseas Trade.* The Hague: Martinus Nijhoff, 1961.

> *A basic discussion of the commerce of Europe's dominant trading state.*

\*Elliott, J. H. *Europe Divided: 1559–1598.* New York: Harper & Row, Publishers, 1968.

> *A panoramic survey of the religious wars of the sixteenth century, good for showing the interconnections between different conflicts.*

\*——. *Imperial Spain: 1469–1716.* New York: St. Martin's Press, 1964. Lynch, John. *Spain Under the Habsburgs.* Vol. 1, *Empire and Absolutism: 1516–1598.* New York: Oxford University Press, 1964.

> *Two recent in-depth accounts of Spanish institutions and policies by recognized authorities.*

\*Friedrich, Carl J. *The Age of the Baroque: 1610–1660.* Rise of Modern Europe Series. New York: Harper & Row, Publishers, 1962.

> *An excellent factual account that finds baroque art the prevailing symptom of the era's tensions.*

\*Geyl, Pieter. *The Revolt of the Netherlands.* New York: Barnes and Noble, 1958. ——. *The Netherlands in the 17th Century: 1609–1648.* Rev. ed., vol. 1. New York: Barnes & Noble, 1961.

> *These replace the classic account of the Dutch Republic by John L. Motley with a fundamental reevaluation and deemphasis of the role of Calvinism in determining the outcome of the Dutch revolt.*

Hamilton, Earl J. *American Treasure and the Price Revolution in Spain: 1501–1650.* Cambridge, Mass.: Harvard University Press, 1934.

> *This study demonstrates that inflation was related to bullion imports, but in this and other writings Hamilton exaggerates the role of bullion in producing the "price revolution" and economic growth.*

Heckscher, Eli F. *Mercantilism.* 2d ed., 2 vols. New York: The Macmillan Co., 1955.

> *A much-criticized attack on mercantilism; however, it provides basic facts on economic policies and conditions in the continental monarchies.*

Lea, Henry C. *A History of the Inquisition of Spain.* 4 vols. New York: The Macmillan Co., 1906–7.

> *A heavily documented indictment of the Spanish Inquisition; volume 4 pertains to this period.*

Mattingly, Garrett. *The Armada.* Boston: Houghton Mifflin Co., 1959.

*Good literature and excellent history, assessing the significance of England's naval victory over Spain.*

Merriam, Roger B. *Six Contemporaneous Revolutions.* Oxford: Clarendon Press, 1938.

*A study of the revolutions at the end of the Thirty Years' War; a pioneer in the comparative history of revolutions.*

Mosse, George L. *The Holy Pretense.* Oxford: Basil Blackwell & Mott, 1957.

*This demonstrates that English Puritans condemned Machiavelli's principles but implemented them under religious terms.*

Neale, John E. *The Age of Catherine de' Medici.* London: Jonathan Cape, 1943.

*A particularly valuable study of Calvinism as an international revolutionary movement.*

————. *Elizabeth I and Her Parliaments: 1559–1581.* New York: St. Martin's Press, 1958.

*This outlines Elizabeth's relations with Puritans in Parliament and the compromises behind the "Elizabethan Settlement."*

*Neff, John U. *Industry and Government in France and England: 1540–1640.* Ithaca, N.Y.: Cornell University Press, 1957.

*A comparative history of mercantilist industrial regulations and their enforcement, emphasizing England's lack of a centralized bureaucracy as a major factor in the decline of English mercantilism.*

*Ogg, David. *Europe in the Seventeenth Century.* 8th ed. New York: The Macmillan Co., 1962.

*An old but useful survey that does not consider England part of Europe.*

Palm, Franklin C. *Politics and Religion in Sixteenth-Century France.* Boston: Ginn and Co., 1927.

*A political biography of Montmorency-Damville, a leader of the politiques.*

Redlich, Fritz. *De Praeda Militari: Looting and Booty: 1500–1815.* Wiesbaden: Franz Steiner Verlag, 1956.

*Legal study that provides reasons why mercenary warfare was economically deleterious.*

Reynolds, Robert L. *Europe Emerges: Transition Toward an Industrial Worldwide Society: 600–1750.* Madison, Wis: University of Wisconsin Press, 1961.

*Basic for the expansion of early modern Europe, Europeans' advantages over non-Europeans, and economic policies.*

Roberts, Michael. *The Military Revolution: 1560–1660.* Belfast: Boyd, 1956.

*A lecture on military adoption of firearms, new tactics, and discipline by the foremost biographer of Gustavus Adolphus.*

Rowse, Alfred L. *The England of Elizabeth: The Structure of Society.* New York: The Macmillan Co., 1950.

*An exceedingly well-written social history.*

Simpson, Alan. *The Wealth of the Gentry: 1540–1660*. Chicago: The University of Chicago Press, 1961.

*A most definitive attack on Tawney's thesis that the gentry was rising economically. Simpson finds that the law and officeholding were more remunerative than agriculture.*

*Steinberg, S. H. *The Thirty Years' War and the Conflict for European Hegemony: 1600–1660*. New York: W. W. Norton & Co., 1966.

*A revisionist survey that puts the Thirty Years' War in the context of a general European struggle for power and attacks older German views of its effects on the empire.*

*Stone, Lawrence. *The Crisis of the Aristocracy: 1558–1641*. Abr. ed. London: Oxford University Press, 1967.

*A thorough social and economic analysis of the English aristocracy before the civil wars.*

Supple, B. E. *Commercial Crisis and Change in England: 1600–1642*. Cambridge: Cambridge University Press, 1959.

*This study derives "mercantilism" from government efforts to remedy specific commercial crises rather than from an ideology of power.*

Tapié, Victor-L. *The Age of Grandeur: Baroque Art and Architecture*. New York: Grove Press, 1960.

*A stimulating art history that relates baroque artistic tastes to the social, political, and religious milieu of the Catholic Reformation.*

Tawney, Richard H. *The Agrarian Problem in the Sixteenth Century*. London: Longmans, Green & Co., 1912.

*One of several works in which Tawney presents economic arguments for the rise of the English gentry.*

Trevor-Roper, Hugh, ed. *The Age of Expansion; Europe and the World: 1559–1660*. New York: McGraw-Hill Book Co., 1968.

*A profusely illustrated folio volume with well-written summary sections written by experts.*

Unwin, G. *Industrial Organization in the Sixteenth and Seventeenth Centuries*. Oxford: Clarendon Press, 1904.

*An old but useful analysis based on England.*

Wedgwood, Cicely V. *Richelieu and the French Monarchy*. London: English Universities Press, 1949.

*A useful short political biography.*

———. *The Thirty Years' War*. London: Jonathan Cape, 1938.

*A standard English account from the emperor's point of view, now under revisionist attack.*

Wernham, R. B. *The Counter-Reformation and Price Revolution: 1559–1610*. The New Cambridge Modern History, vol. 3. Cambridge: Cambridge University Press, 1968.

*A reference work incorporating the latest scholarship on political and economic topics.*

Asterisk (*) denotes paperback.

# CHAPTER IV

# Governments and Societies in the Age of Absolutism

For centuries the custom of inherited routine had been the principal regulator of people's lives and institutions in western Europe. In rural villages each generation followed the procedures of its forebears in ploughing, planting, harvesting, pasturing, worshiping, and celebrating. Each locality had accumulated its own precedents for making and implementing decisions that were binding on the whole, and each town stood in a special relationship with the central government as defined by charters and recorded compromises. Other corporate institutions such as guilds, religious foundations, courts, and diets had their own privileges, rights, legal jurisdictions, and exemptions. These arrangements were reinforced by vested interests as well as custom. Most people, when they thought about them at all, believed them to be part of a divine order of the universe. Hence even the idea of premeditated change seemed to be a kind of sacrilege.

Within the framework of supposedly timeless and changeless custom, innovations were represented either as the restatement of long-recognized principles or as the restitution of an older authority or model. Thus under the guise of the restitution of an older authority, Italian jurists revived Roman law beginning in the eleventh century; Renaissance humanists modified the medieval heritage with other classical precedents; and although the Protestant reformers of the sixteenth century broke the religious uniformity of western Europe, they too used a norm of the past to reorganize creed and church polity. Indeed in early modern times most major innovations were cloaked and limited by precedents of the past.

Out of the crises of both the Renaissance and the Reformation emerged authoritarian governments that claimed to be arbiters of society and thought. By 1660 divine-right kings were trying to obtain absolute control over military, political, legal, economic, and cultural affairs; thus the label *absolutism* has often been used to describe this type of regime. These kings —with their standing armies, their bureaucracies, and their control over established churches—attempted to impose domestic order and extend their hereditary domains. In theory, divine-right kings acknowledged no earthly limitation; they were accountable to God alone. But the societies that they ruled still followed medieval customs that conferred privileges on the higher social, political, and ecclesiastical orders. In part, royal absolutism came into being to defend the "liberties" that the privileged orders could no longer by themselves maintain against rival groups. When the nobles, clergy, and urban oligarchies turned to their kings for protection of their traditional prerogatives, they often had to surrender their political autonomy to divine-right absolutism. Some absolute monarchs, however, were not content to protect privileges: strengthened by the new powers surrendered to them, they attempted to reshape their society, making it dependent on their personal will. But in doing this they jeopardized their alliance with the old aristocracy by elevating commoners to the highest offices. After 1660 the most effective monarchs—Louis XIV of France, Frederick William I of Prussia, Leopold I of Austria, and Peter the Great of Russia —had to deal with an alienated nobility. Their successes and failures are our main concern in this chapter.

Other monarchs claimed, but did not attempt, to wield this kind of unlimited authority. They cooperated with the privileged orders whose political and social claims they respected, and their kingdoms, which remained firmly in the grip of custom, shall be referred to here as "aristocratic monarchies."

Only a few seventeenth-century states were outside the political mold of absolute monarchy. These included oligarchic Venice, the Imperial Free Cities of Germany, and the Swiss Confederacy; but the two most important ones were the Dutch Republic and England. The Dutch fought off absolutism in the "Eighty Years' War" against Spain (1576–1648). England escaped it in 1688 by revolution. These two states went furthest in developing new constitutions, but their revolutions were still far from complete at the beginning of the eighteenth century. In both instances commercial expansion and the growth of large commercial and professional middle classes attended the overthrow of absolutism, but in the Dutch Republic the impetus of commercial expansion subsided after 1660. In decline, the Dutch Republic became a tightly closed oligarchy, as had other once-thriving commercial cities such as Venice and Nuremberg. In England the commercial classes continued to expand with the nation's commercial growth, but they shared power without ruling. Almost everywhere else in Europe this commercial motor of social and political change was not running.* Banking, trading, and manufacture were either stagnant or in decline.

* One small exception was the German city of Hamburg, the banking and transshipping point for English, Dutch, and French trade entering Germany. Revolting against an exclusive patriciate, Hamburg's townsmen established a more broadly based constitution in 1712.

## A. The Nature of Absolutism

### THE ALL-POWERFUL MONARCHY IN THEORY AND PRACTICE

In the late thirteenth and the fourteenth centuries civil lawyers, clergymen, and royal publicists began to claim autocratic powers for kings who traced their descent from feudal times. In opposition to papal claims to sovereignty, they misconstrued feudal monarchy as a lord-subject relationship, neglecting the mutual rights and obligations of feudal contracts and thereby helping to transform late medieval monarchies into governments run according to the absolutist principles of imperial Roman law. In fact the feudal lord–vassal relationship had been based on reciprocity between rights and duties. John Locke and Thomas Jefferson were later to make this reciprocal contractual concept into a revolutionary weapon. But royal absolutists looked back to the late imperial Roman law, in which they found the precept that "the will of the Prince has the force of law." Well buttressed by Roman law, kings were able to delegate some of their powers to personal officials, set up personal courts to enforce their will, and exclude all but themselves and their favorites from the "mysteries of state." They were reinforced by theologians of the Renaissance and the Reformation, who argued that kings had their authority from God alone, that they were in fact God's agents, against whom resistance was resistance to God himself. In their capacity as God-anointed kings they could heal disease, and many a sufferer knelt in line for the king's touch, expecting a miraculous cure.

It was only a short step from such an exalted and sacramental view of kingship to the divine-right doctrine that became prevalent by 1600.

Roman Catholic and Protestant clergy appointed by kings cited Scripture, especially the Old Testament and Romans 13, to prove that kings were direct agents of God, that their power was subject to no limitation except him and his revelation, and that resistance to a divinely ordained ruler was a cardinal sin. If these kings ruled tyrannically, they were only punishing human wickedness for God. A few monarchist propagandists, such as Bishop Bossuet in France, added still another argument—a secular and modern one—for authoritarian rule. They accepted the premises of Jean Bodin and Thomas Hobbes that complete centralization of state authority was rational, necessary, and natural. But this theory was frowned on as being too secular—until "enlightened despots" of the eighteenth century made it their own. Seventeenth-century advocates of royal absolutism instead depicted their kings as ruling in the image of God, simultaneously manifesting traits of feudal and classical heroes.

Absolute monarchs built royal supremacy into the machinery of their governments. Their new standing armies provided security from invasion and put in royal hands the only armed forces permitted within their states; the feudal nobility was forced to abandon its claim to self-help, the right to make war on their king. Frequently the triumphant kings substituted chains of military command for civil administration. The nobility continued its bellicose traditions, but these were directed against rival dynasts away from civil wars. To equip, supply, and pay their soldiers, monarchs sought the power to tax their subjects without interference from traditional representative assemblies. When these assemblies resisted, they and their members were excluded from affairs of state as thoroughly as other subjects. The various *cortes* of the Iberian peninsula, the Estates General, and many German diets, for example, were no longer summoned. With the powers to tax and to maintain standing armies, autocratic kings conducted foreign affairs subject only to the limits of their own ambitions and available resources; thus the age of absolutism was marked by nearly continuous warfare; and royal diplomats served as the agents of aggrandizement. Imitating a Venetian custom, kings sent permanent resident agents equipped with pensions and gifts to buy their way into favorable agreements and information. For workaday espionage and fraud they employed secret agents who could be disavowed when caught. Royal control over military and foreign affairs set precedents for executive discretion that long survived the demise of monarchical forms of government.

In domestic affairs, however, absolutism was more often a superficial facade than a reality. No absolute monarch had as much control over his subjects as did the King and Parliament of England, both of which exacted only semivoluntary obedience. Absolutism was effective in dealing with nonprivileged subjects, but on the broad front of domestic affairs it

was hemmed in by numerous practical restraints. A backward technology was a major curb on royal absolutism, and slow transport and communications limited its range to the vicinity of capitals and provincial administrative centers. Agrarian economies could not support armed forces or bureaucracies proportionate to those of either England or the Dutch Republic. Moreover the officers who served the throne were often more devoted to personal gain than to royal authority. Rather than as public trusts, offices were generally considered private property. In France, for example, the king could remove by judicial process officials 'who acted independently of his direct supervision, but he was obliged to compensate most of them for their loss. Still more important in limiting royal authority were the vested interests of the privileged classes and the strong hold of custom among the masses; no monarch could completely eliminate these restraints.

## THE BRAKES OF CUSTOM, PRIVILEGE, AND POVERTY

Strikingly absent from the configuration of absolutist society were the large commercial middle classes—bankers, merchants, and entrepreneurs—comparable to those in England and the Dutch Republic; the rest of Europe remained primarily agrarian. Only France had an extensive professional and commercial middle class, and even its ambitions were set by the aristocracy. In Brandenburg-Prussia, Poland, Russia, and the Habsburg Danubian monarchy, no such class existed except for officials.

Throughout Europe peasants made up the great bulk of the population, differing widely in status. In western Europe they were for the most part legally free, but, unlike the leaseholders of England and the

Dutch Republic, they were still subject to manorial services, monopolies, and restrictions, and they had only a limited access to royal justice. In most instances taxes, tithes, and various services took more than two-thirds of their gross incomes and energies. Western European peasants, particularly in France, were obtaining *de facto* ownership of their holdings, but east of the Elbe River serfdom during the seventeenth century was taking a firmer hold and expanding. Eastern European lords worked their estates with forced labor and had legal powers of life and limb over their serfs, who were bound to the soil as personal property. Power to exact peasant services, dues, and rents belonged primarily to the nobility, the state, and the Greek Orthodox and Roman Catholic churches. Even though the clergy and aristocracy (the two principal privileged orders) no longer dominated government, they continued to dominate absolutist society in eastern and western Europe respectively.

Royal absolutism was the political antithesis of decentralized feudalism because it subordinated the nobles to the king. But even when absolute monarchs facilitated the rise of commoners into the aristocracy, they still used their political powers to preserve the hierarchical social order. Formal division of society into the estates of the late Middle Ages—nobles, clergy, and commoners—lasted until the French Revolution. Besides maintaining their traditional social ties with the monarchy, the nobles became officers of the royal army and held the most prestigious offices in the state and the Church, thus sharing power with titled and privileged officials, themselves on the way to becoming nobles. In these ways absolute monarchy remained basically, although not entirely, a conservative social force. At the apex of the social pyramid stood the king, who alone had the power to promote limited numbers of men of ability or

*An officer and musketeer of the French Guards.*

wealth. But he lacked the power, and usually the will, to make so many commoners nobles that he made nobility meaningless or to invade and destroy existing privileges and vested interests.

In the simplest kind of hierarchy, as for example in France, the established clergy retained its preeminent position among the estates. In Roman Catholic kingdoms the clergy retained its prestige as the first estate and continued to educate the nobility's offspring; its ranks were staffed at the top by noblemen or commoners elevated by the king and at the bottom by ill-educated, usually impoverished priests. Protestant churchmen were more likely to come from professional ranks, especially as sons of the clergy. The Reformation had produced religious minorities too large to eradicate without civil war, but the still prevalent belief that religious uniformity was necessary for domestic peace was

*A procession of French clergy.*

reflected in the universal acceptance of established churches, formal adherence to whose tenets was necessary to enter honorable professions. By teaching the common people obedience to divine-right rulers, the established churches supported royal absolutism as long as it was consistent with clerical privileges. "No king, no bishop; no bishop, no king" was a commonplace formula. In Roman Catholic countries such as France and Spain, where the Church retained great wealth, the established hierarchy also made considerable contributions to the royal treasury.

Among the privileged laymen, highest honors and preferment went to the nobility, itself a hierarchy of ranks. Law and custom recognized two different types of noble patents—nobles of the sword descended from knights who had performed military service and nobles of the robe who had received titles (or were descended from nobles who had) for nonknightly service. Despite rivalries between

them, nobles of the sword and nobles of the robe shared common traits: they held landed estates, rights to local milling and baking monopolies, power to collect tolls, legal jurisdictions over peasants, and exemption from common taxes; and they believed that acts of manual labor and trade in goods not produced on their own estates were degrading. In many countries such activities by nobles were also illegal. In France the minority of nobles that engaged in commerce failed to overcome this tradition. Despite their different origins and the reluctance of the older noble families to accept new nobles of service on terms of equality, nobles of the sword and nobles of the robe intermarried, and scions of robe families often attempted to demonstrate their military prowess. Both took great pride in their lineage and honor. Although fighting wars was the occupation with the most prestige, nevertheless military undertakings often proved too costly for noble resources forc-

*An English nonconformist minister.*

western Europe lived the bourgeoisie, the town dwellers who enjoyed corporate rights such as tax exemptions, exemptions from military service, and legal immunities. At the top of the bourgeoisie were the professionals, bankers, and great merchants who, aspiring to attain to nobility, acquired office and land with manorial rights, privileges such as tax exemption from royal and municipal offices, and occasional patents of nobility from the king which were available to those able to purchase them. Like nobles, they disdained and avoided manual labor. They, along with the clergy and nobility, were the only representatives to the provincial and central diets that managed to survive. From their ranks kings, overriding resistance from the older nobility, recruited the most aggressive centralizers among the

ing noble families to negotiate despised marriage contracts with wealthy commoners.

Territories as well as social status groups had privileges that were zealously defended, and local estates and courts maintained their "liberties" against incursions by royal officials. These liberties consisted of the privileges and political or legal autonomy of the local clergy, nobles, and bourgeoisie as incorporated in law codes and customs and as preserved and bolstered by local diets and courts. These groups usually thrived on the periphery of the monarchy outside the range of effective centralized control. The absolute monarchies never supplanted this maze of economic and legal localisms and always retained a strongly federal, provincial aspect.

On the fringe of privileged ranks in

*A French lawyer with robe.*

*A merchant and his accounts.*

royal bureaucrats. Also, bourgeois adventurers from the West often entered the service of monarchs in eastern Europe and received privileges and titles there. The leading absolute rulers of the late seventeenth and early eighteenth centuries ennobled more commoners than the older nobility would tolerate, but after the kings' deaths the nobles recovered much lost ground. Nevertheless commoners continued to enter the ranks of the nobility.

A hierarchy also existed within the bourgeoisie, ranging from councillors, landholders, and wealthy merchant bankers at the top through officials, notaries, merchants (wholesale and retail) and masters of corporate guilds. These master craftsmen inherited their status but were considered less respectable if they actually worked with their hands. Within town walls journeymen, apprentices, domestic workers, day workers, and agriculturalists constituted a majority subject to excise and other taxes. They were forbidden to band together for mutual political or economic advantage, even if they desired to do so. For them rapid ascent was difficult if not impossible, but compared to rural workingmen they must still be reckoned among those who held some degree of privilege in absolutist society.

In the hierarchies of all classes the hereditary family—not the individual—was the unit of society. Hereditary rights were most conspicuous among, but not limited to, families of political rulers, whose right to rule was inherited as an indefeasible, inalienable right. Among them marriages sealed treaties, and conflicting claims arose when male lines died out. The principle of heredity also prevailed among the nobility and bourgeoisie: families sought marriage alliances to increase their fortunes or status. Since private and public rights were not sharply separated, dowries and legacies included offices of church and state, profitable legal jurisdictions, and manorial dues, as well as lands and securities. Money enough to give a daughter a large dowry or a son an education was the principal means of social ascent. At the middle level of the townspeople, guild masterships passed almost exclusively by inheritance and marriage. By voluntary or compulsory systems similar to the nobility's entails—which prevented the division of estates among heirs—even landholding peasants prevented the division of their estates. Normally the individual's status was determined for life by the position of the family into which he was born, and the social order strengthened family control over him.

Seldom could kings break through the bulwarks of family loyalties and class privileges, but they were no less constrained by the inertia of custom that prevailed in the countryside. More than 80 percent of Europe's population was rural; usually it was over 90 percent. Even where personal movement was not legally prohibited, most village people lived, worked, and died without leaving the same villages that their ancestors had inhabited since time immemorial. Tradition ordered their daily lives much the same as it had the lives of their forebears, and it made novelty an object of fear.

The villages of the countryside also had

*A master silversmith's shop, ca. 1700.*

*Concluding an arranged marriage.*

their hierarchy based on access to land. Western European leaseholders held full, half, quarter, or lesser estates formally or allotted to a single family. The system of entails that prevented the division of estates among heirs left all but the eldest sons to become squatters on the commons, to work in domestic industries or as day laborers, to wander, to plunder, or to enter the army. Similar differentiations existed among the serf populations of eastern Europe; but even the larger leaseholders of western Europe often lacked the means of supporting their families, especially after droughts. The peasantry lived on the brink of famine not only because its obligations to state, church, and lord claimed the greater part of its pro-

ductivity, but also because agriculture was bound by tradition to backward methods.

The peasants' only method for replenishing the soil was to let one-third to one-half of the land lie fallow each year. This alone could not prevent the soil's eventual exhaustion, and more and more tracts became wasteland. Cereals—the basic foodstuff for man and beast and the best source of calories per acre of cultivated land—seldom returned more than five times their seed in good weather on good soil. Twofold or threefold harvests were most common. Until seed grasses were introduced to provide cold-weather forage, large numbers of cattle could not be kept over winter. Manure for fertilizer was therefore short. Thus agriculture was tied

*Peasants harvesting.*

to a cycle of diminishing returns, and periodically subsistence fell catastrophically short.

Good harvests one after another supported a growth of population, but short harvests brought local and regional famines. France was one of the most productive and prosperous continental states of the seventeenth century, but there were large regional famines there in 1629–30, 1648–51, 1660–61, 1693–94, and 1709–10. No year of Louis XIV's 72-year reign was without famine in some province. Starvation or malnutrition brought death first to the weaker members of the lower classes: children, women, old persons, and beggars. (Half the children died before the age of one year.) Average longevity was probably not more than 25 years, certainly not over 30; peasant women were withered and old at that age, and at 40, village men were often graybeards. Upper-class persons who reached adulthood lived longer, averaging perhaps 50 years. Paradoxically, country folk suffered more than town people from food shortages. Town governments stocked grain in warehouses, but even so famine caused deprivation and unemployment within their jurisdictions. High grain prices consumed greater proportions of spendable income and shrank markets for industrial goods. Craftsmen as well as peasants were obliged to sell tools and equipment—their capital goods—to subsist during protracted shortages, and they were perennially in debt.

Using force to prevent the redistribution of wealth, authoritarian rulers maintained stability at the top of the social order. But at the lower levels of town society, food shortages were the most common cause of riot and disorder. Peasants, on the other hand, seem to have accepted famine with greater resignation, although they frequently revolted against new or heavier taxes; in France and other absolutist kingdoms, especially Russia, such revolts spread across entire regions. Despite the relatively small population there was much unemployment. Officials tried to compel the unemployed to work, but in vain; the capital to provide them with jobs was either lacking or being put to other purposes.

Basic poverty thus curtailed the absolute ruler's credit and revenues. It also set limits upon his militarism. Louis XIV could muster the largest army in western Europe since the Roman Empire, but its range was limited by a lack of fodder and oats for its horses. This was true even though the French monarch geared his policy for power rather than his subjects' welfare.

## ECONOMIC POLICIES OF ABSOLUTIST STATES

The continental monarchies were preoccupied with raising money for war. The policies followed by royal officials to increase revenues were later described as *mercantilism;* but this has become an ambiguous word. On the Continent it departed significantly from the mercantilism practiced by England and the Dutch Republic, which relied upon commercial economies.

Many continental rulers tried to achieve the mercantilist goal of a favorable balance of trade, and they waged economic warfare to secure it. Still, they had to work within the framework and limitations of their feudal traditions. Some of their officials, like Louis XIV's principal finance minister, Colbert, had long-range visions of economic expansion. Colbert tried to facilitate commerce by standardizing production methods, tariffs, and commercial law for the whole kingdom. Such efforts have been depicted as a phase of "state building": a response to the need created by international power politics for more economic centralization. Usually such policies—and Colbert's were no exception—amounted to intensified collection of traditional taxes rather than basic reform. State building might make the regime militarily stronger, but its emphasis upon centralization, industry, and commerce trod on the toes of privileged interests and offended traditional sensibilities. Meanwhile kings persisted in waging wars that their mercantilist officials considered economically ruinous. Even under the strongest autocrats, mercantilism became at most a compromise between aggressive foreign policies and the inertia of tradition.

Nevertheless governments did intervene extensively in the domestic economy. On larger estates in western Europe, peasants—important as taxpayers, billeters of troops, and suppliers of military transportation—were protected against the nobility. Wage rates were fixed at low levels to make domestic products more competitive in foreign markets. Demanding more work, rulers reduced the number of religious holidays, enacted repressive measures against idleness, suppressed some monasteries and boarding schools, and encouraged the growth of population. Industrial production codes prescribed universal standards of quality, but they soon became mere devices to collect inspection fees and curb innovations harmful to craftsmen's monopolies. In the interests of local, provincial, and national self-sufficiency, governments also regulated the grain trade. Some mercantilists favored the removal of restrictions on grain shipments, but the persistence of famines reinforced demands for local control.

Self-sufficiency was a major objective of mercantilist policy. To create military independence and to check the outward flow of hard money, governments established enterprises to produce luxury goods and founded royal arsenals. Tariffs checked the importation of all goods competing with domestic products. To secure colonial products unavailable at home, governments with access to the ocean chartered monopolistic trading and colonizing companies. In England and the Dutch Republic such companies—the East India companies, for example—accumulated capital, lowering interest rates so that the state could borrow at low rates, but elsewhere they required the spur of state initiative and capital.

Rather than concentrating power in the hands of the state, these chartered companies gave public power to private groups of merchants. The same was true of the practice of farming tax collection out to private contractors and establishing monopolies to raise revenues from the sale of such necessities as salt. Thus absolute monarchies often extended the range of economic privilege to private individuals and families. But because mercantilist policies were secular and because they accorded greater prominence to merchants, they tended to undermine the religious and social foundations of the regimes that practiced them.

## B. The Effective Absolutist Regimes

If every European monarch aspired to unlimited authority, only a few came close to realizing it, and those that did were engaged in almost continuous warfare. The pacesetter for authoritarianism in all of Europe was Louis XIV. The Austrian Habsburgs, the Hohenzollerns, and some smaller German princes charted courses similar to his. Eastern Europe also boasted its great autocrat, Peter the Great, who thrust Russia into European affairs and built up his power at home by borrowing technology and institutions from the West. The absolutists' struggle for power turned Europe into a series of armed camps and made peace the exception rather than the rule during the later seventeenth century.

### THE FRANCE OF LOUIS XIV

After the Peace of the Pyrenees in 1659, France replaced Spain as the most powerful and resplendent absolute state of western Europe; in population and resources (except commercial wealth) it exceeded all others. France's army and diplomacy dominated European politics, and its language became the *lingua franca* of upperclass Europe. French manners, fashions, music, art, and court life were aped as far east as Russia. Behind this great expansion of influence lay not only the work of Louis XIV and his ministers but the organization built by his Bourbon predecessors and the Cardinal-Ministers Richelieu and Mazarin.

By ending the struggle for the French crown and then issuing the Edict of Nantes (1598) to pacify the Huguenots, Henry IV had brought peace to France. His chief minister, Sully, had begun to build a royal bureaucracy that subordinated the provinces to the king. But this incipient absolutism waned with Henry's assassination in 1610 and the resurgence of the aristocracy under the regency that ruled during Louis XIII's childhood. Thereafter Louis's principal minister, Cardinal Richelieu (1624–42) and his hand-picked successor, Cardinal Mazarin who served Louis XIV until 1661, proceeded to suppress opposition to a royal autocracy.

Following a revolt by the Huguenots and nobility, Richelieu revoked those parts of the Edict of Nantes that granted the Huguenots autonomous political and military rights. He also displaced the rebellious nobility from critical decision-making and command posts in the central government. The office of *intendant,* staffed by appointees of common birth (who could be removed by the crown), represented royal authority in the provinces. Among other things the intendants brought royal governors (who were local nobles) under surveillance and reported on their conduct of affairs.

Similarly Cardinal Mazarin worked to enhance the authority of the boy-king Louis XIV, extending his power of taxation to finance the latter phases of the Thirty Years' War. As lover, perhaps even husband, of Louis XIV's mother, he handled royal affairs as a family matter, and his military successes secured his political position even further. Nobles and holders of hereditary offices resented Mazarin as an Italian adventurer who trampled on their privileges and enriched himself in office. But the *Fronde,* a prolonged revolt beginning in 1648, failed to unseat him, to check royal taxation, or dislodge the system of intendants. When Mazarin died after concluding the long war with Spain by the Peace of the Pyrenees (1659), he

bequeathed intact to Louis XIV's personal control the machinery of absolutism that he and Mazarin had developed.

## The King's Personal Monarchy

Having just come of age, Louis XIV reacted against Mazarin's tutelage by resolving to have no prime minister, but he attempted to fulfill and improve upon Mazarin's paternal control over France. The civil wars of the 1640s increased his determination to exclude the nobility from making high-level decisions. When queried by a Church official wanting to know to whom he should address himself on question of public affairs after Mazarin's death, Louis replied "To myself." Like his Bourbon predecessors, he considered the state his private inheritance.

Kings [he wrote] are absolute seigneurs [lords], and from their nature have full and free disposal of all property both secular and ecclesiastical, to use it as wise dispensers, that is to say, in accordance with the requirements of their State.[1]

The statement traditionally attributed to him—"I am the state"—is apocryphal, but it illustrates his attitude. A Venetian ambassador once reported:

The King maintains the most impenetrable secrecy about affairs of State. The ministers attend council meetings, but he confides his plans to them only when he has reflected at length upon them and has come to a definite decision. I wish you might see the King. His expression is inscrutable; his eyes like those of a fox. He never discusses State affairs except with his ministers in council. When he speaks to courtiers he refers only to their respective prerogatives and duties. Even the most frivo-

[1] Quoted by Jean Longnon, ed., *A King's Lessons in Statecraft: Louis XIV: Letters to His Heirs,* trans. Herbert Wilson (New York: A. & C. Boni, 1925) p. 149.

*Louis XIV as a chivalric, classical hero.*

lous of his utterances has the air of being the pronouncement of an oracle.[2]

In administering the state Louis proved to be diligent and industrious. After formal court rituals in the morning, he met in the afternoons with his high councillors. Unfortunately for France and Europe, he pursued glory and power for their own sake. The "Sun King" basked in the admiration of his own subjects and the amazement it aroused in neighboring countries. With this advantage, he wrote, there was nothing he could not obtain

[2] Quoted by Louis Bertrand, *Louis XIV,* trans. Cleveland B. Chase (New York: Longmans, Green & Co., 1928) pp. 292–93.

eventually. His wars of aggression were financed, however, by the tax administration that he inherited, and it placed tremendous burdens on the French peasantry. Moreover his aggressiveness repeatedly led other states to form coalitions against him and to frustrate his conquests. His failures and the pressures of his wars on the French people so transformed his image that the appellation "the Great," which his contemporaries used, failed to carry into the future.

Louis continued the Bourbon policy of subordinating the political and economic life of France to the direction of the monarchy. He built a bureaucracy of elevated commoners who owed their positions to the monarch alone, thereby excluding the nobility and high clergy. He set up special courts to discipline nobles, but his greatest thrust at their political power was indirect. At Versailles, a former hunting lodge just outside Paris, Louis constructed a huge palace built at tremendous expense and staffed by nearly 15,000 servants. Apart from the palace's role in setting the court and art fashions of Europe, it served Louis's purpose of gathering the greater nobility around the court. In return for personal services exalting the monarchy, he conferred pensions and made the nobles financially dependent on his favor.

Although this strategy succeeded in converting the higher nobility into politically impotent parasites, the court of Versailles had its drawbacks: it removed the king and his court from the realities of everyday life, and it permeated the court with an air of sycophancy. These results were sources of fundamental weaknesses in the regime.

Louis also threatened the privileged orders by depriving the old provincial assemblies of their functions and by overawing the *parlements* (high law courts). Only once near the end of his reign did the Parlement of Paris assert its claim to nullify a royal law by refusing to register it. Insofar as was possible, the intendants and royal councils carried on the direction of state affairs.

## The Machinery of State

Louis's administration of France became a model for absolutism in other parts of Europe. In deciding matters of high policy the king regularly attended three councils in person—the Council of State, the Council of Dispatches, and the Council of Finance. Administrative officials, especially his four secretaries of state for foreign affairs, war, marine, and the royal household did the work, but the king personally made decisions. Through the Council of Dispatches the secretaries of state communicated these decisions to the intendants in the provinces. ("The intendant," Louis wrote, "is the king present in the provinces.") In practice, however, the king's wishes were often thwarted by provincial institutions, especially the parlements. Although France's centralized government wielded unprecedented authority, there were limits to its functions. Louis XIV was never able to unify the kingdom completely. Over the army and foreign affairs his absolutism was less questionable than over the provinces, but even in the army corruption and traditional privileges tempered his control.

Early in Louis's reign Mazarin appointed and put at the sovereign's disposal a number of outstanding officials: de Louvois over the army, de Lionne over foreign affairs, and particularly Jean-Baptiste Colbert (1619–83). An ennobled draper's son who had been manager of Mazarin's personal fortune, Colbert became controller general of finances in France in 1665. His efforts to strengthen France's economic capacity for war became so familiar that one form of mercantilism is usually designated by his name.

His successes and failures graphically illustrate the gulf between the aims and accomplishments of the royal government.

## "Colbertism"

As finance minister, Colbert worked assiduously to increase tax revenues, expand commerce, and reduce debts and corruption. He hit hard at speculation in government securities, many of them bogus, which passed from hand to hand. He instituted a drastic investigation of the tax farmers, the richest class in France, to force the return of ill-gotten gain.* By administering financial affairs efficiently he nearly doubled revenues within six years and temporarily decreased the basic land tax; by stimulating economic activity he sought further income without raising tax levels. The government took the initiative in encouraging industry—notably silk, lace, drapery, luxury goods, forestry, sugar refining, iron, and glassware—and sponsored colonial trading companies to build an empire in North America and India. To make the quality of French exports uniform and acceptable, Colbert promulgated minutely detailed industrial production codes drawn up by guildmasters. These codes, which specified minimum standards for manufacture, were enforced over the whole of France by the intendants. To stimulate trade and commerce Colbert built roads and canals. He proposed abolition of the provincial tariffs and grain trade regulations that hindered the flow of goods. Foreign goods, especially Dutch merchandise, he sought to exclude by heavy protective tariffs in 1664 and 1667. He strove to make France self-sufficient in grain by prohibiting the export of wheat. Finally, he tried to standardize the legal procedures of the royal courts.

Colbert.

* Tax farmers were men who paid a lump sum to the treasury periodically in return for authority to collect taxes from the king's subjects.

Although Colbert supplied money for Louis's war machine, most of his ventures failed; and war costs mounted faster than revenues. Few basic reforms were implemented. The system of farming taxes to private contractors continued to plague the kingdom until the Revolution of 1789, and private French capital failed to support Colbert's industries and trading companies, turning instead to state bonds (*rentes*). His industrial production codes stifled technological innovations and encouraged craftsmen to maintain the status quo. Only luxury goods and necessities found a ready market, for there was no broad purchasing power necessary to the success of new consumer industries. Furthermore, Colbert's prohibitive tariffs helped precipitate war with the Dutch, who forced their downward revision in the treaty of Nimwegen in 1678. Grain famines and revolts against exorbitant taxes did not cease. Nor did Colbert's attempted revision of the legal system give real unity to France, for approximately 400 different "systems" still existed in 1789. Even his supreme effort to incorporate the "Five Great Farms" in northern France into the largest tariff-free zone in Europe was not a complete success. The rest of France kept its traditional tolls, and extreme confusion over conflicting weights, measures, and tolls left the country an economic hodgepodge until the Revolution swept them away at the end of the eighteenth century.

Although Colbert is often depicted as an opponent of Louis's aggressive wars, he advocated economic warfare: exclusionist tariffs, colonial struggles waged by private companies, and the seizure of Dutch wealth. Moreover he was dedicated to Louis's splendor—"For the king's glory, no sacrifice was too great," he wrote—and his fiscal measures financed his monarch's campaigns. Most of the revenue came from the *taille,* a direct land tax paid generally only by the peasantry. In the recently acquired border provinces that retained their estates it was moderate, but in the older provinces it was particularly burdensome. The *gabelle,* or government salt monopoly, likewise varied according to province. As the pressure of war intensified after Colbert's death, taxes extended to include marriages, births, and deaths. Even in some of the richer areas the peasantry was in a state of semistarvation during Louis's wars.

Royal military expenditures thus exceeded the kingdom's taxable wealth, especially during famines. But without Colbert's management the consequences would have been graver. From the intendants he solicited detailed and precise tax lists and information on business activity, population, and the temper of the people.

Collated in government archives, the intendants' reports constituted a large store of information necessary to policy making.

## The State and the Arts

In charge of royal buildings, Colbert was in a position to regiment architecture and the plastic arts as well as the economy of Europe's most influential state. At the Gobelin royal factory he assembled an army of painters, sculptors, engravers, weavers, cabinet makers, and other artists under the leadership of the painter Charles Lebrun. But Versailles was Colbert's principal artistic concern. As an effort of major construction, it is matched only by the work of the architect Christopher Wren in rebuilding London after the Great Fire of 1666.

Colbert wielded his influence to tame baroque elaborateness with classical simplicity. The Catholic Reformation that had inspired baroque emotionalism was over; classical baroque was dedicated not to an otherworldly religion but to a secular hero, Louis XIV. The Royal Academy of Sculpture and Painting set the tone of official taste, returning to the principles of Aristotle and the Italian High Renaissance. The exterior of Versailles was classical; its gardens were rigidly symmetrical and geometrical; its interior, however, was classical baroque, done in themes drawn from the ancient world but laden with allegorical rather than literal meaning. Lebrun instructed his painters to avoid Venetian models as too colorful, the Flemish and Dutch as too literal and bourgeois. Versailles was designed not for comfort or utility but for magnificence. It was the culmination in grandeur of the courts of the late Renaissance, setting the norm for courtly architecture and furnishings to such a degree that other monarchs felt obliged to imitate it. Likewise its

*Versailles and its classical gardens.*

operas, ballets, and plays set Europe's standards of entertainment.

Besides artists, Louis XIV patronized men of letters. The foremost classical writers—Corneille, Racine, and Molière—were brought to court as willing or reluctant courtiers, and during the first years of the personal monarchy there was a great outpouring of their dramas and satires. Nicolas Boileau-Despreaux (1636–1711), the royal historiographer, more or less set official canons of writing and became the arbiter of literary taste. Attacking the affectations, or "preciousness," of the over-refined and highly personal authors of the Parisian salons, he appealed for good

sense, reason, and rigidly disciplined imagination. He also led in formulating the rules of neoclassicism that spread over Europe.

Under royal patronage, writers—like artists—gained in stature and lost independence. They appealed to a limited audience and scorned the romances, imitative poems and plays, letters, and polemical religious works that most literate Frenchmen read; courtiers looked down upon popular culture as much as upon provincial nobles, and in the quarrel that broke out over the relative merits of ancient and modern authors, they sided squarely with the ancients. Literary advances are often singled out as the most enduring accomplishments of Louis's reign, but they occurred during the years prior to 1685. As the classical "greats" died or retired they were not replaced, for Louis became less generous as he grew older and came under the influence of the pious Madame de Maintenon. As the atmosphere of Versailles, influenced by piety and family misfortunes, turned to cold formality, artistic creativity waned.

## One King, One Church

The Church as well as the arts felt the steely grip of royal absolutism. For a time it appeared that Louis, like the Protestant rulers of Germany, would try to create a national (Gallican) church. The Concordat of Bologna (1516), which the Council of Trent had not nullified, empowered French kings to make most important Church appointments. Thus Louis's appointees supported him against the papacy; but he still lacked the power to name prelates in parts of southern France. During the 1670s he determined to bring these posts under royal sway—an extension of government power that precipitated a sharp quarrel with the pope, who refused to confirm the king's appointments. During the deadlock that ensued, many Church offices fell vacant, and the monarchy collected their revenues. In 1682 a national Church council led by Bishop Bossuet supported the king, reiterating the position of the Gallican church that the pope's spiritual powers were limited to those confirmed by a council. After protracted conflict that cost Louis the diplomatic support of the papacy, he and the pope reached a compromise. Then monarch, pope, and Jesuits joined in common effort against the French Jansenists, a mystical Catholic cult professing Calvinist morals and St. Augustine's theology of predestination. The Jansenists also ad-

vocated a state church, which would have pleased Louis had they not been allied with the parlements and nobility resisting his authority. He destroyed the major centers of their activity but failed to extirpate their spiritual influence. Jansenism survived as an active force in French religion and politics until the late eighteenth century.

Fast abandoning the Bourbon policy of toleration, Louis also attacked the Huguenots. Here too he yielded to the pressure of the clergy and his advisors, who after 1655 demanded the complete elimination of Protestantism. Noble families of "political Huguenots" went back to the Roman church. Financial inducements were offered to apostates, while church closures canceled their privileges and narrowed the range of toleration. Then dragoons were stationed in Huguenots' homes to harass them, while royal troops forced nominal conversions in the public squares of southern towns. Finally, using the specious argument that there were few dissenters left in France, the king revoked the Edict of Nantes in 1685.

Louis forbad the Huguenots to emigrate, but more than 200,000 of them fled the kingdom. Their numbers included skilled artisans, scholars, merchants, soldiers, and professional men, whose talents thereupon enriched Prussia, the English colonies, and other new Protestant homelands. After their emigration, Protestant states were solidified against Louis's foreign policy. Moreover, this episode momentarily reinjected religion into Europe's dynastic power struggles: by abandoning toleration, Louis convinced non-Catholic peoples that Roman Catholics could not be trusted.

## Louis XIV and Europe

The France of Louis XIV epitomized aggressive diplomacy during a century in which warfare decisively influenced institutions. During the Thirty Years' War France's standing army had borrowed tactics from the Dutch and the Swedes in order to defeat Spanish formations that had been invincible for a century and a half. As personal ruler, Louis lavished resources and attention upon the army. Under de Louvois the army adopted improved artillery, bayonets, and a faster-firing muzzle-loading handgun; officers donned uniforms and were given a serious military education; and the administrators centralized command and devoted great attention to supply. Marshal de Vauban, an engineering genius, devised scientific ways to reduce fortresses that were precise enough to predict the time of capitulation. Upon occasion the king, following such predictions, assembled the court, complete with orchestra, to witness the fall of an enemy. Indicative of the strict discipline in Louis's armies, his inspector-general's name, Martinet, became synonymous with insistence on rigid military regulations thereafter. Nobles filled the officer corps, whereas commissioned recruiting captains, often corrupt, hired or impressed the common soldiery. By 1678 the standing army reached 279,000 men, a formidable and expensive force, and one that continued to grow.

Louis sought first to conquer those territories in the Spanish Netherlands that had escaped Mazarin's grasp during the Thirty Years' War. When the queen's father, the king of Spain, died in 1665, Louis claimed the Spanish Netherlands as her inheritance. Catching Spain diplomatically isolated, French armies under de Condé and de Turenne swept through a series of Flemish forts and Franche-Comté in 1667 and 1668. French diplomats forestalled interference by the Austrian Habsburgs by promising them generous slices of Spanish territory upon the death of the sickly Spanish king, Charles II. The task of organizing resistance to French expansion fell to Jan DeWitt, grand pensionary of

Holland, who brought England and Sweden into a triple alliance with the Dutch Republic. Louis opted for peace, retained his conquest in the Low Countries, and then set his diplomatic corps the task of dissolving DeWitt's defenses. In 1670 he detached Charles II of England, who was at loggerheads with Parliament, from the alliance. Charles accepted a French subsidy, joined France against the Dutch Republic, and promised to announce his adherence to Roman Catholicism as soon as possible. In 1672 Sweden also switched sides. And in Germany a horde of diplomatic agents well laden with gifts neutralized all of the princes except the elector of Brandenburg. Thus did Louis prepare for the next onslaught.

Without a declaration of war French armies invaded Lorraine and Holland in 1672. The overwhelmed Dutch met all of Louis's demands, but the king raised his terms for peace. Desperation and fear of defeat brought William of Orange to power in the Dutch Republic. The Dutch opened dikes and flooded fields to stop the invasion. William enlisted foreign assistance: he allied with Brandenburg, Austria, Spain, Denmark, several German states, and—eventually—with England. In 1675 Brandenburg defeated Louis's only remaining ally, Sweden. Although French forces had meanwhile reconquered Franche-Comté, the war had become a stalemate. The French secured peace by making a separate settlement with the Dutch at Nimwegen in 1678; the Dutch received favorable trade arrangements and the restoration of their territory. Spain ceded to France Franche-Comté and a chain of forts extending from Dunkirk to the Meuse River. France, which had been militarily strengthened but had lost an irreplaceable general (de Turenne), was faced with revolts against war taxation in several provinces and would have to live with the marriage alliance between English and Dutch royal houses.

Having acquired Franche-Comté,

## FRANCE OF LOUIS XIV

■ Territorial expansion 1648–1715

Treaty of Westphalia 1648
Treaty of the Pyrenees 1659
Treaty of Aix-la-Chapelle 1668
Treaty of Nimwegen 1678–1679

Ryswick • Nimwegen •

Dunkirk, 1662
1668

FLANDERS
1678
1668
ARTOIS
1659
1678
1659

NETHERLANDS

Scheldt R.
Meuse R.
Moselle R.
Rhine R.

Aix-la-Chapelle •

1678

1642
VERDUN
1648
1661

1659
1661
1680
1661

1648

LORRAINE
Held 1670–97

ALSACE
Strassbourg

La Hogue • (1692)

Somme R.

FRANCHE COMTÉ
1678

1684

1648

SWITZERLAND

Provinces with Estates

• Parlements

Arras •

Rhine R.

• Rouen

Seine R.

Metz •

⊙ Paris

• Nancy

Colbert's Tariff Union

Colmar •

• Rennes

Loire R.

F R A N C E

Dijon •
Besançon •

• Bordeaux

Garonne R.

Grenoble •

Rhone R.

DUCHY OF SAVOY

BARCELONETTE, 1713

ORANGE, 1713

AVIGNON

• Pau
• Toulouse

Perpignan •

• Aix

S P A I N

0    50    100 mi.

S P A I N

ROUSSILLON
1659

0    50    100 mi.

Map by J. Donovan

France was mistress of her eastern frontier. Now Louis XIV's ambition, heightened by success, extended to the Rhine itself. He paved the way with clever diplomacy and inflated legal claims based on the Peace of Westphalia, which had ceded ambiguous rights to France in Alsace in 1648. Now French jurists laid claim to full sovereignty before specially constituted "Chambers of Reunion," courts set up in frontier cities. As the courts consistently rendered decisions favorable to France, the French army occupied its territorial awards. Theoretically, by taking advantage of outdated feudal relationships, the Chambers of Reunion could have pushed

French claims progressively across most of Germany.

Meanwhile French diplomacy—which was setting the language and procedures, open and secret, for all of Europe—was disarming German resistance to this creeping expansion. The French king posed as the protector of the "liberties" of German princes against the emperor; in fact, by 1683 Louis himself had hopes of being elected emperor. By the same date he had reconstructed an alliance system consisting of Sweden, Poland, Turkey, Brandenburg, Saxony, Bavaria, and Hungarian leaders in revolt against the Habsburgs. When the Turks laid seige to Vienna in 1683, Louis played a waiting game hoping to save Europe from the Turks at Austrian expense. But he miscalculated; the Habsburgs drove the Turks from Vienna. Then they purchased temporary peace in the West by recognizing the work of the Chambers of Reunion. They used the time thus gained to turn the Turkish retreat into a rout. Belgrade fell in 1688. Louis, fearing the loss of his Turkish ally, invaded and devastated the Palatinate.

As Louis came to the peak of his power in Europe after Nimwegen, his personal life and the tone of his court were changing. His shapely, vivacious mistress, Madame de Montespan—"as wicked as the devil himself"—gave way in royal favor to Madame de Maintenon, governess of the royal bastards. With the advent of de Maintenon, whom the king married secretly in 1684, puritanical winds blew through the royal corridors. Comedy was banned at court, and the atmosphere at Versailles became sober and stiff. During the same years the king turned to persecuting the Huguenots. Thus the complement of aggressiveness abroad was suppression at home.

By 1685 Louis, expanding along the Rhine, revoking the Edict of Nantes, and reviving French colonial and commercial power, had again lost his allies. William of Orange began organizing the League of Augsburg. In 1688 Louis again miscalculated when he did not oppose William's ascension to the throne of England as coruler with James II's daughter Mary.* Louis thought that civil war would overtake and neutralize Great Britain; instead, William assumed rule over a united country in a bloodless revolution. France was now opposed by a coalition of the empire, the major German states (including Brandenburg), the Dutch Republic, Spain, Savoy, and England. The exhausting War of the League of Augsburg (1689–97) was the first major European struggle to extend to the rest of the world; in the English colonies of North America it was known as King William's War. The League succeeded in turning back French expansion, and at Ryswick in 1697 the terms of peace substantially restored prewar boundaries in addition to giving Emperor Leopold peace in the West again, thus allowing him to drive the Turks eastward until, once again suspicious of France, he called a halt in 1699.

## The War of Spanish Succession

Louis made peace in 1697 because he could not risk being at war with Spain upon the death of the feeble, childless Charles II (otherwise he might forfeit his claims to Charles's empire). By accidents of birth and death there were three dynastic claimants to this, the largest European empire: the French Dauphin, the duke of Bavaria, and Emperor Leopold I.† The struggle among these came to pose the chief threat to peace in Europe. Louis

* James II was forced into exile; when he died his son became the new Stuart pretender under the name of James III.

† *Dauphin* was the designation of the French king's eldest son or heir apparent. The Spanish mothers of both the French and the Bavarian claimant had renounced their rights of succession.

*Charles II, the end of a line.*

negotiated first with England and the Dutch Republic, and together these three states drew up a partition treaty in 1698 that substituted a balance of power for the strict system of legitimate succession. By its terms the weakest contender, the duke of Bavaria, would have received Spain, her colonies, and the Spanish Netherlands. Thus no one dynasty would have monopolized power in Europe. But the treaty was never carried out. The Austrian Habsburgs refused to recognize it, and the Bavarian duke died before Charles II did.

Again Europe faced the threat of general war over the Spanish throne. In 1699 a second partition treaty among the same parties allotted those lands previously promised to Bavaria to a branch of the Austrian Habsburgs. France was to receive Naples, Sicily, and Milan, the last to be exchanged for Lorraine. But Leopold of Austria was not content with only part of the loaf; he preferred to claim the whole. Similarly, the Spanish court opposed partition. Just before his death in 1700, Charles II drew up a will—a "crop of dragon's teeth"—that bequeathed the entire empire to Louis's grandson Philip. If he and his younger brother refused the inheritance, all of Charles's domains would then go to an Austrian archduke. A more devastating threat to peace could scarcely have been contrived. Louis was now faced with the most difficult choice of his reign. To accept the will was to violate the second partition treaty and to secure Spain as an ally in a war against Austria, Great Britain, and the Dutch Republic. To reject the will meant war with both Austria and Spain, with the dubious assistance of the commercial powers. Since he had to fight in either case, the temptation of defiantly taking the whole proved too strong to resist. Needlessly provoking the English and the Dutch, Louis announced the eventual union of the Spanish and French thrones, recognized James Stuart (James III) as the legitimate king of England, issued a series of strong decrees regulating Spanish colonial trade—at the expense of both the English and the Dutch—and seized Dutch-controlled forts in the Spanish Netherlands. Again a grand coalition formed against France. As allies Louis had only Spain, Portugal, Cologne, and Bavaria.

The war for Charles II's inheritance, called Queen Anne's War in England's American colonies, spread overseas between 1701 and 1713. It remained isolated, however, from a contemporary Great Northern War for Baltic supremacy. France had by now lost the military leadership of de Turenne and de Condé, whereas England and Austria had the outstanding services of the Duke of Marlborough and Prince Eugene of Savoy. In the battle of Blenheim (1704) Marlborough drove French forces back across the Rhine; following the battle at Ramillies (1706), he forced them out of the Spanish Netherlands; meanwhile Prince Eugene expelled them from Italy. As France suffered defeats unmatched in the past two centuries, Austria overran Bavaria; Gibraltar fell to the English; and Portugal was detached from Louis's camp. French morale fell very low during the extremely cold winter months of 1708 and 1709. As early as 1706 Louis had decided upon peace, but his foes, as their fortunes improved, raised their demands. Finally in 1710 he offered to surrender Alsace and Lorraine and to supply money to drive his grandson from the throne of Spain. But the allies demanded that Louis himself drive Philip from Spain during a two-month truce. He rejected this demand, and France and Spain began to rally.

At the same time, the anti-French alliance disintegrated. In 1711 the Austrian claimant to Spain died, and his rights reverted to the Habsburg emperor. England found itself fighting to unite the Spanish and Austrian thrones, a union that would upset the balance of power as much as if Louis seized the whole domain. Weary of war, concerned about commerce, and fearful of Austrian Habsburg dominance, a peace party—the Tories—took charge in England and negotiated a separate peace with France. Two treaties— Utrecht (1713) and Rastatt (1714), known together as the Peace of Utrecht—halted the devastating war. Louis's grandson Philip retained possession of Spain and her colonies on the condition that the French and Spanish thrones would never be joined. The Austrian Habsburgs received Naples, Sardinia, Milan, and the Spanish Netherlands, where the Dutch were granted the right to garrison forts in order to forestall any new French invasion. The house of Savoy received Sicily and the status of kingdom. The Hohenzollern ruler of Prussia was allowed to take the title of "king," and he received a small territory (Guelderland) along the lower Rhine.

The lion's share of the spoils of war went to England, which retained Gibraltar, Minorca, Newfoundland, Acadia, St. Kitts, and Hudson Bay. In Spain's American colonies British merchants gained a limited right to trade, which served as an entree for large-scale smuggling. The South Sea Company also obtained a monopoly of the Spanish colonial slave trade (*Asiento*). In subsequent decades Spain was to upset the peace arrangements in Italy, and France was to obtain Lorraine (1739). Despite these changes, however, the Peace of Utrecht stands as one of the most important territorial settlements in modern European history.

## Epilogue to Glory

Louis XIV's death in 1715 brought to a close Europe's longest single reign. He had raised France to a peak of glory, but his reputation for greatness did not survive even the latter part of his reign. Deeply tired of Louis's wars, clergymen, intellectuals, disaffected nobles, merchants, and even military leaders like de Vauban criticized him severely. Louis outlived many critics and silenced some with censorship. But after his death the aristocracy was able to reassert its influence. Despising his "reign of the vile bourgeoisie," the resurgent aristocrats played upon popular desires for peace and stability and took advantage of the minority of Louis XV to assume more control over public policy. In exalting the monarchy, Louis had provided explosive ammunition to its opponents, who now had at their disposal the lines of cultural communication that he had laid across Europe. Subsequent generations of critics could extend their assault on absolutism far beyond the borders of France.

**WESTERN EUROPE AFTER UTRECHT, 1721**

NORTH AMERICA

BRITISH

FRENCH

BRITISH

ACADIA AND NEWFOUNDLAND
*(To Britain, 1713)*

FRENCH

SPANISH

TREATY ADJUSTMENTS 1713-1721

To Prussia

To Habsburgs

To Britain

To Savoy

× Barrier Fortresses

K. OF GREAT BRITAIN

★ London

Paris ★

K. OF FRANCE
*(House of Bourbon)*

UNITED NETHERLANDS

*(to Hanover, 1719)* Hamburg

*(1702-1707)* HANOVER BRANDENBURG

*(1720)* PRUSSIA

Berlin ★

K. OF POLAND

Utrecht

AUSTRIAN NETH. 1714

Guelderland
*(to Prussia, 1713)*

SAXONY

HOLY ROMAN EMPIRE

AUSTRIA

• Rastatt

BAVARIA

Vienna ★

K. OF HUNGARY

SWITZERLAND

SAVOY

PIEDMONT

R. OF GENOA

VENETIAN REPUBLIC

MILAN
*(to Habsburgs, 1714)*

TUSCANY

PAPAL STATES

K. OF PORTUGAL

K. OF SPAIN
*(House of Bourbon)*

★ Madrid

Balearic Is.

Minorca
*(to Britain, 1713)*

CORSICA

Rome •

SARDINIA
*(to Habsburgs, 1714)*
*(to Savoy, 1720)*

K. OF NAPLES
*(to Habsburgs, 1714)*
*(to Bourbons, 1735)*

Gibraltar
*(to Britain, 1713)*

*Mediterranean*

*Sea*

SICILY
*(to Savoy, 1714)*
*(to Habsburgs, 1720-1735)*

Map by J. Donovan

## HABSBURG AND HOHENZOLLERN

In the Old Regime dynastic state boundaries were set by births, deaths, and marriages within ruling families as well as by conquest. Ruling families inherited diverse territories with a variety of laws, customs, and constitutions. Provincial diets usually put provincial interests first and tried to prevent outsiders from hold-

ing local positions of power and privilege. This particularism was especially notable in the provinces of central Europe held by the Habsburgs and Hohenzollerns. Compared with them, Louis XIV's territories were contiguous and relatively homogeneous. Hohenzollern lands were scattered from the Rhine to the Niemen rivers, whereas the Habsburgs ruled peoples of diverse languages along the Danube. Despite the disunity of their holdings, these two families tried to administer them as coherent states. Thus they laid the basis for future rivalry over the control of German affairs.

## Absolutism in the Habsburg Danubian Monarchy

The Peace of Westphalia (1648) left the Habsburg emperors of the Holy Roman Empire with an empty title and admitted their rivals, France and Sweden, to direct participation in German affairs. Their authority was further diluted by the growing independence of the larger German principalities—Bavaria, Brandenburg-Prussia, Saxony, and Hanover—which had their own armies and foreign dynastic ties. Against the strength of his competitors, Leopold I (1658–1705) had no chance of recovering imperial authority. To counter French and Swedish designs on Germany, he was obliged to make Hanover an electorate and concede royalty to the Hohenzollerns as kings "in Prussia."

Leopold was Louis XIV's most persistent opponent, but until 1697 his opposition was sporadic and feeble. In 1668 he agreed to divide the Spanish empire with France. In the Dutch War he gave the beleaguered Dutch no assistance until 1673. Then he appeased the French king by allowing France to annex German territory through the "Chambers of Reunion."* And during the War of the League of Augsburg, William III was more conspicuous than Leopold in organizing Europe against French aggression. Irked by the emperor's ineffectiveness in western Europe, the papal nuncio at Vienna even opined that Leopold, who had been trained for the clergy in Spain, should act more decisively and trust less in Providence.

But Austria's relative ineffectiveness against Louis XIV stemmed more from conscious policy than from weakness. Unable to prosecute a long two-front war, Leopold gave first priority to the extension of his domains eastward. While Louis XIV nibbled at Alsace and the empire, the Austrian ruler was engaged in conquering Hungary, driving the Turks from positions they had held for more than a century. Thus the Habsburgs laid the basis for a strong Danubian monarchy that continued to order the political affairs of central Europe for more than two centuries.

When the Tyrol escheated to Leopold in 1665,† he became the first Habsburg monarch personally to rule the whole Habsburg patrimony. Besides the Tyrol there were Upper Austria, Lower Austria, Carniola, Carinthia, Styria, the German provinces, Bohemia, and Hungary. But Leopold controlled only the western quarter of Hungary, a band 40 to 80 miles wide, and the Magyar nobility rendered his hold on even that portion tenuous. Since 1222 this nobility had claimed the right to elect its own king and to resist any monarch who infringed on its privileges; in fact the nobles refused to submit to any authority. Their restiveness under foreign rule, Habsburg or Turkish, gave each power ample opportunity to intervene in Hungarian affairs at the other's expense.

In 1663 a revived Ottoman military machine conquered Transylvania, selling 80,000 captives as slaves. This event caused the Magyar nobility to join Austria in defeating the Turks at St. Gotthard. But Leopold struck an immediate truce with the invaders. Interpreting this truce as a device to reduce them to submission as Bohemia had been subjected to Vienna after 1620, Magyar nobles conspired to establish an independent state. They were fully justified in suspecting Austrian motives, but they conspired in vain. In 1683

† *Escheat* was a feudal law that provided for the reversion of a territory to its overlord when the vassal line of rulers died out.

* For their activities see pp. 219–20.

the Ottomans launched a major invasion aimed at the conquest of Vienna. Stopped at the gates of that city by King Jan Sobieski of Poland in the defenders' eleventh hour of endurance, the Turks were finally driven out of Hungary. Leopold, who had found a capable general in Prince Eugene of Savoy, terminated the eastern drive in 1699. The Treaty of Karlowitz in that year recognized Habsburg authority over Transylvania and almost all of Hungary. Despite her heavy contributions to the victory, Poland received only one small territory. Leopold now turned his attention westward to deal with the impending crisis over the Spanish succession.

Using the stability gained in the East to strengthen his position in the West, Leopold now made a bid for his sons to inherit the whole Spanish empire. In this he failed, but the Peace of Utrecht awarded to his successor the old Spanish Netherlands, Milan, Tuscany, Naples, and Sicily. Historians have joined the papal nuncio in deriding Leopold for indecisiveness, but he succeeded in enlarging Habsburg domains far more than Louis XIV expanded those of France. After Utrecht, Prince Eugene of Savoy returned to the eastern front to turn back a renewed Turkish counterattack. The Treaty of Passarowitz (1718) confirmed Turkish losses of 1699* and marked the demise of the Ottomans as an offensive threat to the newly established Habsburg empire on the Danube.

Leopold I admired the power and prerogatives of Louis XIV and tried to imitate them by being his own first minister. Like his opposite number in France, he made the higher nobility dependent on the court for its honors and privileges. His central government was compartmentalized into a privy council, a war

council, an imperial treasury, and an imperial chancery; but these were considerably weaker than the institutions of France. The German provinces retained their privileged estates. In order to raise money and troops Leopold had to negotiate with each diet, which then supervised its own levies. The privy council remained an advisory rather than an executive body, and the imperial treasury's revenue was limited to mineral rights and indirect taxes.

In the chancery a group of officials called *cameralists* stood ready to assert the authority of the crown more rigorously than Leopold himself. At the outset of his reign their authority was effective only in Bohemia, which had been reduced to direct control by the Viennese court in the 1620s. Reconquered Hungary seemed ready for the same fate. In 1687 Leopold summoned the Magyar estates to Pressburg to ratify an absolutist constitution that abolished their rights to elect and resist the king. The Diet of Pressburg further equated Protestantism, long associated with political dissent and the religion of many dissident nobles, with treason.

Unlike the Bohemian nobles, the turbulent, ungovernable Magyars were not displaced. In the eastern part of the Habsburg realm only Transylvania was ruled directly from Vienna. For one thing, the Habsburg monarchy lacked a middle class from which to draw loyal bureaucrats. Hungary's administration remained in the hands of the nobility, but its finances were subjected to central control. In order to enforce the Pressburg settlement, the Habsburgs were obliged to garrison Hungary with 30,000 troops during the War of Spanish Succession. Joseph I (1705–11) and Charles VI (1711–40) succeeded in winning over some rebel leaders, and in 1713 Charles VI's Pragmatic Sanction proclaimed that Hungary was an integral part of a unified Habsburg administration. Thus absolutism was firmly

---

* In addition, the Ottomans ceded the remainder of Hungary, western Walachia, and parts of Bosnia and Serbia.

entrenched in the eastern, non-German part of the monarchy. In the German provinces, however, a centralized state with officials comparable to the French intendants did not take form until the reign of Maria Theresa after 1740.

## The Rise of Brandenburg-Prussia

Hohenzollern lands were even more scattered than those of the Habsburg patrimony, but within a few decades the rulers of Brandenburg, who had the title

## RISE OF BRANDENBURG-PRUSSIA

- ■ BEFORE 1648
- ▦ 1648–1680
- ▨ 1713–1720

Map by J. Donovan

*Baltic Sea*

*Niemen R.*

FARTHER POMERANIA
1648

Königsberg
PRUSSIA
1618

HITHER POMERANIA
1720

*Elbe R.*

BRANDENBURG
Fehrbellin
Berlin

*Vistula R.*

P O L A N D

MINDEN 1648

RAVENSBERG 1614

MAGDEBURG
1680

CLEVES
1614

SAXONY

*Oder R.*

SILESIA

UPPER
GELDERLAND
1713

MARK
1614

HALBERSTADT
1648

HALLE
1648

*Rhine R.*

B O H E M I A

"Elector of the Holy Roman Empire," instituted a more effective absolutism. After the Thirty Years' War the Hohenzollerns ruled Cleves, Mark, Ravensburg, Halberstadt, Cammin, Minden, Magdeburg, Brandenburg, Eastern Pomerania, and Prussia—all as separate principalities. Each had its own diet and customary law. In the first half of the seventeenth century the elector's power over these diets had reached its nadir; a long series of economic crises had enabled the nobility to humble city, peasant, and ruler alike. The electors had been forced to side with the nobles (Junkers), who dominated state and society, thus reducing formerly free peasants to serfdom and towns to decadence. But the Junkers were undone by military weakness and depression during the Thirty Years' War.

During that war the Junkers resisted taxation and failed to provide for defense. Fiscal weakness and poverty (Brandenburg was known as "the sandbox of the Empire") left Hohenzollern domains to the mercies of foreign invaders. The war precipitated a conflict between the electors and their noble-dominated diets over the electors' desire to administer, defend, and expand their dynastic terri-

tories as a single state. The war forced some efforts along these lines: a central privy council for all Hohenzollern lands was established, and during the 1630s a centralized war commissariat began to develop independently of the local assemblies. But these diets were still wed to parochial interests and privilege, and Frederick William, the Great Elector who acceded to power in 1640, was forced to cooperate with them temporarily.

In 1653 Brandenburg witnessed the first test of strength between an elector and a provincial diet. Frederick William confirmed the old privileges of the nobles and granted them full power over the peasantry. He also acknowledged their tax exemptions and their privilege of importing and exporting their products duty-free, prerogatives that weighed heavily on townsmen and peasants. In return, the Junkers pledged Frederick William a long-term grant of money. Actually, the diet had unwittingly voted its own extinction when it abdicated financial control, for the outbreak of the Baltic War (1655–60) enabled the elector to secure further taxes without its consent. After 1653 no full diet met again in Brandenburg. In 1667, acting on his own authority, Frederick William

The Great Elector (*by Andreas Schlüter*).

imposed excise taxes on production and trade. His tax collectors were soon administering the cities, but urban crafts were prohibited in the countryside, and control remained in the Junkers' hands.

The elector used his new powers in Brandenburg to wrest concessions from other provincial diets. Taxes supported his standing army, and the army in turn collected the taxes he needed. When peace was signed in 1660, Frederick William did not disband his army as had been the custom; he maintained it and used it to further centralize the Hohenzollern state. Like Brandenburg, Prussia also lost its diet; the Great Elector broke its power during a war with Louis XIV from 1672 to 1678, when the War Commissariat collected military and excise taxes, pushing aside the diet and local officials. Still, as in Brandenburg, the Junkers in Prussia preserved their power over the peasantry, their administrative offices, and exclusive rights to trade in grain.

As in the eastern Hohenzollern lands, autocratic military rule superseded civil-

*A Prussian military parade in Berlin.*

ian control in the smaller territories of north-central Germany such as Magdeburg. But along the Rhine in Cleves and Mark, stronger towns, diets, and a less downtrodden peasantry blunted the thrust of electoral absolutism. Here the War Commissariat obtained large taxes but little administrative power. The Great Elector exempted the nobility from taxation and gave it extensive legal jurisdictions, but the Rhenish provinces retained their assemblies and never conformed to the eastern pattern of autocracy, serfdom, and suppression of town life.

Between 1653 and 1688 the Great Elector became one of Europe's most powerful rulers; his standing army and its administration made this development possible. At the end of the Thirty Years' War the Privy Council had been the highest legal and administrative body for both military and civil matters, but in 1660 it lost control of military affairs to the War Commissariat. This organization had originally been responsible for assembling, equipping, provisioning, and financing the army, but it steadily encroached upon civilian affairs, stripping local diets of fiscal power; and its agents extended their authority over guilds, town government, and courts. It also came to control taxes, trade, settlement of the Huguenots, and numerous other matters.

Hohenzollern absolutism paralleled many developments in France. Agents of the War Commissariat had powers resembling those of Louis XIV's intendants, and its bureaucracy operated under military regimentation. Corruption was less widespread, although family influence and nepotism were common. The Hohenzollern government also gained greater cooperation from the nobility than the French rulers ever enjoyed. It is true that both the Great Elector and Frederick William I placed commoners in positions of high authority; however, noblemen filled most of the offices at all times, and they kept control of the countryside and the army. Their political loyalty shifted away from the local diets to the monarch; still, that loyalty was conditioned by their own interests, to which the Great Elector made important concessions. Nevertheless absolutism stopped at the gates of the landed estates; the Junkers were exempted from all its controls except military conscription. In return for the nobles' service in the military bureaucracy, most of the population was abandoned to their rule.

The Hohenzollerns guaranteed to the Junker class a control of both rural and urban affairs, a guarantee that proved very costly. Taxes per capita were probably double those of France, draining potential capital from the economy and thereby undercutting the Great Elector's mercantilist policies, which were designed to stimulate economic growth. The taxes actually crippled the growth of towns, commerce, and industry.

Under the Great Elector's successors, Frederick (1688–1713) and Frederick William I (1713–40), Prussian absolutism became increasingly centralized. The military bureaucracy grew as the Hohenzollerns struggled to contain Louis XIV along the Rhine and to assume supremacy in the Baltic area. In 1723 the General Directory was formed, uniting civil and military chains of command into a single body. Created to save the state from near bankruptcy, it became the nucleus around which the power of the eighteenth-century Prussian state was built.

Frederick William I devoted special attention to the army; indeed Prussia was sometimes referred to as "an army with a state." At great expense he recruited giants from all over Europe for his palace guard at Potsdam. To Frederick II, who succeeded him in 1740, he therefore bequeathed a large army (80,000 men) and a centralized bureaucracy. The one great chink in the absolutist armor was the power and degree of independence that aristocratic officials enjoyed. Furthermore, the nobles resented the tax that Frederick William I imposed on them in order to help support his army. As the nobility had risen up in France after the death of Louis XIV, so the nobility of Prussia renewed its bid for power when Frederick William died.

## THE EMERGENCE OF RUSSIA AS A EUROPEAN POWER STATE

By the eighteenth century Russia came to resemble Brandenburg-Prussia as a society composed of serfs and lords and governed by a military bureaucracy. Ever since English and Dutch traders had made contact with Russia in the sixteenth century, Russian rulers had borrowed technology from the West to undergird their military power. Peter the Great (1682–1725) accelerated this Westernization and by territorial expansion brought Russian power to bear upon western and central Europe. Absolutism in Russia, however, rested upon political, social, religious, and intellectual traditions quite different from those of any western or central European state.

### The Muscovite Tradition

Forged by the grand dukes of Moscow, the Russian state never experienced that feudal decentralization which gave nobles, churchmen, and town councils in the West legal and political autonomy. No diets defended the vested interests of privileged Russians. Ivan III (1462–1505) stripped the autonomous city-state Novgorod of its republican institutions and dispersed its commercial families. Ivan IV (1533–84)—"the Terrible"—dealt similarly with the city of Pskov. When the government later fostered industry and trade, it was only under paternal state direction.

The grand dukes could suppress urban autonomy more easily than aristocratic

*Frederick William I reviewing his "giant guards."*

power. Ruling an agrarian state and short of money, they were obliged to reward their servants with land and privileges that became hereditary. To undermine the growing influence of the hereditary nobles—the *boyars*—Ivan IV (the first czar) called a representative advisory assembly, the *zemski sobor,* but this body never achieved the status of a Western diet. He also attempted to replace the boyars with a new nobility of service wholly dependent on his own person. When these measures failed, Ivan broke the boyars' power by using secret police and a system of extraordinary courts, both of which engaged in assassination and torture. But eventually the service nobility, too, acquired hereditary privileges that threatened his power. Although the struggle between czar and nobility persisted, the Russian aristocracy remained considerably weaker than its Western counterpart.

The Russian Orthodox church was another potential rival to the czar. Russian Christianity derived from Constantinople (Byzantium) where caesaropapism—the subordination of the Church to secular rulers, or caesars (hence czars)—was well established. During Moscow's wars of expansion Russian churchmen nationalized Orthodoxy into the doctrine that the czar was the only Christian king and Moscow, the "Third Rome," the only capital of pure Christianity remaining on the face of the earth. (Thus the Muscovites claimed to inherit the role of Constantinople, the "second Rome," which, like the first, had corrupted the faith.) This messianic doctrine made holy crusades of Moscow's wars; and the hold that religious leaders assumed over the Russian masses threatened the secular ruler who aimed to concentrate all power in himself.

Russian Orthodoxy and the heritage of Tartar rule* set thought and customs in Russia apart from Western traditions. Orthodox theology remained impervious to scholastic efforts toward reconciling faith with reason, and Russian thought was untouched by the Renaissance revival of classical languages and literatures. Prior to Peter the Great the country had but one printing press and no universities or intellectuals to foster Western culture. Russian

* The dukes of Muscovy overturned Tartar suzerainty in 1480.

clothing and customs (such as the seclusion of women) struck the inhabitants of western Europe as Oriental and alien.

## The Early Romanovs

Ivan IV did not establish internal security or a stable succession of rule by his reign of terror against the nobility. When his son died, in 1598, the male line of the Muscovite house became extinct, and Russia plunged into chaos. The last czar's father-in-law, Boris Godunov, tried to restore order and to found a dynasty, but after he died, in 1605, the army unseated and killed his heir. From 1605 to 1613 Russia was beset by a "Time of Troubles"—bitter faction, fighting, foreign invasion, internal brigandage, and famine. Swedish and Polish troops entered Moscow and vied to make their candidates czar. Finally in 1613 the zemski sobor selected Michael Romanov, who secured order and drove out the Poles and Swedes. His dynasty lasted until another time of troubles and social disintegration in 1917.

Michael's son, Alexis, waged wars of expansion and followed policies that foreshadowed the social regimentation completed by his son, Peter the Great. Tax associations of townsmen were organized to support the army; the royal treasury imposed an excessive salt tax and debased the coinage. These measures provoked riots and disorder and were undermined by the large-scale embezzlement by tax farmers. But popular resistance failed to check Alexis's progressive oppression of the peasantry and the church.

Before the advent of the Romanovs the Russian peasantry had been divided among free farmers, bondsmen, and slaves, but the freer peasants had been losing status since the thirteenth century. By 1550 they were on their way toward chattel serfdom, and as their condition deteriorated, many of them sought freedom and land by escaping to the borderlands in the Don, Dnieper, and Ural river valleys, where they formed egalitarian "Cossack" republics that bore the brunt of frontier fighting. Russian authorities then severely restricted peasant freedom of movement. A new law code in 1649 declared them to be a homogenous mass of serfs bound to the soil. By this time the Cossack areas were losing their attractiveness, for Cossack leaders were beginning to imitate Russian nobles. Soon the czars were ruling the Cossack territories and enforcing serfdom. Discontented Cossacks revolted repeatedly, and during the seventeenth and eighteenth centuries their uprisings spread to old Russia. Between 1667 and 1671 the Cossack Stenka Razin led the whole lower Volga in rebellion before he was captured and executed.

In reasserting czarist control over the church, Alexis had to deal with Nikon, patriarch of Moscow. Nikon urged liturgical reforms that would have facilitated Russian annexation of Greek Orthodox Slavs living under Polish and Turkish rule. But because the Patriarch challenged the czar's supreme authority he was banished. Alexis continued the reforms, however, against the determined opposition of the "Old Believers," Russians who insisted upon keeping the faith of their fathers as it was. Thousands of dissenters were executed or exiled; others burned themselves to death rather than submit. Many Old Believers, sure that the end of the world was at hand, found convincing proof that Alexis's successor, Peter the Great, was the Antichrist. This schism weakened the church, and Peter ultimately reduced it to a department of state under lay control.

## Peter the Great (1682–1725)

Peter transformed Russia from an isolated, landlocked state into a major Euro-

*Peter the Great.*

pressed with the streltsys' contribution to order, Peter set out to consolidate all power in his own hands. He devoted himself to military exercises by commanding a play regiment of grooms and servants (later, soldiers supplied from the arsenals of Moscow). From the foreign, or "German," quarter of Moscow he acquired a mistress, a fascination for Western technical skills and languages, and rowdy companions. At the age of 16 he married a nobleman's daughter, but he preferred shipbuilding, sailing, military exercises, and life in the German quarter to life with her.* In all of these unconventional exploits Peter was accompanied by Menshikov, a courtier of low birth who

* Eventually she retired to a convent to care for their son, Alexis, who was nurtured on her grievances. Peter then married Catherine, a gifted Lithuanian and former servant girl whose charms had attracted the court. Catherine later succeeded Peter to the throne. Alexis became involved with Peter's traditionalist opposition and, accused of treasonable plotting, was tortured to death.

pean power. Petrine Russia adopted Western technology, built a navy, and entered into diplomatic relations with Western chanceries. At Peter's death it extended from the Baltic Sea to the Kurile Islands north of Japan. These rapid changes were mainly the work of the eccentric giant who became czar in 1682.

The young czar was unconventional by any standards. Nearly seven feet tall, he further attracted attention by a jerky walk and nervous facial contortions. A drunken tutor from the bureaucracy gave him a meager formal education, but he learned mainly from experiences that left him disrespectful of the conventions of Russian society and gave him the tastes of an artisan proud of his calluses. At the outset of his reign his elder half-sister, Sophia, manipulated his half-brother and co-czar, Ivan V, intriguing with the palace guard, the streltsy, to purge Peter's relatives and many old boyars. Sophia became regent over both Peter and Ivan, but when she made a second bid for power in 1689, she was confined to a convent. Little im-

*Satirical cartoon of Peter's order to clip beards.*

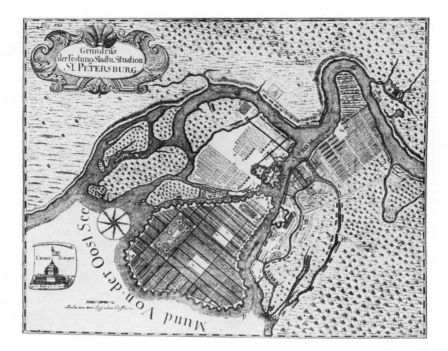

*Layout of St. Petersburg in 1738.*

remained his principal advisor. Fired by exuberant energy, the czar always kept moving. And he drove his people as hard as himself.

In 1695 Peter began to apply his acquired skills by launching an attack on Turkey, then engaged in war with the Habsburgs. Aided by Russia's first fleet, which Peter assembled on the Don, his army took Azov. The courts of Europe took note of this victory, and their curiosity increased when the czar made his "Grand Embassy" to the West. Ostensibly it was to arrange a coalition against the Turks, but its primary purpose was to acquire the technical knowledge that Russia lacked.

## The Czar Westernizer

The events of Peter's itinerary were most extraordinary. Traveling incognito as "Mein Herr Peter Mikhailov," an uncommissioned officer in the party, he put his disguise aside at the courts, insisting on being received with the honors of state. At one German court he mistook his dancing partner's unfamiliar corset stays for protruding ribs; in London he and his rowdy companions left the house of their host a shambles; in the Netherlands he discussed the Quaker religion with William Penn. But his mission was to acquire technology that he could apply in Russia upon his return. In England he visited factories, arsenals, and shipyards, taking copious notes; in the Netherlands he even served as a shipwright carpenter; in Vienna, where he stopped to negotiate an alliance against the Turks, news reached him that the streltsy had revolted again. Stopping only to negotiate with Augustus, elector of Saxony and king of Poland, Peter hastened home.

Peter's ferocity in putting down the

## WESTERN EXPANSION OF PETRINE RUSSIA

**Legend:**
- Acquisition of Alexis, 1667
- Acquisition of Peter the Great
- Invasion route of Charles XII
- Shipyard
- Iron & armaments — Under Peter the Great
- Textiles

SWEDEN

FINLAND

KARELIA

White Sea

Archangel

Dvina R.

RUSSIA

Ural Mts.

Viborg

ESTHONIA

Narva
1700

INGRIA

St. Petersburg

Riga

LIVONIA

Novgorod

Pskov

Volga R.

Ekaterinburg

POLAND

Smolensk

Moscow

Volga R.

Ural R.

Kiev

Dnieper R.

Poltava
1709

Caspian Sea

OTTOMAN

Bender

Ochakov

EMPIRE

Don R.

Azov
1696-1711

Sea
of Azov

Crimea

Caucasus Mts.

Black Sea

0   100   200   300 mi.

Map by J. Donovan

streltsy and the radicalness of his new reform edicts expressed his determination to imitate western European absolutism. In quelling the revolt he and Menshikov punished the innocent with the guilty in order to break the guards' power permanently. The czar then ordered courtiers to shave their beards and adopt Western dress; peasants and priests could escape the order only by paying a special tax. But to Orthodox Russian Christians beards were a sacrosanct part of the human body, created in the image of God. Politically the assault on beards and Oriental dress was a thrust at the Old Believers who had sympathized with the streltsy. To gain revenue Peter also affronted the traditionalists by promoting the use of (taxed) tobacco. Most of his subjects considered smoking no less a defilement of the human body than the shaving of beards. These two official acts augured a more comprehensive effort by the czar to introduce foreign, Western culture into Russia during the remainder of his reign.

## Peter's Foreign Policy

Constant warfare filled the rest of Peter's reign, and military demands became the primary motive for the subsequent reforms that are so closely linked to his name. He fought on all frontiers, making Russia an empire; but his overriding goal was to gain unimpeded access to the Baltic and Black seas.

Peter first launched a new fleet against the Turks while they were at war with Austria. But at Karlowitz in 1699 Austria made peace, leaving Russia to fight the Turks alone. Peter finally secured a truce in 1700, after having allied his country with Denmark, Poland, and Saxony for the purpose of partitioning Sweden's Baltic empire. On the same day that he learned of the Turkish truce he declared war on Sweden; but also on the same day King Charles XII of Sweden eliminated Denmark from the war. At Narva, on the Estonian border, Peter massed 60,000 raw recruits under the command of foreign officers. With only 8000 men Charles XII dealt the Russians a terrifying setback. Luckily for Peter, Charles chose not to prosecute his victory, turning instead to pursue Augustus into Poland.

The czar spent the years between 1700 and 1709 feverishly training a new peasant army with which he conquered Ingria and Livonia, the two Swedish possessions nearest Russia. These territories gave him access to the Baltic and provided the site for the city of St. Petersburg, the czar's window on the West, founded on a barren moor in 1703. Built by forced labor at a tremendous sacrifice of life, St. Petersburg became the capital of Russia, a monument to its namesake's Western orientation.

By 1708 Charles XII had moved into the Ukraine on an ill-fated expedition: in vain he sought alliances with dissident Cossacks and Turks; the winter of 1708 depleted his forces, and the local population, maltreated at his hands, launched guerrilla warfare against him. Peter cut off Charles's supply and reinforcement columns, and at Poltava in 1709 the czar's larger army decisively defeated the Swedes. Charles fled to Turkey, where he intrigued for a new Turkish attack on Russia. Meanwhile Peter reconstructed his northern alliance against Sweden, conquering Karelia and more of Livonia and laying claim to Courland on the Baltic; but in the south he lost his earlier gains: in 1711 the Turks forced him to surrender the territory gained in 1700 that gave Russia access to the Black Sea.

Russia fared better in the Great Northern War for Baltic supremacy. Using his refurbished navy, Peter took Finland and threatened Sweden itself. He hoped to gain the Swedish crown by marriage and widen his grip on northern Germany by diplomacy, which, however, began to falter as his occupying armies turned the German princes against him. After Charles XII's death in 1718, England prevented Russia from overrunning Sweden, but the Treaty of Nystad in 1721 forced the Swedes to cede most of their Baltic empire to Russia. Although this treaty restored Finland to Sweden, it recognized Russian possession of the Baltic coast from Riga to Viborg. Peter had acquired not one, but nine, ports and bases on the Baltic. Russia seemed about to become a major naval and maritime power; however, after Peter's death the fleets deteriorated rapidly.

## Russian Administrative Absolutism

Keeping the war machine going on all frontiers took immense manpower and money and necessitated administrative reorganization. In order to maintain his huge standing army the czar conscripted the enserfed subjects of his nobles. (His recruiting system, with its 25-year term of enlistment, lasted until 1874). His campaigns also required conscript labor, whose losses often equaled those of the army. Peter relied on nobles and foreign adventurers to lead the army and bureaucracy, forcing the nobility to share preferment with newcomers. In 1722 the czar instituted a Table of Ranks to determine the status of his servants. It organized the army, civil service, and the court into fourteen parallel grades. Children of nobles were obliged to start at the bottom grade, but all became nobles upon appointment to the lowest officer rank in the army or upon promotion to the eighth rank in the court or civil service. Those attaining noble status were granted lands, the exclusive right to own serfs, and other privileges that later became hereditary. In order to equip themselves for service the children of the nobility were required to attend state schools, another of Peter's innovations. But the schools were few, and resistance to them debilitatingly strong. Like his predecessors, Peter could not regiment all classes for state service without great opposition.

In a country lacking commercial capital and banking institutions the raising of money to finance administration and wars was a major undertaking. Because the treasury had no credit all expenses had to be met currently. The Great Northern War brought a financial crisis that led to a host of new military and indirect taxes; in fact, tax revenues trebled during Peter's reign, and he had to employ "revenue-finder" boards to discover new taxable items.* His government established monopolies to raise revenue on such items as salt, tobacco, cod liver oil, potash, and coffins; it also commandeered monastic revenues and once more debased the coinage. These measures were in addition to the traditional direct tax on households and implements.

The levy on households, which had been the principal source of revenue, began to dry up as householders evaded it, fled, or were conscripted. The government replaced it with a head, or "soul," tax, applicable to all male peasants. The backbone of the revenue structure until 1886, this tax was collected by the lords of the village communes. Since anyone enrolled on their tax registers was automatically a serf, this tax system helped spread serfdom. Nevertheless the treasury did not reap the principal benefit from the new taxes, for officials, embezzling this and other public money, apparently took as much as 70 percent of all collections.

Peter's effort to introduce Western mercantilist policies fared no better than his tax reforms. In order to encourage industry, mining, and commerce under paternal direction of the state, he enacted high protective tariffs and leased state-built factories to private individuals on favorable terms. Entrepreneurs who copied Western technology were given tax exemptions, interest-free loans, and the coveted privilege of owning serfs. Peter also sent technicians abroad for training and wooed skilled immigrants. Overall, his program of economic development

* The list grew to include lands, rents, sales, horsecollars, hats, boots, horsehides, beehives, hot baths, chimney stacks, beards, moustaches, nuts, watermelons, and cucumbers.

failed, even though the country became self-sufficient in some areas of industry and exported iron and sailcloth. Capitalists, distrustful of officials and regulations, failed to meet Peter's expectations. Rather than increasing revenues, his mercantilism added to state expenditures.

Repeated attempts to reorganize the central administration also failed. In practice the central government was more often represented by military commanders than by civil authorities. In most of Russia the local nobles constituted the only government. Neither military rule, savage punishments, decentralization, nor secret informers eliminated the bribery and corruption that riddled the bureaucracy from top to bottom. The most notorious offender was Prince Menshikov, Peter's closest associate, who accumulated a legendary fortune without losing favor. Against the bureaucracy and military authorities, the public resorted to fraud and violence on a local—sometimes a general—scale.

However Peter did succeed in bringing the Orthodox church, the largest organization in Russia, under secular control. When the patriarch died in 1700, Peter named no successor. Several years later the Holy Synod, a collegiate board headed by a lay procurator, assumed control of the church. The state thus silenced, to some extent, clerics who opposed such reforms as secular education, limited toleration, and the Julian calendar. The Holy Synod itself was charged with dispelling ignorance and superstition by improving education, but the regulation establishing this disclosed still another, more important, purpose: the elimination of the patriarch as a competitor of the czar for the spiritual allegiance of the masses. The subordination of the church to the state served Russian autocracy until 1917.

Peter's impact upon Russian society and government was decisive and long-lived. Despite its failings, in practice the struc-ture he built held firm until the nineteenth century, much of it until 1917. He brought absolutism to its highest point with the undoing of the old nobility, the elimination of the zemski sobor (Russia's only representative institution) and the assertion of the czar's right to name his own successor. However he did not implement a system of succession, failing even to name a ruler to follow himself. Violence and intrigue continued to determine who would hold the reins of power. The strongest force in the state was an immense standing army, and the palace guard decided the fates of the czars and czarinas who followed.

Peter gained a reputation as a westernizer. Conservative nativists accused him of despoiling the Russian soul with heresy, rationalism, and foreign values. Certainly he borrowed institutions, techniques, and outlooks from France, Sweden, England, and the Dutch Republic. St. Petersburg remained the capital and the center of intercourse with the West. By dynastic marriage and intrigue the Romanov dynasty became basically German, and the petrine state assumed a lasting place in the European state system. Nevertheless Peter's westernization was selective; it mainly modified and strengthened existing institutions that resisted deep penetration by Western culture. The army was modernized, but it remained the basic tool of administration. Serfdom was extended and riveted into law and practice by the state. Some of the higher nobles eventually accepted Westernization, but over the larger society of enserfed peasants and boorish lords it lay as a shallow veneer. The question remains whether Peter really wanted to westernize or whether he instead borrowed European technology to defend Russia against Western encroachment. In either case his experience pointed up the limitations of absolutism even in a state where organized opposition was not possible.

## C. Aristocratic Monarchies

Alongside the divine-right kingdoms that we have discussed stood other monarchies whose rulers laid equal claim to unlimited authority but whose effective power was too weak to be considered absolute at all. Some of them—Spain and Sweden for example—had been Europe's leading states but were now in decline. None of them had the strength to hold its own in the dynastic power struggles of the second half of the seventeenth century. In all of them the trend of political development was toward decentralization, away from absolutism.

### SPAIN AND ITALY

There was a close relationship between the rising star of France in western Europe and the falling star of the Spanish Habsburg Empire. Spain emerged from the Thirty Years' War and the Bourbon-Habsburg conflict with an immense empire—still Europe's largest—and great imperial pride; but its men and materials had been overcommitted and overexpended during a previous century of warfare. The efforts of Philip IV's war minister, de Olivares, to revitalize Spain and shunt some of the burdens of empire onto kingdoms other than Castile had come to naught. To put down revolts against de Olivares's "Castilianization" the king was forced to confirm the territorial privileges of the Catalans. The Portuguese, whose revolt in 1640 opened a second front in the Iberian peninsula until peace was signed with France in 1659, slipped away completely. Thereafter Louis XIV denied the exhausted Habsburgs any respite from his encroachment on the Spanish Netherlands and along France's eastern frontier.

During the final phases of the Thirty Year's War Spain suffered an acute depression, and evidence of recovery was hardly perceptible for the rest of the century. Inflation reached dizzy heights prior to 1680, when a particularly severe deflation occurred. Imports of bullion from the New World came to a halt, and foreign smugglers, abetted by monopolistic colonial trade laws, paid no duties in Castile's inadequately defended empire. Although the ruined middle classes recovered somewhat in Catalonia, they were displaced in the rest of the empire by French, Dutch, and English merchants, who dominated Spain's economic life and monopolized its trade with the Americas.

Meanwhile depression deepened the great gulf between the poor and the wealthy, privileged minority. By 1700 nobility, Church, and Crown held an estimated 95 percent of the land. The shepherds' guild (*Mesta*) maintained its privileges at the expense of Spanish agriculture, but its flocks were mere shadows of what they had once been. Seignorial oppression of the peasants went unchecked, and vagabondage and banditry became alternative ways of life. Increasing numbers found a living within the Church. The aristocracy failed conspicuously as a ruling minority, and both courtiers and impoverished *hidalgos* abhorred the manual labor, commerce, and economic investment that the crown tried to make respectable in 1680. Educated churchmen likewise failed in leadership, cherishing contemplative passivity and disdaining the practical application of reason to Spain's pressing social, economic, and political problems.

The postwar government of Philip V momentarily arrested Spain's decline. To some degree he imitated Louis XIV in subordinating the Church and the nobility to central control, restoring authority and commerce in the empire. Yet he could not fundamentally cure the hardening of Spain's social and political arteries, and his schemes of reform failed without exception. By and large the empire remained impervious to contemporary commercial change, rational government, secular science, and speculative thought. And failure to cope with these developments hastened the empire's relative decline.

Like Spain, whose decaying and corrupt authority still dominated the peninsula, Italy was caught in a midcentury depression. Her cities, population, and trade continued to decline until by 1700 most Italian principalities were completely agrarian. Venice, still a maritime state independent of Spain, was beset by a long series of wars with the Turks, and its capital resources flowed steadily from commerce to land. And while commercial life still flickered in Lombardy, Tuscany, and Piedmont, their societies were dominated by the routine of petty courts. Intellectual life and even the arts, save for music and baroque architecture, were in a state of decay. Italy was still a major stopping point on the "grand tour" of every young European aristocrat, but it had become a museum for the greatness of the past

rather than a showplace of vitality for the present.

## THE HOLY ROMAN EMPIRE

The Peace of Westphalia ratified the fragmentation of the Holy Roman Empire into hundreds of petty states. Kings of France, Sweden, and Castile—all princes of the empire—worked against coordinated action, and no imperial bureaucracy existed. When, in 1663, the Reichstag (Imperial Diet) went into permanent session as an assembly of delegates instructed by their states, effective business practically ceased. The Imperial High Court was notorious for the jurisdictions exempted from its authority and for delays of a half-century or more in deciding cases, long after the original litigants had died. Political theorists began to dispute both the Holy and the Roman origins of this empire, considering it instead a contractual republic of princes. In any case, politics were determined by the particularism of innumerable states.

Individual German princes were inspired by Louis XIV, and a number of them built smaller versions of Versailles near their capitals. But not all German principalities became little "absolute monarchies." In some of them the diets remained active and standing armies small. Some German diets became the sole preserve of the landed nobility, while others, privileged oligarchies that they were, preserved traditions that later joined with parliamentary government.

Economic decline accompanied particularistic politics. Seeking fat revenues and self-sufficiency, German princes crisscrossed the empire with a maze of rigid barriers to commerce and production. These barriers delayed the recovery of the economy from the disasters of the Thirty Years' War. As late as 1668 one official reported: "There is hardly any trade and enterprise, all commerce is ruined, no money is to be found either among the great or among the small people."[3] It was more than a century before the empire regained its 1618 level of prosperity, and during its prolonged period of weakness German towns fell more completely than before into princely hands. Even closed urban oligarchies in the Imperial Free Cities accepted the aristocratic dictum that trade was ignoble. Many governments pursued mercantilistic policies as a means of spurring economic activity, but since their taxes sapped the capital and initiative of their productive subjects, it is debatable whether they should be praised for sponsoring production or condemned for making consumption impossible. The same question, of course, applies to the effective absolute regimes such as Brandenburg-Prussia and Russia.

## NORTHERN AND EASTERN EUROPE

### Denmark, Sweden, and Poland

In Scandinavia the political pattern was more uniform than in the empire. Sweden was a major power in control of most of the Baltic coast between 1660 and 1710. Its warrior-king, Charles XII, tried also to acquire Poland but lacked the population and resources for such a large-scale enterprise. After Charles was killed and Sweden was defeated in the Great Northern War, noble factions dominated political life there. Similar factions controlled the kingdom of Denmark, which was exhausted by generations of dynastic warfare with Sweden.

Poland, however, furnished the classic case of aristocratic decentralization. Ex-

[3] Quoted in the *New Cambridge Modern History*, vol. 5, *The Ascendancy of France 1648–1688*, (Cambridge: Cambridge University Press, 1961), p. 434.

tending from the Baltic almost to the Black Sea in the fifteenth and sixteenth centuries, it was now surrounded by aggressive neighbors who took advantage of its internal weakness to invade it repeatedly. An exceedingly numerous nobility, the only class represented in the local and central diets, crushed town interests, the peasantry, and the authority of the elective monarchy. Political life centered on the conflicts of a few great noble families, behind which the lesser nobles arrayed themselves in factions. By the middle of the seventeenth century decisive action by the central government was hardly possible. Furthermore, the diet kept the army ridiculously small. Foreign-sponsored candidates (Augustus the Strong of Saxony was one successful example) vied for the empty honor. By the infamous *liberum veto* any delegate to the central diet could, and on critical occasions did, rise to end further deliberations and to nullify all previous measures passed by the current diet. Only the inability of its foes to cooperate preserved Poland from dismemberment until the late eighteenth century.

### The Ottoman Decline

By virtue of its hold on the Balkan peninsula and the southern Ukraine, the Ottoman Empire was a major European power with its base in Asia Minor and the Near East; nominally the sultans also ruled North Africa from Egypt to Algeria. Formidable as this imperial giant seemed, internal decay and failure to keep pace with its opponents were sapping its relative strength, as its retreat before the Habsburgs showed. A long succession of capable sultans had come to an end in 1566. Thereafter strong leaders rose in times of crisis, but the roots of deterioration were beyond their power to extirpate. Ottoman power had rested on a feudal cavalry and the famed Janissary corps of infantry, recruited as tribute from Balkan Christian communities. No longer terror-inspiring, the Janissaries were becoming a self-perpetuating and privileged Muslim force that made and unmade sultans and officials as harem intrigues and bribery dictated. They neglected the navy and spurned new military inventions such as the bayonet.

Devoid of commercial safeguards and improvements, the Ottoman economy got along no better than the government. Western merchants, backed by their governments, preyed on Turkish commerce and, unsupported by protective tariffs, native production remained at the handicraft level. Whereas the rural population formerly enjoyed a better life than most European peasants, it now fell into the bondage of the privileged orders. Intellectually the Turks remained pre-Renaissance, and the dead weight of tradition stifled innovation. Even by using terror, reformers were unable to check the decline.

Ottoman power was temporarily revived by the Kiuprili dynasty of grand viziers, the sultans' chief administrators. Believing that territorial conquest and the seizure of slaves could generate vitality, they resumed military pressure on the Danube. Venice, Poland, and Russia joined Austria in a holy league to drive them from Europe.* The results we have seen in the Treaty of Karlowitz.† Freed from fear of Ottoman aggression, Europe now took up the "Eastern question." To what state or states would the territories of the weakened empire fall? Because Europeans could make no answer, the Ottoman Empire lived on for nearly two more centuries. Nevertheless its losses of territory and internal trade indicated Europe's continued expansion to the east.

* One casualty of this war was the Parthenon, which the Turks used as a powder magazine in defending the Peloponnesus from Venetian invasion.
† See p. 225.

# D. The Maritime States: England and the Dutch Republic

Declining monarchies and former commercial centers remained most heavily caked with custom, governed by the aristocratic and clerical traditions of medieval times. Competitive power struggles forced some innovations upon absolutist states, but they nevertheless continued to preserve social privileges and a hierarchical society. Neither the effective absolutist regimes nor the aristocratic monarchies made fundamental changes in their socioeconomic structure or introduced new concepts of government. Such changes were peculiar to the maritime states—England and the Dutch Republic, and even they retained much that was traditional or even medieval, especially the notion that government should be limited or contractual in nature. But they instituted a broader governing class and set constitutional limits to the powers of the state. As a result these governments commanded more voluntary obedience from their subjects than they did absolutisms, which arrogated all initiative to the Crown or to aristocracies of birth.

In both England and the Dutch Republic absolutism yielded to the political demands of aristocratic and commercial groups

One Evins a Welch man was lately comited to New-gate for saying hee was Christ

*Iesuit*

*Hears one blasphemously
Thathee was christ did say
Such spirits were foretold
To rise ith latter daye*

*Arminian*

*Ante Scripturian*

*Soul Sleeper*

*Anabaptist*

*Religious diversity: a derogatory view of sectarianism.*

whose strength lay in trade, finance, industry, and market-oriented agriculture; by their wealth and credit they created more military resources than any impoverished absolutism ever enjoyed. Significantly, geography partially guaranteed both countries protection from foreign invasion. England was protected by the sea, the Dutch Republic by its system of rivers, canals, and floodable fields. Thus they could escape from the two primary instruments of absolutism: a permanent standing army and extraparliamentary taxation to finance it. From their relative abundance these maritime states probably spent more per capita on arms than any absolute monarchy, but their money went largely for navies, which

were difficult to deploy against domestic foes, and for mercenary armies raised for specific occasions.

These states diverged from authoritarianism not only politically but also in their religious and intellectual activity. The prevailing formula of the Reformation (the religion of the prince determines the religion of the people) gave way to compromise with limited toleration. Religious pluralism undermined rigorous censorship and divine-right kingship. Although often precariously, radical sectarians maintained their existence, and secular humanists could resume Renaissance speculation about politics and society, which had been interrupted by the Reformation and the religious wars. As

Arian      Adamite      Libertin

Familist      Seeker      Divorcer

refuges for exiles and as establishers of freer societies for their own subjects, England and the Dutch Republic, as well as the English colonies of North America, became the seedbeds of those liberal and humanitarian heresies that flowered during the eighteenth-century Enlightenment.

## THE DUTCH REPUBLIC

Constitutionally the Dutch Republic was a confederation of disparate provinces whose diets sent instructed delegates to the common States General. In Guelderland feudal nobles ruled over subsistent tenant farmers. In Utrecht authority was vested in Protestant canons who had replaced electors of the former Roman Catholic bishop. The richest and most powerful provinces were the commercial states of Zeeland and Holland, ruled by regents—families who lived from investments rather than trade and who made governing a hereditary profession. Led by Jan DeWitt, the grand pensionary of Holland, the regents coordinated the Republic's affairs from 1650 to 1672, defending its aristocratic, decentralized constitution. Favoring the humanistic Calvinists (Arminians) in religion, the regents nevertheless had the tacit support of both Roman Catholics and the sectarians, whom they protected from Calvinist persecution.

Jan DeWitt was locked in a political tug of war with the House of Orange, which traditionally had filled the chief executive, judicial, and military office of stadtholder

*Jan DeWitt and the mob that lynched him.*

in each province. Behind the Orange faction stood the orthodox Calvinist clergy, the discontented urban poor, and most of the local authorities in the rural provinces. To check the monarchical ambitions of the House of Orange, DeWitt secured acceptance in all seven provinces of an eternal edict (1670) barring the young William of Orange from the stadtholderates. But failures in foreign policy brought about the fall of DeWitt and the regents' government. Orangist revolutionaries murdered him in 1672 when the French took advantage of his lack of military preparations to invade the country. William of Orange did not become a monarch and establish a court, but after 1688, working through favorites, he directed Dutch affairs as king of England until his death in 1702. After the War of Spanish Succession the regents' oligarchy again took power, but by then the Dutch Republic's economy and politics stagnated.

Experimenting with a compromise between liberty and order, the Dutch Republic of the seventeenth century became a haven of personal freedom in absolutist Europe, a laboratory of liberalism. But as its commerce declined, its political evolution followed the earlier course of Venice. Dutch greatness had filled the interim between Spanish and French hegemony on the Continent. After 1650 its economy ceased to expand, and in the latter half of the century it consolidated its previous gains and defended them against its greatest rivals, the merchants and navy of England. Between 1652 and 1678 the Republic fought a series of commercial wars with England on even terms, but at the end of the War of Spanish Succession it failed to share in the commercial spoils, which fell instead to England.

In great part the Dutch Republic declined because its resources and population were insufficient to compete with stronger rivals. Internal decay was also responsible. At its peak the Dutch economy pioneered in commercial agriculture and adopted technical skills and techniques for sustaining a dense population; and the Republic's level of education was probably the highest in Europe. But even when commerce was expanding, the lower classes could barely subsist and were burdened by heavy excise taxes. Despite extensive organized charity, hunger was widespread and prompted many youths to enlist in the navy and the merchant marine. By the end of the seventeenth century the Dutch had lost their technological leadership. Investment flowed into banking, insurance, life annuities, state debts, and foreign plantations; yet such investments did not provide domestic employment. Amsterdam remained the financial capital of Europe, but the domestic economy had lost its dynamism.

## THE TRIUMPH OF THE ENGLISH PARLIAMENT

England, Europe's other major maritime power, had also experimented with republican government after the execution of Charles I in 1648. Three years later Oliver Cromwell proposed a union of the two kingless states, England and the Dutch Republic, but instead of uniting they fell to fighting for control of sea-lanes. Becoming less and less popular at home, Cromwell's government deteriorated into a military dictatorship, which his son and political heir was unable to maintain. As the people of England grew impatient with the rule of Puritan saints, Parliament in 1660 invited the Stuarts to return. An able monarch coming to the throne on a wave of religious and political reaction against the Puritan revolution, Charles II soon posed a serious challenge to parliamentary authority. But the Restoration proved to be only an interlude before Parliament took control of the royal succession and, ultimately, most of the powers of the Crown itself.

## The Stuart Restoration

Charles II, the Stuart Restoration.

Like his Stuart predecessors, Charles II was an absolutist in outlook. But England differed sharply from the conditions that fostered autocracy in many continental kingdoms. Economically the English lower classes may have been no better off than the French peasantry, but they enjoyed at least a modicum of civil rights and had left behind them for good the servile conditions of much of the continental peasantry east of the Rhine. Not popular rights but the organized power of the upper classes, however, had been and continued to be the great barrier to Stuart absolutism—Parliament, the common law courts, and the unpaid justices of the peace who came from the gentry. Moreover the social distance between the enlarged merchant classes and the lower aristocracy was smaller than in the continental kingdoms.* The two groups were tied by intermarriage and were repre-

sented in the same house of Parliament, where their participation in affairs of state had given them a national outlook.

Still Charles II had great political abilities; had he lived longer he might have been able to put Stuart concepts of government into effect. The Restoration Settlement was moderate enough not to create a large number of foes for him. Crown and church lands were restored, but confiscated Cavalier estates that had been resold often remained in the hands of Cromwell's followers. Only about twenty persons, who had not been quick enough to declare for the Stuarts, were executed for their part in the civil wars. The least moderate part of the Settlement was a series of laws designed to break Puritan power forever, the Clarendon Code. These laws removed Puritan clergymen from their benefices, barred Puritans from political activity, and prohibited nonconformist teaching and worship assemblies.

* English landlords who improved and managed their own estates enjoyed respect that only the court nobility, for example, held in France.

But the Clarendon Code was the work of the "Cavalier Parliament," not the king.

Benefiting from popular reactions against Puritan rule, Charles's partisans in Parliament protected royal authority, giving him broader treason and censorship laws. They empowered him to select those acts of the interregnum that he wished to retain as binding laws. Parliament also granted him revenues for life, which, fed by commercial prosperity, yielded him greater incomes than anyone anticipated. Charles used his power to add Bombay and New Amsterdam (present-day New York City) to England's commercial empire. His diplomatic alignment with Louis XIV was unpopular, but French subsidies made him more independent of Parliament, which was offended by his suspension of penalties against Catholics and Protestant dissenters. Although his court was a moral affront to Puritans, it catered to science, art, and literature. Many a powerful pen supported him while his radical opposition, led by the Earl of Shaftesbury, discredited itself by republican tendencies, involvement in plots that revived the specter of civil war, and the use of unsubstantiated evidence to secure the execution of Catholics accused of conspiracy.

The most irreconcilable issue between King and Parliament was religion. Charles had Catholic sympathies and a French Catholic queen. His brother and heir apparent—James, Duke of York—was an open Catholic. Suspicion that the king had bound himself to Louis XIV to restore Catholicism in England was founded in fact; the secret Treaty of Dover (1670) had just such stipulations. By exempting Catholics and Protestant dissenters from the penalties of law, Charles aroused religious ire and the constitutional objection that he was setting himself above the law. Parliament rebuffed him with the Test Act of 1673, which required officeholders to denounce the Roman Catholic form of communion and to take the Anglican sac-

rament annually. Anglicanism became the necessary badge for political privilege and advancement; even the Duke of York was forced out of the Admiralty by its terms. But did its provisions extend to the Crown itself? James's heir apparency inevitably raised that question in English politics.

Bills to exclude the Duke of York from succeeding to the throne failed in Parliament, but they became the issue around which political factions formed. The Whig party—composed of progressive landlords, merchants, and Protestant dissenters—originated these bills. The Whigs' opponents were the Tories, a court party whose religious views were High Anglican and whose viewpoints represented the more conservative landed gentlemen. Committed as a matter of religious conscience to the passive obedience of subjects to legitimate kings, the Tories supported Charles II and received offices and favors from him. Fighting for principles rather than following practical politics, radical republican and Whig plotters pushed conservative Whigs into the king's camp also, and with their support Charles was empowered by a corporation act to revoke municipal charters, a power that he also used to replace Whig with Tory councils. Meanwhile trade expanded and with it royal revenues. At his death in 1685 Charles was at the peak of his power. For the moment, parliamentary government had ceased to function.

## James II and the "Glorious Revolution"

James II inherited the throne, Charles's revenues, and his brother's conflicts. His accession was contested by the Duke of Monmouth, Charles II's illegitimate son, who, counting upon Whig support, led an insurrection against James. Bloodily suppressed, the revolt put a standing army at the king's disposal. James was embold-

*James II, an unwelcome king.*

ened by his easy victory and appointed Roman Catholic officials in violation of the Test Act in addition to reviving the Court of High Commission to deal with religious offenders. He acted rapidly to remove recalcitrant judges, maintain his standing army, and force suspension of legal penalties against Catholics and Protestant dissenters. These actions opened old and tender sores, but Englishmen would probably have put up with him if he had had no male heir. In 1688, however, the queen bore a son, James.

Threatened with an eventual Roman Catholic succession, prominent Whigs and Tories cooperated in inviting William of Orange and his wife, Mary (James's Protestant daughter by an earlier marriage) to the throne. Others organized conspiracies in the army and navy in order to disarm the king. Committed to divine-right monarchy, the Anglican Tories were caught in a serious dilemma, but their qualms with respect to overturning James II were eased when he elected to flee rather than fight. Officially he was held to have abdicated. But there still remained his legitimate son and heir.

On this issue the Tories salved their consciences by believing the myth that a commoner child had been smuggled into the queen's chamber in a warming pan. The royal heir did not exist! After the Revolution of 1688 many Anglicans who had participated in it refused to take oaths to the new monarchs as legitimate sovereigns; some even became Jacobites—that is, Stuart counterrevolutionaries who wished to give the throne to James III.

## The Revolutionary Settlement and After

The "Glorious Revolution" of 1688 established the constitutional supremacy of Parliament. The Bill of Rights in 1689 confirmed Parliament's past demands against Stuart kings. It limited royal authority over a peacetime standing army to a specific number of years and defined treason more narrowly, thus making this crime more difficult to prove in court. James II's bid for support from religious dissenters had forced Anglicans to promise them toleration, although not political and civic rights; an act of 1689 exempted all except Roman Catholics and Unitarians from punitive penalties. Formal censorship, but not stringent libel laws, lapsed in 1695.* The Crown, whose succession Parliament now determined, retained considerable powers. After the judiciary's independence was confirmed by an act of 1701, the English constitution had a balance and division of executive, legislative, and judicial powers. But royal prerogatives gradually dwindled. Queen Anne (1702–14) was the last English monarch to wield a royal

*The press became freer in England's American colonies because libel was much more narrowly construed.

veto. During the eighteenth century executive and legislative functions began to merge in the cabinet, a committee standing between Crown and Parliament.

Clearly Parliament was replacing the court as the source of both favor and corruption, an unmistakable indication that power had shifted. But Parliament was an oligarchy, part of the same oligarchy from which local justices and jurists were drawn. To some extent individual rights were protected by the division of the oligarchy into factions of Whig and Tory; but when these were in solid agreement, as upon economic and social policy, their sympathies were distinctly aristocratic. Parliament—not the people—was sovereign, and its two houses were substantially under the same coterie of agrarian and commercial interests.

Having men of means involved in politics marshaled unexpected power behind the English government. As distrust dissolved between King and Parliament, the latter's purse strings loosened. Royal debts became state debts and after 1694 were handled by the Bank of England. The accession of William and Mary marked a revolution in English foreign policy. England became the foremost opponent of Louis XIV, both in Europe and overseas, and for her increased power she was amply rewarded at the end of the War of Spanish Succession with colonial territory and commercial concessions.

Thus in cooperation with the central government, men experienced in trade, finance, and administration were laying the basis for England's colonial and commercial supremacy during the eighteenth century. Unlike trade and production in the Dutch Republic, British commerce continued to expand until the end of the eighteenth century, when it became the basis for urban industrialization.

## E. Interpreting Absolutism: a Paradox

German historians of the nineteenth century made conventional the interpretation that divine-right monarchy was an evolutionary stepping stone to the "modern nation-state." Thereafter absolutism is generally treated as an episode in the centralization of political power that delivered coups de grace to the local power of nobles and churchmen. Historians have also considered absolutism as a part of the "rise of the middle class," who served as officials to kings and as beneficiaries of mercantilist economics. Furthermore, some have tied mercantilism and the absolute state's large-scale purchases of military supplies to the growth of capitalism. Taken together these interpretations conceive of absolutism as a force working for modernization, a necessary step in the transition to the liberal-national state of the nineteenth century.

Individual parts of these interpretations have merit, but as a whole they tend to confuse the *ideology* of absolutism with a *reality* that was quite different. Some absolute regimes did indeed develop trained central bureaucracies, which modern states have imitated; but more generally they established standing professional armies that were authorized monopolies of violence within the state. Both army and bureaucracy took autonomy away from the old nobility, but no monarch stripped the aristocracy of its economic and social privileges. Instead, most absolute rulers multiplied the number of privileged offices and granted hereditary rights to new office-holders. Such newly created privileges were indistinguishable from traditional medieval privileges that limited the powers of absolute kings. Under these officials, new and old, not uniformity but endless diversity prevailed in domestic affairs. Jurisdictions were ill-defined, many, and confused; villages and towns ignored or defied orders and edicts; even taxes—the principal point of contact between state and subject—varied drastically according to social status and locality. Uniformity was more characteristic of religion, for the established churches were the most centralized institutions. In the aristocratic monarchies executive authority had little centralizing effect and commanded even less obedience.

As we have noted, absolutism has often been cited by historians as a major factor in the rise of the middle class and capitalism. But this alleged connection is tenuous if not misleading. It is a blunt fact that the two capitalist commercial states, the Dutch Republic and England, rejected royal absolutism and that divine-right kings flourished in agrarian societies. If absolute monarchs promoted commerce and industry, it was for the purpose of revenues under the aegis of paternal bureaucracies and within the framework of privilege. Merchants becoming officials ceased being merchants and adopted aristocratic social codes that made commerce demeaning. Even in the declining mercantile city-states this tendency of the merchant to become an aristocratic official was manifest. In order to stimulate commerce some absolute monarchs attempted to make commercial and industrial investment respectable, but their edicts had no effect: they were nullified by the nobility, whose privileges the same monarchs preserved. Crown and court reached accommodations with bankers and merchants, but prevailing attitudes under absolutism repudiated commercial society. Royal tax policies favored the aristocracy further. Outside England and the Dutch Republic, nobles, clergy, officials, and privileged wealthy commoners were not taxed except as a last resort, and then seldom successfully. Burdens of state instead fell primarily on the working classes, those engaged in production. Taxes thus cut deeply into the spendable income of the common people and reduced markets for consumer goods other than luxuries and bare necessities, thereby constricting economic development. Rather than being challenged by a new class of capitalist entrepreneurs, absolute monarchs were threatened by the privileged officeholders they had created.

Power presumably was the preoccupation of absolute kings. But the paradox of absolutism is partly that the maritime states, with no centralized bureaucracies, were more efficient in creating and marshaling power. France's hegemony on the Continent was attributable as much to its numerical superiority as to Louis XIV's organization. Louis was great as long as his potential foes were weak and divided; but he was checked on land and defeated at sea when the maritime states with smaller populations combined against him after 1689. Absolutism may have been stronger than the kingdoms dominated by the aristocracy, but it was proportionately weaker than the sociopolitical order of England and the Dutch Republic.

Finally we are led by events to question the permanence of absolute monarchy as an effective type of government, apart from dominating personalities. After the major power struggles of East and West closed at the beginning of the eighteenth century, the leading absolutisms reverted to governments by aristocracy. The "enlightened despots" attempted to revive centralized authority in the second half of the century, but the aristocratic monarchies and republican oligarchies, rather than Louis XIV or Peter the Great, prefigured the dominant political trend after 1715.

Where rapid economic growth and revolution did not occur as it did in the mercantile states, the cake of custom held firm and absorbed the innovations of the most powerful authoritarians of the "age of absolutism."

### Selected Readings

Ashley, Maurice. *Louis XIV and the Greatness of France.* London: English Universities Press, Teach Yourself History, 1957.

*A very readable, short account of the "Sun King's" reign.*

* Beloff, Max. *The Age of Absolutism: 1660–1815.* London: Hutchinson University Library, 1954 (paperback: Harper Torchbook).

*An interpretation that considers societies, rather than governments, decisive in the age of absolutism.*

Boxer, Charles R. *The Dutch Seaborne Empire: 1600–1800.* The History of Human Society, edited by J. H. Plumb. New York: Alfred A. Knopf, 1965.

*A social history of both the Dutch Republic and the Dutch Empire.*

Carsten, Francis L., ed. *The Ascendancy of France 1648–88.* Vol. 5. The New Cambridge Modern History. Cambridge: Cambridge University Press, 1961.

*An exhaustive study of Europe in the age of Louis XIV, this work is useful for reference.*

* Church, William F. *The Impact of Absolutism in France: National Experience under Richelieu, Mazarin, & Louis XIV.* New York: John Wiley & Sons, 1969.

*A collection of illuminating sources and commentaries raising the question how beneficial absolutism was to the French people. It makes clear how "reason-of-state" arguments have been used to justify injustice and exploitation as the price of Louis XIV's greatness.*

Clark, G. N. *The Later Stuarts, 1660–1714.* Oxford History of England. London: Oxford University Press, 1949.

*A dispassionate, scholarly account.*

Cole, Charles W. *French Mercantilism: 1683–1700.* New York: Columbia University Press, 1943.

*One of the author's several detailed works on French mercantilism that is especially informative on the industrial production codes under Colbert.*

Davies, R. Trevor. *Spain in Decline, 1621–1700.* New York: St. Martin's Press, 1957.

*A rambling posthumous work useful in assessing the causes of decay in the aristocratic monarchy of Spain.*

Fay, Sidney B. *The Rise of Brandenburg-Prussia to 1786.* New York: Henry, Holt and Co., 1937.

*A short, classic description of the consolidation of Prussian military absolutism that needs to be supplemented by the works of Carsten.*

Figgis, John N. *The Divine Right of Kings.* 2d ed. Cambridge: Cambridge University Press, 1922.

*An analysis of the major ideology of royal absolutism.*

Holborn, Hajo. *A History of Modern Germany: 1648–1840.* New York: Alfred A. Knopf, 1966.

*A lucid treatment based on recent scholarship; part of the author's three-volume study.*

King, James E. *Science and Rationalism in the Government of Louis XIV, 1661–1683.*

*A detailed interpretation of the reign of Louis XIV that links efficient government with the rational viewpoint of contemporary science.*

* Lewis, W. H. *The Splendid Century, Life in the France of Louis XIV.* Garden City, N.Y.: Doubleday & Co., Anchor Books, 1957.

*Aspects of French society, omitting institutions that the author considers tedious to write about.*

Lough, John. *Introduction to Seventeenth-Century France.* London: Longmans, Green & Co., 1960.

*A literary approach to the period; well illustrated, it unfortunately carries key points in French.*

Maland, David. *Europe in the Seventeenth Century.* New York: St. Martin's Press, 1966.

*A new, exceptionally well-balanced textbook of the period by a British scholar.*

Nussbaum, Frederick L. *The Triumph of Science and Reason: 1660–1685.* New York: Harper & Brothers, 1953.

*A general account emphasizing intellectual developments and recognizing absolutism as a facade of aristocratic society.*

Petrie, Charles. *Earlier Diplomatic History: 1492–1713.* London: Hollis & Carter, 1949.

*A short manual of exceedingly complex diplomatic relationships; the second half is applicable to this chapter.*

Rosenberg, Hans. *Bureaucracy, Aristocracy and Autocracy, The Prussian Experience: 1660–1815,* Cambridge, Mass.: Harvard University Press, 1958.

*A sociological investigation of the Prussian bureaucracy and its rivalry with the monarchy and the aristocracy.*

Schevill, Ferdinand. *The Great Elector.* Chicago: The University of Chicago Press, 1947.

*A political and institutional biography of Frederick William, the founder of Prussian absolutism.*

Sumner, B. H. *Peter the Great and the Emergence of Russia.* London: English Universities Press, Teach Yourself History, 1956.

*Another short, moving account in this series; it emphasizes the military basis of Peter's administration.*

Trevelyan, G. M. *The English Revolution, 1688–1689.* London: Butterworth & Co., Home University Library, 1938.

*A well-written study by the author of several well-known works on the Stuarts.*

* Wilson, Charles. *The Dutch Republic.* New York: McGraw-Hill Book Co., World University Library, 1968.

*This volume surveys the Dutch Republic in its heyday, emphasizing its technological and cultural impact on seventeenth-century Europe.*

* Wolf, John B. *The Emergence of the Great Powers: 1685–1715.* The Rise of Modern Europe. New York: Harper & Brothers, 1951.

*An account of the power struggles in which seventeenth-century absolutism culminated.*

\* ———. *Louis XIV*. New York: W. W. Norton & Co., 1968.

*An exhaustive, sympathetic biography that narrates the monarch's life interestingly and leaves open the interpretation that he may have been acting out a role.*

See also the works by J. H. Elliott, Eli Heckscher, David Ogg, and George N. Clark in *Selected Readings*, volume 1, chapter 14.

Asterisk (\*) denotes paperback.

# CHAPTER V

# The Secularization of Thought: the Seventeenth and Eighteenth Centuries

We saw in the preceding chapter that power struggles between divine-right monarchs whittled away otherworldly concepts of society and politics. Constrained to mobilize force, heads of state had to take stock of their resources and to press first and foremost for revenues. At the end of his wars Louis XIV, the epitome of divine-right absolutism, had to reconcile himself to the secular principle of the balance of power in international relations. At home absolute rulers and their courts became secular in outlook long before the bulk of their subjects, who were mainly peasants bound by tradition to established churches. But during the seventeenth and eighteenth centuries a large section of the intellectual elite also lost its attachment to otherworldly concerns.

The new tone of politics was only one indication of a growing interest in worldly matters; the other great secularizing forces were the accumulation of wealth through commerce and technology, the continued vitality of humanism, the impact of scientific advances, and the stimulus of travel literature.

Secularization first penetrated deeply those areas of northwestern Europe where the pursuit of wealth and comfort were primary social goals—England and the Dutch Republic. Although they retained established churches, they did not forcibly impose religious uniformity as did most absolutist states. The fact that different religious groups could live together peacefully bred religious tolerance. At the same time, trading profits enlarged the mercantile classes, which began to set their own goals independently of the aristocracy and the established churches. English and Dutch farmers became more market oriented, and many villages began to produce goods for commercial entrepreneurs. As the English and Dutch governments catered increasingly to commercial interests, their effective power became stronger than that of any absolutist regime. Their strength, however, derived from the voluntary action, wealth, and private initiative of their subjects rather than from royal paternalism and doctrines of resignation to divine will. Finally, in the more open commercial societies science and technology imparted a sense of control over nature.

Overseas commerce combined with missionary activity added another dimension to this secularization. Travel literature reporting the customs of non-Europeans became common, especially in northwestern Europe. How far this literature in itself helped to break down European parochialism is difficult to assess; nevertheless, because it seemed to demonstrate that "noble savages" could live naturally and happily without Europe's Christian institutions, critics of European conditions used it to bolster their assault on the otherworldly foundations of authoritarianism.

The seventeenth century produced a more secular humanism than that of the Renaissance. The "new" humanism was more involved in the problems raised by scientific development than in the ideas of classical literature. Hence it, too, contributed to the secularization of thought.

More than any other single factor, the demonstrable success of seventeenth-century science brought past authority into doubt and provided the intellectual foundation for new world views. Science did not openly undermine tradition until philosophical conclusions were drawn from its discoveries and methodology. However when this happened—by the second half of the eighteenth century—popularized science and secular humanism merged into the qualified optimism of the Enlightenment, whose popular writers competed with the clergy in defining morality, religious doctrine, and the goals of society. Theirs was a new secular gospel, which they hoped to spread through national systems of education oriented toward natural sciences, modern languages, economics, and modern history. This goal was eventually realized; but it was not until a century later, and then only where industrialization and urbanization were firmly rooted.

The writers of the Enlightenment were not without effective foes in their own day. In traditional agrarian societies, social and religious safeguards functioned without fanfare. More vocal opposition came from Protestant revivalists who sought to salvage the primacy of spirit and revelation from the secular onslaught. Seen in historical perspective these revivalists were the progenitors of nineteenth-century romantics, who taught that feelings are the fundamental guide to life and truth. But in some respects even this outlook indicated that the salvation of souls was no longer the predominant goal of religion and society.

# A. The "Scientific Revolution"

By breaking with the prevalent Western intellectual tradition science became a revolutionary force. This break did not come about suddenly, nor was it always overt. Indeed, no clear distinction existed between natural science and natural philosophy before the end of the seventeenth century. Until the seventeenth century, when it became universally important to intellectuals (still a small minority of the population), the study of nature had been cultivated for centuries by isolated scholars. Yet fourteenth-century schoolmen in England and France had already questioned Aristotle's explanation of motion; and during the Italian Renaissance the University of Padua had become the center for Aristotelian scientists seeking natural causes for natural phenomena. Meanwhile literary humanists were rediscovering Greek and Hellenistic scientific works, including parts of the writings of Euclid and Archimedes; in 1543 the publication of Archimedes' theories contributed significantly to the revival of science.

These ancient works increased both Europe's store of knowledge and its supply of misinformation; but they also undermined faith in the version of Aristotle that philosophers and theologians had propagated, because they revealed that the ancients had disagreed on fundamental conclusions. In trying to decide among conflicting authorities, some early natural philosophers were driven to make their own analyses and observations. On the basis of their own experience artists and engineers, such as Leonardo da Vinci, also questioned prevailing authorities. Although the influence of their work was restricted, the impetus toward new investigations was growing. Navigators needing more and better instruments slowly demonstrated anomalies in prevailing Ptolemaic astronomy, as did an increasing number of persons who, dissatisfied with the Julian calendar, wanted a reliable system for dating Easter and other significant events.

# FROM COPERNICUS TO NEWTON: SCIENCE COMES OF AGE

## Copernicus's Challenge to Ptolemaic Astronomy

The discoveries in astronomy illustrate how slowly early modern science progressed. Traditions prevailing in 1500 stemmed from Aristotle and Ptolemy, who asserted that a stationary earth occupied the center of the universe. According to them stars, sun, planets, and the moon were held in circular orbits around the earth by crystalline spheres. The source of motion was an alleged "prime mover," identified with the Christian God. In the heavens where Dante and lesser men had located paradise, perfection was expressed in circular motion and immutability, and it reigned as the supreme law. On earth, at whose center hell was popularly pictured, quite different physical laws governed motion, for here imperfection was expressed in irregular vertical and horizontal motion and degeneration. But the low prestige of earth was redeemed by theology. According to the Christian epic, earth was the stage for the unique drama of creation, incarnation, and redemption that gave cosmic significance to human life. Thus physics, astronomy, and theology were integrated into a consistent cosmology, or description of the universe, and this Christianized version of Aristotle's physics completely dominated the thought of medieval schools. As Copernicus learned, any effort to reformulate this cosmology was difficult, and by the seventeenth century it was dangerous as well.

Nicholas Copernicus, a Polish-German churchman, had probably come to doubt Ptolemaic astronomy as a student in Italy. Its increasingly asymmetrical explanations were disturbing to his belief that God's handiwork should be simple, orderly, and explainable. He made few observations (these without the aid of a telescope); instead he applied his brilliant mathematical talents largely to older observations to argue in favor of a simplified and more symmetrical scheme, in which the planets, including the earth, revolved around the sun within an envelope of fixed stars. Copernicus still held firmly to the notion that heavenly motion was circular, befitting its perfection, but his model, or theory, of the universe explained why planets at times appeared to be moving backward, a problem that had troubled the Greeks. He published his description of the universe, *On the Revolutions of the*

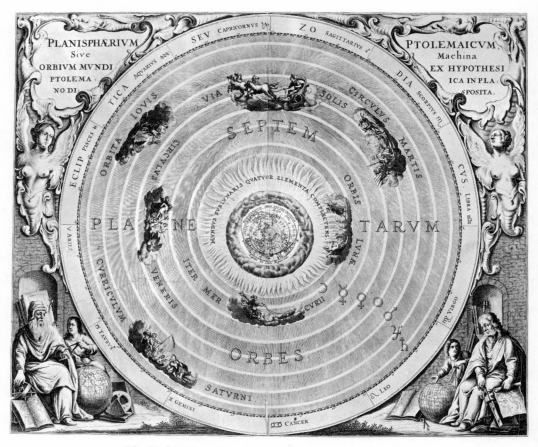

*The Ptolemaic system.*

*Heavenly Orbs,* in 1543, the year of his death. The preface, written anonymously by a Lutheran clergyman, described Copernicus's conclusions as merely mathematical hypotheses, which they were. But they were sufficiently in conflict with specific passages in Scripture to lead Luther to condemn their author as "the fool who would overturn the whole science of astronomy." In the Roman Catholic world Copernicus's thesis was brought into disrepute by the case of the philosopher Giordano Bruno. In addition to asserting the existence of many inhabited worlds and the infinity of the universe, Bruno adopted the concept of a sun-centered cosmos. For advocating these and other

"heresies" he was burned at the stake in 1600. In 1616 Church authorities placed Copernicus's book on the *Index of Prohibited Books,* where it remained for more than two centuries. Copernicus, whose strongest argument was the greater simplicity of his explanation, also failed to win contemporary academicians. They raised pertinent objections, some of which were not explained satisfactorily until the nineteenth century.

Astronomers could not long avoid the issues that Copernicus had raised. The heavens themselves enlivened the cosmological debate in 1572 when a new star appeared and again in 1618 when a new comet came into view. In the past comets

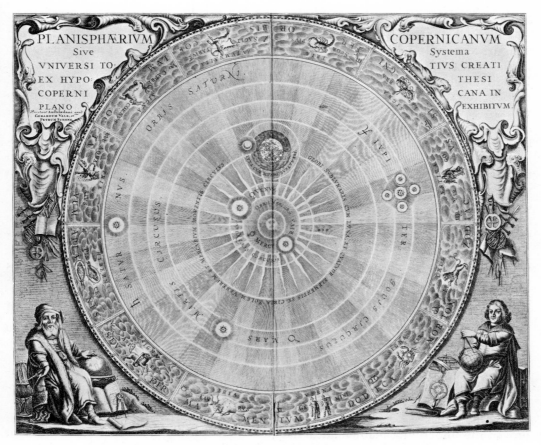

*The Copernican system.*

had been interpreted as divine signs of impending doom. So was this one. But it also caused astronomers to question the existence of crystalline spheres supporting the planets and to doubt the sharp distinction held to exist between the immutable heavens and the mutable earth.

Vindication for Copernicus's sun-centered hypothesis, but not other parts of his system that proved untenable, awaited the accumulation of observations by Tycho Brahe (1546–1601), the improvement of his theory by Johannes Kepler (1571–1630), the invention of the telescope, and the later achievements of Isaac Newton (1642–1727) and his generation.

In the thirty-year course of accu-

mulating a mass of exceedingly accurate observations with the naked eye the Danish astronomer Tycho Brahe proposed a mathematical theory of the solar system that still put the earth at its center. Kepler obtained Brahe's great store of recorded observations, but he found that they gave more support to a sun-centered explanation of the solar system than to Brahe's own conclusions. Inspired by scientific zeal, astrology, and fantasies of the esthetic orderliness of the universe (which he related to the harmonies of the musical scale), Kepler energetically worked out a series of laws describing planetary motion. He discovered that the planets' paths were elliptical, and this discovery constitutes his first law of planetary motion. Although this may seem rather uninspired, we must keep in mind the unwillingness of all the early astronomers, even Kepler, to abandon the idea of circular motion, for they assumed that God had utilized the circle—the most perfect of forms—in constructing his perfect cosmos. The data of Mars's orbit, observed night after night, forced Kepler to admit that its path traced out an ellipse with the sun at one focus. Because planets speed up as they approach the sun and slow down as they move farther away in their elliptical orbits, a mathematical relationship to describe that fact had to be discovered, whence Kepler's second law: a line from the sun to the planet sweeps out equal areas of the ellipse in equal times. Finally, he showed in his third law that the distances of the planets from the sun and their orbital speed are mathematically related, distance cubed being proportional to the square of the time needed to make a complete revolution. While these laws laid the foundations for Newton's astronomy, their importance to Kepler was that they proved the underlying mathematical harmony of the universe, and delighted his mystical soul.

Brahe's observations and Kepler's mathematical analyses destroyed Ptolemaic concepts of the universe, but they failed to answer fully the question what held it together or governed its motion. Ptolemy had fallen into disrepute, but there was as yet no complete alternative.

## Galileo's Contributions to Modern Science

While Kepler worked in Prague, Galileo Galilei (1564–1642) and his successors pursued another line of scientific development in Italy. Here knowledge of Hellenistic scientists, notably Archimedes, had been revived, and Italian science seemed destined to succeed to the glory of Italian art. An industrious student and mathematical genius, Galileo began his career in physics and mechanics in opposition to Aristotelian teachings. By mathematical description and analysis he worked out laws of ballistic trajectories, pendulum movements, and uniform acceleration. He worked at a highly abstract level, considering neither causal theories nor observable effects of resistance. His conclusion that the velocity of a body falling freely in a vacuum was proportional to the elapsed time of fall laid the foundations for mechanics. That field of natural phenomena was most productive of seventeenth-century scientific methodology.

Galileo's studies of motion and falling bodies were directly related to controversies over Copernican astronomy. Anti-Copernicans argued that if the earth were in motion and turning on its axis, terrestrial motion would be distorted. In meeting their objections Galileo partially formulated the concept of inertia. He carried his astronomy much further, however, with a new instrument—the telescope. Learning of its invention in the Netherlands, he built such an instrument for his own use, and with it he detected sunspots, saw the four satellites of Jupiter, followed the phases of Venus, studied the mountains and valleys on the surface of the moon, and noted that the Milky Way was a dense cluster of stars. All these observations were new, and some of them explicitly refuted Aristotelian astronomical physics by demonstrating that the heavens were not immutably perfect but rather subject to change. In 1610 he published the *Message of the Stars,* which demonstrated that the same laws applied both to earth and to the heavens and that Aristotelian natural philosophy was as unreliable in astronomy as in mechanics.

Galileo's fame spread, but he aroused intense opposition in the universities and churches. Scholars who had devoted their lives to examining nature within an Aristotelian framework rejected his conclu-

*To view other worlds: Galileo's telescopes.*

or the authority of the Church. For defying the latter he was summoned before the Inquisition in 1632, forced to retract his conclusions, and put under house arrest for the remainder of his life. Protestant authorities were also hostile toward Galileo: individual clergymen denounced him, and Protestant schools used anti-Copernican textbooks throughout the century. Spectacular as Galileo's accomplishments were, he merely initiated (and not entirely accurately) the broad lines of inquiry that were left to a new generation to follow up.* And follow them up it did. Isaac Newton, the great synthesizer of the new cosmology, was born in 1642—the year in which Galileo died.

## The Organization of Science: Scientific Societies

Spurned by the universities and official scholarship, Galileo and his successors could tie themselves to no existing institution to coordinate or disseminate their work. Men of disparate interests who shared a common enthusiasm for the "new philosophy" banded together in informal groups that evolved into formal scientific societies. Galileo himself belonged to the new Roman *Accademia dei Lincei*, which sponsored his reports on sunspots in 1613. When that society disappeared in 1657, it was temporarily replaced by the *Accademia del Cimento* (Academy of Experiments), which flourished in Florence under Medici patronage only from 1657 to 1667.

sions and even refused to look through his telescope. By 1616 a board of inquiry appointed by the Roman Inquisition had enjoined him to make only hypothetical statements concerning cosmology. Even so, in 1632 he published in Italian for a lay audience the *Dialogue on the Two Principal Systems of the Universe, the Ptolemaic and the Copernican.* Technically the Aristotelian, Simplicio, won the debate with the Copernican, but his victory was undeserved from the evidence used by his opponent. The *Dialogue* revealed that Galileo possessed remarkable literary talents as a propagandist for the new science. He had support within the Church (Pope Urban VIII himself likely supplied the tract's title), but the publication set off a controversy similar to that stirred up in the nineteenth century by popularizers of biological evolution. Clearly Galileo's criterion for scientific truth was not the Bible

* In fact Galileo's *Dialogue* failed to clinch his argument that the earth rotated about the sun, for his best proof was not technically demonstrable for almost two centuries. To prove the earth's rotation, the *Dialogue* referred to the ebb and flow of the tides, an argument that was old and erroneous. Ignorant of Kepler's contemporary work, which was embedded in an impossible literary style, he continued to follow Copernicus's theory that the planets followed circular orbits.

*Louis XIV at the Paris Observatory, 1662.*

Longer-lived and more important were the societies given official sponsorship in France and England. The French *Académie des Sciences,* founded in 1666, received financial support from the French crown. And in 1662 Charles II of England chartered, but did not subsidize, the *Royal Society of London for the Promotion of Natural Knowledge.* Other scientific societies were founded later in Russia and in a few German states.

These societies varied somewhat in their organization, but they performed similar functions. Their members experimented individually and in groups with new instruments; duplicating the experiments of others, they verified or corrected previous findings. Through corresponding secretaries and published monographs and journals they disseminated detailed reports of their work to foreign scholars, irrespective of political or sectarian boundaries. The Accademia del

Cimento, for example, working with the first physical laboratory in Europe, repeated and extended Galileo's experiments, employed the barometer invented by Torricelli, studied vacuums, computed the velocity of sound, and engaged in unproductive studies of the digestive processes of animals. The French society succeeded in computing the approximate speed of light, measured the length of a degree of latitude, and applied the telescope to angular measurement in surveying. The Royal Society of London reached a high level of prestige as Isaac Newton and his contemporaries completed the mathematical synthesis of seventeenth-century astronomy and physics. Although the scope of the societies' interests extended to natural history and medicine, their greatest achievements during the early years lay in the field of physics; here their advances eventually carried them beyond the point where amateurs could make contributions.

Seeking to formulate universal natural laws, the scientific societies set secular, often utilitarian goals. Open for membership to men of accomplishment without regard to birth, they encouraged clarity and precise objective description, choosing to avoid philosophical speculation beyond what was observable and definable in the world of nature. Robert Hooke, curator of experiments for the Royal Society of London, has left us a succinct statement of the leading society's objectives:

To improve the knowledge of naturall things, and all useful Arts, Manufactures, Mechanik practices, Engynes and Inventions by Experiments—(not meddling with Divinity, Metaphysics, Moralls, Politiks, Grammar, Rhetorick, or Logick).

To attempt the recovering of such allowable arts and inventions as are lost.

To examine all systems, theories, principles, hypotheses, elements, histories, and experiments of all things naturall, mathematicall, and mechanicall, invented, recorded or practiced, by any considerable author ancient or modern. . . .

In the mean time this Society will not own any hypothesis, system, or doctrine of the principles of naturall philosophy, proposed or mentioned by any philosopher ancient or modern, nor the explication of any phenomena whose recourse must be had to originall causes (as not being explicable by heat, cold, weight, figure, and the like, as effects produced thereby): nor dogmatically define, nor fix axioms of scientificall things, but will question and canvass all opinions, adopting nor adhering to none, till by mature debate and clear arguments, chiefly such as are deduced from legitimate experiments, the truth of such experiments be demonstrated invincibly.[1]

Not all of these societies, however, were as aloof from nonscientific influence as Hooke's statement would indicate. Governments urged that more attention be given to "useful discoveries" in navigation or war machinery, and the French society was apparently influenced by politics, as were the Berlin Academy (founded in 1700) and the St. Petersburg Academy (1724). Nevertheless, by consciously standing apart from politics and traditional religious metaphysics, the scientific societies caused eyebrows to be raised. The Accademia del Cimento—and Italian leadership in science—lapsed in 1667, when its Medici benefactor became a cardinal and one of its members was indicted by the Inquisition. Traditionalists also attacked the Royal Society of London for trying to subvert religion, but Thomas Sprat, who became an Anglican bishop, answered the charges in his celebrated history of the society in 1667. Unlike the Italian societies, the Royal Society survived unscathed.

[1] Quoted by Martha Ornstein, *The Role of Scientific Societies in the Seventeenth Century* (Chicago: The University of Chicago Press, 1928), pp. 108–9.

## Scientific Instruments

The rapid expansion of scientific knowledge depended in part on the invention and elaboration of instruments that extended the senses. For aid in building such instruments, scientists turned to skilled craftsmen. In the seventeenth century these craftsmen and scientists developed the telescope, the microscope, the thermometer, the barometer, the air pump, and the clock; in the eighteenth century they built electrometers and delicate scales, which helped to open new fields of physical and chemical research.

In studying Galileo, we have already noted the effects of the discovery of the simple telescope. Kepler laid down plans for an improved refracting instrument, and Isaac Newton developed a reflecting model. The development of both types drew upon the same optical and glass-grinding skills as were required for the microscope, which was first produced in the Netherlands. But the usefulness of both the telescope and the microscope was limited at first by color distortions of lens images, incomplete optical theory, and imperfect lens-grinding techniques. When Newton's telescope was improved in the eighteenth century, it extended the astronomers' range beyond the solar system; but the lenses of the compound microscope were not corrected until the nineteenth century, when biological studies were at last able to flourish. Meanwhile Otto von Guericke's air pump was employed in experiments to defy Aristotle's dictum that "nature abhors a vacuum." Primitive thermometers and barometers both originated in Italy.

Another critical instrument, the pendulum clock, which was essential to quantitative measurement, was not developed until 1657 by the Dutchman Christian Huygens. His invention partially solved the difficulties Galileo had experienced using a primitive and inaccurate water

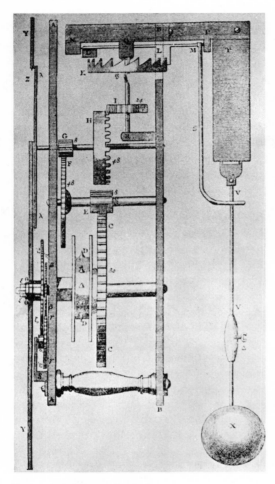

*Exact time: Huygen's clock.*

work whose operations were regular, repetitive, and predictable, reducing God to the position of the master clockmaker who had designed and set it in motion. Later, especially after the outset of industrialization, the clock would assume a central role in the coordination and organization of complex societies. In rural villages bells could summon men for collective enterprise with little regard for accurate timing, but as the interrelationships of modern society have multiplied and speeded up, men have become ever more dependent on the precise timing first provided by the scientifically constructed clock.

## Mathematics and the Completion of the Copernican Revolution in Astronomy

Much of the data that physical scientists collected were neither useful nor intelligible until mathematics (which developed rapidly during the seventeenth century) made it possible to incorporate these data in theories. The symbols of multiplication, division, addition, and decimals as we use them today were standardized after 1600, and in the same period the Scotsman John Napier invented logarithms (1614). Henry Briggs provided one of the most useful innovations for rapid calculations: the slide rule, based on logarithms. In France in the 1650s Pierre de Fermat and Blaise Pascal opened another new line of mathematics—the study of probabilities. To solve problems of motion European mathematicians learned to apply the algebra that they had borrowed from the Arabs to geometry, producing analytical geometry; the French philosopher René Descartes led the way in this field. Equally indispensable for the study of motion, and hence for the Newtonian theories in celestial mechanics, was the concurrent invention of the calculus by Newton and Gottfried Wilhelm von

clock, but for navigation at sea accurate spring-driven clocks were still needed. Several governments offered substantial prizes, and a number of men devoted much attention to the problem. After 60 years of work, practicable chronometers were developed in the eighteenth century, thus making possible for the first time accurate determination of longitude, a great boon to navigation and commerce.

In many ways the clock became the most expressive symbol of new mechanistic concepts of the universe and society. Popularizers of science and scientists described the universe as a gigantic clock-

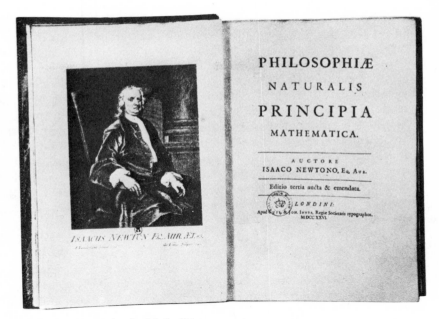

*Newton and his classic third edition.*

Leibniz (1646–1716). Leibniz's system of notation was adapted for general use outside England.

Mathematics, combined with the experimental work of astronomers and physicists after Galileo and Kepler, laid the basis for a more systematic explanation of the solar system. Both men had given impetus to the notion of an orderly, mechanistic universe, but neither had provided answers to fundamental questions. What kept the planets in motion? What held them in their orbits? Or, assuming some gravitational force as Kepler did, what kept them from plummeting to the center of the universe? Many men furnished partial answers to these questions. Among them Descartes formulated a law of inertia that explained the planets' continued motion, and Christian Huygens described the mathematical principles of centrifugal force. From these principles Robert Hooke of the Royal Society developed a working theory of gravitational attraction. However, credit for mathematically demonstrating the operation of gravity in the solar system belonged not to Hooke but to his colleague, Isaac Newton, a genius among the giants of the Royal Society.

Newton was born and trained at the very time when mathematics and physics were ready for a synthesizer of his ability; in the less well developed fields of optics and chemistry, to which he devoted more time, his contributions were fewer. After graduating from Cambridge, Newton spent a momentous year in the country (1664–65). During this time he formulated the calculus, discovered the compound nature of white light, and arrived at the essentials of the law of gravitation. In 1687 he finally published his magnum opus, *Philosophiae Naturalis Principia Mathematica* (*The Mathematical Principles of Natural Philosophy*).

This complex treatise explains natural mathematical principles of matter in motion but cautiously refrains from speculation on ultimate causes. The best-known part of it describes the celestial mechanism in terms of mass, attraction, and the laws of motion, in addition to incorporating Kepler's laws of planetary motion into a general mathematical model. Newton's model for matter in motion was to remain "valid" until challenged in the late nineteenth and early twentieth centuries by the theory of relativity. So sweeping was his concept of the constitution of the "world machine" that intellectuals soon found themselves in a universe from which animistic spirits seemed to have been banished. Although Newton believed that his investigation supported religion, it seemed to be at war with the traditional view of the world given by theology.

After publishing the *Principia*, Newton's enthusiasm for science, which had never been zealous, flagged. On two occasions he served in Parliament; later he became master of the mint when the Whig government was replacing the coinage during the early phases of the War of Spanish Succession. He spent part of his energies in a personal conflict with Leibniz over who had precedence in the invention of the calculus: each charged the other with plagiarism. From 1703 to 1709 he served as president of the Royal Society, during which years he published the *Opticks*, an influential summary of his work on the physical properties of light. His last scientific publication suggested hypotheses to explain the phenomena of light, gravitation, and the composition of matter. Upon his death he received honors previously reserved to royalty.

## THE EXPANSION OF SCIENTIFIC DISCIPLINES

### Electricity

After Newton, scientists devoted themselves largely to the elaboration of his principles in physics, astronomy, and mathematics. The Royal Society lost its practical interests and became an aloof club of pure scientists, leaving technical undertakings for industry to new associations; and the somnolent universities of the eighteenth century made almost no scientific contributions. Nevertheless, science progressed. The study of heat, conceived primarily as a fluid rather than energy, became important, and Fahrenheit formulated tables of specific heat for various substances. But the most striking development of eighteenth-century physics lay in the field of electricity.

Certain aspects of electricity had been studied by William Gilbert (1540–1603), a physician at the court of Queen Elizabeth. The extent to which electricity was conceived as static can be seen from the fact that he derived the term from the Greek word for amber after observing that amber rubbed on fur attracted hair, straw, and other small objects. Gilbert also worked with magnetism, particularly the dip or inclination of a magnetic compass needle, which he sought to make serviceable to mariners. But in order to study electricity further, investigators had to learn how to generate and store a charge. Otto von Guericke, who had already invented an air pump and demonstrated the force of atmospheric pressure, made some advance in this direction with a machine that generated static electricity by friction. The first major breakthrough came in 1745, when a Leyden jar was invented for storing static electrical charges. Although electrical attraction and repulsion had been noted earlier, Benjamin Franklin first set forth the theory of negative and positive electrical charges. This was a far more basic contribution than his famous kite experiment of 1752, which demonstrated that lightning was electricity.

A further breakthrough in the study of electricity came in 1800 when a northern Italian, Count Alessandro Volta (1745–1827) invented a primitive "wet cell" battery that produced a steady supply of current. Joseph Priestley (1733–

*An early experiment with static electricity, 1774.*

1804) and other English experimenters soon learned of Volta's achievement and used it for the electrolysis of water into hydrogen and oxygen. Shortly thereafter Sir Humphry Davy began to develop a theory that explained the chemical origins of Volta's electrical current. Not only was the development of electricity thus highly international in character, but it also formed a bridge to modern chemistry.

## The Birth of Modern Chemistry

Traditional natural philosophy did not recognize physics and chemistry as separate studies. All earthly things were considered imperfect compounds of four elements—earth, air, fire, and water—each of which had inherent propensities for movement. Alchemy, which in one of its aspects is the esoteric art of changing one substance into another, thus seemed a reasonable pursuit to most men of learning. In their trial-and-error pursuit of new remedies, doctors sometimes worked with a different set of assumptions. So did metallurgists. Gradually there developed the basis for a pure science of chemistry; but until the generation of Robert Boyle and Robert Hooke, all chemists lacked the apparatus and ideas needed to overturn sterile traditional notions.

Robert Boyle (1627–91), son of an English earl, was one of the first and most influential members of the Royal Society. He set out to apply the basic concepts of Galileo and Descartes to chemistry. Although his chemical experiments failed to explain the composition of matter, he did destroy the notion that there were only four elements and that all substances could be compounded from them, as the alchemists taught. He concluded that something in the air was necessary for combustion, but he could not think of a way to isolate and identify oxygen. His success was greater in formulating laws describing the behavior of gases, and his works, notably *The Sceptical Chymist* (1661), did provide a basis for subsequent research.

For several generations after Boyle chemists stumbled over the problem of relating gases to solids and fluids, many of them misled by the "phlogiston theory," which emanated from Germany. This theory was designed to explain the heat and light given off by combustion and the weight gained by certain substances when they were burned. Phlogiston was an imaginary fluid of negative weight given off by a burning object. This theory, although it offered explanations for some phenomena, reflected the lack of knowledge about the active chemical role of gases, a subject pursued with success in England and Scotland by Henry Cavendish (1731–1810), Joseph Black (1728–99), and Joseph Priestley. They succeeded in producing and differentiating gases such as oxygen and hydrogen, and their discoveries concerning the active chemical role of gases seriously undermined the old theory.

The French chemist Antoine Laurent Lavoisier (1743–94) finally overthrew the phlogiston theory. In contact with Priestley and others, Lavoisier by 1778 developed the new theory of oxidation. He explained that weight gained by the residue of an "oxidized" object was due not to an elusive fluid but to the fixation of oxygen during the process. Meanwhile Cavendish analyzed the ratio of hydrogen and oxygen in water (1782), thus adding to the emphasis placed upon quantitative measurement by Lavoisier. In 1787 Lavoisier gave his theory a new and lasting terminology for the known elements. His work indicated great progress, but in some fields of technology such as metallurgy craftsmen were using procedures for which no scientific explanations had yet been developed.

## Biology

Biology was even slower than chemistry in responding to new scientific concepts: at the beginning of the modern era it was too enmeshed in methods and concepts that explained little and resisted change. Its inheritance included the fixity of species, animistic concepts of the "soul" of plants, and the belief that certain animals represented moral virtues and vices, concepts as firmly rooted as the geocentric theory of the universe had been. Early modern biologists were primarily catalogers of types of plants and animals, but they lacked an overall system of classification that would give order to their catalogs.

With the microscope investigators extended their range of knowledge concerning the complexity of living things. Marcello Malpighi, an Italian anatomist, used this new instrument to examine body tissues. Anton van Leeuwenhoek's unexcelled microscopic work revealed the existence of protozoa, bacteria, and red corpuscles of the blood. The Englishman Nehemiah Grew, a contemporary of Malpighi and Leeuwenhoek, observed the sexual reproduction of plants.

This sexual aspect of plant life was further developed until Carolus Linnaeus (1707–78) of Sweden finally used it as the basis for classifying the plant kingdom into genera and species. In early editions of his *System of Nature* (1735 et seq.)—which included animal, vegetable, and mineral categories (minerals were thought to "grow" in the ground)—Linnaeus supported the concept of the fixity of species. In the nineteenth century his work was to be used by religious fundamentalists as an authoritative argument against Charles Darwin. Ironically, by 1760 he himself had conceded that new species can rise from stable hybridization, and by the end of the century other biologists also disputed the fixity of species, notably the Frenchman Georges Buffon (1707–88). Buffon seems to have been a precursor of Darwin, but he did not make evolutionary change into a synthesizing principle as Darwin did. Thus the added element of evolutionary change in biology did not appear to upset the concept of the Newtonian world machine until the nineteenth century.

## Medicine and Public Health

Medicine was retarded until microbiology had progressed beyond the primitive concepts that had characterized it in the seventeenth and eighteenth centuries. Meanwhile the Hellenistic medicine of Galen and, to a less extent, of Hippocrates, dominated medical thought and practice. According to traditional Greek medicine the health of the body was dependent upon the balance of the four humors: blood, phlegm, yellow bile (choler), and black bile. As long as this theory prevailed through the nineteenth century so did the general practice of bleeding as a medical treatment. In the nineteenth century this theory also gave rise to the name *cholera*, on the presumption that that disease was caused by a surfeit of one of these humors, choler. Early modern remedies were prescribed according to "signatures": a liver-shaped plant was used for diseases of the liver; an Indian wood was given to cure an

"Indian" disease such as syphilis. The list of popular remedies included the exorcism of spirits and the "royal touch" of kings for the cure of scrofula. Alchemy and astrological cures (hence *influenza*, from the purported "influence" of the stars) also figured in medicine. Neither physician nor patient understood cause and effect relationships; practitioners who proceeded by trial and error were the first to approach such an understanding.

One early rebel against the authority of traditional medicine was Paracelsus (1493–1541), a German physician and alchemist. With a stream of invective he attacked contemporary doctors for using logic rather than experience. This iconoclast introduced a medical chemistry steeped in alchemy but nevertheless empirical to a degree. Driven from his teaching post in the medical school at Basel and condemned by Catholic and Protestant clergymen, the wandering Paracelsus left behind him a succession of medical practitioners who relied on chemical cures.

A more cautious revolt grew out of the Italian medical schools, where dissection was practiced in order to illustrate the texts of Galen. Unfortunately Galen had used animals rather than human cadavers for his descriptions, but his authority was more difficult to overturn than Aristotle's physics. For one thing, doctors of medicine lectured from texts, leaving actual contact with cadaver, dissection knife, and most patients to barber-surgeons who lacked the prestige of having had a philosophical education. Renaissance artists sometimes practiced dissection illicitly and achieved far greater detail than anatomists. Their realism was reflected in Andreas Vesalius's *On the Fabric of the Human Body*, which was published in 1543, the same year that Copernicus's major work appeared. Vesalius, a Fleming who had worked at Paris, Padua, Bologna, and Pisa, threw his work together hastily

*Bleeding a gentleman in the sixteenth century.*

without any intention of assaulting Galen's authority. But his attempt to describe human anatomy part by part, layer by layer, inadvertently piled up evidence against Galen. Facing a hostile reception, Vesalius suspended his work to become court physician to Charles V. Nevertheless anatomy was the earliest medical science to be emancipated from speculative philosophy and the authority of the ancients.

Other advances were made by men who tackled new problems. Immediately after the discovery of America virulent strains of syphilis swept across Europe. In addition, the mortality rate from scurvy among sailors on long voyages was astoundingly high. Doctors had to deal with these problems as well as gunshot wounds, the by-product of new military weaponry. Especially noteworthy was the uneducated military surgeon Ambroise Paré

*Empirical anatomy: Vesalius.*

(1510–90), who discovered by chance that cauterization of wounds with boiling oil was less effective than ligatures and dressings.

The generation of doctors following Paré produced a significant synthesis in the field of physiology. After an education at Padua, William Harvey (1578–1657) demonstrated—insofar as he could do so without a microscope—the circulation of the blood. Inspired by analogies between mechanics and the operations of valves in the veins, he described the heart as a mechanical pump forcing blood through the arteries whence it returned through the veins. Thus he displaced Galen's assumption that two types of blood—one emanating from the liver, the other from the heart—ebbed and flowed within the veins and arteries. Harvey worked on this hypothesis for ten years prior to publishing his conclusions in 1628. Another generation or two passed before medical scientists accepted it. Not until Malpighi used a microscope to discover capillaries connecting arteries and veins in the tissues of a frog's lungs was Harvey's thesis of circulation empirically confirmed.

Despite Harvey's achievements, most attempts to proceed solely on mechanical principles failed. Members of the Royal Society showed that part of the air inhaled into the lungs was essential to life and that combustion and breathing were similar processes. As blood was viewed as a vehicle for carrying air and nourishment, scientific societies attempted inconsequential experiments with blood transfusions, usually from animals to humans. For further success the life sciences depended on the advance of chemistry, microscopy, and clinical medical observations. But they also lacked organizing ideas with which to establish meaningful relationships between known facts. No theory of the origin of disease was forthcoming until the nineteenth century.

Public health remained primarily a local and humanitarian concern. Isolated doctors produced descriptions of epidemics and treatises on occupational diseases. Local governments ordered the cleaning of streets and the provision of water (usually by undersupervised private companies), but in neither case were the standards used nor the level of enforcement sufficient to eliminate the continued threat of epidemics. Control of rats by 1720 brought the end of bubonic plague epidemics except in the jails, but other urban epidemics, including diseases totally new in western Europe, still took heavy tolls. Humanitarian reformers, especially the Quakers in England, concerned them-

Compound microscope, 1665.

selves with "jail fever," the treatment of the mentally ill, and high infant mortality; they built hospitals, some of them specialized. With all its shortcomings, improved public health probably accounted in part for Europe's rapid increase of population after 1750.

Once bubonic plague was curbed, progress in the control of smallpox began. After 1722 upper-class Englishmen began to use inoculation—a practice of long standing in the Near and Far East—to give the patient a mild case as a means of achieving immunity. Using this dangerous procedure was preferable to contracting a virulent case, but inoculation was not practicable for most people because it required isolation. Nevertheless it became popular when Voltaire and others proclaimed its utility on the Continent. At the very end of the eighteenth century Edward Jenner, an English country doctor, discovered a vaccine of cowpox serum for the disease. Jenner had become interested in milkmaids' immunity to smallpox after they had contracted cowpox, and, after

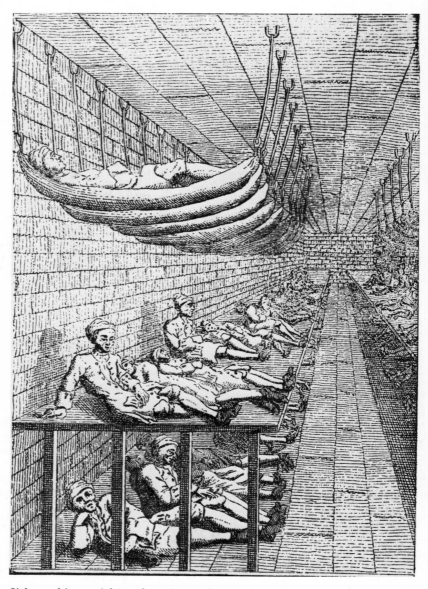

*Sick ward in an eighteenth-century prison.*

long study and discussion, first vaccinated a small boy in 1796. The experiment succeeded in yielding immunity. After Jenner published his findings, in 1798, vaccination for smallpox spread through the Western world and substantially reduced the death rate.

## THE METHODOLOGY OF SCIENCE

Because age-old authorities were overturned in so many fields, it is usually assumed that a revolution in scientific methodology had taken place—a "scientific revolution." Both scientists and their propagandists consciously rejected philosophers' concerns with things beyond (meta) nature (physics) as speculation. "We are to admit," Newton wrote, "no more causes of natural things than such as are both true and sufficient to explain their appearances." This conscious shaking loose from theological authority appears to have been part of that revolution, as was the scientists' spurning of the allegories that theologians used to reconcile science with sacred texts.

But scientific spokesmen did not speak with one voice in defining scientific methodology. The English philosopher Francis Bacon saw it primarily as empiricism, the use of inductive logic to give meaning to direct observations. But René Descartes, author of a classic essay on method, emphasized the necessity of first having a set of hypotheses, even a completely new metaphysics, before empirical testing could take place. Both Bacon and Descartes, who were intimately connected with scientific developments, were immensely impressed with contemporary discoveries. Subsequently, however, Western man has gone through further such revolutions within the same branches of science. These additional "revolutions" have inspired both philosophers and historians to inquire more deeply into the nature of scientific changes, as a result of which historians of science have come to view the new syntheses of this period less as absolute changes than as recurrent aspects of scientific methodology itself.

Purged of magical and animistic beliefs held by primitive peoples, modern science was a continuation of man's efforts to predict natural phenomena, to make them useful to human comfort and survival, and to satisfy curiosity. Since ancient times "natural philosophers" have developed theories or models for that purpose;

whether they conform to ultimate reality is a problem for philosophical speculation. Historically, routine scientific research has gone on within the framework of such theories and models until one of them failed to make new or previously neglected data meaningful. Then a crisis occurred, which lasted until someone conceived a new model. Although the new model gained credence by eliminating anomalies in the old one, it would nevertheless retain the "valid" parts.

The coincidence of several such crises during the seventeenth and eighteenth centuries gave rise to the somewhat exaggerated idea that a "scientific revolution" had occurred: scientists and popularizers of science were certain that they had found a new criterion of *ultimate truth*. Yet experience was to demonstrate that in contrast to the timeless absolutes claimed by traditional theology and philosophy, "natural laws" were authoritative rather than authoritarian. Authoritarians assumed that the premises from which they derived all knowledge, natural or supernatural, were unquestionable. For many of them the existence of awesome, unresolved mysteries was proof of the gulf separating puny man from his omniscient, sovereign, and inscrutable God. In propagating their doctrines, authoritarians relied on indoctrination protected by censorship and coercion. Popularizers of science also usually quenched the human thirst for absolutes with a similar authoritarianism, and even early modern scientists often assumed that their ideas described ultimate reality unconditioned by the human mind and the position of the observer relative to the thing observed.

But the operation of scientific methodology has depended upon quite different conditions. Scientific laws or rules have constantly had to stand the test of new evidence and new concepts for interpreting old and new facts, and, in order for such an interchange to operate fully, freedom of inquiry and communications has been indispensable. Ultimately scientific authority rests upon intellectual assent of peers in the field. Thus scientific "truth" is secular and open-minded rather than a fixed body of doctrine.

Although natural philosophers disavowed metaphysics, certain implicit or explicit metaphysical assumptions were eventually drawn from their ideas and general approach. These assumptions, which belong to the philosophy of science, were at variance with both Catholic and Protestant concepts of divine immanence in the world. Behind the superficial chaos of observable natural phenomena science presupposed regularity rather than supernatural intervention: mathematically regular "natural laws" came to be set in opposition to arbitrary miracles. Although scientists like Newton specifically disavowed this conclusion, it was inherent in their mechanistic approach to nature. They justified their probing into this world as the unveiling of a "second scripture," or the laying bare of God's handiwork. But their deity was a "constitutional" sovereign, since his power was circumscribed by immutable natural laws that the human mind could make progressively more intelligible.

## B. Scientific Philosophy and the New Humanism

At first quietly, the application of new scientific concepts overturned one old authority after another. Only exceptional persons like the English poet John Donne perceived that even man's self-image—as the special creation dwelling at the center of a cosmically purposeful universe—was crumbling before the onslaught of the Copernican revolution during the seventeenth century. From Donne's time to the present, critics of science and technology have shared his lament that

> . . . [the] new Philosophy calls all in doubt,
> The Element of fire is quite put out;
> The Sun is lost, and th'earth, and no man's wit
> Can well direct him where to looke for it.[2]

The new humanists were optimists who foresaw progress in the future if reason were applied to nature and the fetters of the past thrown off. Their humanism was grafted onto the older humanism of the Renaissance. In the sixteenth century humanists like Jean Bodin had learned to study institutions—and even deities—of the past in relation to their historical environment. Some Renaissance humanists had also anticipated progress through the use of reason and the study of nature; but science more than classical letters would confirm this attitude henceforth. In the new humanism science became an idol, a myth. Bernard de Fontenelle, secretary of the

[2] From *An Anatomie of the World* (1611) in the *Complete Poetry and Selected Prose of John Donne and the Complete Poetry of William Blake* (New York: Modern Library, 1941), p. 171.

French Academy and popularizer of its members' achievements, sensed this: "Pure physics," he wrote, "is being elevated into a new kind of theology."

Thinkers who drew their premises from mechanical science were preoccupied with questions raised by the "scientific revolution." They gave Aristotelian philosophy short shrift, arguing that past thought was no aid but rather a prejudice to be overcome, a burdensome ballast to be jettisoned. Still there remained the inexorable question of the relationship of science to religion: what role could divine miracles play within a mechanistic universe governed by mathematical natural laws? When traditionally accepted truths were replaced by scientific and mathematical axioms, questions about the origin and validity of human knowledge became inescapable. What role could man's mind play? Was it the repository of innate self-evident laws or merely an associative device responding to its environment? To what fields was scientific methodology applicable? Could quantitative measurement be applied meaningfully to social phenomena as well as to matter in motion? Most of those who thought that it could, went no further than to postulate certain axioms of social relationships and to cloak them in words of mechanistic science, such as the "balance of power" or the balance of property. A few ventured into the collection of primitive statistics. According to some observers, European thought began to take on a quantitative quality greater than that of any other civilization of the past.

Scientific philosophers who followed the new models of natural philosophy were unanimous in repudiating—even scoffing at—Aristotelianism. They used concepts, terms, and problems produced by contemporary science, but they failed to agree on conclusions drawn from these common roots. They began by denying the authority and categories of scholasticism, which had survived both the Renaissance and the Reformation only slightly scathed. The catchwords of scientific philosophy in the seventeenth and eighteenth centuries were "reason" and "nature." These two terms became as integral a part of new mechanistic world views as divine law and deductive logic had been to scholasticism, or as solitary, irrational faith had been to Protestantism. But "reason" and "nature" became volatile words employed by sharply differing schools of thought: not only did various philosophers define them in varying ways in the seventeenth century, but men of the Enlightenment were to redefine them in the eighteenth century. And in the nineteenth century, romantics and evolutionists were to revise their meaning drastically again.

Most seventeenth-century scientific philosophers held that with reason men could set all past and present prejudices aside. Mathematics seemed to have demonstrated that fundamental truths could be found within the mind itself. For *rationalists* the "nature of things" could be deduced from innate ideas in the mind. Although they sometimes lauded empirical investigation, they relied upon *innate* ideas (called *Platonic* after their first champion, Plato), usually conceived in mathematical terms, as the key to understanding and explaining the world of nature. *Empiricists*, on the other hand, although no less committed to reason and nature, considered knowledge to be the mind's response to *external* stimuli. At most the mind was an associative device that would sort out clear and distinct ideas from the more reliable types of sensation. Like scientists, which they themselves often were, scientific philosophers usually pursued a middle course between pure rationalism and pure empiricism. In practice, however, these categories were more theoretical than actual, and both refuted major traditions of the past.

# SCIENTIFIC RATIONALISM

## The Platonic Tradition

Seventeenth-century rationalists self-consciously proclaimed a revolution. But their zeal for innovation obscured their close ties to the Platonic philosophy of the past.

The thought of the Italian pantheist Giordano Bruno (1548–1600) illustrates the link between Platonism and the newer rationalism. To Bruno physical nature was a visible manifestation of divinity expressed in laws of nature that man could understand without the aid of revelation. (Moreover, it could be manipulated by magic, provided the magician was sufficiently erudite.) Nature was the creation of God, and by the very nature of his unlimited powers he would have created every conceivable level or degree of being, perfect and imperfect. Creation must therefore consist of an infinite universe, an infinite number of worlds, and a physical order representing a great unbroken chain of being descending from the Creator to the lowest inanimate thing. Even if evil, each finite being in this chain reflected the full power of God. Thus nature reveals God by its harmony, beauty, fullness, and orderliness.

As we have seen, Bruno adopted Copernicus's concept of a sun-centered universe; but he died at the stake before Galileo published his major works and before Newton was born. Instead, he drew upon the Platonism of the Italian Renaissance, the same philosophy that inspired Copernicus and played a major role in Kepler's esthetic and geometrical view of the universe.* Later it was to merge with the rationalism of Spinoza† and Leibnitz.‡ Intellectually radical, because in pantheism men found a religious sanction for

* See pp. 259, 262.
† See pp. 279–80.
‡ See p. 282.

revolutionary science, this Platonic rationalism did not offend the existing social order. Rather it shored up that hierarchic order, as it had done in the Middle Ages, with a cosmic rationale.

## The Cartesian Revolution

René Descartes (or des Cartes, hence Cartesian)—not Bruno—was the first person since Aristotle to start afresh in building a philosophical system. A budding mathematical genius disgusted with the authorities taught in the universities, Descartes in 1619 developed the notion of applying mathematics to all nature. This would also be an antidote to skeptics who denied the existence of any authentic human knowledge. In the following decade he worked to found a complete metaphysics based on the premise that ultimate reality would have to be explained theoretically before meaningful experimentation could take place. The starting point for his new system was the one reality he could not refute by systematic doubt: "I think, hence I am." Although he advocated experimentation, he preferred the ultimate certainty of such "clear and distinct" ideas arrived at by introspection and deduction to the chaotic complexities of experience. From his central single axiom he proceeded to deduce the existence of God and of a material world in motion. Besides this material world and sharply separated from it was the realm of the human mind, which obtained real knowledge of the external world by innate ideas such as the concept of God, the axioms of mathematics, and common notions of space, time, and motion. Mind and matter did not interact in Descartes's universe save in the human brain: accepting Galen's erroneous statement that only man had a pineal gland, Descartes concluded that it was the cosmic meeting point of mind and matter. The supernatural intervention of God was required to hold this dualistic universe together. Descartes's dogmatic system thus saved the prestige of man and insulated religion, politics, and moral affairs from empirical study.

Nevertheless Cartesianism offended traditionalists, and Descartes's works were placed on the Roman Catholic Index of Prohibited Books. Once the shock of his iconoclasm passed, however, many clergymen of Europe's established churches invoked Descartes's principles as a means of preventing scientific philosophy—especially empiricism—from making further inroads into politics and morals over which theologians claimed authority.

Despite the conservative uses to which his ideas were put, Descartes did much to popularize scientific discoveries and methodology on the Continent, especially through his *Discourse on Method* (1637). As a mathematician Descartes was at the very center of the "scientific revolution." He set forth logical steps of analysis—that is, the breaking down of complex questions into simpler parts and the progressive solution of simpler to more complex questions. Descartes also gave general currency to certain scientific discoveries, but on some points he was scientifically behind the times. For example, he continued to deny the possibility of a vacuum. His metaphysical speculations concerning the mechanics of the universe contained fertile concepts, but their actual details were of no use to Newton. Descartes's emphasis upon rational hypotheses may have been healthy for science, but his methodology was generally invoked in the seventeenth and eighteenth centuries to obstruct, rather than assist, empiricism.

## Dutch Rationalism and Baruch Spinoza

For most of his mature life (from 1629 to 1649) Descartes took refuge in the Dutch Republic, the outpost of personal freedom and crossroads of heterodoxy in seventeenth-century Europe. Besides Descartes other prominent antitraditional thinkers stayed or at least visited there: Pierre Bayle of France, John Locke of England, and Leibniz of Germany. Native Dutchmen such as Christian Huygens were in the forefront of the scientific revolution. In addition, prominent Dutch statesmen speculated on statistical approaches to taxation and insurance. Classical humanism flourished, and radical religious movements with antimetaphysical bents were tolerated: Quakers, Mennonites, and Unitarians. Among educated and secure townsmen, the ethical and tolerant spirit of Erasmus and Sebastian Castellio had lived on through the Reformation. In other words, major solvents of tradition were at work in the Netherlands. At some point Baruch Spinoza (1632–77) drew upon them all.

Born in Amsterdam of well-to-do Jewish-Portuguese immigrant parents, Spinoza became involved with a Mennonite group, Cartesian philosophy, prominent scientists such as Huygens, and friends with radical economic and political views. Excommunicated by the Jewish community, he renounced business to become a lense grinder near The Hague, where he lived in a garret and produced political and philosophic writings until his death. In his youth Spinoza was deeply involved with utilitarian statistical approaches to social and political problems, but he was disillusioned by the French invasion of 1672, when his republican party lost power. Thereafter he turned more exclusively to a contemplative rationalism that culminated in his *Ethics*, published posthumously.

In the *Ethics* Spinoza sought to establish absolute certainty by rigid mathematical reasoning: the work laid down theorems and axioms and demonstrated ethical principles like a Euclidean textbook of geometry. It was probably the most rigorous application of what the French philosophers called *l'esprit géométrique.* Everything would be better done, they argued, at the hands of a geometer. But Spinoza was an original thinker who went beyond French Cartesianism.

Mind and matter he held to be two coordinate aspects of a pantheistic God who was united mystically with nature. Led by the intellectual love of God, morally free man could rise above his passions by understanding them for his own greater enjoyment. "An emotion which is a passion," he wrote, "ceases to be a passion as soon as we form a clear and distinct idea of it." Spinoza's highest level of knowledge permits the intellectual to rise above the limitations of time, to view life dispassionately "under the aspect of eternity." But on the question of immortality, Spinoza's geometrical proof broke down; it required a leap of faith. With Bruno, Spinoza saw no cosmic viciousness in a natural world filled with both good and evil. He took it for granted that the universe was infinite and that there were many worlds in it. These heresies plus his point-by-point rejection of Calvinist asceticism endeared him neither to Calvinists nor to Jewish authorities.

## EMPIRICISM

Rationalists were inspired by the successful use of mathematics in science. For them mathematical truths found in the mind itself seemed to correspond to the structure of the universe. Banish passion, prejudice, and traditional error, they said, and reason could provide keys to understanding the universe. Empiricists also condemned prejudices, passion, and tradition, but they disputed the existence of innate ideas in the mind. For them the mind was not a storehouse of such master ideas but, in John Locke's phrase, a *blank tablet* on which experience wrote. The mind was a device that sorted and associated the data of experience derived

from the senses. In fact, however, seventeenth-century empiricists did not maintain this view consistently. Instead they started with nonempirical assumptions and made room for the compelling authority of what was "clear and distinct," or "self-evident," even while consciously rejecting innate ideas. Boundaries separating rationalists from empiricists were geographical as well as methodological. On the Continent Cartesianism swept the field as Spinoza's career illustrates. But an empirical tradition maintained itself in revolutionary seventeenth-century England.

### Francis Bacon

An early spokesman of English empiricism was James I's lord chancellor, Francis Bacon (1561–1626), who called for a new science that would establish man's dominion over nature. Since the Renaissance, isolated writers had hailed and lauded new inventions, but Bacon optimistically predicted that if the universities were overhauled and scientific societies for cooperative research founded, the mysteries of the universe could be unveiled in a single generation. (He shared this optimism with Descartes, who thought that a single genius—himself—could accomplish the same goal in a single lifetime.) As a first step, Bacon set out to dispel the "idols," or harmful mental habits, that had perverted reason and led to the repetition of error in the past. He spoke against the Idol of the Tribe—the desire of men to see only what they wanted to believe. Another snare was the Idol of the Cave—the transformation of personal prejudices and limited personal experience into universal principles. In labeling the Idol of the Market Place, Bacon referred to confusion resulting from the different meanings of words. Lastly, he denounced the Idol of the Theater—the stubborn commitment to particular

*A voyage to new logic: Bacon's* Novum Organum.

schools of thought that had become untenable.

Bacon said that men, in order to become free of these idols, had to disentangle science from theology for the mutual benefit of both. He denied that nature was Satan's bailiwick; the created world was, he affirmed, a second Scripture whose study would reinforce religion. "It is . . . most wise to render unto faith the things that are faith's," he wrote in the *New Logic*, but it was apparent that he left it to the scientist, not the theologian, to define the boundary between science and religion.

Bacon was a popularizer of science rather than a scientist, and his influence was limited. In his lifetime he remained a lonely clarion. He sought but failed to reform the universities' curriculum; a proud place-seeker and a political absolu-

tist, he was impeached and deposed by Parliament on charges of bribery. During the English civil wars science tended to be identified with Puritan revolutionaries, his opponents, but the restored Charles II put part of Bacon's cherished plans for a scientific society into operation 34 years after his death. Committed to the utilitarian application of science, the Royal Society's early members touted Bacon as its intellectual father.

## Thomas Hobbes

Bacon lived and wrote without knowing the works of Galileo. Such was not the case with Thomas Hobbes (1588–1679), who made mechanistic science the basis for a materialist philosophy. To him only matter and motion were real, and sense perceptions, conveying the motion of matter to the mind (itself a special kind of matter), were the source of all knowledge. Believing that he had destroyed the basis for transcendant knowledge, Hobbes argued that man was distinguished from beast by his ability to use symbols and language. Hobbes's political philosophy made use of still another device borrowed from science—the concept of a "state of nature." In a state of nature life was "nasty, brutish, and short." But man escaped the natural "war of all against all" by creating a state establishing a political contract. Under this contract the state, by imposing a uniform ideology, was empowered to secure order.

## John Locke and His Conflict with Leibniz

Hobbes's empirical "psychology" was modified by John Locke (1632–1704), the Whig theorist of the English Revolution of 1688. A member of the Royal Society, Locke was a physician and the secretary of the Earl of Shaftesbury, a radical Whig who led the fight against the accession of James II. From discussions within these radical intellectual circles, Locke concluded that conflicts over terminology and contradictory assertions arose because men carried their inquiries beyond the mind's possible experience.

After considering the origins and validity of human knowledge for 20 years, Locke published *An Essay Concerning Human Understanding* in 1690. In it he states that the mind derives its ideas from sensory data. They are recorded as on a blank sheet of paper, and their range is limited to areas of human sensation and experience. No room is left for Platonic universal ideas existing within the mind. Moreover, valid sensations are not sensible qualities such as color, but the mathematical, physical primary qualities of solidity, extension, form, and motion. Yet Locke did not maintain that the mind was wholly passive. He accorded it the ability to originate ideas through active reflection, repeating, comparing, and uniting sensations in an almost infinite variety of ways. But the mind could not formulate metaphysical realities, knowledge of which might be obtained from Christian revelation, subject always to the test of reason.

In *An Essay Concerning Human Understanding* Locke accepts the compelling validity of "clear and distinct," or self-evident, ideas. Among these are the natural rights that justified revolution in his political philosophy. He also anticipates the development of a system of mathematically demonstrable ethics. In contrast to Hobbes, who wanted the state to enforce uniformity of opinion, Locke wanted an exchange of ideas, which required limited religious toleration.

Locke's dedication to empiricism and his denunciation of innate ideas endeared him to many thinkers of the eighteenth-century Enlightenment. More immediately, however, he was refuted by continental rationalists, especially by the math-

ematician Gottfried Wilhelm von Leibniz.

Leibniz was the brilliant German mathematician who had discovered infinitesimal calculus at the same time as Newton. He upheld innate ideas and based a comprehensive metaphysical explanation of the universe upon them. Like Bruno he postulated a created universe composed of an infinite number of substances (*monads*) arranged in a cosmic hierarchy or chain of being. Each monad was self-contained and totally isolated from all others, but all were directed by innate mind or spirit in harmony with the order preestablished by God (the "monad of monads"). Believing that harmony was the essence of the universe, Leibniz labored to negotiate a religious reunion between Catholic and Protestant, proposed a confederation of European states, and worked on a universal language. All of these dreams failed, but Leibniz's confidence in the power of reason to heal human schisms was reflected in the eighteenth-century Enlightenment. Reformers, however, had difficulty accepting his dictum "that this is the best of all possible worlds," which was commonly given a conservative interpretation.

## SCIENCE, POLITICS, AND RELIGION

### The Politics of Reason

Whether rationalist, empiricist, or a combination of both, scientific philosophers of the seventeenth century broke from the otherworldly religious creeds of the sixteenth century. So did political theorists who reacted against the general violence during the religious wars. They discredited warring creeds as a basis for political life and bequeathed a doctrine of natural law to subsequent generations. Humanists like Jean Bodin in the sixteenth century and Hugo Grotius in the seventeenth replaced theology with secular concepts of sovereignty and the commonweal, basing their theories not on divine revelation but on rational natural laws. Borrowing terms from the physical sciences, English empiricists went further in putting politics on a secular, utilitarian footing. Their analyses substituted the "state of nature" for the Garden of Eden and contractual relationships between the ruler and the ruled for authority by divine right. This new political philosophy was a compound of humanism and contemporary science. By the eighteenth century, concepts taken from mechanics such as "balanced government" and "the balance of power" became general in western Europe.

Political philosophers of the seventeenth century demonstrated that their new premises could be used to support revolution, confederation, or absolute states. But even those who, like Descartes, advocated absolutism were at variance with traditional concepts.

To prevent further civil warfare of the kind he had witnessed in England and France, Thomas Hobbes prescribed a thoroughgoing absolutism. Convinced that men would never cease warring against one another in a state of nature, he proposed in his *Leviathan* of 1651 to make the state a "mortal god" with the unlimited power to set all moral and religious values. It would be contractual, rational, and utilitarian in origin. Once entered into, the contract between state and people was irrevocable. In international relations, however, Hobbes foresaw no contract that might curtail wars. Rather he believed that the nations were trapped in a state of nature and would carry out an insatiable struggle for power that would cease only in death.

Most advocates of divine-right monarchy received Hobbes's rationale for absolutism coldly. It was too bluntly this-worldly, materialistic, and utilitarian, leaving no grounds for asserting the divine origins of political authority. Some

Title page of Hobbes's Leviathan, 1651.

enlightened despots of the eighteenth century, however, aimed at Hobbes's model.

No less secular was another theorist of the English civil wars, James Harrington. A contemporary and admirer of Hobbes, Harrington was preoccupied with the distribution of property. Whereas Hobbes found the basis of the state in absolute legal power, Harrington advocated republican government under written constitutional law, since he believed that an imbalance between economic and political power perverted the constitution and could cause revolution, as it had in seventeenth-century England. His ideal commonwealth, detailed plans for which he set forth in *The Commonwealth of Oceana* of 1656, should be a government of laws, not men. Among the devices to secure this end were secret ballots, a separation of policy-making and consultative powers, and rotation in office (which he compared to the circulation of the blood). Harrington's legacy fell primarily to radical Whigs in England and to the American Revolution.

Still a different concept of government based on natural law emerged in the Dutch Republic and the empire. In rebelling against Spain in the sixteenth century, the Dutch had appealed to both natural law and chartered rights. Government in the Dutch Republic became a confederation recognizing individual and corporate rights. Johannes Althusius, a German theorist, formulated a concept of divided sovereignty in which families, communes, associations, and provinces were granted enough strength to set limits to the power of the central government. The Dutch humanist Hugo Grotius (1583–1645) concurred, asserting that associations might limit central government. He conceived of the state as an agreement among individual holders of rights whose autonomous associations could coexist within it. But his concept of revolution did not go beyond the *fait accompli* represented by the Dutch Republic. Grotius's main concern, however, was with international relations, a field in which he exerted considerable influence. Reacting against the religious wars, he tried to detach politics from theology. His major work, *On the Law of War and Peace,* set down the principle that relations between sovereigns should be governed by reason and natural law; their own self-interest and preservation dictated restraint. Grotius considered natural law to be as self-evident and as self-enforcing as the axioms of geometry.

In England John Locke made natural law a revolutionary doctrine. Prior to his writing, English colonists in North America had demonstrated their ability to institute government by voluntary compact, an accomplishment that contradicted the premises of contemporary authoritarianism.

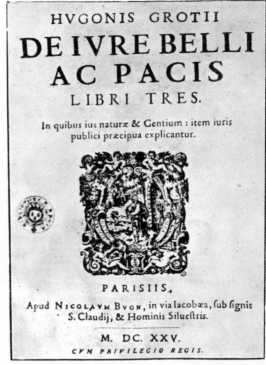

Title page of Grotius's On the Law of War and Peace, *which explained the law of nature and of nations.*

In England itself Locke's radical circle worked against the Catholic Stuart absolutism of James II, and Locke wrote a justification for the Revolution of 1688. Like Hobbes, the English philosopher assumes an initial "state of nature." But to him natural man was neither fallen—as theological politics assumed—nor brutish, as Hobbes had said. Instead Locke agreed with Harrington that man possessed a certain sociability. To guarantee natural rights—life, liberty, and property—men in a state of nature entered into a social contract. Locke could not demonstrate empirically either the existence of these rights or the formation of a contract. Nevertheless, they furnished the basis for asserting that natural rights were anterior to government. Government was instituted, Locke argued, by a second contract with a ruler. Should the ruler flagrantly transgress upon individual rights, the ruled might revoke the contract—that is, revolt. In this way Locke provided a justification for overturning James II, and in so doing he shifted the emphasis of political theory away from indefeasible rights of rulers to the inalienable rights of subjects.

Locke appropriated from Hobbes the ideas of a state of nature and a contractual government, but he used them to refute Hobbes's absolutism. Rather than a monolithic state, Locke advocated a balance of social and political powers. From the revolutionary thinkers of the Puritan Commonwealth he borrowed the notion of a separation and balance of executive and legislative powers, which was as prominent a part of his political theory as the right of revolution.

The idea of a "balanced government" whose primary function was the protection of property (the only natural right that Locke discussed at length) was far more congenial to the thought of the eighteenth century than was his rationale for revolution; it was forgotten that he defined property as life, liberty, and the fruit of labor. His precepts of balanced government were invoked on behalf of the English constitution as a perfect balance of aristocracy, monarchy, and democracy. But his doctrines could also serve the cause of revolution, as American colonists demonstrated in 1776. In any case, whether given a conservative or revolutionary interpretation, Locke's legacy was secular rather than religious.

Natural-law theorists were primarily concerned with domestic rather than international politics. They left foreign affairs in a state of nature regulated only by the doctrine of rational self-interest, which was increasingly supplemented by the notion of a balance of power, an idea borrowed from physics. The Peace of Utrecht (1713) deepened western Europe's commitment to a balance of power and weakened the tradition of inheritance by divine right. Subsequent to that treaty the Western powers intervened diplomatically in other wars in order to prevent any one state from gaining dominance.

## Rational Religion

World views based on revelation and supernatural intervention could not be reconciled with the premises of scientific philosophy and natural-law politics. A collision was inevitable. Whether its outcome would be endless hostility or a satisfactory compromise remained to be seen. When the contest began, traditional theology had a strong hold on intellectuals, but it could scarcely remain firm during civil and military conflicts in which religious truths were decided by the strongest battalions. Rulers and theorists reacted to this situation by making internal peace more important than confessional partisanship. Classical humanists responded by deepening their thought and expanding their influence. Men who had studied the genealogy of the ancient gods were, in effect, acquainted with comparative religion, and from the Renaissance onward some of them had formed a "Deistic" point of view. Behind varying and perhaps inconsequential rituals and creeds they discovered general moral precepts. For humanists such as Jean Bodin and Hugo Grotius, these precepts, themselves imperfect manifestations of natural law, constituted real, or natural, religion.

Commerce and colonization also worked to undermine traditional religious creeds. Christian merchants traded with heretics wherever a profit was to be made, often even in wartime. Their societies seemed to benefit as a result. Entrepreneurs likewise defied prohibitions on usury—the taking of exorbitant interest. Missionaries coming into contact with other religions had to broaden their points of view. The Jesuit order, formerly the shock troops of aggressive Catholic reform, publicized native customs and mores. A few of them even proposed merging Buddhism with the Roman Catholic church. Such a suggestion obviously fell upon deaf ears in Europe, but it was indicative of one important result of European expansion: for the mercantile people who profited from increased trade salvation was no longer a solitary goal. They now sought secular happiness also.

Thus in many parts of Europe conditions were ripe for a redefinition of doctrines that would include humanism, a secular ethic, and the new world view of science and scientific philosophy. But this redefinition was less radical in the older commercial states, where secularization was already far advanced in practice and where a certain stability had been achieved. It was stated most uncompromisingly by intellectuals who admired these societies but whose environment was still the Old Regime. In elaborating ideas and ideals—often borrowed from the more secular, commercial societies—these intellectuals broke more decisively with past religious traditions than did the intellectuals of the Renaissance or the Reformation.

Early scientists such as Copernicus, Kepler, Galileo, Boyle, Pascal, and Newton saw no conflict between their work and their religion. Kepler, for example, was certain that proving the existence of an orderly mechanistic universe would increase the glory of God. Boyle and Newton conceived of God as the giver of laws and the imparter of motion within the divine plan of creation. Newton left this "clockwinder God" with the function of making occasional repairs. On the basis of Old Testament genealogy he assumed with contemporary clergymen that creation had occurred about 4004 B.C. Their calculations did not differ appreciably from those of Francis Bacon or Blaise Pascal, who accepted scientific methodology in the physical realm but relied upon revelation for religious truth. Nevertheless these scientists no longer relied on theology to explain natural phenomena. Since science continued to expand, the boundaries between religion and science would not prove easy to maintain.

As new generations sought to interpret the scope of modern science they raised more and more questions about the nature of religion. Were scientific methodology and conclusions relevant to religion? Did traditional religion uphold Newton's principle that natural law is simple? Was the record of miracles that supported revelation genuine? Or could miracles occur at all in a mechanistic universe? How could the many competing claims of absolute truth, both in Europe and overseas, be reconciled? Given the limitations of human knowledge, could absolute truth be known and enforced? Would it not be discovered by reason from nature rather than from traditional authoritarian institutions and records? Could all the ethical standards in Scripture be considered just or even moral? Particularly in England and the Netherlands, where religious unity was lacking, attempts to answer such questions led to the emergence of a rational religion that gradually transformed faith in revelation into faith in reason or piety.

Humanists led this transformation. In 1627 Hugo Grotius proposed an Erasmian Christianity based on piety rather than doctrine alone. His *Concerning the Truth of the Christian Religion* adhered to Scripture but interpreted it according to its environment at the time of its composition. Thus the Bible became merely another historical document. An Englishman, Edward Herbert of Cherbury (1583–1648), went further in the direction of universality. Through the study of comparative religion and through introspection he set out to find universal religious principles on which all rational men could agree. He eliminated the sacraments and the concept of God-chosenness, whether of nation or of the predestined "elect," his emphasis falling instead on the worship of a Supreme Being, on conscience, and on piety. In the Netherlands Spinoza arrived at similar conclusions. Later in the century Pierre Bayle (1647–1706) began publishing from the Netherlands the *Historical and Critical Dictionary* in the same year that Louis XIV revoked the Edict of Nantes (1685). The *Dictionary* lashed out against superstition, intolerance, and dogmatic assertions, appealing to the primacy of moral conscience over all Scripture that seemed to command violent behavior. At the same time Locke was reconciling faith and reason in his *Reasonableness of Christianity*. Locke defined reason as "natural revelation," which served as a check on recorded miracles. According to him, those who had not been exposed to Christianity could learn moral law by the light of nature. In Germany Johann Semler (1725–91) followed a similar course in biblical criticism, treating the Scriptures as historical evidence rather than as divine revelation.

All proponents of rational religion pressed toward universality, minimized dogma, and emphasized morality. Few followed Hobbes and Spinoza in making faith a function of politics and the social order. Nevertheless all rationalists had replaced revelation with reason in determining ethics. Their outlook, which led to a more explicit scientific Deism in the eighteenth century, appealed primarily to the educated upper classes. It made a deep impression on the more open-minded clergy of several established churches. But it elicited little enthusiasm from the uneducated masses, who often joined emotional fundamentalist revolts against it.

As the new science and philosophy spread, the premises of religious rationalism became increasingly those of scientific natural law. Locke and others had set the main lines of Deistic thought, but it came more into vogue and became more secular as Newton's concepts of a mechanistic universe were popularized.

By 1789 Newton's *Principia* had run through 18 English editions, and no fewer than 40 books describing his accomplishment had appeared in that language alone. Many of these popularizations carried the conviction that Newton had banished mystery from the universe, making it entirely explainable by mathematical laws. Alexander Pope quipped,

> Nature and Nature's laws lay hid in
>     night:
> God said, Let Newton be! and all was
>     light.

Newtonian science provided the two principal Deistic arguments for the existence of a Supreme Being: (1) that he was necessary as the first cause of the universe, and (2) that the flawless order of that universe presupposed an intelligent creator. Since the laws of the universe were uniform and universal, the Deists rejected miracles and relegated prophecy and rites to superstition. They professed a faith in immortality primarily as a sanction for ethics, since the focus of their interest was on this world. They examined traditional Christianity for ethical utility and humanitarianism and found it seriously lacking in both. Their faith was set upon the existence of a Supreme Being who seldom intervened in the affairs of men but also upon man's capacity to reform.

The new humanism of the seventeenth century bequeathed to the Enlightenment of the eighteenth a belief in the possibility of human progress: through reason man could discover and use the laws of nature that applied to him and his society. The Supreme Being was a constitutional sovereign subject also to the laws of nature; as he assumed less responsibility for daily affairs, man assumed more. Resignation gave way to reform, orthodoxy to benevolence, heaven to posterity. Thus the progressive secularization of thought remade religion, and this has continued until the present time.

## C. The Enlightenment   FOUNDATIONS OF EIGHTEENTH-CENTURY LIBERALISM

In the eighteenth century the effort to popularize science and the new humanism and to use these new outlooks as a basis for improving the political and social order was known as the Enlightenment. French publicists who called themselves *philosophes* led this effort. Rapidly expanding its commerce and caught up in new social and political tensions, France produced intellectuals who were receptive to the radical thought of the previous century. Disillusioned with existing institutions and outlooks, the philosophes were attracted to views based on Newton's science and Locke's psychology. Together with travel literature, some of which they edited, their writings helped break down European parochialism. And their works made France, whose cultural and social standards had begun to dominate the Continent under Louis XIV, the radiant center of the Enlightenment. England and the Netherlands provided few new stimuli to radical eighteenth-century thought. But Scots, Italians, Germans, and other European intellectuals, who constituted a cosmopolitan rather than a national sort of elite, joined the philosophes in their mission of enlightening their contemporaries and posterity with new knowledge. They even found some followers in benighted Spain.

### The Prominence of the French Philosophes

Among the publicists of the Enlightenment the most prolific were the philosophes of France. Writers elsewhere wrestled with the same problems, often making basic contributions, but it was such men as Montesquieu, Voltaire, Condillac, Diderot, and Condorcet who set the Enlightenment's basic tone. Unlike previous continental intellectuals, they depended for their livelihood not on patronage of church and state but on a reading public of middle class, clergy, and aristocracy. The tastes of their public were those of the salons, where the influence of women, the requirements of urbanity and wit, and the atmosphere of pleasure-seeking and graceful behavior prevailed. Intermittently the authorities censored the works of the French philosophes, but the inconsistency of this censorship only sharpened demands for the forbidden books, advertised the philosophes' plea for intellectual freedom, and encouraged them to disguise their criticisms by means of satire and ridicule.

Many philosophes had both a humanist education and scientific interests. They became simplifiers and popularizers of scientific discoveries and the views based upon them, and, their interests being primarily social, they proclaimed a challenging and relatively new objective, a *science of society*. They assumed that societies operated in accordance with natural laws as axiomatic and binding

*Voltaire (hand raised), expounding to friends.*

as the mathematical laws that governed the physical universe. They championed empiricism, but they more often used reason than research as a tool. Without becoming slavish imitators, they advocated borrowing foreign, especially English, institutions that seemed to conform to the laws of nature.

The philosophes assumed that these laws could help rational men improve their lot and accepted or rejected existing institutions solely on the basis of their social utility; and they rejected theological sanction, vested interests, or mere historical survival as justifications for the continued existence of these institutions. Without adopting Locke's ideas of natural rights, they brought many of the institutions of their time into question whose usefulness to society could no longer be demonstrated. For the most part, however,

they sought not their destruction but their redirection to propagate the Enlightenment's faith in human betterment.

Without being consciously revolutionary, the philosophes took positions squarely at odds with inherited institutions. According to them, the reform of society required that freedom of thought replace authoritarian censorship and indoctrination by the Church. They condemned the priesthood for using coercion and manipulating popular hopes and fears. They attacked clerical obscurantism as the most serious threat to social progress. Although they provided no blueprint, it was clear that the French church, made vulnerable by doctrinal warfare between Jesuits and Jansenists, would have to be remodeled. Some philosophes wanted its conflicting doctrines replaced by a universal natural Deism without sac-

*"Noble savages" negotiating with William Penn (by Benjamin West).*

raments and rites. All of this "reformism" meant that they rejected the doctrine of the depravity of man; by education at least the upper echelons of society could be transformed. Education, a key part of the philosophes' program, should pass from the Church to the state and be oriented toward citizenship, science, practical arts, and modern languages.

Discredited by foreign defeats, financial crises, and internal conflicts, the French state was especially vulnerable to criticism. All of the philosophes denounced arbitrary government and the violation of rights of property and person. They also opposed economic regulations, clerical influences, and systems of forced labor. Their ideal enlightened ruler would legislate according to the dictates of natural law or social utility to advance the arts, the sciences, and the general welfare. Against

the divine prerogatives of the monarchy and the Church they appealed to nature and the natural goodness of man.

Along with "reason," the word "natural" became the philosophes' touchstone for testing institutions. Unfortunately that word was (and still is) used in a variety of confusing and contradictory ways. Among other things it meant (1) the ideal determined by reason—what ought to be; (2) the customary, the usual—what was, or was done; (3) the worldly as opposed to the supernatural, thus making miracles unnatural; and often (4) the primitive or untarnished original state of nature inhabited by the "noble savage" and reported by travel literature. Thus the repeated proposition that man should discover the laws of nature and conform to them was ambiguous. The philosophes believed that "nature," unmolested by arbitrary authority, would operate harmoniously as a unifying force.

Most of the philosophes considered "social science" an instrument of progress. Past history made some of them pessimistic; Voltaire, for example, believed that progress would always be limited. Condorcet, however, believed that perfectability was an inexorable law of nature that would replace divine providence. In either case the golden age for man was to be found in the future rather than in revelation or in a past era of excellence. (As Fontenelle had explained earlier, moderns were really the ancients, for they had at their disposal the experience of those who had gone before them.)

The philosophes assumed that knowledge of nature would make men virtuous, but as another part of their program for progress they called for sweeping humanitarian reforms. Following in the footsteps of the Quakers, they attacked slavery, torture, secret accusations, arbitrary imprisonment, cruel and unusual punishments, treatment of the insane as criminals, and the inferior status of women. Many also attacked war and militarism. Although they advocated a state in which the individual had a stake in property and civic rights, their patriotism was cultural and not based on emotional hatred or disparagement of foreigners. As a means of curtailing warfare they relied upon enlightened self-interest, working through a balance of power. Rarely did the philosophes think that reason should be supplemented by institutions to resolve international conflicts; they were cosmopolitans rather than internationalists.

## Montesquieu and Historical Empiricism

Rational criticism of the existing regime in France had begun during the reign of Louis XIV, but it first obtained wide currency and general significance with Montesquieu. During the aristocratic resurgence following the death of Louis XIV, Baron de Montesquieu (1689–1755) opened an era with *The Persian Letters* (1721). This satire placed caustic comments on French government, religion, and manners on the tongue of a visiting oriental. Then, after many years of research and travel, Montesquieu published in 1748 *The Spirit of the Laws.* Here he tried by inductive methods to go behind the apparent diversity of governmental systems to find a natural law of constitutional and social structure. His sources were both ancient and contemporary. In the England of his own time he found a political freedom that contrasted with the "tyranny" of Louis XIV. That freedom, he concluded, was guaranteed by a separation of the executive, legislative, and judicial powers and by the maintenance of the hereditary nobility with the power of veto over legislation. Everywhere he found constitutions conditioned by climate and environment to which wise legislators were obliged to adjust specific enactments.

*The Spirit of the Laws,* although blemished with naive associations of cause and effect and with rambling formlessness, was one of the most influential political treatises of the century. At first it became the political bible of European nobles struggling against royal autocracy. Later, in the era of revolution, it became a fountainhead of constitutions that embodied the principle of a separation of powers as well as a system of checks and balances of those powers. Thus, besides it serving the nobles, it served the liberals, who opposed direct popular rule as well as the nobles.

In Italy Giovanni Battista Vico (1668–1744) manifested independently of Montesquieu a similar sense of history and a similar attempt to get at the "spirit" behind differing external forms of government and society. Vico traced an evolutionary cycle of intellectual and institu-

*Montesquieu's chateau near Bordeaux.*

tional development, which he considered to be universally characteristic of all societies. He saw them passing through an initial stage of savage emotion characterized by a theocratic state, an imaginative stage with aristocratic government, and a third phase of knowledge and civilization with monarchical or republican government.

Vico's evolutionary approach and his treatment of institutions as projections of a group mind made little impact on his contemporaries, but his works belie the charge of nineteenth-century romantics that the Enlightenment lacked a historical sense and that it preached purely rational abstractions. In addition to Montesquieu (who also wrote on the fall of Rome) and Vico, the Englishman Edward Gibbon and the Scotsman David Hume were avid historians, as was Voltaire. In fact Gibbon's *Decline and Fall of the Roman Empire* became a classic of English historical

letters. Far from ignoring history, the philosophes used it to show up their traditionalist opponents as contributors to barbarism. Like Italian Renaissance humanists, with whom they shared so much, they invoked the past to lead men into a new era of cultural enlightenment.

## Voltaire and Humanitarian Rage

Whereas Montesquieu represented the enlightened nobility, Jean François Marie Arouet—better known as Voltaire (1694–1778)—the undisputed prince of philosophe letters, expressed the antiaristocratic viewpoint of the middle class. A political realist who praised English constitutionalism and considered absolutism appropriate for Russia, Voltaire differed sharply with Montesquieu about what was best for France. There he championed an enlightened despotism that would curb the nobility. A promising poet who was twice imprisoned in the Bastille at a nobleman's instigation, Voltaire crossed the Channel and imbibed English philosophy, literature, science, and Deism. Returning for 15 years to the Duchy of Lorraine on the French frontier, he popularized Newton, Locke, and the whole English social system as sharp contrasts to contemporary French thought and institutions. A star of the salons and a confidant of princes—notably Frederick the Great of Prussia—Voltaire finally settled in 1758 at Ferney, an estate on the French-Swiss frontier, where he spent most of the remainder of his life writing, supervising his estates and factories, and entertaining guests who made their pilgrimage to him. He produced a flood of plays, histories, essays, satires, letters, and Deistic sermons, filling nearly 90 volumes of collected works. His work conveyed the Enlightenment's message of free thought, common sense, and hatred of fanaticism, ignorance, persecution, and war. He also took up individual cases of injustice with his sharp and witty pen. Hostile to revolution and aloof from democratic sentiments—at least until his old age, he urged rulers to enact the philosophes' program of civil rights and freedoms for their citizens.

*Voltaire (by Houdon).*

Voltaire displayed a humanitarian rage toward intolerance and inhumanity. In this vein his name is most closely linked with criticism of organized Christianity. *Écrasez l'infâme*—"crush the infamous thing" (namely intolerance)—he wrote. He held the organized church largely responsible for the ignorance, superstition, servility, and fanaticism of the masses. He deplored its role in perverting justice and supporting cruelties. Purged of its evils, however, the Church could serve a useful social purpose.

As a moralist-historian Voltaire flayed the past for its follies. He also introduced Far Eastern subjects into universal history: his amateurish effort served mainly to compare Frenchmen unfavorably with the rational Chinese; still, it indicated a universal point of view. Although much of Voltaire's work was clever, witty, superficial, and borrowed, his literary power carried the Enlightenment to its widest audience.

Many indignant voices carried the Enlightenment's gospel of humanitarianism, but an Italian, the Marchese Cesare di Beccaria, produced one of its most cogent treatises on a common theme. His *Crimes and Punishments* of 1764, a systematic indictment of contemporary court procedures and penal codes, became a classic in enlightened criminology. He denied the efficacy of increasingly severe penal codes, torture, and unusual punishments as deterrents to crime. Criminals would be more effectively curbed, he argued, simply by punishment that was certain and proportionate to the offense.

## The Enlightenment's Problem of Knowledge

By denying divinely implanted innate ideas as the source of truth, the leaders of the Enlightenment proceeded to secularize thought drastically. Distrusting rationalist systems of all kinds, they followed Locke's empiricism in setting limits on human knowledge by excluding innate ideas. According to Voltaire, "Locke has set forth human reason just as an excellent anatomist explains the parts of the human body." Denis Diderot, another outstanding *philosophe,* said: "Nothing is in the intellect that was not first in the senses." By the middle of the eighteenth century fundamental dilemmas appeared in the philosophes' empirical doctrine of knowledge. Locke had acknowledged the disparity between sensory data—which could be misleading—and what he took to be the external reality of extension, motion, weight, and so forth. But did these Lockean categories actually conform to reality in the external world? Or were they entirely subjective forms imposed by the mind or human passions?

During the first half of the century Locke's authority was little questioned by enlightened writers, but as early as 1709 the Anglo-Irish bishop George Berkeley had pushed empiricism to its logical extreme, thereby exposing the dilemmas it created. If only specific triangles were real, then there could be no true "abstract genuine idea" of *triangle.* On the other hand, things not perceived had no meaningful reality. "To be is to be perceived," he concluded. Berkeley opted for a complete subjective idealism. He accepted only other minds as being real without being perceived.

David Hume, a Scottish philosopher in revolt against all rationalist systems, adhered to a thoroughgoing empiricism; he questioned all knowledge except individual sensory experience. He assigned supernatural knowledge insufficiently attested by miracles to the realm of subjective hopes and fears. At the same time he doubted the reality of cause-and-effect relationships; they were mental habits. Likewise he attacked self-evident propositions, rational religion based on the assumption of a universal human nature, and rational morality. No man, Hume said in effect, had ever observed a "state of nature"; hence, assumptions drawn from such an idea could not be verified. For the purpose of discovering human nature he urged the study of psychology, history, and anthropology. And since reason was a slave to the passions, sound human relations could not be based on it; they could rest only on an ethic of moral sentiment or on the ability to put oneself in the shoes of another. Hume thus divorced "reason" from "nature" and substituted an alliance between "nature" and "feeling."

French philosophes also had to take up the problem of knowledge in order to support their empirical position, and among them Étienne de Condillac wrestled with it most systematically, beginning in 1746 with *The Essay on the Origin of Human Knowledge* (or *Sense Perceptions*). Condillac was primarily concerned with the "natural history of the soul," the progressive development of the mind. In a famous illustration he compared this development to a statue acquiring human mental capabilities. According to Condillac knowledge came from the senses, but it was the passions that determined their primacy and their impact on the mind. In short, with Condillac and Diderot (who also wrote on the same problem), the Enlightenment began to abandon the rationalist faith in reason's ability to command emotions and to seek to direct the passions in the direction of human happiness and social usefulness. Voltaire's "humanitarian rage" was one illustration of such use of passionate feeling, but his position failed to secure unanimous support. In the later Enlightenment the philosophes' differing views on the origin of knowledge and the role of the passions contributed to diversity of thought and conflicts among them.

## DIVERGENT QUESTS FOR A BETTER TOMORROW

### Diderot and the Encyclopedists

Not all the philosophes' work was individual; their crowning collective achievement was the 17-volume *Encyclopédie,* published between 1751 and 1780 under the principal editorship of Denis Diderot (1713–84). It had no less a purpose than to "bring together all the knowledge scattered over the face of the earth, to lay its general system before the men with whom we live . . . so that our children will know more, and so that they may at the same time be greater in virtue and in happiness." Its contributors included such men as Montesquieu, Turgot, Rousseau, d'Alembert, Holbach, Voltaire, and especially Diderot. In order to pass the scrutiny of the censors, the political and religious articles were orthodox, but the *Encyclopédie*'s columns carried the Enlightenment's assault on existing institutions and values in unsuspected places. The *Encyclopédie* was much more than a philosophic compilation; it became the outstanding work popularizing the Newtonian revolution and Bacon's ideas of inductive science. Its technical articles and plates, drawn to reproducible specifications and intended to show not only how things were actually done but also how they should be done, provided a store-house of skills, for technology's future social significance was not lost on Diderot and his collaborators. The *Encyclopédie* was too large, too unwieldy a work to be as effective as Voltaire's tracts. Nevertheless as a vehicle for spreading the Enlightenment, it reinforced the activities of the salons, the Masonic lodges, and the increasing number of scientific societies, newspapers, public libraries, and museums that appeared both in Europe and America.

The Encyclopedists carried faith in empiricism and in the influence of environment to its limits. Diderot explained human conduct entirely in natural terms and occasionally concluded that environment determined it. On a similar basis Claude Helvétius built up a morality based on people's aversion to pain and attraction to pleasure. His political doctrine was *utilitarianism*—the greatest good for the greatest number. These ideas were later expanded in England by philosophic radicals led by Jeremy Bentham. French materialism reached its culmination in the works of Baron d'Holbach (1723–89), whose *System of Nature,* published anonymously in 1770, explained everything in terms of matter and motion and denied the existence of free will, soul, and God. In stressing the emotions as wellsprings of human behavior these philosophes sought to redirect antisocial feelings into useful paths. In so doing they put natural forces above any deity as a basis of morality.

### Condorcet and Progress

Although the outbreak of the French Revolution has sometimes been blamed on subversion by the philosophes, only the Marquis de Condorcet (1743–94) lived until its early phases and had the opportunity of translating their thoughts into action once the monarchy had given way. A mathematician who had become a popular philosopher, Encyclopedist, anticlerical advocate of economic freedom, and activist for antislavery and feminism, Condorcet turned his home into a salon, whose visitors included Thomas Paine, Thomas Jefferson, and Adam Smith. A constitutional monarchist at the outbreak of the Revolution, he helped pen the French constitution of 1791. As the Revolution progressed, his thought became more and more democratic. But he was eventually put in jail; he died—perhaps a suicide—during the Terror of 1794. During his last few weeks, which he spent hiding from the revolutionary authorities, he penned a celebrated work on progress, *Sketch of the Intellectual Progress of Mankind.* This selective account of the human past predicted the spread of the Enlightenment and the perfectability of man in a world of equal states and equality of individuals. The vehicles of such progress were to be democratic revolution, technology, and the accumulation of knowledge.

Condorcet's main counterpart as an advocate of progress as an inexorable law of nature was Joseph Priestley, the English chemist. Priestley, a founder of modern Unitarianism, seconded and elaborated upon Condorcet's concept of progress as a law of nature.

The idea of progress as expressed by Condorcet and Priestley has sometimes been taken as typical of the Enlightenment as a whole. Most philosophes, however, thought only of limited or conditional progress. Pessimistic with respect to the lower classes becoming enlightened, not a few thought that savagery was a natural state from which men could escape only temporarily. For still others, progress was a temporary, cyclical phenomenon. Yet it is fair to say that a conditional faith in progress typified the Enlightenment even though men like Rousseau denied the faith of Condorcet and Diderot that it could be achieved by expanding technology and knowledge.

## Rousseau and the Emancipation of Passions

Although many writers of the Enlightenment shared the idea of harnessing the emotions, or passions, to useful ends, it was Jean Jacques Rousseau (1712–78), Genevan born and a self-educated wanderer, who brought it to a climax. A plebeian misfit in the exaggerated refinement of Parisian salons, Rousseau became the prophet of revolt against the philosophes' rationalism and materialism. In 1749 he bounded into fame by winning an essay contest on the question "Has the Restoration of Sciences and Arts Tended to Corrupt or Purify Morals?" By charging that luxuries and cities had corrupted man, he attacked the cherished assumption of many philosophes that increased knowledge automatically brought progress. In the *Discourse on Inequality* (1755) he broadened his criticism to indict the morally corrupting influence of society and rule by and for the rich, thereby questioning the existence of a natural harmony between self-interest and society. According to Rousseau a moral revolution was the first prerequisite for progress.

Rousseau sketched the path that this moral revolution should take in his *Social Contract* (1762). If existing government corrupted natural man, then government ought to be transformed into an expression of popular will so that it would preserve as much as possible man's natural quality, virtues, and freedoms. For Rousseau only the "general will" could legitimately bind men to law and government; therefore the *Social Contract* could be construed as a call for popular revolution against monarchical and aristocratic government. Perfect democracy, however, could exist only in small states such as his native Geneva; for large states such as France, he proposed a sovereign restrained from tyranny through required submission to periodic provincial assemblies of the populace. This was to be a direct check on the executive, for Rousseau had no use for representative institutions like the Parliament of England. Rather his chief concern was to maintain civic spirit and curb materialistic self-interest, and to this end he wanted citizens to be indoctrinated with group pride and civic religion. This proposal seemed to contradict his commitment to the individual's moral autonomy and conflicted with his contemporary tract on education, *Émile,* which advocated a natural spontaneous education of youth apart from artificial social contacts.

The life and writings of Rousseau abound in paradoxes, different sides of which have been adopted by the most diverse schools of politics. An unfettered individualist, he would surrender all individual rights to the state—once its authority had been made legitimate. Although contributing to a revolutionary climate that considered the status quo immoral, he considered revolutionary cures worse than the disease.

Rousseau's *Confessions* provides a possible key to his thought and personality. In this autobiographical sketch he portrays at length his moods, reveries, and feelings. His ideal norm for human societies is the better but unrealized nature of Jean Jacques himself, tortured by his own shortcomings to preach social virtues. His idea that a moral revolution must precede progress gave unity to his thought; his intuitive approach, his denial of natural harmony, his refusal to equate virtue with knowledge, and his uncompromising conclusion that contemporary society and its spokesmen were corrupt made a break between him and the philosophes inevitable. In his declining years his belief that he was being persecuted became a mania. Nevertheless Rousseau's approach admirably suited the tastes of those who wanted governments responsive to their peoples and who sought immediate solutions to practical problems that the Enlightenment's intellectualism failed to provide. As a diverse and fertile writer, he stands as the fountainhead of such nineteenth-century movements as the religious revival, democracy, romanticism, socialism, and especially nationalism. For the divine right of kings he substituted the natural rights of peoples. This principle called the legitimacy of all existing governments into question, but it contributed less to the development of an effective substitute than Montesquieu's constitutionalism which had its roots in representative government.

Meanwhile some of Rousseau's younger contemporaries perverted his emphasis on the emancipation of the passions. The Italian adventurer and gambler Casanova, who at one point associated with the philosophes in Paris, made a profession of libertinism and boasted the fact in his memoirs. The Marquis de Sade, whose works became popular at the end of the century, gave a peculiar rationalization to perversion and the pursuit of personal pleasure alone; he equated virtue with inaction and argued that the strong man must be wholeheartedly evil. Yet even extremists like Casanova and Sade were not wholly out of accord with the Enlightenment's resurrection of naturalism in opposition to the doctrine of the depravity of man.

## Kant and Moral Consciousness

An admirer of Rousseau far removed from the libertinism just described was Immanuel Kant, the greatest thinker of the German Enlightenment. A philosopher also trained in mathematics, physics, and theology, Kant tackled head-on the conflict between empiricists and rationalists that had emerged from the scientific revolution of the seventeenth century, believing that he was effecting a second Copernican revolution, this one in philosophy. Kant reversed Locke's doctrine that the mind was a blank tablet on which experience writes, assuming instead an active and synthesizing mind. It was the mind, not external reality—"things in themselves"—that provided sense perceptions with such categories as time, space, and causation. Without such categories imposed on "things in themselves," perception by the senses was blind, yielding nothing meaningful. Having thus vitiated empiricism, Kant scathingly criticized the rationalists' claim that innate ideas give an accurate picture of reality, for "concepts without percepts," he wrote, "are empty." Neither reason nor sense perceptions alone could produce scientific certainty; only a combination of both could do that, and even so "things in themselves" might never be known. But beyond this combination, pure reason detached from sense perceptions yields self-consistent "ideas" that, even though they are not verifiable, could be used to systematize knowledge. Nevertheless such ideas could not be used to validate traditional speculations about the universe or the existence of God.

Siding with the rationalists against the empiricists, Kant did regard one such "idea" as a fact—the experience of moral obligations, or a sense of duty. This common obligation implied that the will was free to make moral decisions despite man's being subject to binding laws of nature. Stimulated by the priority that Rousseau gave to morality as the essence of man, Kant sought a universal compulsory law as its foundation. He discovered it not in individual actions of practical experience, which often violate moral law, but in reason completely detached from existing practices. This was his "categorical imperative" for testing moral maxims: "Act as if the maxim of your action were to become through your will a universal law of nature." A variant of the imperative commanded that all men be treated as ends in themselves, never merely as tools or means to an end. This was a morality of self-determination, for the subjects of the moral law were its creators. Not surprisingly Kant observed and approved both the American and French revolutions. Yet it was reverence for duty, not the philosophes' quest for happiness or pleasure, that characterized his rigorous moral consciousness.

He also departed from the philosophes in making religious faith intellectually respectable, but his was a rational faith subordinated to morality in which all external rites were idle. Although Kant honored Christianity, it was only the morality of the New Testament that he accepted; immortality and the existence of God he demonstrated not from revelation but from the assumptions behind his rational moral code.

Kant's thought, a critical summary of the Enlightenment's repudiation of tradition, did effect a revolution in philosophy, particularly moral theory. Protestant theologians, romantics, idealists, existentialists, and logical positivists, among others, have found at least parts of it relevant. His impact was also felt in political theory, especially in democratic and internationalist schools of thought. But as a rigorous moralist, he had little taste for the Enlightenment's material concerns; consequently he stood almost totally aloof from its emphasis on economic doctrine and the ethic of self-interest that it championed.

## ECONOMIC THOUGHT OF THE ENLIGHTENMENT

### The Philosophes

Insofar as it was not mercantilist or traditionalist, eighteenth-century economic thought reflected the economic and social changes taking place in the more prosperous Western countries. Like the more specialized economic theorists, the philosophes wanted to replace medieval property rights with concepts of private ownership. When "enlightened" economic writers spoke of property, most of them meant landed, rather than commercial, wealth. The philosophes idealized the English colonies of North America and England, where restrictions on exchange of land had partially broken down in the sixteenth century. They assumed that if property could be exchanged freely, it would naturally be dispersed among greater numbers of owners. This distribution would be facilitated by abolishing laws restricting full rights of ownership and by requiring the division of estates in inheritance. Tax reform and state guarantees of property rights were also essential. Property therefore was central to the philosophes' social theory; they considered it the social counterpart to the physical law of gravitation: property held society together by giving men a stake in it and by involving them in political affairs. A few successors of Rousseau devised socialist plans for distributing wealth, but most economists of the Enlightenment left its distribution to the unhindered operation of "natural" laws.

Eighteenth-century economic thought was directed against mercantilism no less than against older forms of property rights. Encouraged by their own economic strength and harassed by complicated regulations, entrepreneurs and landlords in England and France became critical of governmental paternalism. Using analogies from the physical sciences, they argued that "natural" economic forces, given free play, would establish their own beneficial harmony. Whereas mercantilists depended upon government supervision and national antagonisms, economics of the Enlightenment emphasized the natural harmony that would prevail when individuals and states pursued their enlightened self-interest. Governments should abandon intervention and allow the self-regulating mechanism of the market, which operated according to "natural" laws, to work for the common good.

## The Physiocrats and the Formulation of Laissez-Faire

The first "scientific" school of political economy, the Physiocrats, arose in France among the followers of François Quesnay (1694–1774), who claimed that they had discovered the self-evident laws regulating the flow of money. Apart from supporting governmental regulation of interest rates, the Physiocrats advocated leaving the economy to natural laws of supply and demand and to man's enlightened self-interest (laissez-faire). Government, which they would vest in an absolute monarchy, should guarantee the natural and limitless rights of property, security, and (economic) liberty. The Physiocrats agreed with many mercantilists that internal trade barriers were intolerable, but the greater part of their outlook was a reaction against the policies of Colbert. They denounced restrictive industrial production codes, guild regulations, protective tariffs, commercial wars, and the mercantilist emphasis upon industry and foreign commerce. Sympathetic to manorial estate holders, they publicized their new agricultural techniques and accorded the holders full rights over the communal property of peasant villages. Only agriculture and extractive industries, they asserted, produced wealth; manufacturing and the professions were "sterile." As a substitute for forced peasant labor and the cumbersome tax structure of the times they advocated a single tax on the land's net product produced by free labor. This reform would have swept away many existing administrative cobwebs and inequalities.

*Business, politics, and coffee: Lloyd's in the eighteenth century.*

## Adam Smith

Prior to the French Revolution the Physiocrats' influence was small. In 1776 Turgot, Louis XVI's reforming minister of finance, was dismissed for championing their views. In that same year Adam Smith, who had praise as well as criticism for the Physiocrats, published a more comprehensive explanation of economic phenomena, *An Inquiry Concerning the Wealth of Nations.*

In this classic treatise Smith (1723–90) shared the Physiocrats' optimistic faith in the natural harmony of the economic mechanism, provided that men recognized their true self-interests. But in contrast to the Physiocrats, Smith emphasized trade and labor—especially the division of labor—as principal sources of wealth. To government he assigned three tasks: (1) national defense; (2) the administration of justice with the purpose of protecting each member of society against oppression by any other member; and (3) the construction and maintenance of essential public utilities. Traditionally Smith's name has become more closely identified with laissez-faire economics than has that of any other man. Yet his criticism of certain business practices on moral grounds sets him apart from many later adherents and practitioners of laissez-faire who used this principle to justify such practices. Smith's edifice rested upon the premise that the greatest social benefits would result when each individual was allowed to pursue his own rational self-interest. Despite his moral stricture he insisted that natural economic processes need be guided only by the "invisible hand" of natural law, the name he applied to the mechanistic self-regulating characteristics of supply and demand. Although he did not break completely with the mercantilists on navigation acts and tariffs, he warned against the political dangers of high protective tariffs, and he roundly criticized monopolistic corporations, such as the East India Company, that exercised governmental powers.

Smith's advocacy of laissez-faire was

seconded by Jeremy Bentham, in whose utilitarian morality egoism (the securing of pleasure and the avoidance of pain) was the motive force behind individuals and societies. But Bentham also advocated inheritance laws and other reforms to lessen the inequality of economic relationships, always providing that property rights were not disturbed. Other advocates of laissez-faire such as Edmund Burke believed that traditional property rights and economic relationships were regulated by evolutionary laws of nature and God. Whatever form they took, laissez-faire economic theories made inroads only in western Europe, where a prosperous middle class had risen or where landlords became restive about communal agriculture. As refutations of religious paternalism, these theories were an outstanding example of the secularization of thought.

## D. Popular Religious Reactions to Science and Reason

As "world views"—explanations of the universe and man's place in it— rationalism, Deism, and sceptical empiricism satisfied only part of the educated classes. The conservative rationalism that upheld the social hierarchy penetrated the established Protestant churches teaching resignation to the status quo as "the best of all possible worlds." But rationalists chastened by the religious wars to decry "enthusiasm" in all its forms could not hold the loyalty of those who craved a "religion of the heart," an emotional experience of conversion, and a humanitarian morality. Already in revolt against the narrow creeds of the Reformation, several emotional religious movements also spurned the new secular world views taken from science; but even so, their doctrines were less otherworldly than past creeds of salvation in that, although putting more emphasis on moral precepts of human conduct, they were creeds of secular "works" as well as of faith.

### QUAKERS IN ENGLAND AND AMERICA

The English civil wars of the seventeenth century spawned several new religious sects that sponsored secular reforms. Among them the Society of Friends—or Quakers—was at the same time the most spiritualistic and worldly. Rejecting a professional clergy— whom they identified as "hirelings of princes"—tithes, sacraments, and the external paraphernalia of worship, the Quakers emphasized a private faith for living that transcended the boundaries of creed, nationality, race, and social class in the same way that natural law did for scientists and secular philosophers. Although a small sect, the Quakers included a disproportionate number of wealthy businessmen who devoted much time and money to the relief of poverty, unemployment, alcoholism, slavery, scandalous prison conditions, and inadequate medical facilities. In Pennsylvania the Quakers established a government that invoked the death penalty for only two offenses (treason and murder), in contrast to hundreds of capital offenses on the statute books of European states. Pennsylvania's fame as the most prosperous English colony in North America made many philosophes use it as an example of the benefits of humanitarianism. In short, the Quakers set the humanitarian ideal that Western man still professes to see in himself except that they insisted further upon nonviolence and international political organization.

## EMOTIONAL FUNDAMENTALISM

### The German Pietists

In the aftermath of the Thirty Years' War another religious sect, the German Pietists, had also begun to reject the rationalism and scholasticism of the "stone churches." Although the Pietists repudiated both science and reason, they were

*Evangelism in a home: John Wesley.*

not wholly outside the secular currents about them, finding a moral sense within the heart than enabled men to achieve salvation. Theirs was an emotional faith of personal experience, contrition, and conversion. Conversion was expected to transform the individual's private life. Since separatist churches were illegal in the German states, the Pietists founded lay associations for worship and workhouses to serve the unemployed and impoverished. Others migrated to Pennsylvania.

Pietism formed the basis for an emotional religious revival that spread over the Protestant world during the eighteenth century. Against the mechanistic world view of Deism the Protestant revival asserted "fundamentalism"—that is, absolute faith in the literal meaning of the Bible. The number of dogmas inherited from the Reformation was pared down to a few basic ones, but those that were retained reasserted the active in-

tervention of divine spirit in human affairs. Unlike traditional orthodoxies that checked emotion and denied all conscience except that sworn to their own doctrines, the eighteenth-century revivalists emphasized piety and taught that salvation depended not upon predestination or sacraments but upon the individual's religious and moral rebirth. In the eighteenth century the German Pietists turned more directly against science, cosmopolitan French culture, and aristocratic social norms. Their lower-class sympathies stimulated the foundation of philanthropic institutions and schools that were designed to train the heart more than the intellect. German Pietism shared with the philosophes an emphasis upon individualism, but its individualism was more compatible with, and merged into, romanticism.*

* See p. 413.

## The Wesleyan Revival

In England and British North America Methodism challenged the drift toward rationalism. This new revivalist sect was organized by George Whitefield and the Wesley brothers, John (1703–91) and Charles. Calling passionately for personal conversion, these early Methodists revived fundamental doctrines of man's utter depravity, of the Atonement, and of divine intervention. They revived Puritanism in England, particularly among the industrial workers and miners. Neglected by the established church, these urban laborers were inoculated by their religion against revolutionary doctrines of natural rights. Like the German Pietists, they too identified themselves thoroughly with nationalism during the wars of the French Revolution. In North America the revival initiated by Whitefield and the Wesleys was redefined by Jonathan Edwards (1703–58), a prophet of the "Great Awakening." Edwards combined an emotional appeal with Calvinist theology, a combination of intellect and emotion that he shared with the leaders of the American romantic movement. Temporarily he had great success as a popular preacher, and the revival movement followed the frontier westward.

Protestant revivalism in Europe recruited principally from those members of the middle and lower classes who were at odds with their theologically liberal, but socially conservative, establishment. To some extent it was, like the Enlightenment, subversive of the status quo, pressing for humanitarian reforms, the extension of literacy among the lower classes, and a combination of self-help and mutual assistance. These ascetic fundamentalist movements promoted dedication to hard work and disciplined labor; they were also vehicles of religious nationalism, which was ultimately to threaten the legitimacy of princely continental states. In England their revival tactics were later to be copied by agitators who denounced agricultural tariffs (corn laws) and the unreformed House of Commons before urban audiences.

## E. The Impact of Science and Enlightenment

Within two centuries European thought had gone far towards a secular outlook, especially in assuming natural causes for natural phenomena. This was true not only of explanations of the heavens' movements but also of the human body and the organization of society. Humanists had charted this secular course, but it was the scientific revolution that gave it its major impetus. As the frontiers of the unknown were pressed back, mysterious and spiritualistic explanations receded.* In this sense the scientific revolution gave birth to those outlooks that today are usually reckoned "modern." Its impact was sufficient to force even religious diehards opposed to science and secularization to abandon some of their tenets.

The new thought of the seventeenth and eighteenth centuries deserves emphasis because of its overwhelming importance for the future. Yet it left a varied and confused legacy, no more providing a

---

* Except among small pockets of fundamentalists and traditionalists, especially Calvinist areas, belief in witchcraft, for example, died out.

*Scene from a slave ship.*

unifying ideology than the religious authoritarianism that had preceded it. Some empiricists, like Hobbes, were authoritarian, whereas others, like Locke, advocated constitutional government. There was no common standard of values. Many scientific philosophers were certain that a self-evident standard of ethics was not only possible but immediately forthcoming; but no such standard appeared, and voices like Hume's soon arose to question the validity of the quest. Moreover, as Hume foresaw, scientific "natural laws" were subject to constant revision; and metaphysical assumptions deduced from the natural sciences and applied to society could be as shifty as traditional concepts. Nevertheless, humanitarianism gained wider currency than in any previous period of Western history. Indifferent toward heaven and convinced that life on

earth could be improved, the publicists of the Enlightenment popularized reform as a social goal. As the philosophes knew, this trail had been blazed before them by religious sectarians, especially the Quakers and Anabaptists; it now also attracted contemporary religious movements, even those that rejected rational and mechanistic world views.

Although humanitarianism was professed more widely than before, secularized thought had not yet deeply penetrated European society. It remained the property of a narrow, albeit powerful, elite. Even in France the philosophes converted only a minority of the clergy, nobles, and literate middle classes. Literate Frenchmen apparently did more reading in works that reconciled traditional religious doctrines with popularized science than in the *Encyclopédie*. And dissatisfied peasants knew nothing of the philosophes. In eastern and southern Europe the Enlightenment was hardly felt at all. In fact, most Europeans had little reason to take an optimistic view of this world: optimism was generally the prerogative of those who benefited from commerce or royal patronage, and even among them deep pessimism was common.

Many major social and political trends of the eighteenth century ran counter to the hopes of the Enlightenment. Although progress in commerce and technology increased the total wealth of France and England, rapid population growth aggravated poverty, vagabondage, and infanticide even in prosperous areas. The philosophes condemned slavery, but the slave trade had never been brisker. In order to implement their reforms most enlightened thinkers counted upon converting monarchs who, they assumed, would have the power to carry them out. But monarchical power in eighteenth-century Europe was contested by a resurgent nobility whose interests conflicted with

"enlightened despotism." Kings themselves were unreliable converts, and renewed power struggles consumed their principal energies. In short, law and persuasion—the favored means of implementing the philosophes' "new design for living"—gave way to revolution by the end of the eighteenth century. The fate of the philosophes' "search for humanity" was to be determined by foreign and domestic struggles in their own and subsequent centuries; again and again reactionaries were to attack their goals and values. In the twentieth century those conflicts were to be fought with unprecedented violence as fascists mobilized traditionalists and manipulated the "silent" masses to banish the Enlightenment's influence from Western society. For eighteenth-century men, however, the new world view of a rational, mathematical universe did much to undermine the religious and intellectual foundations of divine-right monarchy. At the time that the philosophes were writing, that type of traditional absolutism was in serious decline.

## Selected Readings

*Becker, Carl L. *The Heavenly City of the Eighteenth-Century Philosophers.* New Haven: Yale University Press, 1932.

*A popular series of essays propounding the dubious thesis that the philosophes were reconstructing medieval philosophy with more up-to-date materials.*

Beer, Max. *An Inquiry into Physiocracy.* London: George Allen & Unwin, 1939.

*An analysis of the doctrines of early laissez-faire economists that links them to practices of the medieval towns and exposes weaknesses in their methods.*

Boas, Marie. *The Scientific Renaissance: 1450–1630.* New York: Harper & Row, Publishers, 1962.

*This surveys the early history of science in all fields.*

Brinton, Howard. *Friends for 300 Years, the History and Beliefs of the Society of Friends since George Fox Started the Quaker Movement.* New York: Harper & Brothers, 1952.

*A brief sketch of the Quaker organization, doctrines, and social action. Chapter 8, "The Meeting and the World," is especially pertinent.*

* Bronowski, J., and Mazlish, B. *The Western Intellectual Tradition from Leonardo to Hegel.* New York: Harper & Row, Publishers, 1962.

*Brilliant intellectual history of Europe from the Renaissance to the early nineteenth century, particularly sensitive to the impact of science.*

* Bury, J. B. *The Idea of Progress, An Inquiry into Its Growth and Origin.* New York: Dover Publications, 1955.

*An older discussion, with some omissions, of early advocates of the idea of progress.*

* Butterfield, Herbert. *The Origins of Modern Science: 1300–1800.* New York: Free Press, 1965.

*A history of the "scientific revolution" by an author who considers science the most influential force making the modern world.*

* Cassirer, Ernst. *The Philosophy of the Enlightenment.* Boston: Beacon Press, 1955.

*A classic account that rehabilitates the philosophes as serious thinkers.*

———. *The Question of Jean Jacques Rousseau.* New York: Columbia University Press, 1954.

*A probe of Rousseau's fundamental ideas that confirms his claim that all of his works had a consistent theme; indispensable for distinguishing Rousseau from the French philosophes.*

Cobban, Alfred. *In Search of Humanity, the Role of the Enlightenment in Modern History.* New York: George Braziller, 1960.

*A sympathetic account and an appeal for a return to the Enlightenment's humanitarian principles.*

Feuer, Lewis S. *Spinoza and the Rise of Liberalism.* Boston: Beacon Press, 1958.

*One of the few detailed works in English relating seventeenth-century Dutch thought to its environment.*

Gay, Peter. *The Enlightenment: An Interpretation.* Vol. 1, *The Rise of Modern Paganism.* New York: Alfred A. Knopf, 1966.

*Plumbs the pagan classical roots of the Enlightenment, stressing the similarities between the humanists and the philosophes. A second volume deals with the latter's science of society.*

———. *The Party of Humanity, Essays in the French Enlightenment.* New York: Alfred A. Knopf, 1964.

*Interpretative essays rescuing the philosophes, especially Voltaire, from charges of frivolity and utopianism and dissociating them from the rhetoric of revolution.*

*Gierke, Otto. *Natural Law and the Theory of Society, 1500–1800.* Boston: Beacon Press, 1957.

*A detailed exposition of early modern social and political theory by a German critic of rational natural law.*

* Hall, A. R. *The Scientific Revolution: 1500–1800, The Formation of the Modern Scientific Attitude.* Boston: Beacon Press, 1954.

*A narrative manual of scientific developments organized according to subject.*

*Koyré, Alexandre. *From the Closed World to the Infinite Universe.* New York: Harper & Brothers, 1958.

> *Traces the destruction of the conception of the cosmos as an earth-, or man-centered, finite, hierarchically ordered whole by the new philosophy and science of the seventeenth century.*

Kuhn, Thomas S. *The Structure of Scientific Revolutions.* Chicago: The University of Chicago Press, 1962.

> *An attempt to acquaint nonscientists with scientific methodology; particularly helpful in emphasizing the role of conceptual models in scientific advances.*

*Lovejoy, Arthur O. *The Great Chain of Being, A Study of the History of an Idea.* New York: Harper & Row, Publishers, 1960.

> *Traces a basic assumption of classical and medieval thought through the rationalism of the seventeenth and eighteenth centuries.*

Manuel, Frank E. *The Eighteenth Century Confronts the Gods.* Cambridge, Mass.: Harvard University Press, 1959.

> *Explores explanations, by the men of the Enlightenment, of popular religious beliefs, especially the making of the gods in the past.*

More, Louis T. *Isaac Newton, a Biography.* New York: Charles Scribner's Sons, 1934.

> *A factual biography of the leading scientist of the period.*

Morley, John. *Diderot and the Encyclopedists.* London: The Macmillan Company, 1923.

> *Old account of the Encyclopedists by a Victorian Liberal who also wrote on Voltaire and Rousseau.*

Palmer, R. R. *Catholics and Unbelievers in Eighteenth-Century France.* New York: Cooper Square Publishers, 1961.

> *Treats Jesuit and Jansenist opposition to the philosophes, showing that the Jesuits shared much of the latter's faith in natural law.*

Pinson, Koppel S. *Pietism as a Factor in the Rise of German Nationalism.* New York: Columbia University Press, 1934.

> *A study of the political implications of emotional fundamentalism in the German states.*

Robbins, Caroline. *The Eighteenth-Century Commonwealthman.* Cambridge, Mass.: Harvard University Press, 1959.

> *An in-depth examination of the transmission of English radical thought from the civil wars through the eighteenth century.*

Santillana, Giorgio de. *The Crime of Galileo.* Chicago: The University of Chicago Press, 1955.

> *An investigation of the quarrel between the Church and Galileo, with an eye to political measures taken in the United States after World War II against outspoken scientists.*

Schapiro, J. S. *Condorcet and the Rise of Liberalism.* New York: Harcourt, Brace and Co., 1934.

> *A sympathetic biography of the only philosophe who lived to participate in the French Revolution; a study in activism.*

Smith, Preserved. *The History of Modern Culture.* Vol. 2. *The Enlightenment.* New York: Henry Holt and Co., 1934.

*A detailed, comprehensive account that neglects the continued force of tradition.*

Vyverberg, Henry. *Historical Pessimism in the French Enlightenment.* Cambridge, Mass.: Harvard University Press, 1958.

*A necessary corrective to the notion that unqualified optimism dominated the thought of the Enlightenment.*

* Willey, Basil. *The Seventeenth-Century Background; Studies in the Thought of the Age in Relation to Poetry and Religion.* New York: Columbia University Press, 1952 (paperback: Anchor Books).

* ———. *The Eighteenth-Century Background; Studies on the Idea of Nature in the Thought of the Period.* New York: Columbia University Press, 1953 (paperback: Beacon Press).

*Lucid works based on English thought that show drastic changes in the meanings of the slogans "reason" and "nature" and that emphasize conservative uses of rationalism.*

Wolf, A. *A History of Science, Technology and Philosophy in the Sixteenth and Seventeenth Centuries.* London: George Allen & Unwin, 1950.

*A standard detailed account, useful for reference.*

See also the relevant sections of the volumes by Friedrich, Nussbaum, Wolf, Roberts, and Gershoy in the *Rise of Modern Europe* series, edited by W. L. Langer.

Asterisk (*) denotes paperback.

# CHAPTER VI

# The Decline of Divine-Right Monarchy: 1720–1787

Divine-right monarchy came to a climax in the great wars that engulfed Europe at the beginning of the eighteenth century. The great warrior kings discredited themselves in them, and in their wake these wars left financial exhaustion and a weariness with conflict that temporarily curbed the expansion of royal absolutism. In a sense, Louis XIV's extremism had proved fatal to divine-right monarchy in the West.

Other factors helped to lengthen this momentary pause in the growth of royal power in many European states. A series of succession crises weakened many of the major dynasties, and local aristocracies exploited this weakness to make renewed bids for power and consolidate their positions. The resurgence of aristocratic opposition to central executive authority was general during this century. In themselves, war-weariness, financial exhaustion, and aristocratic aggrandizement may have been sufficient to account for a general decline of absolutism; but especially in western Europe two other significant factors were operative. One of these—the erosion of the otherworldly religious ideology of the divine right of kings—we have traced in the preceding chapter. The other was the rapid growth of commerce, which gradually created a social basis for a democratic response to the revival of the aristocracy late in the century.

Succession crises were a perennial source of weakness in the institution of hereditary monarchy, but the early eighteenth century produced so many of them that they had a cumulative and general impact. The Hanoverians of Britain, represented in the person of George I, were a new dynasty whose succession was tenuous even after the failure of a Stuart counterrevolution in 1715. Until he begot an heir, undisputed succession in France hinged on the precarious health of the young Louis XV. Charles VI of Austria had only a daughter to succeed him to thrones that law customarily reserved for males. And in Russia after the death of Peter I in 1725, instead of strict succession, intrigues at court and among the palace guards made and unmade rulers. Their domestic insecurity made these weak dynasts reluctant to go to war; they much preferred the tedium of diplomacy to armed conflict, which could produce unlooked-for and unwanted results at home. In domestic affairs, continental rulers still claimed authority by divine right, and they retained a formidable arsenal of arbitrary powers, but they were unable to check a slow aggrandizement by the aristocracy.

The aristocratic character of society gave this segment of the eighteenth century a distinctive stability and an aura of fine living. Mediating between sovereigns, or central governments, and commoners, the aristocracy served to give society a certain balance; but in its claims to autonomous privileges and its virtual monopoly of social power, it was as absolute as any king. In France immediately after 1715 titled peers tried and failed to replace Louis XIV's central government with a series of aristocratic executive councils, called collectively the *Polysynodie;* but instead ennobled officials and magistrates succeeded where these failed. Local affairs in central, eastern, and southern Europe were firmly in the hands of nobles and gentry. In the Dutch Republic, the German Imperial Cities, and the Italian city-states, "Venetian oligarchies"—consisting of urban patricians even more exclusive than the aristocracies of monarchical states— filled offices and judicial benches. Even in commercialized England, Parliament was filled almost exclusively by landed gentry. Nor were these local privileged oligarchies easily dislodged. Following the outbreak of general war again after 1740, "enlightened despots" of the continental monarchies attempted with some success to reassert absolute executive powers. However, the aristocracies were so firmly entrenched that they were able to block or dilute much enlightened reform and, while their despots were preoccupied

with making war, they occasionally exacted further concessions from them.

For western Europe this period of declining absolutism was an age of empire and trade as well as of aristocratic dominance. Trade expanded more rapidly than during any previous commercial revolution. Among the colonial products that formed the major sources of new wealth were sugar, slaves, tobacco, dyestuffs, tea, coffee, and precious metals. In both Britain and France great commercial companies gained so much wealth and influence after the War of Spanish Succession that they attempted to assume and manage the inflated debts of their respective states. Both experiments ended in "bubbles," or financial panics, but solid commercial gains continued unabated. England united with Scotland in 1707 to become Britain and emerged as the world's greatest colonial and imperial power, but it was not the only beneficiary of the expanding commercial sector of the European economy. France, whose foreign trade expanded nearly fivefold during this period, entered more positively into the ranks of the maritime states. Others—notably the Austrian Habsburgs, the Prussian Hohenzollerns, and the Bourbons of Spain—also sought to add commercial profits to their power. Spain still held a large empire, but the dynamic rivals for an overseas empire were Britain and France. After 1740 their imperial conflicts again merged with the dynastic struggles of the Continent.

The vast colonial and commercial expansion of this century had profound consequences for the European world. It enlarged the boundaries of an Atlantic civilization whose distinctive features set it increasingly apart from older European societies; in many cases its water routes of communication brought its parts closer together than adjacent continental points that were dependent upon expensive and difficult overland transportation; and commercialization created new problems and strains on the domestic institutions of the mother countries and on the mercantilist ties between them and their colonies. Britain's commercial and industrial cities became centers of agitation for radical reform. In France conflicts between aristocrats and the monarch were complicated by the growing ranks of the economically influential commercial bourgeoisie. Those whose profits and livelihood were tied up with commerce became impatient of old institutions and policies that were no longer appropriate to their needs. This alienation from tradition was even clearer among the British colonists of North America: on the outer fringes of Western civilization, they took advantage of imperial rivalries to forge a revolutionary challenge to both oligarchy and absolutism. And their example proved contagious. Still, it was France—where renewed power struggles caused deepening financial difficulties—and not the North American colonies, that became the wellspring of European revolution in the generations after 1789.

# A. The Era of Aristocratic Stabilization: 1720–1740

## THE COMPETITIVE STATE SYSTEM

After Louis XIV failed to create a personal European empire negotiators at Utrecht restored the balance of power. Ignoring a plan for a federation of states, the major powers agreed instead to consult regularly in diplomatic congresses. This machinery for the peaceful settlement of international disputes was stillborn, however: it failed to replace the competitive system in which each state pursued its own interests individually or collectively. On the other hand, in the years following Utrecht several major powers did work in concert, based on alliances to preserve the general peace.

That peace and concert, which successfully prevented general war until 1740, rested on a minor diplomatic revolution—an alliance between recent foes, Britain and France. An understanding between these two powers, each of which had been of pivotal importance in their earlier hostile alliances, was considered a sure guarantee of general peace. The architect of the alliance was Lord Stanhope, a belligerent Whig soldier who involved Britain everywhere in continental affairs. The agreement secured both dynasties, which were momentarily weak, and Stanhope extended it to include other major powers. In combination with the Dutch, who joined the alliance in 1717, Britain and France cooperated to frustrate an invasion of Habsburg Italy by Spain in violation of the terms of Utrecht, the aim of the Spanish court being to secure a throne for Don Carlos, the infant son of Philip V. Reacting against this invasion and desperate to secure the consent of other powers to the eventual succession of his daughter to the throne, Charles VI brought Austria into the alliance in 1718. In 1720 the allies thrust Spain out of Italy, although Don Carlos did receive rights to succeed in Parma, Piacenza, and Florence. Spain was then more or less forced to join the allied powers, who meanwhile were intervening to bring an end in 1721 to a potentially dangerous war between

Sweden and Russia in the Baltic, which at one point had threatened to involve many other states.

The concert now had five members; but by 1725 it had almost collapsed. Spain, still harboring designs on Italy, withdrew in that year and now sought to accomplish its goals by a diplomatic alliance with Austria herself. In addition to its annoyance with the maritime powers because of their opposition to her Italian plans, Spain was resentful of the British occupation of Gibraltar and bitter over both British and French smuggling in Spanish America. Charles VI of Austria, for his part, was increasingly unhappy with his dependence on the maritime powers (England and the Dutch Republic) for subsidies, and was eager to share in the immense profits of overseas commerce. He irritated France, which had an effectual monopoly on the Mediterranean trade with the Levant, by developing Trieste for trade with the Levant, and he alarmed both England and the Dutch Republic by chartering a new commercial company, the Ostend Company, to trade with the Far East from the Austrian Netherlands. Spain protected the company's ships, but the Dutch preyed on them at every opportunity. The Austro-Spanish alliance, combined with an Austro-Russian accord of 1726, led to the formation of a rival league, including Britain, France, Sweden, and Denmark. By 1727 war clouds once again spread over Europe. Since no one desired war, lengthy negotiations finally led to a peaceful solution in 1731. Charles abandoned the Ostend Company and his alliance with Spain, and the maritime powers in return recognized Maria Theresa as his heir. Reluctantly and temporarily Spain recognized Britain's treaty rights to trade in Spanish America and gave up hopes of recovering Gibraltar. Thus the Mediterranean problem, one of the great threats to peace of the post-Utrecht period, appeared to have been resolved.

Events in Poland, however, soon disrupted this fragile settlement. In 1733 Augustus the Strong, the ambitious dynast who ruled both Saxony and Poland, died. The Polish throne was an elective one, and the death of a king invariably invited the interference of foreign powers—Austria, Sweden, Russia, and, lately, also France—who sought to bribe the Polish electors to choose for the throne a man favorable to their own interests. In this case, reacting against Austrian and Russian intervention, the Polish nobles selected not Augustus's son—the Austro-Russian candidate—but the French candidate, Stanislas Leszczynski, father-in-law of Louis XV. The French had only a navy to assist the installation of their man; the Russians used troops to put their candidate, Augustus III, on the throne. This they did without great difficulty. Nominally this row caused the so-called War of Polish Succession (1733–36), but it was not fought over Poland or by Poles. Rather it was a dreary war of maneuver, involving old grievances as well as new, in which France and Spain fought Austria (who had some Russian support) in northern Italy and along the Rhine. France conquered Lorraine from Austria, and Stanislas, forced to abdicate from the Polish throne, was made duke of Lorraine. In a comic opera of diplomacy, the previous duke of Lorraine was transferred to Tuscany, whose own grand duke had conveniently just died without heirs. Lorraine was to revert to French control upon the death of Stanislas. Don Carlos of Spain surrendered his northern Italian duchies to become ruler of the new Bourbon Kingdom of the Two Sicilies.

Perfunctory as it was, the War of Polish Succession heralded the close of the period of relative stability by pitting the major powers against each other. The end of that stability became clear with the outbreak of the War of Austrian Succession in 1740, the first of a series of general wars. In the meantime, however, the relative peace that it provided had un-

*British press gang at work.*

dergirded a generation of reconstruction, which laid the foundations for aristocratic dominance during the eighteenth century.

## THE POLITICS OF OLIGARCHY AND STABILITY

Against efficient absolute monarchs, aristocrats reacted by reasserting claims to positions of enhanced honor and power. Many of the aristocrats involved in this movement were not of the old feudal nobility of the sword, who could trace their titles to past centuries. Rather, the bulk of them were officeholders, magistrates, and councillors whose aristocratic lineage was recent and, in many cases, purchased. In (kingless) republics, self-perpetuating "constituted bodies," staffed by the same families from one generation to the next, were no less common than in the monarchies. Since titles and offices were not subject to purchase, republican oligarchies were more closed to new blood and the influence of new riches than were the monarchies that practiced venality (the sale of offices). In both republics and monarchies, however, these aristocratic bureaucracies claimed considerable power over their subjects. Theirs was an inherited right to rule, and they usually traced their authority back to medieval origins. Drawing incomes from manorial revenues, loans to the state, and the emoluments of public office, these oligarchies were the backbone of a "cult of stability" in domestic affairs.

This cult predominated in a world half modern, half medieval, and the interests of both central governments and commoners were sacrificed to it. Entrenched bureaucratic power led such men as Voltaire in France and John Adams in America to conclude that a strong central executive was necessary to defend the interests of the many against the few. Later in the century such power was the target of both enlightened despots and democratic revolutionaries.

*Bank note issued by John Law.*

## France

In calling no Estates General, in curbing the provincial estates, and in restricting the *parlements,* Louis XIV had trampled upon the institutions and prerogatives of the older aristocracy. Titled peers led the first counterrevolution against his government after his death in 1715. Louis XV's regent, the Duke of Orleans, fearful of his own shaky position, permitted them to dominate the government from 1715 to 1718 through their ascendancy in a series of central councils (Polysynodie). Lacking technical competence, however, they became bogged down in ceremonial trivia and jurisdictional disputes, which finally put an end to this experiment. Leadership of the aristocracy then passed to educated nobles of the robe, especially the jurists of the parlements, most of whose old powers were now restored. So alarmed was the regent by their power that he contemplated abolishing all hereditary privileges. Instead, however, he turned to the expedient of centralizing financial power in accordance with a plan submitted to him by John Law, a Scottish gambler, adventurer, and financier of unusual talents. Law's scheme had the double merit of promising to cope with both war debts and problems of power.

On no matter had the old aristocracy floundered worse than in handling royal debts. Accounts were chaotic, and there was no budget. Speculators had bought government annuities on terms exceedingly disadvantageous to the Crown.

Repudiation of debts was the only solution that most of the nobility could suggest; but that, of course, would ruin credit in the future. France had no centralized financial institution comparable to the Bank of England, which had been eminently successful during the past war. After petitioning several European governments without success, Law gained the Regent's favor and established a central, note-issuing bank in France in 1716. Then he founded the Company of the West (Mississippi Company) to trade with Louisiana. Soon it absorbed all other French chartered companies, gaining a monopoly of French colonial trade. Law had promised the Regent that he would extinguish the royal debt; the company now accepted certificates of debt in partial payment for its shares. It planned to pay off these debts through trading profits and by acquiring a monopoly on the collection of internal indirect taxes.

The scheme was not a total failure. Law's bank notes stimulated trade, as he had promised, but the purchase of shares in the company became a speculative mania in which the price of shares skyrocketed to many times their real worth. In 1720 the "Mississippi Bubble" broke, taking many investors from paper riches to rags. In the disillusionment that followed, the Parlement of Paris canceled Law's charters. Only his original trading company survived and continued to prosper. The Regent was convinced that Law's downfall was the work of rival financiers, but the unfortunate Scot was driven from the country nevertheless. Not until after the Revolution of 1789 did the French people overcome prejudices—which the Mississippi Bubble had ingrained more deeply—against central banking, bank notes, and even joint stock ventures. Nor were the government accounts in any better order as a result of Law's scheme.

Unlike Louis XIV, the new French monarch had no taste for affairs of state. After he came of age in 1726 Louis XV turned

*Contemporary satire of the Mississippi Bubble in which Folly and Chance run down True Commerce.*

them over to the 72-year-old Cardinal Fleury. A cautious administrator who avoided offending vested interests, Fleury worked for retrenchment and recovery; he stabilized the coinage, provided security for highways, and built better roads than England's. Tax farming was not abolished, but the cardinal kept taxes down by avoiding the expenses of war. Although he worked for stability at home and abroad, his policies did not check the growing power of the nobility of the robe, whose obstructionism eventually crippled the central government and made "French absolutism" a misnomer.

The nobility of the robe was composed of men or descendants of men who had gained patents of nobility from the king for nonmilitary service such as administrative and judicial offices. A century earlier the older nobility of the sword, who claimed descent from the feudal warriors of the Middle Ages, had considered nobles of the robe part of the bourgeoisie, the class of commoners from which they sprang. After 1715 the ascent of the nobles of the robe into full-fledged aristocrats was indicated by their social merger with the older nobility. Better educated and organized, they proved to be better defenders of aristocratic interests than were the nobles of the sword, whose tastes, views, and interests they gradually acquired. They bought up legal jurisdictions, manors, state loans, and profitable survivals of the manorial system. Rigorous

*Cardinal Fleury.*

collectors of these obligations, they became an integral part of the "feudal reaction" that began to exacerbate relations between landlords and peasants around midcentury. In their religion they supported Jansenism, a puritanical Catholicism that opposed papal centralism and the Jesuits. Supported by the parlements against the central government, the Jansenists engaged in doctrinal brawls with the Jesuits that discredited the French church and made it vulnerable to attacks by the *philosophes* of the Enlightenment. By portraying themselves as defenders of liberty against arbitrary government, the nobles of the robe, who constituted the membership of the parlements, also discredited the monarchy. But at the same time, they blocked reforms. More than any other group, the nobles of the robe protected the provincial and social privileges that made France's nominal absolutism a contradiction in terms. But prior to 1789

their refurbished feudalism could offer no substitute for it.

In a distinctly separate compartment of French life (but coincident with the aristocratic resurgence) was the development of an overseas empire and colonial trade. In Martinique, Guadeloupe, and Santo Domingo, French planters had the most productive sugar islands of the West Indies. French traders vied with English companies for illicit trade with the Spanish empire, encroaching upon the decrepit Portuguese empire in India and increasingly coming into hostile contact with the English East India Company. Marseilles was a prosperous port for trade with the Levant, which French merchants made almost entirely their own. As a result of the War of Spanish Succession, France had lost part of North America to Britain. French efforts to build a self-sustaining society in Canada and Louisiana failed, but merchants traded with the Indians and returned a profitable supply of furs. French commerce thrived during the first half of the century, but it affected a smaller proportion of the population than was the case in England.

## Britain

It has been said that eighteenth-century England was a federation of country houses—the ancestral seats of the gentry who, as in the past, filled most of the offices and the benches of the House of Commons. Titled nobles were few in number and lacked privileges that continental nobles enjoyed, such as tax exemption.* Among the governing classes social class lines were not tightly drawn, but coteries of families, knit together by intermarriage and personal acquaintanceship, formed the basic units of political life. Within the aristocracy Whigs and Tories,

* The English lords who exploited Ireland were the nearest parallel to the continental nobility.

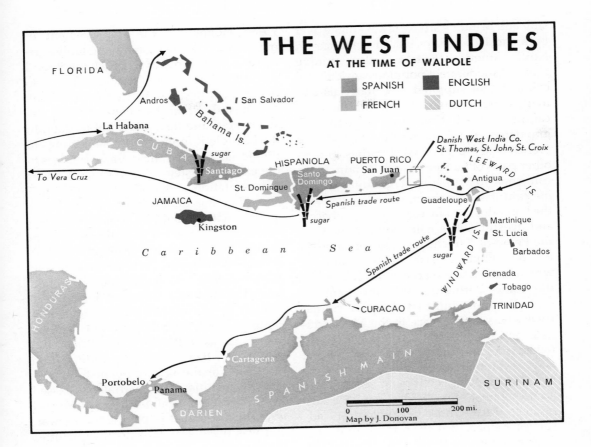

The West Indies at the time of Walpole. Map by J. Donovan.

and factional subdivisions of each, contended for positions of power and prestige.

In addition to being a constitutional kingdom dominated by the gentry, England was fast displacing the Dutch Republic as Europe's principal *entrepôt* of colonial trade. Merchants as well as "improving landlords" had social respectability and influence, and younger sons of the aristocracy entered trade and married heiresses of mercantile fortunes. Thus the aristocracy was attentive to trade and harkened to publicists such as Daniel Defoe, who attributed England's manifest wealth to commerce:

. . . Trade is the Wealth of the World; Trade makes the Difference as to Rich and Poor, between one Nation and another; Trade

nourishes Industry, Industry begets Trade; Trade dispenses the natural Wealth of the World, and Trade raises new Species of Wealth, which Nature knew nothing of; Trade has two Daughters, whose fruitful Progeny in Arts may be said to employ Mankind; namely

MANUFACTURE
and
NAVIGATION.[1]

With respect to both commerce and industry, Defoe was not wide of the mark. Better balanced and protected than French commerce, British overseas trade increased rapidly during the century. The growth of western ports such as Liverpool, Bristol, and Glasgow reflected this expan-

[1] Quoted by J. H. Plumb, *England in the Eighteenth Century* Baltimore: (Penguin Books, 1950), p. 21.

sion and Britain's strategic advantage over both the Dutch Republic and France. In North America, Britain had a unique series of moderately populous agricultural colonies that supplied raw materials and markets but did not fit well into the mercantilists' mold. Their lines of commerce gravitated more naturally toward the French and Spanish West Indies and to other parts of Europe than to Britain. More congenial to British strategic interests, as mercantilists saw them, were Jamaica and the Barbados, producers of sugar, tobacco, and dyestuffs. The half-century following the Peace of Utrecht was also prosperous for the English East India Company, which vied with the French for primacy in the former Portuguese mercantile empire in India and southeast Asia. A similar rivalry was taking place in the Mediterranean and in the Levant, where Dutch and Italian markets and influence were giving way to French and English merchants. Naval bases such as Gibraltar secured this trade against Spaniards and Barbary pirates. Meanwhile technological advances helped British traders undersell their competitors in all areas; cheap coal, which early steam pumping helped to obtain, was one such factor. Also, by 1750 British craftsmen had overtaken the Dutch in the art of finishing cloth and could produce calicoes that equaled the native Indian cotton product. In other words, the technological advances that would later blossom into the "industrial revolution" were already working to enhance Britain's strategic advantages by the middle of the eighteenth century.*

By 1720 Britain had accumulated large reserves of capital from commerce. This relative abundance of investment funds brought interest rates down† and pro-

vided money for the improvement of other sectors of the economy, notably agriculture and industry. To channel and direct the flow of that capital Britain also had a major financial institution, the Bank of England, which handled exchange, issued notes, and floated the public debt. In the last role it funneled private savings to public use and tied the moneyed classes to the existing system of government. Their representation in Parliament gave assurance that the debt would not be repudiated, that it would be considered a national, not just a royal, obligation. Even though the interest rate declined from five percent to three percent between 1717 and 1749, the debt rose from about £1 million when the bank was chartered to about £80 million by the middle of the eighteenth century. Bank certificates were readily taken up as gilt-edged securities. But despite the Bank's effective mobilization of capital for the War of Spanish Succession, its facilities were partially bypassed in 1720 by political leaders confronted with the difficulties of paying for the war.

It was these scandal-ridden difficulties that brought the fall of the radical Whig, Stanhope, and the rise of Robert Walpole, who stood for stability and peace. Stanhope's aggressive foreign policy alienated Walpole and other Whigs; he was defeated in Parliament when he tried to liberalize government policy by removing civic disabilities from Dissenters and to strip the Crown of its power to create new peers.* Then came the "South Sea Bubble," an episode that paralleled the Mississippi Bubble in France and led to a reshuffling of the Whig ministry.

Walpole established a sinking fund to retire part of the debt at reduced rates of interest, and its bonds became prized securities among investors. However in 1720 directors of the South Sea Company ob-

* Industrialization is discussed in greater detail in chap. 6.

† It will be recalled that large supplies of capital had had a similar effect in the Dutch Republic of the seventeenth century.

* That power had been used to push through Parliament ratification of the Peace of Utrecht, which Stanhope considered a betrayal of British victory.

tained authority to assume other parts of the debt, exchanging company stock for the bonds. Walpole opposed the scheme, but the directors liberally plied leading politicians and the king's mistresses with stock. The company had its way, and a mania of speculation in its shares followed. In 1720 the "Bubble" broke into a financial panic. No general depression of commerce occurred, but Parliament reacted by restricting the incorporation of banks, a measure that eventually became a serious obstacle to Britain's industrial expansion. Uncompromised by the scandal, Walpole served as a "screen" to save the dynasty and drove the implicated Whigs from office.

A landed gentleman who had married into a family trading in Baltic timber, Walpole was a representative of the cult of stability, not of Stanhope's radical Whiggery. "I am no Saint," he wrote, "no Spartan, no Reformer." He considered the nobility an indispensable element of any free government. Preferring to "let sleeping dogs lie," he cautiously avoided offending any great interest except those who pressed for war. To merchant entrepreneurs he gave a free hand by forbidding labor to organize. Toward the North American colonists his policy was "salutary neglect." Parliament regulated trade, but the "prime minister," as Walpole was called by his opponents (much to his own discomfort), neglected to enforce a tariff on foreign molasses imposed on the colonies by Parliament in 1733. His reluctance to offend great interests became even clearer the same year when he abandoned a bill to extend excise duties to colonial products sold in England. Intended to relieve tax rates on land, the Excise Bill evoked a storm of protest in London. Led by Lord Bolingbroke's popular press, opponents of the tax depicted it as a step toward tyranny, a monster that would enable officials to ride roughshod over common people. Threatened with insurrection in London, Walpole retreated and withdrew the proposed taxes.

But Walpole's reluctance to confront great opposition must not be misunderstood; he dominated British politics more thoroughly than any previous minister. He is considered by many to be the first British prime minister to work with a cabinet: following the scandal of the Bubble he joined the inner circle of royal advisors and administrators who wielded real power in Britain's government, officials such as the secretaries of state and the chancellor of the exchequer. This early committee of ministers, the precursor of England's modern cabinet, was responsible to both Parliament and king, even though it met in the absence of the king and drafted the laws that Parliament voted. Meetings were informal, often at dinner, and no records were kept; one man, Walpole, acted to secure the king's assent to measures they agreed upon collectively. For this purpose he found George I's favorite mistress and George II's queen, Caroline, most useful. His power over England's political machinery, however, was not along the lines of cabinet government that developed during the nineteenth century. It rested instead on the duke of Newcastle's control over patronage, that is, the power to make appointments, influence the letting of contracts, and so on.

The powerful but colorless Newcastle made loyalty to Walpole an unconditional qualification for appointments to offices of church and state. Through his patronage he controlled Parliament. Bishops in the House of Lords and Scottish M.P.'s were absolutely under his command. Indirectly, so also were a majority of other members, for, apart from appointment to offices, Newcastle controlled nominations for Parliament from the counties. After 1733 Walpole became increasingly unpopular, but as long as Newcastle and George II supported him, he continued to hold power.

In tying his policies to powerful vested interests, Walpole failed to respond to

*Master of patronage: the Duke of Newcastle.*

lations as aggression against British honor. Walpole took the accurate but unpopular view that boarding English vessels for customs inspection was within Spain's treaty rights. Much of the public debate focused on atrocity: the story of a Captain Jenkins who had lost an ear during a boarding, an ear whose desiccated remains he carried about in a box. Agitators for war with Spain seized on his plight, and the war that followed was popularly known as the War of Jenkins's Ear. As France supported Spain in trying to limit British trade in her colonies, other powerful English leaders turned against Walpole's pacific stance. William Pitt the Elder joined the chorus for war, depicting French prosperity and prestige as the cause of British poverty. When Newcastle and George II also came out for war, Walpole was forced to change his policy. War was officially declared in 1739 and soon became general. Forced to fight against his will, Walpole resigned in 1742.

new problems brought by social changes. At the top, British society was remarkably stable and uniform; at the bottom of the social pyramid riots, looting, vagabondage, unpaid debts, drunkenness, and ever-present death and crime were festering. Officials responded with penalties more and more severe, filling prisons and constantly employing the gallows, but they failed to get at the roots of poverty and unrest. Politically, however, the lower segments of society were inarticulate and impotent. Walpole's downfall had to come from quarters quite different and more powerful.

His foremost critic had been Lord Bolingbroke, a Tory who had joined the Stuart pretender abroad for a time after 1715. Bolingbroke's London press had raked the "prime minister" for corruption and a lack of patriotism. During the War of Polish Succession this line of attack gained other powerful supporters. British merchants engaged in wholesale smuggling in Spanish America condemned enforcement of the Spanish customs regu-

## The Prevalence of Aristocratic Stabilization

France and Britain furnish only two examples, albeit major ones, of stabilization under aristocratic oligarchies between 1720 and 1740. Nearly everywhere else in eighteenth-century Europe a similar consolidation was also taking place.

The most dramatic shift from absolutism to aristocracy occurred in Sweden. Exhausted by Charles XII's catastrophic aggressiveness, Swedes looked back upon his reign as a national disaster that had lost an empire, and they imposed a restrictive constitution on the monarchy in 1720. Nobles used the occasion of royal disrepute to lay claims to all offices and to oppress the peasantry. Their "era of liberty" (during which they divided into factions that catered to foreign bribery) lasted until a royal counterrevolution in 1772. When that royal coup d'état oc-

Polling at an Election (*by William Hogarth*).

curred, it had the support of the burghers, the peasantry, and the clergy.

Poland set the pace of aristocratic resurgence among the nobles of eastern and central Europe. There the nobility assembled in provincial diets and a national diet (*Sjem*) representing them. The government was essentially a republic of serf-owning lords, where a single vote in the Sjem was sufficient to veto any piece of legislation and to undo all previous acts of the Sjem's current session (the *liberum veto*). Too jealous of executive authority to entrust taxes, an army, or even a bureaucracy to their elected king, in practice the lords were ungovernable. Although Poland was in anarchy and little respected as a state, its nobles were the idols of aristocrats of other states.

On the heels of Peter the Great's autocracy Russian nobles secured the succession of women rulers whom they hoped to control. Reaction to autocracy went so far that in 1726 Prince Golitsyn, who had read John Locke, led a movement aimed at restricting the Czarina in the same way that the English Whigs had limited the authority of William and Mary after 1688. But in Russia this attempt was not much understood or supported, and a counterrevolution by Empress Anne (1730–40) took advantage of the nobles' divisions to assure her own succession. Nevertheless, she was obliged to exempt the privileged nobility from compulsory service to the state.

In Habsburg lands the Polish example attracted the dissident nobility: Hungar-

*A. The Era of Aristocratic Stabilization: 1720–1740*

ian officials drawn from the gentry and titled families refused to bow to Habsburg officials from Vienna. Great serf-owning landlords of Hungary, Bohemia, and the German Habsburg duchies monopolized power in local diets. Charles VI brought many of them to court to serve as imperial officials, but in winning over a part of the great nobles he secured neither cooperation from the provincial aristocracy nor harmony among the great noble officials. Because it signified that the dynasty's prerogatives took precedence over provincial constitutions, his greatest domestic achievement was to obtain the diets' acceptance of Maria Theresa as his heir; but while factions wrangled at court, the power of the Austrian state waned.

To a degree Bourbon Spain under Philip V was an exception to the general decentralization of authority seen elsewhere in Europe. Slowly and patiently the new king renovated the administration, setting up provincial administrative organs—the intendancies—on the model of France. But for the most part, the condition of maintaining his theoretical absolutism was that he refrain from exercising it. Philip greatly enlarged the number of grandees and titled noblemen, who lived from revenues collected by bailiffs who exploited one of the most impoverished peasant populations in Europe. In Spain, an oligarchic balance between clerical and noble lords was not so much a novelty as it was the conservation of the immediate past.

## Prussia: an Exception

While one continental autocracy after another lurched in the direction of inefficient oligarchy or even in some cases aristocratic anarchy, Prussian absolutism under Frederick William I reached its prime.* Like previous great absolutists,

* For his consolidation of power immediately after the Great Northern War, see p. 231.

the elector-king continued to compensate the aristocracy with economic and social favors while using talented commoners as his highest advisors and administrators. Frederick William was never able to overcome all rivalry between these administrators and the local Junker-dominated governments, but he mobilized Prussia's meagre human and material resources to build a "Sparta of the North." His state served as the headquarters and magazine for central Europe's largest army, but after the Great Northern War, which ended in 1721, it fought no battles under his rule.

Although the elector-king held his growing military power in reserve, its very existence tipped the balance of power in Prussia's favor. Realizing this, his successor, Frederick II, determined to exploit the advantage for the immediate seizure of Silesia, because as he assessed Europe's power relationships he thought that he could carry this off with impunity.

## Aristocratic Stabilization and the Arts

Before examining the renewed power struggle that Prussia launched in 1740, it is worth noting that the aristocratic resurgence affected the arts as well as politics. After the building of Versailles France continued to set the continental tone of architecture, painting, and interior decoration, and her artists influenced aloof England as well. As a result of the costs of Louis XIV's wars, the French state could no longer afford art on the grand scale of the past; but the court and provincial aristocracy did imitate it as far as their more limited resources and tastes permitted. Concerned with furnishing their chateaus and town houses (*hôtels*) for gracious, intimate, and comfortable living and as salons, they bent the baroque style into an ornamental refinement called by its later detractors *rococo*.

Rococo, if it meant anything at all,

*Nature-art of the French court: Boucher's* Spring.

meant elegance and refinement. It emphasized interior decorating with elaborate
chandeliers, plaster bas-reliefs, porcelain
and terra cotta statuary, and ceilings that
were joined to walls by elaborate decoration that obscured their junctions. It was
an age of elaborate craftsmanship in the
making of furniture, internal furnishings,
and tapestries, and its influence radiated
over the courts of Europe, including
northern Italy. Some of its most extreme
forms occurred in southern Germany, notably Bavaria.

In rococo painting preference went to
smaller pictures as distinct from the wall-
sized canvases of the baroque. Themes
were distinctly secular, often frankly erot-
ic. At first rococo painting was dominated

by the Flemish-French work of Jean Antoine Watteau (1684–1721), in whose
paintings nymphs, goddesses, and heroes
displaced saints and biblical characters.
He portrayed the aristocracy in gay finery,
often in forest or rural scenes, and his *Em-
barkation for the Isle of Cythera,* now in the
Louvre, won him major recognition as a
depicter of gallant festivities. French rococo came to a peak in the work of
François Boucher (1703–70) at about midcentury. An engraver and celebrated deco-
rator of salons, Boucher gave dominance
to gay and hedonistic elements within the
classical themes he was wont to portray.
Frankly sensual in such works as *Diana
after the Bath* (1742), he was favored by
Louis XV's mistress, Madame de Pom-

padour. By the end of the century, when a neoclassic revival occurred, this type of work came to be associated with the empty frivolity of court life, hence the derogatory name *rococo* was given to it to indicate that it was playful, immoral, and insubstantial. Surviving rococo artists then fell into obscurity.

Anyone who was "somebody" in this aristocratic age desired a flattering portrait. In England, where the Puritan Revolution had succeeded in confining painting to portraits, such work offered paths to fame to the two leading artists of the renowned and well-to-do, Sir Thomas Gainsborough (1727–88) and Sir Joshua Reynolds (1732–92), both of whom drew some inspiration from France. But in both England and France middle-class patrons were also coming to have more influence on art. By moralizing upon the vices and follies of man William Hogarth (1697–1764) had already found a ready reception, as did lesser-known French artists who followed the Dutch tradition of Vermeer in portraying domestic scenes of extraordinary realism.

By midcentury scientific philosophy, sentimentality, and naturalism were having an impact on the arts. So was classicism, which had a strong revival in France during the reign of Louis XVI and which already had a hold on English architecture. It was a symptom of rapid transition that the leading French sculptor of the eighteenth century was not of the rococo school but a neoclassicist executing busts of the greats of the Enlightenment and of the American Revolution, Jean Antoine Houdon (1741–1828). In architecture as well, the rococo modification of the baroque began to give way to a neoclassic movement. One prominent illustration of this is the Pantheon (1764), originally built as a church in Paris under the stimulus of English neoclassic models. Thus aristocratic stabilization failed to hold art in a fixed rococo mold, just as it failed to hold politics in a state of equilibrium.

## B. International Conflicts after 1740

Compared to the religious wars of the past and the nationalist revolutionary wars of the future, eighteenth-century warfare was conducted leisurely. On both land and sea it followed rigid conventions established during the era of aristocratic stabilization that made warfare primarily a matter of defensive maneuvering. Standing armies and great warships represented investments too heavy to be risked. Moreover balance-of-power wars were the affairs of kings, not of peoples. Common soldiers and sailors were forced into service by press gangs or hired; lacking ideological motivation, they were likely to desert at the first opportunity. Therefore savage discipline was considered necessary to keep them subject to orders, but even this was not adequate to secure their loyalty on operations that took them beyond the immediate direction of their officers. For both civilians and combatants, the scourges of war were reduced to a level not duplicated since, and many philosophes were convinced that militarism was in its death throes.

But after 1740 the pace of conflict quickened, due largely to the new militarism of Frederick II. In his youth he upset the old conventions by trying to strike quickly at the heart of the enemy's power, winning decisive victory by battle. Frederick's new tactics failed to transform the nature of eighteenth-century warfare (he reverted to old patterns later in his reign), but for a generation they challenged the existing balance of power.

# THE RENEWED STRUGGLE FOR POWER: 1740–1763

## The War of Austrian Succession

In 1740 occurred the event toward which Charles VI had aimed his reign—his death. As Maria Theresa ascended the thrones of the Habsburg inheritance, a peaceful succession seemed assured. All the major European powers and the Habsburg diets themselves had given advance approval of Charles's Pragmatic Sanction that enabled a woman to rule all except the Holy Roman Empire. But this assurance and Europe's short respite from armed power politics were destroyed by Frederick II. Laying specious dynastic claim to Silesia, he suddenly set the Continent ablaze by wresting that province from the young Habsburg princess. By 1741 France, Bavaria, Spain, Prussia, and Saxony had agreed to partition the Habsburg empire, leaving Maria Theresa only her eastern Austrian and Hungarian provinces. Meanwhile the war for overseas trade and empire, which Britain initiated in 1739 with the War of Jenkins's Ear, merged with the continental dynastic struggle. There followed a series of wars lasting until 1748, collectively known as the War of Austrian Succession.

Led by Louis XV and tradition-minded noblemen, France undertook to lead the apparently irresistible coalition against Austria, but Maria Theresa proved to be resourceful in defending its patrimony, and the allies were racked by mutual jealousies. To avert French hegemony and avoid sharing the spoils of war, Frederick II repeatedly deserted his allies; and, although tied by a Bourbon family compact, France and Spain could not agree on a common policy for the conquest of Italy. France's preoccupation with war on the Continent diverted its resources from fighting its real enemy, Britain. The French court sought to win overall victory on land, making gains on the Continent that could be exchanged for imperial territories at the peace table. This strategy worked as French armies conquered most of the Austrian Netherlands, which Britain tried vainly to defend in 1745. But Britain gained victories in the colonies and on the seas that canceled French gains in Europe. American colonists and the British fleet took Louisburg, the fortress that commanded the mouth of the St. Lawrence River, the indispensable gateway to French Canada. Thus both sides waged an exhausting war without gaining a clear-cut victory.

In 1748 financial exhaustion—or fear of it—brought both the dynastic and the imperial conflicts to an end in the Peace of Aix-la-Chapelle, which restored boundaries as they were before the war, except that Frederick II retained Silesia. But it did nothing to assuage the imperial antagonisms between Britain and France, nor did it reduce Maria Theresa's resolve to retake Silesia at the first favorable moment. For these reasons Aix-la-Chapelle endured only as a truce, not as a lasting pacification.

## The Seven Years' War: 1756–1763

Hostilities first began again in the race for overseas empire. In both Britain and France publicists ascribed prosperity to the rapid increase in colonial trade. The port cities and planters of both kingdoms displayed the wealth of colonial commerce, and each echoed the conviction that greater wealth and security were to be had by eliminating the competition represented by the other. The Anglo-French conflict now encircled the globe; it focused on West Indian plantations, slave-shipping stations in Africa, trading "factories" in India, and control of the North American continent. The plantations produced a cash crop of great economic importance—sugar. They imported foodstuffs, clothing, and—because the life expectancy of slaves was short—an ever-increasing amount of "black gold." In India conflict grew out of expansionist policies by rival East India companies. When the French company's profits lagged, Dupleix, its director, subdued the native states of the Deccan and subjected them to taxes and tributes. Officials of the English company backed rival native rulers, thus precipitating warfare between native protégés of the two companies; abandoning strictly commercial objectives for the assumption of political authority, the two were locked in a war for the domination of India. This occurred while their European governments were officially at peace; but in 1756 their colonial war merged with the Seven Years' War.

Hostilities broke out in North America two years before the main war began in Europe, and, unlike India, they involved government troops of both countries. In North America the issue was not so much markets or prized colonies as it was a struggle for strategic locations for an empire.

After the War of Spanish Succession France developed Louisiana and began linking it to Canada by forts and settlements along the north-south river systems. With the erection of Fort Duquesne (present-day Pittsburgh) in 1754, the chain of forts was completed. Manned by royal troops, the French positions initially had superior military strength. But lacking on-the-spot resources and population, they were too weak, even with the aid of the Indians, for a long war of attrition. To no avail the French government cared for its colonies with expensive paternalism. Private investment was slight, for French investors preferred state annuities or offices to hazardous North American ventures, especially after the Mississippi Bubble. Nor did Frenchmen emigrate to North America in great numbers. Religious dissenters were excluded, and the lower classes were discouraged by efforts to reconstitute the manorial system of France in America. Most French settlers were trappers, traders, churchmen, and soldiers. Cut off from the mother country by British naval power, New France could not support large military forces.

Although militarily disorganized, the populous agricultural and commercial mainland colonies of Britain had greater endurance and easier access to Europe. Their interests clashed most sharply with the French in the Ohio River valley over trade, Indian loyalties, and, especially, land. In the first clashes of 1754 and 1755 the French and Indians drove off the British and their Indian allies. Then both home governments committed themselves to a greater collision by reinforcing their respective colonial claims. When prowar forces in Britain were able to promote raids against French shipping in 1755, maritime hostilities became inevitable. In part, then, the world war that followed was a struggle for control over the American mainland east of the Mississippi River and north of Florida.

Despite their bellicosity overseas, neither the French nor the British government wanted war on the Continent. But this was not true of Maria Theresa, who would not be reconciled to the loss of Silesia and to the possibility of Prussian hegemony in the empire and in central Europe. Her foreign minister, Count von Kaunitz, operating on the assumption that the traditional Austro-French antagonism had lost much of its importance in the face of a new threat from Prussia, had worked diligently at Versailles since 1749 to align France with Austria against Prussia, but without success. During a few months of

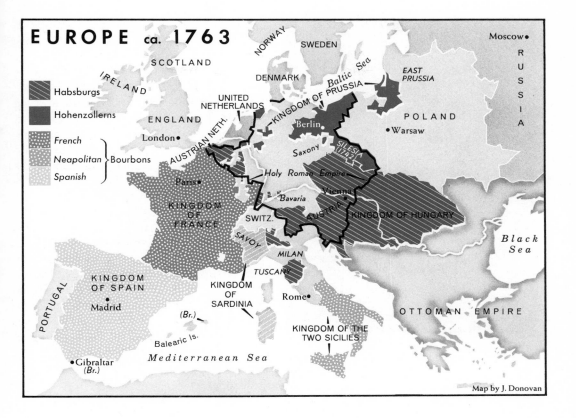

EUROPE ca. 1763

Habsburgs

Hohenzollerns

French

Neapolitan } Bourbons

Spanish

*Map by J. Donovan*

1756, however, Kaunitz's aims material-
ized into a diplomatic revolution, to
which Britain, by negotiating a subsid-
iary treaty with Russia, inadvertently
and indirectly contributed. Caught between British-ruled Hanover and Russia,
Frederick became alarmed; discounting
France as a serious ally and contemptuous
of her performance as a partner in the last
war, he hastened to tie himself to Britain
as protector of George II's principality of
Hanover. Motivated by pique with
Prussia and Britain, French and Russian
diplomats now bound their countries to
Austria against Prussia. Immediately
plans for the reduction of Prussia were
drawn up, with Russia and Austria taking
the lead. When Frederick became aware of
this, he seized Saxony in a surprise attack
and held it during the remainder of the
Seven Years' War as a tribute-producing

vassal state. Again, Frederick's precipitous action begot a general continental
war, which merged with the Anglo-
French struggle for empire overseas.

As in the War of Austrian Succession,
continental warfare diverted French energies from an all-out effort in the colonies. In the previous war France had salvaged her colonial losses by seizing parts
of the Austrian Netherlands as hostage
territories, to be bargained with at the
conference table. But this time Austria
was an ally. The same strategy could now
work only by taking enemy territory in
Hanover, but it was too far away and
too well defended. Unless Prussia were
destroyed, France was committed to a war
she could not win.

The destruction of Prussia was an aim
less of France, however, than of Austria
and Russia, and they missed achieving it

*Lord Clive (after a Gainsborough portrait).*

commoner, Pitt came to power after the older Whig ministry had suffered reverses. With national pride as a basis for popularity and with the support of aggressive merchants, Pitt became almost dictator of wartime Britain; certainly, and by popular consent, he became the absolute manager of a war for imperial expansion.

In contrast to Britain's unity of command and power France was racked by internal conflicts and inability to raise adequate taxes. French hopes of victory ultimately came to hinge on plans for an invasion of Britain, but the naval power to reach English shores was lacking. By 1760 Canada fell to Britain and her colonists; parts of the French West Indies were lost; and French forces in India yielded to British sea power and the resourcefulness of the East India Company's agent, Robert Clive. Although saddled with heavy war debts, Britain prospered while French shipping, commerce, and credit suffered disastrously.

Attrition and Russian withdrawal from the war made peace necessary. In Europe the Peace of Paris of 1763 restored prewar boundaries and therefore did not resolve the rivalry between Austria and Prussia. Colonial peace came as a result of domestic British politics. In an attempt to unseat the Whig oligarchy that had ruled since 1715, George III replaced Pitt with Lord Bute. Bute, apprehensive of Britain's immense successes and not quite able to believe them in any case, granted lenient peace terms, but Britain retained the preeminent power that it had gained during the war. France was driven from the North American continent, retaining only two offshore islands and fishing rights. To placate Spain for the loss of Florida to Britain, France ceded Louisiana to it. The French West Indies were restored, but in India France retained only unfortified trading stations; its political power there was definitely broken.

France's humiliation and the discrediting of her Bourbon monarchy were not

by only a narrow margin, putting Frederick's military prowess to its supreme test. The allied sovereigns' failure to cooperate, however, allowed him for a time simply to defeat each in turn. But his position became so precarious, due to massive demands on manpower, money, and supplies, that he even contemplated suicide early in 1762. Russia's sudden withdrawal from the war saved him. Peter III, who succeeded the Prussophobe Empress Elizabeth in January 1762, very much admired Frederick and turned from foe into ally. Catherine II, Peter's wife and successor (she had her imbecilic husband done away with after only a few months of his reign) did not resume the war against Prussia, thus enabling Frederick to survive.

While Prussian and other British-subsidized German troops pinned France down on the Continent, Britain reaped great gains overseas. Rallied by William Pitt the Elder, British forces swept away most of the French colonial empire. A

the only legacies of the Seven Years' War. Its scope and intensity challenged the philosophes' optimistic antimilitarism, for it demonstrated that within the competitive state system enlightened self-interest was insufficient to stop wars. Rather, reason had become an adjunct of *raison d'état* ("reason of state"), a tool of predatory states justifying aggression as a way of increasing the state's security.* The war also demonstrated that Britain's parliamentary regime, antimilitaristic at home but the largest spender on arms, had proved more than a match for the declining absolutism in France. The price of victory for Britain, however, was the loss of all its allies on the Continent. Previously it was the Austrian court that had become disillusioned with "perfidious Albion"; now it was Frederick II who deserted England for an alliance with Russia. Against British predominance, the balance of power now worked to isolate Britain completely, generating universal suspicion, hostility, and jealousy, which helped to make the American Revolution successful. The war also gave impetus to a new form of absolutism cast in the secular language of the Enlightenment—"enlightened despotism." In a sense, both of the two major radical political programs of the late eighteenth century—enlightened despotism and democratic revolution—were offsprings of the midcentury wars.

## THE WAR OF THE AMERICAN REVOLUTION

As we shall soon see in greater detail, the American Revolution was simultaneously a civil war and a national revolt against Britain; but its success was also the result of renewed imperial rivalry that aligned France and the other major powers against Britain. Whetting the long knife of revenge, the French court stood ready to give the rebellious colonists immediate covert aid. As soon as the colonists' victory over Burgoyne at Saratoga demonstrated their resolve to pursue independence seriously with force, France concluded a permanent alliance and a commercial convention with the new republic in 1778.

French aid was the foreign mainstay of the American Revolution,† but it was not the only assistance the Colonies received. When Spain joined France against Britain in 1779 (but not as an ally of the colonists), Britain lost control over the seas. At great loss to its trade, the Dutch Republic made loans to the Continental Congress and became an active, but ineffective, belligerent in 1780. Russia and several other continental countries in 1780 formed the League of Armed Neutrality, designed to stop British search and seizure on the high seas. Only the general hostility toward Britain within the context of continental rivalries can fully explain the paradox of the aid given by Europe's absolute and aristocratic states to this republican revolution. Even France had no intention of creating a powerful new state in North America. When American negotiators became aware of this fact, they violated their alliance with France in order to accept Lord Shelburne's offer for a separate peace.

The war among the European powers that the American Revolution started did not come to an end with the preliminary peace between Britain and the United

---

* Frederick II, a favorite of many philosophes, repeatedly epitomized this application of reason to aggrandizement when he calculated that the alignment of European powers would allow him to get away with the seizure of Silesia (1740), Saxony (1756), and, later, parts of Poland. These were all areas to which he could lay little or no claim on the basis of dynastic inheritance.

† The battle of Yorktown in 1781 illustrated the impact of this aid. French forces aided the Americans on land, while at the same time a French fleet offshore prevented relief of the beleaguered and encircled British troops.

*Shipbuilding at Toulon.*

States. Thereafter Britain won a naval war with France and Spain in West Indian waters. Undiverted by the continental war, France had lost its last bid for empire under the Old Regime, and its defeat paved the way for the Peace of Paris in 1783, which recognized American independence, but which also transferred Florida from Britain to Spain, an unmistakable indication that more than a colonial revolt was involved in the war.

## EASTERN POWER STRUGGLES AND THE FIRST PARTITION OF POLAND

While France and Britain fought for empire overseas, Austria, Prussia, and Russia annexed territories shorn from Poland and the Ottoman Empire. Poland's misfortune was to be the buffer between the three great Eastern powers. Because of internal weakness, Poland, territorially the third largest state in Europe, incited the appetites and mutual distrust of its stronger neighbors, who, prior to their actual partition of the kingdom, worked to preserve the nobles' "freedoms"; that is, they maintained the constitutional anarchy that virtually disarmed the kingdom and made it subject to their manipulation. Russia was particularly successful in this. In 1763 Catherine II installed as king her former lover, Stanislas Poniatowski, who succeeded Augustus III, another Russian nominee. Content with this almost complete control over Poland, Catherine in 1768 launched an invasion of the Ottoman Empire to secure the northern shores of the Black Sea, territories that Peter the Great had first won, then lost.

With an uncanny political eye, Frederick II perceived that the Russian invasion of the Ottoman Empire provided him with the opportunity of taking part of Poland. Russian gains along the Black Sea would rouse Habsburg fears of Russian power; if the two powers began hostilities, he might even be dragged unwillingly into war with Austria. By a power play, however, he might avoid such a war and force Catherine II to partition Poland, giving him West Prussia, a territory that would form a land bridge between Pomerania and East Prussia. Hoping thus to consolidate his eastern territories into a

*Europe's great carve: the Polish Cheese.*

single block, Frederick proposed the partition of Poland to Catherine in 1772. To pacify Maria Theresa, she, too, would share in the spoils. Catherine reluctantly agreed. The plan shocked Maria Theresa, but as Frederick noted cynically, "The more she wept for Poland, the more she took of it." Frederick got his land bridge, Catherine took White Russia, and Maria Theresa annexed Galicia. A revolutionary act, the first partition of Poland had only *raison d'état* to justify it. In no way could monarchical legitimacy—the underlying theory of absolutism—be invoked in its defense.

The rape of Polish territory neither

checked Russia's war on Turkey nor reconciled Austria with Prussia. Catherine's peace with the Turks in 1774 resulted in Russian acquisition of Azov, permitted Russian ships to operate on the Black Sea, and placed Christians within the Ottoman Empire under a vague Russian protection. Far from satisfying Catherine, this limited success whetted her desire for more. She turned to Maria Theresa's son and successor, Joseph II, with plans for a joint partition of all Ottoman territory in Europe. The acquiescence of Frederick II, who had just frustrated Joseph's plans to round out his domains by exchanging the Austrian Netherlands for part of Bavaria, was to be purchased by suggestions of a further partition of Poland. Russia began the war by invading the Crimea and territories between the Black and Caspian seas. Weakened by internal resistance to his enlightened despotism, Joseph II did not field an army until 1788. Meanwhile Catherine parried a futile bid by Sweden's enlightened despot, Gustavus III, to regain the Baltic empire lost in 1721. This series of power plays in eastern Europe did not cease until Poland was entirely absorbed by two further partitions in 1793

and 1795, but it was halted temporarily by the aggressive expansion of revolutionary France after 1793, which directed the Eastern powers' attention westward.

## C. The Politics of Enlightenment

### ENLIGHTENED DESPOTISM

The great wars of the midcentury decisively affected the domestic policies of several monarchs as they tried to reconstitute and streamline their authority and central institutions. This new impetus to centralization came at the same time that the French Physiocrats and many other philosophes were calling for "enlightened despots" to reform their states in accordance with the enlightened standards of Reason and Nature. In practice the autocratic implementation of the Enlightenment's "laws of nature" bade fair to strengthen the central power of the state. As a result, eighteenth-century rulers and officials pursued both enlightened despotism and power politics with little sense of contradiction. Some centralizers—Maria Theresa, for example—abhorred the Enlightenment and its secularism; on the other hand, Catherine II, a devotee of enlightened principles, pursued traditionalist policies. Thus the boundaries between the older form of absolutism and enlightened despotism were often blurred and confused. But with a few exceptions, it was true that most eighteenth-century absolutists viewed their states as secular rather than otherworldly entities. They agreed with Frederick II that "the king is the first servant of the state," a phrase that implied that the state was a secular bureaucratic machine rather than an instrument of divine will.

The idea that society should be managed by philosopher-kings was as old as Plato, but eighteenth-century rulers had a rather specific program of enlightened policies in mind. First and foremost was the centralization of administration and justice in separate, parallel institutions whereby all subjects would be under the same laws, taxes, and officials. Such uniformity entailed revision of the serfs' status to give them legal personalities, rendering them more directly subject to the state than to their lords and, incidentally, subject also to conscription. Made uniform within, the state would also use its power to simplify its boundaries, making its territory compact and thereby rationally manageable. Clerical orders such as the Jesuits, who transcended the state's boundaries, had to be abolished or subordinated to secular authority. Enlightened domestic policy also required that the established churches relinquish control over censorship, education, welfare, and family affairs. Under secular officials there would be intellectual freedom—except in politics—and a freer exchange of goods. Compared to absolutism of the past, enlightened rulers placed more emphasis on humanitarianism and economic well-being. All initiative, however, lay with hereditary monarchs. Enlightened despots would do everything *for* the people; nothing would be done *by* the people except under royal supervision.

## Maria Theresa and Joseph II

Charles VI's Pragmatic Sanction securing Maria Theresa's succession bound all Habsburg territories permanently under a single ruler for the first time. Nevertheless it was still more appropriate to speak of a Habsburg *dynasty* than a Habsburg *state*. A congeries of duchies and kingdoms gathered together by dynastic marriage and the fortunes of war, the Habsburg empire was inhabited by Germans, Hungarians, Czechs, Slovenes, Slovaks, Croats, Flemings, Walloons, Italians, and, by the end of the century, Poles and Ruthenians also. Unlike their Hohenzollern rivals in Prussia, the Habsburgs had retained provincial diets that shared executive powers with the cosmopolitan court in Vienna.

As a result of her conflict with Prussia, after 1740 Maria Theresa sharply modified this policy of collaboration with local nobles and churchmen in the diets. For the sake of efficiency she set out to build a military state; around her she established an advisory council of experts headed by Count von Kaunitz and Count von Haugwitz. Under their guidance she introduced new royal officials comparable to the French *intendants,* who gave her domains more unity. So did a tariff union between Bohemia and the German provinces. To strengthen her power, the first female Habsburg ruler taxed the nobility, limited nobles' jurisdictions over, and dues from, the peasantry, laid plans for a system of state education, and had the laws codified in a more humane, orderly, and secular direction. Above all, she reorganized the army in order to cope with Prussia.

Total consolidation of the Habsburg empire, however, posed too many problems for her to accomplish. Preoccupied with waging war and retaining her patrimony, Maria Theresa made no determined effort to impose her centralization on Hungary, the Austrian Netherlands, and northern Italy. To the Hungarians in

*Empress Maria Theresa.*

particular she made concessions of local autonomy in order to secure their military assistance and acceptance of her authority.

Maria Theresa was too pious to sympathize with the secular philosophes; never could her attitude be described as "enlightened." But Joseph II, her son and coruler from 1765 to 1780, took over the reins of government and was determined to make "philosophy" the legislator of the empire. Undaunted by the power of his opposition, Joseph undertook to reduce the power of the clergy, nobles, and chartered towns throughout the empire. The assault on privilege was the reflection both of his personal enlightenment and of his desire to increase the state's vitality and power. Deliberately bypassing the provincial diets (the defenders of privileged interests), he divided the realm into administrative districts supervised directly from Vienna. He had the civil and penal laws codified for application to all subjects alike. In conformity with the Enlightenment's humanitarianism, these codes substantially reduced the number of capital offenses. More than did his mother, he threatened the nobility with a land tax and the abolition or reduction of peasant dues.

Since the Catholic Reformation the Habsburg dynasty had identified itself with an intolerant Roman Catholicism. Impatient with clerical resistance, Joseph turned this traditional policy upside down and embarked upon anticlerical religious policies derogatorily dubbed "Josephism," which aimed at a thoroughgoing secularization of the monarchy. In general he sought to bring the Church under state control: the Jesuits, who operated directly under papal authority, were expelled; papal bulls now required his approval; and the clergy had to take an oath of allegiance to the emperor. Joseph further curtailed the Church's autonomy by stripping it of control over education, personally appointing prelates, taxing the Church's lands, abolishing many monastic orders, and reducing the number of bishoprics. In some instances "Josephism" also entailed state regulation of ritual and clerical education. Except in political matters, which remained under stringent censorship, he decreed intellectual freedom. To Protestants and Jews Joseph extended toleration of private worship, but his enlightenment was not sufficient to overcome his Catholic piety to the point that he could tolerate Deists and atheists. Revenues taken from the Church were assigned to a system of free compulsory state education, to charity, and to newly founded medical facilities at Vienna. Catholic reaction to "Josephism" was severe, and in the Austrian Netherlands was the core of a revolution designed to frustrate the emperor's policies.

In order to protect her source of taxation of the peasantry, Maria Theresa had curbed the nobility's power to increase their receipts from the peasants. Joseph went much further. Initially he proposed free peasant schools, the freedom to buy and sell land, and the opportunity of commuting forced labor into payments of money. Eventually he tried to emancipate

The "revolutionary emperor," Joseph II.

all peasants from the remnants of serfdom—to give them freedom of marriage, enable them to move, improve their land tenure, and reduce their total obligations and dues. Surveys by his officials indicated that peasants had been paying about 73 percent of their gross incomes to Church, landlord, and state. Joseph proposed to reduce it to 30 percent; but when he attempted to implement these reforms, the privileged orders resisted with force. He utterly failed to free the peasants under noble and clerical lords. Only those living on the royal domains, which in Hungary were practically nonexistent, were freed during his reign.

The emperor's policy toward the peasantry was part of a more comprehensive general economic reform, which entailed restriction of the guilds, reduction of industrial controls, and the removal of internal trade barriers. He revived Charles VI's project of founding a commercial company in the Austrian Netherlands, but foreign opposition and war expenses negated his efforts.

As a theory of government, enlightened despotism was predicated on the prince's absolute sovereignty—his ability to alter society by edict. To execute his reforms, Joseph needed an immensely larger bureaucracy than he possessed, and one more committed to his goals than were the aristocrats who filled most of the important official posts of his government. No such supply of men existed, and, even had they been available, it is unlikely that they would have succeeded, for the emperor simply lacked the power and public support to decree and implement the overturn of existing privileges and property relationships. Hungarian nobles revolted successfully against all of his reforms. Belgian towns took to arms also. His reforms for the peasantry stirred up revolts but little effective support for his policies. Moreover pressures of taxation and conscription to prosecute the Turkish war after 1788 forced him to reverse his own stance. In 1790 he died a disillusioned man. "Here lies a prince whose intentions were pure," he ordered inscribed upon his tombstone, "but who had the misfortune to see all his plans miscarry." Joseph painted the picture too darkly. His administrative reorganization, legal codification, emancipation of the peasants on the royal domains, and stimulus to medical research in Vienna survived the aristocratic counterattack that followed. But his brother-successor, Leopold II, former enlightened despot of Tuscany, was forced to cancel most of Joseph's other changes. Ironically, the reaction had at its disposal the same central institutions, including secret police, that Joseph had created to implement his reforms. During the French Revolution admirers of Joseph's policies were arrested and imprisoned for professing their political views.

## Frederick II (1740–1786)

Frederick II of Prussia was more the heir than the builder of an efficient bureaucratic absolutism. Most of his "enlightened" reforms were simply continuations of his predecessors' policies. This is not to say, however, that he was not a child of the Enlightenment. Far from it. As a youth he defied the traditions of his dynasty. A devotee of French culture and educated by a French tutor, Frederick dabbled in arts and letters, played the flute well, wrote histories and bad verse in French, and even penned an essay attacking Machiavelli and his conception of statecraft. His relationship with his father, Frederick William I, was particularly stormy. On one occasion the elder Hohenzollern ordered his son shot as a deserter, but settled for temporary confinement. Nevertheless after 1732 Frederick served as a commander of a regiment of grenadiers, and for the rest of his life he made the code of the barracks his own guide to life. From his personal experience and education he effected a peculiarly Prussian fusion of tradition, reason, custom, and enlightenment, which he enforced on his subjects as the head of the Prussian state.

From the French Enlightenment Frederick took a completely secular attitude toward life: neither religious nor political passions had a legitimate place. Revealed religion he held to be an "absurd system of fables," but his Protestant state was tolerant rather than anticlerical; it even opened its doors to the Jesuits driven out of Catholic Austria. Describing himself "to a certain measure pope of the Lutherans," he abandoned the label "Christian magistrate," which his predecessors had proudly displayed since the Reformation.

*Frederick II reviewing his troops at Potsdam.*

mestic policies were based on clever, detached analyses of human motivations, and he mistrusted and despised all men as hopelessly depraved. Only the nobility was partially redeemed by virtue of its military valor and relative detachment from selfish worldly concerns. The nobles best conformed to his military doctrine that the object of battle was not to win by maneuver but to attack and destroy the enemy, preferably at the center of his power. Frederick was as much a military commander as a civilian administrator. State power, not individual well-being, was his overriding concern, although he tended to see the latter as realizable only through the former. In a real sense, his enlightened ideas were secularizations of the religious doctrines of church, state, and society that had prevailed during the religious wars. The one great exception was his hostility to enthusiasm and emotional passion. His regime was founded on a rational royalism; violence was to be constrained by reason, the reason of state.

Frederick's redefinition of enlightened values did not prevent him from collecting leading European intellectuals at Sans Souci, his palace at Potsdam, in an attempt to make his court the literary and scientific center of Europe. His closest intellectual ties were with the continental rationalists, but for 40 years he maintained contact with Voltaire. Although punctuated with quarrels, his patronage of the great philosophe enhanced his reputation, for Voltaire gave him favorable publicity as a beacon of light in the midst of clerical obscurantists. Rousseau, to be sure, denounced him as a fraud, but Frederick's sponsorship of free speech and religious tolerance put him in good stead with influential makers of public opinion throughout his reign.

Hohenzollern strength had grown through an unbroken succession of able administrators on the throne. Frederick's reign was no exception. The king dis-

Moreover he also denied that the state was the personal property of the dynasty; rather, it was something above and beyond both king and people, something to which all owed their lives and fortunes.

Reason was to order state, church, society, economics, and high policy. But for Frederick the rule of reason was severe, a deterministic providence that made statesmen and soldiers stoic marionettes. Their duty was not to humanity in general but to the concrete historical state; and self-interest, not international agreements, determined the relationships between states. "The fundamental principle of great states at any time," he wrote, "is to subordinate all in order to expand their own power without ceasing." In 1740, therefore, he felt secure in invading Silesia without diplomatic preparations or alliances, because he calculated that the self-interests of the other states would force them either to join him or to accept the outcome. It was his harsh duty to exploit Prussia's opportunity; equally harsh necessity would force others to recognize this. Frederick's foreign and do-

played phenomenal energy as he conducted journeys of inspection (often incognito) and issued reports and instructions that flowed down to every level of his bureaucratic machine. With the possible exception of establishing more direct contact with serfs on private estates, he needed no innovations to introduce the legal absolutism demanded of conventional enlightened despots.

In economic policy Frederick made no breach in the mercantilistic tradition of his predecessors; his main concern, like theirs, was to raise revenues for the army. Frederick made no change in the tax and toll structure that sharply separated town from country and gave privileged exemptions to the Junkers, the noble landlords. He retained the tightly administered system of exploiting revenues from the royal domains, which in Prussia were very extensive; but his wars consumed far more revenues than the Hohenzollern lands produced. Subsidies from England and levies on conquered territories gave only partial relief. To expand economic activity and to enable war-devastated areas to recover, the king enlarged the role of the bureaucracy in economic affairs. And to secure a favorable balance of trade and tariff revenues, heavy duties were placed on foreign goods, especially luxury products and Saxon textiles. In addition to supporting military industries, the state threw its weight behind the production of such luxuries as silk and porcelain, and in 1765 the government founded a bank to finance new industries. Monopolies were established for colonial products that were particularly in demand, such as coffee and tobacco. The acquisition of Silesia added a territory rich in textiles, iron, lead, and coal. Some of these industries, especially luxuries, continued to grow. By 1783 Prussia was exporting about one-third of its manufactures.

Agriculture was still Prussia's basic occupation, and devastation during the Seven Years' War dealt the rural economy a serious blow. Frederick's government provided seed and stock for its recovery; travelers were sent to England to observe and report on new procedures; skilled foreign peasants ("colonists") were brought in to occupy wastelands and new areas recovered from swamp and forest; and the government advertised the cultivation of new crops such as potatoes. But Prussian agriculture did not undergo an "agricultural revolution" comparable to that of England in the eighteenth century. Customary methods of farming and land tenure were little touched.

Because revenues continued to flow into the treasury and because Prussia became an exporting state, Frederick's mercantilism has generally been considered a marked success. The growth of population from about two million to six million, partly as a result of conquest, is often cited to demonstrate the point. There is, however, another side to all this, one that suggests that Prussia was headed toward a major socioeconomic crisis.

State capitalism and bureaucratic paternalism crowded out individual enterprise at every level. There was, for example, a state bank, but no large private banks survived. Because state taxes were heavy and the landed aristocracy largely exempt, peasant and urban incomes were sharply reduced by taxes, which left little capital for productive investment. Frederick proposed the emancipation of the peasants, whom he sympathetically described as "the beasts of burden of human society," but like Joseph II he could free only those on the royal domains. Their emancipation did not result in any reduction of army and billeting services, taxes, and cartage (the obligation to put teams, wagons, and drivers at the service of the state).

In the cities wage rates were fixed by law at a low level, and most craftsmen were forbidden to practice outside the towns. Commoners lacked the purchasing power to buy heavy industrial or luxury goods, and while these industries produced more than their markets could absorb, general consumer industries failed. However, probably sustained by high-priced colonial commodities such as sugar and the cultivation of potatoes, the population increased rapidly: between 1757 and 1805 births are estimated to have exceeded deaths by 30 percent; and Silesia grew especially fast in spite of major famines during the 1770s. Pressure of youth upon "places" in society hit all classes. Even the Junkers became heavily indebted in trying to provide for their more numerous surviving offspring. Unemployment, vagabondage, and crime increased, and authorities tried in vain to repress them with more severe laws. Frederick's economic policies certainly had areas of success, but they could not cope with this rapid increase in population. Those in positions of power within the bureaucracy responded to this population pressure by forcefully maintaining the traditional social order. But a disinherited "surplus population," which plagued other states of the Old Regime also, provided one of the dynamic social forces behind the revolutionary and romantic assault on reason in the following generation.

Unlike Joseph II, Frederick did not attempt to alter the distribution of wealth, power, and privilege. On the contrary, he gave the nobility more authority in the bureaucracy than it possessed under his predecessors. The law code he ordered to be compiled preserved intact the medieval legal differentiation of the nobility from the commoners. The nobles' accrual of power within the bureaucracy enabled them to resist basic reforms, and when Frederick died childless and with no one trained to succeed him, decay set in. The reign of Frederick William II (1786–97) was one of reaction against the Enlightenment. Fundamental reform awaited the shock of the Napoleonic invasions.

*Catherine II: despot, enlightened or otherwise.*

## Catherine II

Catherine the Great was one of the trio of best-known enlightened despots who ruled major states of Europe in the eighteenth century. But practical application of the Enlightenment's principles in Russia had even less chance than in Prussia. After Peter the Great's death, Western influences had continued to affect the narrow intellectual circles at the court, the nobility, and the bureaucracy; through foreign travel, tutors, and literature they became attached to French culture, rococo art, and the writings of the philosophes. On no one did the Enlightenment seem to make a deeper impression, however, than on the obscure German princess who became the slighted wife of Peter III. Upon his removal and murder in 1762, she became Catherine II, empress of Russia.

Herself widely read, Catherine sponsored French culture, wrote Russian histories, and maintained a lively correspondence with such philosophes as Voltaire, d'Alembert, Baron d'Holbach, and Diderot, enticing the latter to come to St. Petersburg. The climax of her enlightened idealism came in setting forth an Instruction for a convention called in 1767 to prepare the way for a new codification of Russian law. Justifying autocracy but adopting the principle that "people do not exist for the ruler, but the ruler for the people," the Instruction borrowed most of its contents from Montesquieu and Beccaria. Among other things it advocated equality before, and freedom under, the law, denounced torture and serfdom, and criticized the concentration of ownership of large estates in a few hands.

This convention, the first real Russian deliberative assembly, represented all social classes except serfs under private landlords, which were about half the population. But as a vehicle for translating Catherine's intentions into concrete proposals it was a dismal failure. Long sessions repeatedly failed to achieve agreement on particulars. Noble delegates construed "freedom" to authorize the extension of their power over the peasantry and denounced critics of serfdom as "traitors to their class"; townsmen interpreted "equality" to mean their equality with nobles in sharing privileges such as the holding of serfs. Although Catherine denounced these perversions of enlightened principles and instigated discussions of serfdom, she failed to define clearly the convention's function. In 1768, long after she herself had ceased to take them seriously, the sessions were suspended, and by 1774 the committees ceased to meet. Apart from stirring up discussion of controversial subjects, the convention had no practical significance.

Catherine's enlightened principles can also be seen at work in a variety of specific measures: she was instrumental in establishing foundling hospitals, medical facilities, a public library, and the practice of inoculation against smallpox; and in 1764 she secularized most of the land belonging to the church. Her most lasting reform was probably the reorganization of local government along lines that remained essentially unchanged until 1917. In 1775 she ordered the establishment of 50 identical provincial governments, each with a noble governor. At both the provincial and district level an attempt was made to separate justice from administration and, within justice, civil from criminal jurisdiction. Local authorities had power over all classes, but the administrators were drawn from the nobility alone. Thus the nobles, now free from compulsory service to the state, became the legal masters of the provinces. The towns, allowed to hold land in 1766 and chartered for their own self-government in 1785, seemed to have been an exception to noble dominance. But in fact the privileged urban classes, who controlled the town governments, lacked financial and police powers and found themselves subordinated to the nobility.

To portray Catherine as a faithful executrix of the Enlightenment would be to distort the major weight of her reign's significance for Russian development. She was more concerned with an aggressive foreign policy than with the worsening condition of most of her subjects' lives. As avidly enthusiastic for Machiavelli as for the philosophes, she adopted the traditional Russian political system of intrigue among favorites. (Diderot once characterized her as a combination of the soul of Brutus and the charms of Cleopatra.) From the time she, a non-Russian, seized the throne, she played that system as a master. It is difficult to see how, had she been sincerely and primarily devoted to enlightened principles, she could have carried out reforms and kept power. As a matter of practical politics, she was dependent on an ascendant nobility for provincial and local government; and since the death of Peter the Great this nobility had secured almost total exemption from obligations. The state, lacking a trained and obedient

*Flogging of a Russian peasant.*

bureaucracy, had assisted the nobles' reduction of the mass of the Russian population to their will.

Instead of ameliorating the deep social ills of Russian society Catherine legitimized and extended them. The nobles secured confirmation of their gains during the previous half-century in a Letter of Grace of 1785, which constituted them henceforth as "an estate . . . separated by its rights and privileges from the rest of the people." Exempted from military service, personal taxation, and corporal punishment, they were confirmed in their rights to buy and sell land freely, to trade, and to operate mines and factories. To the hereditary nobility was given the exclusive privilege of owning serfs, a privilege that was becoming the foundation of Russian society and its chief curse.

Despite the state's interest in the serf as the principal source of taxes, he became almost a chattel slave: not only was the lord his overseer, tax collector, and landlord, to whom he owed undefined amounts of labor and fees, but the lord (or his bailiff) also served as policeman, judge, jury, and sometimes (as a result of beatings) executioner. With this boundless power, lords eroded peasants' rights to the use of the land. While exactions in labor and fees were increased, peasant appeals to the government were forbidden by law. Individual lords were forbidden to emancipate their serfs, who on occasion were detached from their land and sold at increasing prices at public auction. Although administrators of the central bureaucracy occasionally protested against the nobles' usurpations, laws defining noble-serf relationships were not passed; instead administrative practice acquiesced in the serfs' declining status. Even though Catherine herself could denounce serfdom and its advocates, she did nothing to mitigate the condition of peasants on church lands that the government confiscated and turned over to private lords. Moreover, for the convenience of tax collection through noble lords the government granted to magnates in newly acquired districts similar powers over their peasants. Thus serfdom reached its apogee in the late eighteenth century.

With all the avenues of political expression blocked off to the peasantry—an estate sunk in ignorance, superstition, and tradition—the only reaction to its worsening condition could be resignation or rebellion. Numerous peasant conspiracies and revolts threatened Catherine's rule, but all channels of discontent merged in the massive Pugachev Rebellion of 1773–75, during which peasant restiveness loosed itself in a furious counterattack. Pugachev, a Don Cossack veteran encouraged by Old Believer priests,* organized nomads, adventurers, and disgruntled peasants into a great army. Sweeping along the Volga River and the Ural Mountains, they terrorized the nobility and clergy. Defeated at first, government forces finally caught Pugachev and executed him after famine had sapped the strength of his forces. Pugachev's suppression firmly reestablished noble superiority and snuffed out all further thought of reform.

The riveting of servitude on the peasantry became the most salient feature of Russian czarist society. Squeezed by exactions of both state and nobility, the serfs could neither improve their lot on present lands nor migrate to others. Yet neither the state nor the nobility appears to have profited from the system; despite increased taxes and dues, Catherine's government went deeper into debt. The greater part of the nobility became unproductive administrators, dwelling often in towns as absentees from their estates. As the social distance between peasant and noble increased, the nobility lost its sense of reality. It repudiated its Russian environment in favor of French ideas, clothes,

* See p. 233.

fashions, manners, and language. In fact so cut off from actual conditions were Russian recipients of the Enlightenment that they would have been impotent to change the system even had they desired to do so. Moreover commercial urbanization bringing social, economic, and intellectual changes in western Europe was arrested in Russia by the lords' absolute rights over the peasants and by their pronounced economic and trading privileges. Both tended to hinder the growth of the tiny indigenous middle class. At Catherine's death the urban population constituted not more than four percent of the total population. The path of gradual change was thus almost entirely closed on the eve of the gigantic population increase that was to come during the nineteenth century.

## Enlightened Despotism in the Lesser States

The major states had no monopoly of enlightened despots. Indeed, the chances for their success seem to have been greater in the smaller states that had neither the resources nor the desire to become embroiled in major wars.

Latin Europe produced several cases of secular anticlerical reform similar to the program attempted by Joseph II. In Savoy the Old Regime was overhauled by uniform laws, curtailment of the Church, emancipation of the serfs, and reorganization of taxes and administration. In Tuscany Joseph's brother Leopold successfully carried out a similar set of policies. Don Carlos, who became Charles III of Spain in 1759, reorganized the administration of the Kingdom of the Two Sicilies along the lines of Bourbon France. From 1759 to 1788 he made Spain the seat of a reform movement designed to revive Spanish power. Hindering both centralization of secular authority and reform were the Inquisition and the Roman Catholic clergy. Charles curbed both, centralized his administration in a council of state, proclaimed economic reforms, and attempted, with only small success, to break the landholding monopoly of nobles and clergy. But Charles did revitalize Spanish power in Europe and the New World. Meanwhile Portugal had a brief period of reforming absolutism under the police-state measures of the able Marquis de Pombal, who served as the king's chief minister. In expelling the Jesuits Pombal initiated what soon became a universal aspect of enlightened despotism in Catholic states.

Among the many smaller German states there were instances of enlightened rule. The dukes of Baden and Saxe-Weimar followed such formulas, giving some slight roots to German liberalism and the basis for a cultural renaissance involving such important literary figures as Johann Gottfried von Herder and Johann Wolfgang von Goethe.* Other German despots followed quite unenlightened courses: the landgrave of Hesse-Cassel, for example, made a fortune by selling his subjects as soldiers ("Hessians"), a practice that others followed on a smaller scale. Within the Holy Roman Empire there was no general pattern of enlightened despotism.

Earlier in the century Sweden had provided the most spectacular shift from absolutism to aristocratic oligarchy. In 1772, with the coup d'etat of Gustavus III, Swedish politics shifted as decisively back to absolutism. But Gustavus coupled reform with an ill-fated attack on Russia to recover the Swedish Baltic empire. Denmark, too, had its absolutist reformer in the person of Johann Friedrich von Struensee, a royal doctor who cared for the debilitated king. Taking control of the administration and of the queen, whose lover he was, he issued a flood of decrees in his brief tenure in office. Both he and Gustavus III were killed at the instigation of nobles who re-sisted the drastic curtailment of their powers that absolutist reform entailed. Struensee was executed by judicial decree in 1772; Gustavus was assassinated in 1792.

## THE COLLAPSE OF ABSOLUTISM AND THE RISE OF DEMOCRATIC MOVEMENTS IN THE MARITIME STATES

Enlightened despotism was one of two major responses to the resurgent aristocracy during the eighteenth century. With varying degrees of success enlightened despots contended with aristocrats in agrarian kingdoms whose commerce and industry were relatively backward. Such "revolutions" as occurred in these states were either counterrevolutions of the privileged classes against enlightened reforms or hopeless uprisings of the peasantry. In the more commercially developed societies, especially in the Atlantic maritime states, a different evolution led to the second response: demands for the democratization of political institutions and the social structure. In Britain's older North American colonies, where semi-democratic institutions were indigenous, this movement became overtly revolutionary after the Seven Years' War. In Britain itself democratic elements sought means short of revolution to reverse the growing oligarchic trend of British institutions, especially the English and Irish parliaments. There were also democratic movements that led to open revolution in Geneva and the Low Countries. Except for the American Revolution, whose success was due partly to the diplomatic alignment of Europe, all of these movements failed—but by 1787 French absolutism was on the point of collapse because of rapidly deepening financial crises and the obstructionism of the aristocracy. France had not fully become a maritime state, and

* See pp. 417–19.

*William Pitt the Elder (earl of Chatham).*

before 1787 the democratic movement was more latent than actual, having not yet become distinct from the rebelliousness of the aristocracy. As events proved, however, France had developed the potential for the most significant of the revolutionary democratic movements.

## The Failure of the Democratic Movement in Great Britain

Walpole's fall in 1742 brought no change in the methods he had used to manage Parliament. Backed by the Duke of Newcastle, his successors disposed of proposed reforms as easily as he had done. Charges of corruption were widespread, but no reform in the parliamentary system occurred until after the Seven Years' War.

This delay came in part because discontented elements pinned their faith on William Pitt, a prophet of empire, and on war with France, all of which detracted from interest in reform. As early as 1746 Pitt considered proposals to conquer Canada and ruin French commerce. Immensely popular in London, he was not acceptable to George II as head of the government until the Seven Years' War. Under his direction in that war Britain carried the day in one theater of war after another: North America, India, North Africa, and on the seas in general. The trade and the industry that supplied Britain flourished as the victories mounted. While British debts, taxes, and nationalistic fervor grew, Pitt would not make peace. After his resignation in 1761 over the question of the conduct of the war, that task was undertaken by Newcastle on terms that Pitt denounced as too lenient. Although the peace was unpopular in London, it gave the small but vocal movement for parliamentary reform a new impetus.

Revived agitation for reform coincided with a long period of government weakness and embarrassment in foreign affairs. George III, who ascended the throne in 1760, replaced Newcastle—who had been the real power behind the scenes since Walpole's emergence—with Lord Bute, who was not a member of Parliament, and whose appointment stirred its opposition. Parliament began to assert its independence of the Crown on the one hand and its abhorrence of popular reform movements on the other. Newcastle's dismissal disrupted the patronage system that ministers had used to control Parliament, and when the lever of patronage ceased to be an effective means to secure unity between Crown and Parliament, the controlling Whigs broke into rival factions. George III searched in vain for a stable coalition until he found it temporarily under Lord North, appointed in 1770. George meanwhile attempted personally to use the temporarily disorganized system of patronage and influence in order to build up in Parliament a body of supporters loyal to himself and thus to reestablish the integrity of the executive powers of the Crown within the constitution as he interpreted it. The unpopularity of this royal bid for increased influence contributed to a near revolutionary situation in Britain in 1780. So did Britain's entry into the American revolutionary war with no allies and with the British people themselves sharply divided on the justice of the war. These two factors resulted in the temporary coincidence of two different reform movements. One, largely within Parliament, sought to strip the Crown of its control over "placemen" (those who enjoyed the benefits of government patronage) in the House of Commons; it would make no concessions to democratic control over the House. The other, mainly outside Parliament, aimed at making the House of Commons more representative of the population.

The extraparliamentary movement was led by radicals from the new industrial bourgeoisie, many of whom were religious dissenters who were being discriminated against under the present system. While the decadent universities were firmly wed to things as they were, dissenting academies taught science, economics, and history, as well as rational religion and more modern approaches to new social problems. Joseph Priestley, a chemist and a founder of modern Unitarianism, and Richard Price, later to be the target of Edmund Burke's polemics for teaching the doctrine of natural rights, were among their teachers and leaders. Literate men, whose practical and political interests were not served by parliamentary representation as then constituted, also formed technical societies, clubs, and workingmen's associations, which joined in the campaign to democratize Parliament.

Early popular discontent with Parliament's oligarchy centered around the personality of John Wilkes, a townsman of recent wealth who founded a newspaper, the *North Briton*, in 1762. When it attacked

*Portraiture of the English oligarchy:* Mrs. Grace Dalrymple Elliott (*by Thomas Gainsborough*).

Bute's "ministerial despotism" with a more than merely implied slap at the king himself, the Crown tried to suppress the paper by arresting Wilkes, a member of Parliament, and his staff. The courts declared the general warrants on which Wilkes and his associates were arrested illegal, but Parliament expelled him. His leadership among dissenters was weakened by discovery of a lascivious essay on women among his personal papers, but after a short stay in France Wilkes was elected—and reelected—to Parliament. When that body consistently refused to seat him, his case became the cause of public meetings and agitation against Parliament. Elected mayor of London, he secured the city's support in publishing the debates of Parliament for the first time—a

*Mob firing Newgate Prison during the Gordon Riots.*

major step in the subjection of Parliament to public scrutiny. Finally admitted to Parliament, Wilkes introduced an abortive bill for universal manhood suffrage, but he gradually disappeared from prominence during the American Revolution.

British democrats perceived in that revolution many of the same elements of the fight that they were waging at home. A Major Cartwright, for example, refused to serve in America and proposed home rule for the colonies and thorough democratization of Parliament. When the popular reform movement organized local "associations" and called for a national General Association—a representative body that might rival and perhaps even displace Parliament—it alarmed parliamentary

Whigs and country gentlemen alike. In 1780 the Association Movement, which had its counterpart among Protestants in Ireland, was badly compromised by the Gordon riots in London.* Ignited by mild but extremely unpopular parliamentary concessions to Roman Catholics and by lower-class frustrations, these riots destroyed sections of unpoliced London. More destructive of property than any single episode during the French Revolution in Paris, the Gordon riots revealed the latent violence at the bottom of Britain's social order and also demonstrated the gulf between the lower classes themselves and the would-be reformers of Parliament, for Priestley's house was destroyed and Wilkes tried to quiet the disturbance.

After the Association Movement petered out, bills to reform Parliament also failed. Between 1782 and 1785 the younger Pitt introduced a series of bills to redistribute parliamentary seats and to broaden the suffrage. They failed without exception.

The only successful reform was the parliamentary one for which Edmund Burke was spokesman, and its success weakened the executive still further. He introduced bills that reduced some corruption by barring certain placemen and contractors from sitting in Commons. These measures, although weakening the executive, did not democratize the legislature. Threatened by a new and radical urban society, Whig and Tory lords drew together to preserve their own power—but they relied on their own control of Parliament, not on the authority of an absolute monarch, to secure that goal. Burke himself, although sympathetic to the American Revolution, now turned to defending the existing British constitution as perfection itself.

* Named after an eccentric Scotsman, Lord George Gordon, the riots followed his presentation of a petition to the House of Commons protesting reduction of penalties against Roman Catholics.

## The American Revolution

Meanwhile the 13 mainland colonies of Great Britain in North America succeeded in breaking free from the empire. Only those colonies that had been most successful in transplanting European populations and civilization overseas were involved. In 1700 they had a population of 200,000; by midcentury there were nearly two million in these 13 colonies, over two-thirds of them native-born, and their birth rate was prodigious. In Philadelphia, New York, and Boston they possessed commercial cities of significance; in the middle and northern colonies shipbuilding, distilling, and commerce (including the slave trade) flourished; Pennsylvania, the most prosperous and populous colony, was a world leader in the production of raw iron. Unlike the colonists in the West Indies, the mainlanders had apparently unlimited opportunities for expansion. Land speculation was rampant among the wealthy, whereas less fortunate elements could find new opportunities on the frontiers. They had at hand well-rooted, if not oligarchic, institutions: each colony possessed a legislature with a popularly elected house, paralleling the British House of Commons. These legislatures used their power to blunt the authority of royal officials. In short, the mainland colonies had developed to a point at which they were able to articulate local interests with considerable success. Once the French barrier was removed by the Seven Years' (French and Indian) War, their dependence upon the British for military protection, already weak, diminished still more.

The growing colonial self-confidence assured that if the empire were to remain a harmonious body, constitutional means of resolving divergent interests within it would have to be found. Before 1775 Americans had based their resistance to unpopular British enactments on their rights as Englishmen guaranteed by local charters and grants; thus they defended themselves as part of the corporate structure of the British constitution. Despite non-English immigration and geographical isolation from Europe and from each other, their culture, governmental systems, and principal trading relationships were English. The common British connection was useful in mediating local conflicts resulting from each colony's pursuit of its own particularist course. Overlapping territorial claims, differing religious institutions, divergent economic and trade patterns, and local loyalties discouraged cooperation in common enterprise, all of which was extremely exasperating to the British government in wartime. Nor were relationships within each colony without conflicts such as those between debtors and creditors, orthodox and nonconformists, and frontier and tidewater interests. For reasons that varied in different colonies, discontented elements challenged the commercial, family, and religious oligarchies whose control over government and its spoils mitigated the democratizing effect of broad suffrage. During the decade of discontent that preceded the American Revolution part of the colonial leadership (the radicals, or patriots) came to espouse separation from Britain as a necessary step in the realization of their own goals.

## The Colonial Rift
## with Britain: 1763–1775

Parliament claimed full sovereignty over the colonies as "dependent corporations," but until the midcentury wars, the implications of this claim were muted by Britain's failure to enforce its authority fully: Americans paid fewer taxes than any people except the Poles; only a few colonial laws were disallowed or vetoed by the Privy Council; some customs were collected, but smuggling, often with the connivance of officials, was commonplace.

After the Seven Years' War, the North American customs service actually cost more to operate than it collected.

Resulting from the experience of that war, the British policy of "salutary neglect" gave way to a "new imperial policy." Britain had failed to secure close coordination and cooperation among the colonies, whose legislatures had met requisitions for supplies and money sporadically or not at all. And colonial traders had persisted in trading with the enemy. At the end of the war, taxes in debt-ridden Britain were high enough to stir internal unrest. Parliament balked at providing further outlays for America and demanded that the colonists share the expenses of the empire. These expenses were immediately increased by Pontiac's Indian uprising of 1763, which captured all but one of the ceded French forts north of the Ohio River. The British government sought to pacify the Indians by regulating and restricting westward expansion by means of negotiated treaties, a measure that gave rise to great dissatisfaction among various elements of colonial society, especially settlers and land speculators. They also sought to station in the colonies troops financed by the colonists themselves. To raise customs duties for this purpose Parliament first lowered duties on molasses imported from the foreign West Indies—the colonists' principal source of hard money—but then, in contrast to its earlier relaxed attitude, ordered strict enforcement of customs collection. Specie was already critically short because the balance of payments ran heavily against the colonies, depriving them of circulating coinage; further acts of Parliament made the sterling shortage worse; and Parliament forbad the colonies to mint their own money or to pay their debts with (depreciated) currency Although colonists paid scant taxes to their provincial governments, compliance with these acts was exceedingly difficult. Britain's new policies were challenged be-

*Rioting against the Stamp Act in New York.*

fore the bars of law and public opinion, but resistance to assuming a share of imperial burdens did not become general before the Stamp Act of 1765.

This attempt to raise taxes for colonial administrative and military expenses did not really threaten the local currency supply, but it did set off a decade of constitutional debate. Providing for an excise on newspapers, business records, and legal documents (much lower, incidentally, than a current stamp duty in Britain itself), the Stamp Act stepped on the toes of the most articulate, educated, and influential segments of the population. Riots prohibited its enforcement, while a Stamp Act congress representing nine of the colonies met in New York to protest formally. The congress denounced "taxation without representation" but rejected representation in Parliament as impracticable. It affirmed American loyalty to Brit-

ain but offered no substitute, as Britain had requested, for requisition as a means of raising revenues. Parliament repealed the tax, but both the issue of the right to tax and the means of supporting the colonial army and administration were left unsettled.

Quartering acts and subsequent customs measures met a similar rebuff. Against the Townshend tariffs of 1767 a boycott enforced by local "Sons of Liberty" threatened sales by British merchants. Again Britain yielded by repealing most of the acts, but it reaffirmed the principle of parliamentary taxation by sustaining a tax on imports of tea. A period of relative quiet followed until 1773, when the home government sought to relieve the financial distress of the foundering East India Company by selling taxed tea at reduced prices that even smugglers could not meet. Colonial port authorities quietly refused to unload the British tea, but in Boston radicals started a chain of events that led to violence and open pronouncement of revolutionary aims.

Following a minor collision between British troops and local citizens in 1770 (the "Boston Massacre"), revolutionary leaders had gained increased power over public opinion and government in Massachusetts. Now they disguised themselves as Indians and dumped cargoes of tea into Boston harbor. This destruction of property by the "Boston Tea Party" alienated many moderate and conservative colonists, but more significantly it drew from the home government, which had vacillated between strict enforcement and concessions, a series of coercive acts: it closed Boston's harbor until the tea was paid for, altered the government of Massachusetts Bay to make the council appointive rather than elective, and suspended the town meetings, where such radicals as Samuel Adams held sway. Adams and John Hancock then began to organize the collection of arms, and in 1775, when British troops tried to seize them and their supplies, armed clashes occurred at Lexington and Concord. Coercion of the Massachusetts Bay government and bloodshed gave the radicals their most convincing demonstration that Britain was bent on tyranny, something that they had seen as the intent of every act of the British government, including its belated fulfillment of its 1763 treaty obligations to recognize French law and Catholicism in conquered Quebec. Neither side had planned a war, but the outbreak of armed hostilities brought the constitutional debate to a climax in an atmosphere favoring American advocates of total independence.

After the Stamp Act the constitutional positions of the colonial leaders fell into three general categories. Some held parliamentary sovereignty to be indivisible and therefore competent to tax and regulate commerce. Although they opposed specific measures as examples of bad policy, they were Loyalists from the start. Others invoked English constitutional precedents to deny tax and tariff powers to Parliament, but they advocated an American legislature that would be equal to Parliament under the British Crown. Prominent colonists, some of whom later became Loyalists as well as some revolutionaries, were in this camp: Franklin, Jefferson, James Wilson, and Joseph Galloway. A third group, the radicals—best represented by Patrick Henry in Virginia and Samuel Adams in Massachusetts—described any authority outside the local legislatures and courts as tyranny and slavery. They organized "committees of correspondence" to coordinate their efforts and wielded effective propaganda through the press. They also set the tasks for the local "Sons of Liberty." In the absence of local police these groups enforced boycotts and intimidated their opposition by threats and violence. Their aim was not just local autonomy but the breaking of British ties that supported entrenched oligarchies.

In 1775 the radicals gained control of the Second Continental Congress, which met to organize colonial resistance. Within individual colonies they carried out revolutions that produced state constitutions curtailing executive authority, curbing existing oligarchies, and providing bills of rights. Their campaign for independence was reinforced by the writings of Thomas Paine, a recent radical immigrant from England who there had agitated unsuccessfully for reform of the British constitution. The success of the radicals became clear when the Second Continental Congress opened American ports and adopted the Declaration of Independence, which, drafted by Jefferson, invoked a natural universal right of revolution whenever existing governments persistently trampled on the natural rights of the governed to life, liberty, and the pursuit of happiness. To demonstrate the Revolution's legitimacy, the Declaration at-

*A Colonial antidote for Loyalists.*

tributed to George III, heretofore praised as the one accepted link between Britain and America, a long list of tyrannical acts. In reality, Parliament was primarily responsible for them.

Powers accorded to the revolutionary Congress reflected the radicals' opposition to any central government, British or American, possessing power to tax or regulate commerce. The same was true of the Articles of Confederation, which operated as the first American constitution between 1781 and 1789. The radicals devoted their attention largely to the state governments, whose failure to cooperate fully had made the Continental Congress's task of prosecuting the war reminiscent of Britain's experience during the French and Indian War.

## The Achievement of American Independence

From the point of view of materials, industry, wealth, and manpower, the colonists' revolt against the world's strongest maritime power was inauspicious; but the colonies had the advantages of geographical remoteness and British reluctance to proceed vigorously. Also, as we have seen, the revolt caught Britain isolated diplomatically, giving the colonists the opportunity of harnessing imperial rivalries for their own purposes.

Independence left the radicals in control under the new Articles of Confederation. The unicameral Congress representing the confederated states had some successes: the Northwest Ordinance of 1787, for example, provided a new method of territorial government that repudiated slavery and provided for the admission of new states on equal terms with the old. Problems of the postwar years, however, undermined the new government: as the Loyalists had predicted, the new country was excluded from world markets; the expenses of the war, largely financed by depreciated paper money and loans, went unpaid; and the newborn nation was caught in a depression aggravated by the uncoordinated commercial policies of the different states. After the revolutionary ferment abated, state constitutions were rewritten more in accordance with the British past, incorporating stronger executive power and devices to insulate part of the government from direct popular control. The states' failure to restore confiscated Loyalist estates in accordance with treaty commitments seemed a dangerous precedent for property relationships. In several states sharp conflicts between factions of debtor-farmers and creditor-merchants broke out. By 1787 conservative and national forces joined hands to replace the Articles of Confederation with a new constitution, which provided for a federal government wielding the power of taxation, controlling commerce, and protecting property from expropriation in the future without due process of law.

Although the drafters of the Constitution of 1787 were obliged to compromise with advocates of a bill of rights defining individual rights and states' rights against the central government, the new instrument represented a mild resurgence of conservatism. Nevertheless American conservatism had been weakened by the permanent exclusion of the Loyalists, who found new homes in Canada, England, or elsewhere. Finally, the Constitution's espousal of popular sovereignty made it a distinctly radical document. It was, after all, the product of a democratic revolution, a precedent that soon inspired other revolutions.

## The Failure of French Absolutism (1743–1786)

The difficulties of the British government at home and abroad were matched by a more gradual, but in the long run even more serious, disorganization of the royal government in France. After the competent but superannuated Fleury died in 1743, Louis XV took personal charge of the government but without giving it direction. Affairs of state drifted dangerously for more than a decade. Frederick II quipped astutely that France in this period really had four kings—the four secretaries of state—whose policies contradicted one another. Their disagreements were to some extent a direct result of the policy of Louis, who deliberately chose rival personalities as ministers in order to prevent the possibility of ministerial conspiracy. For the king these were years of growing unpopularity. His personal lassitude and disinterest in governmental and administrative affairs introduced a creeping paralysis into the central government. He was particularly vulnerable to the charge that his mistress, the Marquise de Pompadour—an upstart commoner—was manipulating decisions and appointments behind the scenes. Worse still, France lost heavily as a result of the Seven Years' War. Some very able and progressive administrators, especially among the *intendants* of the provinces, were able to check some of the chaotic tendencies of the center but not the slow disintegration of absolute royal command.

Louis's unpopularity, however, was not entirely his own doing. His administration was obstructed by the *parlements* while their members, armed with Montesquieu's aristocratic arguments, raked him for tyranny. In such attacks they appealed to the nation over and above the king and presented themselves as its true representatives. In actuality they represented the old hierarchical and corporate structure of the privileged orders of French society, which commercialization was steadily undermining and whose legal safeguards Louis's ministers were beginning to dismantle. The parlements cooperated to interfere with royal administration in numerous ways. In 1770 they were implicated in a successful court intrigue to dismiss Choiseul, the able royal minister who had been responsible for breaking the guilds' legal hold over domestic industry and for opening trade to the Indies by private traders. The king then took the momentous step of abolishing the troublesome parlements and replacing them with panels of nonhereditary jurists appointed on the basis of merit. This reform of the courts, primarily a political measure, was also intended as a prelude to the establishment of uniform codes of civil and criminal law. But the monarchy did not justify its action in secular, utilitarian terms; instead it merely made a blunt declaration of the monarchy's divine right. Far from settling the conflict, this judicial reorganization initiated a period of heightened discontent that lasted until the accession of Louis XVI in 1774.

Louis XVI, a good-hearted but none-too-intelligent man, immediately terminated the crisis by an appeasing act of weakness: he restored the parlements with all of their traditional rights, including the power to register new laws and taxes and to remonstrate with the king on decrees they regarded as detrimental to the country (or their own interests). Ultimately, taxes became the nub of their renewed conflict with the royal government. Although commercial wealth was accumulating in private hands, monarchical finances were rapidly approaching bankruptcy; even the expediency of heavy borrowing was becoming difficult except at ruinous interest rates, which reflected the government's failing reputation among the financial community. Louis's controller-general of finance, the one-time intendant Turgot, might have saved the situation when he was called to office in 1774. He abolished costly sinecures, tried to curb the waste and corruption that allowed half the revenues collected to find their way into private hands, and sought to abolish clerical and noble exemptions from a new single tax on land. Turgot abolished the guilds and instituted free trade in grain. However, famine, speculation, and skyrocketing grain prices undid this last act, and the other acts were opposed by the offended privileged orders, which denounced and conspired against him. In 1776 Louis dismissed Turgot and recalled almost all of his reforms. Thereafter France entered the American Revolution, an action that Turgot rightly predicted would bankrupt the royal treasury.

Turgot's successor, Jacques Necker (who held office from 1776 to 1781), a Protestant Genevan banker, faced a hopeless task. First, relying on his reputation as a banker, he floated vast new loans to finance the new war and to gain time for more thorough reform. Subject to increasing attacks from the privileged classes as well as some from financial circles, Necker sought to protect his position by publishing in 1781 the famous *Account Rendered to the King,* which purported to make public the details of royal financial administration. By juggling figures Necker contrived to show a surplus in the treasury; in reality, the government's indebtedness was greater than ever. Nor did this publication have the effect Necker intended. By revealing to the public the tremendous sums spent by the monarchy on gifts and pensions to the parasitic court nobility it not only deepened popular distrust of the government but also called down on Necker's head a fury of opposition from the court, which forced his dismissal in 1781. His successors, including the able Calonne, resorted to one expedient after another but were unable to make any dent in the budgetary deficits of the government. Failing to secure consent to increased but also more equitable taxation from the parlements, clergy, and nobility, their efforts were doomed. The rapidly deepening financial crisis proved to be the undoing of the Bourbons' nominal absolutism, for it enabled the ascendant privileged orders to make a revolutionary assault on royal authority in the years after 1786.

For the years ahead both the American Revolution and the phenomenon of enlightened despotism presented alternative solutions to the problems of eighteenth-century political and social life. In their different ways, both had the same objective: the strengthening of the secular power of the state to overcome the power of traditional corporate "intermediate bodies" between the state and the individual. In this sense new revolutionary governments would effect the centralization of authority that absolute monarchs had heralded ideologically and implemented imperfectly with limited bureaucracies. But neither divine-right monarchy nor even its modern cousin, enlightened despotism, was a genuinely evolutionary stepping-stone toward the establishment of a parliamentary government responsible to the governed. The aristocratic resurgence after 1715 again gave evidence that under normal circumstances the successors to the great absolute monarchs were special interest groups whose privileges the throne had created or maintained. In theory, enlightened despotism marked a departure from this pattern by its assaults on social and economic as well as political privileges. But its practical results in this direction were scanty. Joseph II's failures testified to the weakness of monarchical fiat in overcoming vested interests. As matters of practical power politics, both Frederick II and Catherine II yielded still greater political powers to the privileged. And in France even the emergence of enlightened despotism was largely blocked by the coincidence of royal timidity and the obstructive power of the higher orders of society. Here and there, to be sure, enlightened despots scored some successes that tended toward the benefit of society as a whole, but they did not lead in the direction of popular government.

Eighteenth-century experience indicated that without fundamental alterations in the nature of society itself, something that enlightened despots were unwilling to consider, governments had little ability to legislate basic changes in the distribution of power and prestige. Even where external conditions were seriously undermining the basis of the traditional social structure, as in France, there was no guarantee that the monarchy could adapt to, or appropriate, such conditions for its own purposes. The same uncertainty hung over entrenched oligarchies like the English Parliament, which claimed powers scarcely less sovereign than those of the enlightened despots.

But in contrast to enlightened despotism the parliamentary reform movement in England and the American Revolution were on courses that would reconcile greater individual liberty and initiative with stronger government based on legal equality and the active consent of the governed. Both Britain and its mainland colonies already had some degree of popular participation in their constitutional fabric; but the task of expanding that participation proved to be much easier in America than in Britain. Indeed, the ease with which the American revolutionaries succeeded in establishing their "new order of the ages" gave birth to illusions. They had no powerful neighbors except Britain to threaten counterrevolutionary intervention, and the balance of power worked in their favor to offset any threat from that quarter. They had no entrenched feudal order to contend with, and the violence-laden miseries produced by population growth in Europe were outside their ken. In Britain economic growth and the existence of popular elements in the constitution made an accommodation to change possible so that Britons would not follow America's revolutionary example. But the succeeding age of revolutions demonstrated that conditions on the Continent were so different that the American experiment could not be duplicated easily.

## Selected Readings

*Anderson, M. S. *Europe in the Eighteenth Century: 1713–1783.* New York: Holt, Rinehart, & Winston, 1961 (paperback: Galaxy Books).

*Up-to-date textbook written as comparative history.*

Barber, Elinor G. *The Bourgeoisie in Eighteenth-Century France.* Princeton: Princeton University Press, 1955.

*An analysis of the social stratification of prerevolutionary France. Good for indicating bourgeois imitation of the nobility, but it becomes the prisoner of its preconceived social theories.*

Blum, Jerome. *Lord and Peasant in Russia from the Ninth to the Nineteenth Century.* Princeton: Princeton University Press, 1961.

*An authoritative history of the Russian peasant in the bondage that reached its apogee in the eighteenth century.*

*Bruun, Geoffrey. *The Enlightened Despots.* New York: Henry Holt and Co., 1929.

*A brief, comprehensive summary well suited for the beginning student.*

*Dorn, Walter L. *Competition for Empire, 1740–1763.* New York: Harper & Brothers, 1940.

*A comprehensive account of the renewed power struggle, well-balanced between colonial and continental rivalries; also excellent on the thought of the Enlightenment.*

Ford, Franklin L. *Robe and Sword, the Regrouping of the French Aristocracy after Louis XIV.* Cambridge, Mass.: Harvard University Press, 1953.

*This book demonstrates the growing community of interest between the two major branches of the French nobility during the eighteenth century.*

*Gagliardo, John G. *Enlightened Despotism.* New York: Thomas Y. Crowell Co., 1967.

*A good, brief analysis of the reforms of the enlightened despots, based on the most recent research.*

*Gershoy, Leo. *From Despotism to Revolution, 1763–1789*. New York: Harper & Brothers, 1944.

> *One of the best accounts in English; part of the* Rise of Modern Europe *series.*

*Gipson, Lawrence H. *The Coming of the Revolution: 1763–1775*. New York: Harper & Brothers, 1954.

> *Presents the origins of the American revolution from the point of view of the British Empire.*

Gooch, George P. *Maria Theresa and Other Studies*. London: Longmans, Green & Co., 1951.

> *One of the author's several biographical studies of the period, which tend to be rather old-fashioned.*

Goodwin, Albert, ed. *The European Nobility in the Eighteenth Century*. London: A. and C. Black, 1953.

> *Studies of the nobility in each of the major states, showing that "enlightened despots" in eastern Europe actually favored the nobility.*

Kluchevsky, V. O. *A History of Russia*. Translated by C. J. Hogarth. 5 vols. New York: Russell and Russell, 1960.

> *Volume 5 treats the reign of Catherine II; this work is particularly clear in establishing serfdom as the basic social institution of Russia.*

Lindsay, J., ed. *The Old Regime, 1713–1763*. The New Cambridge Modern History, vol. 7. Cambridge: Cambridge University Press, 1957.

> *A thorough reference work, particularly good for diplomatic and general military developments.*

Link, Edith M. *The Emancipation of the Austrian Peasant: 1740–1798*. New York: Columbia University Press, 1949.

> *Critical for an understanding of peasant conditions in central Europe and for the aims of Joseph II.*

Namier, Lewis B. *England in the Age of the American Revolution*. 2d ed. New York: St. Martin's Press, 1961.

———. *The Structure of Politics at the Accession of George III*. 2d ed. New York: St. Martin's Press, 1957.

> *Both are detailed analyses of British political life that focus on the personal connections of its factions.*

*Ogg, David. *Europe of the Ancien Regime: 1715–1783*. New York: Harper and Row, Publishers, 1965.

> *A new conventional history distinguished by its recognition of geographic factors in political and economic developments.*

Palmer, Robert R. *The Age of the Democratic Revolution, A Political History of Europe and America 1760–1800*. Vol. 1, *The Challenge*. Princeton: Princeton University Press, 1959.

> *This work lucidly sets forth the consolidation of aristocratic power against which both democrats and enlightened despots contended.*

Pares, Richard. *War and Trade in the West Indies, 1739–1763*. London: F. Cass, 1963.
*The standard account of the subject.*

Petrie, C. A. *Diplomatic History, 1713–1933*. London: Hollis and Carter, 1946.
*A manual of diplomatic events that sketches the balance of power in the eighteenth century.*

*Plumb, J. H. *England in the Eighteenth Century*. Baltimore: Penguin Books, 1950.
*A social, cultural, and technological summary by the leading biographer of Robert Walpole and the elder Pitt.*

Priestley, Herbert I. *France Overseas through the Old Regime: A Study of European Expansion*. New York: Appleton-Century-Crofts, 1939.
*A survey from the beginning of the French empire through Napoleon.*

Reddaway, W. H. et al., eds. *The Cambridge History of Poland*. Vol. 2. Cambridge: Cambridge University Press, 1941.
*The major large-scale study of Poland in the English language, edited by a major contributor to the history of the eighteenth century.*

Ritter, Gerhard. *Frederick the Great: A Historical Profile*. Berkeley: University of California Press, 1968.
*An edited English translation of a classic German study of Frederick's reign that sought to justify his power politics.*

*Roberts, Penfield. *The Quest for Security, 1715–1740*. New York: Harper & Brothers, 1947.
*A basic study of the oligarchical politics of stability in the Rise of Modern Europe series.*

Thomson, Gladys Scott. *Catherine the Great and the Expansion of Russia*. London: The Universities Press, 1959.
*A short, readable, and scholarly treatment of Russia under an "enlightened despot" in the Teach Yourself History series.*

Williams, Basil. *The Whig Supremacy, 1714–1760*. London: Oxford University Press, 1936.
*A competent survey in the Oxford History of England series.*

Wilson, A. M. *French Foreign Policy during the Administration of Cardinal Fleury, 1726–1743*. Cambridge, Mass.: Harvard University Press, 1936.
*A monographic study, one of the few modern scholarly histories of the reign of Louis XV.*

See also the works by Boxer, Holborn, and Rosenberg listed at the end of chapter 1 and the great work on mercantilism by Elie Heckscher cited at the end of volume 1, chapter 14.

Asterisk (*) denotes paperback.

# CHAPTER VII

# A Generation of Revolution: 1787–1815

On the heels of the American Revolution a wave of political and social upheavals swept through Western societies. In France the most populous and powerful state on the Continent,* the balance between the social classes was disrupted, the old political order shattered, and the king himself executed in a rapid and often violent series of events between 1787 and 1792. In Sweden and in the Dutch Republic rulers who had withstood the threats of reforming minorities in the 1780s lost their places in the next decade when the revolutionary leadership of France exerted its influence. Gustavus III of Sweden fell, murdered by his own nobility in 1792, and the House of Orange was driven into exile from Holland in 1795. In Poland and Ireland—unstable neighbors of two staunchly antirevolutionary powers, Russia and England—large minorities welcomed the course of revolution and openly sought French military aid to achieve it. In German-speaking and Italian-speaking lands, lawyers, teachers, and other intellectuals banded together to discuss and plan the revolutionary pattern. Not even England, where the monarchy was more secure and political institutions more venerated than in most countries, escaped a wave of radical protests against the old order.

No single pattern of events, no short list of causes, no simple division into forces of revolution and forces of counterrevolution encompasses these European upheavals in the generation after the achievement of American independence. The influence of the American victory itself is difficult to assess. Polish patriots and liberal French noblemen returned from the New World inspired to secure written constitutions and the guarantee of certain inalienable rights in the Old, but other Europeans expressed their discontent in phrases that were native to the Continent. By the time the American Constitution, ratified by conventions that represented popular sovereignty, went into effect in 1789, counterrevolutionaries aided by major foreign powers had snuffed out revolts in

* In 1787 approximately one of every seven Europeans was French.

Geneva, Liège, and the Dutch Republic. In the long run the American experience could not simply be transferred to Europe, because the social composition and the political power of the factions differed greatly on opposite sides of the Atlantic.

We saw in chapter 6 that the second half of the eighteenth century was characterized by a three-way division of contending forces. Kings and ministers, in the best tradition of enlightened despotism, sought to preserve their deteriorating positions by reform programs. Broader in base, often more conservative, and relying on historic claims to an exalted place in the constitution were the aristocratic groups. These "constituted bodies" sought not only to dominate reform movements but also to protect their privileges against despot and democrat alike. They included the two houses of the British Parliament (which were essentially alike in representing the great landowners' interests), the leading members of the French sovereign courts, or *parlements,* and the patrician "Estates" party of Belgium, which drove out the Austrians and declared a United States of Belgium in 1789. The third part was composed of democrats in the political sense only—men usually of relatively high social standing (lawyers, bureaucrats, journalists, teachers, businessmen) who sought to broaden existing political institutions. Although these "democrats" were not all middle-class,

they usually came from the elite of the Third Estate, which was below the ranks of clergy and nobility. In France and elsewhere they suffered from inexperience in politics but enjoyed high expectations of participation. Dutch Patriots, Belgian revolutionary democrats (called "Vonckists" after the name of their leader who proposed to expand representation to the estates of Brabant), and Genevan "representatives" all aimed at popularizing their constitutions; in city-state of Geneva the struggle of 1768–82 was waged between aristocrats and democrats, with no monarchical element present.

From the vantage point of 1815 it is difficult to assess the exact roles of the three great factions. The subjugation of the most expansionist and revolutionary power (France) by a congress of states dedicated to Christian, legitimate monarchy (Austria, Prussia, Russia, and England) would seem to indicate that counterrevolution had triumphed. Yet within each nation the revolutionary virus had left an infection. Below the level of courts and ministers, institutions had changed, especially the bureaucracies and the military establishments. The map of Europe, particularly of Germany, had been redrawn. A new spirit of national self-determination and pride in lingual and cultural achievement had arisen to shatter the easy cosmopolitanism of the eighteenth century.

## A. Deepening Revolution in France: From Monarchy to Republic

### ABSOLUTISM OVERTURNED

#### France on the Brink of Revolution

Despite its ideology of "one king, one faith, one law," divine-right monarchy had failed to unite Frenchmen politically, religiously, or economically. France's society was still divided into formal estates inherited from the Middle Ages; its institutions were the product of time, not of the human reason that the *philosophes* and enlightened despots had tried to implement.

Territorially the kingdom was composed of historic provinces, which, in the heyday of absolutism, had been subordinated to 34 intendancies, or generalities. Superintending justice, tax collection, and economic activities, the *intendants* had crowded out noble governors of the provinces, making them figureheads. But the provinces that retained their own assemblies of estates—located largely on the frontiers—preserved their local privileges and deprived the intendants of most of their powers. In the later days of the Old Regime the intendants had become largely nobles, to whom the central government ceased to give direction; thus conflicts of authority and jurisdiction were rampant. Absolutism in the sense of centralized authority had become an illusion, for France had gone far in the direction of an administrative feudalism that operated for the profit of the great office holders, particularly the great families attached to the court. Although administrative authority was arbitrary, it did not have the power to overturn the fundamental law of the kingdom, which guaranteed the legal confusion that undermined effective administration.

The same type of conflicting authority and jurisdiction was true of the administration of justice: the court system was a hodge-podge of overlapping jurisdictions filled by judges who had bought or inherited their offices, and at the appellate level there were 13 parlements staffed by an office-owning judicial aristocracy. Standards of justice differed in different parts of France, and geographical jurisdictions were not defined. In general, Roman law prevailed south of the Loire, but north of that river some 300 different customary codes of law were followed. Nominally, all justice flowed from the king, but it was confused, uncertain, slow, and expensive. When the king intervened, it was often for the sake of privilege and at the expense of justice. Moreover the parlements, headed by the Parlement of Paris, claimed the right to pass upon the constitutionality of royal legislation and administrative actions, using their vast powers to protect vested interests and privileges, which meant the preservation of inequality, inefficiency, and confusion, which in turn led to endless litigation. Generally, the boundaries of administration, justice, and financial districts overlapped chaotically.* Commerce was impeded by varying local standards of weights and measures and by tariffs levied on goods going from province to province and from country to town. In addition, the Church, which attended to many civil functions, had its own administrative districts and its own courts.

Socially France was rent into hostile interest groups each with its own privileges. At the top were a few hundred great families of nobles and wealthy parvenus clustered about the court, where they filled the ministerial posts and drew profits from both commerce and agriculture. This power elite was superimposed on the traditional pattern of privilege that made both the clergy (the First Estate) and the nobility (the Second Estate) states within the state. The clergy, however, was divided between the noblemen, who held almost all the highest and remunerative posts, and the lesser clergy recruited from the ranks of commoners. This schism reflected the success of the resurgent aristocracy at the end of the Old Regime in laying claim to the highest offices in both the Church and the state. In addition to monopolizing the prelacies, the nobility filled almost all the councils of the state, and in 1781 it secured a law barring commoners from securing commissions in the army without passing through the ranks. By waivers and falsified genealogies wealthy commoners could still attain nobility, but dowries demanded of commoners for

* See map, p. 375.

noble wives rose to astronomical heights. Jealously divided among court nobles, nobles of the robe (such as the judges of the parlements), provincial nobles, and decayed families with little save their pretensions to rank, the Second Estate stood together in defending its privileges. Economically many of the nobles had much in common with the upper bourgeoisie, investing in commerce, industry, and mining; on the other hand, wealthy burghers bought up manors, legal jurisdictions, tolls, and privileged offices. Indeed, the bourgeoisie was often more successful in escaping taxation of its wealth than was the nobility, whose land was taxed after 1749. Yet, despite their affinities and mutual privileges, there was a social rift that was growing, a gulf defined by birth that excluded the bourgeoisie from the nobles' honorific privileges, and it caused resentment among the bourgeoisie, whose ranks swelled during the commercial expansion of the eighteenth century.

Together, the two most highly privileged orders—the clergy and the nobility—comprised little more than 2 percent of the population. The rest were commoners belonging to the Third Estate, and of these a small minority lived in the towns. As a whole, the Third Estate was a disparate group, with privilege and wealth defining its hierarchy. At the top were financiers, tax farmers, officeholders, merchants, guildmasters, and professionals, many of whom had vested interests and some privilege under the status quo. Most townsmen, however, were small shopkeepers, guild employees, and wage earners hard pressed by taxation and by prices that spiraled far beyond wages in the last decades of the Old Regime. Since France was predominantly rural, the overwhelming majority of the Third Estate— more than 20 million—were peasants. The peasantry encompassed a hierarchy of its own, ranging from semi-free serfs, through hired laborers and sharecroppers, to those who were both sharecroppers and owners of small scattered plots. Although serfdom still existed here and there, most of the rural population had escaped formal bondage; indeed, many were landowners or at least had transferable rights to the lands that they worked in the village tracts. Nevertheless most of the proprietors' holdings were too small to support them and their families, and they were still subject both to paying transfer fees on their property to the manor lord and to the use of the lord's monopolies such as baking ovens and wine presses. Furthermore their landhunger was intensified by a rapid growth of the population after about 1750. Because other classes had privileged exemptions, most of the government's tax burden fell on the peasants. During the eighteenth century they were still paying for the glory of Louis XIV through taxes that went to pay off the debts that his wars had incurred. The tithes of the Church also fell upon the peasants. Most grievous of all to the peasants' sense of independence, however, were their obligations to the lords of the manors (nobles, clergy, or bourgeoisie), who were in charge of their communal villages. During the latter part of the eighteenth century the lords exploited these obligations to increase their incomes. Old obligations that had lapsed were revived, and current ones were rigidly enforced. Poisoning the relationship of lords and tenants, this "feudal reaction" was a major source of discontent for a peasantry that was rarely far from hunger's door.

These conditions of governmental inefficiency and social tensions form the backdrop of the French Revolution at its outset, but similar conditions elsewhere failed to provoke a similar revolution. Consequently historians have argued about the general causes of the upheaval in France ever since it took place. Certainly the criticism of the philosophes, who rejected revolutionary solutions unanimously, contributed to the feeling among

*Cartoon of a French peasant holding up the privileged orders.*

the educated that the status quo was immoral or at least against the laws of nature, thereby helping to create a revolutionary situation. Churchmen in exile were among the first to blame the subversive ideas of political philosophers such as Rousseau and critics of the Church such as Voltaire for the seduction of an entire population. The evil genius of the Enlightenment still lurks in the writings of many conservative Frenchmen today. For such critics the concept of a fanatical minority seizing power while right-thinking men acted too slowly looms large, but it has been entertained not only by modern opponents of the Revolution—the "Right"—but also by those on the "Left" as well. Since 1917 socialist critics accepted this thesis that a few leaders, the precursors of Lenin, attempted to seize power on behalf of the masses. But in fact, it was members of the ruling classes—discontented educated classes—who first raised the standard of revolt.

The current generation of less doctrinaire scholars, primarily university scholars on both sides of the Atlantic, have held that the deteriorating economic and social conditions in France from about 1770 were responsible for the popular unrest that produced a revolutionary situation. In the 1930s, beginning with the work of such influential professors as Ernest Labrousse and Georges Lefebvre in Paris, historians have come to recognize the picture of a nation in an era of erratic harvests and poor communications that was overpopulated for its food supply and subject to inflated prices. A revolution in agricultural productivity comparable to that in contemporary Britain did not occur, for it was precluded by the system of communal agriculture, which the courts and administration upheld as a matter of peasant privilege. After 1786 a full scale depression set in, and by the winter of 1788–89, following a disastrously poor harvest, the landless peasantry was fleeing unemployment in the countryside to join the relief projects of the city, while working-class families in Paris were spending almost nine-tenths of their budget on bread. The wealthier classes also suffered after 1786. Businessmen in such cities as Bordeaux and Marseilles, lacking a central bank and other institutions of credit, and yielding control of government funds to court speculators, found their customers at home impoverished and their markets overseas—especially in the West Indies— overcrowded with competition. Textile manufacturers in Rouen and Lille watched their sales dwindle and laid off many workers. Producers of wine and cereal grains faced a long-term decline in prices after about 1770, yet the poor harvest years of the late 1780s so reduced their crops that few buyers could afford them. There were few Frenchmen without serious economic grievances by 1787. If the country bailiff or the city notary was doing a good business, many more rural and urban people had begun to live an existence bordering on starvation. And the state, deprived of revenues by the depression and near bankruptcy due to the expenses of the War of the American Revolution, found its financial position utterly untenable.

Poverty does not account for the actual succession of events after 1787, however. If economic conditions alone had given rise to action, then Spain, East Prussia, or Russia might have laid claim to the great revolution of the century. Nevertheless it was a potent factor, for in France the overt break with the past occurred when Louis XVI and his finance minister, Calonne, tried to forestall government bankruptcy with a thorough set of reforms. The fiscal crisis provided the opportunity for factions of the nobility and the Third Estate to force their own versions of reform on the nation. The threefold revolutionary pattern, partially realized in the 13 American colonies, in Geneva, and in the Low Countries, appeared in full dress in France. But it was the aristocracy, or at least an aggressive part of it, that took the initiative in exploiting the Crown's fiscal embarrassment in order to bring Louis XVI's absolutism to its knees.

## The Revolt of the Nobility

As 1786 came to a close Louis XVI and his ministers realized that they could no longer ignore the growing state deficit. Calonne, the controller general, announced that the total deficit was well over 100 million livres (French pounds)— almost one-fourth of the yearly revenue. The old tax structure, which put the burden so heavily on peasant income and on consumer goods, would stand no further increase in a time of depression, and the interest on short-term loans already accounted for almost one-half of the royal treasury's payments. Calonne proposed large reductions in the operation of the royal household, abolition of many internal taxes, free trade in grain, the extension of a stamp tax, and a single income tax based on the yield of the land in each harvest. Provincial assemblies were to administer the new tax. Such a program would have reduced royal debts, provided steady income, and alleviated the discontent of the rural masses. The program was in the best tradition of enlightened despotism, recalling the brief career of Turgot as reforming minister (1774–76).*

A serious question of tactics now presented itself. Would the privileged bodies of the land, especially the bishops of the Catholic church and the nobility of the 13 parlements, acquiesce in such sweeping changes? The clergy, rich in land and income from feudal dues, paid no individual taxes but granted a "free gift" to the Crown every fifth year. Noblemen were exempt from the *taille,* a direct land tax, as were the clergy, the bourgeoisie, and others who had bought exemptions. To summon the Estates General of delegates from the clergy, nobility, and commoners seemed risky, even though the last Estates had met in 1614. The nobility still insisted on a quasi-constitutional right to approve taxation when meeting in such an assembly; and a royal edict proclaiming needed reforms would likely be blocked by the Parlement of Paris. Consequently Louis XVI decided to summon a special advisory group, the *Assembly of Notables,* to convince them of the necessity for reform. A few were liberal noblemen, such as the young Marquis de Lafayette who had recently returned home from the American wars. But one-fourth of the 144 members were magistrates of the parlements, and the majority of the others—including the king's two brothers—were suspicious of reform. Calonne himself became the first victim of these suspicions when he announced that Necker, the supposed financial genius of the late 1770s, had lied in his published accounts of 1781.† Calonne foolishly lost the support even of Lafayette and his "patriots" when he addressed the Parisian populace on the evils of privilege. For his rashness he was replaced in May 1787 by Brienne, arch-bishop of Toulouse, who was an advocate of clerical reform but who was more trusted at court than Calonne.

Nevertheless the Notables were sufficiently impressed with the seriousness of the financial crisis to accept equal taxation in principle—but not Calonne's specific tax proposals—and the king for his part showed his good will by cutting the army pension list and reducing the queen's expenses. Both king and ministers accepted the principle that taxes should be raised only to satisfy actual needs, which led one critic to remark that the king of France had become the king of England, who was obliged to assemble his people yearly to approve taxes. The granting of civil status to Protestants (legalizing marriage and inheritance, legitimizing birth), which became law in November 1787, was another edict that originated in this period. Less popular and more a product of zealous ministers was reform of the parlements, which restricted their jurisdiction in civil and criminal cases, enforced a minimum age for members, and ended the use of torture after conviction.

It was, in fact, the magistrates of the sovereign courts, not the nobility of Versailles or the country squires, who revolted against the royal reforms. Reflecting socially the merger of sword and robe families, the parlements were the epitome of an aristocratic body. Although a few of their members followed Lafayette in the hopes of a constitutional change along English lines, the large majority were more determined to protect their fiscal and political privileges than to accept a ministerial reform program, even a good one. Eloquent in their own defense, they were violently opposed to the Enlightenment (with the exception of Montesquieu) and to those ministers inclined toward enlightened despotism. Many of the parlement members were young, under 35. In theory their offices were for sale, but after midcentury they had

* See p. 353.
† See pp. 353–54.

increasingly excluded commoners from their ranks. Finally, they had already taken the lead in opposing royal absolutism, censuring it for its tyranny, a line of attack that proved quite popular with the people.

In the summer of 1787 the Parisian magistrates refused to register the new tax edicts and began to call for an Estates General as the only acceptable vehicle for reform. When the taxes were proclaimed despite their protests, they told the king that his program was against the national interest. By mid-August Louis XVI felt that he had no choice but to banish the Parlement from Paris; yet the monarch and his ministers had no real party of their own to support this measure for badly needed revenue. Late in September the government agreed to give up the idea of new taxes, and the Parlement of Paris, enjoying the enthusiastic support of most Parisians, was allowed to return. An Estates General was promised for some time in the next five years, but the ministers clung to the hope that an Estates would only solemnize the royal will.

The first victory of the Parlement only increased its intransigence. By January of 1788 the Parlement of Paris freely discussed aspects of royal power that were not included in the reforms, attempting to subvert the new provincial assemblies instituted by Calonne. Most dangerous of all for the monarchy was the fact that provincial parlements sympathized with their Parisian colleagues. In a minor coup d'état early in May 1788 the king and his chancellor struck at the offending bodies. The Parisian court system was replaced with a plenary court that was well laced with notables, and the provincial parlements were suspended. The Parisian magistrates, however, successfully defied the king in refusing to hand over their leaders. Meanwhile their popular supporters in Paris and Rennes (Brittany) threatened royal officials, while in Grenoble (Provence) four men died in street fighting. The disgrace of the ministerial solution was complete when Brienne was forced to admit, early in August, that the treasury was almost empty. The plenary court was abandoned and the parlements reinstated. The Estates General, which was feared by the ministers but hailed as a panacea by most factions of the nobility, was promised for May of 1789. Jacques Necker, the bourgeois Protestant financier, was recalled to replace Brienne. The nobles' revolt seemed to have taken command.

Yet the parlements saw their prize slip from their hands in the next six months. Although they offended liberals by proclaiming that the Estates General would be assembled and composed as in 1614, the judicial nobility really bowed before the aspirations of the Third Estate.

## The Emergence of the Third Estate

The Estates General as the historic form of a national representative body was only a fiction in terms of the French population in 1789. In past Estates General the clergy and the nobility, sitting separately as the First and Second Estate respectively, each cast one vote. Thus the representatives of this tiny privileged minority cast two votes, while all other Frenchmen, the commoners, cast but one vote through their representatives. By 1789 that single vote was to represent 25 million people. Although the ranks of the nobility and clergy included rich and poor alike, the variation of social classes within the Third Estate was staggering. It may be argued that the sharecropper accepted the judgment of his clerical or noble landlord, and that the wholesale merchant often sought to imitate the titled nobility. Yet bourgeois lawyers, journalists, and other professionals were highly critical of noble privilege and of the venality of the 130 bishops, all of whom were noblemen in 1789. Many businessmen and independent farmers were ambitious for a role in the reform movements in their own localities and within their own Estate. Criticism of privilege was at heart a moral position, however. The most outspoken detractor of the Versailles nobility was the liberal nobleman the Comte (Count) de Mirabeau. The pamphleteer who made his mark attacking noble and clerical privileges and arguing that the Third Estate demanded a place in politics commensurate with its talents was the Abbé Sieyès, a highly placed church administrator. Although one was a noble, the other a cleric, they were both elected to sit with the Third Estate in 1789.

In the autumn of 1788 Parisian and provincial lawyers attacked the pretensions of the parlements and urged the "doubling of the Third" so that the number of commoners' delegates would equal those of the first two orders together. This "doubling of the Third" would have little practical effect if the three estates continued to sit separately and each cast a single vote, but this demand for enlarging the commoners' delegation was often tied with proposals for voting individually by head rather than by estate. Press censorship was suspended to allow the nation to advise the king how to convoke the Estates General. Political pamphleteers swamped the government with hundreds of advisory tracts, but one came to stand out above all others as the "Catechism for the Commons": *What is the Third Estate?* by Abbé Sieyès. Commoners were everything in France, it argued, but in the past they had counted for nothing. In language reflecting Rousseau's *Social Contract* Sieyès demanded that the Third Estate, expressing the general will, meet as a national assembly to draw up a constitution for France. A flood of petitions from the cities convinced Louis XVI to accept the principle of double representation; in so doing he followed the advice of his subjects at large, not that of his aristocratic notables. But he and Necker refused to

The first page of What is the Third Estate?

answer the more difficult question whether the Estates should vote by order or by head, with one vote for each delegate.

Elections to the Estates took place in the spring of 1789. Although a nearly universal male suffrage existed within the Third Estate, a complicated series of electoral assemblies within the old administrative districts unbalanced the representation in favor of urban interests. Each electoral assembly, even at the lowest levels of guild and country parish, drafted a "notebook of grievances." There was broad agreement among the orders on the need to guarantee civil rights and impose fiscal equality. However, the nobility, which elected only a small minority of liberals among its 270 delegates, demanded a return to archaic social practices and the protection of seigneurial (manor lords') rights. The clergy was more clearly divided, because the parish priests outnumbered the bishops five to one. The notebooks of grievances produced by the Third Estate's assemblies, in which the humbler citizens had little influence, displayed great variety in their discussion of local economic conditions. The commoners occasionally used phrases borrowed from the philosophes, went further in their demands for civil liberties and constitutional government, and demanded the surrender of ancient privileges conveyed by birth. Two-thirds of the 648 deputies to the Third Estate were lawyers or former royal bureaucrats. Only one in seven was a businessman, and one in ten was a country-dweller. No more than one was a peasant.

When the Estates General met at Versailles on May 5, 1789, the deputies were given little indication that they were to participate in decision. No reform program was offered to them. The commons found themselves treated as inferiors, left to deliberate as a separate assembly without assurance that they might later vote by head. Then for five weeks they urged members of the nobility and clergy to join them in one great assembly. Although only the delegates from Dauphiny had had any experience in the fusion of the three orders, the commoners' determination soon split the clergy, some of whom crossed over to join the Third Estate on June 15. Two days later this already mixed group assumed the title of the *National Assembly,* representing the nation as a whole. If the king were to dissolve their new Assembly, the deputies declared, no taxes would be valid. With this step the constitutional history of France took a new and profound turn. On June 20 the Assembly, finding itself locked out of its hall, retired to the royal tennis court where it took a solemn oath not to disperse until a constitution of the realm should be on a firm foundation. The first great symbolic act of the Revolution was thus consumated; it is immortalized on David's canvas.*

Faced with the commoners' revolt, Louis XVI listened to his courtiers' advice. Three days after the Tennis Court Oath he assembled the orders and informed the National Assembly that its resolutions were void. He offered penal and fiscal reform, and he offered to raise no loans or taxes without consent. He made it clear, however, that the first two orders alone would discuss their special privileges and immunities. The king did not realize that it was too late to settle the crisis on his own terms; the Third Estate claimed parliamentary immunity and refused to leave the hall. On the next day the majority of the clergy defected, and on the following day almost 50 noblemen walked out on their order. On June 27 Louis reluctantly ordered the remnants of the orders to merge with the National Assembly. An English traveler who knew France well was moved to write in his diary that "the whole business now seems over, and the revolution complete."[1]

## Completion of the Bourgeois Revolt

The revolution of the politically aware Third Estate was far from complete. The court party began at once to move troops (including Swiss and German regiments) into the vicinity of Paris, probably not so much to occupy the city as to prepare to dissolve the Assembly. Meanwhile within

* Jacques Louis David (1748–1826) was the most famous artist of the Revolution. His dominance of the arts signified a turn to classicism that characterized the art of the Revolution.
[1] Arthur Young, *Travels in France and Italy During the Years 1787, 1788 and 1789* (New York: E. P. Dutton & Co., 1915), p. 147.

The Oath of the Tennis Court (*by Jacques Louis David*).

the city itself the electors of the Third Estate remained sitting as an informal new government for Paris, while more daring journalists sought to win over the French Guards from the court. Finally, the city lay in readiness for a typical eighteenth-century urban riot; food prices soared, and the lives of grain merchants and bakers were endangered.

The crisis broke on July 11. At Versailles Necker was dismissed; in Paris customs posts were systematically demolished and documents burned. On July 12 the insurrection became more general when groups of marchers forced the royal garrison to withdraw from Paris. The electors quietly took over the city hall in an attempt to curb the popular agitation, but by the night of July 12–13 crowds were looting houses in a search for weapons. The electors tried unsuccessfully to control the ferment by announcing the formation of a National Guard, a militia for the respectable bourgeoisie. On the morning of July 14 the shortage of arms and gunpowder led the crowds first to an arsenal, where they removed 30,000 muskets, and then across the city to the Bastille. The old fortress for state prisoners was said to be another arms depot, and its guns commanded the neighboring suburbs. There in the east end of Paris the first bloody act of the Revolution was played out. The governor made concessions to the crowd, but he ordered his men to fire to prevent it from gaining forcible entry to the fortress. Ninety-eight of the civilian attackers—laborers and master craftsmen for the most

*The creation of a revolutionary symbol: the fall of the Bastille, July 14, 1789.*

part—died at the Bastille. Seven of the defenders were murdered after the governor capitulated; his head and the mayor's were paraded through the city on pikes.

The Bastille became "the shot heard 'round the world" of 1789, and the National Assembly was saved. Louis XVI even journeyed to Paris to recognize the electors as a municipal council, Lafayette as commander of the National Guard, and the tricolor as the symbol of the new regime in Paris. Necker was recalled, and

many court extremists, including the two royal brothers, fled the country. If the National Assembly had not been involved in the fighting it nonetheless shared power with the lower elements of the Third Estate who had saved it from being suppressed by Louis XVI's troops.

In much of France political power in the cities changed hands in the summer of 1789. The provincial bourgeoisie responded first to Necker's dismissal and then to the Bastille. Although the timing of these urban revolts varied, in most cases a civilian National Guard effectively held the military balance while a political elite of merchants and lawyers took control. In a few cities the old corporation merely expanded its ranks. Other cities, including Bordeaux, replaced their old governments with the electors of the Third Estate, as Paris had done. Many cities, Dijon and Rouen among them, installed men new to politics. The primary effect of these changes was to drive out royal officials and weaken the king's authority.

In the countryside agitation was far less organized. Rural riot was endemic to France after 1775; beginning with the fall of 1788 there had been sporadic violence and protest against game laws, royal taxes, and feudal (manorial) dues. After the Bastille fell waves of rumor affected much of the country: the peasantry envisaged imaginary oppressors—brigands, Poles and Spaniards, aristocrats. The exact relationship between this "Great Fear" and the economic condition of the peasantry is unclear. There is little doubt that the smaller leaseholders, sharecroppers, and wage earners in the countryside were severely affected by obsolete methods of agriculture, overpopulation, and taxes. But instead manorial records and houses were the principal targets of peasant action in 1789. Perhaps the peasants believed that they were carrying out the king's reform program in attacking the seigneurial privileges of the nobility. At any rate, the Great Fear was the signal for a magnanimous gesture by the liberal aristocracy and the clergy.

Lacking the power to suppress the peasant uprising, the Assembly was obliged to consider peasant grievances. In an emotional session on the night of August 4, 1789 the liberals led the Assembly in renouncing personal services, hunting rights, seigneurial justice, venality of office, and plural benefices. Tithes were also abolished. The National Assembly declared that it had destroyed the entire "feudal system," and its resolutions put an end to the principle of aristocratic privilege in France. What the nobility and clergy would not give up in May they surrendered in August in response to the peasant uprising.*

Later in August the Assembly turned to more positive principles in what amounted to a preamble to the forthcoming constitution. On August 26, 1789 the Assembly proclaimed the Declaration of the Rights of Man and Citizen. Basically a document of the Third Estate, the Declaration made private property "a sacred and inviolable right" along with freedom of conscience, freedom of press, and freedom of the citizen from arbitrary arrest. Equality in the Declaration meant equality before the law and in eligibility for office. But economic equality and state obligation to the poor were not mentioned; and, although citizens were invited to take part in lawmaking, no specific rights of suffrage were granted. The Declaration was expressed in good eighteenth-century universals: law was held to be "the expression of the general will," and there were marked similarities to the American declaration of 1776. For those who idealize history, the French Declaration reads as strong philosophy. For its authors, it prepared a nation for the constitutional changes to come.

No discussion of a constitution could be fruitful, however, until the king's powers were more carefully defined; but he refused his assent to the August decrees and to the Declaration of Rights. Moreover a

* In the committee that framed the laws to implement these resolutions many seigneurial and service obligations were abolished without compensation, but others, especially fiscal obligations, required indemnity payments by the peasants. Most peasants, however, resisted paying this compensation until the revolutionary government of 1793 abandoned the attempt to salvage manorial rights as indemnifiable property of their owners. Thus, by resisting the National Assembly the peasantry increased its vested interest in the preservation of its own autonomous revolution.

*Lafayette as Commander of the National Guard.*

faction within the Assembly that embraced both commoners and nobility wanted an "English" constitution, with an upper chamber and a royal absolute veto. This first clear division of political attitudes had its effect on Paris, where there was talk of marching on Versailles. The more radical group in the Assembly won its point in mid-September when the king received only a suspensive veto, the power to veto legislation only temporarily. The king, still convinced that he was the first defender of privilege, showed his disapproval by allowing Versailles to become a hotbed of emotional demonstration for the monarchy.

Paris had soon had enough of insults to the tricolor, the symbol of its revolutionary movement. On October 5, 1789 a group of women from the central markets set off in the rain to Versailles to demand bread from "the baker"; then Lafayette's National Guard took the road following them to Versailles. Historians will probably never know just how spontaneous the expedition was. It had been preached in the radical press for weeks, but it is difficult to identify its leaders or its connections to the Assembly. The king made haste to sign the decrees and the Declaration, but the crowd was not satisfied. Early in the morning of October 6 the royal quarters were invaded and some of the bodyguard murdered. Louis XVI had no choice but to accompany the marchers back to Paris. Ten days later the National Assembly joined the royal family there.

The last of the great days of 1789 ended all hope of a compromise between the royal party and the more determined reformers. The king and queen henceforth felt themselves prisoners, as they secretly wrote to their friends abroad. The "English" faction was driven from the Assembly. As it set forth to give France a constitution worthy of a revolution, the middle class found itself indebted to the masses for victory over the aristocracy and the court, and this uneasy alliance was to characterize the next six years of the Revolution.

## THE CONSTITUTIONAL MONARCHY: 1789–1792

### The National Assembly

The National Assembly took two years to produce a constitution as well as a series of laws that were among the most constructive of the decade. Although the Assembly was in fact a permanent constitutional convention, the planning of the new regime was not confined to the narrow hall near the royal palace where the "Constituent" sat. Editors and polemicists came into their own as political journals flourished, and the range of opinion covered the aristocratic (the Swiss Mallet du Pan's *Mercure de France*), the patriotic (Brissot's *Patriote Français*), and the democratic (Marat's *L'Amie du Peuple*). Political clubs, which had sprung up in the cafes of Versailles, now dotted the neighborhood of the Assembly.

Often taking their names from the vacated monasteries and convents in which they met, the clubs reviewed the agenda of the Assembly and sought favorable legislation through petitions. The Club de Cordeliers, frequented by radical journalists and politicians such as Jacques Hébert and Georges Danton, had low dues and even accepted a few artisans as members. The Cordeliers challenged the Parisian government and adopted as the club's symbol the single eye of vigilance. The most famous organization of its kind was the Society of the Friends of the Constitution, or Jacobin Club. At Versailles the group had paid high dues and included Sieyès and Mirabeau. By 1791 the Jacobins of Paris had more nominal dues, an upper middle-class membership, and about 400 provincial affiliates. The deputies from Paris dominated debates, although few were as outspoken in support of civil liberties as a young provincial lawyer turned Parisian journalist, Maximilien Robespierre. As the Jacobins committed themselves to increasingly radical causes —republicanism, for example—their more conservatives followers seceded to form other clubs such as the Feuillants who were dedicated to constitutional monarchy and whose membership included Lafayette and Sieyès.

Although more than 200 clergy and 50 nobles sat in the National Assembly—a body of more than 1000 deputies—the electoral arrangements made for the future Legislative Assembly were, to judge by first appearances, quite liberal. Citizens were divided into "actives" and "passives." The vote in primary assemblies was reserved for active citizens—males of 25 years or more who were domiciled for a year and paid a direct tax equivalent to three days' wages. This primary electorate of about four and a quarter million (two-thirds of the adult males) was by far the largest in Europe, but final election of deputies was reserved for electors, one to

*Meeting of the Jacobin Club.*

be selected for every 100 active citizens, and they were required to be men of greater means. Actual political participation, however, was restricted further in practice by such factors as the lack of local polling places—which compelled voters to travel to regional polls—and the necessity of leisure for political service. Thus national officeholding tended to be confined to a small moneyed class.

In economic policy the Assembly's bourgeois character was evident. Although service dues were abolished gratis, the peasant was obliged to pay an indemnity in order to extinguish certain rights of the manorial lords to their property, and their redemption price was high—at least 20 times the annual cash payment. As was noted above, a majority of the peasants affected simply refused to pay any compensation. The establishment

of unitary metric weights and measures and the abolition of internal customs and monopolistic trading companies suited private commerce. Guilds and workingmen's associations were abolished also, opening up all crafts, professions, and trades to those who could learn them. The prohibition of all forms of association by employers and employees in June 1791 (the Chapelier Law) was designed to prevent political agitation, but such zealous liberalism pleased manufacturers more than workingmen. Piece by piece the Assembly was dismantling the restrictive status groups of the Old Regime which had restrained the economy by rewarding privilege rather than talent or wealth; their end was most clearly signaled by the abolition of titles and hereditary nobility.

In line with the Enlightenment's quest for orderly natural law and its evaluation

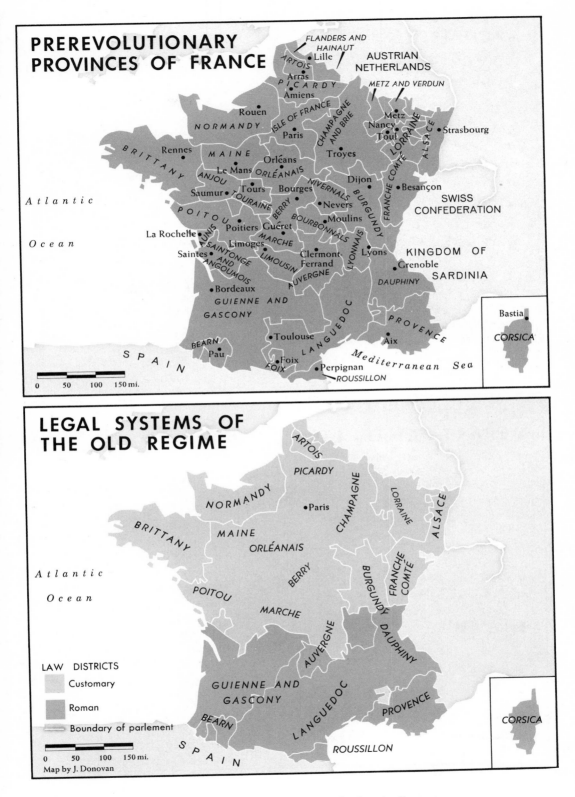

# PREREVOLUTIONARY PROVINCES OF FRANCE

FLANDERS AND HAINAUT

ARTOIS

• Lille

AUSTRIAN NETHERLANDS

• Arras

PICARDY

METZ AND VERDUN

• Amiens

• Rouen

NORMANDY

ISLE OF FRANCE

• Paris

CHAMPAGNE AND BRIE

• Metz

• Nancy

• Toul

LORRAINE

ALSACE

• Strasbourg

*Atlantic*

BRITTANY

• Rennes

MAINE

Orléans

• Le Mans

ANJOU

ORLÉANAIS

• Troyes

• Dijon

NIVERNAIS

BURGUNDY

FRANCHE COMTÉ

• Besançon

SWISS CONFEDERATION

• Saumur

TOURAINE

• Tours

• Bourges

BERRY

• Nevers

BOURBONNAIS

• Moulins

*Ocean*

POITOU

AUNIS

• La Rochelle

• Poitiers

• Guéret

MARCHE

SAINTONGE

• Limoges

LIMOUSIN

LYONNAIS

Clermont-Ferrand

• Lyons

KINGDOM OF

• Saintes

AND ANGOUMOIS

AUVERGNE

• Grenoble

SARDINIA

DAUPHINY

• Bordeaux

GUIENNE AND GASCONY

LANGUEDOC

PROVENCE

BEARN

• Toulouse

• Aix

• Pau

*Mediterranean Sea*

S P A I N

• Foix

FOIX

• Perpignan

ROUSSILLON

Bastia •

CORSICA

0   50   100   150 mi.

# LEGAL SYSTEMS OF THE OLD REGIME

ARTOIS

PICARDY

NORMANDY

• Paris

CHAMPAGNE

LORRAINE

ALSACE

BRITTANY

MAINE

ORLÉANAIS

*Atlantic*

BERRY

BURGUNDY

FRANCHE COMTÉ

*Ocean*

POITOU

MARCHE

DAUPHINY

AUVERGNE

LAW DISTRICTS

Customary

Roman

Boundary of parlement

GUIENNE AND GASCONY

LANGUEDOC

PROVENCE

CORSICA

BEARN

S P A I N

ROUSSILLON

0   50   100   150 mi.

Map by J. Donovan

375        A. Deepening Revolution in France

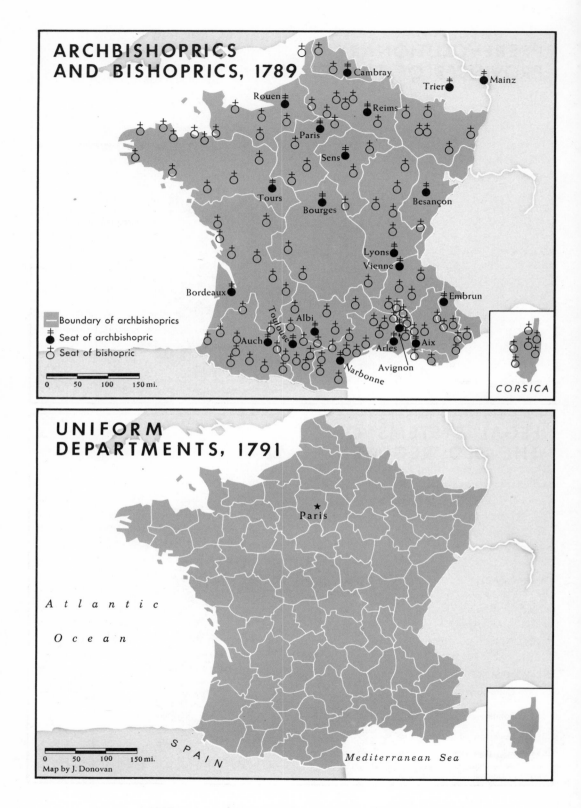

# ARCHBISHOPRICS AND BISHOPRICS, 1789

Cambray

Trier

Mainz

Rouen

Reims

Paris

Sens

Tours

Bourges

Besançon

Lyons

Vienne

Bordeaux

Embrun

Toulouse

Albi

Auch

Arles

Aix

Narbonne

Avignon

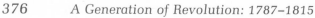

Boundary of archbishoprics

Seat of archbishopric

Seat of bishopric

0   50   100   150 mi.

*CORSICA*

# UNIFORM DEPARTMENTS, 1791

Paris

*Atlantic*

*Ocean*

*SPAIN*

*Mediterranean Sea*

0   50   100   150 mi.

Map by J. Donovan

of institutions by utility rather than their mere historical survival, the National Assembly revealed its concern for rationality more than for class interests in redrawing the map of France. Eighty-three *départements* (administrative subdivisions), which were approximately equal in size and named after natural phenomena, replaced the unequal historic provinces. Each département was subdivided into districts, but the real foundation of local government lay in the communes, in which active citizens voted directly for councils. France became a federation in which village and town politics played an especially important part in training men for national life.

Following the suggestions of Montesquieu and the precedent of America, the Assembly separated the judiciary from the executive. Parlements and seigneurial courts disappeared and were replaced by tribunals at municipal and departmental levels. Magistrates were compensated for the loss of their offices.* Justice was free and equal, and judges and criminal juries were elected.

In two areas the problems facing the Assembly were more profound and the solutions more ephemeral. The replacement of the old fiscal system with a new land tax and income taxes had failed to produce the revenue to meet old debts and current expenditures. The left wing of the Third Estate and many reforming clergymen had singled out the lands of the Catholic church, estimated now at about ten percent of the country's surface, as a potential national resource as early as August 1789. With clerical members such as Talleyrand† leading the way, it was decided in December to sell some Crown and Church

property in order to obtain 400,000,000 livres. Anticipating the proceeds from such sales, the government issued interest-bearing *assignats,* or bonds, to holders of the long-term debt. This solution to the government's financial crisis so intrigued the government that by 1790 all Church holdings of rural and urban property were ready for the auction block. In practice, however, the first issue of assignats failed, forcing the Assembly to make them legal tender. Historians are still tracing the sales of Church property, but it seems evident that the bourgeoisie bought more lands and houses than the peasantry or former nobility. As for the assignat, it relieved a currency shortage in 1790 but by the end of the next year the money had lost one-third of its nominal value. Afterward it depreciated more rapidly.

## The Assembly and the Church

The most divisive issue facing the National Assembly proved to be religion, particularly the reorganization of the Catholic church. Losing its exclusive role when the Assembly granted freedom of worship to Protestants and Jews was one sign that the Church's prestige was waning. That the contemplative orders had lost their spiritual justification, that plural benefices were an abuse, and that the parish clergy's income was far too low were evils recognized by many prelates as well as laymen. The majority of the clergy even accepted the inevitable conclusion that they had to become salaried state servants once their land was gone. But lay and clerical members of the Assembly fell into fundamental conflict over ratification of the new Civil Constitution of the Clergy, which was approved by the king in August 1790.

Most laymen were able to accept the fact that the National Assembly was empowered to remake all institutions. How-

* As many of them worked for the restoration of the Old Regime, however, as accepted the compensation.

† Charles Maurice de Talleyrand-Périgord (1754–1838) went on to become the leading cleric to accept the Revolution and a perennial official in one regime after another until his death.

ever, without the approval of the papacy or of a national synod the clergy could not accept the redistribution of parishes and dioceses, the reallocation of income in favor of the lower clergy, the reduction of bishops from 130 to 83 to correspond with the départements, and popular election of bishops and parish priests. When, by November 1790, no such approval seemed possible, the National Assembly declared the Civil Constitution of the Clergy to be in force and required a loyalty oath to the nation from bishops and priests. The confrontation of spiritual and temporal authority was all the more tragic in a nation that was not noted for its religiosity. Only seven bishops took the loyalty oath, and in some parts of the country, especially in Brittany and in Alsace, as much as 90 percent of the priests would not join the new state church. Pope Pius VI condemned the arrangement in the spring of 1791. The newly elected constitutional clergy was regarded by the devout as blasphemous, and the "nonjurors," or refractory priests, were considered by the patriotic to be potential counterrevolutionaries. The refractory priests often led their congregations into deep hostility toward the new regime.

## Seeds of Counterrevolution

Other signs of danger had appeared by 1791. Across the border on the east there lived small groups of noblemen, including many army officers, who had emigrated from France and were bitterly hostile to the Revolution. The emigrés at Turin (Savoy) and Coblenz and Worms (west of the Rhine) were seeking foreign support and even beginning to form a counterrevolutionary army. Unemployment was returning to Paris in the spring of 1791. The Cordeliers Club and its affiliates were moving into open opposition against the restrictions on suffrage, which excluded about two million French male adults with insufficient property.

It was the treason of Louis XVI that broke the precarious balance. The king chose the night of June 20–21, 1791 to flee Paris and attempt to reach the emigré garrisons over the northeastern frontier. Marie Antoinette and her Swedish lover had planned the escape badly, however, and the royal family was detected at Varennes, close to the frontier, and brought ignominiously back to Paris. The king could no longer be seen as a weak monarch with good intentions. His repudiation of the regime very nearly produced his suspension, and the Cordeliers Club called for a republic. Agitation turned into tragedy in mid-July when the National Guard broke up a meeting of would-be republicans on the Champs de Mars, killing about 50 petitioners. Varennes had an international effect, too, because the rulers of Austria and Prussia joined in the Declaration of Pilnitz on August 27, 1791, threatening the restoration of the old order in France.

By this time the image of the Revolution abroad was already ambiguous. German poets and philosophers, such as Wieland, Kant, and Herder,* had hailed the fall of the Bastille. In England the young poet Wordsworth and the scientist Priestley thought that the first several months after the Estates General had been as glorious as 1688. In 1789 the liberal Polish nobility formed a sympathetic philosophical club, while many of the towns banded together to ask for burgher rights. Since the Polish gentry dominated the diet, however, there was ground for conflict between the entrenched aristocracy and the ambitious bourgeoisie. Yet in 1791 this conflict was avoided in the constitutional reforms that terminated the free veto of the great magnates and gave burghers access to nobility; and the towns were granted self-government. More than other Europeans the Poles needed the French example of

* For discussions of Kant and Herder see pp. 297–98 and 417–18.

sharing privileges in the name of individual liberties in order to survive aggressions by their expansionist neighbors.

Another strand of thought, however, was skeptical of the changes in France. By 1790, when the confiscation of Church property and the emigration were under way, these critics turned into enemies, the most famous of whom was the British statesman Edmund Burke. Formerly a champion of American independence and of Irish rights, Burke was unable to sanction events in France. He was genuinely fearful for the fate of the court and the clergy by the time he published his *Reflections on the Revolution in France,* in November 1790. Burke's opposition to change in France rested on grounds that have made him one of the pillars of European conservatism: the French experiment was dangerous, irreligious, and bound to fail because it proceeded from abstract principles, he argued. Politics is not a manipulation of contracts, but the indissoluble partnership of succeeding generations in eternal society. The "Rights of Man" were a blind substitution for the experience of the landed, ruling classes. Burke's *Reflections* opened a great debate on the French Revolution, for he was challenged in 1791 by the Anglo-American pamphleteer, Thomas Paine. There were soon self-styled counterrevolutionaries and revolutionaries in Europe. Although the latter were often of the urban middle classes, dissenters from religious orthodoxy, and democrats in political affairs, the debate was at heart ideological rather than social.

## The Legislative Assembly and the Constitution of 1791

In September 1791 the constitution was presented to the king for his assent, and elections to the new government took place. The unicameral Legislative Assembly, like its predecessor, over-represented urban areas, and its social composition was almost the same. Approximately two-thirds of the 745 deputies had some experience in local government or in the courts, but they were all new men on the national scene, since a self-denying ordinance had prevented reelection of members of the Constituent National Assembly. Men such as Robespierre and Danton had to confine their political ambitions to the clubs, which now took on new importance.

The political elite that was most in evidence was a loose coalition of provincial deputies, known to posterity as the Girondins (from the river of their native Bordeaux), although contemporaries often called them after their principal spokesman, the impulsive journalist Brissot. Their inspiration was the imaginative Madame Roland, who yearned to make of revolutionary France another, more virtuous Rome. Brissot and the other Girondins rapidly moved to secure strong measures against refractory clergy and emigrés, including death sentences for nobility who assembled against the nation. But it was as war hawks that the Girondins left their mark on revolutionary politics.

## The Girondins and the Outbreak of War

Brissot and his friends viewed the idea of a war against France's eastern neighbors, Prussia and Austria, as a crusade to spread revolution against wicked kings. They also sought to use the war issue to gain important posts in the ministry. Austrian and Prussian support for the emigrés abroad and the French queen at home, the sister of the emperor, added both moral fervor and a diplomatic case for war to the Girondin stance. Robespierre, at the Jacobin Club, feared that Marie Antoinette would turn an Austrian war into a trap. Brissot's followers carried the day, however, and on April 20, 1792

France declared war on Austria. In response Austria's ally, Prussia, declared war, and Catherine the Great of Russia promised to send troops.

Foreshadowing events to come, the war went badly for France from the start and led to political upheaval at home. The Prussian forces began a steady advance against a French army that had been weakened by the emigration of more than one-half of its officers; Parisians rioted over the high cost of provisions; and rumor grew that the Queen had formed an "Austrian Committee" to surrender the nation. The king tried to stem the rush of events by using his veto against a plan to bring 20,000 National Guards to Paris to celebrate the "Federation Day" on July 14, anniversary of the fall of the Bastille. When Louis XVI dismissed his Girondin ministers in June, an armed band of shopkeepers and artisans invaded the royal apartments and danced about the king as he donned a red liberty cap. Ignoring the royal veto, the Assembly summoned the National Guards to Paris in July. The Marseilles battalion arrived singing a battle hymn that had been written for a northern regiment, but was soon to become a stirring national anthem.

In Paris the National Guards found a militant atmosphere. The assignat had declined further; the distribution of grain was badly slowed, with shortages compounded by requisitions for war; and there was talk in Paris and elsewhere of price controls and the appropriation of large farms. Jacques Roux, a Parisian vicar, demanded the death penalty for hoarders. Poverty began to be equated with virtue, and vice became the inevitable trait of the wealthy. A ringing phrase that summed it up for many Parisians by the summer of 1792 was the negative appellation *sans-culotte*, that is, he who went without the knee-breeches of the upper class. Implying contrast with the high bourgeoisie as well as with the nobility, the term was first applied to those who intransigently

*Sans culotte Parisien.*

*A Parisian sans-culotte.*

demanded the deposition of Louis XVI after Varennes. A type of the sans-culotte was the artisan who had no classical education and who saw issues in black and white. Because of the distinction between active and passive citizens he was not represented politically, although he was often in attendance at the meetings of the Paris *sections,* or wards. The emergence of the sans-culottes marked the response of the disenfranchised lower classes to the rhetoric of the Girondins and Jacobins attacking the court and the Legislative Assembly respectively. They would provide the revolutionary force to carry the revolution deeper than their original spokesmen intended, particularly in the area of economic controls.

In the summer of 1792 the Girondins, who sought to preserve the constitutional monarchy, began to fear that cooperation between the citizens of the sections and the guardsmen might overpower their leadership. By the end of July these fears were realized: 47 of the 48 sections had come out for the abdication of the king. By signing and publishing a manifesto threatening to destroy Paris if Louis XVI or any member of the royal family was molested, the Prussian commander only strengthened the Parisians' will. On the night of August 9–10, 1792 deputies from the sections took over the city government while the Legislative Assembly stood by, paralyzed. Early the next morning the insurgents marched on the Tuileries (the royal palace), while the royal family fled to the Assembly. Bloodshed followed in hand-to-hand and artillery combat, in which the king's defenders, mostly Swiss guards, were defeated.

## The Revolution Revolutionized

The August insurrection turned the Parisian government into a revolutionary Commune, which proceeded to imprison many liberal noblemen and clergy as suspects and to assume direction of the war. The Legislative Assembly was shattered when more than half of its members fled Paris. Louis XVI, in reality a condemned man, was suspended by the Assembly's rump and turned over to the Commune for imprisonment. Following Robespierre's aims the rump announced a National Convention, the deputies to be elected by universal male suffrage. As Lenin was to say many years later after the second upheaval of 1917 in Russia, the events of August 10, 1792 revolutionized the Revolution. In the six weeks before the Convention met France was governed in effect by the revolutionary Commune of

Paris. Its radicalism was apparent in measures that deported refractory priests, ordered emigré property sold by the state, and deprived manorial lords of all their dues without compensation unless they could prove title. As the revolution deepened, the egalitarian form of address "citizen" was adopted, and a distinguished group of foreign intellectuals including Tom Paine was given honorary citizenship.

During these weeks the remnants of the Assembly failed to cooperate with the Commune, but cooperation was needed, for the Prussian advance into France quickened after August 10. By the end of the month the enemy had taken Verdun, only 150 miles away. Thousands of Parisians marched off to the front as the Commune combed the city for arms and for suspects. On September 2 the mood of patriotic frenzy turned to paranoia against the supposed enemy within; popular bands invaded the prisons, took the unfortunate inmates before hastily erected tribunals, and carried out summary executions. The September massacres went on for several days; and between 1100 and 1400 prisoners were slaughtered, including thieves and prostitutes as well as priests and former nobles. The American ambassador reported seeing blood running in the streets. No party would accept responsibility for the massacres, and in reality almost all of the national delegates feared the violence of the city. This was the situation when the new assembly, the Convention, met.

## THE REPUBLIC OF THE CONVENTION: 1792–1795

### The Republic and the War

The Convention celebrated its first session on September 21, 1792 by replacing the monarchy with a republic. The occasion was a triumphant one, for news had arrived of the first clear French victory in the field, which had halted the Prussian advance at Valmy in the Argonne Valley to the north. The battle of Valmy was little more than an artillery duel in the fog, but, as the German poet Goethe remarked, it was to have infinite repercussions. The approach of winter sealed the Prussian defeat: in the next six weeks the French armies "liberated" Savoy, crossed the Rhine to take Frankfurt, and overran Belgium, after a true victory at Jemappes, where 40,000 sans-culottes overwhelmed the enemy while chanting the "Marseillaise."

By mid-November 1792 the Convention was in a position to promise "aid and fraternity to all peoples wishing to recover their liberty." The simple formula was tested in occupied Belgium, where there was a contest between the Estates party (Statists)—victors over the Austrians in 1789 and now considered aristocrats—and the Democrats. After the Convention decreed the confiscation of noble and princely property to pay for the occupation the Democrats, the favorites of the Convention, lost the first election to the Statists. Alarmed by the results of self-determination, the Convention followed the request of the Democrats and annexed Belgium in February 1793. Whether the universal pattern of democratic revolution could be achieved without French soldiers was to remain a vital question throughout the 1790s.

Military victory failed to produce unity at home. Elections to the Paris Commune returned many radicals and most of the Parisian wards were demanding price controls for grain, a policy sharply in conflict with the prevailing economic ideology of the Convention. For the most part the peasants, the mass of the electorate, were satisfied by the revolution at this point, but they were antagonized by the Commune's sending its own commissioners to neighboring provinces to requisition men and supplies. Soon the depu-

ties of the Convention were faced with a virtual rural insurrection south of Paris.

Politics, however, became the great divisive issue in the new republic. The Girondins had aroused the opposition of a small group of deputies from Paris even before the war. Now the Girondins, who were basically men of the provinces, found their opponents from Paris clustered high on the benches of the Assembly and taking for themselves the name of *The Mountain*. Both groups were approximately of the same social class, and there was rough agreement on anticlericalism and economic liberalism. The Mountain, however, could accuse the ministers of federalist tendencies and be less fearful of an alliance with the sans-culottes. The rapid train of events exaggerated ill feelings between the two groups. The harmony of the first days of the republic soon faded before the question of the king.

The fate of Louis XVI marked a clear break between the two factions. The Girondins squandered their initiative in trying to blame Danton and the Mountain for the September massacres. It was Robespierre who had to remind the Convention early in December that either Louis XVI was guilty of treason or they were. Few could doubt the duplicity of the king after a chest with his secret correspondence was found, but the Girondins could question the competency of the Convention to sit as a jury. They lost their point and also failed to prevent the imposition of the death sentence. Louis XVI was guillotined on January 21, 1793. The real victors were the Mountain and their friends in the Jacobin clubs.

Military and diplomatic events took on a new significance. Despite strong libel laws and press censorship English democratic societies alarmed their government by sympathizing with France, for both governments regarded war as inevitable after the French intervention in the Low Countries. In February France declared war on both England and Holland, and a

*Drawing the bluest blood: the execution of Louis XVI.*

month later Spain was in the war along with the Italian states. England became the cornerstone of a coalition of unequal allies that was negotiated throughout 1793. Englishmen such as Burke believed that the First Coalition would save European civilization and the aristocracy. Young William Pitt, a great wartime leader like his father, had a more traditional aim—to restore the political equilibrium and contain France. The continental powers were not as strongly convinced that France represented a real threat, for France and England had fought colonial and naval wars for more than a century.

Coalitions against France never held together for very long in the revolutionary years. Eastern members were bent on ex-

panding their own borders: a Russian army had moved into Poland in May 1792, putting down the year-old regime as a criminal plot inspired by France; Prussia similarly crossed the Polish frontier in January 1793. The two invaders formed a holy alliance against "French democratism," but they also sought to annex more Polish territory. By midsummer of 1793 a conservative restored Polish Diet had, under Russian pressure, ceded large areas of Great Poland (with Danzig) to Prussia and of the Ukraine to Russia. The end of Poland as a nation effectively dates from the Second Partition of 1793, which was the greatest victory of the counterrevolution.*

* See map, p. 332.

## Internal Crises

The coming together of social unrest, political agitation, and unfavorable foreign entanglements had marked the crises of May–June 1789 and July–August 1792. Now late in February of 1793 another rapid series of events left the legislative body torn asunder.

Food shortages, skyrocketing prices, and intensive suspicion of hoarding and speculations touched off enforced sales at prices that were set by the Parisian crowds, often by women. Sectional leaders and journalists such as Marat were not ashamed to accept responsibility for such acts. Radicals such as Jacques Roux, a priest preaching political terrorism and extensive economic measures for the poor, starting with the regulation of grain prices, led their followers enraged by inflationary prices (the *enragés*) to demand an "agrarian law," the subdivision of large estates in favor of small agricultural producers. Thus they added a threat to private property to the sans-culottes' affront to the Convention's economic liberalism. On the front the spring campaign against Holland opened badly. When the Convention, early in March, turned to recruiting soldiers throughout the Republic, a major civil war broke out in the Vendée, west of Paris and south of Brittany; rebel bands of peasantry under noble and clerical leadership fought savagely and soon offered a real military threat to the Revolution at home. As the Vendée turned into a siege of western cities, the French General Dumouriez entered into treasonable negotiations in Holland with the enemy. Early in April French forces were driven from the Rhineland, and the first regiments of English soldiers moved across the English Channel.

The response of the Convention was necessarily in the direction of increased central authority. Deputies from the Convention, dressed in scarlet cloaks and sporting the tricolor, were made "representatives on mission." By early April they were acting as political commissars to the armies. A revolutionary tribunal was created on March 10 especially to judge political cases and the refractory priests, and the public prosecutor could arrest suspects on denunciation by a single person. News of the Vendée led to the death penalty for rebels caught in arms. A similar sentence for all emigrés, and revocation of their sales and inheritances since 1789, followed. The citizenry at large was enlisted in discovering the enemy within by the establishment of committees of surveillance in the communes. The emergency legislation was capped on April 10, 1793 by the creation of a Committee of Public Safety to supervise the executive functions of the state.

The Convention was also the scene of a desperate struggle for power between the Girondins and the Mountain. The struggle was mirrored in many provincial cities, especially in the south, where in Lyons, Marseilles, and Bordeaux the Jacobins were driven out. While the two factions screamed of plot and counter-plot, the enragés and the Parisian sections successfully urged price controls on grain. A rough coalition of sectional leaders, Jacobin Club members, and sans-culotte National Guards put an end to the crisis, purging the Convention of 29 Girondin leaders from May 31 to June 2, 1793. Paris had experienced its third great revolutionary day, but the pattern of conflict between aristocrat and democrat had been left behind. The summer of 1793 was to be the summer of the sans-culottes.

Historians who believe that men do exactly what they want to do write of bitterly opposed groups in that summer. The Girondins retained power in Lyons, and in August the Convention opened siege on this city, which had executed its Jacobins. In Paris the sans-culottes wanted their own militia; instead, the Convention relied on general mobilization—the *levée en masse* of August, which commandeered all lives and resources until France was cleared of enemies. Therefore it stands as a major precedent in the introduction of modern "total warfare," the task that most preoccupied the Committee of Public Safety. Such warmaking also entailed economic controls. The enragés wanted to enforce economic controls by violence; the Convention tried to forestall thorough measures by creating public granaries. The sans-culottes wanted social needs to precede the rights of property; but the new constitution stopped short at state responsibility for employment and education, and it went on to combine absolute property rights with universal male suffrage. The Parisian world of sectional leaders and journalists sought everywhere to challenge the moderates, but in that summer Marat was assassinated and Roux arrested.

Historians who emphasize the impersonal forces of history are less prone to judge the various republicans as entirely responsible for their actions. The assignat fell from 36 percent of value in June to 22 percent in late August; bread shortages were constant; the war went very badly on both northern and southern fronts; finally, the handing over of Toulon and half the navy to the British was the cruelest loss of all. Not until September did the Convention turn back rebel power in the Vendée, and then only with seasoned troops. The argument between historians of plot and historians of circumstances may never end, but the atmosphere of treason, defeat, and assassination in the summer of 1793 prepared for the period of the Terror that followed.

The Convention triumphed over the sans-culottes with great difficulty in the autumn of 1793. The crisis—still another dramatic turning point—came on September 4 and 5, when crowds of workingmen surrounded the city hall and penetrated to the floor of the national legislature, demanding more bread and a revolutionary army. The day was narrowly saved by a promise to pay indigent sans-culottes for attendance at the sections. Before the end of September, the Convention moved to set up a wide system of price controls on more than 40 necessities; wages as well as foodstuffs, fuel, and clothing were affected. With large-scale requisitions of raw materials and labor, city control of the grain trade, and prices set by the districts, government intervention in economic life was complete.

## The Terror and the Republic of Virtue

An even more profound legacy of the struggle for control of the Revolution was the routinization of terror in the fall of 1793. A law regarding suspects listed many vague categories of enemies who were to be imprisoned for the duration of the war. The Committee of Public Safety, which Robespierre joined in July, now received two extremist Parisian deputies. On October 10 the new mood of the committee was expressed by its youngest member, Saint-Just. In a speech justly famous he defined the principles of the Terror. Not only treachery but indifference would be punished. The Republic had but two parties—the people and their enemies. Justice is reserved for the former and iron for the latter. The Constitution of 1793 was to be suspended (to which the Convention assented) and the "provisional government of France" was to be "revolutionary until the peace."

Saint-Just justified the startling transition in dangerously abstract terms, citing the sovereign will of the people. Neither he nor Rousseau 30 years earlier meant a majority rule when they used the term. The sovereign will expresses the fundamental truth of a community; it must always be just and reasonable. To the men who governed France in the winter of 1793 to 1794 the regime had to be absolutely virtuous. To those who so believed, the seeds of totalitarianism remained hidden.

The principle of a single will was soon institutionalized. A decree of December 4, 1793 became the virtual constitution of the new regime. The Convention was to publish its laws within 24 hours. Departmental administrations, suspect of federalism, were shorn of most of their powers. Local surveillance committees, which were busy at purifying popular societies and at screening suspects for the revolutionary tribunals, had to report to the Convention every ten days. The Committee of Public Safety was made officially responsible for war and diplomacy. (Its members and representatives on mission visited the armies, checked on the communes, and presided over military tribunals to try the prisoners of civil war.) Police power lay within the Committee of General Security, which also presided over the political trials. In mid-October Marie Antoinette went to the guillotine; the scene, with her proud figure seated in the tumbrel, was caught in a sketch at the right moment by the artist David. Two other well-known women followed her—a mistress of the old regime (Madame Du Barry) and one of the new (Madame Roland). Twenty-one Girondin leaders were executed in November.

An old view of the period after the passage of the December laws held that the Committee of Public Safety emerged with a despotic hold on France. It allegedly condoned the savage reprisals at Lyons, where one of its members oversaw the massacre by cannonade of 350 moderates, and at Nantes, where Carrier (the representative on mission) was present while 3000 Vendéens were shot and 2000 deliberately drowned in the Loire. The Twelve, the members of the committee, were a remarkable group—young (averaging 37 years) and variously experienced (they included a Protestant pastor, an actor, two army officers, and six lawyers). Until the 1920s Robespierre, the member without

*Marie Antoinette led to execution (by Jacques Louis David).*

portfolio, was described as a deluded and bloodthirsty fanatic, so secure in his own virtue that he could still wear the powdered hair, frock coat, and frilled shirt of the aristocracy. It is now evident that the less dramatic members of the committee, such as Lazare Carnot, an army engineer who was labeled by Napoleon as "the organizer of victory," were more important in the business of governing than were the doctrinaires. Several committee members and the majority of the representatives on mission were genuinely interested in bringing justice and equality to the provinces they inspected.

The committee itself, although temporarily immune from review by the Convention, was opposed on the "Right" by a group that gathered around Danton and on the "Left" by the revolutionary militia and by more radical clubs that were inspired by Hébert, one of history's great yellow journalists. The Committee of Twelve owed its power in 1793–94 far more to circumstances than to cohesion and genius. Their reign after December rested on victory in the civil war in the west and the southeast and on the expulsion of the enemy from French territory. The assignat regained some of its purchasing power by 1794. Through the representatives on mission the committee was associated with the widespread anticlericalism that became a veritable campaign for the dechristianization of France. A republican calendar, in which months were named after the seasons, had already replaced the Christian year, history beginning with the year I, on the day of the declaration of the republic; Sunday became a workday and every tenth day became a lay holiday. Churches were stripped of their ornaments and vessels. By the end of 1793 Parisian churches were closed and a Festival of Reason had taken place in Notre Dame. Priests were urged to marry, and Jesus became a sans-culotte. In the first months of its rule the committee may have been in touch with the mood of the upper classes in matters of religion, but the ultimate effect of dechristianization was to alienate further small communities and the Church from the Revolution.

The apparent rule of the committee lasted only a few months. By April 1794 it had brought about the trial and execution of Hébert on the Left and Danton on the Right. Robespierre and Saint-Just were crying of a "foreign plot," but were prosecuting domestic enemies. Price controls were altered to allow higher retail profits. The committee announced the redistribution of traitors' property to the poor, but failed to convince the sans-culottes of a true desire for social equality. Some measures of social justice were passed—free medical care for the aged, free compulsory primary education, the end of slavery—but Robespierre and Saint-Just were

*Robespierre, spokesman for the Republic of Virtue.*

increasingly preoccupied with moral absolutes. A series of national festivals of republicanism was arranged by David, who was now the "pageant-master." A Supreme Being was invoked to halt the tide of sacrilegious practice, and it was apparent that Robespierre was at heart a warm Deist. More ominously, the procedure of the revolutionary tribunals was accelerated with the law of 22d *Prairial* II (June 10, 1794): the accused was to have no counsel; and moral feeling that the accused was guilty was adequate proof. Only two verdicts were possible— acquittal or death. More than half of the 2639 executions performed in Paris occurred after the Prairial law.

Ironically, the final period of the Terror saw the French armies again on the move into Belgium. But the revolutionary government depended on crisis. Now fatigue and personal animosities could take their toll: in the last weeks of their lives Robespierre and Saint-Just were becoming estranged from their colleagues, and the General Security Committee suspected its rival of seeking to take over the police power. The Commune was largely on the side of Robespierre, but the all-important committees of the sections were divided. On July 27, 1794—the 9th *Thermidor*, or hot month—the Convention was persuaded to arrest Robespierre and his immediate followers. He perished on the guillotine on the following day together with Saint-Just and many of the Commune leaders.

The period of the Terror will forever be weighted by the chilling number of executions. Probably more Frenchmen died in prisons and in summary executions in the year before Thermidor than were guillotined following trial (16,594). Three-fourths of the death penalties were pronounced in the west and in the Rhone Valley, seats of civil war; four-fifths of the charges specified rebellion or treason. Only one victim in twelve was a nobleman and one in sixteen a priest. Almost 60 percent were workers and peasants who were held to be "aristocrats" or other guilty categories because of their beliefs, not because of their social status. Some historians have argued that more Frenchmen died in 1871 (in the suppression of the Commune) than in the Terror, but the power of a revolution as historical myth does not depend on statistics. "Paris in the Terror" still symbolizes a people caught up in moral oppression. Death on the guillotine weighed heavily on men's minds, but equally dominating was the realization that the state demanded complete devotion. Until the enemy without and the enemy within should be vanquished—and only the state could say when that might be—every citizen had to show his dedication. For a few brief months in the Year II of the Revolution, men and women suspended their ordinary interests and changed their civic symbols, their dress, and even their names. Robespierre, in his most important speech, declared that a popular revolutionary government must have both virtue and terror. What he could not realize in the spring of 1794 is that very few ordinary men shared his profound belief that the Revolution could substitute morality for egotism, principle for habit, and right reason for tyrannical custom.

## The Reaction of Thermidor

The republic of the Convention hung on for more than a year after Robespierre's death, but some of the divisive issues of the Terror soon spent themselves. The cult of the Supreme Being passed quickly, and in the autumn of 1794 the constitutional church came to an end, with the state being officially neutral in matters of religion. (There is some evidence of a religious revival among the less educated, and in many towns refractory priests returned to say Mass). The Committee of Public Safety lost its extensive powers and was purged of the remaining original members. The infamous Prairial law survived Robespierre by only three weeks. The Convention negotiated a peace with the rebels of the Vendée and returned their firearms and their clergy, and the puritanism of the Republic of Virtue gave way to a cynical press and theater, to the revival of the salon, and to revealing dress.

But Terror itself, especially political assassination, did not end on 9th *Thermidor*. Former Hébertists and Dantonists stirred up gangs of "gilded youths" against supporters of the Mountain and closed the Jacobin Club. The Parisian sections were purged of lower-class members, including many of the sans-culottes. The reaction from the Right reached its climax in the spring of 1795 in the southeast with the massacre of prisoners at Marseilles and at Lyons, later known as the White Terror.

The most serious unsettled business after Thermidor was the reappearance of inflation after the end of most economic controls in the winter of 1794–95. Price controls ended in December, yet requisition for war continued. By March 1795 the assignat had fallen to eight percent of its value; meanwhile extreme cold added to the misery of the sans-culottes, and the suicide rate rose in Paris. The desperation of the sans-culottes erupted in the spring of 1795. Following a popular threat to the Convention in April, Jacobin survivors were deported. The repression was more severe after an abortive attack during May 20–24, in which artillerymen of the working quarters almost fired on the Convention. A military commission condemned the leaders, and the legislature was further purged; also, sans-culottes were almost wholly excluded from the National Guard. The popular phase of the Revolution came to an end, leaving bourgeois democrats solely in command.

Great success on the military front characterized the year after Thermidor: the army of occupation in Belgium swept into the Ruhr; the Palatinate fell, and Prussia withdrew from the war in April 1795, leaving the left bank of the Rhine to France. Spain withdrew from the coalition in the summer of 1795, and French troops gained the Italian Riviera. The most striking success came in the Low Countries, where the Army of the North had crossed the frozen Rhine delta in January 1795. A Batavian republic was declared; the first of the "sister republics," it was built on the support of the native Dutch Jacobins. The stadtholder of the House of Orange fled to England. Under the Treaty of the Hague (May 1795) the Dutch paid a high price for their independence, joining France as an ally and giving up an indemnity and the mouth of the Scheldt. The Batavian Republic was not to have its constitution for three years, but the French invasion had revealed another genuine group of democrats in Europe, the first to combine in a motto the three key words, "Liberty, Equality, Fraternity." Of the First Coalition, only Britain at sea and Austria on land still challenged France.

Late in the summer of 1795 the Thermidoreans produced a new, more bourgeois constitution, which specified the duties as well as the rights of man and reinstated the system of a qualified electorate. Fear of centralized power led to a bicameral legislature and a five-man executive, the *Directors*. However when the convention tried to ensure that two-thirds of the new legislature would come from its ranks, a royalist revolt in Paris nearly succeeded. Under the poor leadership of Louis XVI's younger brother, the royalists bungled an attempt to link up with a British invasion of Brittany in July 1795. Revolt by the Parisian sections was more dangerous, and the uprising of October (*Vendémiaire* in the revolutionary calendar) 1795 had to be put down with concentrated artillery fire even though the officer in charge of the artillery, Napoleon Bonaparte, would later claim that a "whiff of grapeshot" was sufficient to put it down. In the confused politics of the *Directory* (1795–99), the army was to play an increasing role.

## B. Reaction, Militarism, and Defeat

### THE REPUBLIC OF THE DIRECTORY

### The Bourgeois Republic and Its Enemies

The sans-culottes and their cry for "bread and the Constitution of 1793" had been defeated in 1795: under the new constitution the vote was restricted as it had been in 1791. Property qualifications for members of the two houses (*Council of Five Hundred* and *Council of Ancients*) were higher than before. There were 158 regicides among the council members, but an equal number of royalists were returned. Many of the new men not taken from the Convention were businessmen and speculators. Of the five original Directors only one remained a Jacobin. The Directory was truly the bourgeois republic.

The institutions that the Directory gave to the nation also favored the upper middle class. The Convention in its last days had decreed elite secondary schools, the forerunners of the present *lycées;* now the Directory installed central schools in each département; and a National Institute dedicated to the sciences symbolized government aid to research. Strict accounting procedures were introduced in the administration of relief to the poor and in the preparation of the national budget. The assignat, worthless by the spring of 1796, was replaced by another paper currency, the conversion rates favoring those who still held gold. Bankers and businessmen in the councils prepared legislation for a Bank of France, to be created in 1800.

The Directory weathered an attack from the Left in its first days. François Babeuf, a radical newspaper editor who had seen rural and urban poverty, became convinced of the impossibility of a just regime as long as the protection of private property continued to dominate politics. In the autumn of 1795, as prices in Paris rose 75 percent higher than in 1789, Babeuf prepared an armed "Conspiracy of Equals" to take over the republic. With the aid of former Jacobins and terrorists Babeuf created a secret and highly disciplined organization whose "Manifesto of the Plebeians" ordered the end of private property. The movement has been called "the first attempt in history to establish a communist society by political means."[2] Babeuf was betrayed by a police spy, and the movement was broken up in May, 1796; he and his associates were guillotined a year later.

Royalism was as dangerous to the Directory as Jacobinism, however. Purges followed the yearly elections to the legislatures from 1795 to 1799, recalling the years between the English monarchy of the 1640s and Cromwell's protectorate. In the course of these purges the Directors relied increasingly on the generals and on the

[2] George Rudé, *Revolutionary Europe: 1783–1815* (New York: Harper & Row, Publishers, 1964), p. 172.

loyalty of the troops to their officers. Generals from two major armies made possible the most sweeping change of regime on the 18th *Fructidor* (September 4, 1797), when more than 200 deputies and even one of the Directors were driven out of office, with 65 persons deported to the "dry guillotine" of Guiana.

## The "Grande Nation"

The latent power of the military rested on the great accomplishment of the Directory—the expansion of France and her revolutionary institutions. This expansion was prepared by the many young generals who had been promoted so rapidly after 1792, by the Jacobin sympathizers who acted as commissars to the armies, and by the hundreds of thousands who served in the ranks. Almost one million men had been mobilized by 1796, and about 450,000 were in service when the Directory began. The Directors themselves were content with having broken the First Coalition.* They made little attempt to encourage revolutions abroad, and it was not until the coup of Fructidor allowed more explicit aid to foreign Jacobins that the Dutch democrats of the Batavian Republic gained their written constitution.

It was in northern Italy that the French army proved that its aims went far beyond simple conquest. The brilliant campaign of the spring of 1796, in which the French took Milan in five weeks and neutralized the entire peninsula within three months, was planned and led by the most daring of the young generals—Napoleon Bonaparte. Born in 1769 of a landed Italian family on Corsica, and French by reason of the island's annexation the year before, Bonaparte had been educated in France and commissioned in the artillery. He had distinguished himself in action against the British at Toulon in 1793 and against the

Parisians in Vendémiaire.* He also knew how to mix politics with his military career. A good Jacobin in 1791, he was a moderate in 1795, and by 1796 he saw that he should seek his fortune at the front, away from the corruption of Paris (where, nevertheless, he had just married Josephine de Beauharnais, the former mistress of a Director). In Italy Bonaparte settled down at Milan to cultivate his army's loyalty and to send home bullion and art treasures to placate the Directors. But Bonaparte believed in liberty for the Italians as well as in requisitions. Giving material aid to middle-class revolutionaries in Milan, he announced the Cisalpine Republic in June 1797, the first deliberate copy of the French regime abroad. Bonaparte also ignored instructions in negotiating his own terms with Austria. In October 1797, in the Treaty of Campo Formio, he confirmed French possession of Belgium and sacrificed the ancient Republic of Venice to the Austrians, who withdrew from the war.

The year 1798 has been called "the high tide of revolutionary democracy." Sister republics in Holland, Switzerland, northern Italy, Genoa, Rome, and Naples had constitutions similar to that of the Directory in France. Each contained a declaration of the rights of man, and most specified citizens' duties as well. Each republic was divided into départements and had two legislatures and a five-man Directory. The republics had been founded with the aid of local patriots, and the citizenry voted in primary and electoral assemblies. In 1798 Frenchmen were speaking of the *"Grande Nation"* and the "natural frontiers" of the French people, which included the left bank of the Rhine. On the fourth anniversary of Robespierre's fall a procession wound through Paris honoring Liberty and proudly showing the imperial scope of the republic, a conscious imitation of a Roman

* See p. 383.

* See p. 389.

triumph. A bear from Berne, lions from Africa, and camels from Egypt were followed by the famous Corinthian bronze horses from Venice.

## Defeat and Coup d'État

Many contemporaries and modern historians have come to see democratic revolution at its height in 1798. This seemed clear in France and neighboring territories, but English sailors had mutinied, and the United Irish rose in Ulster—an abortive rebellion to be followed by union with Great Britain. Even the American government, only a few years before the idol of democratic revolutionaries, reacted to the democratic sweep as conservative Federalists in power enacted the Alien and Sedition Acts to stem the spread of Jacobinism. Other historians will admit that revolutionary movements were liberal and bourgeois in character everywhere, but not democratic; only in France did the sans-culottes force their will temporarily on the Revolution.

All historians are agreed that French military power was at its height in 1798, the year the Jourdan Law established universal military service. But military success indirectly brought down the republic. French expansion drove some of the old allies (England, Austria, Russia, Turkey, Sweden) into a Second Coalition. In 1799 Austrian forces drove the French from Switzerland and Germany, while the Russian general Suvorov liberated northern Italy. The young Parthenopean Republic in Naples fell to a conservative peasant uprising. The Directors took the blame for the reversals, and various factions began to plot a military coup d'état. The one that succeeded in bringing Napoleon to power was carried out by two old clerics who were wise in diplomacy, Sieyès and Talleyrand, and a former Jacobin terrorist, Fouché, who went on to become head of Napoleon's secret police.

*Sieyès, the old revolutionary who organized Napoleon's coup d'état.*

After his Italian expedition Bonaparte had gone his own way, avoiding the project of invading England, which he considered too risky. Instead he led an expeditionary force to Egypt, where he intended to undercut the British Empire's communications by seizing the Near East as an imperial base. The expedition also capitalized on growing scientific interest in that area, but it went badly when the British destroyed the invasion fleet and Napoleon failed to take Syria. Leaving his army behind, Napoleon made a dramatic escape through Lord Nelson's fleet to land in southern France in October 1799. The French public overlooked this defeat and failed to note that other commanders had driven the Coalition back in Holland, Switzerland, and Italy. Napoleon was the man of the hour that Sieyès and his conspirators needed to overthrow the Directory and its republican councils.

On the 19th *Brumaire* (November 10, 1799) the two councils were summoned in special sessions and then dissolved at sword's point according to plans laid down by Sieyès and carried out to a great extent by Napoleon's brother Lucien.

Within three weeks the bourgeois republic had come to an end and Napoleon was First Consul under a Caesarean constitution. Ten years of history had come to a close when the consuls proclaimed the Revolution to be ended.

# THE REVOLUTION STABILIZED: 1799–1804

## Early Napoleonic Government

The civilian instigators of the coup of 1799 sought a more powerful executive who shared their fears of popular government. In Napoleon, a second choice, they thought that they had found a man of order without a compromising political past who would be content to name generals and ambassadors and who would be responsible to the Senate, a kind of constitutional jury. Sieyès's proposed constitution called for a triple executive with an equal voice in decisions for each of the three consuls.

But Napoleon refused to play their game; from the outset he intended to exercise full command in France, as he had done in Italy and Egypt. He argued successfully that the First Consul was to have final decisions in all matters, although he took care at first to give the appearance of deferring to his legislature and his advisors. The Constitution of the Year VIII was largely the work of Sieyès and Napoleon. It recognized the principle of universal male suffrage but made it useless by the introduction of complicated electoral machinery; popular sovereignty was recognized only by a plebiscite approving the constitution after it had already been promulgated. The structure of government followed Sieyès's principle that "confidence comes from below, power from above." Four bodies were set up to help the First Consul govern. The indirectly chosen *Tribunate* could discuss legislation but could not vote on it. The *Legislative Corps* could vote on laws but without amendment or discussion. Sieyès put great stake in the *Senate,* which was to select the consuls, the members of the Tribunate, and the Legislative Corps from national lists proposed by indirect elections; it could also veto legislation passed by the Legislative Corps. He and his friends had packed the Senate with men of the Directory, but Napoleon bought its complacent cooperation with grants of estates and with military triumphs. Real power, including the power to initiate legislation, was vested in the *Council of State,* nominated by Napoleon. The Council of State revived the idea of a Bourbon royal council: members were experts in such areas as the Army, Navy, Finance, Legislation, and Internal Affairs. The ministers were subordinate to the council, which also drafted proposals for laws and rules of administration. The council was by far the most efficient part of the constitution, and it is to Napoleon's credit that he worked as hard as his advisors and received long periods of service from most of them.

In local administration Napoleon built upon Jacobin centralization, appointing prefects in charge of each département, subprefects for the département subdivisions, and mayors in the communes. The First Consul even had a crude semaphore telegraph system: he was determined to know the mood of his nation as well as he prided himself on knowing his troops. Napoleon financed his state through rational assessment of taxes and more stringent collection rather than through loans. Physically, the First Consul was worthy of the system: he was tireless in council meetings, unstinting in his tours of the country, and indefatigable in correspondence; there are more than 40,000 of his letters in print, and perhaps as many are lost.

In the first years after his accession Napoleon combined his phenomenal energy and the flexibility of the constitution to move the administration of the state into constructive channels. He had asked for and received a mandate for action at the outset, submitting the constitution to a national plebiscite; between 1800 and 1802 he set up committees to codify civil, criminal, and commercial law. The lawyers combined revolutionary legislation with the ordinances of Louis XIV and produced succinct and well-defined documents. Napoleon attended the meetings often enough to affix his name to the codes collectively in 1807, but the Civil Code of 1804 especially drew its strength from the Revolution. Napoleon leaned on Roman law to tighten procedures on marriage and divorce, but the granting of absolute property rights, the freedom to bequeath a portion of one's property at will, and the abolition of servitude were legacies of the 1790s. Although the codes enforced social conformity—especially the rights of husband over wife and father over children—they were sufficiently adaptable to have influenced the law of Italy, Egypt, Canada, Louisiana, and Japan.

Both old-regime authority and revolutionary equality pervaded Napoleon's social and economic policy. He required workers to carry a passbook, thus hardening the law of 1791 against trade unions. In place of the Directory's secondary schools, with their permissive curricula, he established 45 lycées with state scholarships to train boys for civil service, the professions, engineering, and the army. With the characteristic statement that girls should *believe*, not *think*, Napoleon left their education to religious orders. He conceived of the national economy more in Colbert's terms than those of Adam Smith; he sought a favorable balance of trade with protective tariffs and excluded English goods. The most obvious attempt to strike a balance between old and new was the Legion of Honor, founded in 1802. The First Consul genuinely sought to bestow distinction, without regard to social rank, on individuals for civic achieve-

ment. Yet Napoleon also sought a captive institution named by himself, a kind of republican service nobility.

For reasons of state Napoleon effected a reconciliation with the Church. Although state and church had been separate since 1795, the Directory's attitude toward the nonjuring clergy had wavered. A great variety of religious practices had appeared; Notre Dame of Paris had seen worship by Catholics, Protestants, and Theophilanthropists (an intellectualist cult). Bonaparte's own religious attitudes were tolerant and skeptical, and it was for political and social gains that he negotiated a concordat (or treaty) with the Pope in 1800. As he so often did, Napoleon had the better of the bargain: the Catholic clergy would be named by the bishops, who in turn were nominated by the First Consul and instituted by the pope. The distinction between refractory and constitutional clergy came to an end, and the clergy became once again salaried servants of the state. The pope was persuaded to accept the dispossession and sale of Church lands; but Roman Catholicism was declared to be "the religion of the great majority of the citizens." Papal intervention in France and episcopal control of the diocese were limited by the First Consul and the Council of State. The concordat was published in April 1801. In the long run the bishops rather than the pope or the consul came to control the French church, but in 1802 Napoleon won his gamble that the legislatures and men of liberal opinion everywhere would accept this charter.

## The Pacification of Europe

Napoleon did not betray the popular trust in his coming to power in order to make an honorable peace. To the former general this meant rolling back the enemy to the lines of 1798. The campaign to recover Italy proceeded with a hard-fought victory in June 1800 at Marengo, in Lombardy. Napoleon's legendary reputation was enhanced by his crossing the Saint Bernard Pass. Even more decisive French victories north of the Alps—over the Russians at Zurich and the Austrians at Hohenlinden—left the Austrian emperor with little choice but to sign a peace treaty. The Treaty of Lunéville (February 1801) more than restored the terms of 1797, notably in granting France the left bank of the Rhine from Switzerland to Holland. England was ready to sign a peace 13 months later at Amiens.

Lunéville and Amiens proved to be only a temporary respite for France and Europe. English wealth and maritime power were unimpaired, and a wave of Gallophobia developed in 1802 and 1803 when Napoleon failed to honor the peace treaty and gave every indication of preparing an invasion fleet. When hostilities resumed in May 1803 his military mind argued that self-sufficient France could outlast mercantile and debt-ridden England. The French blockade closed continental ports to English and uncertified neutral ships. Napoleon was also willing to bleed off English wealth by selling smuggling licenses and allowing English captains to purchase French luxuries in return for needed raw materials. Bonaparte's grandiose scheme—to conquer the sea from the land, as he put it—led to the extension of warfare over all of western Europe.

## Termination of the Revolution

Napoleon's restless energy similarly destroyed the balance between revolution and order that he had been creating at home. The First Consul had always been hypersensitive to criticism from his citizens and to opposition from his legislators. At the beginning of his rule most of the Parisian newspapers were shut down and the rest subjected to strong censorship. Madame de Staël and other writers were particularly harassed by Fouché's secret police; and after Lunéville (1801), Napoleon purged the Tribunate. Then, following a royalist attempt on his life, he felt it more expedient to eliminate his enemies on the "Left" rather than to eliminate those on the "Right," so he deported or executed a number of Jacobin opponents. Napoleon's contempt for parliamentary government emerged in 1802: counting on the gratitude of the nation for the Peace of Amiens, the First Consul again used a plebiscite to force his plan on the government; he became Life Consul, able to nominate most senators, to declare war and make treaties, and to designate his successor. Thus the legislative and electoral machinery of the constitution was stripped of almost all meaning. Napoleon's power to make law within a new private council and the large number of appointments that he controlled cast a suspicion of dictatorship over the republic. Ominously, his profile appeared on the coinage for the first time, and he dropped his surname, a pretension to royal grandeur.

By 1804 Napoleon had broken openly with the revolutionary past. His arbitrary arrest and murder of the Bourbon Duc d'Enghien, who was kidnapped from the neutral territory of Baden, shocked European opinion and discredited Napoleon more than did any other of his acts. The same conspiracy that had doomed the Duc d'Enghien and had removed two of the generals who had won the peace—Moreau and Pichegru—was now used as an excuse to provide for the succession. In May 1804, by proclamation of the private council, Napoleon became "emperor of the French," and the populace was given its third (and most meaningless) plebiscite, this one to approve the proposition that "the Imperial dignity is hereditary." Napoleon planned to assume the title in a manner calculated to remove any question

Coronation of Napoleon (*by David, artist of the revolution*).

of Bourbon legitimacy and to humiliate the Habsburgs. He summoned Pope Pius VII north of the Alps for a coronation rite intended to recall that of Charlemagne. The ceremony of December 2, 1804 was less religious than imperial, with Napoleon unwilling to communicate at Mass or to take an oath of dependence to the pope, as the title historically demanded. The emperor crowned himself, bringing to a close the period in which the Revolution in France might have continued.

## THE GRAND EMPIRE: 1804–1815

Napoleon's admirers see the turning point of his career in the military disasters beginning with the invasion of Russia in 1812. The new emperor's treatment of France and the republics abroad, however, indicated from the start that he cared little for the pattern of change that had emerged from the 1790s. A desire to legitimize his family's claim, while he himself had no children to inherit the throne, prompted Napoleon to install his relatives in new monarchies that had once been sister republics. His eldest brother, Louis, became king of Holland in 1804, when the Batavian Republic was abolished. Josephine's son by an earlier marriage became viceroy of the kingdom of Italy, while Lombardy became part of the empire. Another brother, Joseph, went to rule Naples in 1806. Before the empire was complete the youngest brother, Jerome, was established in Rhenish Prussia. Other relatives gained lesser, but significant, posts.* By 1810 Napoleon realized that Josephine, at 46, would not bear him an heir. The marriage, which had been hastily solemnized in the Church on the eve of the coronation, was now put aside by a French ecclesiastical court. Austria supplied the new empress, Marie Louise, who bore Napoleon a son within a year. An imperial court of about 3500 dukes, counts, barons, and chevaliers formed the backdrop for the empire. Old revolutionary officials and generals as well as relatives received Italian, Spanish, and Portuguese estates as imperial fiefs. Using the discipline of the Jesuit order as an analogy, Napoleon placed an imperial university over the entire structure of education. Modern scholars have seen in all of these public actions a private anxiety over the succession. Contemporaries merely saw a man who was insensitive not only to the true meaning of 1789 but even to the aristocratic amenities of the Old Regime.

## French Expansion

The first three years of the empire produced stunning victories on the Continent and a stalemate on the seas. The invasion fleet assembled at Boulogne in the summer of 1805 never sailed, having failed to secure the English Channel. While Napoleon turned eastward with his Grand Army in the autumn of 1805, the British admiral Nelson crippled the Spanish and French fleets at Trafalgar (October 21, 1805), off the southern coast of Spain.

What Napoleon gave up at sea in 1805 he gained on land, in the Habsburg empire. The campaign proved Napoleon's faith in himself, for he carried no baggage trains; nevertheless the French captured more then 20,000 Austrian troops at Ulm in Bavaria on the day before Trafalgar and went on to occupy Vienna. The Austrians and Russians still believed that they could defeat Napoleon in a pitched battle and foolishly engaged him at Austerlitz in Moravia. On the first anniversary of his coronation the emperor cut the allied force in half, thus gaining his greatest victory.

In the Peace of Pressburg that followed, Francis II gave up Venetia and the Tyrol and recognized the kingdoms of Bavaria, Wurttemberg, and the Grand Duchy of Baden as independent states. In 1806 the Holy Roman Empire came to an end, and Napoleon reorganized further German territory in the Confederation of the Rhine, taken from Prussia's western provinces. Frederick William II of Prussia, convinced that Napoleon would soon break the truce, and expecting Russian aid, mobilized his army. In three weeks and two swift battles (Jena and Auerstadt) Napoleon humiliated the Prussians and went on to Berlin, where he decreed that all continental ports under his protection were closed to British ships. In the spring of 1807 Napoleon's army advanced toward the Baltic and defeated Alexander I of Russia at Friedland. The emperor and the czar met at Tilsit in July 1807 to divide Europe into two spheres of influence, Alexander being particularly eager to set his own course against Sweden and Turkey. Prussia lost her Polish districts to a new French satellite, the Grand Duchy of Warsaw. The campaigns of 1805 and 1807

* Only Lucien broke with his brother, refusing the kingdom of Naples in order to keep a wife who had earlier been his mistress.

*Trafalgar, 1805: the eclipse of Napoleon's bid for naval power.*

sealed Napoleon's reputation as a field commander, but it was the failure of the allies to place military cooperation ahead of individual interest that opened the Continent to France.

## The "Continental System"

After Tilsit the emperor was convinced that his conquests would reinforce the blockade against the British Isles—a blockade that was changing from one of protection to that of economic warfare. By 1810 the Atlantic, the Baltic, and even the Adriatic had become untenable for neutral ships caught between French Decrees and British Orders in Council. The Continental System, as some perhaps too-rational historians have called it, hurt British exports to Europe, but new markets in Latin America appeared. Although Britain suffered from inflation, bad harvests, and mass unemployment in 1811, the blockade probably did less damage than did monetary instability, and Britain never lost its continental grain supply. France, too, suffered from a commercial and industrial depression in 1811. Above all, its

neighbors' trading interests were damaged, and the empire began to entail heavy taxes and customs duties.

Napoleon's military reversals also began as a result of the blockade system. Since he needed the Iberian peninsula to seal off trade with the enemy, he set out to occupy Portugal in 1807. Napoleon conspired with Godoy, the royal favorite at the Spanish Court, to share the partition of Portugal, but the emperor's ambitions were drawn to Spain itself. In 1808 he secured the abdication of the Bourbon Spanish king, replacing him with his brother, Joseph, who was transferred from Naples. The Spanish peasantry, which was little affected by the Enlightenment, reacted to French rule as a threat to church and society as well as a violation of nationality. Guerrilla forces drove Joseph from Madrid and defeated two French divisions in the field at Baylen in July 1808. Supplied by the duke of Wellington's British base in Portugal, local militia and juntas fought the savage occupation in scenes that were immortalized by Goya. Until Wellington cleared the peninsula in 1813, the French were forced to commit many thousands of troops to

*The result of Spanish resistance to the French:* The Third of May, 1808, *by Goya.*

the occupation. "The Spanish ulcer," Napoleon later wrote, "destroyed me."

## The Empire at Its Height

Spanish resistance encouraged other continental powers either to resist or to question the obligations to France. Austerlitz had led to patriotic cries for a war of revenge in Austria. By 1808, with troops being pulled back from Germany for the Spanish front, and with Fouché and Talleyrand in dissent at home, Napoleon needed a reconquest of Vienna. The resumption of war between Austria and France was not so one-sided this time, and a peasant uprising in Tyrol lasted for

months. Napoleon went on to cross the Danube and to overturn the Austrians at Wagram in July 1809, but the defeat was not a disaster. The armistice deprived Francis I* of Salzburg and Cracow, but it also led to Napoleon's marriage to Marie Louise of Habsburg. Napoleon's expansion after Tilsit produced its most unfortunate result in Italy, where the Papal States were annexed to the blockade system in 1808. Pius VII, remembering the many issues that Napoleon had already forced against papal authority, moved toward excommunication of the emperor. Napo-

* The Austrian ruler's title was now Francis I because the Holy Roman Empire, of which he had been Francis II, was dissolved in 1806.

NAPOLEONIC EMPIRE
AT ITS HEIGHT

FINLAND
(to Russia, 1809)
St. Petersburg

K. OF DENMARK
AND NORWAY

K. OF SWEDEN

UNITED KINGDOM
OF
GREAT BRITAIN
AND IRELAND
(Act of Union, 1801)

Moscow

Napoleon's route

■ French Empire
▨ Controlled by Napoleon
▦ Allied with Napoleon
▤ Hostile to Napoleon

London

Copenhagen
Friedland
Tilsit

K. OF
PRUSSIA

RUSSIAN
EMPIRE

Berlin
Leipzig
Jena
Hohenlinden
Vienna
Wagram
Waterloo
Paris

CONFEDERATION OF THE RHINE
Rhine R.

GRAND DUCHY
OF WARSAW

Austerlitz

BESSARABIA
(to Russia, 1812)

FRENCH
EMPIRE

SWITZ.

K. OF
ITALY

AUSTRIAN
EMPIRE

Marengo

Danube R.

Black
Sea

K. OF
SPAIN

Madrid

PORTUGAL

Trafalgar

Balearic Is.

Corsica

Elba
Rome

K. OF
SARDINIA

MONTENEGRO

K. OF NAPLES

OTTOMAN EMPIRE

Constantinople

Gibraltar (Br.)

Mediterranean Sea

K. OF SICILY

AFRICA

Malta (Br.)

Map by J. Donovan

leon's reaction was to kidnap the Pope in July 1808. The captivity lasted five years.

Between 1810 and 1812 the Grand Empire reached its height. A total of 131 départements and about 44 million inhabitants fell under French rule. Napoleon's son, the infant king of Rome, ruled directly over a long stretch of the Mediterranean coast and over the Illyrian provinces; the Low Countries and the coastal plain of Germany, including Hamburg, were French territory; and Napoleon's relatives in Italy ruled principalities that conformed to older boundaries. Political lines had been redrawn, however, in Germany and in Poland. His youngest brother, Jerome, ruled over a kingdom of Westphalia that was pieced together from Hanover, Brunswick, Hesse-Cassel, and the

Prussian Rhenish provinces. Prussia was in fact the great victim of the empire's growth, in both west and east, and it was demilitarized between 1806 and 1813.

The Grand Empire never achieved complete unity, but all its parts shared the authoritarian order that was seen in France after 1804. The emperor allowed religious toleration and internal free trade, but he restricted suffrage rights everywhere. He tried to use the Civil Code to destroy the old social order in the empire by secularizing marriage and education and abolishing feudal dues and corporate bodies. His attack on monasteries and his search for administrative unity recalled the enlightened despotism of Joseph II. Wherever the Directory and Consulate had already touched an educated middle

*Napoleon at the Battle of Borodino.*

class with these proposals, the Napoleonic regime evoked no great opposition. In fact, its assimilation was incomplete in the areas across the Rhine and south of Rome. The price of the French mission —taxes, tariffs, recruitment, loss of political liberty—was not fully apparent until after the fateful invasion of Russia in 1812.

## Collapse of Napoleonic Europe

By 1810 the accord that had been reached between Napoleon and Alexander at Tilsit, the cornerstone of French expansion, had worn thin. French and Russian ambitions collided in the Balkans. Napoleon's reconstitution of Poland as the Grand Duchy of Warsaw was intolerable to Alexander, who, on the last day of 1810, renounced the Continental System and began preparations for war. In 1811 the emperor retaliated by assembling in Poland a polyglot "Grand Army" of almost 600,000 men. He recognized the campaign as his greatest gamble, but as usual he counted on a short war, one that could be fought to a successful conclusion in a single great encounter.

In June of 1812 the grand army crossed the Niemen to begin the invasion. Of necessity the czar's army retreated, destroying provisions as it went. In August Napoleon arrived in Smolensk with almost two-thirds of his force dissipated. The expected great encounter took place at Borodino, but the Russian general Kutusov withdrew the Russian army deeper into the great plain. Napoleon entered Moscow in mid-September but found the city deserted and soon in flames. Alexander still refused to negotiate or to engage in a decisive battle. In October 1812 Napoleon gave the order to retreat.

Both armies had wasted away tremendously, but the French retreat through the bitter northern winter finished the destruction of the Grand Army. About 100,000 were killed and another 100,000 imprisoned, and perhaps 200,000 perished of disease, cold, and famine. In December 1812 Napoleon left the remnants of the army and hastened in disguise to Paris, where the "lawyers"—the civilian officials he left behind but whom he despised—awaited him. There was no real threat to the emperor in the winter of 1812–13, but close observers remarked on his utter lack of concern for the army's suffering and on the decline in his physical capabilities.

In the months after the retreat from Moscow Napoleon might have extricated himself from the war on the terms of Lunéville offered by Metternich, the Austrian foreign minister. But the emperor always preferred to negotiate after a victory and not before a campaign. Although forced to restrict his recruiting of men and material to France, Napoleon put together a force of 150,000 for the invasion of Germany. But 1813 was in no way like 1806. German nationalism had been awakened from the Rhine to the Oder by the message of the Civil Code, by the example of what an authoritarian administration could do, and especially, as Jerome Bonaparte put it in Westphalia, by "the crushing burden of taxation.*

The reaction to Jena in 1806 had been further cultural nationalism led by professors and liberal bourgeoisie, but the building of an army to face the French was the work of Prussian ministers. In 1807 Barons Stein and Hardenburg ordered serfdom and feudal obligations abolished,† ended the restrictive allocation of professions and vocations by social rank, and tried to build up a bureaucracy that

would be free of privilege. Hardenburg summed up his program as "democratic rules of conduct in a monarchical administration."[3] The most effective reforms took place in the Prussian army, where Scharnhorst and Gneisenau relaxed barbarous punishments, retired incompetent officers, and made universal military service a patriotic duty. Using a rotating reserve to avoid Napoleon's limit on the size of the army, Prussia trained 150,000 men by 1812.

In February 1813 Prussia allied with Russia and declared war on France. Napoleon gained enough time to field 450,000 men by August, but the Prussian *Landwehr*, or civilian militia, had also become available by that time. Austria broke off negotiations and declared war, and the Swedes sent British-subsidized troops. During October 16–19, 1813, in the "Battle of Nations" at Leipzig, Napoleon was decisively beaten and driven across the Rhine into France.

Napoleon's opponents at first failed to agree on war aims, Metternich being particularly distrustful of Russia. The promise of British subsidy, however, brought the four major powers together at Chaumont in March 1814, binding them to a 20-year alliance against Napoleon and establishing a cordon of independent states around France. Meanwhile Wellington's armies had crossed the Pyrenees into France, and the Dutch had recalled their stadtholder. Napoleon had already precluded any repetition of the nationalist crusade of 1793 with his recruitment (a million men were drafted in 1812–13), requisitions, taxes, and repression of popular movements. The civilian population took the defeat at Leipzig passively and offered little resistance to the allied troops. In Paris the Senate and legislature prepared to restore Louis XVIII, who promised a liberal charter. Napoleon abdicated on

---

* The genesis of German nationalism is discussed more fully in Chap. 8.

† The order was largely evaded by aristocratic officials in charge of its execution.

[3] Quoted in Geoffrey Bruun, *Europe and the French Imperium: 1799–1814* New York: (Harper & Brothers, 1938), p. 174

April 6, 1814, retiring with his dignity intact to the island of Elba, while the allies granted pensions to the entire Bonaparte family.

The Treaty of Paris of May 1814 was generous to France, which kept its frontiers of 1792, losing Belgium, Italy, and the left bank of the Rhine; but there was no occupation, no disarmament, and no indemnity. Talleyrand, the versatile foreign minister, was to join the discussion of Europe's fate at the Congress of Vienna. Meanwhile Louis XVIII's charter had guaranteed the election of two houses by the new nobility and the wealthy bourgeoisie and had assured the rights of land purchasers, bondholders, army officers, and religious dissenters. But its terms did not satisfy traditionalists, for the king's brother, the Count d'Artois, pressed for full restoration of noble privilege and properties. The fact that army officers went on half-pay was another source of bad feeling.

Discontented revolutionaries and soldiers had good reason to rejoice when Napoleon left his island empire, landed on the southern coast of France, and reached Paris on March 20, 1815, causing the flight of the king. After he had failed to arouse national enthusiasm with a new constitutional "appendix," and after he had been labeled an outlaw by the Congress powers at Vienna, Napoleon mobilized and headed for the Belgian frontier. He had been able to raise about 125,000 troops, but the combined forces of Wellington's British and Blücher's Prussians numbered almost twice as many. On June 16, 1815 the allied generals joined forces at Waterloo in time to break Napoleon's attack. The Chamber in Paris refused him a further chance and submitted to Louis XVIII when he was returned by a Prussian escort. The second Treaty of Paris (November 1815) deprived France of Savoy and the Saar, declared an occupation of three to five years, and set an indemnity of 700 million francs. Napoleon became a British prisoner on the south Atlantic island of Saint Helena where he died six years later, not of cruel treatment by his captors as legend once had it, but of intestinal cancer.

## THE CONGRESS OF VIENNA

Before Waterloo the diplomats at Vienna had already agreed on the territorial settlement in Europe; but the Congress had nearly disbanded over the question of Poland in January 1815. Talleyrand, Metternich, and Lord Castlereagh (the British delegate) had drawn up a secret alliance against Russia and Prussia, which were suspected of designs on Poland and Saxony. The issue was settled by one of the great principles of the Treaty of Vienna (June 1815): mutual compensation. Prussia received the Rhineland, part of Saxony, and Swedish Pomerania; Alexander I was entrusted to oversee a constitutional monarchy in "Congress Poland" and was guaranteed his conquests in Bessarabia and Finland. Sweden was compensated for the loss of Finland by Norway, which was taken from Denmark, Napoleon's ally. Austria received Lombardy, Venetia, and Dalmatia, as well as the presidency of a German confederation of 39 lay states. Holland gained Luxembourg and the Austrian Netherlands. Great Britain's colonial territories were increased by Mauritius, Tobago, Saint Lucia (taken from France), Malta (from the Knights of St. John), and Ceylon and the Cape Colony (from the Dutch).

Restoration of prerevolutionary dynasties also helped to destroy the Grand Empire: Bourbons were returned in France, Spain, and the kingdom of the Two Sicilies; the pope was guaranteed his estates in central Italy and a safe residence in Rome. In Portugal the rule of the Braganza king John VI, who had fled to Brazil when French forces occupied his

*Counterrevolution triumphant: The Congress of Vienna.*

kingdom, was confirmed. The Congress powers respected national self-determination no more than Napoleon had. Norwegians, Poles, and Belgians found themselves under foreign rule. Central Europe remained a congeries of dynastic territories rather than unified states. Other provisions of the Treaty have remained more acceptable to modern sensibilities: suppression of the international slave trade and piracy and establishment of freer international waterways.

The Hundred Days of Napoleon's reign after his return changed the orientation of the Congress. The four conquering powers entered a Quadruple Alliance, pledging themselves to prevent a Napoleonic restoration, to enforce the second Treaty of Paris, and to provide contingents to occupy France. Castlereagh then bound all five participants at Vienna to a "Concert of Europe," which was not only to protect the settlement but also to provide machinery to settle disputes without recourse to war. Yet Britain steadfastly refused to support armed intervention in

the internal affairs of other states, and it was unclear from the start whether the Congress System would act against nationalist and democratic uprisings after 1815. For Alexander I the Concert of Europe was not enough. He proposed a "Holy Alliance," or a kind of Christian commonwealth, against the rationalism and anticlericalism of the Revolution. The czar was probably the only serious believer in the scheme, and his recent interest in religious mysticism was well known. All European rulers except the sultan, the pope, and the British regent signed the Holy Alliance, however, and liberals began to identify the Congress System with the counterrevolution.

The Revolution of the 1790s had apparently been overturned at Vienna. Expansionist France was contained, self-determination was denied, and secular ways of thought were refuted—such was the message of the dynastic restoration. Yet the revolutionary generation left a legacy

**EUROPE**
AFTER THE CONGRESS OF VIENNA, 1815

Map by J. Donovan

of profound change in European history. The nature of that change was visible to Napoleon in exile, where he cultivated the legend that the empire had been founded on principles of liberalism, nationalism, and religious toleration.

Liberalism, in its classic sense of the right to make free choices, especially in politics, broadly characterized the hopes of the Constituent Assembly in 1789. The Constitution of 1795 and the Civil Code were perhaps the two most widely imitated documents of the period. Although they promised no great downward redistribution of power in society, each of them was concerned with the protection of inalienable rights. The idea of a career open to talent entered European thinking about governmental administration. Ecclesiastical and seigneurial justice yielded to national courts within the empire. But monarchy was the system of government that was most trusted in western Europe in 1815.

Only a man as egotistical as Napoleon could believe that the generation had given Europe peace. The commercial and dynastic wars of the Old Regime recur in almost epidemic fashion after 1740. Of far more consequence to the future was the conversion of warfare after 1792 from the use of mercenaries and lower-class conscripts under aristocratic officers to the idea of the nation in arms. The emigration of noble officers and the *levée en masse* of 1793 set a pattern for a classless army, although no other nation achieved a base of conscription so broad as that of France in 1805. Even England found itself equipping 300,000 men in the army and half as many in the fleet by 1814. War hardened the conflict of social classes in France after 1792 and helped to destroy the attractions of the empire after 1804. For scholars who see a humanitarian concern in eighteenth-century ideas the wars of the Revolution have been called "the frustration of the Enlightenment."

Nationalism cannot be attributed directly to the revolutionary generation, although after 1808 the reaction against the empire was also a reaction against the French. France under the Convention and western Europe under the empire enjoyed more national institutions, however. Uniform weights and measures, the end of internal customs, and a single educational system all worked to speed communication within cultural units. Nationalist German and Italian historians consider the national awakenings in their countries, which had their roots in native soil but were nevertheless influenced by the French example, as part of a Europe-wide phenomenon of the 1790s.

That Napoleon saw correctly the weakening of the temporal power of the Church may have been due to his personal lack of religious conviction. The counterrevolution was built on a religious revival, especially after the pope's captivity, and was preserved by the French church's looking toward Rome for guidance after the hated revolution was over. But civil marriage and divorce, lay education, the civic oath as a test of morality, and the loss of Church estates won out over Burke's special protection of religion in the unwritten constitution.

Napoleon was unable to appreciate the passing away of two aspects of the generation. Guided by his own star, he could not have realized that aristocratic privilege received its deathblow between 1787 and 1815. There has been more recent historical argument over the nature and extent of social change than over any other problem, but it seems clear that the consti-tuted noble bodies lost much of their personal privilege, if not their political power or their lands, by 1815. The peasantry neither profited very greatly from the redistribution of land nor solved many of its economic problems, but the legal and social status of rural people improved in France, northern Italy, and western Germany. Bourgeois society, defined in terms of economic activity—especially trade and manufacturing—was retarded by the wars. But bourgeois society undoubtedly enjoyed greater prestige in 1815 than in 1787.

The Revolution as a historical myth naturally surpassed the vision of Napoleon. Institutions never received all of the sanctity that Burke had desired after 1789. Written constitutions and declarations of rights became living organisms in France and America by 1791, and most Western societies still venerate these documents more than any other civic artifact except the flag. The use of force by France to achieve legitimate ends became blessed with success too many times to allow Europeans to disregard the history of the period. Terror itself became legitimized in 1793, and every major revolution since then has seen the rationalization—and even glorification—of violence. Few revolutions in history have left such evocative symbols as the sans-culotte and the guillotine. The enigma of the revolutionary emperor haunted Europe for more than a generation after his death, and still defies the historical imagination. Although the immediate goal of European political society was to prevent the recurrence of another Napoleon, the mystique of the Revolution lived on to inspire one revolt after the other against the counterrevolutionary victors in the generation that followed.

## Selected Readings

*Amann, Peter. *The Eighteenth-Century Revolution, French or Western?* Boston: Heath & Co., D.C., 1963.

An introduction to a current debate on the scope and nature of the revolutionary movement(s).

*Behrens, C. B. A. *The Ancien Régime.* New York: Harcourt, Brace & World, 1967.

A short, masterful sketch of the revolutionary situation in France that uses social, political, and ideological analysis to show why the Old Regime led to violent revolution.

*Brinton, Crane. *A Decade of Revolution: 1789–1799.* New York: Harper & Brothers, 1934.

A competent general survey in the Rise of Modern Europe series; the revised paperback edition furnishes differing interpretations of the revolution.

———. *The Jacobins.* New York: The Macmillan Co., 1930.

This describes the organization and activities of the dominant revolutionary republican faction.

———. *The Lives of Talleyrand.* New York: W. W. Norton & Co., 1936.

A sympathetic biography of a celebrated opportunist who served many phases of the revolution and restored Bourbons.

*Bruun, Geoffrey. *Europe and the French Imperium: 1799–1814.* New York: Harper & Brothers, 1938.

A volume in the Rise of Modern Europe series that treats Napoleon as an enlightened despot.

Cobban, Alfred. *The Social Interpretation of the French Revolution.* Cambridge: Cambridge University Press, 1964.

Historiographical essays on the social history of the revolution, raising fundamental questions about all historical writing.

———. *Edmund Burke and the Revolt against the Eighteenth Century.* 2d ed. New York: Barnes & Noble, 1961.

This work sets forth the reversal of Locke's philosophy by Burke and the early romantic poets.

Gershoy, Leo. *The French Revolution and Napoleon.* New York: Appleton-Century-Crofts, 1964.

A standard textbook with an excellent annotated bibliography.

Geyl, Pieter. *Napoleon, For and Against.* New Haven: Yale University Press, 1949.

A collection of judgments passed on Napoleon.

Godechot, Jacques. *France and the Atlantic Revolution of the Eighteenth Century.* Translated by Herbert H. Rowen. New York: Free Press, 1965.

This work fully develops the controversial theme that a general "Atlantic revolution" encompassed the Western World.

Goodwin, Albert. *The French Revolution.* London and New York: Hutchinson University Library, 1953.

*A short, factual account, especially useful for beginning students.*

*Hampson, Norman. *The First European Revolution: 1776–1815.* New York, Harcourt, Brace & World, 1969.

*A sweeping, well-illustrated survey that finds changes less in material economic and social changes than in attitudes, especially a new xenophobia.*

Herr, Richard. *The Eighteenth-Century Revolution in Spain.* Princeton: Princeton University Press, 1958.

*This work discovers a belated Spanish Enlightenment produced by the French Revolution between 1792 and 1801.*

Hobsbawm, E. J. *The Age of Revolution, Europe 1789–1848.* London: Weidenfeld and Nicolson, 1962.

*With Marxist overtones, this presents the thesis that two revolutions, one industrial and one political, remade Europe with global consequences.*

Hyslop, B. F. *A Guide to the General Cahiers of 1789.* New York: Columbia University Press, 1936.

*This discusses the formulation and content of the "notebooks of grievances" compiled by the upper electoral assemblies at the outset of the French Revolution.*

Kaplow, Jeffry, ed. *New Perspectives on the French Revolution, Readings in Historical Sociology.* New York: John Wiley & Sons, 1965.

*A collection of articles on the social and economic pressures behind the revolution, especially those making the lower classes revolutionary.*

*Lefebvre, Georges. *The Coming of the French Revolution.* Translated by R. R. Palmer. New York: Alfred A. Knopf, 1957.

*A superlative short analysis of the events and background of the revolutionary movements of the year 1789.*

*————. *The Directory.* New York: Random House, Vintage Books, 1967.

*One of the few works available on the subject; it presents the Directory as the product of a reactionary bourgeoisie frightened by democracy, royalism, and centralized government.*

————. *The French Revolution.* 2 vols. New York: Columbia University Press, 1962–64.

*A translation of the author's influential work in* Peuples et Civilisations, *an interpretation friendly to the revolutionaries of 1789.*

Markham, F. M. H. *Napoleon and the Awakening of Europe.* New York: The Macmillan Co., 1954.

*A easy-to-read account in the* Teach Yourself History *series.*

Nicolson, Harold. *The Congress of Vienna, A Study in Allied Unity: 1812–1822.* New York: The Viking Press, 1965.

*A short treatment of the wartime treaties and the peace settlement.*

*Palmer, Robert R. *The Age of Democratic Revolution, A Political His-

*tory of Europe and America, 1760–1800.* Vol. 2, *The Struggle.* Princeton: Princeton University Press, 1964.

*This work recounts the revolutionary conflicts; it is especially informative on revolutions outside France.*

———. *Twelve Who Ruled: The Committee of Public Safety during the Terror.* Princeton: Princeton University Press, 1941.

*An analysis of the men and policies of the Terror, which emphasizes military considerations and treats Robespierre as one—not the most powerful —of the Twelve.*

*Rudé, George. *The Crowd in History, A Study of Popular Disturbances in France and England: 1730–1848.* New York: John Wiley & Sons, 1964.

*This analyzes the origin, composition, and motives of preindustrial crowds; the central chapters deal with the French Revolution.*

———. *Revolutionary Europe: 1783–1815.* Harper & Row, Publishers, 1964.

*A new general history, which disputes the Palmer-Godechot thesis of a general Atlantic revolution.*

Soboul, Albert. *The Parisian Sans-Culottes and the French Revolution: 1793–94.* London: Oxford University Press, 1964.

*This work shows differences between the urban lower-class movements and the Jacobins in power.*

Stewart, John Hall. *A Documentary Survey of the French Revolution.* New York: The Macmillan Co., 1951.

*A comprehensive collection of most significant documents up to 1799.*

Sydenham, M. J. *The French Revolution.* New York: G. P. Putnam's Sons, Capricorn Books, 1966.

*A solid analytical survey that ends with the Thermidorean reaction to the Terror.*

*Thompson, James M. *The French Revolution.* New York: Oxford University Press, Galaxy Books, 1966.

*A reliable summary by a biographer of Robespierre and Napoleon.*

Van Deusen, Glyndon G. *Sieyès: His Life and His Nationalism.* New York: Columbia University Press, 1932.

*A biography of an outstanding French nationalist who urged expansion and engineered Napoleon's coup d'état.*

Webster, Charles K. *The Congress of Vienna, 1814–1815.* 2d ed. London: Oxford University Press, 1934.

*A detailed exposition.*

Asterisk (*) denotes paperback.

# CHAPTER VIII

# Reaction and Revolution:
# 1815–1850

## A. The Revolt Against the Enlightenment and Revolution

When French imperialism collapsed with Napoleon's defeat, Europe's war-weary people obtained long-sought repose. But the social, political, and ideological tensions that produced violence in France in 1789 and had spread over Europe were still unresolved, for the counterrevolutionary victory restored to most positions of power the old elite of nobles, clerics, and hereditary monarchs who shunned as dangerous such things as science, intellectual freedom, and secular reform projects.

Challenged by the Enlightenment and by revolution, the old elite had produced a counterideology of conservatism or traditionalism. That ideology asserted that the rights, privileges, and powers that it had acquired in the past were indispensable in governing men depraved by original sin; human experience proved the necessity of such government and providence sanctioned it. Social and political reorganization, natural rights, progress, popular sovereignty, French dominion—these concepts must be repudiated, for they stemmed from the presumptuous aspirations of the bourgeoisie, behind whom lurked rootless urban workingmen and insurrectionary peasants. Fearing that any change would invite renewed revolution, traditionalists refused to share power with leaders drawn from the lower classes, and they used religious principles to justify that exclusion. The traditional monarchical governments restored to power in 1815 proudly proclaimed the union of Throne and Altar, and they would not tolerate criticism of that union—it was sacrilegious as well as subversive for the lower orders to question it.

411

Not surprisingly, such repression precipitated a renewed struggle with the bourgeoisie, dissatisfied intellectuals, urban workers, and, eventually, the peasantry, whose growing grievances had not been redressed. In 1820, 1830, and 1848 this struggle erupted in waves of revolution that became progressively more liberal-national in nature. First and foremost, liberals demanded constitutional, parliamentary government that would provide civic freedoms to the many and political rights to those who held property. Most liberals were convinced that such a regime was possible only when a single nationality constituted the body politic, hence they were nationalists, men who advocated the formation of states by people who shared a common body of historical and political myth. Not all nationalists were constitutionalists, but the two groups conjoined after 1815 to try to overthrow the Old Regime, which the Concert of Europe had reimposed on Europe. Both groups sought to substitute a new elite and establish new purposes for society. Also engaged in these revolts were a smaller number of socialist intellectuals and urban workingmen. They were not primarily interested in individual liberties or the securing of property rights but instead sought the creation of a regime that would guarantee social justice and distribute more widely the fruits of industrial productivity. For these purposes they naturally believed democratic government was best suited. In general, however, economic depression—not political or social ideology—kindled revolution among the urban lower classes during these years. The same was true of the peasantry still under old manorial obligations: they had their own grievances, which population pressure and depression rendered more unbearable. When liberal-nationalist revolutionaries proved unsympathetic to their economic problems, the peasants, still the great bulk of Europe's people, staged their own autonomous revolutions, especially in 1848.

By midcentury the bourgeoisie had gained power in most of western Europe; only in Britain and France were the middle classes seriously challenged by urban labor. In southern, central, and eastern Europe, however, military establishments usually came to the aid of the traditionalists and kept them in power.

Superficially these nineteenth-century struggles appeared to be waged between traditionalist defenders of the Old Regime on the one side and heirs of the Enlightenment and the French Revolution on the other. Although this generalization contains a large kernel of truth, it is much too simple, because both sides—and shades of opinion between them—were deeply imbued with romanticism. Traditionalists certainly fought to maintain the inherited social order; but in elaborating their defense of the Old Regime they mingled perceptive observations of society with a species of romanticism. Liberals fought for constitutional government under which policy would be determined by the outcome of rational debate. But they, too, invoked irrational sentiment—romantic nationalism—in their quest for power to reorganize society. Thus neither side rested its case solely on the precedents of the previous generation of revolution and counterrevolution.

Before turning to the renewed struggle of the liberals to remake Europe and the actions of the traditionalists to prevent it, we must, then, give some detailed attention to the admittedly confusing—indeed often baffling—impulse that we call "romantic."

## THE ROMANTIC IMPULSE

### The Many Faces of Romanticism

In its broadest sense romanticism meant reliance on the emotions or intuitive feelings to determine what is real and true. It appealed especially to intellectuals who reacted negatively to the "cold rationalism," scientific analysis, and material environmentalism of the Enlightenment. Thus it held great attraction to a generation torn by revolution, a generation that had failed to find the *philosophes'* simple, precise, rational solutions to pressing problems. Although the philosophes themselves had emphasized feelings as a motive force for constructive work along lines laid down by reason, the romantics of a frustrated generation made the stimulation of intense feelings an end in itself, the way of coming into contact with ultimate reality.

Using passionate emotion as a guide to life has been a perennial aspect of human experience, but its origins as an accepted, respectable outlook lay in the literature of the late eighteenth century. Popular chivalric tales; the novels of Fielding, Sterne, and Richardson, which adapted lower-class heroes and heroines to romantic themes; the studied, natural simplicity of Robert Burns's poetry; the mystical symbolism of William Blake; and especially the *Confessions, Emile,* and *The New Heloise* by Jean Jacques Rousseau, in many ways the "father of romanticism"*—all of these fed the rising tide of the cult of sentiment and emotion that considered reason without intuitive feelings sterile. Emotional religious revival movements such as the Pietists and Wesleyans also contributed to the same tide with their emphasis on "religion of the heart."† As early as 1756 Edmund Burke, the later counterrevolutionary writer, added a philosophic dimension to the romantic assault on the Enlightenment and neoclassical forms of expression with his *Philosophical Inquiry into the Origin of Our Ideas on the Sublime and Beautiful.* In conscious opposition to

the explicit classical ideals of such eighteenth-century painters as Reynolds and Gainsborough, Burke argued that man's deepest, most sublime emotions are not aroused by witnessing scenes of proportion, unity, serenity, and decorum. Rather they were stimulated by disintegration, dissolution, and distortion awakening horror and incomprehensibility. Instead of turning to classical rules and reason, the early romantics relied on genius, intuition, and emotions that stirred the soul intensely.

Romantics self-consciously repudiated the Deists' mechanistic view of the universe, which conceived God as a detached author of mathematical, mechanical laws operating in the same way everywhere. Instead of conceiving the cosmos as a creation finished at a given time in the past, they saw it as a "growing world," in which ever-increasing diversity expressed the essence and divine direction of nature. Whereas the philosophes found nature's God expressed in uniformities, the romantics found evidence of their deity in uniqueness, in the ever-growing differences that separated every individual part of creation from the rest of it.

They found support for their idea of a "growing world" in some contemporary scholarship and science. Research by medievalists, philologists, anthropologists, theologians, and legal scholars pointed to the historical *evolution* of languages, states, and concepts of God that gave each social organism its peculiar cultural individuality. As geologists explained the formation of the earth's crust over vast periods of time by processes that were still going on, physical and biological sciences began to turn to evolutionary hypotheses. Paleontologists, for example, discovered that forms of life had changed and that some of them had even become extinct. A half-century before Darwin's biology appeared, the idea of evolutionary change through time was "in the air." In

* See pp. 296–97.
† See pp. 302–3.

this scientific milieu the romantics first made the idea that an evolving spirit gives form and meaning to the material universe (conceived as a vast organism) the heart of a new world view.

If nature was a grandiose spirit-filled living thing whose whole was greater than its parts, mathematical laws of rational analysis could not express its essence; only feeling or intuition could perceive the spirit dwelling within it. Nor did the spirit dwell only within the external world organism. Self-made worlds were no longer consigned to childhood fantasies, for they, too, were part of experience and added to the diversity of the spirit's manifestations. Nominally individualistic rebels against all rules, the romantics inclined toward collectivism when they assumed that the individual was always subordinate to the organic whole of which he was a part. That whole—whether village, tribe, or nation—made him, they said, what he was.

In effect the romantics substituted a spiritual environmentalism for the material environmentalism of the Enlightenment. To them, man's material creations, instead of being his glory, somehow seemed degenerate. Anything done for individual self-interest would spoil natural spontaneity. Venting the frustrations and anguish they felt for the commercialization, urbanization, and industrialization of their own contemporary world, they dreamed of an idealized past, usually the Middle Ages. In doing so they heaped praise on (but never adopted!) the life of the peasantry because it was presumably least corrupted by human invention and artifice. And they spent great literary energies popularizing medieval chivalry in tales laden with selfless devotion to an altruistic ideal. Again and again the romantics took pains to demonstrate the miraculous power of inspired heroic will or character to triumph over the limitations of its physical environment.

Romanticism was more than a specific ideology; it was a method of confronting the universe and answering questions of every kind. In politics and social theory romanticism cut across every ideological boundary and gave particular force to varying kinds of nationalism—the identification of self with the nation, the greater whole. Anarchists, who proclaimed the iniquity of every restraint on natural freedom, were romantics, it is true, of one particular sort; but so were collectivists, whose fundamental assumption was that the individual possessed no reality apart from—and no higher duty than to—the nation. Between these two poles there were liberal, humanitarian romantics who divided their loyalties among state, church, family, inherited rights, and the individual's separate identity.

## The Romantic Break from the Classical Mold: Art and Music

Romantic individualism reigned most freely in the creative arts, where it took the form of the revolt of genius against the restrictive rules of composition and form that were imposed by neoclassicism, a revolt that culminated—in the nineteenth and twentieth centuries—in impressionism and expressionism. This romantic impulse was most strongly felt in music and literature. Some neo-Gothic architecture appeared—the British Houses of Parliament, for example; some painters (the "pre-Raphaelites") took as models the preclassical greats of the Italian Renaissance; "wild" landscape painting flourished; and painters such as Goya and Delacroix depicted the idealized writhing emotion of civil war and atrocities. But neoclassical standards continued to dominate architecture, sculpture, and painting as they had done during the late eighteenth century.

While Franz Joseph Haydn (1732–1809) and Wolfgang Mozart (1756–91) were the

*Classicism in painting: Jacques Louis David,* The Death of Socrates.

favorite guests of major courts, simplicity and formality dominated musical fashions. But the compositions of Ludwig van Beethoven (1770–1827)—notably his "Eroica," or Third Symphony, of 1804— initiated a break from "classical form" to meet the demands of expressing such psychological qualities as heroic strength and vitality, fear, horror, terror, grief, and endless longing. Other modes of musical feeling were created—the adaptation by Franz Schubert of lyric poetry to art songs, and the tone poems and symphonic poems of Felix Mendelssohn (1809–47), Robert Schumann, and Frederic Chopin. This generation used a wide variety of new devices to explore tone and color, and their experiments, coupled with the adoption of folk sagas as operatic themes in Germany, opened an era of romanticism for the following generation.

## Literature

Romantic writers concentrated on lyric poetry, novels—especially historical novels of the Middle Ages—and confessions of personal experiences. Early English novelists had written with sentimentality, but not to the degree that such English romantic poets as William Wordsworth (1770–1850), Samuel Coleridge (1772–1834), and John Keats (1795–1821) did. Choosing natural pastoral or exotic subjects, they evoked emotions ranging from childhood memories to the far-off mistiness of Kublai Khan in Xanadu (Coleridge). Theirs was an attempt to communicate directly and intuitively with nature through inner spirit. At the hands of Sir Walter Scott (1771–1832) history was transformed from the philosophes' record of the follies, vices, and manners of man-

*The attraction of Gothic and unspoiled nature: John Constable,* Salisbury Cathedral.

kind into the idealized and legendary local color of King Arthur's court. In America, where the grandeur of a medieval past was lacking, James Fenimore Cooper attempted to penetrate the imagined "inner soul" of the American Indian, presenting him as the truest son of unspoiled nature.

As we have seen, prerevolutionary France had its romantic prophet in Jean Jacques Rousseau, but his influence was more international than national. During the Revolution Madame de Staël (daughter of Jacques Necker) popularized romanticism by reporting on the land where it had its most extreme and permanent development, Germany, where a surfeit of unemployed young intellectuals were re-

pudiating the canons of classicism and rational natural law.

German literary romantics revolted against the petty, cramped court society of local princes, against French cultural dominance among aristocrats, and against the stringent rationalism of pulpit and university. Nowhere else had the classical ideal become such a fetish as among the university scholars of Germany. When a new generation of intellectuals (mostly from the middle and lower-middle classes), impotent to change the conditions of real life, shook off the classical spell, they veered to the opposite extreme, defying all conventions and restraints during a period of "Storm and Stress"

(*Sturm und Drang*), which spent its force between 1770 and 1789. Thereafter Goethe (1749–1832), Friedrich Schiller, and Johann Gottfried Herder strove for a delicate balance in drama and poetry between a rational desire for knowledge and the turbulent spiritualism of romanticism. Having welcomed the French Revolution, they were disillusioned with it by the end of the century and took flight into an idealism having little contact with everyday reality. Fed by Rousseau, English novels, and a revival of baroque literature, the German poets and dramatists Friedrich Schelling (1775–1854) and Friedrich von Schlegél (among others) turned to creative poetry to express an unrequited yearning for an "absolute" beyond the limitations of everyday life. From poetry and drama they turned to folktales and histories, especially the history of the Middle Ages. Casting aside all pretensions to scientific detachment, they made history bear witness to the manifestations of a World Spirit (*Weltgeist*) in successive "spirits of the time" (*Zeitgeiste*) and to the working out of beneficent purpose behind the violence and bloodshed that marked their own time. In rejecting the Enlightenment they praised all that it had condemned: religious fanaticism, the Middle Ages, the baroque, and spirited enthusiasm or faith. As former anarchists such as Johann Gottlieb Fichte switched from literature to politics under the impact of the Napoleonic wars, the boundaries between literature, religion, and politics ran together into a nationalism closely akin to French Jacobinism.

## Romantic Politics, Law, and Philosophy

Germany was the fountainhead not only of the literature, but also of the social philosophy, of romanticism. Herder's work preceded both the French invasion and the circulation of Burke's writings in

*Johann Gottfried von Herder, patriarch of cultural nationalism.*

German. One of the most influential writers for German—if not Western—civilization, Herder developed a cultural nationalism that laid the foundations for subsequent nationalist politics.

Herder conceived of each nationality as a living organic being with its own peculiarities and myths. In its primitive stages each had its own divine revelation from the World Spirit to its "founding fathers." According to Herder Germany's national spirit or genius (its *Volksgeist*) had its origins in late medieval folk poetry, which he tried to revive as popular literature. He was a cosmopolitan who conceived of each such genius living side by side with every other in harmony. Accordingly, he popularized early Slavic as well as German literature, laying a basis for Slavic cultural nationalism. But his premise that each nationality had the duty of developing its

*Hegel lecturing, University of Berlin.*

own peculiar spirit was also capable of being turned into a bigoted creed at the hands of traditionalists and nationalists.

During the Napoleonic invasions Fichte demonstrated the ease with which romantics could switch to collectivist nationalism. Formerly an anarchist who would accept no law to which he himself did not assent, Fichte began to preach the establishment of a German Jacobin state to repel the invader. Within that state the individual was to find freedom by total absorption into the nation-state, which would minutely regulate every aspect of life, including economics. Fichte and his fellow nationalists recognized only two realities—God and country (nation). And after 1815 some of his disciples considered only Germans capable of holding to either. Friedrich Ludwig Jahn, who organized a patriotic gymnastic society largely for dissatisfied college students, was one of these. In terms anticipating twentieth-century Nazis Jahn vehemently denounced extranational influences on Germany by such people as the Jews and the international bourgeoisie. But except for youths who had found no suitable "place" in society Jahn won few converts to his strident nationalism.

Political control in the German states rested not with publicists such as Jahn but with absolute princes and nobles, who found their principal spokesman in Friedrich Carl von Savigny (1779–1861). His first work on jurisprudence in 1814 justified the rulers' cancellation of the Code Napoleon wherever it had been introduced. Advocating the restoration of traditional legal systems based on the inequality of social estates, Savigny founded the "historical school" of legal and political theory that was dominant in Germany for the rest of the century. Repudiating natural rights as a pipe dream, this school of law subordinated the individual's identity to the hierarchical social order and to officials obedient only to the monarchy.

German evolutionary philosophy and social theory—the two became one—was expounded in its most classic form by Georg Friedrich Hegel (1770–1831). For him human affairs were ordered by an evolving World Spirit, which human reason could only intuitively "understand" or contemplate, for this idealistic, nonmaterial metaphysical force was beyond rational control. Embodied most perfectly in a succession of dominant states, this World Spirit would eventually reach fulfillment in the Absolute, a state of perfection. Meanwhile conflict would rage within existing, imperfect reality. Historical experience was the unfolding of a dialectical clash between opposites, a "thesis" and an "antithesis," which in collision would produce a new synthesis. This synthesis would in turn be a new thesis generating a new opposite, or antithesis, and the dialectical process of conflict would be repeated, frustrating all aspirations for human happiness. The younger Hegel saw this conflict primarily between economic and social classes, which only a reign of absolute law could quell. Later he saw it primarily as warfare between different states, each bound to assert its peculiar genius against others. Therefore in this spiritual dialectical clash that reflected the ultimate principle of the universe itself it was military leaders like Napoleon who made the real stuff of history.

Hegel's contemporary Prussian rulers were puzzled whether to consider him a revolutionary or an absolutist. Clearly he gave sanction to their tradition of militarism, and in one breath he identified the Prussian autocratic monarchy with perfection. In another, because the present was imperfect, his scheme indicated that change was both necessary and inevitable. His system was sufficiently ambiguous to serve those whose sentiments ranged from radicalism to reactionary absolutism.

In one sense Hegel secularized the Protestant doctrine of providence by advocating the contemplation of a new spiritual force that it was also beyond human ability to change, but French romantic social theory was closer to traditional theology. The principal theorists of the restoration—Chateaubriand, Joseph de Maistre, and Louis de Bonald—burned with religious zeal to restore universal papal authority. They believed that man, evil by nature, could be made sociable only by the inherited union of Throne and Altar, divinely sanctioned institutions wielding force. Because the Jacobins had been zealous users of force, they both admired and hated the revolutionary terror, for the executioner, one of them wrote, was the "savior of society." Romanticism proved too volatile, however, to sustain their authoritarianism, and after 1820 several prominent romantics, including Chateaubriand, turned to liberal causes and social reform, vainly hoping that the Church would follow their leadership.

## Romanticism, Religion, and the Restoration

French political thought of the Bourbon restoration was one of many indications that the Roman Catholic church, after reaching the nadir of demoralization during the Enlightenment, had revived during the era of revolutionary wars, when it even regained prestige in Protestant countries as a bulwark against revolution. From the fashionable skepticism of the Enlightenment most of the aristocracy returned to the fold of the Church, and restored Catholic monarchs, who showered churchmen with favors, proclaimed the union of Throne and Altar as the only legitimate basis for secular authority. For a time the revival carried overtones of the sixteenth-century Catholic Reformation. The Jesuits were reestablished, and in Rome and Spain the Inquisition and *Index of Prohibited Books* were resurrected. Moreover romantics who repudiated liberalism and the revolution were attracted by the Church's symbolic rites, art, music, traditions, and organic social doctrines. Many of them—including Chateaubriand, Joseph de Maistre, Louis de Bonald, and the German Novalis—became converts or publicists for a new international order under the papacy.

But papal support of political and social reaction cut short the postwar Catholic revival. Because he feared its blindness and lack of savoir faire in dealing with old revolutionaries, even Prince Metternich of Austria shied away from clerical reaction. In the course of time, however, memories of the revolutionary era dimmed, and as they did, one practical reason for the Church's recent popularity declined. Also, the spread of science and industry undermined the Catholic resurgence because high churchmen found it difficult to come to terms with modern, urban society.

At the end of the revolutionary wars some Protestant romantic foes of the Enlightenment were attracted to Roman Catholicism. Although belated (1845), the most conspicuous conversion was that of John Henry Newman, a prominent leader of the Oxford Movement in England that after 1833 began to stimulate religious enthusiasm by emphasizing the continuity of Anglicanism from medieval Catholicism. More common in the Protestant countries, however, were continuations of the emotional religious revivals of the

*Friedrich Schleiermacher, prophet of religious nationalism.*

eighteenth century, the Pietists on the Continent and the Wesleyans in England. German Pietism, in particular, merged with romanticism and nationalism, especially in the influential writings of Friedrich Schleiermacher (1768–1834). For Schleiermacher religion consisted not of dogmas nor in the quest for immortality but rather in the loss of self in the pure contemplation of the universe. For him the essence of religion was an extension of man's own consciousness, an intuition that answered a deep human need. Thus the Enlightenment's search for a universal natural (rational) religion was all wrong. "If you want to grasp the idea of religion as a factor in the infinite and progressive development of the World Spirit, then you must give up the vain and empty desire for one religion."[1] Cosmopolitanism

[1] Quoted by Koppel S. Pinson, *Pietism as a Factor in the Rise of German Nationalism* (New York: Columbia University Press, 1934), p. 73.

would disfigure the uniqueness of the individual and his national group. Christianity commands attachment to the nation, and Schleiermacher would make the nation-state the mediator between God and man.

Many Pietists refused, however, to follow Schleiermacher's fusion of religion and nationalism. Considering the war against Napoleon a holy crusade against the anti-Christ, several such groups called for abdicating sovereignty to a supranational government in order to obtain a new era of peace. In eastern Europe Bible-reading societies propagated such hopes. Some of their converts gained the ear and confidence of Alexander I, who tried to incorporate a supranational state into his Holy Alliance, but it was rejected by the Congress of Vienna.

More influential on the terms of peace were the English Wesleyans, who closely resembled the continental Pietists in emphasizing an inner religious experience, spiritual rebirth, and emotional faith. They also shared a qualified humanitarian outlook that sought to alleviate human misery, even though the roots of that misery—original sin—could not be eradicated. Foes of the rational natural-rights philosophy of the Enlightenment and the French Revolution, the Wesleyans became English nationalists during the wars with revolutionary France. Largely at their instigation the Congress of Vienna adopted provisions to bring the international slave trade to an end.

## POSTWAR POLITICS

At the conclusion of the Napoleonic wars the peacemakers' immediate concern was to contain future French aggression. The Concert of Europe, created by the Quadruple Alliance of Britain, Prussia, Austria, and Russia had maintained that purpose, but by 1818 Bourbon France had demonstrated its monarchical respectability. Thereafter the Concert changed its primary goal from the containment of France to the repression of liberal and national revolts. French entry into the alliance—now the Quintuple Alliance—clearly signified that change.

Conforming to the principle of restoring a balance of power, the Congress of Vienna had proceeded with moderation as far as territorial awards were concerned, moderation that laid the basis for a lasting peace. There was no major war before 1854 and no general war until 1914. But with respect to internal politics the Concert, headed by Austria, worked to keep in power regimes that were reactionary and often vindictive. To maintain themselves the restored rulers had at their disposal centralized bureaucracies, including secret police and *agents provocateurs*.* The Revolution had intensified their fears of the lower classes; consequently, wartime promises of constitutional or social concessions were forgotten or emasculated. Piety and fear of all innovations set the tone of the restored governments, which were beset with immense postwar problems. A few aristocrats like Metternich could still appreciate Voltaire, but the wit, frivolity, repartee, and openness of the Enlightenment were gone. When discontent erupted, the restored elites tried to stamp it out resolutely and forcibly for fear that a revolutionary movement would again get out of hand. In doing this they precluded the development of constitutional machinery capable of adapting to social and economic change.

Nevertheless for a time reaction had broad acquiescence if not popular support. For a generation the prestige of having beaten Napoleon put halos around the triumphant aristocratic leaders. Moreover most people on the Continent were still peasants uninterested in politics. Except in western Europe, liberal and national revolutionary leaders could count on little popular support, and by 1815 even in western Europe they were on the defensive if not quiescent. Their surest aid in producing new revolutionary situations was the reactionary policies of the restoration governments themselves.

## "Austria Over All"

The pivot of continental diplomacy, and therefore of internal policies enforced by it, was the Habsburg Empire. This multinational conglomeration was held together by its sovereign, the well-intentioned but inflexibly reactionary Francis I. He presided over an uncoordinated central bureaucracy that relied heavily on the army and a network of secret police. Although the Habsburgs had suffered much from the French Revolution, they were little influenced by it. The directors of this "absolutism tempered with inefficiency" simply concluded that reform did not pay. Francis I sounded the dominant note of the court when he wrote:

I do not want any novelties; all that needs to be done is to apply the laws in a fair way; they are good and satisfactory. The present is no time for reforms. The nations are dangerously wounded. We must avoid provoking them by touching their wounds.[2]

During postwar famine and depression Francis showed signs of benevolence, but his policies at home and abroad were tailored to the maintenance of the status quo. He restored, but seldom called, provincial diets dominated by nobles and clergy. He rejected Metternich's proposals for administrative reform even though Metternich himself was not committed to any basic social change beyond strengthening the landed aristocracy. Since rapid economic growth, liberalism, and nation-

---

* Undercover police agents who led illegal activities in order to entrap the participants.

[2] Quoted by Hans G. Schenk, *The Aftermath of the Napoleonic Wars* (London: Kegan Paul, Trench, Trubner and Co., 1947), p. 69.

*Prince Metternich, diplomat of stability and reaction.*

powers. Between 1807 and 1820 the Prussian king promised a constitution on five occasions, but Austrian warnings and royal vacillation prevented fulfillment. Four southern princes defied Austria by calling constitutional assemblies, but although all four constitutions gave ample protection to aristocratic privileges, Austria considered them dangerous concessions to liberalism.

As elsewhere, the Napoleonic wars left behind depression and stagnation disastrous to all social classes in Germany. But German economic problems were aggravated by traditionally anarchic standards of money, weights, measurements, and tolls. Some Germans emigrated to the United States, but the peasant majority of the population remained passive until 1848. Articulate agitation for national unification, constitutional government, and economic reform came primarily from the urban middle classes, some university professors and students, and a few nobles and officials.

Student societies (the *Burschenschaften*) and patriotic societies such as the *Tugendbund* (Virtue Union) and *Turnverein* (Gymnastic Association) led the agitation for national unification. Despite their meager following they aroused the authorities' fears. In 1817 the Jena student society led a rally at the Wartburg Castle near Eisenach to celebrate Luther's break from Rome as a great national act. The celebration—the first public protest against the settlement of 1815—ended with the burning of the Napoleonic Code and the symbols of restoration society, for both were regarded as impositions by foreign powers. In 1819 student radicals caused still greater fears when one of them assassinated a czarist agent.

Reacting sharply to this nationalist agitation, local monarchs invited the German Confederation to intervene. In the Carlsbad Decrees of 1819 it banned the student and patriotic societies, established rigid newspaper censorship,

alism threatened the social and political structure of the empire, Metternich's foreign policy (as well as Austrian domestic policy) was intended to squelch their emergence anywhere for fear that they might spread. As Austrian foreign minister, he understood their implications well and conceived it his duty to preserve a doomed order—to "hold the fort"—as long as possible.

## Unrest in Germany

After the war Austria was predominant in Germany and Italy. The Austrian chancellor presided over the German Confederation, which otherwise lacked real executive, military, or local administrative power. The Congress of Vienna had promised diets to the German states, but Austria worked to maintain the princes'

barred the employment of "objectionable" professors, and put informers in lecture rooms and some churches. In Mainz the Confederation set up a central investigating committee to snuff out subversive revolutionary ideas, but it uncovered no evidence of an organized revolutionary movement. Finally the Austrian-dominated Confederation guaranteed the sovereignty of its princes against limitation by the adoption of constitutions. But the more liberal monarchies of such states as Baden, Wurttemberg, and Saxe-Weimar, which already had constitutions, were restive under Austrian leadership, and by 1819 Prussian officials had already started a customs union, the *Zollverein*. By eliminating local tolls between Prussia and her neighbors the Zollverein facilitated commerce and, eventually, political unification under Prussian, not Austrian, leadership. Sponsorship of the Zollverein gave Prussia a reputation for economic progressivism that contrasted with, and thus emphasized, the handicaps that Austrian dominance preserved in the rest of Germany.

## Repression in Italy

After Austrian ascendancy replaced French hegemony in Italy in 1815, secret police and troops under Austrian control secured political conformity, but economically and administratively the peninsula was as divided as it had been before the French Revolution. In the south Ferdinand I (restored Bourbon ruler of the largest state, the kingdom of the Two Sicilies) committed himself to respect French reforms, but he also secretly pledged to Austria that he would allow no further constitutional changes. In southern Italy aristocrats and clerics continued to wield great power. This situation combined with corruption, inefficiency, and censorship alienated the middle classes and the army. Although one of Europe's largest cities—Naples—was situated in the kingdom, it was economically backward and plagued with nearly universal illiteracy, poverty, and brigandage. Feudal and theocratic traditions were still more dominant in the restored Papal States. Cardinal Consalvi, papal secretary of state, secured stable finances and refurbished the city of Rome, but there, too, the middle classes were alienated by censorship of the press, exclusion from government, and public disorders that fed anticlerical sentiments throughout Europe.

In the old city-states of northern Italy enlightened despots and French rule had removed the last remnants of manorial and noble jurisdictions, but Habsburg princes now ruled Modena, Parma, Lucca, and Tuscany. Lombardy-Venetia—whose geography provided strategic control over the peninsula—was administered directly from Vienna. These areas were managed efficiently, if somewhat despotically, and some concern was shown for commerce. Least under Austrian control was the kingdom of Piedmont-Sardinia, enlarged to form a buffer against French expansion, where enlightened despotism, a generation of French rule, and the annexation of Genoa provided institutions and interests that contested the Old Regime's return. But throughout the peninsula political reaction as well as clerical and papal resurgence marked the postwar years.

## Bourbon Spain

Conservatives like Metternich, Louis XVIII of France, and the duke of Wellington feared that flagrant misgovernment by vindictive restored rulers would provoke further revolution. Their worst fears were first realized in Spain. With the possible exception of Russia, no European kingdom had been less influenced by the philosophes and revolutionary thought. Still, Ferdinand VII proceeded against political dissent as though it were a huge threat. Clerics and nobles tried to erase not only the effects of the revolutionary epoch but also all changes of the eighteenth century. After the counterrevolutionary victory the privileges of the Old Regime were restored, the government identified itself with the Jesuits and the Inquisition, and only two newspapers were authorized—both devoted to the weather and religious subjects.

Ferdinand, zealous in pursuing opposition, was incapable of organizing an effective government. During the postwar commercial and agricultural depression (which was aggravated by revolts in Latin America) state finances collapsed, public services lapsed, and the army and navy went unpaid and underfed. The clergy successfully resisted taxation of its holdings, which the papacy had nevertheless been willing to concede in order to save the regime. Despite the narrow social basis of Spanish liberalism the first open revolution against a government recognized as legitimate at Vienna occurred in Spain.

## Restoration France

Even though Louis XVIII shared the clergy's belief in divine-right kingship and the union of Throne and Altar, he proved to be the most circumspect and practical of the restored monarchs. In 1814 he granted a constitutional charter that created a two-house legislature similar to the British Parliament. Most of the badly divided French population was probably prepared to accept any government that brought peace and guaranteed the liberties gained in the Revolution. This Louis was willing to do, for he tried to promote a royalist movement that would accept the charter of 1814. To suppress agitation for further changes he drove the republicans and liberals underground, but nevertheless his greatest opposition came from recalcitrant nobles and clerics, leaders of the "Ultras," whose aims were more similar to the policies of other restored monarchs than those of Louis XVIII.

Headed by the king's brother, the Count d'Artois, the Ultras had the only open political organization besides the king's. During the first elections the Ultras loosed a bloody "white terror" against former revolutionaries, Bonapartists, and Protestants, thereby securing an irreconcilable Chamber of Deputies "more royalist than the king and more Catholic than the pope." They denounced legal equality as blasphemy against God and attacked Louis XVIII as "a crowned Jacobin," because of his royal constitutionalism. In their vindictive attack on the Revolution and all its works they pushed through the assembly laws for administrative arrest and detention and for military courts removed from royal clemency. They also provided for preliminary censorship of the press and the abolition of divorce. And they successfully pressed for the execution of Marshal Ney, a prominent Napoleonic general whom they had charged with treason.

Affronted by Ultra opposition in the legislature, Louis dissolved it and, with an electorate broader than England's, secured a moderate royalist assembly in its stead. By 1818, in cooperation with the king, this assembly had put finances in order, raising loans to pay the war indemnity. It also secured the evacuation of occupation troops and relaxed censorship. Attempting to "nationalize the monarchy and royalize France," the king reconciled the old nobility, some of the Bonapartists, and part of the upper bourgeoisie, but he failed to placate either liberals or urban labor, whose efforts to organize during the economic crisis of 1816–17 were sternly repressed. Factions in the new assembly that assailed the ministry from both "Right" and "Left" gained at the expense of the middle. The Ultras grew particularly alarmed at liberal gains in the election of 1819, but they were unable to do anything about it until the Duke de Berry (son of the Count d'Artois, who was in the line of succession) was assassinated in 1820. The shock of his assassination enabled the Ultras to launch still another offensive. They doubled the votes of the wealthiest electors, appointed officers to supervise elections, and secured a renewed crackdown on the press, and they were even able to send French troops to suppress a revolution in Spain. When Louis XVIII died in 1824, making way for the Count d'Artois as Charles X, the Ultras' leader gained the throne itself. However, the events after Louis XVIII's reign belong to a new era of revolutions, since he was the last crowned monarch to die on the French throne.

## Russia

One outcome of the Napoleonic wars was that Britain and Russia—on the periphery of battle—suffered little decline as compared to the war-torn continental states, and both emerged from the wars with large territorial acquisitions. Neither suffered direct onslaught of revolutionary reorganization—Napoleon's invasion of Russia had been purely military—and both remained little touched by revolutionary ideology. As victors, they saw their traditional institutions acquire the prestige of demonstrated superiority.

The institutions of the Old Regime remained more vitally alive in Russia than in any other state. Catherine the Great's shallow enlightened despotism had yielded to the economic and political power of the serf-owning and landed nobility: at the outbreak of the French Revolution she banned everything French, forbad travel to France, and banished critics of serfdom and internal institutions who used words that the Empress herself had uttered previously. Catherine's unstable son, Paul (1796–1801), reverted to reform plans—suspending

nobles' privileges, limiting forced labor, fixing succession to the throne in the male line; but he was strangled in 1801 as the result of a conspiracy to which his son, Alexander I (1801–25), was privy.

Educated by a Swiss Jacobin tutor, Alexander was a late product of the Enlightenment and of religious pietism. Disliking class privilege, he ordered the drafting of a constitution, set about reorganizing the government, and laid plans for serf emancipation and education. He fostered intellectual and religious freedom, and founded three universities and many urban public schools. He also encouraged manufacturing and commerce, and forced serf holders to humanize peasant labor conditions. Theoretically the czar wielded unlimited power, but in practice Alexander was repeatedly frustrated. Nine-tenths of the people were illiterate serfs, turbulently dissatisfied, but undemanding of constitutional change. Townsmen, a potential source of discontent, were few in number, for Russia had only two cities of note, Moscow and St. Petersburg. That part of the aristocracy, bureaucracy, and army which had been exposed to European ideas and institutions was reform-minded; but the czar was dependent on irreplaceable administrators who detested reform and were subject to pressure from like-minded landed nobility. Understandably, perhaps, Alexander came to the conclusion that liberty in Russia depended upon unquestioned obedience to royal will.

When Czar Alexander I's domestic reforms had come to nothing by 1804, he turned more exclusively to foreign affairs where entrenched interests were less obstructive. In making proposals for an international postwar government, his cosmopolitan diplomatic corps served the self-interest of the nobles who had lost their foreign grain markets due to the war. At first Alexander had lauded the French Revolution and its principle of national self-determination while deploring its excesses and armed expansion, but now he proposed an international government (the Holy Alliance) that would restrict state sovereignty. Realists everywhere rejected the scheme except for the usefulness of its moral and religious principles to justify intervention against revolutionary change.

After the Congress of Vienna the czar's hands were tied at home but relatively free in territories ceded to him. He allowed the Finns to keep their traditional institutions and emancipated the peasantry in Russian-held Baltic provinces. To "Congress Poland" he granted a constitution ostensibly more liberal than that which existed in France and Britain. In several countries his agents worked with secret societies causing his wartime allies to fear that he intended to export this liberalism outside his own dominions. But in reality Alexander's liberalism was partly hollow, for the Baltic peasants failed to receive land and the Polish Diet had no control over the Russian-directed budget or army. "Alexander wants everyone to be free on condition that everyone obey him blindly," lamented a Polish aristocrat.

Repeatedly disillusioned by his allies abroad and conditions within Russia itself, Alexander came round to Metternich's repressive conservatism. After 1818 Russian policy became decidedly reactionary, and in Russia proper Count Aleksei Aracheev (1764–1834) and the monk Photius secured sufficient power to undo earlier reforms and apply repression. By 1815 Aracheev had already begun to establish military colonies for soldiers and their families, all subject to military discipline and exorbitant work and drill. By their agricultural production these colonies were to make the army self-sufficient; failing in this, they became nuclei of discontent. Despite a mutiny in 1820, the program of military colonies went on, and by 1825 an estimated one-third of the army was so deployed. Veterans who im-

bibed Western ideas began to form secret societies, draw up reform programs, and engage in elementary adult education. Alexander was probably ignorant of the colonies' worst features, but he was aware of the secret societies and their objectives. He did not suppress them presumably because their leaders had been his friends during his liberal youth. But especially after Alexander's death in 1825, Russian policy was directed by men who upheld the nobility as agents of a divine sovereign and threatened all dissent with exemplary displays of force.

## Conservatism in Britain

Paradoxically, Britain, whose institutions and liberties inspired revolutionary discontent on the Continent, became as absolute during the revolutionary wars as any other monarchy, and the freedoms on which its liberal reputation rested were not restored at the wars' close. By the end of the eighteenth century the entire political-constitutional apparatus was controlled by mercantile families and members of the landed aristocracy. Although it assimilated new wealth, the elite in Britain became nearly as closed as the aristocracies on the Continent. Legislation favored the squires and commercial magnates, while population pressure, early industrialization, and the French wars coincided to generate intense social difficulties.* One symptom of landlord dominance was the rash of enclosure acts —private acts of Parliament that consolidated and enclosed common lands—that deprived cottagers of access to land, making them (especially between 1794 and 1804) wage laborers heavily depen-

---

* An account of the Industrial Revolution and the increase of population in Britain appears in chap. 6.

*Bread riot, House of Commons, 1815.*

dent on relief.* Producing under the protection of agricultural tariffs, or "corn laws," landlords increased their profits after 1770—and spectacularly after 1793—at the expense of English consumers, who had to pay higher prices for food as a result. To finance the wars the government relied on indirect taxes and, to a much greater degree than in France, on loans. No concessions were made to the reform-minded, who were no longer represented in Parliament. Almost unbroken warfare from 1793 to 1815 enabled

* By 1795 local justices of the peace met the social crisis by adopting the "Speenhamland system" of relief, which provided aid to underpaid or unemployed workers at rates dependent on the price of bread and the size of the recipients' families. The government praised the "system" as a deterrent to revolution, but its operation reduced the mobility of labor and was detrimental to the wage system of remuneration.

the Tories to dominate the government, identifying domestic reformers with external revolutionary foes. To encourage this identification of reform with treason, the ministry employed *agents provocateurs*, newspaper subsidies, and packed juries, and cultivated conservative clergymen to crush the English "Jacobins." Parliamentary reform was thus postponed until 1832, and the English model of Montesquieu and Voltaire became an effective tyranny in ways that war alone did not explain.

Basking in the prestige of victory but faced with intense postwar problems, the Tory government continued repression after Waterloo. Victory proved little more prosperous than defeat, for Britain shared Europe's three postwar years of poor harvest; and while wages fell and prices and landlord incomes rose, heavy indirect taxes were used to retire the state's debt.

*The charge at "Peterloo."*

Especially in the textile trades unemployment of artisans rose due to market fluctuations, technological displacement, and the return of soldiers and sailors. In some parishes one-half of the population is estimated to have been on relief. During the depth of the crisis (1816–17) there were strikes, bread riots, machine-breaking demonstrations and rural incendarism. Cheap newspapers, reaching the lower middle classes for the first time, occasionally used revolutionary language. But in Parliament Whig critics went no further than to complain about using secret agents. Fear, whipped by the ministry's investigation reports, gripped the upper classes.

The government did little more than to check agitation and expand the Anglican establishment, but a few key Tories such as Castlereagh and Wellington sought to relieve social pressures by expanding trade. Probably because harvests were better, the tensions of 1817 fell short of revolution, but another crisis (a commercial depression) followed in 1819 after a period of rampant financial speculation. As part of a policy to repress all opposition outside Parliament, government cavalry charged a crowd that had illegally assembled at the new industrial city of Manchester, which was not represented in Parliament. Following this "battle of Peterloo," Parliament enacted the Six Acts, most of which were intended to be permanent. They further curbed public meetings, forbad unauthorized military exercises, provided drastic punishments for offenses against public order and libel laws, and authorized broad powers of search and seizure. Despite all the tensions within the world's leading commercial, colonial, and industrial nation, such popular reformers as the journalist William Cobbett had few followers prior to 1820.

During the 1820s new men began to form an opposition group in Parliament. Putting more emphasis on commercial and agricultural expansion, they relieved part of the population's grievances. In 1819 they obtained an initial but impotent factory act, and in 1824–25 they lifted some restrictions on trade unions. Later in the decade political disabilities were removed from religious dissenters, but this amelioration did not alleviate the grinding submission of Catholic and Protestant Ireland to British rule and exploitation. Both the labor laws and the religious emancipation acts, however, reflected the growth of humanitarian sentiment and organizations. Notably they attacked slavery, the abusive care of orphans, and conditions in factories, mines, and prisons. Humanitarian laws and the reform of parliamentary representation were probably the fundamental reason that Britain escaped the waves of revolutions that invested the Continent in 1830 and 1848.

## B. A Generation of Dissent: 1820–1848

Revolutionary elan and liberalism seemed dead after the Napoleonic wars. The victorious counterrevolutionary governments drove their remnants into underground conspiracies and secret societies by censorship, secret police, and surveillance, but active discontent survived, mainly among business and professional men, urban labor, displaced or unemployed artisans, intellectuals, and youth. Veterans who remained on active duty but whose prestige and income fell sharply after Waterloo also had significant grievances.

Part of the general discontent resulted from circumstances beyond governmental control: the end of wartime contracts, heavy war debts and taxes, incomplete reassimilation of vast armies into civilian life, poor harvests caused by bad weather, and the flooding of continental markets with British goods. Indeed, the masses became revolutionary only during times of economic depression. Nevertheless, inefficient government and discriminatory economic policies were major causes of the weak, sporadic disturbances that began in 1820.

Once stability was restored, dissent gained a broader base. This was particularly true where expanding economies produced a growing middle class, chafing under paternal restraints on its production and profits. Liberalism and nationalism, the two ideologies weakly represented by the revolts of 1820, gained increasing momentum and erupted in a more significant round of revolutions and constitutional changes between 1830 and 1832, especially in France, Belgium, and Britain. These liberal successes whetted desires for similar changes in the rest of Europe. A climactic series of revolutions and constitutional revisions blanketed the Continent from 1848 to 1850 with varying degrees of success and failure. The failures resulted in part from divisions within the revolutionary movement. Differing objectives between liberal constitutionalists and romantic nationalists came to light in eastern and central Europe, where militant nationalists, whose desires for national unification and self-determination were unsatiated, outstripped liberals, who were divided between constitutional monarchists and republicans. In central Europe the peasantry entered on a course that was independent of both. Urban workingmen in the more industrialized areas such as northern England, Paris, and Brussels also challenged the bourgeoisie's brand of liberalism. These divisions crippled the revolutionary movement; but despite them, the generation between 1820 and 1848 secured a more general extension of social and constitutional reorganization than had been won between 1787 and 1815.

## THE RESURGENCE OF LIBERALISM AND NATIONALISM

The liberals' watchword was individual freedom—under law enacted by representative, constitutional government. Nationalism was the belief that ultimate authority should be accorded to the nation-state. The *nation*—a new word in the century's vocabulary—was defined by language, cultural kinship and, above all, by a subjective feeling of "we-ness." Liberals and nationalists shared some common assumptions such as self-determination of peoples. Historical circumstances joined them in opposition to the Concert of Europe, which forcefully represented monarchical legitimacy, the divine right of kings. As a result of the experience after 1815, when nationalism and liberalism were closely associated, these two precepts have been frequently considered inseparable features of a new urban culture. But further experience has amply demonstrated that nationalism has combined with far more ideologies than liberalism. Even in this period czarist Russia, hardly an urban or a liberal state, proclaimed a highly xenophobic nationalist doctrine of Russian uniqueness and mission. By 1848 several European nationalist movements had proved incompatible with liberalism. Nevertheless the revolts between 1820 and 1848 were sufficiently interfused with the two "isms" to be categorized as "liberal-national" affairs.

## The Many Mansions of Liberalism

Liberalism presupposed the individual's rationality, aiming at a rationally directed social-constitutional structure without legal curbs on individual development or on the disposition of labor and property. Within the environment of traditional authoritarianism its first tasks were to secure free speech, a free press, religious toleration, and the removal of legal restraints on economic activity. This required changing to a constitutional monarchy or a republic whose legislative authority would be lodged in a representative assembly of those who were capable of independent thought—that is, those who were economically independent of others. Where representative assemblies already existed, liberalism was reformist and evolutionary; where king, noble, and priest jealously guarded their monopoly of power, it was necessarily revolutionary and anticlerical. Once in power, liberalism's formula was civic rights for all who accepted its constitutional order and political rights (such as the right to vote) for those capable of rational, independent decisions—that is, men of means and education.

Early nineteenth-century liberalism was preeminently the outlook of the bourgeoisie, who lived from investments, professional services, large-scale farming, or industrial management. Hence it is usefully called "bourgeois liberalism" to differentiate it from the "democratic liberalism" put in practice during the second half of the century and from the "social liberalism" of the twentieth century. Fearing the political influence of the urban lower classes and the peasantry, most

## MAJOR LANGUAGES OF EUROPE

Map by J. Donovan

**INDO-EUROPEAN**

- Germanic
- Germanic intrusions
- Romance
- Slavic
- Greek
- Greek remnants
- Celtic
- Baltic

**NON INDO-EUROPEAN**

- Basque
- Turkish
- Albanian
- Finnish, Estonian, and Magyar

bourgeois liberals withheld the franchise from them. Conservative bourgeois liberals, like François Guizot of France, considered democracy inherently socialist, and all liberals considered socialism abhorrent. Radicals like Jeremy Bentham, on the other hand, envisaged a democratic republic based on an educated electorate. Whatever the hue of their creed, liberals reacted against authoritarianism and its religious sanctions, appealing instead to natural secular laws. In effect, power in their state would fall to leaders of commerce, industry, and the professions, which they held to be the dynamic elements of society.

At least in the realm of economic pro-

duction bourgeois liberals considered all governments necessary evils at best. The state's authority should be limited to justice, defense, and a minimal number of public utilities; above all it should enforce contracts and protect property, retaining (if necessary) a strong monarch to do so. Theirs was a society based on contract and wealth rather than inherited legal status, but under their version of laissez-faire the state was to encourage production and distribution by standardizing weights and measures, eliminating internal tariffs, tolls, staple rights, and monopolies, and dissolving guilds and labor organizations. Then each individual, pursuing his own rational self-interest, could serve the commonweal, since the natural laws of supply and demand were self-regulating.

By curtailing economic regulation, state police powers (those dealing with health, welfare, and morals), and the harsh legal codes of the Old Regime, liberals would ostensibly establish a weak government narrowly limited in its functions. But the liberal state's reputation as a "watchman state"—Thomas Carlyle dubbed it "anarchy plus the constable"—proved transitory, because in fact it was legally more "absolute," although not more arbitrary, than "absolute" monarchies. Its legal equality under uniform laws meant the elimination of the intermediate jurisdictions of nobles, clerics, manor lords, and guilds, thereby bringing every citizen into direct contact with the central government which alone could then command the ultimate loyalties of the individual citizen. Relying on the consent of a widening segment of the governed, it could count on a greater degree of voluntary obedience than could any "absolute" monarchy. Historically bourgeois liberals founded representative institutions over which they partially lost control as large urban lower classes became literate and politically self-conscious. Ironically this happened as a direct sequel to the rapid economic growth which the bourgeois liberals themselves fostered, and as the social base of the liberal state expanded it began to enact comprehensive economic codes over the opposition of the bourgeois liberals who adhered to their original principles.

Major liberal theorists—Jeremy Bentham, Benjamin Constant, and François Guizot—flourished where parliamentary government already existed and the bourgeoisie already had economic and political power. In southern, central, and eastern Europe the liberals' only available channels were secret societies, conspiracies, and the use of force—which contradicted and weakened their own adherence to constitutional procedures. Also, in central and eastern Europe existing governments were either petty provincial states or multinational empires, and in such a setting romantic nationalism propagated by literary figures rather than experienced political leaders, came to overshadow liberalism.

## Nationalism

Liberals regarded the self-determination of peoples as the only legitimate basis for government. But while their outlook was based on this-worldly individual self-interest, romantic nationalism was a religious attitude that looked to the nation-state as the agent of moral regeneration. Nationalism was ethnocentric and demanded self-sacrifice. In Herder's footsteps, most nationalist theorists before 1850 professed a cosmopolitan humanitarianism that would be advanced as each nationality put its own house in order. Some even viewed the achievement of national unity as a stepping-stone to international federation; but others cherished the prospect of exerting their collective military power as the supreme moral good. Either way, the romantic nationalists shared with Giuseppe Mazzini (1805–72), leader of the Italian unification movement after 1831, the view that the nation was "the God-appointed instrument for the welfare of the human race." Thereby each particular nationality was the messianic agent for redeeming mankind. Nationalist literary men, journalists, historians, and linguists focused public attention on formative periods of national character and eras of past national glory, instilling in their youth a longing to reclaim lands held in the past. Scholars in both France and Germany, for example, probed their medieval pasts, laying the basis for conflicting claims to Lothair's "middle kingdom" of 843; many Greek nationalists wanted to restore the old eastern Roman Empire; Serbs strove to revive their fleeting greatness of the Middle Ages; and so forth. Thus romantic nationalists would not only break up supranational empires but also would engage in mortal combat with other "emancipated nationalities" whose territorial claims, based on "historic rights," overlapped their own.

## THE EUROPEAN
## REVOLTS OF 1820–1821

### Spain and Portugal

Before liberalism and nationalism became broad revolutionary movements, discontented soldiers, officials, and townsmen toppled traditionalist regimes in the Iberian and Italian peninsulas. On January 1, 1820 troops embarking from Cadiz to suppress revolts in Spanish America* mutinied against Ferdinand VII. Soon Madrid and other major cities (which were economically depressed) joined the rebels, and a provisional government proclaimed anew the revolutionary Spanish constitution of 1812, a copy of the French constitution of 1791, which Ferdinand had suppressed in 1814.

But most of the population, which was largely illiterate, remained apathetic. Moreover the inexperienced liberal minority in power was split between constitutional monarchists and republican radicals. The revolutionary military commander supported the radicals. The provisional government's actions quickly stirred opposition among nobles, clergy, and peasants, who denounced freedom of the press and legal equality. When the new civilian authorities suppressed the Inquisition, confiscated some Church lands, and abolished some monasteries,

Giuseppe Mazzini, cosmopolitan Italian nationalist.

they met greater resistance than they were able to deal with. And by granting amnesty to former Bonapartists and changing inheritance laws, they only made matters worse. Effective power passed from the *Cortes,* or parliament, to the army. By 1822, when French invasion was imminent, the army was the sole defender of the revolution. The following year French soldiers, acting in the name of the Concert of Europe, restored Ferdinand, who, in the name of religion and stability, suppressed the rebels ruthlessly. But Spain was torn for two generations thereafter by controversies over the succession. This struggle pitted Ferdinand's traditionalist-oriented brother Don Carlos against his daughter Isabella who was forced to rely on the towns for support.

Meanwhile in 1820 a revolt in Portu-

* See p. 437.

# UPRISINGS OF THE 1820s

St. Petersburg 1825

RUSSIAN EMPIRE

PRUSSIA
★Berlin

K. OF

Paris★
FRANCE

Troppau
★Vienna

EMPIRE OF AUSTRIA
•Laibach

1821
PORTUGAL

PIEDMONT
1821

1820
★Madrid
K. OF
SPAIN

SERBIA
1815-1826
(Successful)

1820
NAPLES

GREECE
1821-1829
(Successful)

SICILY
1820

Map by J. Donovan

liberal revolutionaries remained dependent on the vacillating support of the army to maintain their power.

## Italy

Repeatedly the example of one uprising spurred others. News of the Spanish revolt set off a similar one near Naples among discontented military detachments, who were joined by the militia and members of the *Carbonari* ("charcoal burners"), a secret society composed mainly of well-to-do landholders, professionals, liberal nobles, and judges. Alienated by inept administration and heavy taxes, they also decried the government's use of lawless secret bands to check organized brigandage and thievery—a cure as bad as the malady. On the mainland of the Kingdom of the Two Sicilies the rebels' victory was ridiculously easy. While it threw the central government into confusion, upper-class leaders demanding self-rule led a revolution in Sicily. Only there did serious fighting occur when Neapolitan forces tried to put down Sicilian separatists.

The victorious Neapolitan revolutionaries proclaimed the Spanish constitution of 1812, which few if any of them had read, and whose provisions had nowhere provided stable government. The single-chamber parliament was filled by moderate inexperienced lawyers, doctors, clerics, officials, and nobles, who were more capable of debating than governing. Their problems were immense: rifts between moderates and radicals divided them; the masses of the population were illiterate and indifferent; public order was wracked by brigandage; and the treasury was empty. In early 1821 Austria delivered the coup de grace to the revolution by sending an army at the request of King Ferdinand. Prior to his return to Naples the king allowed a conservative terror to purge the kingdoms of rebel leaders.

gal overturned the Braganza's regency council.* The rebels pressured John VI into returning from Brazil to proclaim a constitution and laws similar to those in Spain. But by 1823, when Brazil declared its independence of the revolutionary government and French troops entered Spain, counterrevolutionaries led by the king's son gained the upper hand. Spanish and Portuguese absolutists joined forces and received aid from Piedmont-Savoy, but Braganza rule was disturbed by factional conflicts over the succession and by occasional intervention by Britain and France on behalf of the liberals.

In both Iberian kingdoms political instability continued for the remainder of the century. Since economic expansion was insufficient to change the social structure in favor of the middle classes, both kingdoms proved too obdurate for a liberal-national victory. In both kingdoms

---

* Since 1807, when he fled French occupation troops, John VI maintained his residence in Brazil. Reflecting the extent of Britain's aid in driving out the French, his regency council in Portugal was dominated by a British officer.

Restored Bourbon rule in the Two Sicilies now gained the reputation of being the worst rule in Europe. It was kept in power and given a measure of stability by the Austrian army, whose garrisons remained (at Neapolitan expense) until 1827. The occupation costs, underwritten by loans that Metternich secured from the Rothschilds, proved ruinous to state finances. Although Metternich feared the repercussions of Ferdinand's mismanagement, his only suggested remedies were to improve administrative efficiency and apprehend dissident agitators. No fundamental problems of trade, agriculture, customs, industry, or education were tackled, and brigandage went unsuppressed. Although the Neapolitan revolt had been liberal, it was provincial rather than national, but the mode of its suppression could not have been better calculated to turn reform aspirations into nationalist, anti-Austrian channels.

In crushing the Neapolitan revolution Austria made one of its many moves to dominate the Italian peninsula. Another occurred in 1821 when rebelling liberal aristocrats, intellectuals, army officers, and students in Piedmont were immediately put down by Austrian arms, which the new king of Piedmont-Savoy, Charles Felix, had requested. Although the Piedmontese insurgents failed to coordinate their efforts with the Neapolitan rebels, their announced intention to unite all of Italy was significant for the Italian unification movement of the future.

## Turkey and Greece

The revolutions of 1820 and 1821 in Latin Europe succumbed to internal divisions and hostile intervention. Except in the minor Portuguese Revolution, no outside power supported the rebels diplomatically or militarily. In both the Balkans and Latin America, however, major powers belonging officially to the Concert of Europe actually supported revolutions against the status quo when it was in their interest to do so.

One area where major powers aided such a revolution was the European part of the Ottoman Empire, whose institutional decay and political disintegration invited outside interference. Russia, France, Britain and Austria were all interested parties, but Austria was temporarily preoccupied elsewhere. During the Napoleonic wars Russia had taken territory from the sultans and helped the Serbs achieve autonomy. In 1821, while Russia and the Turks were engaged in a dispute over treaty terms, Ypsilanti, a Greco-Russian general, led a body of Greek troops into Walachia and Moldavia, expecting Russian aid. Then a more general revolution broke out among the Greek peasants of the Morea and Aegean Islands.

Greek nationalism had been fostered by Greek merchants, whose wartime prosperity was reduced by the Viennese peace. The merchants, who had little in common with the illiterate, economically backward, clerically-led peasantry, had imbibed revolutionary European ideas. They revived Greek linguistic culture in their schools and founded a secret society, the *Hetairia Philiké* (Friendly Brotherhood), which spread among the mercantile colonies of the Black Sea and Aegean ports. The society's aim was to oust the Ottomans from the Balkans and resurrect the Greek medieval empire. While the peasants' war degenerated into a national-religious struggle of mutual extermination, Greek leaders proclaimed a constitutional government whose separate existence Britain recognized in 1822. But jealousies between leaders vying for political and economic spoils split the revolution into factions, and in 1825 it began to collapse before Turco-Egyptian forces.

At this point Greek freedom became the celebrated cause of a liberal romantic (Philhellene) movement in Europe and America, which urged governments

# LATIN AMERICAN INDEPENDENCE
### ca. 1824

TEXAS

*Atlantic Ocean*

*Gulf of Mexico*

MEXICO

Havana  C U B A *(Sp.)*

• Mexico City

SANTO DOMINGO

BRITISH HONDURAS

HAITI   PUERTO RICO *(Sp.)*

GUATEMALA
SALVADOR  HONDURAS
NICARAGUA

*Caribbean Sea*

CENTRAL AMERICA
*(Independent, 1821)*
*(Divided, 1838)*

COSTA RICA

Panama

Caracas •

TRINIDAD *(British)*

*VENEZUELA 1830*

BRITISH GUIANA
DUTCH GUIANA
FRENCH GUIANA

*Pacific Ocean*

Bogotá •

*Equator*

Quito •

*ECUADOR 1830*

GREAT COLOMBIA *1819-1830*

*Amazon R.*

PERU *1824*

Lima •

EMPIRE OF
BRAZIL
*1822*

B O L I V I A *1825*

La Paz •

*Chaco dispute*

PARAGUAY *1811*

Rio de Janeiro •

C H I L E *1818*

A R G E N T I N A *1816*

*Patagonia*

Buenos Aires •
Montevideo •

URUGUAY *(Independent, 1828)*

---

### ca. 1790

VICEROYALTY OF NEW SPAIN

CAPTAINCY-GENERAL OF CUBA

CAPTAINCY-GENERAL OF SANTO DOMINGO

HONDURAS *(Br.)*

JAMAICA *(Br.)*

CAPTAINCY-GENERAL OF GUATEMALA

VICEROYALTY OF NEW GRANADA

DUTCH GUIANA
FRENCH GUIANA

VICEROYALTY OF PERU

VICEROYALTY OF BRAZIL
*(Portuguese)*

VICEROYALTY OF BUENOS AIRES

0   100   200 mi.

Map by J. Donovan

0   50   100   150 mi.

whose nationals were economically involved in the area to intervene. In 1827 British and French naval forces destroyed the Turco-Egyptian fleet at Navarino Bay. In the following year France interdicted further Egyptian military operations against the Greeks, and Russia launched an invasion that culminated in the conquest of Adrianople in 1829. Foreign intervention thus forced the sultan to concede Greek independence. This was the first triumph of the principle of nationality in Europe since 1815. But the independent state that resulted was confined to the southern tip of the peninsula; by no means did it satisfy the thirst of revolutionary leaders for either self-determination or restored empire.

## The Latin American Revolts

Before Greek independence was finally recognized most of Latin America had successfully broken from Europe. The American revolutions were colored by sharp social cleavages that, as was not the case in Europe, involved racial distinctions. Tensions between the pure-blooded European Creoles born in America and the mixed, ostracized *mestizos* had erupted prior to the French Revolution; so had conflicts between the Creoles and officials sent from the mother countries who were at the top of the social-economic ladder of privilege. A few uprisings had occurred among the Indians, but this most grievance-laden class largely remained inert.

The Creoles were decisive for the Latin American revolutions, but their course was not consistently liberal or national. In the late eighteenth century many of them rallied to the Enlightenment, but when the French Revolution became radical and aggressive, they reverted to orthodox monarchism. Except in Mexico, where a social-political revolution was under way, the Spanish Creoles broke with Napoleonic

Spain in the name of Ferdinand VII. Royalist Brazil received the Portuguese royal family in exile. Then certain radical Creoles such as the wealthy, aristocratic Simon Bolívar, an admirer of both the French and American revolutions who had led repeated revolts for the independence of Venezuela, took to arms to secure total separation from Europe.

Expulsion of Spanish authority was largely the work of Bolívar in the north and José de San Martín, liberator of Argentina, in the south. After 1815 Bolívar's fortunes declined sharply, but when the Spanish Revolution broke out in 1820, he drove Spanish garrisons from present-day Venezuela. From there he pushed southward into Ecuador and Peru, the center of Spanish power, where he met San Martín leading liberation forces from Argentina and Chile. The southern revolution had begun in Buenos Aires, an area that Britain had unsuccessfully sought to annex as early as 1806. Ten years later a revolutionary government in Buenos Aires declared its independence. Thereafter, amid anarchic political conditions the southern portion of the Spanish empire in South America crumbled into local states. Carrying the revolution beyond Argentina, San Martín joined with Chilean revolutionaries and proceeded to Peru, where he retired in favor of Bolívar. By 1824 Spanish America had driven out its European officials, and Brazil had become independent of Portugal under Pedro I, eldest son of John VI.

Latin America secured its independence with the aid of Britain who reaped commercial rewards for its efforts. While British freebooters and veterans gave San Martín provisions, men, and direction, British trade and investments flowed into the whole Ibero-American area. At first the independence of the new states was recognized only by Great Britain and the United States, who engaged in weak competition with one another for the area's trade.

## The Collapse of
## the Quintuple Alliance

The revolutions of 1820 and 1821 tested the resolve of the Quintuple Alliance of 1818 to keep Europe peaceful and conservative. Metternich's Austria, by its geographical position and interests, was destined to lead the alliance in the crushing of liberal-national uprisings. The Spanish revolt of 1820 presented the first challenge. But Spain was remote, and Metternich hoped that the revolution would burn itself out. Naples, on the other hand, was too close to ignore. At Troppau in 1820 the three Eastern members of the Alliance met with observers from Britain and France to consider these revolts, and Metternich completed Alexander I's conversion to conservative interventionism. Thereafter Austria, Russia, and Prussia agreed to the Troppau Protocol justifying intervention against liberal-national revolutions:

States which have undergone a change of government due to revolution, the results of which threaten other states, *ipso facto* cease to be members of the European Alliance, and remain excluded from it until their situation gives guarantees for legal order and stability. If owing to alterations, immediate danger threatens other states, the powers bind themselves, by peaceful means, or if need be by arms, to bring back the guilty state into the bosom of the Great Alliance.[3]

Lord Castlereagh, whose country supported constitutional governments for their stability and openness to British trade, rejected the Troppau Protocol as an illegitimate extension of the postwar treaties. At a subsequent congress at Laibach (in present-day Yugoslavia) the issue of intervention in Italy came to a head. Austria secured authorization (although not from Britain) to destroy both the Nea-

[3] Quoted by W. Allison Phillips, *The Confederation of Europe*, 2d ed. (London and New York: Longmans, Green & Co., 1920), pp. 208–9.

politan and Piedmont revolutions. Britain eventually approved this intervention in Italy—as an act of Austrian self-defense, not as a general principle.

To deal with the Spanish, Latin American, and Greek revolts, the powers next assembled in 1822 at Verona in Venetia. Czar Alexander, who had provided a reserve army to back up the Austrians in Italy, pressed for authorization to send his forces across Europe to Spain. But his proposal stirred fears of Russian expansion. For Metternich, French intervention in Spain was a palatable substitute. Furthermore the expedition fitted into domestic French politics as a way of reconciling both the Ultras and the army (bored with inactivity) to the government of Louis XVIII. Once more Britain, fearing further intervention in Latin America under French auspices, stood aloof.

The crushing of the Spanish Revolution in 1823 was the Concert's last victory. Britain's new foreign minister, George Canning, welcomed the return to a situation of "every nation for itself and God for us all." Already he was involved in aiding the Greek and Latin American uprisings. To forestall intervention in Latin America he turned to both the United States and France. He proposed to the United States a mutual declaration guaranteeing Latin American independence and pledging both countries not to acquire territory for themselves; from France he secured a formal disclaimer of intent to intervene. The American President, James Monroe (who was advised closely by John Quincy Adams), spurned Canning's proposed joint declaration in favor of a unilateral declaration, later known as the Monroe Doctrine, in which he warned that the Americas were not to be considered subject to further European colonization.* For good measure he asserted American noninterference into the fundamentally different political system of Europe. The

* Monroe was also concerned with Russian territorial expansion on the Pacific coast of North America.

Monroe Doctrine exhilarated America's sense of national pride, but for the time being it was the British fleet and Canning's pledge from France that were the surest guarantees of Latin American independence.

Reduced to the three Eastern monarchies of Austria, Prussia, and Russia, the Concert continued to function in attenuated form. The formal machinery of cooperation established at Vienna was further weakened, however, by the Greek revolt. Metternich was able to prevent Alexander I from active participation, but after the czar's death in 1825 Russia joined with Britain and France to help the Greeks win their independence.

### The Decembrist Epilogue

Alexander I's death in 1825 provided the occasion for Russia's one fleeting revolutionary experience in the nineteenth century. Discontent within the army among officers recruited from the nobility and men who were inspired by Western liberalism broke into open revolt in December 1825. A southern group headed by Paul Pestel (1793–1836) agitated for liberation of the serfs, abolition of class privilege, a republic based on manhood suffrage, and the forcible assimilation of non-Russian minorities. Simultaneously a northern secret society, which included noble landlords as well as soldiers, took Bourbon France as a model. Neither group had a significantly large following, and both organizations were transient, their revolt more a matter of unexpected opportunity than of planning. When Alexander died, the succession was not clear because Constantine, the next in line, had secretly renounced the throne. During the three-week interregnum military units in St. Petersburg attempted a coup d'état under the slogan "Constantine and Constitution." As Nicholas I took the throne, both insurrections were quickly smashed. Sub-

sequent would-be revolutionaries would later study the Decembrists' naïve tactics for knowledge how *not* to conduct a revolution.

### TREMORS OF CHANGES: 1830–1832

None of the risings of 1820 and 1821 had survived without foreign assistance, and the Italian and Spanish revolutions had collapsed when met with force. But by 1830 conditions had begun to change perceptibly: the Concert of Europe was in disarray, and ecclesiastics no longer presented a solid counterrevolutionary front. In France a liberal Catholic movement had started, and in Poland and the Belgian half of the kingdom of the Netherlands local churchmen openly opposed the status quo. Romantic liberals and nationalists were gaining converts through an expanding press, education, and the popularization of causes such as Greek independence. Although most of Europe remained as agrarian and economically backward as it had since the Renaissance, an agricultural revolution was beginning to uproot inherited relationships in the countryside. Expanding commerce and industry bred discontent among businessmen and guildsmen. In 1830 only France sustained a revolution without foreign aid, but the revolts of 1830 and the peaceful constitutional changes that occurred in Britain, some Swiss cantons, and a few German states by 1832 indicated a much broader liberal-national base of support than had prevailed in 1820 and 1821.

### Bourbon Rule Deposed in France

France (or more specifically, Paris) was the epicenter of the revolutionary quake beginning in 1830. Charles X, whose ac-

# REVOLUTIONS AND REFORMS
## 1830 - 1832

*North Sea*

DENMARK

*Baltic Sea*

UNITED KINGDOM OF
GREAT BRITAIN AND IRELAND

K. OF THE NETHERLANDS

HANOVER

PRUSSIA

Berlin ★

K. of Poland

Warsaw ●

RUSSIAN EMPIRE

Reform Bill of 1832

London ★

BELGIUM

K. OF

HESSE

SAXONY

★ Paris

FRANCE

local reforms
SWITZERLAND

AUSTRIA

Vienna ★

German Confederation

Budapest ●

AUSTRIAN EMPIRE

Turin ★

Constitutional
reforms

Revolutions

Unsuccessful

Successful

K. OF
SARDINIA

Corsica

PAPAL
STATES

Rome ★

Naples ★

OTTOMAN EMPIRE

SERBIA

MONTENEGRO

*Adriatic Sea*

KINGDOM OF THE
TWO SICILIES

0    100    200    300 mi.

Map by J. Donovan

cession Louis XVIII prophetically feared as the doom of the Bourbon dynasty, could not keep a moderate ministry working under the Charter of 1814. The court, ministries, and legislators were under Ultra influence. At the court, medieval pageantry and the practice of the king touching subjects to miraculously cure them of disease were revived. Ministers openly counted on divine assistance for their policies, and laws initiated by the assembly were seemingly designed to restore the Old Regime. New laws cut down the number of voters already sub-

ject to pressure from appointive officials, eliminated jury trials for critics of the government, and extended clerical education. In 1825 the government reduced the interest paid to bondholders in order to compensate *emigrés* for land that had been confiscated during the revolution. Stern penalties for sacrilege—the despoiling of Church properties and objects of worship—were instituted. Another measure would have restored inheritance by primogeniture among the nobility, but the Chamber of Peers—the upper house of the legislature—which contained Bonapartist

*The last of the Bourbons: Louis XVIII (seated) and the Count d'Artois, the future Charles X (left).*

elements rejected it. And courts mitigated the censorship laws by acquitting persons accused of treason under them.

Liberal opposition fanned by journalists mounted as influential bankers and intellectuals, who hitherto had usually kept aloof from the conspiracies of secret societies, joined in denouncing the government. Hostility to the Bourbons was the major cause of resentment, but there were also economic grievances that made workingmen revolutionary. Lower-class Parisians suffered from a lack of work, low wages, and the high price of bread. Instead of the "dangerous classes," however, it was the more solid artisans who formed the backbone of the revolutionary crowds as they had in 1789, but these crowds were not much interested in the constitutional issues that inspired the liberals. Charles X and his ministers, discovering that mild appeasement failed to satisfy liberal agitators, turned to vain expedients. As a distraction from domestic tensions and as an appeal to nationalists, Charles began an invasion of

Algeria. When liberal dissent continued to swell, he resorted (July 1830) to a series of ordinances that provoked a popular revolution in Paris.

The July Ordinances, although promulgated without military precautions, gave popular credence to the charge that Charles intended to restore royal absolutism: they dismissed an elected assembly before it met, forbad further publication without prior government authorization, reduced the electorate, and placed Ultras in high office. Journalists, however, defied the censorship and denounced the ordinances as violations of the charter, while Talleyrand (among others) negotiatied with leading bankers and citizens of the capital to plan a new government. Constitutional monarchists emphasized that no social-economic upheaval was in the making. Paris, however, still nourished a small republican movement that was socially more radical. The revolt began when employers freed their workers to take up arms. The republicans made the first show of force, but they were promptly left

The Charter or Death, *Parisian poster of 1830.*

stranded when Lafayette, their political idol, attached himself to the dominant revolutionary faction: the constitutional monarchists. Their candidate for the throne was Louis Philippe of Orleans, himself a Bourbon, but one who had participated in the early stages of the French Revolution and who now accepted its symbols.

Louis Philippe, replacing the fleeing Charles X, gave up royal power to issue decrees, recognized Catholicism as the religion of the majority (he himself was a Deist), made civil liberties more firm, and lowered voting qualifications slightly. As in England in 1688, divine-right monarchy was replaced by the rule of an elite defined primarily by wealth. Louis epitomized the ideals of his principal supporters—thrift, investments, and dedication to order; the ideological spokesman

for the July, or "Bourgeois," Monarchy was a historian—François Guizot—who held office during most of Louis' reign. Guizot's histories and policies identified the interests of the bourgeoisie as the golden mean, the *juste milieu,* between royal absolutism on the one hand and, on the other, democracy, which he considered a stepping-stone to abhorrent socialism. Attuned to bourgeois liberalism, his policies alienated the republicans, Bonapartist advocates of power politics, and urban workingmen to whom the government made few concessions.

Because the Parisian revolution of 1830 overturned a key provision of the counter-revolutionary peace of 1815, the restoration of the legitimate line of Bourbon kings, it excited both conservatives and liberals across Europe. Metternich, a constant prophet of doom, judged it as being the end of his life's work. Eager to intervene, Nicholas I of Russia assembled troops in Poland, but he was too far away. Louis Philippe reassured the conservative powers that he had no intention of exporting revolution, but in fact the French example caused revolutionary and reform movements to spread out in an emotional wave. It precipitated uprisings in Belgium, Italy, and Poland and stirred agitation for constitutional changes in Switzerland, Britain, and several German states. One revolution encouraged agitation for another, and the fact that several revolts were going on at the same time gave them the effect of diplomatic coordination, for the revolts in eastern and central Europe pinned down the military forces of the Eastern empires, precluding their intervention in the West.

## Belgium Achieves Independence

Prior to 1830 there had been no general agitation for Belgian independence, but since the forced Dutch-Belgian union of 1814, latent grievances had been accumulating among the Belgians. More numerous and less indebted than the Dutch, they had to share equally with them in representation and combined debt, and the administration, although enlightened, was Dutch. It laid much of the basis for Belgium's subsequent rapid industrialization, but Belgian critics attributed the problems of the middle and lower classes to their Dutch officials—particularly to their low, agriculturally oriented tariffs. The religious rift was more serious: Belgian Catholics opposed the state's monopoly of lower education, and Catholic conservatives resented forced freedom of conscience. The revolt in Paris brought dissatisfaction with the House of Orange to a head. In August Belgian leaders presented the king with demands for reform, but his concessions came too late. A provisional government declared Belgium independent—a clear violation of the peace settlement at Vienna, and in 1831 the new state adopted the most liberal constitution in Europe. It provided for popular sovereignty, local self-government for provinces and towns, and basic freedoms (press, assembly, religion, and education —albeit clerical education). The constitution contained no restrictions on the suffrage, although later statutory enactments limited voting to the wealthy.

To declare independence, however, was not the same thing as achieving it. William of Orange confidently anticipated assistance from the Eastern powers, but Britain and France adhered to the principle of no counterrevolutionary intervention. After the outbreak of a revolt in Poland in November 1830, they secured international recognition of Belgian independence and its perpetual neutrality. When Orangist troops moved to recover the Belgian provinces, both France and Britain intervened to prevent them. Not until 1839 did William, still absolute in the Dutch provinces, acquiesce in Belgian independence.

## Uprisings that Failed: 1830 and 1831

The remainder of the uprisings of 1830 and 1831, whose leaders counted vainly on French assistance, occurred in eastern and central Europe and ended in failure and renewed reaction. The largest and most significant of these was in Poland. In reaction to the repressive policies of Nicholas I, nationalism flared in "Congress Poland" among the aristocracy, army, and intellectuals. A secret society, established in Warsaw at the army officers' school in 1828, was first in effectively organizing discontent. When rumors spread that Polish troops were to be sent to France and Belgium, soldiers and students rebelled. Then, after Russian troops withdrew, the aristocratic Polish Diet declared Nicholas

*Polish revolutionary forces, 1831.*

deposed. The aristocrats, fearing radical nationalists who desired social reforms, tried to negotiate with the czar. This social division weakened the revolt, as did the spread of Europe's first cholera epidemic. Russian troops took only from February to May of 1831 to suppress it. Vengeance followed. The universities were closed; lands were confiscated, and the intellectual elite of Poland emigrated en masse to western Europe (especially Paris) and to the United States. In new homelands they helped paint Russia's image as the major suppressor of human liberties.

Revolts in northern Italy—Parma and Modena—and the northeastern Papal States challenged Austria's hold in Italy in 1830. Although literary nationalists revived Dante and Machiavelli and recalled Italy's glory in resisting German rule during the Middle Ages, these revolts were local rather than national; the Carbonari, who organized them, seldom aspired to more than provincial independence. Playing upon local rivalries, Austria crushed them one by one in 1831. For Italian nationalists this experience reconfirmed the lessons of 1820 that Italian disunity was responsible for the peninsula's subjection to Austria.

The reaction that followed was significant for both Italy and Europe. The papacy, in whose states revolts had occurred, condemned liberalism unconditionally in 1832; liberal Catholics were denounced for supporting freedom of conscience, freedom of the press, separation of church and state, and "other harmful errors of those who, possessed by an undue love for liberty, do their utmost to undermine authority." This position sharpened the cleavage between liberalism and the Church, and it encouraged nationalists to uphold their creed as a rival religion. The Italian fiasco of 1831 also discredited the old secret societies. Now Giuseppe Mazzini's Young Italy took the lead. Its tactics were secret and conspiratorial also, but its religious nationalism intended to unite all of Italy by concerted action.

## Nonrevolutionary Changes (1830–1832): The Great English Reform Bill

The liberal-national surge of 1830, either because it was weak or because authorities made concessions, did not lead to violence everywhere. Slavic and Magyar nationalists were reviving their literatures and histories. Eventually their cultural nationalism led to political self-consciousness, but, for the moment, the Habsburg government, which ruled most of the nationalities involved, kept it in check. In Hesse and a few other German states the revolts of France and Poland served as a goad for constitutional reform. Saxony and Hanover adopted laws that totally emancipated the peasantry from inherited dues and services, but in most of Germany this revolutionary period produced more agitation by professors, students, lawyers, and writers than immediate concrete achievements. Again, as in 1819, the German Confederation thwarted constitutional changes and curbed dissent. Individual Swiss cantons were able to show more liberal results by 1832: local constitutions now provided for popular sovereignty, a broader suffrage, and secular education. Agitation also occurred in Scandinavia but, except for the establishment of consultative assemblies in Denmark, no institutional changes occurred. England's Reform Bill of 1832 was the main nonrevolutionary constitutional change in Europe. By 1830, when the first bill to alter Parliament was introduced, industrialization had drastically altered Britain's economic, social, and demographic structure, while the basis for representation in the House of Commons was still that of the seventeenth century. Wealthy landed persons, sometimes a single family in a "pocket borough," elected members to the House of Commons or appointed representatives for towns that had ceased to exist, while populous industrial cities like Manchester were totally unrepresented and industrial counties like Yorkshire had only its usual two seats. Conservative defenders of the existing constitution claimed that under the old system all Englishmen were "virtually" represented by men of wisdom. Tory repression, however, failed to check pressures for reform. During the 1820s young humanitarian Tories including Robert Peel, George Canning, and William Huskisson cooperated with moderate Whigs to break the Tories' solid front. But moderate reform did not become a real issue until the Whigs adopted it as a party program. This occurred during the excitement produced by the July revolution in Paris.

Newspapers and popular orators generated public support for the bill that Lord Grey, the new Whig prime minister, submitted to Parliament. But Grey and his titled cabinet ran into a flurry of opposition from the older Tories and higher churchmen. When the House of Lords blocked the bill in 1831, mobs patrolled the streets of Bristol and other cities. Armed organizations appeared, and the Bank of England was threatened with a run on its gold reserves. When the Duke of Wellington tried to form a die-hard cabinet, Britain came close to civil war. When Wellington failed, the king agreed to threaten the Lords with the mass creation of new peers favorable to the bill. In 1832 the Tory peers decided to let the bill pass

*A Union Jack for the Reform Movement, 1832.*

worst abuses of the old system without a thorough revision of the electoral machinery, taking seats from smaller boroughs and transferring them to the industrial towns and counties of the north and west; it also extended suffrage to the upper middle classes. Landed and commercial wealth still dominated the House of Commons, but the admission of wealthy industrialists to political power challenged the Tories and established a balance of power that utilitarian radicals and humanitarians exploited in order to secure reform. Both Whigs and Tories considered the Great Reform Bill "final." Its sharing of power between aristocracy and middle classes provided the axis of politics known as the "Victorian Compromise."* Instead of being final, however, it had broken the principle that only landed property holders could participate in politics. Thereafter no easily defined principle separated the one property holder in thirty already entitled to vote from the one in four or five whom universal manhood suffrage would enfranchise.

* The workings of the Victorian Compromise as well as its revision and eventual destruction are treated in Part III, chap. 4.

rather than risk civil war or dilution with new peers. Thus British conservatives and particularly the king demonstrated greater flexibility than Continental traditionalists. The conservatives, erroneously predicting that reform would cause a revolution, yielded peacefully to popular pressures.

The reform bill cut away some of the

## C. The General Revolutionary Sweep of 1848–1850

Constitutional changes between 1830 and 1832—by evolution and revolution—drew a boundary between a liberal West and an absolutist East and Center. The major Western states were no longer part of the Concert of Europe. In 1833 the monarchs of Prussia, Russia, and Austria consolidated their triumph at München-grätz by reasserting their collective right to intervene against revolts outside their borders. For their severity in repressing liberal revolts, Western liberals denounced the Eastern regimes. Subsequent diplomacy eased this East-West rift, but a crucial question remained to be tested by the next wave of revolutions: how far would the Western states go to aid uprisings against the Eastern empires?

A dispatch from the British foreign minister, Lord Palmerston, to the British ambassador to Russia in April 1848 made clear how transitory the defeat of most of the revolutions of 1830 had been. Palmerston wrote that (with the exception of Belgium) Britain and Russia "are at present the only two Powers in Europe . . . that remain standing upright." Especially for central Europe, the 50-odd revolutions of 1848–49 brought to a climax and exhausted the ideology of the French Revolution.

Social and economic conditions in that part of Europe were more similar to pre-revolutionary France than to industrializing Britain or traditionalist Russia. There were only a few pockets of industrialization, railroads, and improved communications. As in the great revolution of 1789 a combination of problems older than industrialization coincided to make a broad section of the central European populace revolutionary—at least for a time.

Burgeoning liberalism and nationalism were only partly responsible for stirring the people up, for these ideologies motivated only a small minority—albeit an important outspoken revolutionary minority, the middle classes and the intelligentsia. With respect to the less articulate lower classes rapid population increase, followed by a general crop failure in 1846, heightened unrest. Inclement weather and the potato blight shriveled the peasantry's store of staple foodstuffs from Ireland to central Europe, creating a subsistence crisis. The resulting famine was responsible for the collapse of commerce and credit in 1847. Skyrocketing food prices during depression put rural and urban workers and guildsmen in acute distress, and in a few areas this distress was magnified by the replacement of craftsmen by machines. Discontent among the lower classes (especially the peasantry) paralyzed existing governments, making the liberal-national intellectual minority freer to work than they were in 1830. With remarkably little violence central Europe seemed won over for liberalism and nationalism at the peak of the revolutions of 1848. Yet much more than liberalism and nationalism was involved in shaping the course of these revolutions—their causes, temporary victories, and especially their failures.

The liberals' apparent power was a temporary illusion, for they represented only a small segment of the forces working to sustain the revolution. The peasants ceased being revolutionary when they secured release from their old manorial dues and services. When anticapitalist workingmen asserted themselves in France and Germany in early summer, the bourgeoisie recoiled in horror, leaving further revolutionary activity to a narrow segment of radical republicans. The revolutionary wave ebbed further as nationalist animosities arose to prevent cooperation between different revolutionary movements. Counterrevolution had another unexpected ally in the cholera epidemic, which struck preferentially at the densely populated cities, debilitating its surviving victims and terrorizing the spared, since contemporary medicine was helpless against it. As the older authorities regained their nerve and the will to use force against their inexperienced foes, the liberals' early bubble of success broke before a new wave of reaction. The most durable gains were not theirs but the peasants'.

# FRENCH REVOLUTION AND COUNTERREVOLUTION

## The Toppling of Louis Philippe's Bourgeois Monarchy

Between 1846 and 1848 restiveness caused by the economic depression was general, but it first boiled over into revolutionary riots in January 1848 in Palermo, Sicily, where the Carbonari were instrumental in fanning resentment to Austria's repressive domination. Within a month similar riots swept almost all of the

PUT OUT!

*Liberty extinguishes Louis Philippe's candle.*

with the continuing conquest of Algeria, Bonapartists derided the government for its disregard of national prestige and glory. Frequent attempts were made to assassinate the king. And François Guizot, his principal minister from 1840 to 1848, found it difficult to hold the loyalty of the minute electorate—about three percent of the adult males—whose unpaid representatives he manipulated by appointing them to profitable government offices. This narrow bourgeois government not only aroused conservative opposition but also, by a callous policy toward urban labor, contributed to the rise and influence of socialist intellectuals, whose plans to reorganize the economy will be discussed in chapter 7. Most of the early socialists—whether advocates of violence such as Auguste Blanqui or humanitarians such as Saint-Simon, Louis Blanc, Victor Hugo, and George Sand—agreed that a democratic republic must succeed Louis Philippe's government. If opposition to the Orleanist monarchy was alarmingly widespread, the divisions rending that opposition were equally ominous for the erection of a stable substitute.

Supporters of deputies in opposition to the monarchy, forbidden to hold political meetings, began holding banquets with political toasts and interminable speeches. After the Italian revolts began they planned a massive banquet and demonstration in Paris on February 22, 1848. When the government ordered it cancelled, prominent sponsors and members of the assembly withdrew. Although the banquet was never held, the government ban stirred resistance, which in turn was answered by repression. Students and workers clashed with the police, and rioting inspired by martyrs continued for several days. Reluctant to provoke further bloodshed, Louis Philippe successively dismissed Guizot, called off military suppression, and, after barricades were thrown up in the working-class districts, abdicated.

major Italian cities and Ferdinand II was forced to grant the Neapolitans a constitution, a precedent other Italian rulers were soon obliged to follow. Also within a month Louis Philippe's opposition in Paris started open agitation that came to a head in his abdication. Italians first set off the revolutionary powder train of 1848, but their efforts were soon overshadowed by events in France, a major power whose aid other revolutions counted on.

Louis Philippe's government had lost the support of one major segment of the population after another. The French Revolution of 1830, which Victor Hugo described as a "revolution stopped half way," left the republicans totally without influence and hostile to the regime. Also in opposition to Louis were the Legitimist Bourbons, whose dissent split and weakened French conservatism. The governments' Voltairean anticlericalism also alienated Roman Catholics. Unsatisfied

Republicans and socialists (mostly journalists from two capital newspapers) joined together in proclaiming a provisional government, France's Second Republic. Prodded by the people of Paris, a nonindustrialized city of more than one million people that had increased by one-third since 1830, this government proclaimed universal manhood suffrage, absolute freedom of the press, and other radical measures. Slavery, imprisonment for debt, and capital punishment for political offenses were abolished. For urban lower classes it guaranteed a right to work at livable wages, reduced the work day from about 14 to 10 hours, set up an employer-worker council, and authorized the establishment of producer cooperatives as a substitute for private capitalism. However, the provisional government inherited an empty treasury and an economic crisis that soon became catastrophic. As wealthy Parisians emigrated by the thousands, credit dried up, banks closed, the markets slumped, shop closures swelled unemployment, and the cooperatives (Louis Blanc's National Workshops) seldom got beyond unproductive relief projects. Inexperience and the substitution of zeal for skill plagued the new government.

The provisional government's most severe weakness was its narrow urban basis of support. Election by universal suffrage, even at the height of revolutionary fervor, produced a majority of republicans, monarchists, and clericals determined to wipe out concessions to urban labor that were being financed by rural taxes. The constituent assembly, elected in April, removed Parisian radicals from positions of power and utilized the National Guard—a bourgeois "honor society"—to thwart pressures from working-class districts. Its decision to abolish workshop relief, giving recipients the choice between draining pestilential swamps in the provinces or joining the army, provoked open warfare between the popularly elected government and the Parisian workers. During the "June Days" (June 23–26) more than 50,000 workers, whose leaders were in jail for having organized previous risings, took to the barricades. Unlike the liberal cry of "liberty or death," theirs was "bread or lead." The assembly gave full authority to an Algerian veteran general, a republican—Cavaignac—who used the new telegraph and railway system to gather troops from the provinces. Waiting to attack until the insurgents had completed their barricades, Cavaignac reduced them by withering artillery fire. Thus the workers' defeat was the bloodiest suppression of a popular revolt thus far. According to official statistics, whose adequacy is subject to serious question, 1460 lives were lost, including prisoners summarily executed at the end. Of more than 11,000 prisoners, nearly 500 were still being held in 1850. The bloodshed of the "June Days" sealed the doom of a social democratic republic, for the insurrection's affront to the government of the Second Republic, which represented popular sovereignty, produced a shock wave of reaction that revoked all social concessions made to the working classes during the revolution. This schism among revolutionary factions ensured the triumph of a conservative counterrevolution.

## The Fall of the Second Republic

Cavaignac's victory inspired conservatives throughout Europe, and in France initiative shifted from the divided republicans to clerical monarchists and frightened bourgeoisie. The new constitution promulgated by the constituent assembly in November 1848 added further to the republic's woes by creating a power stalemate between a strong elected unicameral assembly and a strong elected president that resulted in the breakdown of constitutional procedures. The subsequent election in December of a Bonapartist

*Procession of Napoleon's ashes at the Arc de Triomphe, 1840.*

president, who promptly appointed a monarchist ministry, and the election of a monarchist assembly in January sounded the republic's death knell.

In electing Louis Napoleon (nephew of the great emperor) president, the voters—largely peasants enfranchised by the republic's new universal male suffrage—repudiated the socialists, radical republicans, and even the conservative republican, Cavaignac. Louis Napoleon's past smacked of comic opera, but he bore the great general's name and exploited the legend that Napoleon I had been the champion of peace and the common man.* To the "Left" he posed as a socialist; to the "Right" he appealed as a disciplinarian of labor, an apostle of authority and order.

* In addition to the writings of Napoleon himself Louis Napoleon had contributed to the making of that legend. In 1840 Louis Philippe had the emperor's remains returned to Paris and interred (with much ado) in the Dôme des Invalides.

Ironically for democratic liberals, universal manhood suffrage in a society that was still basically agrarian had produced a government less liberal than that of Louis Philippe. Led by clerical monarchists, the new assembly proceeded to purge urban radicals from the electorate, give the Church an enlarged role in primary and secondary education, and join with Louis Napoleon in destroying the short-lived Roman Republic in 1849.* But by reacting against radicalism more than public opinion warranted, the assembly armed Louis Napoleon with the popular support to destroy it: when the assembly refused to amend the constitution to allow him to succeed himself as president, he staged a coup d'état (on December 2, 1851—the anniversary of Napoleon I's great victory at Austerlitz). After suppressing republican uprisings he obtained authority by

* See p. 456.

# MAJOR REVOLUTIONS AND REFORMS

## 1848-1849

Constitutional reforms
Revolutions

Mediterranean Sea

0    100    200    300 mi.

Map by J. Donovan

---

plebiscite to write his own constitution. Once again a revolutionary French republic had given way to a Napoleon on horseback.

## HABSBURG HUMILIATION AND TRIUMPH

The Parisian uprising of 1848 was far more provocative than the July revolution of 1830. Not only did it produce a republic that was feared, but one that, while pledging no aggressive war, disavowed the treaties of 1815 and claimed the right to intervene to protect other revolutions against foreign suppression. But the pace of change in 1848–49 was so rapid that, instead of aiding revolutions abroad, France became conservative and acted only to preserve peace and to put down the Roman Republic in 1849. As for intervention by the Concert of Powers in France, the series of uprisings that invested central Europe made any such plans completely useless. So many revolutions occurred in such a short period of time that only the more strategic ones can be discussed here. Probably the most significant revolt of the series was the one that toppled the Habsburg bulwark of counter-revolution in central Europe.

## Habsburg Paralysis: The Viennese Revolt

Institutionally the Habsburg bureaucracy had become frozen in the state that reaction to the reforms of Joseph II and the French Revolution (1789) had left it. It was a rigid, centralized absolutism, dependent entirely on the monarch's person for its coordination, and was unresponsive either to social-economic changes or to the burgeoning demands for provincial or national autonomy. Until his death in 1835, Francis I rejected Metternich's proposals to reform the wooden bureaucratic machine. But even Metternich lacked a sense of urgency for domestic reform. Moreover he (who once quipped that he had sometimes ruled Europe but never Austria) lost influence in domestic affairs under Francis's weak-minded successor, Ferdinand. The upper aristocracy—a self-contained social world insensitive to the pressures for change among its subjects—dominated the bureaucracy, pursuing policies inimical to the provincial German diets, the peasantry, and nationalist movements in the non-German provinces where a majority of the monarchy's population lived. Its repression of the interests of the middle and lower urban classes jeopardized Habsburg economic development, but its failure to cope with the peasant problem was worse, since it alienated both nobles and peasantry.

Before 1848 some landlords adopted changes in agriculture that upset inherited relationships on the manor. Demand generated by a rapid increase in population led large landholders, usually organized in agricultural societies, to introduce new crops such as sugar beets and potatoes. They developed more productive strains of cattle, brought old and newly reclaimed lands into more intensive production, and improved transportation to markets. Their greatest needs were twofold: credit for capital investment and an efficient supply of hired labor in place of inefficient forced labor. Provincial diets dominated by progressive landlords petitioned the government to establish credit institutions. They also wanted a form of peasant emancipation that would give them a ready labor supply and control over peasant lands. These landlords were willing to surrender feudal jurisdictions and some peasant obligations gratis, but they insisted that emancipated peasants pay for their land and for release from labor, dues, and fees.

Under the existing system the peasantry, which constituted about four-fifths of the population, owed as much as 70 percent of the product of its labor to Church, state, and landlord. The peasant accepted the idea of emancipation gladly, but balked at paying for it. An uprising in Galicia in 1846, when peasants refused to perform services and pay dues, seemed to forecast general revolt not only in Habsburg areas but in the whole of north-central and eastern Europe. Fearing that freed peasants would become dangerous bands of idlers and cease paying taxes, the bureaucracy refused to consider emancipation.

A crisis sparked by economic depression had been germinating in Vienna and Budapest for several months prior to the revolutions in Italy and Paris. Then, beginning in early March, popular movements gained progressively greater concessions from the Habsburg government. First, the court dismissed Metternich, symbol of the era just past. He took refuge in Britain. Then the emperor promised a constitutional convention, agreed to revolutionary Hungarian laws, and promised administrative autonomy to the Bohemians. Stirred by nationalism and liberalism, Croats, Serbs, Slovaks, Czechs, Moravians, Galicians, and Rumanians were also demanding constitutional rights and local autonomy. Late in April the emperor promulgated a centralized constitution based on the Belgian constitution of 1830. Slavs distrusted it as being pro-German, and the populace of Vienna rightly suspected that the emperor was insincere, but further pressure forced him to fulfill his promise of a constitutent assembly. Soon thereafter the court left the capital, and a popular government took the place of imperial authorities. This precipitous collapse of Austrian central authority encouraged revolutionaries in Italy and Germany and gave the Habsburg liberals and nationalists an illusory sense of power.

In July of 1848 the revolutionary constituent assembly, composed mainly of urban liberals, proclaimed emancipation of the peasants but postponed a decision on indemnities. The peasantry—the greatest social force behind the whole revolutionary movement—had no interest in constitutions or liberal government; thinking that the victory was won, they withdrew support from the revolution, leaving the liberals and nationalists to fight their own battles. But the liberals' and nationalists' concept of property closely paralleled that of the nobility. A law passed in September 1848, and retained by the counterrevolution, required that the peasants pay for release from old obligations in kind, labor, and cash. The outcome was an unmerited double victory for the Habsburg court: first, the peasantry had withdrawn from the revolution at a critical point; second, the provincial German aristocracy had lost its principal economic grievance against the bureaucracy. Now the two could work more closely together.

## Slavs and Magyars

In the non-German Habsburg provinces nationalism, as much as the peasants' revolt, caused the breakdown of central

Metternich's flight, a caricature.

authority. Hungarians had long resisted Habsburg encroachments on the noble Diet's autonomy. In 1825 the Diet vindicated its power to levy troops and taxes. Modern liberalism and nationalism shaped its resistance after 1830, even though Hungary's political, economic, and intellectual life remained almost entirely in the hands of a medieval aristocracy.*

* The Magyar aristocracy had clung more tenaciously than any other in Europe to semifeudal privileges. Together with the clergy the aristocracy enjoyed the exclusive right to own land; the right to hold peasants and administer justice over them; exemptions from taxes, tolls, and penal laws; and participation in the Diet. The Diet was divided between the magnates and the exceedingly numerous untitled gentry. The magnates held great conglomerations of landed estates which passed intact from generation to generation due to laws preventing their division among heirs. They joined with the clergy to form the upper house of the Diet and laid exclusive claim to the major offices of state, church, and army. The gentry, whose economic and social position varied widely, formed the lower house of the Diet: the Table of Deputies.

*Louis Kossuth in the Hungarian Diet.*

At first the liberal-national Magyar movement was cultural and economic; then it became political. The Magyar language was revived and, in 1844, was made the official language of the kingdom. Count Czecheny (1791–1860), a great noble, worked to imitate western Europe's economic development and to institute gradual political reform. An agrarian-based liberalism spread rapidly among the gentry and, in 1847, carried the lower house of the Diet. The liberal majority passed on to the upper house of magnates bills to reorganize the Hungarian state and society, providing for a constitutional government responsible to parliament, a large list of personal freedoms, the compensated emancipation of the peasantry, and termination of rigid entails that prevented the division of inherited estates; but they were blocked in 1848 by the magnates and the court.

As revolution swept Europe, Hungarian leadership passed to the radical Louis Kossuth (1802–94). While the Habsburgs were weakened by the revolt in Vienna, Kossuth secured royal approval of the liberal reforms. Liberalism, however, was the lesser half of the Hungarian reform program. And nationalism, the greater goal— the will of the ruling Magyar minority to impose its language, culture, and rule upon the entire kingdom—immediately alienated the Slavic Croatian and Rumanian majority. Therefore the Croatians helped the Habsburgs suppress Hungarian independence, which was weakened by the failure of the Hungarian gentry, considering itself the whole nation, to win support of its own peasantry. Thus its narrow, aggressively intolerant nationalism played into the hands of the Habsburgs who, with Russian assistance, crushed Kossuth's newly proclaimed Hungarian Republic in 1849.

Nationalist movements posed less of a threat to the Habsburg court than to the Magyar bid for independence. Some Slavs, notably the Bohemians, demanded cultural and political autonomy, but no major Slavic group attempted to secede from the Habsburg orbit. Political circumstances dictated otherwise. Divided geographically by Magyars and penetrated by islandlike settlements of Germans, the Slavs' main concern was to avoid being ruled as subject peoples by either German or Hungarian nationalists. To resist these pressures the Czechs and Moravians took the initiative in organizing a Pan-Slav Congress in Prague in June 1848, whose objective was a federated empire of equal nationalities. Its leading spirit, Francis Palacky, a historian who glorified Czech independence prior to Habsburg rule, firmly committed himself to the political consolidation of central Europe. He wrote that if the Austrian Empire did not exist, "in the interest of Europe, nay of humanity, it would be necessary to make haste and create it."

While the Pan-Slavs met in Prague, riots expressing stronger desires for democracy and autonomy broke out among the city's people. The outcome was disastrous to both Czech autonomy and the Pan-Slav Congress. Prince Windischgrätz, a thoroughgoing absolutist whose wife had been an accidental victim of the rioting, turned loyal troops on the revolutionary movement. After reducing Prague and Bohemia to a military dictatorship, the Prince then prepared to move on Vienna. His action marked the first successful reconstruction of "pre-March" Habsburg authority.

## Italian Revolution
## and Counterrevolution

Soon thereafter in Italy another imperial general, the aged but able Joseph Radetzky, defied the court's orders and began a military rout of the revolutions that had swept the Italian peninsula earlier in the year.*

Austria's grip on Italy had begun to waver prior to 1848. A popular book on political prisons had kept alive resentment of the reprisals of 1831, and the Lombard-Venetian population was restive under the arrogance and Germanizing tendencies of their officials appointed from Vienna. Hatred of Austria had become a religion for angry young men lacking wealth and social position. They heeded Mazzini's call for assassination and guerilla warfare as a means of uniting and regenerating Italy and of establishing republican freedom. After 1840 moderate constitutional monarchists competed with Mazzini for influence. One group hoped that Charles Albert of Piedmont-Sardinia would lead a crusade for unity; another formed around the plan of Abbé Vincenzo Gioberti of Turin, who proposed a federation under the papacy. Gioberti's scheme became popular after 1846, when a new pope, Pius IX, named a lay advisory

* Ironically, the revolutionary government in Vienna ordered him to take the offensive against Italian revolutions.

council, adopted plans for gaslights and railroads, and resisted Austrian troop movements in 1847 and 1848.

Before Metternich's fall in 1848, riots and revolts radiated throughout the peninsula from Sicily, causing rulers in Naples, Florence, Turin, and Rome (Pius IX) to introduce constitutions. One of these, the *Statuto,* issued by Charles Albert of Piedmont-Sardinia—a royal grant of parliamentary government, individual rights, and a very narrow suffrage—eventually became the constitution of united Italy.

Following Metternich's dismissal, Austrian hegemony quickly collapsed. In a five-day war against Radetzky's garrison the Milanese drove Austrian troops from their city, and before the end of March the Austrian dukes had been evicted from Parma, Modena, and Tuscany. Charles Albert, hoping to extend his dynasty, declared war in late March, helping to drive Austrian garrisons from most of Lombardy and Venetia. They retired to the security of their northern fortifications.

But in June and July the tide began to turn. The king of Naples used Swiss mercenaries to break the Neapolitan parliament, enabling him to withdraw his troops from the north. Under Austrian pressure Pius IX also withdrew his troops. Radetzky, rejecting his government's plans to abandon Lombardy, reorganized his troops and began to recover one Venetian town after the other, although not Venice, whose republican government did not fall until August 1849. Even as disillusionment with liberal ineffectiveness spread, radical republican movements came to the fore, taking power in Rome and Florence, and Charles Albert was induced to reenter the war. But the spread of radicalism alienated the moderates, notably the patriotic Pius IX, whose civil powers in Rome were seized by republicans, causing him to flee to the protection of the king of Naples. When Charles Albert was quickly defeated again, the remaining revolutionary governments were left on their own resources to resist Austrian counterrevolutionary arms. Under the military leadership of Giuseppe Garibaldi, the Roman Republic held out until the end of June 1849, when it succumbed to French forces sent to restore the pope. Starved and ravaged by cholera, Venice, the last pocket of revolutionary resistance, fell to Austrian seige at the end of August. Apart from the Piedmont constitution, no positive vestige of the revolution survived the vengeful reaction which again reigned in Italy.

## Habsburg Recovery

Counterrevolution in Italy restored Austrian power, coinciding with its success in the older Habsburg domains. During the summer and fall the liberal-national tide began to ebb as rapidly as it had risen. Dissipation of pent-up emotional energies, the ruinous impact of political uncertainty upon the economic crisis, and liberal fears of urban lower-class movements partly explained the debacle that began during the summer. However three interrelated, underlying factors account better for the liberal demise:

(1) Conflicting noble and peasant programs for peasant emancipation previously rejected by the government were resolved in July, so that both parties assumed victory and stopped opposing the government.
(2) Local national movements that had defied the central government became mutually antagonistic after the revolution began.
(3) A breakdown in the bureaucracy of military conservatives, who were more politically experienced than the liberals, mended during the summer and fall.

The ascendant court banished the constituent assembly from Vienna to the Moravian town of Kremsier. In March 1849 the assembly completed a federal, parliamentary constitution with guarantees to individuals and minorities. The Kremsier Constitution proved to be the empire's last chance to avoid nationalist disruption; however, it remained a dead letter because Radetzky's absolutist favorite, Prince Schwarzenberg, gained control of Habsburg affairs. Securing the accession of Francis Joseph I (1848–1916!) who had made no promises to the liberals, Schwarzenberg canceled all concessions and grants except peasant emancipation. He proclaimed his own centralized constitution, whose provisions for popular representation were never implemented and whose equality was of subjects instead of citizens. Successfully crushing the Hungarian Republic with Austro-Slav and Russian assistance, he built a new, modernized bureaucracy, which trampled asunder every local and inherited aristocratic privilege that stood in the way of centralized absolutism. Thus, under military auspices he remedied the breakdown of the "pre-March" administration. While carrying through reforms almost as thorough as the Napoleonic Codes, Schwarzenberg successfully contested Prussian dominance in the German states, where revolutions had also failed.

## THE LIBERAL-NATIONAL MISCARRIAGE IN GERMANY: 1848–1850

Like Italy, Germany lacked an existing central government that liberal-national forces could take over, for the Diet of the German Confederation represented Austrian influence and illiberal local German princes. Liberal-nationalists were therefore obliged to operate simultaneously on two competing levels: (1) changing local monarchies and oligarchies while (2) creating a central parliamentary government. The first level divided revolutionary

*Hungarian surrender to the Austrians.*

energies and led to conflict between local and national reformers. The second level was difficult because it required the destruction of the German princes' dynastic rights and because German boundaries were ill defined.

Following revolutions in Paris and Vienna the people of nearly every German capital and major city demonstrated in order to secure greater popular participation and rights. Where parliamentary institutions already existed (as in the Rhineland and some imperial cities), republican movements with proletarian support stirred and spread. Except for a peasant uprising in the Neckar Valley (which troops quickly suppressed) and the revolt in Berlin, almost no violence occurred. No strong conservative power checked liberal gains by force, since Austria was tied down at home, and the Prussian government, which flirted incon-

stantly with liberal and nationalistic policies, was itself the most significant victim of the German revolutions.

## Prussia in Revolt

Prussia's course was critical for the German liberal-national movement, for the Hohenzollerns ruled one-third of all Germans. The strength of their army overawed other members of the Confederation, including Austria, and their political-economic policies served as a magnet for popular nationalism that was only remotely "liberal." In 1844 the *Zollverein* —a General Customs Union across northern Germany—was completed, welding together Prussian leadership, and a national school of economic reformers founded by Friedrich List advocated high tariffs and state assistance to transportation and industry to initiate progress. But he also repudiated Western liberalism as being materialistic and cosmopolitan, and urged Germans to use their power to civilize the "barbaric" countries of the world. Another indication of Prussian goals was the plan of the Prussian foreign minister in 1848 to make war on Russia in support of a Polish revolution. His aim was to unite the Germans under Prussia, but the Prussian king and French opposition killed the project.

Catholic liberals from the Rhineland and more orthodox liberals everywhere objected to Prussian bureaucratic and militaristic authoritarianism, but their misgivings were eased by the pronouncements of Frederick William IV (1840–61). In his romantic quest to restore the purity of medieval institutions the Prussian king called Prussia's first General Diet in 1847, a body divided into houses corresponding to medieval estates, since the king believed this to be the only natural Christian order. The purpose of calling the estates—the raising of a loan to build a railroad desired by the eastern Prussian aristocracy (Junkers) to market the grain from their estates—was distinctly modern, however, and the king also conceded some liberties to the press. Refusing to become a rubber stamp of the king, the Diet demanded a constitution before granting the loan, and the press reported the Diet's proceedings, opening this impasse to public scrutiny. Thus the press prepared the way for a revolt of Berlin's citizenry against the army's administration of the city in March 1848, following the king's dissolution of the Diet.

Repulsed by the idea of insubordination and civil war, Frederick William IV attributed the uprising to the activities of foreign agitators among "my dear Berliners." Much to the army's chagrin, he ordered its withdrawal, made repeated liberal concessions including the election of a constituent assembly, and embraced the national cause by declaring that "Prussia will henceforth be merged into Germany." Agitation by workmen and guildsmen,* however, scared the intellectuals and middle classes, who left the capital in droves.

A radical conservative coalition of Junkers, army officers, and Lutheran clergymen posed a graver threat to the revolution, for it counted on peasant support for suppressing both liberal and urban lower-class agitation. While a combined Prussian constituent assembly and parliament sat during the summer, the conservative coalition edited a newspaper and formed a secret ministry that worked to undo every concession made by the official government and to win the king to their policy of military suppression. Among them was Otto von Bismarck. Meanwhile the parliament-constituent assembly suffered from inexperience, ministerial instability, peasant passivity toward its constitutional objectives, and failure to control taxation and the army (the two traditional levers of monarchical absolutism). It passed only eight laws. In the end the king complained that the assembly always gave way to the mob, and he returned to his conservative supporters, whose theories of government were his own. Following the army's recapture of Berlin and the proclamation of martial law in December 1848, he proclaimed his own constitution.

This constitution, gradually amended into final form in 1850, drew from the constituent assembly's work but retained royal initiative. It created an upper house of hereditary lords and an assembly

* The industrial workers' organizations were national in scope. Besides political democratization they demanded unemployment insurance, consumer cooperatives, free secular schools with free books and elected teachers, housing, income taxes, a ten-hour day, a ministry of labor, and equality for women. Guildsmen, who also began to organize nationally during the summer, wanted a return to their guaranteed position of the past. Neither organization agitated for the liberal demands of a free press, an armed militia, or commercial reforms.

elected by universal manhood suffrage. Initially its broad suffrage rallied rural sentiment behind the monarchy, but the Crown retained a veto, prevented the Diet from controlling the ministry and tax collection, and established an indirect electoral college based on tax payments—in other words, wealth. The electoral system for the lower house was so ingeniously constructed that the upper two electoral colleges (representing, respectively, four and fourteen percent of the electorate) were able to outvote the lower electoral delegates sent by the other 82 percent of the voters by a vote of two to one. This "sham parliamentary system" lasted in Prussia until 1918. Other German states, the Habsburg Empire, and Russia (1905) borrowed its features to grant the form of universal suffrage without abandoning political control to the electorate.

## Abortive Unification at Frankfurt

While the local German revolutions ran their course from early success to triumphant reaction, the first all-German parliament in history met at Frankfurt-am-Main. Its purpose was to formulate a constitution and to take direction of German affairs. Dubbed "the professors' parliament" by its detractors because it represented a plethora of scholars to the exclusion of seasoned statesmen, its membership was almost exclusively middle-class lawyers, administrators, judges, and professors. There was a slight sprinkling of landowners and still fewer businessmen. But the Assembly lacked more than experience; it lacked a machinery of government and a populace obedient to it. Although it tried to establish a provisional executive, an army, and a navy, the dynastic states (whose forces it commissioned for specific tasks) followed its direction at their own discretion. As a government,

*Frederick William IV taking oath to the Constitution, 1851.*

the Frankfurt Assembly therefore functioned in a vacuum. After the revolutionary movement receded, a narrow majority tried to enlist Prussian support by making the Prussian king the constitutional monarch of Germany. But Frederick William refused to accept "a crown of filth and mud"—that is, one based on popular sovereignty. Mortally wounded by this rejection, the Assembly disbanded after an existence of 11 months. A republican remnant, which transferred its seat to Stuttgart, was eventually disbanded by force.

Despite its impotence, the Frankfurt Assembly was significant as a source of constitutional innovations. Parts of its stillborn federal constitution were adopted by the North German Confederation of 1867 and by the Weimar Republic of 1919.

*Execution of a revolutionary in Germany.*

or "civilize" other nationalities—overrode the professed goal of national self-determination of peoples whose practical implementation in east-central Europe was an ethnographer's nightmare. Even more difficult for the deputies at Frankfurt was the question of the inclusion or exclusion of the Austrian Germans. The Greater German (*grossdeutsch*) radicals would have disrupted the Habsburg empire by annexing the Austrian Germans and their Czech subjects. The Smaller German (*kleindeutsch*) party favored the exclusion of Austria altogether. For the time being the question was settled by the failure of both the German and the Austrian revolutions, but the basic issue remained.

Later the kleindeutsch approach dominated Bismarck's unification of Germany around Prussia in 1871, while the grossdeutsch solution triumphed with Adolph Hitler's annexation of Austria to Germany in 1938 and the incorporation of the German population living in Czechoslovakia (the Sudetenland) in 1939.

Factions also formed in the Assembly around constitutional and social issues, but the great majority adhered to constitutional monarchism, considered property inviolate, and rejected the philosophy of natural rights in favor of historically acquired rights. Nevertheless the Frankfurt Constitution would have abolished nobility, patrimonial courts, and entail. Neither the constitutional monarchists nor the republicans favored working-class programs: the Assembly rejected a government-guaranteed right to work and called on Prussian and Austrian troops to put down a national organization of trade unionists at whose headquarters in Frankfurt disorders designed to influence the Assembly broke out. Still, on other issues the republicans were at odds with the constitutional monarchists. By vain new revolutions in Baden, the Palatinate, and Saxony in 1849, the republicans sought to preserve the life of the Assembly against

More immediately the Assembly served as a mirror of attitudes within the German liberal-national movement as practical problems arose. Constitutional deliberations were interrupted by circumstances requiring a definition of the German nation-state's frontiers. In June 1848 the Danish sovereign tried to recover the rebellious duchies of Schleswig-Holstein and incorporate Schleswig, whose population was a mixture of German and Danish, into Denmark. At that point the Assembly commissioned Prussia to drive the Danes out, unsuccessfully asserting German sovereignty over the duchies. In a more difficult boundary situation between the Germans and the Poles, the Assembly overwhelmingly voted to approve both Prussian rule over wholly Polish districts and rule by German minorities in mixed areas. In both the Polish and Danish episodes, nationalism—the will to dominate

reaction. But they were forcibly dispersed.*

## Failure of German Unification

· As Frankfurt's attempt to unify Germany collapsed, princes took the initiative in appealing to nationalist sentiment. In May 1849 Hanover, Saxony, and a number of smaller states signed a Prussian agreement for political union. But the larger southern states turned to Austria, whose victory over Hungary had put Schwarzenberg's government in a position to challenge the Prussian union with a reformed Confederation Diet. During a revolt in Hesse-Kassel in 1850, a showdown between Austria and Prussia occurred as battle-ready troops of the Confederation Diet and Prussia—both claiming counter-revolutionary jurisdiction—confronted each other. But Russia, trying to maintain the balance of power that a united Germany would overturn, threw its weight behind Austria. At Olmütz, in the same year, Prussia backed down and gave up its union—the "humiliation at Olmütz"—the outcome of which was a standoff between Austria and Prussia. Thus Germany remained as before a loose confederation of 38 states. As a result of these failures of 1848 nationalists became disillusioned with pacific parliamentary procedures. In the next decade most of them became "realists," ready to follow Bismarck in unifying Germany by "blood and iron."

At both the national and local dynastic levels the German revolutions of 1848 and 1849 utterly failed to transfer political initiative from kings and their ministers to parliamentary assemblies dominated by the middle classes. No dynasty was un-

seated; whatever constitutional changes followed were granted by sovereigns, who usually allowed the nobility and upper classes a strong voice, although more in an advisory capacity than as directors of affairs. At the same time programs of workingmen received no recognition whatsoever.

As in Habsburg territories, the peasants, not the urban populations, gained in legal status. In a few western German states legal emancipation was far advanced in 1848; in others it had hardly begun. The revolutions of 1848 forced the aristocracy out of its intermediary role between the peasants and the state. Subject to long-term redemption fees from the peasantry, old feudal-manorial obligations were canceled. At the same time steps were initiated to break up the communal holding of lands under control of the village, which had controlled agricultural activities for centuries. The impact of reform was more than to increase the material well-being of the peasants; it was to throw the countryside open to capitalist agriculture, which provided foodstuffs for expanding urban populations. Legal emancipation also made the peasantry mobile and more easily drawn into urban industry in subsequent decades. Ultimately, urban industrialization more than legal freedom decreased the pressure of population in the countryside, which had contributed heavily to the crisis of 1848. In specific instances reaction after revolution narrowed peasant gains, but nowhere could it thwart the basic change.

# THE LESSER REVOLUTIONS AND EVOLUTIONARY CHANGES

Revolution visited several other European areas in 1848 and 1849 with little success. Poles in the duchy of Posen prepared for a Prussian-backed war of unification,

---

* Following suppression of these revolts many of their surviving leaders emigrated. In the United States "Forty-Eighters" such as Carl Schurz subsequently played leading roles in American liberal politics.

*London slums, a source of upper-class fears (by Gustave Doré).*

which failed to materialize when Prussia changed her policy. Rumanians in Transylvania revolted unsuccessfully against the Magyars. Other Rumanians in Walachia and Moldavia, led by intellectuals returning from western Europe, also revolted but were crushed by Turkish and Russian troops.* A revolt in Greece scored

---

* Russian troops stayed on in these principalities, becoming one of the causes of the Crimean War (1854–56).

no gains, and an enfeebled revolution in famine-ridden Ireland was no more successful.

The most successful smaller revolution occurred in Switzerland. In 1847 liberals and Protestants won a 25-day war against a conservative league of Catholic cantons before France and Austria could intervene. The victors gave Switzerland economic unity and a federal constitution modeled largely on the Constitution of the United States.

During the mid-century revolutionary sweep some governments introduced liberal changes that were sufficient to forestall revolutionary popular uprisings. Belgium successfully checked riots and radical movements by doubling the electorate to include most of the middle classes, while public works and poor relief sufficed to prevent revolts by workingmen. In 1848 King William II of the Netherlands permitted his wealthier citizens to elect a parliament that could initiate laws and choose the ministry; in 1849 the king of Denmark conceded a national assembly with an elected lower house, but initiative did not clearly pass to popularly elected representatives for the remainder of the century. Unrest under enlightened despotism in Sweden also led to minor popular concessions between 1844 and 1859, but a modern parliamentary system was not established there until 1866. Thus the states that acquired successful democratic governments in the twentieth century were evolving in that direction in 1848. Significantly, they escaped the military reactions that plagued liberalism in the revolutionary states.

During the crisis years 1848–50 the two major peripheral states, Britain and Russia, had neither revolution nor progressive political evolution. Although the middle classes were badly scared by the Chartists, Britain escaped a revolution.* In part that escape was due to economic concessions that the functioning parliamentary system made in order to check discontent among the lower and middle classes. Moreover Britain had long before passed through the agricultural crisis that rocked central Europe in the middle of the nineteenth century. Perhaps as important, population pressures found release in Britain (although not in Ireland) and Russia. In this connection British industrialization played a significant role, and British people were also emigrating to the colonies and the United States in great numbers. Meanwhile the Russian frontier expanded rapidly into central Asia. Finally, for a variety of reasons the upper classes, who wielded political power in both countries, remained united and conservative.

* For the Chartist Movement see Part III, chap. 4.

# D. The Struggle for Social and Political Power: A Summing Up

After the French Revolution the contest between liberalism and nationalism on the one hand, and traditionalism on the other, became a struggle of the educated middle classes against kings, nobles, and clerics entrenched in power. By mid-century the middle classes were holding or sharing power in Britain, Belgium, the Netherlands, Switzerland, Piedmont-Sardinia, and the Scandinavian kingdoms; their hold on the political institutions of France slipped temporarily with the rise of Louis Napoleon. And their bid for liberal institutions in central Europe failed. Although Western liberals sympathized with these ill-fated revolts, their governments failed to intervene. In fact Britain even sanctioned Russian intervention in Hungary, which was decisive in breaking the Hungarian Republic. Europe continued to be divided between a liberal West, whose orbit was expanding, and a conservative, monarchical East and South.

In theory Western liberalism held a concept of the self-determination of nationalities that it would substitute for the dynastic state. Where national cultural boundaries and the dynastic state approximately coincided, self-determination could be achieved by the evolutionary or revolutionary transformation of existing governments. But in Germany and Italy national unity required the expulsion of the Habsburg power and the elimination of existing petty states. Within the Habsburg Empire self-determination meant either federation of equal, autonomous nationalities (the Pan-Slav approach) or the total disruption of the empire into separate states (the radical Hungarian position). In this environment collectivist romantic nationalists gained the upper hand over the liberals.

During and following the revolutions of 1848 tough-minded nationalists jettisoned all pretence of universal humanitarianism. Reaping a harvest of disillusionment from parliamentary failures of 1848, they became willing allies of radical conservatives and "national liberals," who subordinated the goals of individual liberty and responsible government to the cause of unification by "blood and iron"—power politics abroad, and coercive uniformity at home. The liberal catastrophe of 1848 marked the end of an era in which publicists envisaged nationalism as a stepping-stone to international cooperation. Free, unrestrained nationhood had become the highest good.

The year 1848 also became a landmark in social conflict. Politically conscious artisans and workingmen entered the struggle for status and power, and the "June Days" in Paris indicated their willingness to use force. With few exceptions their political and social programs aimed more at "social welfare" than at "socialism" or "communism." Nevertheless they inspired fear, condemnation, and forcible repression by an alliance of the bourgeoisie, peasants, and traditionally privileged classes. The bourgeoisie, frightened by what the then obscure Karl Marx called in 1847 "the specter of communism," compromised with conservatives, clerics, and nationalists to preserve the existing distribution of property and its benefits. At mid-century the urban labor movement was a small minority of the population, slow to achieve self-consciousness. Potentially, however, when industrialization on a par with Britain and Belgium became general, it would constitute the largest segment of society. Urban industrialization meant the transformation of the mobile peasant into an urban wage earner. In 1850 conservatives could count upon the peasants' support, but would this support survive the transition to an industrial society?

## Selected Readings

*Artz, Frederick B. *Reaction and Revolution, 1814–1832.* New York: Harper & Brothers, 1934.

*A general account in the* Rise of Modern Europe *series, revised in detail by more recent research.*

Babbitt, Irving. *Rousseau and Romanticism.* Boston: Houghton Mifflin Co., 1919.

*This work assaults root and branch the premises and methodology of the romantic thought attributed to Rousseau and his successors.*

Barzun, Jacques. *Classic, Romantic and Modern.* London: Martin Secker & Warburg, 1962.

*A romantic who believes that twentieth-century critics have vilified his tradition rehabilitates romanticism, narrowly defined.*

Blum, Jerome. *Noble Landowners and Agriculture in Austria, 1815–1848: A Study in the Origins of the Peasant Emancipation of 1848.* Baltimore: Johns Hopkins Press, 1948.

*This sets forth the agricultural changes that caused peasant grievances and moved many secular landowners toward a form of emancipation.*

Brinton, Crane. *Political Ideas of the English Romanticists.* London: Oxford University Press, 1926.

*This work demonstrates parallels between German romanticism and the English romantic poets.*

*Bruun, Geoffrey. *Revolution and Reaction, 1848–1852, A Mid-Century Watershed.* Princeton: D. Van Nostrand Co., 1958.

*A short introduction to the impact and sequel of Europe's most general revolution of the nineteenth century.*

Bury, J. P. T., ed. *The Zenith of European Power, 1830–1870.* The New Cambridge Modern History, vol. 10. Cambridge: Cambridge University Press, 1950.

*An exhaustive work useful for reference.*

*Butler, Eliza M. *The Tyranny of Greece over Germany.* Cambridge: Cambridge University Press, 1935 (paperback: Beacon Press).

*This portrays the rigid idealized classicism that dominated German esthetics, against which an exaggerated romanticism was in revolt.*

Englebrecht, H. C. *Johann Gottlieb Fichte, A Study of His Political Writings with Special Reference to His Nationalism.* New York: Columbia University Press, 1933.

*A monograph that sketches Fichte's drastic change from romantic individualism to collectivist nationalism in response to the French invasion of Germany.*

Ergang, R. R. *Herder and the Foundations of German Nationalism.* New York: Columbia University Press, 1931.

*A basic work on the fundamental formulator of modern nationalism.*

Evans, David Owen. *Social Romanticism in France, 1830–1848.* London: Oxford University Press, 1951.

*This traces the origins of republican socialism in France, especially in literary circles.*

Halevy, Elie. *A History of the English People in the Nineteenth Century.* 2d rev. ed., 6 vols. London: Ernest Benn, 1949–52.

*A celebrated study by a perceptive French scholar.*

*Halsted, John B. *Romanticism.* New York: Harper & Row, Publishers, 1969.

*A representative anthology of well-chosen quotations with a very intelligent introduction.*

Hayes, Carleton J. H. *The Historical Evolution of Modern Nationalism.* New York: The Macmillan Co., 1955.

*A study that identifies and describes several different kinds of nationalism.*

Herring, Hubert C. *A History of Latin America from the Beginnings to the Present.* 2d rev. ed. New York: Alfred A. Knopf, 1962.

*A standard textbook, excellent for the revolutionary period.*

Hovell, Mark. *The Chartist Movement.* New York: Longmans, Green & Co., 1918.

*Presents an account purely factual and descriptive.*

Kissinger, Henry A. *A World Restored; Metternich, Castlereagh and the Problems of Peace 1812–1822.* Boston: Houghton Mifflin Co., 1957.

*Both a general theoretical and a historical account that finds much to admire in the balance of power established at Vienna.*

Marcuse, Herbert. *Reason and Revolution, Hegel and the Rise of Social Theory.* 2d ed. New York: The Humanities Press, 1954.

*An attempt to absolve Hegel of fascist implications, interpreting him as a rational critic of the status quo.*

*May, Arthur. *The Age of Metternich, 1814–1848.* New York: Henry Holt and Co., 1933.

*A good short summary in the* Berkshire Studies in European History, *designed for beginning students.*

*Namier, Lewis B. *1848: The Revolutions of the Intellectuals.* Garden City, N.Y.: Doubleday & Co., 1964.

*This work finds evidence that nationalism was overcoming liberalism in Germany.*

*Robertson, Priscilla. *Revolutions of 1848: A Social History.* Princeton: Princeton University Press, 1952 (paperback: Harper Torchbooks).

*A general study that finds social class lines often more significant than economic and political categories.*

*Ruggiero, Guido de. *The History of European Liberalism.* Translated by R. G. Collingwood. Boston: Beacon Press, 1959.

*A detailed historical analysis.*

*Schapiro, J. Salwyn. *Liberalism: Its Meaning and History.* Princeton: D. van Nostrand Co., Anvil Books, 1958.

*This work is excellent for differentiating strains of bourgeois, democratic, and social liberalism.*

Schenk, Hans G. *The Aftermath of the Napoleonic Wars, the Concert of Europe—an Experiment.* London: Kegal Paul, Trench, Trubner & Co., 1947.

*This deals with postwar difficulties, including economic problems, briefly and well.*

Schroeder, Paul W. *Metternich's Diplomacy at its Zenith, 1820–1823.* Austin: University of Texas Press, 1962.

*This work uses archival evidence to demonstrate the exploitative nature of Austrian dominance in Italy, thus refuting apologies such as the one that follows.*

*Viereck, Peter. *Conservatism Revisited.* Rev. ed. New York: Crowell-Collier Publishing Co., Collier Books, 1962.

*A vindication of Metternich whose argument turns on an undefined and misleading usage of the word "constitution."*

Walzel, Oskar. *German Romanticism.* Translated by A. L. Lussky. New York: G. P. Putnam's Sons, 1932.

*A comprehensive survey covering political views as well as literature.*

Asterisk (*) denotes paperback

# Credit List for Part II

I.–6: Historical Pictures Service. 12: The Metropolitan Museum of Art, Dick Fund, 1925. 15: Cliche des Musees Nationaux, Louvre. 18: The Granger Collection. 20: Johann Jakob Simmler Collection-City Library of Zurich. 21: Historical Pictures Service. 22: The Metropolitan Museum of Art, Fletcher Fund, 1933. 23: Alinari-Art Reference Bureau. 24: Both Alinari-Art Reference Bureau. 25: Both Alinari-Art Reference Bureau. 26: Cliche des Musees Nationaux, Louvre. 27 (top): Alinari-Art Reference Bureau; (bottom) Huntington Library, San Marino, California. 28: Staatliche Kunstsammlungen, Dresden. 29: Both Alinari-Art Reference Bureau. 30: Alinari-Art Reference Bureau. 35: Brussels Library. 38: Alinari-Art Reference Bureau. 46: Museo del Prado, Madrid. 50: Historical Pictures Service. 52: Historical Pictures Service. 53: Historical Pictures Service. 66: Vatican Museum.

II.–74: Both Bayerische Staatsbibliothek, Munich. 77: Staatsbibliothek der Stiftung Preubischer Kulturbesitz, Marburg. 79: The Granger Collection. 82: Bettmann Archives. 85: Crozer Theological Library. 93: Historical Pictures Service. 95: Museo del Prado, Madrid. 97: Bibliotheque publique et universitaire, Geneva. 100: Bibliotheque publique et universitaire, Geneva. 102: Bettmann Archives. 107: Historical Pictures Service. 109: Bettmann Archives. 113: Museo del Prado, Madrid. 117: Walters Art Gallery, Baltimore. 120: Historical Pictures Service.

III.–131: American Museum of Natural History. 132: Historical Pictures Service. 133: Historical Pictures Service. 139: The National Library of Wales. 140: The Huntington Library, San Marino, California. 144: The Metropolitan Museum of Art, Dick Fund, 1925. 147: The Metropolitan Museum of Art, Bequest of Annie C. Kane, 1926. 148: Prints Division, New York Public Library. 149: Historical Pictures Service. 152: Kunsthistoriches Museum, Vienna. 162: Propriete du Musee cantonal des beaux-arts a Lausanne. 164: Museum of Fine Arts, Boston, Gift of Gordon Abbott and George P. Gardner. 166: Kuperstichkabinett, Basel. 169: The National Gallery, London. 181: Essex Institute Collection. 186: (top): Alinari-Art Reference Bureau; (bottom) New York Public Library Picture Collection. 187: Alinari-Art Reference Bureau. 188: The Metropolitan Museum of Art, Bequest of Mrs. H. O. Havemeyer, 1929. 189: Copyright Fotocommissie Rijksmuseum, Amsterdam. 193: New York Public Library Picture Collection.

IV.–203: Historical Pictures Service. 204: Historical Pictures Service (from a painting by the Le Nain brothers in the Louvre). 205: Both Historical Pictures Service. 206: Bettmann Archives. 207: Bettmann Archives (from the

469

Bagford Collection, The British Museum). 208: Historical Pictures Service (engraved after a painting by Jan Steen in the Braunshweig Gallery). 209: Historical Pictures Service. 213: Bettmann Archives (painting by P. Mignard in the Chateau de Versailles). 215: Historical Pictures Service (painting by C. Lefevre in the Versailles Museum). 217: Historical Pictures Service. 222: Bettmann Archives (painting by Claudio Coello). 229: Bettmann Archives (from the Bridge of the Elector, Berlin). 230: Bettmann Archives. 232: Historical Pictures Service. 234: Both Bettmann Archives. 235: Historical Pictures Service. 244–245: Historical Pictures Service. 246: Historical Pictures Service. 247: Historical Pictures Service. 249: Bettmann Archives.

V.–260: American Museum of Natural History. 261: American Museum of Natural History. 263: Historical Pictures Service. 264: Historical Pictures Service. 266: Historical Pictures Service. 267: Historical Pictures Service. 269: Bettmann Archives. 271: Bettmann Archives. 272: Historical Pictures Service. 273: Historical Pictures Service. 274: Bettmann Archives. 281: Historical Pictures Service. 283: Bettmann Archives. 284: Historical Pictures Service. 289: Historical Pictures Service. 290: Pennsylvania Academy of Fine Arts. 292: Historical Pictures Service. 292: Historical Pictures Service. 300: Historical Pictures Service (Courtesy of Lloyd's). 302: Historical Pictures Service. 304: Bettmann Archives.

VI.–313: Historical Pictures Service. 314: Historical Pictures Service. 315: Historical Pictures Service. 316: Bettmann Archives (painting by Rigaud in the Wallace Collection, London). 320: Historical Pictures Service. 321: Historical Pictures Service. 323: The Frick Collection. 328: Historical Pictures Service. 330: Historical Pictures Service. 331: Bettmann Archives. 334: Historical Pictures Service. 335: Historical Pictures Service. 337: Bettmann Archives. 339: Historical Pictures Service. 341: Historical Pictures Service. 344: Historical Pictures Service. 345: The Metropolitan Museum of Art, Bequest of William K. Vanderbilt, 1920. 346: Historical Pictures Service. 349: Historical Pictures Service. 351: Bettmann Archives.

VII.–363: Bettmann Archives. 367: Historical Pictures Service. 369: Bettmann Archives (Versailles Museum). 370: Historical Pictures Service. 372: Bettmann Archives. 374: Historical Pictures Service (Bibliotheque Nationale, Cabinet des Estampes). 380: Historical Pictures Service. 383: Bettmann Archives (after Manet). 386: Bettmann Archives. 387: Photo Bulloz (Carnavalet Museum). 392: Historical Pictures Service. 396: Historical Pictures Service (Louvre). 398: Bettmann Archives (painting by Clarkson Stanfield in the Royal United Service Institution, London). 399: Museo del Prado. 401: Historical Pictures Service. 404: Bettmann Archives.

VIII.–415: The Metropolitan Museum of Art, Wolfe Fund, 1931. 416: The Frick Collection. 417: Bettmann Archives. 418: Historical Pictures Service. 420: Bettmann Archives. 422: Bettmann Archives (painting by Sir Thomas Lawrence). 427: Historical Pictures Service. 428: Historical Pictures Service (drawing by George Cruikshank). 433: Historical Pictures Service. 441: Historical Pictures Service. 441: Historical Pictures Service. 442: Historical Pictures Service. 444: Historical Pictures Service. 446: Historical Pictures Service. 448: Historical Pictures Service. 450: Marburg-Art Reference Bureau. 453: Historical Pictures Service. 454: Bettmann Archives. 457: Historical Pictures Service. 459: Historical Pictures Service. 460: Historical Pictures Service. 462: Bibliotheque Nationale, Paris.

seventeenth century, 41, 176-183; triumph over king, 246-250
Parma, Duke of, 153, 155
Particularism, in Holy Roman Empire in fourteenth and fifteenth centuries, 54; in sixteenth century, 76
Pascal, Blaise, 266, 286
Passarowitz, Treaty of, 226
Paul III (Pope), 33, 105, 110, 111
Paul IV (Pope), 105, 107, 108, 112
Paul, Czar of Russia, 425
Peace of Westphalia, 171-172
Peasantry, affected by potato blight, 447; in Brandenburg-Prussia, 228; on brink of famine, 208-209; and Calvinism in France, 161; civil rights in England, 247; decline at end of Renaissance, 40, 41; disinterest of, in liberalism, 447, 453; in early Russia, 233; in Eastern Europe, 56; emancipation of, proposed by Frederick II, 338; emancipated by French Revolution, 371, 406; emancipation of, in Germany, 454, 461; under enlightened despotism, 333, 338; fails to support constitutional government in Russia, 425; flight of, to French cities (1788-1789), 364; Great Peasants' War, 84-86; in the Habsburg Empire, 167, 452, 453; in Holy Roman Empire, 77, 172; idealized by romantics, 414; independent course of (1848), 429; under noble privileges in Hungary, 226; in Ottoman Empire, 243; in Poland, 242; policy of Joseph II regarding, 335; power of custom over, 199; restiveness of, after 1815, 412, 421, 429; revolts of, during Renaissance, 35; rights of French lords over, 362; Roman law and, 77; in seventeenth century, 202-203, 207, 208, 210, 233; near slavery in Russia, 341-342
Peasants' Revolt (1524-1526), 77, 80, 84-86, 88
Peel, Robert, 445
Penn, William, 235
Pennsylvania, 301-302, 347
Persecution, religious, 86, 87-88, 90, 94, 101, 119, 121, 151, 153, 161, 178
Perspective, linear, 31
Peru, 437
Pestel, Paul, 439
Peter I (the Great) of Russia, 200, 233, 234-239, 252, 309, 321, 330, 339, 340
Peter III, Czar of Russia, 327, 339
"Peterloo," 428
Petition of Right (1628), 177

Petrarch, Francesco, 4, 8
Petrine Doctrine, 61
Philip II of Spain, accession, 91; Armada and, 155-156; attempts to expand empire, 146-148; Escorial and, 148; government of, 147-150; Inquisition and, 150; Requesens and, 153; revolt in Low Countries, 151-154; England and, 96, 155-156, 160; war with Turks, 150-151
Philip III of Spain, 155-156, 165
Philip IV, the Fair, of France, 60
Philip IV of Spain, literature in the reign of, 190; painting in the reign of, 185; revolts and, 173-174; Thirty Years' War and, 165, 170, 172, 174
Philip V of Spain, 222-223, 241, 311, 322
Philip the Bold of Burgundy, 52
Philip the Good of Burgundy, 53
Philip of Hesse, 84, 86, 88, 90
Philippines, 133
Philosophes, 288-301, 302, 303, 304, 305, 339, 361, 362, 413
Physics, 254, 267, 268, 297
Physiocrats, 299, 300, 332
Pico della Mirandola, 11
Piedmont-Sardinia, 423, 435, 455
Pilgrimage of Grace, 93
Piracy, 151, 153, 155-156
Pisa, Council of, 61
Pitt, William (Earl of Chatham), 320, 327, 328, 344, 383
Pitt, William (the Younger), 347
Pius II (Pope), 62
Pius IV (Pope), 112
Pius IX (Pope), 454
Platonic Academy (Florence), 11
Platonic Rationalism, 278, 282
Poland, alliance of, with Louis XIV, 221; alliance of, with Peter the Great, 234, 237; anarchy in, 242, 330; churchmen of, against status quo, 439; Grand Duchy of Warsaw, 397, 401; invaded by Russia, 175; in Northern War, 175-176; in sixteenth century, 102, 115, 166; union with Lithuania, 115; as issue at Congress of Vienna, 403; lack of middle class in, 202; partitions of, 330-332, 383; preserved by division of enemies, 242; revolution of 1791, 378-379, 383; revolutionary stirrings in, 360, 458, 461-462; troops of, in Moscow, 233; and turning of Turks back from Vienna, 225; uprising of, in 1830, 443, 444; War of Polish Succession, 312, 320; war with Sweden, 175
Political theory, Calvin and, 99; divine right of kings, 89, 121-

122; humanists and, 282-283; in the seventeenth century, 282-285; in the eighteenth century, 291, 296-298; Lutheran doctrine of passive obedience, 89, 121; Machiavelli and, 17-19; Reformation and, 193-194
Politiques, 106, 163, 169, 193
Poltava, Battle of, 237
Polysynodie, 314
Pombal, Marquis de, 323
Pompadour, Madame de, 303-304
Poniatowski, Stanislas of Poland, 310
Poor Law (1601), 144, 158
Population, 209, 305, 338-339, 355, 364, 447, 452, 463; colonial, 133; decrease in early Renaissance, 34; effects of Thirty Years' War, 172; and "Price Revolution," 141-142; recovery during Renaissance, 36; in seventeenth century, 129, 192
Portugal, 222, 343, 403-404, 433-434, 435; Brazil and, 132; commercial empire in sixteenth century, 36, 131-132, 143, 146; independence movement, 173; Olivares and, 173; origins, 44; Philip II succeeds to throne, 146
Positivism, 298
Potato, 339
Prairial Law, 387, 388
Pressburg, 226, 397
Price, Richard, 345
"Price Revolution," 77, 94, 141-142, 153, 191
Priestley, Joseph, 268, 269, 296, 345, 347, 378
Prince Henry, "the Navigator," 131
Printing press, 232; in Deventer, 65; early printed works, 20, 65; and English civil wars, 20, 181; impact on governments, 41; impact on Reformation, 64, 80-81; invention of, 19-21
Privilege, and absolute monarchy, 199, 200; acquisition of, by service nobility in Russia, 232; assaulted by Joseph II, 335; assaulted by Turgot, 228; of corporate bodies in the seventeenth century, 205; defense of, by parlements, 353, 365; extension of, by absolute monarchs, 211; in French Revolution, 368, 409; held by "constituted bodies," 354-360; of Junkers in Prussia, 228-230; as limit on royal authority, 202, 206; multiplication of privileged offices, 251; of nobility in Britain, 316; in